Compensation Management in a Knowledge-Based World

EIGHTH EDITION

Compensation Management in a Knowledge-Based World

Richard I. Henderson

Professor Emeritus, Georgia State University

Prentice Hall, Upper Saddle River, New Jersey 07458

VP/Editorial Director: James Boyd
Editor-in-Chief: Natalie Anderson
Editorial Managing Editor: Melissa Steffens
Assistant Editor: Hersch Doby
Executive Marketing Manager: Michael Campbell
Director of Production: Michael Weinstein
Production Manager: Gail Steier de Acevedo
Production Coordinator: Maureen Wilson
Permissions Coordinator: Monica Stipanov
Manufacturing Buyer: Natacha St. Hill Moore
Senior Manufacturing and Prepress Manager: Vincent Scelta
Cover Design: Bruce Kenselaar
Cover Art: Margie & Howard Fullmer/Stock Illustration Source, Inc.
Full Service Composition: Omegatype Typography, Inc.

Library of Congress Cataloging-in-Publication Data

Henderson, Richard I.
    Compensation management in a knowledge-based world / Richard I. Henderson.—8th ed.
      p. cm.
    Includes index.
    ISBN 0-13-086682-2
    1. Compensation management.   I. Title.
HF5549.5.C67H46 2000
658.3'14221—dc21

99-046496

Prentice-Hall International (UK) Limited, London
Prentice-Hall of Australia Pty. Limited, Sydney
Prentice-Hall Canada, Inc., Toronto
Prentice-Hall Hispanoamericana, S.A., Mexico
Prentice-Hall of India Private Limited, New Delhi
Prentice-Hall of Japan, Inc., Tokyo
Prentice-Hall (Singapore) Pte Ltd.
Editora Prentice-Hall do Brasil, Ltda., Rio de Janeiro

Printed in the United States of America

10 9 8 7 6 5 4 3 2 1

Contents

vii

Preface

The last decade of the twentieth century witnessed monumental changes in social, political, and economic systems throughout the world. This book takes a pragmatic look at one of the most controversial and critical issues facing all kinds of organizations in all kinds of political systems—that is, how to compensate employees for services rendered.

Designing and administering a compensation system that rewards employees fairly while stimulating them to provide goods and services that satisfy customer demands and permitting the organization to operate profitably is the focus of this book. This book recognizes the critical role played by compensation in modern organizations. Although the book concentrates on how organizations design and administer their base pay programs for most employees, it also reviews and discusses in lesser detail what organizations are doing today to expand their base pay opportunities with incentive awards resulting from various productivity or performance measures and the complex and ever-expanding area of benefits.

Since the mid-1960s, the subject of compensation has received increased stature and recognition by all kinds and sizes of organizations. It is not unusual for even medium-sized organizations to have a director of compensation and a director of benefits. Although this book includes pay, incentive awards, and benefits within the field of compensation, many organizations will physically separate pay and benefits because of the different knowledge and skills required to properly manage both areas. In addition to focusing on the technologies related to the establishment of base pay programs, the book discusses and describes all the parts of a compensation system. Compensation is recognized as a broad, complex system in which organizational revenues for labor costs can be distributed in many ways. The compensation professional must be able to integrate organizational mission and policy with employee compensation demands in a manner that leads to improved organizational productivity and employee performance.

What must be recognized is that employee compensation may be as small as 10 percent of organizational expenditures, or it may consume more than 80 percent of expenditures. Whatever the percentage, no other major expenditure component has a greater influence on organizational profitability than employee compensation. This is true even for nonprofit and public-sector organizations that do not have a "profit" motive. These organizations must provide a wide variety of goods and services, and both the quality and quantity of goods and services provided relate directly to their compensation programs.

This book is separated into three parts:

Part I provides a macro or "big picture" review of compensation management and the reward system of an organization. It analyzes some of the major factors that influence compensation opportunities.

Part II contains the "nuts and bolts," or microanalysis, of compensation in organizations. It includes a step-by-step discussion of the processes involved in establishing the base pay program of an organization. This part informs the reader how job requirements are identified, defined, and valued. It then describes how to recognize marketplace forces and how these various processes are integrated into a pay system.

Part III combines a macro- and microanalysis by explaining how a base pay program is expanded into a total compensation system that includes various short- and long-term incentives. It discusses the ever-increasing importance of benefits programs that not only protect employees and their dependents but provide a wide variety of lifestyle enhancement opportunities that add enjoyment and pleasure to the lives of workers and their families. It discusses how the compensation components made available to each employee are based on such criteria as membership in the organization, tenure, or seniority with the organization, responsibilities related to the job, quality of job performance and the results achieved, and overall organizational success and profitability. This part also includes an in-depth look at the short- and long-term pay and incentives offered to executives and the special compensation programs developed for employees in foreign locations.

A Model for Compensation Management: Rewarding Performance

A Macro View	*A Micro View*	*A Macro–Micro View*
Chapter	*Chapter*	*Chapter*
1. Compensation in a Knowledge-Based Global Economy	6. Job Analysis	13. Measuring and Paying for Performance
2. The Reward System: Compensation and Noncompensation Dimensions	7. Job Description	14. Short-Term Incentives
3. The World of Pay and Compensation	8. Job Evaluation	15. Long-Term Incentives and Wealth Building
4. Organizational Structure: Strategic and Tactical Compensation Issues	9. Job Evaluation: Two Point-Factor Methods	16. Executive and International Compensation
5. Legislation and Compensation	10. Surveying Market Pay and Compensation Practices	17. Benefits and Services
	11. Designing a Base Pay Structure	18. Pay Delivery Administration
	12. Team-Based Pay in a Knowledge-Based World	

SUPPLEMENT PACKAGE

The supplements to accompany *Compensation Management* have been thoroughly revised for the eighth edition. Available through Prentice Hall are an Instructor's Manual and a Windows-based Exercise Book with Interactive Software. The Instructor's Manual includes solutions to assignments, an overview of each chapter within the text, and objective questions for examination purposes. The Exercise Book contains experiential exercises, which provide the student with the opportunity to use knowledge gained from *Compensation Management* to solve real-world problems.

ACKNOWLEDGMENTS

I deeply appreciate the ideas and efforts of the many people who have contributed to the concepts developed in the eight editions of this book. I especially want to thank Ron Adler, John Chandler, Matthew Doster, Dean Grant, Gene Hamilton, Ron McCage, Terry McCreanor, Theresa Mees, Greg Melia, John Menefee, Peggy Metz, Gordon Morse, Pat Nielsen, Waino Suojanen, Joe Tajcnar, Dave Thomsen, Mike Thompson, and Dave Wessinger.

I also appreciate the help of the reviewers of this edition: Brian Murray, University of Texas–San Antonio; Deborah Knapp, Cleveland State University; Shawn Carraher, Indiana University, Northwest; Rick Labib-Wood, National University–San Diego, CA; Russel Kent, Georgia Southern University; Ed Arnold, Auburn University, Montgomery; Oliver Mulford, Mankato State University; Craig Tunwall, SUNY–Utica; Daniel Gallagher, James Madison University; Robert A. Figler, University of Akron; L. G. Gill, Southwest Texas State University; and Fraya Wagner, East Michigan University.

Richard I. Henderson

PART

I

Macroeconomic Compensation Concepts

CHAPTER 1

Compensation in a Knowledge-Based Global Economy

CHAPTER 2

The Reward System

CHAPTER 3

The World of Pay and Compensation

CHAPTER 4

Organizational Structure

CHAPTER 5

Legislation and Compensation

The rise in importance of global markets over the last two decades of the twentieth century has placed greater stress on organizations regarding their ability to compete and be profitable. The need to be competitive is critical to all organizations—profit and nonprofit, privately owned or government operated. To be successful, these organizations must provide high-quality goods and services to their clients in a cost-effective manner. A major cost for all organizations in providing needed goods and services is their labor costs. This book discusses the design and administration of the labor cost function of organizations of all kinds and sizes.

Part I includes a number of discussions concerning organizational strategy. Each chapter of the book discusses a particular component of a total compensation program. The beginning of each chapter contains a brief discussion of a compensation strategy that relates to the content of that chapter. For a particular organization, the compensation strategy(ies) may have to be more specific in supporting its strategic plans.

Chapters 1 through 5 provide the reader with a macroview of the reward system of an organization, assisting the reader to understand and recognize the opportunities available to organizations to attract and retain competent workers through their compensation systems. Organizations accomplish this goal by offering employees something they want and need. The rewards provided by employers vary by kind and amount and are combined in widely different packages, but these different packages must have one common purpose—to direct employee behavior toward the accomplishment of organizational objectives and goals.

Chapter 1 focuses on the importance of money in a capitalistic–democratic society. Particular attention centers on differences in lifestyle opportunities for all members within a seven-class social structure.

Chapter 2 introduces the reader to the compensation and noncompensation dimensions of the reward system of an organization. Chapters 3 and 4 provide current and useful pay data on the earnings of employees by various characteristics, including (1) kind of job, (2) geographic location of job, (3) industry of employer, (4) competition facing employer, (5) degree of unionization, (6) government legislation regarding compensation, and other major demographic criteria.

Chapter 5 focuses on the requirements placed on a reward system by legislation. In some manner, every component of the compensation system is directly influenced by legislative mandates. After completing the first five chapters, the reader should have developed a conceptual model of compensation system design and should be ready for a microview of how to design and implement the major basic subsystems that provide the foundation for a compensation system.

CHAPTER

Compensation in a Knowledge-Based Global Economy

Learning Objectives

In this chapter you will learn about:

1. The importance of a rapidly growing global economy.

2. The relationship between labor costs and organizational competitiveness and profitability.

3. The contribution of organizational compensation to the lifestyle opportunities of employees and their families.

4. Income levels that determine social-class structure for inhabitants of the United States.

5. The relationship between levels of education, knowledge and skills, and work-related income.

Compensation Strategy

Develop a compensation program that recognizes the lifestyle and standard of living of all employees.

Ever since the end of World War II, social, political, and economic systems have moved toward a world economy. In the past 20 years, however, this move toward a more complex and competitive world has accelerated at a rapid pace. Today and into the future, there will be an expanding focus on market forces and international resource allocation. Although a global economy focuses on such macroeconomic factors as inflation, gross domestic product, monetary policies, trade tariffs, and international resource allocation, there is one microeconomic factor that has been and will continue to be of critical importance within a global economy. That factor is labor costs.

Labor cost issues affect the efficiency and even the survival of both public- and private-sector organizations. Long before the advent of a global economy concept, governments in some manner developed various approaches and efforts to redistribute

3

income to the poorer members of their society. It has been recognized that if some kind of subsistence level of income or necessary goods and services is not provided to the poor, a belligerent society develops with constant warfare between the "haves" and the "have-nots." One major method of providing for the poor promoted some kind of welfare payments in the form of money, food, housing, health care services, even clothing. Another method was for government agencies—Civil Service—to provide jobs and job-related paychecks. In many countries, all kinds of nongovernment service and goods-producing organizations were stimulated to hire as many workers as possible. A major problem with these hiring practices was that many jobholders made little or no constructive contributions to the output of the hiring organization. Not only did these practices result in drastically overstaffed organizations, but also the overall performance of these organizations was poor and inefficient. Providing jobs and paychecks to un-needed, nonproductive workers not only leads to overstaffing but most often results in inefficient operations and promotes cronyism and corruption.

To survive in a complex, competitive global economy, all organizations, both private and public, must be able to focus on the effective and efficient delivery of the products they are designed to offer. A key factor in promoting effective delivery of essential goods and services is the provision of a performance-based remuneration system to all workers. *Compensation Management* provides a step-by-step approach for designing a remuneration system that recognizes job requirements, employee-related knowledge and skills, and performance-related incentives that link individual, team, work unit, and organization performance. Total remuneration also includes a host of benefits that protects and expands the lifestyle and health of the worker and his or her family. The total of these contributions by the organization represents its labor costs. On the one hand, these costs should contribute to improved employee performance and, on the other hand, expanded productivity so that an organization can be competitive and profitable in providing its goods and services within a global economy.

CAPITALISM AND KNOWLEDGE IN A GLOBAL ECONOMY

It is not often that world events have a major influence on organizational support operations. With the fall of the Soviet empire and worldwide decline in communism, however, interest in capitalism has risen to an all-time high. The political-social-economic battle between capitalism on one side and communism-socialism on the other side has focused renewed worldwide attention on jobs, employee income from job-related efforts, organizational profitability, ability to compete in global markets, and income distribution in the United States and throughout the world.

To gain appreciation of the influence of these worldwide events on the role of compensation professionals and managers, it is helpful to start with a brief explanation of capitalism and the dynamics that support it as a viable economic solution to global problems. A critical factor underlying capitalism as an economic theory is that profit is OK; it is neither wicked nor unacceptable to make money. For capitalism to succeed, however, there must be a strong, direct, and supportive relationship between work and the monetary rewards available through work. Today, more than ever before, there is recognition all over the world that if an organization is to succeed, it must have a motivated workforce that has joy in working and is dedicated to successful operations. In a capitalistic world, employees must respect money and the challenges of their work to gain satisfaction from work performed.

The move of capitalism into a knowledge-based world centers attention on an enlightened society. The importance of knowledge demands a predisposition toward continuous self-improvement. To be successful in a knowledge-based capitalistic world, there must be a passion for learning that includes a recognition of the need for education.

A major problem facing the United States and its leadership role in a capitalistic-democratic world is an increasing and unacceptable difference between the income of the lower-paid and the higher-paid members of the workforce. The growing disparity of income between the lower-income and the higher-income members of society relates directly to the increasing influence of higher levels of knowledge and skills in pay determination. Those members of society who do not have an adequate or acceptable level of education are going to find themselves in a very unenviable position regarding current and future income opportunities. The pay and compensation for those with acceptable levels of knowledge and skills will rise, whereas those with minimal levels of required knowledge and skills will see their income opportunities stagnate, even decline.

More than ever before, the compensation professional must be able to support all activities that will make the organization more successful. In the past decade, there have been widespread activities to reduce the size of the workforce—downsizing or reduction in force (RIF)—and the elimination of entire levels of management structure—reengineering. These efforts have been very successful in decreasing organizational costs and increasing profitability. For some employees, it has meant increased workloads with minimal to no change in pay. To others, it has meant the loss of well-paying jobs.

From the very beginning of these organizational redesign efforts, compensation professionals have been called upon to identify jobs in which worker efforts can be combined, unneeded jobs, and possibly jobs in which incompetent, obsolete, or unneeded employees are being hidden. In addition, these same compensation professionals are being asked to redesign compensation and reward programs that can improve employee morale and motivation while keeping labor costs within specified limits.

To assist their organizations to compete while functioning within these often conflicting requirements, compensation professionals have had to increase their knowledge and skills dramatically. Because of these advances in knowledge and skills, the importance of the compensation profession has risen in the managerial-professional world.

COMPENSATION AND ORGANIZATIONAL STRATEGY

To develop a competitive advantage in a global economy, the compensation program of the organization must support totally the strategic plans and actions of the organization. The individuals occupying the executive positions of the organization are responsible for establishing and developing the strategy of the organization. The overall strategic plans inform all of its members of the direction the organization wishes to take. Management and organizational specialists review these strategic plans and take the actions necessary within their domain to ensure accomplishment of plans.

For the human resources/compensation specialist, the assignment to ensure accomplishment of organizational strategy begins with determining (1) the work that must be performed by some work unit or individual, (2) the kinds and levels of knowledge and skill required, (3) the quality of people needed to promote organizational success, and

(4) the rewards the organization can offer to its members that promote a work culture that ensures accomplishment of organizational strategy.

A human resources/compensation strategy that fulfills the preceding four requirements will provide a competitive advantage to the organization. Of equal importance, these efforts assist in developing an organizational structure that promotes effective use of all available resources.

INTEGRATING KNOWLEDGE AND SKILL REQUIREMENTS, ORGANIZATION COMPENSATION, AND EMPLOYEE INCOME

To be successful in a knowledge-based world, each organization must make full use of available technologies. The efficient and effective use of these technologies requires a workforce that has the needed knowledge and skills. Recognizing that available technologies are constantly changing and expanding, the masters of these technologies must also have constantly expanding levels of knowledge and skills. The ability of the individual to interact with ever-changing technologies places boundaries on work assignments. The issues of work boundaries and work-required knowledge and skills are a major part of the discussions in this book regarding the setting of base pay and the design of compensation systems.

The major point presented in this chapter of *Compensation Management* is that work does pay off. However, to be successful, the worker must be willing to accept challenges—to solve problems. In solving problems, job opportunities expand, which leads to the need to take risks and accept challenges. In these situations of uncertainty, there must be a focus on correctness to minimize the chance and cost of improper action. Change is inevitable in the knowledge-based world. Living and successful adaptation to change requires the continuous expansion of knowledge and skills.

Although organizations are constantly searching for ways to keep labor costs within acceptable limits, they must recognize that employee satisfaction relates directly to income obtained from work performed and the lifestyle opportunities made available to the workers and their families from this work-earned income. To gain an appreciation of the relationship between work-provided pay and employee work satisfaction, it is very helpful to gain an understanding of social class, class lifestyle, and income in the United States.

LIFESTYLE AND COMPENSATION

For at least the past 50 years, behavioral scientists and economists have discussed at length the two critical forces of pay—the absolute and the relative. As the United States moves into the twenty-first century, its future survival, let alone growth, focuses on these twin factors of pay.

Gone are the days when anyone would, or could, think that money-pay is NOT a motivator. It exerts a powerful influence on human behavior. As the famous English poet, John Milton, said over 300 years ago, "Money brings honor, friends, conquests, and riches." As with any force that is available to one individual to direct or redirect the behavior of other individuals, money and its workplace counterpart, pay, must be used with skill and integrity if they are to accomplish their mission of directing behavior in a positive manner. To better understand how to direct or influence human behavior with money, it is critical to recognize the relationship between lifestyle and social class. The first step in understanding social class is to define it. A *social class* consists of a group of people of roughly equivalent status in an unequal society. Various criteria are normally used to measure status to differentiate social classes. These criteria are income, property, occupation, and education. Typically, society is divided into three classes—upper, middle, and lower.

PAY AND SOCIAL CLASS

From the dawn of civilization, humanity has been divided into at least two social classes—the haves and the have-nots. As families merged into tribes and tribes into governments, a small, insignificant social class emerged between the haves and the have-nots. Members of this middle group were government and religious administrators, military officers, artists, entertainers, traders, and merchants. During the past 500 years, as democratic practices began to emerge, this middle social group moved from a minority to a majority in a small number of industrialized nations and became the driving force to spread democratic concepts throughout the world.

Almost from its start, the United States has flourished within a democratic, middle-class environment. Today, with the continued prosperity, let alone survival, of the nation in peril, it is important to recognize the relationship among pay, earnings and income, and social structure within the country.

Social Structure and Income

For hundreds of years, those involved in the identification of social classes have used a variety of criteria for determining who should be in a particular social class. Today, in capitalistic-democratic America, one criterion can be used to determine the class of an individual or family unit, and that is income. Most adults in the United States must depend on their job-related pay or earnings for their income. The typical upper-, middle-, and lower-class divisions can be further separated into seven subsets. Each of these subsets defines a significantly different standard of living based on family income. The three classes, seven subset classes, and annual family income intervals are shown in Figure 1–1.

FIGURE 1–1 Seven Classes of Society in the United States

	Class	*Family of Four Annual Income**	*Percentage of U.S. Population*
UPPER	Ultrarich	Over $1,000,000	Less than 0.5 of 1
	Wealthy	$250,000 to $1,000,000	Less than 2
MIDDLE	Upper Middle	$90,000 to $250,000	6
	Middle Middle	$50,000 to $90,000	25
	Lower Middle	$30,000 to $50,000	37
LOWER	Working Poor	$18,000 to $30,000	17
	Poverty	to $18,000	13

*By 1999, about 64 percent of the working-age population held a job. The labor force now includes 75 percent of all men, 60 percent of all women, and 56 percent of all teenagers. These numbers mean that the average family has at least two members working, if not more.

Although to some degree these annual family income intervals are somewhat arbitrary, a review of a wide variety of readily available economic data provides a sound basis for these interval values. Like any data used for making rather sweeping generalizations, for example, placing 272.2 million inhabitants of the United States into seven social classes (Figure 1–1), they are approximate, especially for middle and upper classes in which the income amounts could vary by ±15 to ±20 percent based on geographic location of the family. The plus amounts would recognize significantly higher housing costs and state and local government taxes for urban and suburban dwellers in such high cost-of-living cities as New York, San Francisco, Los Angeles, and Boston, whereas minus amounts would relate to inhabitants in much of rural America, where living costs and taxes are far lower than those for city dwellers.

Establishing Class Family Income Limits

The actual dollar values presented in Figure 1–1 were established from the top-down and from the bottom-up. Poverty-level income statistics generated annually by the U.S. Department of Health and Human Services to determine eligibility for food stamps and other government welfare programs are used to establish the dollar level for the poverty class. Early each year, this federal government agency establishes poverty-level income for single persons, two-member families, and so on. Poverty levels of income in 1999 are shown in the following table.

Family Size	Income	Percentage of 4-Person Family
4 persons	$16,700	100.0
3 persons	13,880	83.1
2 persons	11,060	66.2
Single person	8,240	49.3

Federal Non-Farm Poverty Income Guidelines, March 15, 1999.

The $16,700 family income statistic provides a useful dollar income value for separating the poverty class from the working poor.

Another useful statistic comes from the Internal Revenue Service with its earned income tax credit. Working families making less than $30,095 in 1998 and having at least two children under 18 living at home were eligible for a maximum credit of $3,756. (No distinction is made between one-parent and two-parent families.)

An assumption made regarding the working poor is that at least two members of the family work. Today, one member working full time at minimum wage ($5.15) would earn $10,712, and the other, half-time at minimum wage, would earn $5,356 for a total of $16,068—approaching the bottom dollar income limit of the working poor. This family would still be eligible for a variety of government subsidies, from food stamps to housing subsidies to federal income tax rebates.

A number of valuable statistics are available for establishing the limits of the lower-middle class. A primary statistic is the U.S. Congress upper limit on tax rebates for the working poor—approximately $30,000. The National Association of Realtors® identified a median income of first-time home buyers for 1997 as $46,600. A starter home for 1997 was priced at $108,000. A first-time home buyer would have to have an income of approximately $34,200 to qualify for a loan of $97,200 with a 10 percent down payment of $10,800. The median-priced resale home for 1997 was $121,500 and required a qualifying income of approximately $33,393. The median family income for all home buyers for 1997 was $54,100.[1] The ability to qualify for a home mortgage is one of the first badges of entry into middle class. The transition income from lower-middle to middle-middle class is a gray zone, but somewhere at around $50,000 a family of four begins to truly enjoy the fruits and opportunities available to the middle class.

Federal income tax legislation begins to be very useful in establishing the limits between middle-middle and upper-middle class. Various pieces of tax legislation identify who must be considered the highest-paid 5 percent of the organization. For organizations to qualify their benefit programs, including retirement options, they must meet certain nondiscrimination requirements. Over the years, the federal government has attempted to democratize, if not socialize, employer-provided benefits. It has developed some very stringent nondiscrimination rules regarding the kinds and amounts of benefits an employer can provide to ensure that its plan is "qualified" from the view of the IRS. (*Qualified* in this sense means that both the employer and employee receive certain income tax benefits.)

As an individual moves from the largely inhabited ranks of middle-middle class to the more sparsely inhabited ranks of upper-middle class, the lowest figure provided in IRS pay discrimination regulations uses annual earnings of $45,000 and $50,000 (indexed annually based on increase in the CPI). Here, a two-wage-earning family would be in the realm of at least middle-middle class.

The $250,000 cutoff between upper-middle class and the wealthy class can again use IRS statistics to identify who truly are the "highly compensated." In 1993, the "highly compensated" statistic was $235,840. By 1996, this figure had been reduced to $150,000. A review of the pay of senior executives and top professionals also provides an insight to both the $250,000 bottom limit to the upper class and the $90,000 threshold to the upper-middle class.

The cutoff between the wealthy and the ultrarich is probably the most arbitrary of all the class income interval values. The annual million dollar earnings appear to continue to attract the attention of all kinds of publications, including *National Enquirer, AFL-CIO News, The Wall Street Journal, New York Times,* other major city newspapers, and business magazines such as *Fortune, Forbes,* and *Business Week.* Stories of the rich and famous fascinate many readers. The rich and famous in the United States include a select group of top corporate executives, athletes, entertainers, artists, and professionals.

The various breaks between the seven social classes are the results of analysis of pay for different kinds of work and lifestyle opportunities available through different levels of income. The percentage of members of American society in each social class, again, are approximations using widely available data from the U.S. Bureau of the Census and other reports that identify percentages of the population and income data for various purposes.

Using IRS data, the Tax Foundation of Washington, DC, found that the top 5 percent of all taxpayers had an adjusted gross income (AGI) above $101,202, the top 10 percent of taxpayers had AGIs above $74,978, whereas the top 25 percent of all taxpayers had an AGI of at least $45,833. It must be recognized that the income levels of a family of four as presented in Figure 1–1 are gross income dollars before taking any

---

[1]*The NAR Home Buyers and Sellers Report* (Washington, DC: National Association of Realtors®), pp. 25, 39.

kind of income tax-related deductions. However, a comparison of the Tax Foundation cutoff dollar incomes support this model.[2]

The U.S. Census Bureau compiles income data by quintiles (20th percentiles). This provides a barrier in relating Census Bureau data to the seven-class social structure presented here. Even with this difference, the Census Bureau data do provide some interesting comparisons. For example, in 1997, the median family income for a family of four was $44,508 (toward the middle of lower-middle class). The census "low" income category (bottom 20th percentile) was for families with an income below $18,576 (middle of working poor class). Using data calculated by the Institute on Taxation and Economic Policy, the Citizens for Tax Justice claimed that in 1999, the average family income for the lowest 20 percent was $8,410, and for the second 20 percent, $18,340. The "high" income category (top 20th percentile) was for families with an average income of $138,850. The top 1 percent had an average income of $833,240. This 1999 report noted that changes in income distribution from 1992 to 1999 were marked by an increase in overall inequality.[3] Ever-increasing inequality in income distribution among social classes continues to be a major social and political issue in the United States.

Lifestyle and Social Class in the United States

To appreciate the importance of employer-provided pay, it is necessary to have an understanding of the lifestyle and standard of living dictated by pay, earnings, and income. A 1989 analysis of a survey of 2,387 men and women age 18 or older noted that stress decreases with age and income. The study found that the lower the income, the higher the stress level. People who seemed to be best off had incomes between $45,000 and $50,000. If this study continues to be valid, the income a decade later should be between $55,000 and $60,000.

The Poverty Class   Those who, unfortunately, are members of the lowest-income group in the United States are not enjoying the "good life" available to the majority. Most of the people in this income group do not have full-time jobs. A large number of the individuals are illiterate and are school dropouts. Housing is a critical problem for this group. It is not unusual for families in this group who have housing to spend from 25 to 50 percent of their income on rent and utilities. Many households are headed by single parents, mostly females. Many of the females are or were teenage mothers, with their only income derived from some welfare program such as Aid to Families with Dependent Children. A 1989 analysis by the U.S. Bureau of the Census indicated that among all American children, 24 percent lived in single-parent homes.

Research by the National Center for Health Statistics indicates that children living in nontraditional families have substantially greater health and emotional problems than those living with both natural parents. Within this segment of the population are the truly impoverished—economically, socially, and intellectually. Here reside many of the hard-core poor. Many of the underclass live in urban ghettos where crime and drug selling are common everyday life activities and drug addiction is rampant. In fact, a major underground economy revolves around some kind of criminal activity such as robbery, stealing, and selling drugs. A 1990 study of drug dealers in Washington, DC,

---

[2]Patrick Fleenor, "Top Five Percent of Taxpayers Pay Over Half of Total Federal Individual Income Taxes," *Tax Foundation Report No. 83,* November 1998.
[3]Robert C. McIntyre, Director, Citizens for Tax Justice, personal communication, May 10, 1999.

revealed that the typical drug dealer is between 18 and 40 years old and nets $29,000 a year tax free. Earnings from legitimate, tax-paying jobs for these individuals average $7 per hour, whereas "moonlighting" drug deals earns them an average $30 an hour.

The Working Poor   One feeble and fragile step away from complete destitution are the working poor. Many of these individuals hold part- and full-time jobs that pay a wage equal or close to the government-established minimum wage. Many of these individuals supplement their income with food stamps. They frequently live in government-subsidized, low-income housing and rely on government-assisted medical services. Few individuals in this group have any kind of estates, and major possessions are a well-used automobile or truck, some furniture, and clothing. A major life-improvement goal for those in this group is to move into the lower-middle class, which is made possible principally through a better job that pays at least a dollar or two per hour over minimum wage to the single person, and four or five dollars more per hour than minimum wage to those maintaining a family.

Lower-Middle Class   Lower-middle class families do not have the luxury of wasting their money. When lower-middle class individuals spend their earnings on frivolous pastimes, they are only one short step away from returning to the lower-income class. A family of four earning from $30,000 to $50,000 a year can afford to buy their own house and have their two cars (purchased used), but they are usually deeply in debt. Their mortgage payments and utility bills could consume as much as 40 percent of their income. They have little to no savings and any kind of financial problem can be disastrous. A major financial problem is job loss. Without the earnings coming from one of the jobs, a two-wage earner, four-member family can become destitute quickly. Even with the extra earnings of the second wage earner, the Bureau of Labor Statistics noted that child care and other work-related expenses consumed 20 to 30 percent of the extra income.

In 1992, the U.S. Congress expanded federal grants to U.S. students who needed money for a college education. The family income limit was raised from $30,000 to $42,000 (an income level that would include most lower-middle class families).[4]

Middle-Middle Class   When people talk about middle class in the United States, they are usually referring to those in this group. Once family income exceeds $45,000 to $50,000, the payment of monthly bills does not require extensive manipulation of the family's financial resources. House mortgage payments and utility bills will consume about 14 percent of their family income. The median price of a house in the United States in July 1998 was $133,800. Making a 10 percent down payment and carrying a monthly principal and interest payment of approximately $1000 is not a hardship.

At middle-middle class, a little reserve fuel for rainy days begins to develop. Individuals in this class can begin purchasing extras that make life so enjoyable. A new car every four or five years is possible and no longer a dream. A week or two vacation for the entire family is something to look forward to. Money to pay for some fashionable clothes is available without cutting back on some other essentials. At middle-middle class, children can expect to go to college and have to be neither a top-of-the-line athlete nor in the top 5 percent of the achievement test scores nor a straight-A student. However, even when entering the desired grounds of middle-middle class, job-based income is critical. If anything happens to eliminate the income of the major wage

---

[4]"Student Aid," *Miami Herald*, February 22, 1992, p. 6A.

earner or even one of the wage earners, lifestyle can revert to lower-middle class or even lower-income class. In middle-middle class as well as within those classes lower on the income ladder, a drug habit can quickly make a family destitute or involve members in criminal activities. When this situation arises, chances of jail sentences, injury, and homelessness increase significantly.

Upper-Middle Class   There are some who feel that families of four with annual incomes in excess of $90,000 per year are wealthy. It is easy to see why someone living in a low-income housing unit would feel this way. Those having an annual income in excess of $90,000 can afford the comfortable home in the suburbs, which in the United States has a median price of $176,000, or a house in a well-kept, secure section of the city. Financial investments become of significant concern to these members of society. Ski trips, beach vacations in the tropics, and tours to Europe become part of the lifestyle. Upper-middle class parents no longer worry about finding affordable day care for their preschool children; rather, they worry about the qualifications of their prospective nannies and how to retain them after they have been hired. Options develop regarding elementary and secondary education. Public schools are no longer the sole option. Expensive private schools are a possibility. House furnishings and clothing begin to have the feel of luxury.

The good life of the upper-middle class is made possible through earning $90,000+ a year. Although job security is not an absolute requirement, because individuals holding these kinds of jobs are usually able to find other high-paying jobs, the pay in the new job may not be as high as that in the previous job. A loss of job or change in job may reduce the family to middle-middle class status. From an outsider's perspective, this may not be as dramatic as returning to lower-income class from lower-middle or middle-middle class because of loss of job income, but to those enjoying the fruits of upper-middle class, it can be quite traumatic. The popular book, *The Millionaire Next Door,* by Thomas J. Stanley and William D. Danko, is truly about people occupying the upper-middle class of society in the United States.

The Wealthy   Not too many years ago, very few individuals and an extremely small percentage of families had annual earnings of between $250,000 and $1 million. The numbers and percentages are still very small, but they are growing. Many of those occupying the top five to ten positions in American corporations now have annual earnings well in excess of $250,000. Owners of closely-held small businesses (annual revenue between $1.0 million to $100.0 million) of the 10 highest-paying industries among 35 industrial groups received $202,000 in 1988. The overall median total compensation for executives in these 35 industries was $151,000. Successful professionals (attorneys, physicians, dentists, consultants), entertainers (actors, artists, athletes, authors and writers, models, musicians), and sales personnel can expect an annual income greater than $250,000. With income at this level, most individuals can develop savings and investments that will ensure them the good life for the remainder of their lives. Five to 10 years of earnings at this level can provide protection from loss of job. There is little that life offers that those in this income class cannot afford. Individuals with incomes of greater than $250,000 a year can quickly become millionaires. In the decades of the 1980s and 1990s, it has been estimated that more than 100,000 Americans became millionaires each year.

For the wealthy, a second, or even third, home in exclusive vacation areas is easily affordable. Pursuit of distinctive household furnishings is commonplace. Eye-catching designer clothing and sleek, high-performance automobiles help identify a member's place in the social order. In this social class, it is possible to spend 25 percent of income on leisure activities. Luxury for the wealthy is the way of life.

The Ultrarich   Not a week goes by that the daily news does not inform the world of the pay of the rich and famous. In 1998, the wealthiest person in the United States was William Gates, founder and chairman of Microsoft. In 1986, Lee Iacocca made the headlines with his $41.6 million in pay and stock options; in 1987, Michael Milken made the front page with his half a billion dollars in earnings, and, in 1998, Michael Eisner, CEO of Disney, received a salary and short-term bonus of $5.7 million and exercised stock options worth $569.8 million. The billions accumulated by the late Arkansas merchant, Sam Walton, were well noted each year in *Forbes* magazine. The many entertainers who annually earn more than $1 million receive daily recognition. The executive compensation consulting firm of Pearl Meyer & Partners, Inc. noted that in 1995 the average compensation that included salary, bonus, restricted stock options, and stock grants valued at the time of the grants, plus other long-term payoffs for 30 highly paid CEOs was $4,367,000. From a review of 350 of the nation's largest businesses, William M. Mercer, Inc. reported that the median salary and bonus of CEOs was $1,432,000.[5]

Fortune magazine stated that the top 1 percent of wage earners had pretax incomes for a family of four starting at $350,000. It noted that percentage by occupation in 1991 of the top 1 percent wage earners were corporate executives (31 percent), business owners (18 percent), attorneys (13 percent), doctors and dentists (15 percent), and others such as sports stars, actors, and consultants (23 percent).[6]

Developing an appreciation of lifestyle opportunities further emphasizes the importance of pay and compensation practices in the United States. Because job-related earnings can affect every part of the lifestyle of the wage earners and their families, it becomes readily apparent that pay has both an economic and emotional impact on the wage earner.

Two-Wage-Earner Family

Historically, adult female members of families in the lower class of society performed some kind of work activities in addition to raising the family and performing household duties. During World War II, however, a major change began to develop in the work pattern of families in the United States. As many male members of the workforce joined the military and marched off to war, females who normally would have been housewives staying at home and raising a family joined the workforce to provide the goods and services necessary for a rapidly escalating war machine. By the 1950s, large numbers of females in middle-class households were searching for and accepting permanent employment. Most of these women continued to have children and primary responsibility for family maintenance. The job-related earnings provided the income necessary to move from the working-poor class to lower-middle class, and from lower-middle class to middle-middle, even upper-middle class. The desire to enjoy the lifestyle

[5]Joann S. Lublin, "The Great Divide," *The Wall Street Journal,* April 11, 1996, pp. R1, R4.
[6]Anne B. Fisher, "The New Debate Over the Very Rich," *Fortune,* June 29, 1992, pp. 42–44, 46, 50, 54.

of the middle-middle and upper-middle class became a primary motivator of increasing importance for the two-wage-earner family. The median family earnings of a two-wage-earner family in 1997 was $53,361.[7]

The social and family costs related to the two-wage-earner family are significant. Both the male and female wage earners have to make major adjustments among their work, family, and recreational activities. In addition, these efforts for an improved lifestyle make these wage earners more critically analyze their job opportunities and the pay and compensation they receive from the work they do. These interests and concerns about pay and job opportunities place additional burdens on compensation managers for developing pay systems that treat all employees in an equitable manner. It also requires ever-improving communications between employers, their compensation representatives, and employees regarding all aspects of the compensation system of the organization.

Workforce Demographics

As of December 1998, the following statistics provide a picture of the workforce as it presently exists.[8]

	In Millions
Population of the United States	272.2
Noninstitutionalized Population (16 years and over)	206.3
Civilian Employment	138.5
Unemployed Persons	6.0
Labor Force in Nonagricultural Industries	129.3
Full-Time Employed	109.5
Part-Time Employed	23.3
Employed Husbands	43.2
Employed Wives	33.1
Union Members	13.9
Employed Managerial and Professional Specialty	38.9

The future picture for the United States and its workforce for the first decade of the twenty-first century is now established. Two-wage-earner families have become even more commonplace. Sixty-one percent of working-age women hold jobs, 47 percent of the workforce are female, 61 percent of working women are mothers, and 53 percent of these working mothers have children under 8 years of age. Pressure to raise a family and be productive has increased stress on both employers and employees. Although minimally skilled unemployed workers are available, organizations are constantly searching for skilled and dedicated workers who will be able to perform assignments in knowledge-oriented, service-providing jobs. Many of the most highly trained and dedicated members of the organization are those who want to raise a family. These individuals with joint allegiance to family and employer will need the income

---

[7]U.S. Department of Commerce, Bureau of Economic and Statistical Analysis, *Statistical Abstract of the United States, 1998* (Washington, DC: U.S. Government Printing Office, 1998), p. 474.
[8]*Employment and Earnings* (Washington, DC: USDOL, Bureau of Labor Statistics, January 1999), Tables A-1, A-6, A-7, 10, 40.

from their jobs to survive, let alone enjoy some of the extra things that make life in the United States enjoyable.

See discussion of Economic Theories—appendix 3A in chapter 3 for historical analysis of the development of social classes.

Summary

To survive and be successful in a global economy, an organization must be competitive. A major factor underlying organizational competitiveness is labor cost. Not only must an organization pay its workforce a competitive wage within its geographic region, but also it must vary the kinds and amounts of rewards offered, recognizing differences in individual contributions. A major difference in individual contributions relates to the knowledge and skills the employee brings to the workplace and the interest, effort, and innovative qualities the employee provides in completing work assignments. The pay and reward system of the organization must stimulate acceptable levels of performance from all employees. Money is the name of the game, but the distribution of organizational funds determines who wins the game.

Review Questions

1. What is the relationship among money, labor costs, profitability, and knowledge in the modern democratic-capitalistic society?
2. Briefly describe the three major classes of society and their seven subsets.
3. What is the greatest force for the continuation of poverty in the current democratic-capitalistic society?
4. Will the two-wage-earner family become more or less important in the future?

CHAPTER

The Reward System

Compensation and Noncompensation Dimensions

Learning Objectives

In this chapter you will learn about:

1. Opportunities available to employers to stimulate the productive efforts of each employee.

2. The dimensions of a compensation system.

3. The dimensions of a noncompensation system.

4. The need to skillfully combine the compensation and noncompensation dimensions into an effective reward system.

Compensation Strategy

Recognize and group compensation components so that they influence employee motivation in a positive manner and lead to improved organizational performance and profitability.

People gain satisfaction from their work, but the kinds and the strengths of satisfaction have been difficult to identify, define, and measure with any degree of precision. Furthermore, the individual performer may attain one set of satisfactions from work efforts, whereas the group with which the same individual identifies attains another. Meanwhile, as the individual and the group coordinate their needs and efforts, a third set of satisfactions develops. These satisfactions are those gained by the leaders or employers of the group—those who both receive and offer some form of reward for the services provided by the individual and the group.

This book focuses on the rewards members of an organization receive from their employers. Specifically, it focuses on monetary rewards paid either directly (base pay or cash incentives) or indirectly (employee benefits paid for by an employer). These rewards may be paid in the short term (within one year) or in the long term (beyond one year). Employers use their reward systems to attract and retain those who not only have the desired knowledge and skills, but also have the interest and are willing to put forth the effort needed to link their knowledge and skills to the accomplishment of organizational goals and objectives.

THE REWARD SYSTEM

An organization is formed to accomplish a specific mission. To do this, it must attract and hire people who have certain knowledge, skills, aptitudes, and attitudes. To attract and retain such people, the organization provides rewards. An organization designs and implements a reward system to focus worker attention on the specific behaviors the organization considers necessary to achieve its desired objectives and goals. The behaviors range from simply arriving at work at the scheduled time to meeting specified performance standards and providing innovative contributions that lead to improved productivity. If rewards are to be useful in stimulating desired behaviors, they must meet the demands of the employees whose behaviors they are intended to influence.

Understanding how rewards affect motivation or modify behavior has been the aim of behavioral scientists. Motivational theorists have been most successful when designing models that explain behavior in general. They have been far less successful in developing models that predict the behavior of a specific individual. One great difficulty they face is that the value an individual attaches to a specific reward or reward package may vary significantly over time, and the time span need not be too long. Furthermore, the worth of a reward is greatly affected by any factor that influences the lifestyle of an individual. Because of the almost endless variety of human qualities, workplace requirements, and situational demands, the task of designing and managing a reward system so that it will benefit the organization is a difficult and complex undertaking.

The reward system of an organization includes anything that an employee may value and desire and that the employer is able or willing to offer in exchange for employee contributions. A rather broad classification scheme that facilitates the identification of the various kinds and qualities of rewards provided by employers is to separate the *compensation* components from the *noncompensation* components. That is to say, all rewards that can be classified as monetary payments and in-kind payments constitute the *compensation system* of an organization. Monetary payments can be in the form of coins or paper money, or in the less tangible form of checks or credit cards. They have value in use and they simplify exchange transactions. In-kind payments are goods or services that are used in lieu of money and that provide an equivalent value for what has been offered or received. All other rewards constitute the *noncompensation system*.

COMPENSATION SYSTEM

The compensation system results from the allocation, conversion, and transfer of a portion of the income of an organization to its employees for their monetary and in-kind claims on goods and services.

Monetary claims on goods and services are wages or salaries paid to an employee in the form of money, or a form that is quickly and easily transferable to money at the discretion of the employee. As a medium of exchange, money enables an employee to purchase certain kinds and amounts of a wide variety of goods and services available in the marketplace. The actual kinds and quantity of purchases made depend on the individual mechanisms that motivate choice behavior. Wages and salaries in the form of money may be further subdivided into payments earned and acquired at the present time and payments earned but not acquired until some future time—deferred payments.

In-kind claims are claims on goods and services made available and paid for either totally or in some percentage by the employer. Employees often have little or no opportunity for immediate monetary gain from an in-kind payment. Many employer-provided in-kind payments, however, replace monetary payments of some amount of the employees' income should the employees obtain similar goods and services elsewhere. Organizations purchase these required and usually desired goods and services for their members to take advantage of (1) economies of scale available through group purchasing, (2) the benefits available through tax laws and regulations, and (3) government laws requiring certain services.

The value of any in-kind payment to a specific employee depends directly on the employee's perception of its worth. Individual perception relates to a range of demographic characteristics (age, gender, marital status, education, number and age of dependents, length of service, level in the organization, current wealth, other income), as well as to the physical and emotional state of the employee.

The total compensation package may be described in many ways, but the classification scheme used in this book is based on eight dimensions. Each dimension has a number of compensation components. Each component has a variety of features. Because of different features, one component may relate to more than one dimension. The structuring of features, components, and dimensions into a compensation system is a job for the compensation specialist. Figure 2–1 models the eight dimensions of a compensation system.

This book will discuss in detail the processes and practices related to the first compensation dimension, which provides for current spendable income. The other seven di-

FIGURE 2–1 Dimensions of a Compensation System

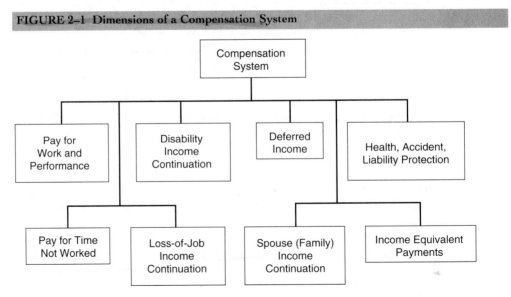

mensions will be discussed briefly. An analysis of each compensation dimension must include a discussion of the many components in that dimension. Table 2–1 presents a list of the major compensation components included within each dimension. Of course, this list can be expanded as innovative reward system designers and employees with insatiable reward appetites identify new and more desirable compensation components that will promote or stimulate acceptable and desired workplace behaviors. Changes in legislation and court rulings will also influence the design of compensation programs.

COMPENSATION DIMENSIONS

A brief description of the eight compensation dimensions and some of their components may help the reader to understand and appreciate the complexity of a compensation system in a modern organization.

Pay for Work and Performance Pay for work and performance includes money that is provided in the short term (weekly, monthly, and annual bonuses/awards) and that permits employees to pay for and contract for the payment of desired goods and services. The amount of money payments provided to employees normally depends on specified job requirements; outputs that meet or exceed quantity, quality, or timeliness standards; innovations that may lead to improved productivity; dependability; loyalty; and some combination of these items. Typical components within this dimension are base pay, premiums and differentials, short-term bonuses, merit pay, and certain allowances.

Pay for Time Not Worked Over the years, there has been a decrease in hours worked per week and the number of days worked per year. During the past 40 years, workers have enjoyed more days off with pay for holidays, longer paid vacations, and paid time off for a wide variety of personal reasons. These components of pay for time not worked significantly increase labor costs and also enhance quality-of-work-life opportunities for most employees.

Loss-of-Job Income Continuation Job security is and always has been the primary consideration for most workers. They want assurance that their jobs and the income derived from working will continue until they are ready to retire. Workers also know that few jobs are guaranteed to continue to retirement. Not only may accident and sickness problems occur, but personal performance or interpersonal dynamics problems may cause temporary layoff or termination of employment. Changes in economic conditions and technology may restrict or even eliminate the need or demand for the product of the employer, resulting in the decline or demise of the firm. A variety of components such as unemployment insurance, supplemental unemployment benefits (SUBs), and severance pay help unemployed workers to subsist until new employment opportunities arise.

Disability Income Continuation The possibility always exists that a worker may incur health or accident disability. Because of these disabilities, employees are frequently unable to perform their normal assignments. Even so, individual and family living expenses continue; and medical, hospital, and surgical bills create additional burdens. Social Security, workers' compensation, sick leave, and short- and long-term disability plans are examples of components that provide funds for employees who are unable to work for health-related reasons.

TABLE 2–1 An Outline of Compensation Dimensions and Compensation Components

Pay for Work and Performance	Pay for Time Not Worked	Disability Income Continuation	Loss-of-Job Income Continuation
Base pay	Holidays	Short-term disability, sickness and accident (S & A)	Unemployment insurance
Base pay add-ons	Vacations		
Length of service	Jury duty	Long-term disability (LTD)	Short-time compensation (work-sharing unemployment)
Long service	Election official		
Market adjustment	Witness in court	Workers' compensation	
Cost-of-living adjustment	Military duty	Supplemental workers' compensation	Supplemental unemployment benefit insurance (SUB)
Geographic differentials	Funeral leave		
Overtime premiums	Paternity leave	Social Security	
Shift differentials	Maternity leave	State temporary disability	
Rotating work schedules	Sick leave	Nonoccupational disability	Guaranteed annual income
Weekend premiums	Wellness leave	Travel accident insurance	
Holiday premiums	Time off to vote	Sick leave	Severance pay (golden, tin, silver, platinum parachutes)
Reporting pay	Blood donation	Supplemental disability insurance	
Call-back pay	Grievance and contract negotiation		
Standby or idle-time pay		Accidental death and dismemberment	
Cleanup and clothes change pay	Lunch and rest periods		Job contract
Dangerous and distressing assignments	Personal leave	Group life insurance	Individual account plan
Isolation	Earned time off	Total permanent disability (TPD)	
Pay for results (short term)	Family illness leave		Trade adjustment assistance
Merit pay adjustment	Tool reimbursement/ allowance	Disability features within various kinds of retirement plans	
Short-term performance awards			Underemployment benefits
Front-end bonus	Relocation expenses		
Professional achievement pay	Health (stay-well) payments		
Skill pay			
Proficiency pay			
Educational incentive pay (tuition reimbursement)			
Safety pay			
Suggestion awards			
Patent awards			
Salary advance payments			
Travel expenses			
Car reimbursement			
Tolls and parking			
Food and entertainment reimbursement			
Clothing reimbursement/ allowance			

Components and component features will differ for the following groups of employees:

Exempt

  Executives   } Senior management
  Senior managers

  Top-level operating managers
  Mid-level operating managers   } Operating management
  Lower-level operating managers

  Professionals
  Administrators
  Sales personnel

Nonexempt

  Salaried   *Regular*   *Temporary*
  Hourly (nonunion)   Full-time   Full-time
  Hourly (union)   Part-time   Part-time

Special Groups

  Employees in foreign work sites
  Board of directors

Deferred Income	Spouse (Family) Income Continuation	Health, Accident, Liability Protection	Income Equivalent Payments	
Social Security	Pension plan	Medical, hospital, and surgical insurance (self and dependents)	**Tax free**	**Tax favored**
Pension plans	Social Security		Charitable contributions	Medical expense reimbursement
Profit sharing (long term)	Life insurance		Giving of gift (less than $25)	Chauffeur-driven car/ bodyguard
Savings and thrift plans	Workers' compensation	Major medical	EAP (employee assistance programs)	Company car, plane, yacht
Keogh plans	Group life insurance	Health maintenance organization (HMO)	Counseling	
Individual retirement accounts (IRAs and SEPs)	Total and permanent disability		Financial	Company-provided facilities and diversions
			Legal	
			Psychiatric/psychological	
			Outplacement	
Stock purchase plans	Features within various kinds of retirement plans	Postretirement medical plan	Retirement	Personal use of credit cards
Stock option plans		Postretirement physical	Family	
Stock grants			Tax preparation	Vacation accommodations
Phantom stock plans	Travel-accident insurance	Hospital services	Child adoption	
Tax-sheltered annuities		Comprehensive health plan	Child/dependent care/elderly care	Special loan arrangements (no interest and low interest)
Tax-sheltered purchases	Funeral arrangements		Subsidized food service	
Investment trusts			Discounts or no cost on merchandise	
Supplemental income plans	Postretirement life insurance	Social Security (Medicare)	Physical awareness and fitness programs	Club membership Athletic club Country club Luncheon club
Supplemental executive retirement plans (SERPs)		Workers' compensation	Athletic leagues	
		Dental	Parking	
Long-term performance awards		Vision care	Transportation to and from work (commuting assistance)	
		Hearing aid	Fly first class	
Job contracts (employment contracts)		Prescription drugs	Professional licenses and certificates	
		In-house medical services	Professional memberships	
Zero net worth limited partnerships		Visiting nurse	Professional meetings	
			Professional journals and newspapers	
Postretirement consulting contract		Group legal	Special moving and relocation allowances	
		Group automobile		
Annuities (insurance based)		Group house	Pay for spouse on business trips	
		Group umbrella liability	Home utility allowance	
401(k) "Salary reduction plan"			Home entertainment allowance	
		Employee liability	Home office equipment	
403(b) Nonprofit organization		Fidelity bond insurance	Home servants allowance (domestic staff)	
Postretirement income adjustment		Hospice services (long-term care)	Season tickets to entertainment events	
		Travel insurance	Use of assistant for personal services	
			Kidnap/ransom protection	
			Security escort service	
			Mobile phone (cellular or car telephone)	
			Executive dining room	

Deferred Income   Most employees depend on some kind of employer-provided program for income continuation after retirement. There are two basic reasons for these programs. First of all, most employees do not have sufficient savings at retirement to continue the lifestyles they enjoyed while working. Various kinds of programs, such as Social Security, employer-provided pension plans, savings and thrift plans, annuities, and supplemental income plans provide income after retirement. Second, tax laws and regulations make deferred income plans more appealing to many employees. Because of tax regulations, employers can often take immediate deductions and employees can defer tax obligations until income tax rates are possibly more favorable. In addition, funds invested in many of these deferred plans draw tax-free interest, significantly increasing the amount of money available upon retirement. Stock purchase, option, and grant plans are components commonly used to achieve tax deduction, estate building, and deferral goals.

Spouse (Family) Income Continuation   Most employees with family obligations are concerned with what may happen if they are no longer able to provide money that will allow their families to maintain a particular standard of living. Certain plans are designed to provide dependents with income when an employee dies or is unable to work because of total and permanent disability. Specific features within life insurance plans, pension plans, Social Security, workers' compensation, and other related plans provide income for the families of employees when these conditions arise.

Health, Accident, and Liability Protection   When a health problem occurs, employees must be concerned not only with income continuation, but also with payment for the goods and services required in overcoming the illness or disability. Organizations provide a wide variety of insurance plans to assist in paying for these goods and services. In recent years, the cost of medical-related goods and services has increased at a greater rate than almost any other good or service desired or required by employees. Medical, hospital, and surgical insurance plans and major medical, dental, and vision insurance are only a few of the numerous compensation components designed to provide such protection for workers.

Because of savings available through group purchasing, organizations are now providing various kinds of liability-related insurance plans for their employees. These plans include group legal, group automobile, group umbrella liability, employee liability, and other insurance plans.

Income Equivalent Payments   A final set of compensation components may be grouped under the title of income equivalent payments. Many of these components are frequently called perquisites or "perks." Employees usually find them highly desirable, and both employers and employees find certain tax benefits in them. Some perks are tax free to employees and tax deductible to employers. In recent years, the Internal Revenue Service (IRS) has required that employer costs for a specific portion of certain perks be considered earned income to employees. In most cases where this occurs, the earned income charge to employees is significantly less than the amount an employee would have been required to pay if he or she had purchased the good or service in the marketplace. Some of the more desirable perks are the use of a company car or a company credit card, payment for expenses to professional meetings, subsidized food services, and child care services.

NONCOMPENSATION SYSTEM

The other major part of the reward system consists of noncompensation rewards. These rewards are much more difficult to classify and their components far more complex than is the case for compensation rewards and components. Noncompensation rewards are all the situation-related rewards not included in the compensation package. These rewards have an almost infinite number of components that relate to the work situation and to the physical and psychological well-being of each worker. In fact, any activity that has an impact on the intellectual, emotional, and physical well-being of the employee and is not specifically covered by the compensation system is part of the noncompensation reward system. Figure 2–2 models the noncompensation system.

The noncompensation system contains many of the reward components that behavioral scientists have been describing for the past 50 years as critical for improving workplace performance. An in-depth analysis of the seven noncompensation dimensions identified in Figure 2–2 reveals a close interrelation between compensation and noncompensation rewards. The line between these two major reward categories may at first glance appear to be sharply defined, but it soon blurs as they interact and blend together.

Enhance Dignity and Satisfaction from Work Performed   Possibly the least costly and one of the most powerful rewards an organization can offer to an employee is to recognize the person as a useful and valuable contributor. This kind of recognition leads to employee feelings of self-worth and pride in making a contribution. Few people want to be simply given something. They would much prefer to know that through their own efforts they have earned and deserved rewards. Every compensation and

FIGURE 2–2 Dimensions of a Noncompensation System

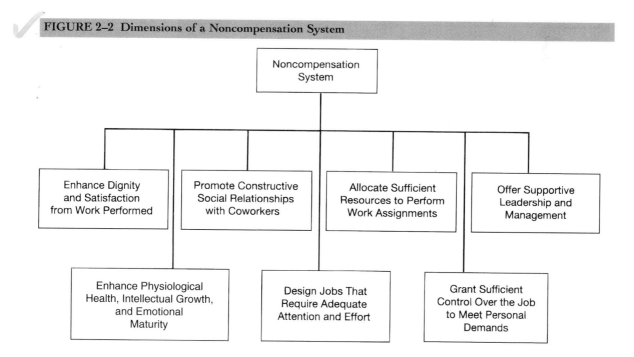

noncompensation reward component should carry with it the message, "We need you and appreciate your efforts."

Enhance Physiological Health, Intellectual Growth, and Emotional Maturity   Considering the number of hours a person spends on the job, on travel to and from the work site, and off the job in attempting to resolve job-related problems, work obviously has a great effect on the health of employees. Health-related problems frequently receive minimal attention until a serious problem occurs. Once this happens, however, it overrides all other employee concerns and activities. Modern health practices recognize the direct relationship between the physiological health and intellectual and emotional well-being of each individual.

A safe working environment has always been a thorny issue between employers and employees. Provision of safe equipment; a work environment that is as risk free as possible; minimization of noxious fumes; avoidance of extreme heat, cold, and humidity conditions; and elimination of contact with radiation, carcinogens, and other disease-related materials and substances—these conditions are expected by all employees. The clean workstation, the cheerfully decorated walls and floors, and the reduction of noise to a tolerable level all provide an enjoyable work environment that enhances employee health.

As important as these physical conditions are, more and more attention is being focused on the emotional strains that result from the extreme specialization of work assignments and the complex interactions caused by this specialization. Additional stress is caused by technological advancements that require rapid changes in the knowledge and skills of workers. Demands for a greater share of the limited resources of both organizations and society as a whole result in further disharmonies that cause additional psychological and emotional problems for workers.

Although these universal problems are almost impossible to overcome, management can recognize their existence and can take action to limit their negative influence on the performance of each employee. Letting employees know what the organization can provide to help them maintain a secure and stable lifestyle will help minimize job-induced stress. Training employees to perform current jobs in an acceptable manner and offering development opportunities that will help employees attain their potential are noncompensation components that can influence this health-related dimension in a positive manner.

Promote Constructive Social Relationships with Coworkers   An old adage states that "One man is no man." Although there are constant reminders of what one dedicated person can achieve, there are even more reminders that one human alone is weak. However, with concerted action, people can accomplish almost anything. In this world of extreme specialization, people need and rely on other people more than ever. One of the most valued rewards gained from working is the opportunity to interact in a socially constructive manner with other people—to enjoy the comradeship of workplace associates.

The chance to communicate and interact with others is another inexpensive but valuable reward. A workplace environment where trust, fellowship, loyalty, and love emanate from the top level of management to the lowest levels of the organization promotes the kinds of social interaction most people need in order to thrive. All parts of the reward system can enhance the establishment of a trusting workplace environment; or they can provide barriers where suspicion, jealousy, and intrigue can destroy any opportunity to productivity-promoting social relationships. The move toward team-based operations is an example of what organizations are doing to improve social interactions among employees.

Design Jobs That Require Adequate Attention and Effort Over the past 40 years, organizational scientists have discussed at length the problems arising from boredom related to work. Specific attention has been focused on "scientific management" efforts to specialize work assignments that were developed in the last quarter of the nineteenth century. Jobs were designed so that workers could quickly be taught how to perform a few highly repetitive tasks. Workers were then required to perform these few tasks for as long as they remained on the job. What first appeared to be an efficient way of melding human resources with machine technology proved to have serious drawbacks.

Many employees soon became bored and dissatisfied. Work-related anxieties and frustration produced employee behavior that led to declining performance. Employee turnover, absenteeism, tardiness, minimal concern for quality or productivity, waste of physical resources, and even theft and malicious damage were behaviors attributed to unacceptable workplace and job design.

Recognizing these problems, behavioral scientists and managers at all levels have been searching for and implementing new approaches to improve the quality-of-work-life. On both an individual and team or group basis, employees are being given more opportunity to have a voice in how their jobs should be performed. Restructuring of job tasks and job responsibilities is receiving top attention. Flexibility in job requirements is being provided by rotating work assignments and by giving employees more opportunity to schedule workdays and workweeks. Managers are being taught to instruct workers to do their jobs and then to leave them alone to perform their assignments in their own ways. This does not mean that managers must abdicate supervisory responsibilities. Rather, they must learn to recognize when to provide needed support, when to tell employees what they are doing right, and when to assist them in correcting their errors.

Allocate Sufficient Resources to Perform Work Assignments Requiring employees to perform assignments for which they have neither the knowledge nor the skills opens the door for problems. Not only is the organization likely to suffer because of outcome failures, but employee job-related interest and satisfaction are apt to break down because of the likelihood or inevitability of failure. Most employees seek a sense of accomplishment from their work. They want some degree of challenge, but they also want to feel reasonably sure that they can succeed.

In addition, when employees are told they must produce certain kinds and quantities of output within a specified time, they want to know that resources are available to help them meet these demands. Possibly the most critical resource is sufficient time available to accomplish an assignment. Does the employee have the time to perform the assignment? Are other assignments making demands on the employee's time that preclude or jeopardize successful job performance? Has the organization assisted or enabled the employee to gain the knowledge and skill necessary to perform the assignment? Are the necessary human, technical, or physical resources available to support and aid the employee in accomplishing the assignment? These and many other questions must be answered by supervisors as they analyze assignments and review performance.

To make work a satisfying, even exhilarating experience, employees must not be placed in a no-win situation. This doesn't mean that an employee should not be expected to stretch and put forth sufficient effort to meet workplace obligations. It does mean, however, that with the proper interested effort, success is likely. The organization must do everything possible to assist the employee in completing missions successfully.

Grant Sufficient Control Over the Job to Meet Personal Demands   From the 1950s to the present time, behavioral scientists have discussed the need to grant employees greater opportunity to participate in organizational decision-making processes. One problem with this participation concept is that organizations are composed of all kinds of people with all kinds of decision-making desires. Some people simply want to be told what to do, to be shown what is an acceptable level of performance, and then to be left alone to do their jobs. A few people in every organization want to tell top management how to run the organization. Between these two extremes is a wide variety of demands for a greater voice in determining how to perform assignments.

One of the most important decisions being made by more and more workers is that of scheduling work activities and, in some cases, of choosing the location of assignments. Over the past two decades, flexible work schedules have been implemented that range from compressed workweeks (for example, 4-day, 40-hour schedules) to the flex-time programs in which workers can work a 7½- to 8-hour day within a 12- to 14-hour interval. With the advent of the personal computer and networking, more employees are allowed to work at home or at a worksite of their choice.

Another advancement in this area allows two part-time employees to share one full-time job. Each of the two may work only 15 to 25 hours per week, but together they share and perform all job responsibilities. Like many other noncompensation rewards, the benefits gained by granting such scheduling privileges frequently outweigh the costs of having an additional employee on the payroll.

Another change to make life easier is the casual dress day. With this option, employees are granted the opportunity to "dress down" or wear clothing of a more relaxed or casual style. In most cases, the organization provides guidelines regarding clothing to be worn.

Offer Supportive Leadership and Management   This dimension is difficult to separate from all other noncompensation rewards, but it is so important that it must be recognized as a unique dimension of the noncompensation rewards and not just a component of the other factors.

Practically all people look to certain individuals for guidance and support. They have a need to recognize and respect those who can help them achieve goals. They look to managers who have influence and can bring about desired changes. Followers must have faith in and abide by the actions taken by their leaders, and the leaders must heed the requests of their followers.

Employee faith and trust in management assist in establishing a workplace environment where job security becomes accepted, where social interaction thrives, and where work satisfaction is possible. Supportive leadership is demonstrated in many ways: skill and interest in coaching and counseling; praise for a job well done; and constructive feedback leading to improvement of job performance. Leaders must be sufficiently flexible with policies, rules, and regulations so that an employee can meet both job and nonjob responsibilities without infringing on the rights and the opportunities of other employees. The selection, training, and promotion of individuals who will later become effective leaders and managers are the cost components of this dimension. Here again, the costs are minimal compared to the benefits.

Summary

As Albert Camus, the French philosopher, stated: "Without work all life goes rotten. But when work is soulless life stifles and dies." For the great majority of people, work is a necessity. As the result of working, people obtain compensation rewards that provide money to purchase a wide variety of goods and services or receive in-kind payments of goods and services that would have required the expenditure of money had they not been provided by the employer. Noncompensation rewards are almost infinite in variety. These rewards satisfy both emotional and intellectual demands. They make people feel good about themselves, permit them to make full use of their talents, and promote interactions with others in a supportive manner.

Through work, employees have the opportunity to improve their lifestyles. The analysis of lifestyle demands and the opportunity for maintaining a current lifestyle and improving it in the future underscore the importance of job-earned compensation. It is no wonder that a major union leader made this statement: "A job is a job; if you don't pay enough, it is a lousy job." Or that another union leader has stated, "The most sensitive artery in the human body is the one going from the heart to the pocketbook."

Review Questions

1. Why should managers be concerned about developing a reward system?
2. What is the reward system of an organization?
3. What is meant by *compensation*?
4. Distinguish between monetary and in-kind payments.
5. Describe the relationship between the compensation and noncompensation subsystems of the reward system.

CHAPTER

The World of Pay and Compensation

Learning Objectives

In this chapter you will learn about:

1. The major components of a compensation program.

2. The variations in base rates of pay for employees performing different assignments within an organization.

3. Factors that influence differences in rates of pay for people doing similar work in different organizations.

4. The increasing importance of different rates of pay within a global economy.

Compensation Strategy

Identify forces that influence compensation practices and promote hiring and retention of a productive workforce.

Prior to the computerization and robotization of manufacturing, the allocation of 40 percent of revenues for labor costs was a good ballpark figure. This meant that for each dollar of revenues generated by a manufacturing company, 40 cents went for base pay and benefits for the workforce. With the move toward heavy capital investment for continuing automation and robotization, labor costs in the manufacturing sector of the economy have been declining from the 40 percent figure. However, employment in the manufacturing economy also continues to decline. Today, less than 20 percent of the workforce is involved in manufacturing; more and more people are working in service-related industries and jobs. Over 70 percent of all workers perform what are considered service jobs. Most service-sector organizations are heavily labor intensive, and it is not unusual for service-related companies to spend 40 cents and sometimes as high as 80 cents of each revenue dollar for employee compensation costs.

THE COMPENSATION PROGRAM

To understand something about these labor costs, a good first step is to identify the major parts that can be included within a compensation program—(1) base wages and salaries; (2) wage and salary add-ons; (3) incentive payments, both short and long term; and (4) employee benefits and services.

This four-dimensional model simplifies the eight-dimensional model presented in chapter 2 (see Figure 2–1). These two models provide different ways of viewing compensation. The model in chapter 2 may be more useful from an employee's perspective, whereas this model is more useful from the perspective of an employer.

Base Wages and Salaries   From the perspective of many employees, the most important part of the compensation program involves the determination and administration of base wages and salaries. The lifestyles of the great majority of workers revolve around their paychecks. The after-tax amount on the paycheck determines the kind and quantity of food, clothing, housing, and transportation a worker can afford. Leisure activities are in many ways restricted or defined by the paycheck. These powerful influences on the lifestyle of a wage earner and his or her dependents underscore both the importance of the job and the pay received by an employee for performing the job.

Wage and Salary Add-Ons   For many employers, this is the least critical of the four major components of the compensation system. It includes overtime pay, shift differentials, premium pay for working weekends and holidays, and other add-ons for being on call or for other demands not normally required of workers. In some cases, overtime pay can add 30 to 50 percent to the base pay of an employee. For employees who perform specific jobs in certain kinds of companies, these add-ons are practically permanent, and the employees can depend on receiving them with a high degree of certainty. Chapter 14 covers these add-ons.

Incentive Payments   Possibly the oldest part of the compensation package is payment for a specified output. For hundreds of years, workers in certain kinds of jobs have received a specific amount of money for a prescribed output. Payment for output reached its zenith in the manufacturing world at the end of the nineteenth and into the twentieth century. Many kinds of factory and mill work fitted neatly into pay for output systems. Individual activities could be defined precisely, daily output could be measured, and pay could be tied directly to the measured output.

With the rising dominance of service jobs in the second half of the twentieth century, including the work of clerks, secretaries, repair and service technicians, administrators, professionals, scientists, and managers, both activities and output vary so much from day to day and from person to person that pay for output systems are frequently neither feasible nor practical. There are, however, certain kinds of service jobs in which output can be measured accurately, such as data entry operators or processing clerks in large banks or insurance companies.

Benefits and Services   This part of the compensation package includes time off with pay, pay when employment has been suspended or terminated, pay when unable to work because of accident or sickness, payments for medical protection and attention, retirement pay, pay to dependents upon death of employee, and provision of a wide variety of desirable goods and services ranging from the company car, to cafeteria services, to tuition reimbursement, to child and elderly dependent care, to recreation activities. Although base pay critically influences current lifestyle activities, benefits and services affect both current and future standards of living.

Benefits and services are of rather recent vintage. Following World War II, many compensation enhancements focused on the area of benefits and services. After rather startling increases during the 1970s and into the early 1980s, the costs of benefits and services briefly leveled off at between 36 and 37 percent of base wage or salary, but by the late 1980s and continuing into the 1990s, had risen to 39 percent.[1] The benefits offered by organizations vary widely in kind and amount. Although 39 percent of payroll is an average cost for a benefits package, the amount can vary from less than 20 to over 60 percent, depending on the organization.

During the 1980s and 1990s, many organizations made strong efforts to limit the rising cost of the benefits package. Health care and retirement costs, in particular, have increased much more rapidly than practically any other part of the total compensation package. In 1996, the United States spent $1,035.1 billion on health care.[2] However, by the mid-1990s, health care costs had started to stabilize. Health care costs accounted for $1,086 of the price of the average vehicle made by the Big Three U.S. automakers. Some 44 percent of the beneficiaries of the automakers' health insurance are retirees.[3] Chapters 15 and 17 describe employer-provided long-term benefits in greater detail.

DETERMINING RATES OF PAY

How are decisions made that determine who will be paid $5.15 per hour and who will receive $3 million for a year's work? Why does an organization consider it reasonable to pay an entry-level clerk $12,000 per year, a star salesperson $3,000,000 per year, and its chief executive $9,500,000 per year? Why should the manager of the junk bond operations for an investment banking firm make $20 million a year, or a TV star $35,000 per series episode? Why should a college senior be offered a contract for $8 million to play professional football, or a newly minted 25-year-old graduate of a top law school be given a starting salary of $85,000 a year? Believe it or not, there are rational and logical reasons for these seemingly exorbitant salaries.

The critical or basic reasons underlying the differences in pay and compensation packages for different employees relate to the following correlates or determinants. Each of these correlates is relatively simple and straightforward, but like most factors influencing compensation decisions, their interactions can become difficult to follow and understand.

1. Kinds and levels of required knowledge and skills
2. Kind of business
3. Union–nonunion status
4. Capital- versus labor-intensive
5. Size of business
6. Philosophy of management
7. Total compensation package
8. Geographic location
9. Supply and demand of labor
10. Profitability of the firm
11. Employment stability
12. Gender difference
13. Employee tenure and performance

---

[1] U.S. Chamber of Commerce, *Employee Benefits* 1995 ed., Table 17, p. 38.
[2] U.S. Department of Commerce, Bureau of Economic and Statistical Analysis, *Statistical Abstract of the United States, 1998* (Washington, DC: U.S. Government Printing Office, 1998), no. 165, p. 118.
[3] "Health-Care Costs Add $1,086 to US Car Prices," *The Wall Street Journal,* February 6, 1992, p. B5.

Kinds and Levels of Required Knowledge and Skills

The most important factor influencing the rate of pay of an employee is the kind of job the person performs. In classifying or differentiating jobs for pay purposes, no one single factor carries greater significance than the knowledge and skills required of the jobholder.

The highest-paid jobholders in the United States and, for that matter, throughout the world are those who are successful entertainers (artists, athletes, actors, models, musicians), business leaders (entrepreneurs and top executives), political leaders, professionals, and salespersons. The highly paid people in these fields all have a common skill—the ability to influence others. They have also mastered skills in their particular disciplines or areas of work that have allowed them to reach levels of eminence and, in return, receive exceedingly high rates of pay for what they do.

For the great majority of workers who perform the relatively mundane, everyday tasks that make life acceptable for most people, knowledge and skills are not the only criteria used to determine job rates of pay. Although these factors continue to be important, other factors such as working conditions, effort, and even seniority also affect rates of pay.

Kind of Business

The nature of the business is also a major factor influencing the pay received by a jobholder. For some jobs (especially higher-level jobs), private-sector businesses provide higher rates of pay than those in the public sector. Profit-motive, private-sector organizations pay their leaders far more than nonprofit private-sector organizations. For example, the range of pay from the lowest-paid to the highest-paid member in a religious organization is normally very restricted, except for some televangelists whose pay relates more to entertainment than to religious services. The lowest-paid full-time clerk in a church may receive $11,000 per year, and the highest-paid administrator may receive $110,000, a 10:1 ratio. On the other hand, the lowest-paid clerk for an automobile manufacturer may receive $15,000 per year, whereas the highest-paid executive may receive a salary of $1.5 million, a 100:1 ratio. What this example shows is that rates of pay for lower-level workers do not vary nearly to the degree that rates of pay for top executives vary.

Not only do private-sector–public-sector, profit–nonprofit characteristics influence and vary rates of pay for certain jobs, but so does the nature of the product. Restaurants, lodgings, and retail businesses have a reputation for being low payers for their operative employees. Transportation, mining, and heavy manufacturing provide relatively high rates of pay for nonmanagement workers; textile and apparel manufacturing are low-paying industries. Table 3–1 provides examples of average rates of pay for workers in different kinds of businesses.[4]

Union–Nonunion Status

Approximately 15 percent of all workers in the United States are unionized. Industries with the highest proportion of unionized workers are in the public sector—federal, state, and local governments (42.5 percent), manufacturing (16.8 percent), construction

---

[4]*Employment and Earnings* (Washington, DC: USDOL, Bureau of Labor Statistics, January 1999), Table B-15.

TABLE 3–1 Average Hourly Earnings of Production Workers by Specified Industry, November 1998 (10 lowest and highest paid by two-digit SIC code)

Lowest Paid		*Highest Paid*	
Eating and drinking places	$6.45	Pipeline except natural gas	$20.99
Apparel and accessory stores	8.54	Petroleum and coal products	20.90
General merchandise stores	8.55	Electric, gas, and sanitary services	20.43
Apparel and other textile products	8.63	Coal mining	19.26
Food stores	9.19	Legal services	18.54
Leather and leather products	9.42	Metal mining	18.46
Miscellaneous retail establishments	9.52	Engineering and management services	18.27
Amusement and recreation services	10.14	Transportation equipment	17.56
Agricultural services	10.18	Services, nec	17.49
Textile mill products	10.49	Communications	17.48

(18.4 percent), and mining (13.4 percent).[5] By 1998, the percentage of unionized members in the private sector had declined to 10.3 percent.

Since the blossoming of unions in the late 1930s, those businesses with the highest rate of unionization have also included some of the highest-paid members of the workforce. In 1982, the United Steelworkers of America (USWA) boasted that its members were the highest-paid industrial workers in the world, earning an average hourly wage of $13.10. In 1982, there were more than 1 million of these highly paid steelworkers; by 1986, the number had dropped to fewer than 700,000, and by 1995, the number was less than 600,000. In 1999, a Job Class 34 steelworker working on an incentive received a standard hourly rate of $18.482 with an incentive calculation rate of $9.868 for a total hourly income of $28.350. Examples of average hourly pay for workers in heavily unionized industries (as of November 1998) are:[6]

Malt beverages	$24.35
Cigarettes	$24.29
Motor vehicles and car bodies	$21.03
Blast furnaces and steelmills	$20.03
Metal cans	$17.84

At the same time, the average hourly earnings of *all* production or nonsupervisory workers in manufacturing jobs were $13.60.[7]

Capital- versus Labor-Intensive

Quite often, businesses that have low labor costs relative to revenues pay employees higher rates of pay. Probably no one cost of business is more controllable and has a greater influence on profits than labor costs. When labor costs are a small percentage

---

[5]*Employment and Earnings* (Washington, DC: USDOL, Bureau of Labor Statistics, January 1999), Table 42, p. 221.
[6]*Employment and Earnings,* 1999, Table B-15.
[7]Ibid.

of revenue—say, around 10 to 15 percent—such as in chemical processing operations, there is a chance that labor costs will not be as tightly controlled as when these costs are 35 to 60 percent of revenue.

Labor-intensive industries also require the employment of larger numbers of low-skilled laborers. As businesses become more capital-intensive, using newer and more sophisticated technology and processes, they require fewer employees; but these employees must have higher levels of knowledge and skills. In turn, these more highly skilled employees will usually demand higher rates of pay.

Size of Business

Large businesses quite often provide higher wage rates than smaller businesses. Profitability and unionization are frequently related to company size. Firms normally increase in size because their products are in demand. With high demand come economies of scale and the opportunity to increase profit with each additional unit of good or service provided. If for no other reason than strictly the psychological factor, a more profitable business is more likely to share some of its profits with workers by increasing their pay.

Unions have traditionally focused on businesses with many employees. Organizing, like any sales activity, is very expensive, and the purpose of organizing is to have as many dues-paying members as possible. Even when a large firm is not unionized, it pays its members rates of pay equivalent to, if not greater than, those received by employees in comparable firms that are organized. This is a fundamental business strategy to keep a firm "union free."

There is also a direct relationship between the size of the salaries and bonuses received by top executives and the size of the companies for which they work. For example, the average pay and short-term bonus of a chief executive officer in a nondurable goods manufacturing firm with less than $25 million in annual sales is approximately 31.3 percent of that paid to a similarly situated executive of a firm producing over $1 billion in sales.[8] In fact, a good rule of thumb is that the pay of the CEO will increase by about 21 percent for each doubling of revenue size.

Philosophy of Management

Some owners and top executives have a philosophical bias toward paying their employees as much as possible. Other owners and managers may have a completely opposite bias. These biases have a definite impact on the amount of pay offered and given to employees.

To employers who have a "no more than necessary" philosophy, such factors as minimum wage laws or existing market-established minimum wage rates significantly influence the rates of pay offered to employees. Currently, the minimum hourly wage of $5.15, as set by Congress under the Fair Labor Standards Act, affects most workers. A few states now require employers to pay more than the federal minimum standard. To keep the federal minimum wage standard current, a proposed idea is to index it at 50 percent of the average hourly earnings of all production workers on private payrolls.

Even with federal or state minimum wage laws, some locations may have a labor shortage that requires companies to offer minimum wages higher than $5.15 per hour.

---

[8]Wyatt Data Services/ECS, 1991/92 *Top Management Report, Forty-Second Edition* (Fort Lee, NJ), p. 47.

An example of a market-driven minimum wage is fast-food restaurants offering $6.00 or more per hour for untrained new hires. It is also important to recognize that pay for more highly valued jobs frequently has a direct relationship to the pay given the lowest-rated or -paid jobs.

On the other hand, there are employers committed to the philosophy of paying their employees above industry or area standards in order to attract and retain the very best pool of skilled workers available. In these cases, rates of pay may be significantly higher than those found in organizations with a more traditional approach.

Total Compensation Package

In 1936, a steelworker received $4.32 per day. There was no time and a half for overtime, no hospitalization insurance, no paid vacations, no paid holidays, and no pensions. The same conditions held true for many other workers, except that they received significantly less per day—around $1. Today, the base wage of a skilled automobile assembler for General Motors (GM) is $20.44 per hour. Pay scales for workers in an automobile assembly plant can range between $19.56 and $24.75 per hour. At the same time, GM pays approximately $25.00 per hour for the employee's supplemental wage package, including vacations, holidays, supplemental unemployment benefits, pension, and life, medical, and hospitalization insurance. This $25.00 cost also includes overtime, shift differentials, and profit sharing, which are typically not included within a benefits package.

Although the GM–United Auto Workers (UAW) worker receives benefits that are the envy of most workers, the benefits packages provided to many other American workers today cost employers more than 38 percent of base wages. Various kinds of incentive plans are further enhancing and also increasing the complexity of the compensation packages of workers in all kinds of companies.

Base pay or annual earnings have been used to compare the compensation packages of employees. With each passing year, this kind of comparison becomes less and less useful. Today, even young, new employees soon become interested in their employer's pension plan, day care assistance, medical and hospitalization insurance, and many other benefits and services. Two clerks doing similar kinds of work for two different firms may receive an hourly wage rate that differs by $1 per hour, or approximately $2,000 per year. The benefits and incentive packages offered to these two employees may differ so significantly that the clerk earning $2,000 less in base pay may be receiving a much larger and more desirable compensation package.

Today, employees have sufficient interest in and knowledge of their compensation packages to recognize the value or worth of its major components. In fact, it is a challenge to management and to compensation professionals to keep employees fully informed of the compensation they receive.

Geographic Location

Employment and unemployment do not affect all sections of the nation equally. The drop in commodity prices between 1982 and 1986 and the increase in foreign manufactured goods had a particularly devastating impact on the 20 contiguous "heartland" states. As high-paying jobs disappeared, workers had to accept lower-paying jobs or move and search for jobs where opportunities existed. The early 1980s witnessed a dramatic decline in farming, mining, and heavy manufacturing jobs, and large increases in service jobs. Then the recession of the early 1990s witnessed a reduction in defense industry-related organizations and service-sector jobs. States with large numbers of defense-related industries and workers had severe economic problems. Many managers and white-collar workers joined the ranks of the unemployed.

Not only do employment opportunities dampen or improve job wage rates, but certain regions have historically paid higher wages than others. States where earnings are the highest are normally states with the highest costs of living. In 1997, the average personal income per person in the United States was $22,713. The seven highest and the seven lowest disposable income levels in the United States are these:[9]

	1997		*1997*
1. Connecticut	$32,177	50. Mississippi	$16,213
2. New Jersey	28,974	49. West Virginia	16,821
3. Massachusetts	27,972	48. Arkansas	17,378
4. New York	27,287	47. New Mexico	17,380
5. Delaware	25,752	46. Montana	17,787
6. Maryland	25,705	45. North Dakota	17,987
7. Illinois	25,024	44. Utah	18,130

Another way of looking at pay from a geographic consideration is to analyze hourly earnings for production workers in manufacturing by state. The five highest and five lowest hourly earnings for workers by state are these:[10]

Five Highest Paid		*Five Lowest Paid*	
1. Michigan	$18.71	50. South Dakota	$10.39
2. Washington	16.03	49. South Carolina	10.57
3. Ohio	16.02	48. Mississippi	10.82
4. Delaware	15.33	47. Arkansas	11.21
5. Wyoming	15.08	46. North Dakota	11.45

Alaska has the highest food and housing costs in the nation. Other high-income states have housing costs and a variety of taxes that normally exceed those found in the low-income states. Rates of pay in the southern states have typically been lower than those offered in other states. These regional differences have been declining over the years, but differences do continue to exist.

Supply and Demand of Labor

Even in times of high unemployment, individuals with certain sets of skills or abilities are in demand. Sometimes the demands are in specific locations; at other times, they are national in scope. Over the past 30 years, for example, there has been a large demand for skills related to electronic (computer-based) data processing. Jobs in high demand are frequently called "exotic" jobs, and those who have the necessary skills can demand and will receive premium wages. But all high-demand jobs that affect existing wage rates are not necessarily exotic. When there is a short supply of unskilled or

---

[9]*Statistical Abstract of the United States, 1998*, Table 727.
[10]*Employment and Earnings* (Washington, DC: USDOL, Bureau of Labor Statistics, January 1999), Table B-18.

low-skilled workers willing to work for minimum or near-minimum wages, the pay offered for these workers will quickly soar over existing federal minimum wage guidelines.

When construction is booming in a region and strong, able-bodied workers are in short supply, hourly wages can escalate from $5 to $10 per hour to attract such labor from other locations. The increase in base pay for fast-food restaurant workers from $5.15/$5.75 per hour to $6.00/$7.00 per hour will influence some individuals to apply when otherwise they would remain among the unemployed. Appendix 3A contains a broad historical review of economic theories, including the critical subject of supply and demand.

Profitability of the Firm

Employees working for highly profitable businesses have a greater chance of receiving higher wages than those working for less profitable firms. The "concession era" that began in 1982 is an excellent example of what happens when profits decline. Until 1982, the idea that a powerful union would agree to give an employer concessions in wages, benefits, and work rules was almost unthinkable. It is true that by 1976 once-mighty Eastern Airlines had gained some wage concessions from its employees and that by 1979 Chrysler had gone to its employees asking for concessions, but these were weak companies on the verge of bankruptcy. Beginning in 1982, literally hundreds of businesses feeling the competitive edge of the lower labor costs of foreign and domestic firms insisted on and received reductions in wages and benefits and changes in work rules. By 1991, Eastern Airlines had ceased to exist, indicating that wage concessions do not always work.

Historically, high-paying firms felt they had an edge in hiring and retaining the best workers by paying above the going rate in their markets. The best candidates took less time to train. Also, by retaining competent workers, many of the costs related to hiring are reduced. In 1986, the American Management Association stated that it costs $50,000 in search and relocation expenses to lure someone for a general management job paying $80,000 a year—a rate of pay received by a relatively high-level middle manager. Temporary living expenses could increase hiring costs to over $100,000.[11] The cost of hiring and training an operative employee can quickly cost a business $20,000. By attracting and retaining employees through higher base wages, these employers feel that they are reducing costs and increasing profits.

Employment Stability

In this time of reduction in workforce, employees become extremely concerned about continuation of employment. Practically all workers want the psychological security of knowing that their jobs will be there as long as *they* want them. The good life consists of not only a car, housing, and clothing, but enjoyable leisure time. These items all have a cost, and frequently a significant part of the cost is absorbed through a credit card that is secured by future employment. To some degree, many workers' current lifestyles require payments over an extended future time. The idea of not having a regular job to pay the many incurred debts and existing living costs is distressing. In addition, many people find the search for employment traumatic. The trauma increases when there are bills to be paid and more than one mouth to feed.

---

[11]*The Wall Street Journal,* June 17, 1986, p. 1.

For these and other reasons, an employee who feels that his or her job is permanent is often willing to take lower pay, knowing that the paycheck will be there as long as the assignments are performed in an acceptable manner. When times are good and jobs are plentiful, workers tend to forget that there are few absolute guarantees of future employment. However, as economic conditions worsen and more people are seeking fewer available jobs, security becomes an almost oppressive demand.

Gender Difference

The gap between male and female earnings has been a major irritant to advocates of women's rights. In industries and jobs in which females dominate the workforce (in excess of 70 percent of all employees are female), wage rates are normally lower than in those cases in which males are the dominant members. Historically, women have earned approximately 60 percent of what men have earned. However, in the 1980s, the gap began to close. In 1998, 54.5 million full-time male workers had median weekly earnings of $614, while 41.8 million full-time female workers had median weekly earnings of $471. This means that by the end of 1998 women were earning 77 percent of what men earned.[12]

Employee Tenure and Performance

When analyzing rates of pay using various kinds of composite data, it is practically impossible to separate two critical employee differences: tenure and performance.

In most cases, an employee's rate of pay increases with years of service. Even employees in low-level, minimal-skill jobs become more valuable with increasing length of service. Through their experience, they become more effective problem solvers. Employers frequently find more senior employees to be more dependable—at a minimum, managers have a better understanding of an individual's behavior patterns—and they find the more senior employee to be more predictable. It is not unusual to find very senior employees being paid double the amount received by new employees for comparable jobs.

Individual performance can also make a significant difference in the pay received by incumbents in similar jobs. Once again, when reviewing rates of pay for individuals doing similar kinds of work in different organizations, there is seldom any way of relating a high rate of pay to unusual or outstanding level of performance. Both senior employees and high-performance employees have ways of enlarging their jobs and increasing their value to the organization. Frequently, the job title and job description do not change, but the employee accepts additional responsibilities and duties and performs existing duties in a manner that changes the value of the job, if not the job itself. But because these changes frequently go unnoticed, they flaw any job match.

JOBS AND PAY IN THE UNITED STATES

The 1960s witnessed the rise of the drug culture, an antiwar movement, and the birth of a New Frontier and a Great Society. A "do-your-own-thing" attitude prevailed. Then came the 1970s. With the Arab oil embargo and Watergate, Americans began to take a good look at themselves, their lifestyle, and the economy. By the late 1970s, two major

---

[12]*Employment and Earnings* (Washington, DC: USDOL Bureau of Labor Statistics, January 1999), Table D-20, p. 159.

businesses, Eastern Airlines and the Chrysler Corporation, were having severe financial problems. For the first time since the Great Depression, employees of major corporations who were also members of powerful unions were asked to make concessions to management. The givebacks requested included reductions in wages and benefits and granting management more freedom in assigning work duties.

By 1991, contracts negotiated with unions provided unionized workers with wage gains that exceeded the rise in the cost of living for the first time since 1982. No 1991 contract settlement called for pay cuts. However, unemployment increased with continued reductions in force as organizations in the United States worked to improve their competitive opportunities. From 1991 to 1995, many negotiated pay increases for unionized workers ranged from 3 to 5 percent, closely approximating annual increases in the consumer price index.

Foreign Competition—The Global Economy

The 1980s started with double-digit inflation. A wide variety of foreign-made products, from automobiles, to VCRs, to apparel, began to dominate their respective markets. Steel mills, automobile assembly plants, and textile mills began laying off employees as they felt the pinch of imports produced by workers receiving significantly lower wages.

While Korean automobile workers cost their employers from $4 to $5 per hour, their counterpart American workers cost GM, Ford, and Chrysler over $27 per hour. Similar variations existed between steelworkers in the United States and those in South Korea and Brazil. American workers and their employers must compete with goods and services produced by workers receiving drastically lower rates of pay. Yet differences between local and foreign labor markets are fast disappearing. In the 1980s, it became more evident with every passing month that U.S. businesses must compete in world markets and that their labor costs cannot continue to be five or ten times greater than those of foreign competitors.

From 1985 to 1988, the U.S. dollar was devalued against the currencies of its major economic competitors. Consequently, industrial workers by 1986 in Germany, the Netherlands, Norway, and Switzerland had become more highly paid than their American counterparts. However, developing industrial nations such as South Korea, Taiwan, Singapore, Mexico, and Brazil did not revalue their currencies upward and continue to be in strong competition with U.S. manufacturers. Table 3–2 shows hourly compensation costs for production workers in U.S. dollars and Table 3–3 shows the exchange rates for U.S. dollars from 1975 to 1997.

Compensation and Global Economy

As U.S. organizations become more competitive, moving production and marketing operations into foreign countries, they must recognize labor costs from a total compensation perspective rather than by simply comparing base pay. The components of a compensation package vary significantly among different regions of the world and even country by country. Two major factors that influence the design of compensation packages are (1) major differences in tax rates and tax deductions from country to country, and (2) government-provided or -directed Social Security and welfare systems.

Taxation   Employers and employees must comply with tax systems that vary significantly from country to country. Low or no taxes on certain organization-provided

TABLE 3–2 Hourly Compensation Costs in U.S. Dollars for Production Workers in Manufacturing, 29 Countries or Areas and Selected Economic Groups, Selected Years, 1975–1997

Country or Area	1975	1980	1985	1990	1993	1994	1995	1996	1997
United States	$6.36	$9.87	$13.01	$14.91	$16.51	$16.87	$17.19	$17.70	$18.24
Canada	5.96	8.67	10.94	15.84	16.43	15.85	16.04	16.66	16.55
Mexico	1.47	2.21	1.59	1.58	2.40	2.47	1.51	1.54	1.75
Australia	5.62	8.47	8.20	13.07	12.49	14.02	15.05	16.52	16.00
Hong Kong SAR[1]	.76	1.51	1.73	3.20	4.29	4.61	4.82	5.14	5.42
Israel	2.25	3.79	4.06	8.55	8.82	9.19	10.54	10.99	12.05
Japan	3.00	5.52	6.34	12.80	19.21	21.35	23.82	20.91	19.37
Korea	.32	.96	1.23	3.71	5.64	6.40	7.29	8.09	7.22
New Zealand	3.21	5.33	4.47	8.33	8.01	8.93	10.11	11.03	11.02
Singapore	.84	1.49	2.47	3.78	5.25	6.29	7.33	8.32	8.24
Sri Lanka	.28	.22	.28	.35	.42	.45	.48	.48	–
Taiwan	.40	1.00	1.50	3.93	5.23	5.55	5.92	5.93	5.89
Austria	4.51	8.88	7.58	17.75	20.16	21.51	25.21	24.66	21.92
Belgium	6.41	13.11	8.97	19.17	21.44	23.07	26.65	25.89	22.82
Denmark	6.28	10.83	8.13	18.04	19.11	20.30	24.07	24.11	22.02
Finland	4.61	8.24	8.16	21.03	16.63	19.06	24.14	23.56	21.44
France	4.52	8.94	7.52	15.49	16.79	17.63	20.01	19.92	17.97
Germany[2]	6.31	12.25	9.53	21.88	25.32	27.03	32.22	31.79	28.28
Greece	1.69	3.73	3.66	6.76	7.23	7.73	9.17	9.59	–
Ireland	3.03	5.95	5.92	11.66	11.89	12.39	13.57	13.85	13.57
Italy	4.67	8.15	7.63	17.45	15.80	15.89	16.21	17.73	16.74
Luxembourg	6.50	12.03	7.81	16.74	18.74	20.33	23.35	22.55	–
Netherlands	6.58	12.06	8.75	18.06	20.08	20.80	24.02	23.08	20.61
Norway	6.77	11.59	10.37	21.47	20.21	20.97	24.38	25.05	23.72
Portugal	1.58	2.06	1.53	3.77	4.50	4.60	5.37	5.58	5.29
Spain	2.53	5.89	4.66	11.38	11.62	11.54	12.88	13.51	12.16
Sweden	7.18	12.51	9.66	20.93	17.59	18.62	21.44	24.37	22.24
Switzerland	6.09	11.09	9.66	20.86	22.63	24.91	29.30	28.34	24.19
United Kingdom	3.37	7.56	6.27	12.70	12.41	12.80	13.67	14.13	15.47
Trade-weighted measures[3]									
All 28 foreign economies	3.83	6.60	6.74	12.33	14.32	15.01	16.38	16.09	15.25
OECD[4]	4.25	7.30	7.39	13.46	15.55	16.27	17.75	17.37	16.40
less Mexico, Korea[5]	4.82	8.30	8.48	15.51	17.78	18.57	20.39	19.90	18.77
Europe	5.10	9.90	7.96	17.31	18.36	19.33	22.10	22.19	20.46
European Union	5.03	9.83	7.85	17.09	18.14	19.05	21.75	21.87	20.24
Asian NIEs	.52	1.17	1.65	3.72	5.19	5.78	6.40	6.87	6.65

Dash means data not available.

[1] Hong Kong Special Administrative Region of China.
[2] Former West Germany.
[3] For decription of trade-weighted measures and economic groups, see the Technical Notes preceding these tables.
[4] Organization for Economic Cooperation and Development.
[5] Mexico joined the OECD in 1994, and Korea joined in 1996.

Source: International Comparisons of Hourly Compensation Costs for Production Workers in Manufacturing 1997 (Washington, DC: USDOL, Bureau of Labor Statistics, September 1998), Table 2, p. 12.

TABLE 3-3	Exchange Rates, 29 Countries or Areas, Selected Years, 1975–1997 (national currency units per U.S. dollar)								
Country or Area	1975	1980	1985	1990	1993	1994	1995	1996	1997
United States	1.000	1.000	1.000	1.000	1.000	1.000	1.000	1.000	1.000
Canada	1.017	1.169	1.366	1.167	1.290	1.366	1.373	1.364	1.385
Mexico	12.50	22.97	256.9	2813	3.116	3.375	6.419	7.601	7.918
Australia	.7647	.8772	1.428	1.281	1.471	1.367	1.350	1.277	1.345
Hong Kong SAR[1]	4.939	4.976	7.791	7.790	7.736	7.729	7.736	7.735	7.743
Israel	.6390	5.124	1.179	2.016	2.830	3.011	3.011	3.288	3.449
Japan	296.7	225.7	238.5	145.0	111.1	102.2	93.96	108.8	121.0
Korea	484.0	607.4	870.0	707.8	802.7	803.5	771.3	804.5	950.8
New Zealand	.8254	1.027	2.010	1.677	1.847	1.685	1.524	1.454	1.509
Singapore	2.371	2.141	2.200	1.813	1.616	1.527	1.417	1.410	1.486
Sri Lanka	7.050	16.53	27.16	40.06	48.32	49.42	51.25	55.27	–
Taiwan	38.00	36.02	39.85	26.92	26.42	26.47	26.50	27.47	28.78
Austria	17.40	12.93	20.68	11.33	11.64	11.41	10.08	10.59	12.21
Belgium	36.69	29.20	59.34	33.42	34.58	33.43	29.47	30.97	35.81
Denmark	5.735	5.629	10.60	6.190	6.486	6.356	5.600	5.800	6.609
Finland	3.665	3.719	6.197	3.830	5.725	5.234	4.376	4.595	5.196
France	4.282	4.220	8.980	5.447	5.667	5.546	4.986	5.116	5.839
Germany[2]	2.455	1.815	2.942	1.617	1.655	1.622	1.432	1.505	1.735
Greece	32.29	42.62	138.1	158.5	229.3	242.6	231.7	240.7	–
Ireland	.4500	.4860	.9379	.6033	.6827	.6680	.6236	.6250	.6595
Italy	652.4	855.1	1909	1198	1573	1611	1629	1543	1704
Luxembourg	36.78	29.24	59.38	33.42	34.60	33.46	29.48	30.96	–
Netherlands	2.523	1.985	3.318	1.822	1.858	1.819	1.604	1.686	1.953
Norway	5.214	4.936	8.593	6.254	7.098	7.055	6.336	6.459	7.086
Portugal	25.45	50.05	172.1	142.7	161.1	165.9	149.9	154.3	175.4
Spain	57.39	71.64	170.0	102.0	127.5	133.9	124.6	126.7	146.5
Sweden	4.142	4.229	8.603	5.923	7.796	7.716	7.141	6.708	7.645
Switzerland	2.581	1.675	2.455	1.390	1.478	1.367	1.181	1.236	1.451
United Kingdom	.4501	.4300	.7708	.5605	.6660	.6528	.6335	.6407	.6106

[1]Hong Kong Special Administrative Region of China.
[2]Former West Germany.
Note: National currency units are: United States, dollar; Canada, dollar; Mexico, old peso (1975–92), new peso (1993–97); Australia, dollar; Hong Kong, dollar; Israel, shekel (1975–84), new shekel (1985–97); Japan, yen; Korea, won; New Zealand, dollar; Singapore, dollar; Sri Lanka, rupee; Taiwan, dollar; Austria, schilling; Belgium, franc; Denmark, krone; Finland, markka; France, franc; Germany, mark; Greece, drachma; Ireland, pound; Italy, lira; Luxembourg, franc; Netherlands, guilder; Norway, krone; Portugal, escudo; Spain, peseta; Sweden, krona; Switzerland, franc; United Kingdom, pound.
Source: International Comparisons of Hourly Compensation Costs for Production Workers in Manufacturing, 1997 (Washington, DC: USDOL, Bureau of Labor Statistics, September 1998), Table 6, p. 12.

benefits and perquisites will result in these tax-favored components being widely used by businesses and highly desirable to the employee. The company car, housing allowances, and company-paid tuition for employee dependents are examples of perquisites whose advantages relate closely to tax laws. Not only are there differences in the taxation of benefits and perquisites, but income tax rates and deductions vary greatly for both employers and employees country by country.

Social Security   Although national Social Security systems have a direct linkage to tax programs, they are such an important part of an employee's benefit program that an analysis of compensation must recognize the costs and features of the Social Security system of each country. For example, most Western European countries provide significantly larger retirement packages to their workers than does the Social Security system of the United States. It is not unusual for a worker in a Western European country to receive a Social Security retirement payment equal to 70 to 90 percent of former job salary. This, in turn, places significantly less pressure on employers to fund a pension plan.

Many Western European countries and Canada provide free or very low-cost universal health coverage to all workers, retirees, and their families. This can reduce employer compensation costs by thousands of dollars per employee. Social Security systems also provide a broad package of maternity and child care services that include (1) payment of the majority of prenatal, delivery, and postpartum expenses, (2) four months or longer paid maternity leave, (3) subsidized day care, and (4) generous annual tax deductions for each child. Employees who lose their jobs because the employer terminates operations or implements a reduction in force may be eligible for severance payments that extend for up to five years.

As global competition becomes important to more and more U.S. businesses, awareness and understanding of the differences in compensation packages will increase. Not only do base pay, benefits, and perquisites vary by region and country, but the use of short- and long-term incentive plans also differs significantly. The amounts paid to members of organizations at various levels also differ. In many foreign countries, the base pay of a top executive will have a ratio from 10:1, at the most, 25:1 from the pay of the average worker. For top executives in large organizations in the United States, it is not unusual for these ratios to exceed 50:1 and at times be greater than 100:1 (see discussion of pay ratios in chapter 4).

Deregulation and Takeovers   Many American firms protected from the foreign import onslaught began to feel a different form of competition. In the late 1970s, Congress had approved deregulation legislation that opened the banking and transportation industries to the pressures of competition. Many heavily unionized airlines became alarmed at the success of nonunionized, low-labor-cost competitors. The same problems faced old-line trucking companies. With the mergers of major banks, management and staff officers found their jobs eliminated.

In the case of the mightiest of all American businesses, American Telephone and Telegraph (AT&T), federal court-imposed divestiture opened many segments of the business to competition. In the meatpacking industry, nonunion businesses operating extremely modern packing plants underpriced the heavily unionized (high-paying) old-line firms.

During the 1980s and through the 1990s, many companies faced not only problems caused by product competition but also pressure exerted by financial raiders seeking to buy these companies and then profit by revamping, reorganizing, and selling all or parts of them. With these changes, top management gave more of its attention to actions necessary to protect the company and its jobs from financial raiders, instead of on their local and foreign product competitors.

Problems related to deregulation, takeovers, and foreign competition continued into the 1990s. Pan American, Eastern, and Midway Airlines disappeared. In 1991, General Motors had its worst financial year ever. Many leaders blamed Japan for the severe economic problems encountered in 1991 and 1992. However, by the mid 1990s, American firms had significantly improved their competitive posture and were regaining their dominance in worldwide business operations. Much of this improvement can be traced directly to tight controls over their pay and benefits programs.

Becoming More Competitive

As organizations throughout the country analyzed their operations in an effort to survive and ensure profitability, it was apparent that a number of issues required resolution. Above all, it was evident that all kinds of businesses producing a wide variety of goods and services must become more competitive. It was equally apparent that labor costs must be brought more in line with those of the rest of the world. In analyzing competitive posture and the opportunities available to American businesses, the following issues dominated:

1. Computer-based technology will drive the production of goods and services.
2. Highly skilled workers will operate these computer-driven technologies.
3. Errors made at any level in the organization can severely damage its profitability, even its survival.
4. Quality products demanded by customers require the effort and attention of a committed, trained, and well-educated workforce.
5. Top management must become more skilled in integrating short-term activities with the long-term directions their businesses must take and be willing to take the risks in moving toward the unknown. Strategic considerations will continue to be an ever-increasing part of the work of top management.

In company after company, dramatic changes are occurring in ways of doing business. Robots in the factories and computer-based workstations in the offices are changing and will continue to change jobs and the tasks people perform while doing their jobs.

Technology, more than ever before, is driving the production of goods and services. Surviving companies must focus on product and customer. Manufacturing companies can no longer afford the luxury of inventories large enough to take care of any contingency. At the same time, they cannot afford to tell a customer they cannot provide the product at the desired time. Quality is also becoming a more important issue as consumers throughout the world seek high quality.

Major disasters of the past decade make it painfully clear that human error at any level in an organization can severely affect its survival. Although Boeing admitted that faulty repair work on the tail area of a Japan Airlines 747 resulted in a crash that killed 520 passengers, it has continued to prosper. Union Carbide still has financial liability problems because of the mistakes made at Bhopal, India. No one died in the nuclear power accident at Three Mile Island, but possibly hundreds, if not thousands, have died, or will, as a result of the nuclear disaster at Chernobyl in Ukraine. These two accidents, which were caused by human error, will continue to have a devastating impact on the nuclear power industry around the world.

No accident in history was witnessed by more people than the explosion of the space shuttle *Challenger* in January 1986. A special committee established by the president of the United States with the charge of investigating the accident identified the fatal flaw as a seal that did not work under low-temperature operating conditions. This problem had been recognized as a potential for disaster for many years. Although changes were initiated to overcome the problem, past successes hid the immediate need to correct it.

A WORLD IN TRANSITION

In 1970, in his book *Future Shock,* Alvin Toffler identified the rise of critical social and economic problems caused by the rapid changes that were occurring in society. Toffler stated that bureaucracy, the formal organizational structure established to direct day-to-day routine activities, is incapable of recognizing and resolving the crises that have the potential to destroy organizations and of recognizing and implementing innovations that can lead them into a successful future.

Problems caused by rapid change are already influencing the operations of organizations. Employees at all levels must daily recognize more variables when solving problems. In addition, less time is available to solve these more complex problems. As fit becomes ever more critical, designed tolerance for errors is constantly being reduced, placing increased demands on correct operations. When errors are made, punishment becomes much more severe both for organizations and for individuals who make mistakes. To operate within these kinds of restrictions, organizations are changing.

Many changes have already occurred in the way organizations are designed, structured, and staffed. Job opportunities and rates of pay have also begun to change. The conditions forcing these changes will not disappear, and their impact on job opportunities and employee compensation will continue to have significant influence. It is and will be a world where (1) economic growth is slow, (2) competition is vigorous, (3) advancement opportunities are few, and (4) wage, salary, and benefit increases are restricted. Recognizing the paradox of restricting, even reducing, employee wages, salaries, and benefits while demanding increased employee awareness and contributions, organizations are now taking other actions to improve reward and compensation programs. An opportunity available to all organizations is to provide employees at all levels with a variety of incentive payments based on individual, team, and work unit performance and organizational productivity and profitability.

Summary

This chapter identifies and briefly describes the different correlates or determinants that influence the rate of pay of each employee. These correlates are (1) kinds and levels of required skills; (2) kind of business; (3) union–nonunion status; (4) capital- versus labor-intensive; (5) size of business; (6) philosophy of management; (7) total compensation package; (8) geographic location; (9) supply and demand of labor; (10) profitability of the firm; (11) employment stability; (12) gender difference; and (13) employee tenure and performance.

Employee compensation and its major component, base pay, vary significantly by kind of job, kind of organization, and environmental factors. At first glance, these differences appear to be inexplicable. However, if the compensation package is analyzed from the perspective of the correlates or determinants of pay, logical and rational reasons for these compensation differences begin to appear. To operate within a competitive environment, organizations must understand how the correlates influence their compensation practices and make the kinds of reasoned decisions that permit them to function both efficiently and effectively.

Review Questions

1. What changes are occurring in the workforce relative to the kinds of work employees are performing?
2. Identify the major parts of a compensation program.
3. What is the most important factor influencing the rate of pay an employee receives?
4. Distinguish between labor-intensive and capital-intensive industries.
5. What is a gender-dominated job?
6. What is an example of a market-driven minimum wage?
7. Are there any relationships between the geographic location of a business and employee rates of pay? If so, explain.
8. What differences may an employer's philosophy have on rates of pay?
9. How are differences in rates of pay throughout the world influencing American employers?

Appendix 3A
Economic Theories

Figure 3A–1 describes the economic theories affecting compensation that have developed over the centuries. At the top of the model, the "social" wage theories are those that seem to have the least effect on the wage levels in a democracy. Coming down the model through the "funnel" are the theories that seem to have a stronger influence on wage levels—the closer to "compensation," the greater the influence of the theory.

MACRO THEORIES

I. The Social Wage Theories, often classified as the Classical Wage Theories, attempt to explain what society "ought to pay" to one of its members, based either upon the need or the "right" of that member. In no case do these theories mention, or appear to consider, the talents of the individual or the quality or quantity of work produced by that individual.

a. Although the fundamental concepts of the *Subsistence Theory of Wages* existed long before the Christian era, David Ricardo is given credit for its development. In about 1817 he proposed this theory, which deals with population rather than labor. This theory suggests that each member of society be provided enough food, clothing, and shelter to continue to exist. It further implies that when the income of workers exceeds their subsistence level, they respond by further procreation, thus increasing the labor force and consequently lowering wages as a

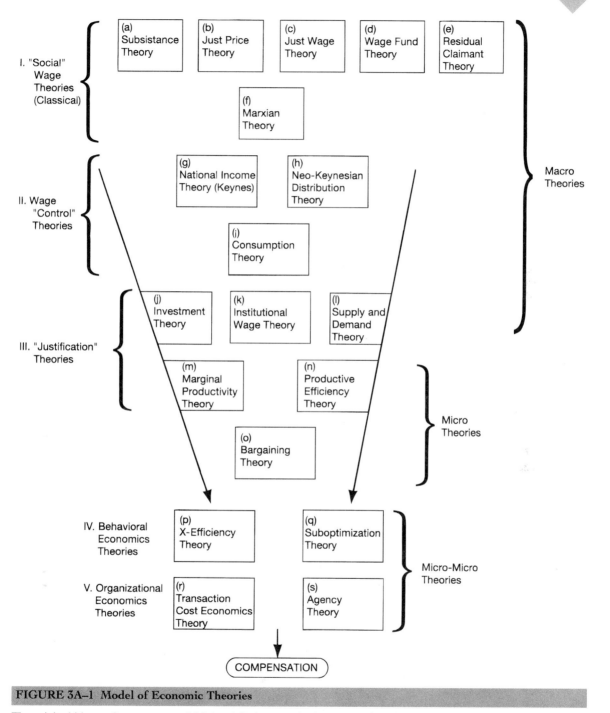

FIGURE 3A–1 Model of Economic Theories

The original idea and component of this model of economic theories was developed by John W. Crim. Crim's original model has been modified by contributions made by Bruce E. Kaufman, Robert Figler, and this author.

result of supply and demand. The earlier works of Thomas Num and Thomas R. Malthus influenced Ricardo in this effort. This theory is also known as the Iron Law of Wages.

b. In the pre-Christian eras of Greece and Rome, early philosophers began developing theories to explain and describe the economic relationships among social groups. The *Just Price Theory,* originally proposed by Plato and Aristotle some 300 years before Christ, suggested that each person born into the world is foreordained to occupy exactly the same status and to enjoy the same creature comforts as did his or her parents. Therefore, society owes these individuals sufficient compensation to maintain exactly the same position of life into which they were born.

This theory defended the role of birthright with an elitist upper class and a lower class that lived at a subsistence level. Nothing is mentioned about a small group between the upper and lower classes that provided the knowledge and skills to make society function and who, through their own wiles, enjoyed a lifestyle that exceeded a subsistence level.

Biblical teachings and the rise of Christianity in Europe continued to defend a basic two-tiered society, with the upper class enjoying both affluence and influence and the lower class living at subsistence level. Little attention focused on an almost silent middle class in existing society.

The Old Testament proposes some form of philosophical equality between the haves (upper class) and the have-nots (lower class) by stating that in heaven the first (upper class) shall come last and the last (lower class) shall come first. In the New Testament, concern about equality and the provision of a subsistence wage is described in Matthew, Chapter 20, verses 1–6, where an employer pays one penny to all laborers regardless of hours worked, conditions endured, and results achieved.

c. The Just Price Theory of the pre-Christian era evolved into a *Just Wage Theory* and became more firmly established during the feudal Middle Ages in Europe. The construction of churches and government buildings and the continued expansion of commercial activities provided more and more job opportunities for artists, artisans, and traders. Like their earlier counterparts in ancient Egypt, Greece, and Rome, the artists and artisans felt that they should receive better wages than the unskilled lower class who provided physical work that required minimal intellectual effort.

The Just Wage Theory received strong church support with the philosophy proposed by St. Thomas Aquinas. He presented the concept of a common Father and the brotherhood of man. He also suggested that the price of any article should be adequate, but no more than adequate to cover the cost of production, which, in turn, is based upon the accustomed standards of living of the producers of the item. Aquinas continued to promote the view that society owes each individual sufficient compensation to maintain exactly the same position of life into which he or she was born. By inference, this theory had no provision for entrepreneurial profit and made no recognition of the differences in productive efficiency between two workers. Economic theory and socioreligious philosophical teachings still did not recognize individual knowledge and skills, differences in individual contributions, and entrepreneurial profits.

Even with the continuing advocacy of a Just Wage Theory, however, the artists and artisans of the Middle Ages and the Renaissance were able to demand and receive better than subsistence wage treatment for their efforts. The upper-class nobility and landholders recognized that there was a shortage of artists and artisans to build their buildings and castles and produce the tapestries and furnishings required for these structures, so the guilds and other collective bargaining groups were able to improve the economic strength of these skilled workers. Marketplace supply and demand began receiving formal recognition in compensation practices, if not in economic theories.

The Renaissance not only witnessed a surge in demand for artists and artisans but, with the invention of the printing press and the advancement of intellectual pursuits, those interested and willing to advance their knowledge in a variety of professional fields, including teaching, medicine, engineering, and trade, found an escape from a preordained life of subsistence to a more enjoyable middle-class lifestyle. The social class in the middle began to increase not only in size but in affluence and influence. For example, by the 1500s, merchants and guild members in Ghent, Belgium, who were the major worldwide manufacturers of tapestries, were powerful enough to question the authority of their king. In the neighboring Netherlands, the merchant class became sufficiently powerful to enable their country to become independent of the Spanish empire.

A relatively large middle class arose with the prosperity enjoyed in England during the 1700s. This prosperity helped to give birth to the Industrial Revolution and the movement of the lower classes from the farms to the factories.

   d. The *Wage Fund Theory,* advanced by John Stuart Mill in the 1830s, suggests that the wages of an employee are paid from a fund, which presumably has been accumulated by the entrepreneur from operations of previous years. This fund, which to some extent was under the control of the entrepreneur, was then divided evenly among all employees. An obvious shortcoming of this theory is that wages are usually paid from current business operations rather than from past operations. However, the theory does seem to possess some validity when applied to not-for-profit organizations such as government and public service whereby the wage fund is actually forecasted and drawn from tax monies.

   e. In the late nineteenth century, Francis A. Walker enlarged upon the concepts developed in David Ricardo's "Theory of Political Economy." He proposed the *Residual Claimant Theory,* a version of the Wage Fund Theory, in which he hypothesized that the wage fund derived, not from previous years' operations, but simply from the residue of total revenues after deducting all other legitimate expenses of business operations such as rent, taxes, interest, and profits. Following this through to its logical conclusion, if the "other expenses" consumed all of revenue, labor, being the "residual claimant," would receive no wages and presumably would not be entitled to them.

   f. The *Marxian Theory* or *Surplus Value Theory* of Karl Marx is essentially the inversion of the Residual Claimant Theory, inasmuch as he suggests that labor is the sole source of economic value and, therefore, labor should exercise the prime claim on revenue. This means that the price of an article consists solely of labor value and any other value collected by the entrepreneur represents unacceptable exploitation of labor. The surplus between labor cost and product price should be paid to labor. Marx further suggests that the displacement of labor, through technological progress, is dysfunctional to the system and will eventually destroy capitalism. This appears to be the ideological basis for the opposition to automation by some segments of the labor union movement.

During the last half of the nineteenth century, Marx continued to have a very pessimistic view of working conditions in the emerging industrial state and of the opportunity of the workers in the lower class of society to improve their economic plight. Marx took Ricardo's Iron Law of Wages one step further through his Surplus Value Theory. Marx stated that workers would receive only subsistence levels of income even though it was through their labor that profits were generated. The surplus created through their labor (profit) would be taken by their employers.

The demons underlying Marx's economic philosophy were the affluent and influential members of a social class of the eighteenth and nineteenth centuries called the bourgeoisie, the predecessor of what today can be grouped within the upper-middle class. Marx felt that this group within middle-class society and the birthright upper class would continue to exploit the lower class and prohibit them from moving out of a life of poverty and subsistence. This perceived lack of upward mobility caused Marx to write his *Communist Manifesto,* urging the working class or proletarians (his title for those working in an industrial society who were members of the lower class) to revolt and form their own classless society.

Marx's pessimistic view of economic opportunities for workers did not stop the generation of economic theories that described the operation of a market-based economy and its influence on the pay of labor. Throughout the nineteenth century, economic theorists began to move away from wage theories based on subsistence levels of income for the lower class to a recognition of the influence of the supply and demand of labor at the marketplace, organizational and entrepreneurial profits, differences in employee contributions, and differences in results achieved.

II. The Wage Control Theories suggest that somewhere between a pure dictatorship and a pure democracy there is room for a mode of government that frankly and openly permits, even demands, some degree of indirect control of wage levels.

g. In the 1930s, John Maynard Keynes recognized that a thriving middle-class economy required full employment. Keynes developed his *National Income Theory,* sometimes called Full Employment Wage Theory or General Theory. This theory states that full employment is a function of national income. National income, in turn, is equal to the total of consumption plus private and public investment. If the national income falls below a level that commands full employment, it is the responsibility of the federal government to manipulate any or all of the three variables to increase national income and return to full employment.

This suggests that government is the one agent powerful enough to control monetary and fiscal policies as well as to enforce direct edicts upon private enterprise, thereby maintaining full employment and, indirectly, the desired wage level.

The National Income Theory appears to treat the labor supply as though it were fixed. Actually, though constantly growing, the national labor force continually varies within rather wide limits. This short-term variation is a result of the fact that a substantial segment of the population can, in the short run, exercise a personal choice as to whether they are actually a part of, or are not a part of, the labor force. This personal choice can be exercised by a second wage earner in the family, by teenagers who have not previously been in the labor force, by older people who may be able to choose whether to be employed or not, by recipients of unemployment compensation who for the short term may actually not be available for alternate employment, or simply by those who are unwilling to work under practically any conditions. Thus, the critics of the National Income Theory suggest that a fault of the theory is the fact that it does not recognize this fluctuating labor force.

   h. The *Neo-Keynesian Distribution Theory*[13] is a refinement, or extension, of the National Income Theory in that it attempts to explain how full-employment conditions can be achieved without conflicting with general living standards or with stable prices. This theory is, therefore, actually a theory of the general wage level, in both the long and short term. It also recognizes the fact that entrepreneurial decisions can determine the general level of wages in the short run. Money wage rates, within limits, are determined by bargaining between the capitalist and the employee. This is a departure from the theories previously mentioned in which economic forces alone determine the wage level. Thus, the ever-changing labor supply is given some consideration in this theory.

To this very day, politicians and economists continue to debate the issue of how to reach and maintain full employment. Full employment involves every segment of society. Politicians, leaders of business and society, those seeking a better lifestyle, and those wishing to maintain an already existing and acceptable standard of living recognize the need for jobs and, even better, well-paying jobs.

   i. By the twentieth century, wage theories became closely linked to employment practices. One of the great industrialists in the United States, Henry Ford, developed the *Consumption Theory,* sometimes referred to as the Purchasing Power Theory. In 1915, Ford unilaterally instituted the $5-a-day wage for workers in his automobile plant. This wage was about double that being paid by competitors at that time.

The pay-related actions of Ford took much of the steam away from Marx's *Manifesto.* Ford's simple philosophy was that higher-paid workers could buy more products that would, in turn, improve their lifestyles. This, in turn, would generate more business and higher profits for entrepreneurs, employers, and stockholders. Ford, better than Marx, recognized the strength of an upwardly mobile middle class that in a capitalistic-democratic society would yearly increase in numbers. Ford, however, operated in a democratic society, whereas Marx lived a half-century earlier within absolute and constitutional monarchies.

Those who defend Mr. Ford's action as a "new wage theory" suggest that high money wages encourage consumption, increase demand for products, and thereby lower commodity prices. This theory is included in Wage Control Theories because, indeed, it involves a macro approach to the general wage level throughout the entire economy. However, the instrument of control is private enterprise itself rather than the federal government.

---

[13]Marjorie S. Turner, "Wages in the Cambridge Theory of Distribution," *Industrial and Labor Relations Review,* April 1966, pp. 390–401.

III. The Justification Theories are so labeled because their authors apparently attempt to explain, or "justify," an individual worker's compensation level. The first three theories approach the wage level from an overall macroeconomic viewpoint, whereas the remaining theories use a microeconomic approach.

j. In the *Investment Theory*,[14] H. M. Gitelman recognizes that labor markets vary in the scope of "worker investment" required for their particular industry. Generally, the wider the labor market, the higher the wage. The individual worker's "investment" consists of the education, training, and experience that the worker has invested in a lifetime of work. Individual workers vary in their desire to maximize income, as do employing organizations vary in their worker investment requirements. Thus, Gitelman hypothesizes that an individual worker's compensation is determined by the rate of return on that worker's investment. This theory has conceptually combined broad economic influences on compensation with the specific means whereby workers may control the level of their own compensation.

k. The *Institutional Wage Theory* attempts to place the "level of compensation" on a "system," or establish an "empirical and quantitative" basis. It is an interdisciplinary approach to compensation to include such considerations as wage experience, variability of wage relationships, latitude of decision makers, the influence of collective bargaining, and so on. It suggests that a wage level depends on a variety of choices of decision makers and that weights can be assigned to these choices. It considers all types of wage structures, such as interpersonal, interfirm, interarea, interoccupational, and interindustry. It suggests that one must analyze compensation from a dynamic, continually changing basis, rather than assuming that we can hold constant all factors affecting compensation while varying only one factor.

l.   A review of selected wage theories would seem incomplete without reference to the classic *Supply and Demand Theory*. Probably the least refuted theory of compensation is this hypothesis that if jobs are few and supply of workers is high, then wages will fall. Conversely, if jobs are plentiful and there is a shortage of workers, wages will rise, and in the long run wages will seek a level at the point at which the demand curve intersects the supply curve.

The last half of the twentieth century witnessed the blossoming of labor economics. Labor economists, like their psychologist and sociologist behavioral scientist colleagues, have been and will continue to be deeply involved in developing theories and designing models that assist managers and compensation professionals to implement the rewards that aid in achieving organizational goals. Even more than behavioral scientists, labor economists view the world of work in the most general manner possible.

Wage determination is at the core of labor economics because the structure of wages and changes in wages over time are responsible for allocating labor efficiently and maintaining a balance between supply and demand in the marketplace. Labor economists develop supply–demand models to identify the wage that balances supply

---

[14]H. M. Gitelman, "An Investment Theory of Wages," *Industrial and Labor Relations Review,* April 1968, pp. 323–352.

and demand in the marketplace. The starting place is the theory of perfect competition. There are five key assumptions in the model of perfect competition:

1. Employers seek to maximize profits and workers seek to maximize utility.
2. Employers and workers have perfect information about wages and job opportunities in the market.
3. Workers are identical with respect to skill and performance, and jobs offered by employers are identical with respect to working conditions and other nonwage attributes.
4. The labor market consists of many individual employers on the demand side and many workers on the supply side and any one employer or employee has a negligible influence on the market. Employers do not collude and workers do not belong to unions.
5. All jobs in the market are open to competition and there are no institutional barriers to mobility of workers from one job to another.[15]

Given these assumptions, the labor economics supply–demand model takes the form illustrated in Figure 3A–2. The diagram shows how the forces of demand and supply determine the rate of pay for a particular type of labor in a specific labor market. The demand curve D_L, slopes downward, showing that employers will desire to hire more labor at a lower wage. The supply curve S_L slopes upward, showing that at higher wages more people will desire to work in this occupation. The key prediction of the model is that the wage at which labor is bought and sold in this market will be W_U, determined by the intersection of the supply and demand curve. At a higher wage of W_U, there is an excess supply of labor (the quantity supplied exceeds the quantity demanded) and the resulting competition for scarce jobs should cause the wage to fall to W_1 where demand equals supply. Otherwise, at a lower wage such as W_L, there exists an excess demand for labor and competition for workers would force the wage to rise to W_1.

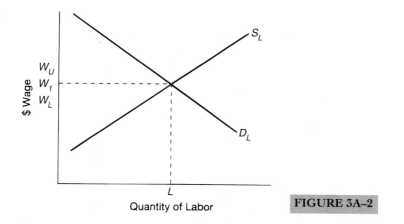

Quantity of Labor

FIGURE 3A–2

---

[15]Paraphrased from Bruce E. Kaufman, *The Economics of Labor Markets and Labor Relations* (Chicago: Dryden, 1986), p. 209.

The assumptions of perfect competition are obviously unrealistic, but the models nevertheless are important for compensation professionals because they highlight the role of market forces in the process of wage determination. Just as market forces cannot be ignored by the compensation professional, neither are they the only determinant of wage rates and the wage structure in a firm because imperfections in real-world labor markets cause them to diverge from the theoretical ideal of perfect competition. Information is not perfect. Mobility is not costless. Economists such as Richard Lester long ago admitted that competitive market forces do not determine one unique wage for each type of job skill or occupation but establish a range with an upper limit of W_U and a lower limit of W_L, within which the firm has discretion over what it pays. The firm cannot pay more than W_U or it will sacrifice too much profit, and it must pay more than W_L, or no one will work for it. Between W_U and W_L, however, is an "area of indeterminacy" in which the firm can formulate its own wage policy.[16]

Because firms have some discretion over the wage they pay, in a labor market it is common to find a distribution of firms with some as "high-wage" firms, others as "low-wage" firms, and the remainder somewhere in the middle. This phenomenon was documented in a famous study of truck drivers in Boston by John Dunlop.[17] In 1953, the hourly wage rate for unionized truck drivers in Boston ranged from $1.27 to $2.49. Dunlop argued that firms in Boston were arranged on "wage contours," with some firms on a higher contour than others for the same type of labor. What influenced which contour a firm was on? Dunlop found that an important influence was the industry or product market of the firm and, in particular, the profitability of the industry and the employer's ability to pay.

MICRO THEORIES

The theories outlined previously are essentially "macro" in nature because each attempts, in some way, to describe or account for the broad economic influences of society that affect the level of compensation of all workers. The following theories have been termed *micro* because they treat the wage structure within a given industry or even a given company, directly involving the bargain and the exchange between employer and employee.

m. In about 1876, Johann Heinrich Von Thuren, a German economist, proposed the basis for the *Marginal Productivity Theory,* which was developed further by Philip Henry Wickstead in England and John Bates Clark in America. According to this theory, the wage that is paid to an employee should be equal to the extra value of productivity that the employee adds to total production. The value of the worker's production is determined by the revenue the employer can realize from the worker's productivity. As the employer hires additional workers, a point is eventually reached at which the last worker hired just produces enough product to pay his or her own wages. The hiring of an additional worker would result in a revenue that did not equal that worker's wages. The latest worker hired is called the "marginal employee," and the increased pro-

[16]Richard A. Lester, "A Range Theory of Wage Differentials," *Industrial and Labor Relations Review,* July 1957, pp. 483–500.
[17]John Dunlop, "The Task of Contemporary Wage Theory," in *New Concepts in Wage Determination,* eds. George W. Taylor and Frank C. Pierson (New York: McGraw-Hill, 1957), pp. 117, 139.

duction attributed to the worker is called "marginal productivity." The wage paid to the latest marginal employee determines the wage of all workers who are doing similar work. Although the theory has come under considerable criticism from students of compensation, it does at least represent the first formal theory embracing the principle that a worker should be paid according to the quantity and quality of work contributed.

n. The *Productive Efficiency Theory* is an offshoot, or refinement, of the Marginal Productivity Theory in that each worker is provided the opportunity to increase his or her wages by increasing his or her productive efficiency. This theory provides the basis for an array of monetary motivational tools such as incentive systems, bonuses, and profit-sharing plans. Many economists feel that, because of its realistic application, the productivity theory is the most constructive of recent wage theories.

o. The beginnings of the *Bargaining Theory of Wages* are found in the writings of Adam Smith. However, it was described more explicitly by John Davidson in the late 1890s. This is the first clear presentation of the simple principle that compensation is instigated by, and dependent upon, a bargain between an employer and an employee. This theory further indicates that the work performed by any employee is an exchange of economic value that balances the original commitment of the employer who is making the bargain. The bargaining theory is based on the assumption that there is no single fixed wage rate for a particular kind of work. Rather, there is a *range* of possible wage rates. The upper limit of this range is determined by the highest wage the employer is able, or willing, to pay, and the lower limit is determined by the lowest wage for which the employee is willing to work. In actual practice in America, this lowest minimum limit that the employee will accept is in effect established by the minimum wage law and/or the prevailing rate of unemployment compensation.

The Bargaining Theory remains, to this day, probably the most practical and valid explanation for the level of a given employee's compensation. When, and if, an employee chooses to designate a union as a bargaining agent with the employer, then this theory becomes the Collective Bargaining Theory. However, the basis of the theory remains unchanged, whether the employee bargains personally, or authorizes an agent to do the bargaining on his or her behalf.

It is important to point out that in appointing a union to act as the bargaining agent, the employee must inevitably forgo, to a degree, some personal rights. As is the case with any group activity, in which each member must subjugate certain personal rights to the good of the whole, union members must also relinquish the right to bargain, on their own behalf, for any better benefits than those enjoyed by their fellow union members.

It is interesting to note that in Smith's brilliant economic analysis he developed the following argument:

> Every regulation introduces some degree of real disorder into the constitution of the state, which it will be difficult afterwards to cure without occasioning another disorder.

This proposition applies equally to the organization. Recognizing its truth and value, organizations should make every effort to develop a theory of compensation that meets its needs, the needs of its members, and the needs of the consumers of its output so that it minimizes the need for external regulations and control with regard to its compensation program.

Economic models of demand and supply and exchange rates highlight several important points for the compensation professional. One consideration they do not adequately emphasize is of equal significance for compensation management: the ambiguity of the term *wage rate*. To the economist, *wage* is a general term used to measure the total cost of labor per hour. To the compensation management professional, however, the cost of labor takes on many different forms. For example, should incentives be added to base pay? If so, what forms should the incentives take? Should any of the pay be deferred? What kinds of benefits should be given? How are these costed out?

MICRO-MICRO THEORIES

IV. Behavioral Economics Theories began to be developed in the last half of the twentieth century. Researchers who developed Behavioral Economics models had become concerned with the lack of behavioral assumptions in earlier economics models. They recognized that many of these economic theories viewed the organization as a "black box" that, in some manner, transformed inputs into outputs. Even with the development of micro theories, minimal attention focused on the functions, structure, and management of the organization. The developers of micro-micro economic theories recognized that management practices could critically influence the output (productivity) of the organization and that internal managerial and compensation management practices must be recognized.

p. H. Leibenstein developed the *X-Efficiency Model* that recognized the influence of internal management practices on organizational productivity. He found that firms operating under competitive market conditions could produce additional levels of output by changing internal work processes without changing the scale of operations or technology. He postulated that the actual output levels of a firm seldom matched its competitive optimal level. The difference, X-inefficiency, was established to recognize the difference between the firm's production attributable to its internal operations rather than the allocative efficiency of the market.[18] Leibenstein felt that the optimizing behavior assumed under neoclassical theories (Wage Control and Justification Theories) was the exception rather than the rule.[19] He further stated that productivity was significantly influenced by the internal structure of rewards and incentives, work effort, individual personality, and the management system of the organization.

q. The foundation of Leibenstein's view of nonoptimal behavior is strongly supported by the work and findings of Herbert Simon. From his research, Simon recognized that managers do not make optimal decisions; rather, they suboptimize. The *Suboptimization Theory* as developed by Simon recognized that managers work under conditions of bounded rationality and they satisfice. Bounded

---

[18]H. Leibenstein, *Beyond Economic Man: A New Foundation for Microeconomics* (Boston, MA: Harvard University Press, 1980), pp. 6, 29–46; *Inside the Firm: The Inefficiencies of Hierarchy* (Boston, MA: Harvard University Press, 1987).

[19]H. Leibenstein, "A Branch of Economics Is Missing: Micro-Micro Theory," *Journal of Economic Literature,* June 1979, pp. 477–502.

rationality occurs because managers seldom if ever have all of the knowledge and facts to select the best optimal action for a specific situation and then, because of actual or even perceived limits on available resources (including time), they satisfice. They act in a manner that is "good enough" but not necessarily the optimal or best way—they suboptimize. What Simon and Leibenstein recognize is that economic behavior is linked directly to individual decision makers and situational-related constraints.

V. A set of theories and models related to behavioral economics that centers on the nature of the firm can be titled *Organizational Economic Theories.* Organizational economics consists primarily of transaction cost economics and agency theory.

r. *Transaction Cost Economic Theory* has been largely associated with the writings of Oliver Williamson, although its primary influences can be traced directly to Frank Knight, J. R. Commons, and Ronald Coase.[20] The theory centers on the nature of exchanges of goods and services among parties; however, unlike earlier economic theories, it assumes complexity and uncertainty in the process of the exchanges, bounded rationality, asymmetrical distributions of information, and potential opportunism of the parties in the exchange. Transaction costs consist of negotiating, monitoring, and enforcement costs that must be borne to allow an exchange between the two parties to take place.[21] Essentially, when these costs of exchange in the market become so great, there is an incentive to remove them from the market and produce them internally. Internalizing these costs requires an internal organizational structure that specifies incentive systems and monitoring activities. From this perspective, it is clear how a well-designed compensation system plays a major role in the operation of the firm. Gomez-Mejia and Balkin suggest that a strategically designed compensation system will take into account these transaction costs and attempt to reduce them.[22]

s. Another contribution to organizational economics is the *Agency Theory.* Of all the theories in the micro-micro/organizational economics framework, the Agency Theory provides the most relevant implications for the design of a compensation system for the organization. Under conditions of imperfect information, divergent interests among stockholders (principals), management (agent), and employees may prevail. The fundamental compensation problem is how to develop either an explicit or an implicit incentive-reward contract that aligns the interests of management with those of the stockholders.[23] For example, stockholders (principals) who desire that the value of their investment in a firm be as great as possible will often provide management (agent) with some form of compensation (profit sharing) based on firm performance in order to assure an alignment of interests. The costs for forming, monitoring, and enforcing such a contract are termed *agency costs.* The primary theme of agency theory and effective compensation policies suggest that "the firm owners can utilize moni-

[20]Oliver Williamson, *The Economic Institutions of Capitalism* (New York: The Free Press, 1985), pp. 1–68.
[21]G. R. Jones and C. W. L. Hill, "Transaction Cost Analysis of Strategy-Structure Choice," *Strategic Management Journal,* 1988, vol. 9, p. 160.
[22]L. R. Gomez-Mejia and D. B. Balken, *Compensation, Organizational Strategy and Firm Performance* (Cincinnati, OH: South-Western Publishing Company, 1992), pp. 126–129.
[23]Ibid., p. 21.

toring and incentive alignment mechanisms to induce managers (and their subordinates) to engage in those behaviors that improve shareholder wealth."[24]

Although not presented in this model of economic theories, three other organizational economics models could assist in linking current compensation practices to economic theories that extend over a period of 2,500 years. They are (1) Property Rights Theory, (2) Implicit Contract Theory, and (3) Evolutionary Economic Theory.[25]

The theories drawn from the micro-micro/organizational economics framework do not replace or denigrate the importance of earlier presented economics models. However, this final group expands one's understanding of the variability in organizational strategies and structures and, by implication, the multitude of compensation practices that are encountered in the real world. They have the potential for providing the field of compensation management with a theoretical foundation for its practices. Furthermore, the diversity and complexity of this last stage of development simply mirror the nature of the problems and challenges facing general management and compensation practitioners.

Economic Theory Bibliography

A further discussion of economic theories and their impact on wages may be found in the following books:

Barney, Jay, and William G. Ouchi. *Organizational Economics*. San Francisco: Jossey-Bass Publishers, 1986.

Clark, John Bates. *Distribution of Wealth*. New York: The Macmillan Company, 1899.

Davidson, John. *The Bargaining Theory of Wages*. New York: G. P. Putnam's Sons, 1898.

Dunlop, John T., ed. *Theory of Wage Determination*. New York: St. Martin's Press, Inc., 1957.

Ford, Henry. *My Life and Work*. New York: Doubleday, Page & Company, 1922.

Heneman, Herbert G., Jr., and Dale Yoder. *Labor Economics*, 2nd ed. Cincinnati, OH: South-Western Publishing Co., 1965.

Hicks, J. R. *The Theory of Wages*, 2nd ed. New York: St. Martin's Press, Inc., 1963.

Kaufman, Bruce E. *The Economics of Labor Markets and Labor Relations*. Chicago: Dryden, 1986.

Keynes, John Maynard. *The General Theory of Employment, Interest and Money*. New York: Harcourt, Brace & Company, Inc., 1936.

Leftwich, Richard H. *The Price System and Resource Allocation*. New York: Holt, Rinehart & Winston, 1966.

Marshall, Alfred. *Principles of Economics*. London: Macmillan & Co., Ltd., 1947.

Milgrom, Paul, and John Roberts. *Economics, Organization & Management*. Englewood Cliffs, NJ: Prentice Hall, Inc., 1992.

Smith, Adam. *An Inquiry into the Nature and Causes of the Wealth of Nations*. Scotland: Adam and Charles Black, 1863.

Taylor, George W., and Frank C. Pierson, eds. *New Concepts in Wage Determination*. New York: McGraw Hill Book Company, 1957.

Whittaker, Edmund. *A History of Economics Ideas*. London: Longman's Green & Co., 1940.

Wooton, Barbara. *The Social Foundations of Wage Policy*. New York: W. W. Norton & Company, Inc., 1955.

---

[24]Ibid., pp. 165–168.

[25]Joseph T. Mahony and Rajendran J. Pandian, "The Resource-Based View within the Conversation of Strategic Management," *Strategic Management Journal*, 1992, p. 369; Sherwin Rosen, "Implicit Contracts: A Survey," *Journal of Economic Literature*, 1985, 23, pp. 1144–1175.

CHAPTER

Organizational Structure

4

Strategic and Tactical Compensation Issues

Learning Objectives

In this chapter you will learn about:

1. The principal activities required in the development of an organization.

2. The relationships among pay satisfaction, job satisfaction, and organizational satisfaction and their effect on individual behavior.

3. The major employee groups that make up an organization.

4. The variations in rates of pay among the different major groups of employees.

5. Exempt and nonexempt employees.

6. Pay equity and pay ratios and their influence on employee performance.

7. The importance of relating pay to the strategy and tactics of the organization.

Compensation Strategy

Support organizational mission and strategy through compensation strategy and tactics that integrate major organizational groups of employees.

Organizational leaders, including those occupying the executive suites and those in charge of human resources and compensation practices, must be able to recognize and integrate long-term strategic objectives of the organization with its short-term tactical requirements. An understanding of how organizational strategy and its related tactics interact and become integrated is becoming increasingly important to managers at all levels performing various organizational assignments.

To improve cost and quality competitiveness in an environment where social and political problems are becoming increasingly more sensitive and complex, where masses of data and information are readily available, and where information overload is a problem facing all organizations and their employees, information regarding work requirements, performance standards, and organizational recognition and rewards programs must be readily available, complete, and accepted. The compensation system, therefore, must be able to transmit a message understood and accepted by all employees that they are valued contributors to organizational success and that the organization is willing to share the revenues from its products in an equitable manner with all members.

To develop and operate a compensation system that promotes fair treatment, an organization should consider compensation strategies such as:

1. Relating job worth to differences in job requirements
2. Recognizing the worth and value of employee knowledge and skills
3. Rewarding employee contributions and the results achieved
4. Promoting employee continued acquisition and upgrading of knowledge and skills
5. Supporting team and work unit cooperative efforts
6. Designing compensation plans that successfully compete within established labor markets
7. Aligning compensation of all employees with objectives and goals of the organization
8. Providing a compensation package that enhances current lifestyles and provides long-term protection for employees and their dependents

DEVELOPMENT OF AN ORGANIZATION

The process modeled in Figure 4–1 identifies the major functions in developing an organization that achieves both its short- and long-term goals. The organizational "seed" is an idea in the brain of an individual. From the time the organization is only a seed of an idea until it is actually producing an output, a sequence of human activities occurs.

Underlying any human action is a value system. A value system is a composite of everything an individual understands or has learned. It takes the form of guidelines or limits that direct thinking and behavior. These guidelines express both internalized likes and dislikes and rational and irrational judgment.

An idea originates and develops in the brain and through the thinking process of an individual. As the idea begins its journey from the brain to a specific output requiring the efforts of more than one person, a production process starts. When this output of a good or a service requires the efforts of more than one person, groups are formed. In some manner and to some degree, coordination and direction of effort become essential if the groups are to be successful in producing their desired outputs. The value systems of the group leaders and the group members critically influence the direction and the intensity of productive effort. The expression of the value system becomes identifiable through the philosophy of the organization.

The Philosophy of the Organization

Although many organizations do not have written philosophy statements, the oral expressions and the actions of leaders establish their operating philosophy. The philosophy of the organization, expressed either in written form or through the behavior of its

```
┌──────────────────────────────────┐
│     Establishing a Philosophy     │
└──────────────────────────────────┘
                 │
                 ▼
┌──────────────────────────────────┐
│       Identifying the Mission     │
└──────────────────────────────────┘
                 │
                 ▼
┌──────────────────────────────────┐
│         Developing Policy         │
└──────────────────────────────────┘
                 │
                 ▼
┌──────────────────────────────────┐
│  Formulating Organizational Strategy │
└──────────────────────────────────┘
                 │
                 ▼
┌──────────────────────────────────┐
│    Determining Objectives and     │
│     Subobjectives or Goals        │
└──────────────────────────────────┘
                 │
                 ▼
┌──────────────────────────────────┐
│    Defining Work Unit Activities  │
└──────────────────────────────────┘
                 │
                 ▼
┌──────────────────────────────────┐
│      Grouping Tasks into Jobs     │
└──────────────────────────────────┘
```

FIGURE 4–1 Principal Activities in the Development of an Organization

leaders, establishes general guidelines for decisions and actions to be taken by all members. The statement of philosophy, whether written or unwritten, thus describes the values of top management or the leaders of the organization. Critical to organizational success is the degree of congruence between the values of all its members and the philosophy of the organization. A major roadblock to success frequently arises when members fail to recognize a positive relationship between their own values and the philosophy statements or philosophy-based behavior of their leaders.

The Mission of the Organization

The next step in moving from ideas and values to concerted action occurs with the identification and the description of the mission of the organization. The mission statement describes in broad or general value-laden terms what the organization wishes to accomplish in the long term—the kind of product it intends to provide and *how* it intends to provide it. It details the reasons for the existence of the organization. It defines its superordinate goals, which will provide long-term guides to action. It provides the link between the organization and the environment. The philosophy statement provides standards for guiding employee action; the mission statement identifies desired results that must be translated into action. Mission statements can be considered the criteria used for assessing the long-term effectiveness of the organization. The realization of these requirements assists in ensuring the survival of the organization.

The Policy of the Organization

To ensure proper and acceptable operations in working toward the accomplishment of its mission-identified end results, an organization develops a policy. Policy statements, like mission statements, are broad guidelines for directing action. Those responsible for formulating policy recognize the influence of human behavior and social demands on the accomplishment of desired output. To be effective in directing employee behavior, policy must support the mission of the organization. It must be sufficiently broad to relate to different actions and behaviors required of the various work units and members of the organization, and it must be understood by those members.

The Strategy of the Organization

A primary responsibility of the top management of any organization is the establishment of organizational strategy. Organizational strategy continues the planning process that began with establishing a philosophy, identifying the mission, and developing policy. Strategy provides the foundation for future growth and development of the organization.

In order to be successful in the ever more complex environment within which all organizations exist, strategy must be realistic. In identifying what it wants to accomplish, the organization must recognize the resources that are available and the resources it will need. Organizational strategy must establish realistic expectations. It must have a clear vision of the work culture and provide a common purpose for all members to provide constructive effort in working together for a competitive advantage. From the organizational strategy, substrategies for major financial areas will be developed, and within the various organizational functions and units, tactics will be implemented to promote the accomplishment of the organizational objectives.

The Objectives and Goals of the Organization

The next step in the idea-to-output process is to establish objectives and goals. The primary objective is to translate the broadly developed mission statements into more specific output requirements. These results-oriented statements become further translated into more specific short-term goals for the work units of the organization. At this stage in the process, the organization identifies operational requirements. It begins the establishment of the levels of performance needed to accomplish the mission of the organization. In making the transition from strategic to tactical operations, the organization must determine the most effective and efficient means of accomplishing its mission.

Work Unit Activities

Once the organizational and work unit objectives (subobjectives and goals) have been established, each unit must develop its own function statement. The function statement is, in effect, the charter for the work unit. It identifies the principal activities of the work unit. It further assists in integrating the top-down established organizational objectives and goals with the assignments of each work unit.

Worker Tasks

From the activities assigned to each work unit come the tasks to be performed by the members of that unit. Work unit activities become segregated and assigned to specific individuals. These activities become further identified as tasks, duties, and responsibil-

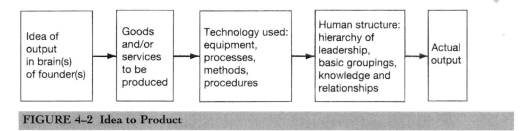

FIGURE 4-2 Idea to Product

ities of a job. The translation process from the idea to the expenditure of human energy that leads to production of a desired output is now under way. Figure 4–2 describes the evolution of an idea into a product.

To influence and direct this effort, the organization must consider how it can reward behaviors and results in a manner that recognizes differences in job requirements. It is through the division of labor that particular tasks are assigned to an individual. These tasks, in turn, require specific knowledge and skills and require that the job be performed under a variety of environmental conditions, which also make different kinds of physiological, intellectual, and emotional demands on the worker.

EMPLOYEES—A CRITICAL RESOURCE

From both a strategic and tactical perspective, the quality and quantity of organizational output depend directly on the skill, interest, and effort of employees. Certainly, the more highly paid may be more critical contributors, but the productive efforts of all employees are essential.

Recognizing the influence of emotion on human behavior, it may be valuable for organizational strategists and tacticians to understand the relationships among pay satisfaction, job satisfaction, and organizational satisfaction and their effects on individual behavior.

Pay Satisfaction

In developing a compensation system, designers must recognize that people make decisions about pay based on comparisons with others. The others for comparison purposes can be an immediate coworker with similar if not identical assignments, other employees in the organization performing different activities, and even workers in other organizations doing similar or different work for similar or different rates of pay. These comparisons are uniquely weighted by each individual. The results of these comparisons, in turn, influence employees to stay or leave, to work at their best, or even to sabotage the organization. Managers and human resource professionals must do everything possible to influence these comparison decisions favorably.

Job Satisfaction

Ability to perform in a proficient manner, recognition of a "job well done," and an opportunity to advance in the current career ladder or even take a bridging job to a new career path all enhance job satisfaction. Although pay and job satisfaction are entirely different, they interact and significantly influence each other. A positive view of one process can improve the view of the other. Just as easily, a negative view of one process can destroy a positive view of the other. Although job satisfaction is not a primary area of responsibility for the compensation professional, involvement in organizational strategic issues underscores the need to recognize and work toward improving employee job satisfaction.

Organizational Satisfaction

The third process, organizational satisfaction, includes the other two processes but is not limited to them. Security in employment for many employees can minimize frustration and stress arising from pay and job dissatisfaction. Recognizing fairness in all kinds of personnel decisions may limit the frustration an employee feels about a specific issue. Recognizing, understanding, and accepting organizational philosophy and policies go a long way toward promoting organizational satisfaction.

Satisfaction: An Employment Perspective

To design, develop, and implement reward systems that lead to improved employee pay, job, and organizational satisfaction, it is critical to understand the meaning of the word *satisfaction* from an employment perspective. First, satisfaction is a process, not a thing. To some, satisfaction means the fulfillment or gratification of a need. However, from an employment perspective, it means the fulfillment of an obligation. The addition of the word *obligation* recognizes that at least two parties are involved in the satisfaction process: the employee and the employer. To be useful in making workplace decisions, satisfaction models or definitions must not only be rigorous and logical but must also apply to the world where work is performed.

To be rigorous and workplace applicable, a satisfaction model must recognize that satisfaction is strongly *individual based*. What causes satisfaction in one person may lead to a high degree of dissatisfaction in another. Possibly even more critical, the model must recognize that satisfaction is a dynamic process—what can cause satisfaction in a person today can cause dissatisfaction tomorrow.

Because satisfaction involves reciprocity, it is important that opportunities to gain satisfaction are viewed and analyzed from the perspective of all parties. This reciprocal relationship means that to gain any benefit from analyzing or even considering satisfaction at the workplace, the satisfaction opportunities for all parties must be recognized and understood. To move satisfaction from the "toolbox" of the witch doctor, magician, or mystic to the toolbox of the manager, organizations must recognize that satisfaction involves a contract between employee and employer. The terms and conditions of the contract must, at a minimum, state to the employee: (1) This is what the organization expects from you; (2) these are the rewards we offer you in exchange for the availability of your skills, effort, and interest.

DIVISION OF LABOR

The ability to take the greatest advantage of dividing labor and specializing work requirements among individuals in a social group has helped the human race to dominate all other life forms. The basis of the employer–employee exchange process is the division of labor, the performance of specialized activities, and the provision of rewards to those who make contributions. The quality and the quantity of rewards normally vary according to the worth of employee contributions as measured by the employer and the value of those contributions as perceived by employees.

Emile Durkheim, the famous French sociologist, recognized the importance of the division of labor when he stated that *what* a person is and *who* a person is depend on and reflect the kind of work a person does. He further stated that the acceptance of a job is the crucial act by which individuals integrate into society and find a definition of self that corresponds to their place in society. Fulfillment and satisfaction from work come from individual achievement and from being a member of a group. However, most people do not subordinate themselves unless they view their work relationships as being legal and just. Organizations require some form of established procedures, specialization of activities, and central direction, which in turn require management to enhance cooperation as it affects collaboration and to minimize the conflicts that result from specialized work requirements.

CREATING AN ORGANIZATIONAL HIERARCHY

One basic approach to distributing rewards focuses on the level of the job in the organizational structure. The higher the level of the job, the greater the responsibility of the incumbent. Once an organization employs 100 or more people, it develops a line structure that is common to organizations hiring hundreds of thousands of people. This structure consists of a board of directors, senior management, operating managers (senior, midlevel, first level), professionals and administrators, and operative employees. Figure 4–3 shows a basic organizational hierarchy with a list of major groups, the limits of exemption status (exempt from overtime requirements of the Fair Labor Standards Act), and the range of unionization in the organization. Figure 4–4 provides another way of looking at organizational groups. Increased responsibilities require broader and more complex knowledge and skills. The more diverse the knowledge and the higher the level of the skill requirements, the greater the compensation.

To gain further insights into the distribution of workers within an organization, Table 4–1 presents the distribution of workers in the United States in 1998. The occupations in this table do not match precisely the occupations presented in Figure 4–4, but there is a very close relationship. The managerial and administrative groups in Figure 4–4 are represented by the executive, administrative, and managerial group in Table 4–1. The professional group in the table includes architects; engineers; mathematical and computer scientists; natural scientists; health diagnosing, assessment, and treatment occupations; teachers and counselors; librarians; social scientists; social, recreation, and religious workers; lawyers and judges; writers, artists, entertainers, and athletes. Individuals identified in the professional and technician groups relate to the paraprofessional group identified in Figure 4–4. The administrative support category in Table 4–1 correlates with the secretarial-clerical classification under the operative group in Figure 4–4.

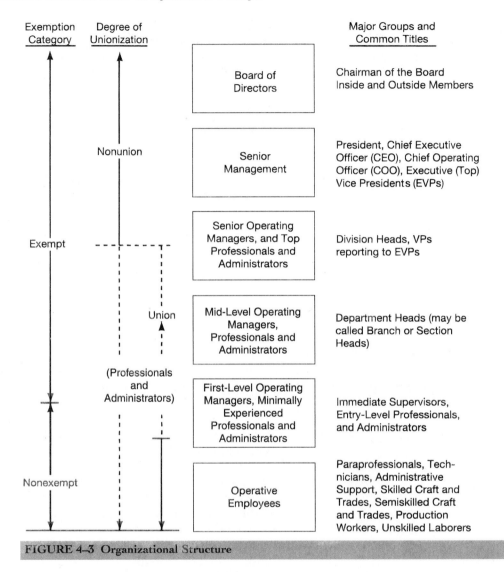

FIGURE 4–3 Organizational Structure

The service occupation includes private household workers, protective services, food preparation and delivery, health services, cleaning and building services, and personal services. These individuals are identified in Figure 4–4 within the operative category. The precision production, craft and repair, and the operators, fabricators, and laborers groups in Table 4–1 include craftworkers of all kinds, machine operators, equipment operators, welders, cutters, assemblers, and transportation and material moving workers who also may be found in the operative group in Figure 4–4.

In 1997, the American labor force produced a gross domestic product (GDP) of $8,079.9 billion. In turn, this workforce received a total compensation of $4,798.0 billion

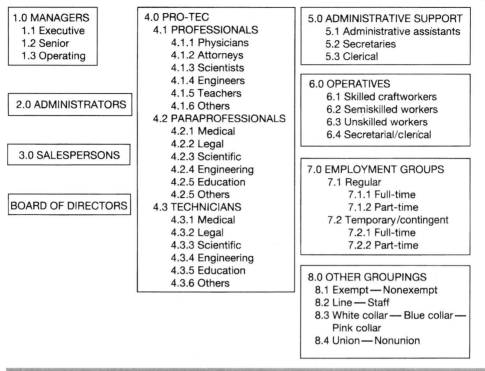

1.0 MANAGERS	4.0 PRO-TEC	5.0 ADMINISTRATIVE SUPPORT

FIGURE 4–4 **Basic Groups for Structure and Organization**

further divided into \$3,877.4 billion in wages and salaries and \$920.6 billion in benefits and services.[1] A brief analysis of these data reveals that

$$\frac{\text{total compensation}}{\text{GDP}} = \frac{4,798.0}{8,079.9} = 59.4\%$$

$$\frac{\text{supplements to wages and salaries (benefits and services)}}{\text{wages and salaries}} = \frac{920.6}{3,877.4} = 23.7\%^{[2]}$$

With almost 60 percent of the GDP of the nation being consumed through employee compensation, it is evident that this cost is extremely important both to the employers

---

[1] In chapter 17 there is a lengthy discussion of the cost of benefits. For major organizations in the United States, benefits cost approximately 39 percent of wages. It must also be recognized that approximately 25 percent of all working Americans do not have employer-provided health insurance coverage and other desired benefits. These GDP figures recognize such differences in the *total* economy.

[2] U.S. Department of Commerce, Bureau of Economic and Statistical Analysis, *Statistical Abstract of the United States, 1998* (Washington, DC: U.S. Government Printing Office, 1998), Table 715, p. 458.

TABLE 4–1 Labor Force by Major Occupational Groups in December 1998 (with percentage and number of women)

	Total Labor Force (in millions)	Percentage by Major Occupation of Total Labor Force	Number of Women (in millions)	Percentage of Women by Major Occupation
Total employed (16 years old and over)	131,463	100.0	60,771	100.0
Executive, administrative, and managerial	19,054	14.5	8,469	13.9
Professional specialty	19,883	15.1	10,602	17.4
Technician and related support	4,261	3.2	2,285	3.8
Sales occupations	15,850	12.1	7,975	13.1
Administrative support (including clerical)	18,410	14.0	14,469	23.8
Service occupations	17,836	13.6	10,614	17.5
Precision production, craft, and repair	14,411	11.0	1,203	2.0
Operators, fabricators, and laborers	18,256	13.9	4,487	7.4
Farming, forestry, and fishing	3,502	2.7	668	1.1

Source: Employment and Earnings (Washington, DC: USDOL, Bureau of Labor Statistics, January 1999), pp. 176, 177.

who make the payments and to employees who provide their knowledge, skill, and energy in exchange for these payments.

The pay and total compensation received by each employee relate almost directly to that individual's level in the organizational hierarchy and the kind of work he or she performs.

BOARD OF DIRECTORS

The board of directors usually consists of 10 to 20 members elected by the shareholders of the corporation. The highest-ranking member of the board is the chairman. In some cases, the chairman of the board also assumes full-time responsibility for directing the operations of the organization. In most cases, however, the chairman directs only the operation of the board. All members are classified as *inside* or *outside* members. *Inside* members are those who are also employees of the corporation—normally, the chief executive officer and other key senior staff officials. *Outside* members are usually knowledgeable and skilled individuals who have considerable business experience or who represent an important segment of society or are major shareholders in the corporation. These individuals may represent suppliers of inputs to or receivers of outputs from the corporation.

In performing their obligations, boards of directors provide certain services. Among the more important are these:

1. Establishing policy for key internal and external operations that permits effective use of organizational resources while complying with social and legal mandates.
2. Ensuring that senior management is properly structured and staffed.
3. Identifying the mission of the organization and the preferred strategic and tactical practices to accomplish the mission.
4. Reviewing senior management actions to ensure that actions are congruent with established policies and plans and that these managers are making best use of available resources and achieving desired results.

To accomplish these major requirements and other collateral assignments, members of the board are being required to spend more and more time preparing for and executing board business. Not only are board members required to have a broader knowledge of business-related activities, they are also being held increasingly liable and financially accountable for what they have done, what they have undone, and what they have not done. Like most people, members of the board recognize the honor bestowed upon them by being offered the position, but they also expect to be compensated for the services they provide.

The compensation package for members of the board usually consists of the following: (1) regular meeting fees for board meetings attended; (2) an annual retainer for board membership; or (3) a set fee that combines fees and annual retainer; and (4) acquisition of stock in the company. A small percentage of organizations provide inside members of their boards with board membership compensation. The regular organizational compensation package recognizes board-related assignments. WWDS noted in its 1998 survey that only 3.0 percent of responding organizations compensated inside members extra for board membership.[3] Larger companies are less likely to compensate inside members. They are also more likely to provide richer compensation packages to their outside members.[4]

Meeting fees can range from $1,000 to $1,500 per meeting with a $1,000 payment most common. Retainers range from $10,000 to well over $25,000 per year with a median retainer fee being $22,200 per year.[5] The median annual compensation to outside directors in 1998 was $33,950, while total compensation, including the value of stock components, was $45,000.[6]

---

[3]Watson Wyatt Data Services, *The ECS Report on Board of Directors Policies and Practices, 30th ed.* (Rochelle Park, NJ: Watson Wyatt Worldwide, 1998/1999), p. 98.
[4]Ibid., p. 294.
[5]*Corporate Directors Compensation in 1998* (New York: The Conference Board, 1998), p. 8.
[6]Ibid., p. 7.

In recent years, the compensation package for many board members has been significantly enhanced through the addition of long-term incentive programs. The two major components of a board of directors long-term incentive plan are (1) non-qualified stock option plans and (2) restricted stock plans.[7] The actual size and amount of long-term incentives received by board members vary according to corporate performance. The following corporate performance measures are being used to determine incentive awards. They are (1) earnings per share, (2) net profits after taxes, (3) return on equity, (4) return on assets, and (5) annual sales or revenue.[8] More and more companies are providing their board members with stock ownership guidelines.[9] In recent years, companies offering stock to board members made the stock offerings every year. In 1998, the median value of a stock option grant to a board member was $58,800, while the median value of restricted stock awards was $15,650.[10]

In addition to the retainer and the fees for attending meetings, most organizations reimburse outside members for all incurred travel expenses and provide director and officer liability insurance (D&O) to indemnify board members for personal losses sustained from legal action arising out of their activities as board members. This has become a highly desirable compensation component.

Some organizations now provide their outside directors with (1) group travel insurance, (2) group life insurance, and (3) accidental death and dismemberment insurance. A few are offering group medical and hospitalization insurance.

A major change in the compensation programs of outside members of the board of directors began to appear in the mid-1990s with the elimination of pension plans for outside directors. A major reason for the elimination of pensions was that lucrative retirement plans encourage outside directors to stay too long and cause them to lose their independence.[11]

In 1996, 30 percent of the companies reporting their plans to The Conference Board had retirement plans. By 1998, the number having pension plans was reduced to 12 percent.[12]

SENIOR MANAGEMENT

Senior management is responsible for the proper organization and operation of the firm. In a small organization, senior management may consist of only the owner or the president. In a larger organization, it will consist of executives and senior managers—those who have responsibility for setting the objectives of the organization, establish-

---

[7]Watson Wyatt, p. 309.

[8]Watson Wyatt, p. 311.

[9]These guidelines inform not only members of the board but also executives and managers about owning shares of stock in their corporations. Many of the stock ownership guidelines suggest a level of ownership based on a multiple of annual salary or, for board members, retainers and meeting fees.

[10]Watson Wyatt, p. 316.

[11]Joann S. Lublin, "Five More Big Companies to Stop Giving Pensions to Outside Members of Boards," *The Wall Street Journal,* February 12, 1996, p. A2.

[12]The Conference Board, p. 27.

ing its operating policies, and defining courses of action through the strategies they develop and approve.

In 1976 Arch Patton, a recognized expert on executive compensation, stated that there were approximately 135,000 employees in American businesses who could truly be identified as policy-making executives.[13] Given a workforce at that time of approximately 85 million, this executive group consisted of approximately one-sixth of 1 percent of the total workforce. Because this is an average statistic, the number of executives in any particular organization may be somewhat larger or smaller. The highest-ranking officer of this group, who may be the chief executive officer (CEO) or the president, is responsible for all operations. Normally, an organization will use only one of the two titles. Periodically, however, an organization will have a CEO as well as a president.

Reporting directly to the CEO is a small number of top executives who have overall operational responsibilities for the organization. The number two person in the organization is often the chief operating officer (COO) and reporting to this individual are key executives who have the titles of senior or executive vice president with functional responsibilities such as controller, manufacturing, finance, marketing, research and development, engineering, legal, and human resources, or they are responsible for the operation of large profit centers. The salary and total compensation package received by these executives and senior managers relates directly to the compensation package of the CEO. Table 4–2 lists the top executives commonly found in U.S. organizations and describes their pay relationships as a percentage of the CEO's salary and bonus. In this table, total compensation includes salary and short-term bonus.

The important message presented in Table 4–2 is that the pay and short-term bonuses of senior managers in U.S. organizations are tied directly to those received by the top executive of the organization. Thus, it is in the best interest of these individuals that their top executive receive the highest possible pay and short-term bonus.

The actual size of the CEO's total compensation package (and, for that matter those of other members of senior management) relates to the size of the organization. For organizations in different industries, the determinant or size indicator varies. The following business activity statistics indicate differences in compensation practices:

Manufacturing, construction, and retail trade	Dollar sales volume
Utilities	Operating revenue
Banks	Total deposits
Insurance companies	Total premium income

Table 4–3 lists total cash compensation of the chief executive officer by industrial categories such as durable and nondurable goods manufacturing, retail and wholesale trade, services, and utilities and energy.

---

[13] Arch Patton, "The Boom in Executive Self-Interest," *Business Week,* May 24, 1976, pp. 16, 20.

TABLE 4-2 Selected Top-Management Compensation Compared to CEO Compensation (CEO = 100%)

	Sales Size Group ($ million)													
	Under $50		$50 to $99		$100 to $199		$200 to $499		$500 to $999		$1,000 to $1,999		$2,000 and Over	
	% of		% of		% of		% of		% of		% of		% of	
Position	S	TC	S	TC	S	TC	S	TC	S	TC	S	TC	S	TC
Chief Executive Officer	100%	100%	100%	100%	100%	100%	100%	100%	100%	100%	100%	100%	100%	100%
Chief Operating Officer	93%	93%	99%	99%	68%	66%	74%	72%	77%	76%	74%	69%	67%	67%
Top Subsidiary Executive	60%	60%	57%	65%	56%	60%	54%	51%	41%	37%	29%	24%	46%	40%
Executive Vice President	77%	81%	67%	64%	60%	61%	57%	55%	60%	57%	59%	52%	54%	50%
Administrative Vice President	61%	54%	58%	47%	56%	57%	48%	45%	41%	37%	39%	33%	36%	33%
Top Group Executive	50%	44%	84%	76%	43%	42%	51%	51%	43%	41%	32%	27%	39%	35%
Corporate Secretary (if not top legal executive)	42%	25%	—	—	30%	29%	30%	25%	33%	31%	25%	20%	20%	15%
Top International Executive	31%	37%	30%	34%	43%	41%	45%	36%	49%	44%	27%	20%	28%	23%
Top Long-Range Planning Executive	62%	65%	51%	37%	40%	36%	35%	30%	37%	32%	32%	26%	25%	21%
Mergers and Acquisitions Executive	—	—	—	—	48%	30%	37%	31%	30%	23%	28%	22%	31%	25%
Top Real Estate Executive	—	—	—	—	65%	60%	34%	27%	44%	41%	29%	22%	23%	19%
Top Total Quality Management Executive	47%	35%	43%	39%	29%	31%	31%	27%	23%	18%	25%	23%	28%	23%
Top Financial Executive	57%	54%	56%	53%	55%	53%	50%	46%	51%	50%	45%	39%	44%	40%
Controller (if not top financial executive)	44%	39%	39%	34%	35%	32%	31%	26%	31%	27%	27%	22%	25%	20%
International Controller	—	—	—	—	25%	25%	31%	19%	25%	21%	13%	8%	16%	12%
Top Risk Management Executive	26%	24%	37%	37%	32%	32%	20%	17%	25%	22%	18%	13%	15%	12%
Top Auditor/General Auditor	41%	26%	—	—	39%	39%	18%	12%	21%	16%	18%	13%	18%	15%
Top Investor Relations Executive	—	—	—	—	—	—	28%	28%	28%	24%	22%	17%	18%	14%
Top Tax Executive	23%	22%	19%	16%	35%	26%	22%	16%	24%	19%	22%	17%	21%	17%
Treasurer (if not top financial executive)	65%	70%	29%	27%	35%	33%	32%	25%	30%	26%	23%	18%	24%	21%
Top Human Resources Executive (with labor relations)	42%	33%	44%	41%	40%	36%	35%	30%	36%	34%	31%	27%	34%	28%
Top Human Resources Executive (without labor relations)	32%	31%	33%	30%	39%	38%	35%	30%	35%	33%	32%	26%	26%	22%
Top MIS Executive	39%	37%	41%	37%	40%	36%	35%	29%	33%	29%	28%	24%	28%	23%
Top Telecommunications Executive	—	—	52%	66%	38%	33%	22%	20%	24%	19%	16%	14%	14%	10%

Sales Size Group ($ million)

Position	Under $50		$50 to $99		$100 to $199		$200 to $499		$500 to $999		$1,000 to $1,999		$2,000 and Over	
	% of		% of		% of		% of		% of		% of		% of	
	S	TC	S	TC	S	TC	S	TC	S	TC	S	TC	S	TC
Top Business Development Executive	60%	64%	49%	42%	53%	46%	46%	42%	49%	45%	35%	29%	36%	38%
Top Facility Management Executive	33%	33%	—	—	35%	34%	35%	33%	27%	23%	19%	14%	18%	13%
Top Marketing and Sales Executive	62%	62%	56%	51%	58%	55%	49%	44%	47%	43%	39%	34%	30%	25%
Top Advertising Executive	25%	23%	32%	37%	39%	37%	30%	22%	23%	20%	25%	25%	19%	13%
Top Customer Service Executive	39%	38%	37%	40%	44%	42%	29%	23%	28%	22%	24%	17%	19%	15%
Top Marketing Executive (excluding sales)	39%	36%	40%	34%	49%	48%	42%	38%	39%	34%	33%	28%	27%	22%
Top Market Research Executive	—	—	—	—	29%	26%	33%	22%	27%	22%	26%	21%	15%	11%
Top Sales Executive (excluding marketing)	50%	47%	45%	45%	47%	46%	43%	42%	39%	36%	37%	35%	30%	24%
Top Franchising Executive	—	—	—	—	46%	53%	10%	13%	32%	29%	24%	24%	17%	9%
Top Public Relations Executive	30%	34%	—	—	32%	29%	28%	24%	26%	21%	22%	18%	20%	17%
Top Legal Executive	50%	46%	45%	39%	58%	53%	42%	37%	43%	40%	39%	32%	37%	32%
Top Government Affairs Executive	—	—	42%	49%	40%	35%	46%	46%	26%	22%	27%	22%	21%	16%
Top Engineering Executive	65%	60%	44%	40%	47%	45%	44%	41%	31%	27%	25%	18%	24%	18%
Top Environmental Executive	—	—	59%	45%	54%	50%	28%	24%	24%	18%	21%	15%	17%	13%
Top Industrial Engineer	—	—	—	—	28%	22%	20%	16%	12%	11%	—	—	16%	13%
Top Quality Control Executive	37%	36%	38%	32%	28%	25%	28%	23%	23%	14%	34%	27%	18%	11%
Top Research Executive	58%	54%	64%	59%	41%	42%	45%	41%	38%	32%	29%	21%	21%	16%
Top Product Development Executive	52%	51%	51%	46%	40%	37%	41%	35%	36%	28%	24%	19%	23%	23%
Top Manufacturing/Production Executive	50%	48%	55%	50%	47%	46%	45%	42%	45%	40%	31%	28%	34%	30%
Top Operations Executive (nonmanufacturing)	68%	71%	68%	68%	50%	50%	34%	28%	44%	44%	35%	29%	33%	31%
Top Materials Management Executive	44%	43%	31%	31%	27%	21%	37%	33%	34%	28%	23%	18%	22%	17%
Top Distribution Executive	—	—	26%	25%	28%	23%	42%	33%	29%	25%	24%	21%	27%	23%
Top Purchasing Executive	45%	43%	31%	24%	31%	29%	28%	26%	31%	28%	22%	18%	22%	19%
Top Traffic/Transportation Executive	29%	29%	32%	32%	18%	19%	21%	21%	24%	17%	17%	14%	17%	12%
Top Construction Executive	79%	73%	—	—	35%	31%	29%	25%	26%	23%	25%	16%	20%	15%

[a]S = Salary
[b]TC = Total Cash Compensation

Source: Watson Wyatt Data Services, Top Management Compensation, 49th ed. (Rochelle Park, NJ: Watson Wyatt Worldwide, 1998/1999), pp. 967, 968.

TABLE 4–3 Total Cash Compensation Median of Chief Executive Officers

Sales Group ($ millions)	Durable Goods Manufacturing	Sales Group ($ millions)	Nondurable Goods Manufacturing	Sales Group ($ millions)	Retail and Wholesale Trade
Under 75	$197.3	Under 125	$ 301.3	Under 2,000	459.5
50–250	315.0	50–250	350.0	1,000 & Over	987.5
100–450	432.7	200–650	409.5	All Organizations	617.9
250–2,000	635.0	500–2,000	750.0		
1,000–5,000	900.0	1,000 & Over	1,167.6		
2,000 & Over	900.0	All Organizations	452.9		
All Organizations	402.3				

Sales Group ($ millions)	Services	Sales Group ($ millions)	Utilities and Energy
Under 100	$ 263.0	All Organizations	565.9
50–200	317.2		
100–500	420.0		
250–1,000	588.2		
500–2,000	661.4		
1,000–5,000	1,159.0		
2,000 & Over	1,660.3		
All Organizations	425.0		

Source: Watson Wyatt Data Services, *Top Management Compensation,* 49th ed. (Rochelle Park, NJ: Watson Wyatt Worldwide, 1998/99), pp. 62, 64, 66, 67, 68.

OPERATING MANAGERS

Operating managers hold positions with a wide range of titles and also an extremely wide range of pay, although the total compensation package includes fairly comparable components. The employees who occupy positions in the middle of the organizational hierarchy frequently find that their compensation program is critically influenced by the system designed for their subordinates. They are also the beneficiaries of a trickle-down effect of some of the compensation components offered to those at the top level in the organization. However, the true golden carrot placed in front of this group of employees is the information that, through faithful service and superior performance, they will achieve promotion to senior management and that the compensation provided to top-level employees will be theirs.

Employees in the lowest group of operating managers often have the title of foreman, first-line supervisor, or possibly team leader. Moving further up the hierarchy, there are unit, department, or branch managers or functional unit managers such as sales, human resources, accounting, data processing. These managers are frequently called middle managers. At the highest levels of operating management are plant managers or superintendents and store managers. Interspersed among these managers are

TABLE 4–4 Salary and Annual Bonus Data for Different Operating Management Jobs

	Plant Manager					Information Systems Manager				
Total Full-Time Equivalent (FTE) Employment	Salary ($000)			Bonus ($000)		Salary ($000)			Bonus ($000)
	First Quartile	Median	Third Quartile	Median	Sales Group ($ millions)	First Quartile	Median	Third Quartile	Median
Under 500	66.5	76.5	89.0	12.9	Under 500	57.0	70.0	84.7	8.7
500–2,000	72.0	82.1	96.3	15.7	500–2,000	64.4	73.5	81.5	7.5
2,000–7,500	72.3	87.0	100.8	17.9	2,000–7,500	69.0	81.0	99.9	13.4
7,500 & Over	78.2	91.2	116.7	13.7	7,500 & Over	78.9	83.7	101.1	18.2
All Employee Groups	71.3	83.2	96.3	15.3	All Employee Groups	64.4	75.0	87.0	10.5

[a]The overall figure was supplied by participants in response to a separate question; not calculated from other employee levels.

Source: Watson Wyatt Data Services, *Middle Management Compensation,* 47th ed. (Rochelle Park, NJ: Watson Wyatt Worldwide, 1998/99), *Information Systems Manager,* p. 416; *Plant Manager,* p. 1044.

administrators who perform highly specialized services and who may, at the same time, act as supervisors or subordinate administrative staff workers. All operating managers are responsible for meeting daily quality, quantity, and timeliness standards in the goods and services produced by their units.

The base pay of the employees at the lowest levels of operating management is frequently much less than that paid to the highest level of operative employees. (In its 1998/99 report *Supervisory Management Compensation,* WWDS noted that approximately 20 percent of its survey participants required a median salary differential of at least 10 percent between first-line supervisors and their subordinates.) Furthermore, the managers responsible for the operation of large facilities, stores, and major service-producing units receive base pay and have pay-for-performance opportunities that exceed those received by some members of senior management. Table 4–4 provides pay and bonus data for two common operating management jobs: the plant or factory manager, and the data processing manager/director of EDP. Like the pay of executives, the pay of operating managers varies by size of unit managed, measured by dollar criteria and employees supervised.

SALES PERSONNEL

Convincing people to accept and use the output of an organization normally requires the talents of a special group of people. These individuals present the output to potential consumers, then influence the consumers to use it. Output can be a good, a service, or both. It can be tangible (an automobile) or intangible (life insurance). It can be a service provided by a business in a highly competitive industry (time-sharing and data processing) or electricity from a public utility. It can be the output of a profit-making business (General Motors) or a nonprofit organization (the Salvation Army).

In most cases, those responsible for the sales of the product or service are members of a sales or marketing unit. Their primary responsibilities require contact with buyers whom they *must influence* to purchase the goods or services. Frequently, they work independently and perform in unstructured situations. Although the basic duties of a salesperson normally are to make sales, these individuals perform many other assignments. They may identify potential customers, review current products on the market, and identify the degree of competitiveness of major suppliers and their products. They may report on product quality (their own and competitors'). Market analysis is another information-gathering mission they may perform. During times of product shortages, they may be responsible for allocating the product among customers.

Some sales personnel do not directly sell anything; their sole responsibility may be to contact potential consumers or those who direct consumer activities (the doctor who writes a prescription for a patient requiring a particular medicine) and inform them of the strengths and the benefits to be derived from using their good or service. Their main responsibility may be to acquire preferred space in an area where their purchasers will encounter product displays.

Sales personnel may deliver products, set up displays, direct promotional campaigns, provide instruction to customer sales personnel, and give technical advice. They advise on size, color, and style to order, acceptable order quantities, and delivery and reorder date expectations, warranties, and other guarantees. Most sales personnel have to maintain extensive records, and many make frequent, detailed reports. They do this to accomplish company goals and to meet customer demands. The availability of computerized data storage and processing systems signficantly improves and simplifies the work of sales personnel. There is an extensive discussion of the U.S. DOL definition of an outside salesperson for exemption purposes later in this chapter.

There are five basic methods available for paying sales personnel. The first is *salary.* The salary-only method provides a specific amount each pay period to the salesperson regardless of quality of performance. The salary-only plan includes a program in which the organization covers all expenses incurred by the salesperson in the performance of assignments. Slightly more than 20 percent of all sales personnel are paid under a salary-only plan.

The second method is the *sales commission.* In this method, the salesperson receives a commission that is usually a percentage of the net sales price of the product. If no sales are made, the commissioned salesperson receives no money. Success in selling a product, on the other hand, can result in the salesperson becoming wealthy nearly overnight.

The third approach combines salary and commission. In recent years, the *combination plan* has become a popular approach for paying sales personnel.[14] Combining salary with incentives offers advantages to both the company and the salesperson. It provides the salesperson with a certain amount of security because it guarantees income during periods of economic downturn or depressed demand. It removes a certain amount of pressure from the salesperson to make sales and, at the same time, grants the company more opportunity to direct the efforts of the individual toward such activities as customer service and searching for new prospects that may not have an im-

---

[14]Charles A. Peck, *Compensating Field Sales Representatives* (New York: The Conference Board, 1982), p. 12.

mediate impact on sales. These plans are more difficult to design. It may be more difficult for the company to send a message with the plan to its sales personnel because the combination plan usually carries multiple objectives.

The fourth method is to provide the salesperson with a *salary and bonus.* The bonus may be based on individual performance (individual bonus) or on group performance. In most cases, the amount of the earned bonus is tied to some performance indicator (goal), but it is not unusual for the size of the bonus or bonus payment to be at the discretion of senior management (discretionary bonus). The fifth method is to *combine bonus payments with a salary and commission* plan. The bonus provides an additional incentive to accomplish a desired organizational target.

Over the years, these commission and bonus incentives for sales personnel have merged, and it has become difficult to separate them. When requesting compensation information on sales representatives, WWDS now asks for data in two categories: (1) salary only and (2) salary plus incentives. Table 4–5 provides median salary only and salary plus incentive data for sales personnel. Table 4–6 lists the base salary and bonus opportunities of regional sales managers.

The base pay program of personnel in large and complex sales operations using a salary-only plan may relate the pay of all jobs to that of the most senior executive. Such a plan could take this form:

Job Title	Percentage of Pay of VP, Marketing
Vice president, marketing	100%
Division sales manager	70–75%
Regional sales manager	60–65%
District sales manager	54–58%
Sales supervisor	44–48%
Sales representative	32–37%

Sales personnel in a salary plus incentive pay plan may have annual earnings similar to those received by lower-level operating managers—$40,000 to $70,000—to seven figures (millions of dollars). In 1991, the stockbrokers of the nation were paid an average of $93,480, up from an average of $79,000 in 1990. With year-end bonuses, some

TABLE 4–5 Method of Compensating Sales Representatives

			$(000)			
Method	*Sales Representative*	*Senior Sales Representative*	*Account Specialist*	*Government Representative*	*Special Market Representative*	*Telephone Sales Representative*
Salary Only	43.2	60.3	54.9	—	47.6	26.2
Salary Plus Incentive	53.8	72.2	81.2	78.2	74.1	36.4

Source: Watson Wyatt Data Services, *Sales and Marketing Personnel Compensation,* 43rd ed. (Rochelle Park, NJ: Watson Wyatt Worldwide, 1998/99), pp. 67, 87, 115, 125, 130, 138.

Regional Sales Volume ($ millions)	Actual Salary (thousands of $)			Weighted Average Annual Incentive and/or Other Cash Compensation ($ thousands)
	First Quartile	Median	Third Quartile	
Under 5	56.1	64.9	77.1	20.8
5–9.9	60.0	66.3	84.3	18.3
10–19.9	62.5	73.3	86.6	28.1
20–39.9	66.1	73.5	89.1	32.8
40 and Over	82.4	90.9	103.5	24.6

TABLE 4–6   Regional Sales Managers

Source: Watson Wyatt Data Services, *Sales and Marketing Personnel Compensation,* 43rd ed. (Rochelle Park, NJ: Watson Wyatt Worldwide, 1998/99), p. 424.

brokers earned in excess of a million dollars. A St. Petersburg, Florida, securities firm paid the head of its asset management unit a salary and bonus of $2.2 million.[15]

PROFESSIONALS

Professionals are those employees who regularly perform nonroutine assignments requiring originality, discretion, independent judgment, innovative abilities, and analytical skills. Their jobs normally require specialized and prolonged courses of intellectual instruction. They normally hold, at a minimum, an undergraduate degree in some specialized area such as science, engineering, accounting, finance, medicine, or law. Laws or existing practices may require them to have a certificate or license to practice. Their work normally involves the solution of complex technical problems that vary widely and may have a broad range of interpretation. They devote a minimum amount of their time to directing the work of others. An extensive discussion of the U.S. DOL definition of a professional for exemption purposes appears later in this chapter. Table 4–7 contains salary data for five professional jobs—accountant, compensation and benefits administrator, programmer/analyst, mechanical engineer, and attorney.

The design of compensation programs for these professional employees is a problem for many organizations. These employees are easily able to identify with other professionals who have similar credentials and work for themselves or for other organizations. They develop fairly accurate perceptions of the kinds and the quality of work their peers are performing in other kinds of work settings and of the compensation and noncompensation rewards these peers are receiving. From their perception-based measurements (equity theory), either they achieve greater satisfaction from their current jobs or they become dissatisfied with their jobs or work environment.

The compensation of professionals normally follows the same route as that provided for operating management personnel. In fact, their pay opportunities usually

---

[15]Michael Siconolfi, "Return of the Little Guy Helped Fatten Brokers' Paychecks in '91," *The Wall Street Journal,* January 7, 1992, p. C1; "Florida Firm Shells Out Wall Street Style Bonus," *The Wall Street Journal,* January 9, 1992, p. C12.

TABLE 4–7 Salary Data for Five Professional Jobs

	Level	Years of Experience	Average Salary			% Receiving Bonus	Average $ Bonus
			First Quartile	Median	Third Quartile		
Accountant	Level 1	0–2	27.9	30.7	33.6	16.2	1.5
	Level 2	2–5	31.8	35.5	39.9	21.1	2.1
	Level 3	5–8	40.0	43.4	47.8	24.1	3.2
	Level 4	more than 8	48.0	53.2	60.5	24.2	4.6
Compensation and Benefits Administrator	Level 1	0–2	30.1	34.9	38.7	22.0	0.9
	Level 2	2–5	33.9	40.6	45.1	18.8	2.4
	Level 3	5–8	43.1	47.7	56.0	14.0	2.4
	Level 4	more than 8	55.0	60.0	65.5	10.0	9.7
Programmer/Analyst	Level 1	0–1	31.9	35.1	38.8	15.7	1.4
	Level 2	1–3	37.4	41.6	46.0	22.8	2.2
	Level 3	3–5	44.6	49.7	54.7	26.5	3.0
	Level 4	5–8	52.0	55.9	61.5	32.5	3.4
	Level 5	more than 8	59.8	63.9	69.5	32.7	4.5
Mechanical Engineer	Level 1	0–1	36.4	38.6	41.6	19.3	2.3
	Level 2	1–3	40.9	44.4	48.0	30.3	3.0
	Level 3	3–5	48.3	52.9	57.6	28.5	4.0
	Level 4	5–8	55.7	61.4	67.1	24.9	3.4
	Level 5	at least 8	66.3	70.6	79.0	22.1	6.7
	Level 6	more than 10	79.7	84.4	91.3	13.5	11.4
Attorney	Level 1	0–2	40.0	46.5	55.0	7.0	4.5
	Level 2	2–5	52.0	60.0	70.8	27.8	6.4
	Level 3	5–8	70.1	80.0	91.6	30.9	11.3
	Level 4	more than 8	83.6	96.0	112.9	50.9	15.5

Source: Watson Wyatt Data Services, *Report on Professional and Scientific Personnel Compensation,* 13th ed. (Rochelle Park, NJ: Watson Wyatt Worldwide, 1998/99). Mechanical Engineer, p. 830, Compensation and Benefits Administrator, p. 244, Attorney, p. 658, Programmer/Analyst, p. 428, Accountant, p. 68.

"top out" and equal those of jobholders in the middle levels of operating management (currently between $70,000 and $110,000). Frequently, to obtain greater income, professionals move into management positions that are related to their own areas of specialization. Much to the dismay of many organizations, the result is the loss of a good researcher or engineer and the gain of an incompetent manager. In many of these cases, not only does the organization suffer from the twin losses, but the individual does not enjoy the managerial assignments and would much prefer to be working in the professional specialty area.

To retain the services and elicit superior performance from their professional personnel, more organizations each year are offering them bonuses. However, the number of professionals receiving bonuses is still rather small. The next to last column in Table 4–7 shows the percentage of professionals by each occupation currently receiving bonuses, and the last column shows the average dollar amount of the bonus.

OPERATIVE EMPLOYEES

The previously mentioned groups of senior management, operating management, sales personnel, and professionals constitute between 20 and 25 percent of the workforce. The remaining 75 to 80 percent are the operative employees—the people who make it all happen. These employees perform assignments that range from those given by a few specific and easily understood oral instructions to those requiring knowledge of specific trades or skills. The base pay of operative employees can range from the minimum wage (the federal minimum wage is $5.15 per hour) to hourly rates as high as $30 to $40. Operative employees must be paid time and a half when working more than 40 hours per week. Most of the remainder of this book focuses on the design of pay and total compensation programs for this major portion of the workforce.

Paraprofessionals

Paraprofessionals span the gap between the technician and the professional. They do not require the broad, extensive educational background of the professionals, but they are assuming more of the responsibilities that were once the sole prerogatives of the professionals. Poor use of the talents of the professionals and the costs connected with their productive efforts ensure the growth and the future of the paraprofessional. This group is in a stage of rapid transition, and undoubtedly there will be rigid licensing and certification requirements as its members assume roles of increased responsibility and gain commensurate increases in compensation. The rise of paraprofessionals will be particularly noted in the legal, medical, health care, and engineering professions.

Technicians

Technicians are employees who provide semiprofessional technical support in their specialized areas. They perform a variety of activities ranging in scope from something that is simple and routine to activities that are quite complex. Their activities may involve responsibility for planning and conducting a complete project of relatively limited scope, or a portion of a more diverse project in accordance with objectives, requirements, and methods as outlined by a supervisory paraprofessional or professional.

There are limited licensing and academic requirements for technicians. Knowledge acquired on the job or academic programs such as those offered in the two-year community college associate degree courses are usually sufficient for entry-level technicians. There is an overlap between the advanced technician and the lower levels of the paraprofessional ranks.

Administrative Support (Secretarial–Clerical)

In the operative group is a subgroup of employees who fit primarily into the semi-skilled area but who actually have characteristics of both the unskilled and skilled employees. With the increasing expansion of both automation and the service-oriented industries, this large, widespread group of workers requires special recognition. Be-

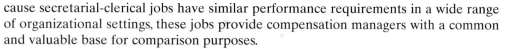

cause secretarial-clerical jobs have similar performance requirements in a wide range of organizational settings, these jobs provide compensation managers with a common and valuable base for comparison purposes.

The secretarial-clerical group performs a variety of office procedures that range from simple manual filing assignments to the preparation of complex reports using automated systems, to secretarial support for high-ranking executives. This group forms the white–pink-collar base of organizations.

Skilled Craftworkers

The identifying characteristics of the skilled craftworkers are their training and education programs. In this group, the novice traditionally moves from apprentice to journeyman to master. This education program has a strong on-the-job orientation, but it is possible to acquire portions of it in an academic environment.

To interface with the technology of their trades, the skilled craftworkers have a rather large stock of skills. Their efforts frequently require originality and ingenuity in performing a wide variety of planning, operating, and control functions with regard to their jobs or those of their helpers. In addition, they know the inherent characteristics of the raw materials common to their work and are capable of training less skilled workers to operate equipment and to use basic raw materials. They frequently interact with professionals and technicians on the best use of technology and the determination of methods and procedures with regard to the material used and the results desired. They also have a high degree of manual dexterity and an ability to work within extremely fine tolerances and precise finishes. This group includes members of the building trades and a wide variety of machinists, mechanics, and makers of instruments and models, as well as those responsible for operating and repairing high-technology equipment.

Semiskilled Workers

Semiskilled workers include those moving through the various educational and training programs that are necessary to achieve skilled status and those who are becoming more skilled on a particular job but are not adding different skills to their inventory. Semiskilled workers perform jobs that range from fairly simple assembly operations to those that require operation of complex equipment within limits set by specific or detailed operating instructions. The members of this group receive brief instructions about their specific assignments. The semiskilled group includes most assemblers, truck drivers, equipment and machinery operators; those who repair standard office and industrial equipment; and material handlers responsible for verifying, stocking, transferring, and recording a variety of materials.

Unskilled Workers

Unskilled employees must be able to follow simple but relatively few verbal (written and/or oral) instructions. Their jobs usually involve substantial physical effort and require minimum education and only basic communication skills. Supervisors frequently review their work while it is in progress to ensure conformance with standards, and they almost always review it upon completion. The unskilled group consists of manual laborers, janitors, and custodians and those who handle simple, routine, material, and processing assignments.

White Collar–Blue Collar–Pink Collar

In recent years, the classification of workers as being white collar or blue collar has attracted much attention. In the 1970s, a third color was added to the grouping: pink. The pink-collar description focuses attention on the kinds of work in which women are the predominant jobholders and in which, in many cases, it is said that their pay is unfairly depressed because women predominate in these jobs.

The white-collar segment of the workforce has historically included the professional, administrative, technical, and secretarial-clerical groups, whereas the blue-collar segment has included the skilled and semiskilled craftworkers, the unskilled laborers, and their first-level supervisors.

The pink-collar classification includes nurses, medical technicians, noncollege teachers, retail sales personnel, secretaries and clerks, apparel-industry workers, food service workers, and domestics. In today's politically correct society, this term may now be an anachronism.

A brief analysis of pay and percentage of women in various industrial settings assists in explaining why women workers as a group earn 65 cents to 75 cents of each dollar earned by men (see Table 4–8).

Union–Nonunion

Another consideration in grouping employees is whether or not they exercise their right to organize and bargain collectively with management. Those members of the organization who select a union to negotiate for wages, hours, and other benefits and working conditions normally become separate from those who do not delegate this activity to an intervening third party. A major reason for employee interest in joining a union has been dissatisfaction with pay.

TABLE 4–8   Average Hourly Earnings of Blue- and Pink-Collar Workers in Selected Industries, and Percentage of Women

	Hourly Rate	Percentage of Women
Blue-Collar Industrial Workers		
Coal Mining	19.26	3.3
Petroleum and Coal Products	20.90	20.7
Construction	16.80	9.4
Mining	17.32	13.7
Pink-Collar Industrial Workers		
Eating and Drinking Places	6.45	55.2
Variety Stores	7.74	68.9
Apparel and Accessory Stores	8.54	73.9
Apparel and Textile Products	8.63	66.4

Source: Employment and Earnings (Washington, DC: USDOL Bureau of Labor Statistics, January 1999), Hourly rates of pay by industry (November 1998), Table B-15; percentage of women workers, Table 18.

With the movement from a strong industrial-based society to a service-based economy, union strength and activity have changed. Between 1945 and 1998, the percentage of the workforce that is unionized has been cut by more than half—from 35 to less than 16 percent. Some of the most powerful unions with the highest-paid members, such as the United Steelworkers (USWA), and the United Automobile Workers (UAW), have seen their membership also decline by approximately 50 percent. The one bright spot in the union movement has been the rapid expansion in union membership among public-sector unions. By the mid-1990s there were more public-sector than private-sector union members. A large number of public-sector employees are both white- and pink-collar employees and professionals.

In the past, the line between union and nonunion members fell between the management group and the operative employees. In recent years, however, there has been widespread unionization among various professional groups. Even higher levels of operating management have indicated interest in unionization, but the Supreme Court recently upheld existing legislation that exempted management from government protection when involved in collective bargaining activities.

Professionals have traditionally grouped together to form associations that can be considered unaffiliated or independent unions, although a number of professionals have joined unions affiliated with the AFL-CIO. Professional associations normally have as their primary mission the transfer and progress of knowledge, but they also provide exceptionally strong job security opportunities and have significant influence on the pay of their members.

Professional associations such as the American Medical Association, American Dental Association, and American Bar Association have, over the years, been extremely strong lobbyists. Through their lobbying efforts, they influence legislation that has an impact on the pay of their members. Athletes, actors, musicians, university faculty, schoolteachers, and airline pilots have been successful in using collective bargaining to improve their financial status. In addition to joining unions for improvements in pay, some professionals are using union membership to improve their technical-professional relationships with their organizations. Contract negotiations may include improved technical support, more independence in the work they perform, and greater opportunity to participate in decisions that relate to project assignments.

Exempt–Nonexempt

Because of exemption from certain requirements of the Fair Labor Standards Act of 1938 (FLSA), as amended, it is necessary to take into consideration the requirements of the U.S. Department of Labor, Employment Standards Administration, Wage and Hour Division, as to what is meant by bona fide executive, administrative, professional, and sales personnel. Employees in these categories are *exempt* from the overtime requirements of the act if they meet the test for each category.[16] Employee exemption

---

[16]A complete description of exemption requirements is found in U.S. Department of Labor, *Executive, Administrative, Professional, and Outside Salesmen Exemptions under the Fair Labor Standards Act.* WH Publication 1363 (rev.) (Washington, DC: Government Printing Office, 1973). The salaries quoted are out of date but, as of 1999, have not been changed.

depends on (1) responsibilities and duties and (2) salary. This dichotomy between the exempt (exempt from certain wage and hour regulations) and the nonexempt is present in almost every organization. Organizations are not required to keep records of hours worked of employees in the exempt categories. In 1983, in its research on pay practices, the Executive Compensation Service, Inc. noted that approximately 20 to 22 percent of all employees are in the exempt category.[17]

The Wage and Hour Division defines an *executive* as follows:

1. One whose primary duty is management of the enterprise, or of a customarily recognized department or subdivision.
2. One who customarily and regularly directs the work of at least two or more other employees therein. (They must work a combined total of 80 hours per week, the combined equivalent of two full-time workers.)
3. One who has the authority to hire and fire, or recommend hiring and firing, or whose recommendation on these and other actions affecting employees is given particular weight.
4. One who must customarily and regularly exercise discretionary powers.
5. One who devotes no more than 20 percent (less than 40 percent if he is employed by a retail or service establishment) of his hours of work to activities not directly and closely related to his managerial duties. [The "20 percent rule" is no longer considered a firm requirement. If the other six requirements are met, it is possible for the employee to spend more than 50 percent of his or her time doing non-managerial-related work.]
6. One who must be paid on a salary basis of at least $155[18] per week.
7. One who receives at least $250 per week and must meet the "shortcut" test requirements.[19]

The exception in item 7 is called an upset or high-salary proviso. A review of these seven recommendations indicates that the term *executive* as defined by the U.S. Department of Labor (DOL) is far broader than that developed in this chapter. According to the DOL definition, practically all managers are executives, although some lower-level managers (supervisors, foremen) may not meet these seven tests. In some organizations, supervisors or working foremen spend a considerable portion of their time performing nonmanagerial activities, and although this is not a sole criterion, it requires close scrutiny on the part of the compensation manager to determine whether such lower-level managers meet the requirements set forth for an executive under DOL regulations.[20]

---

[17]ECS, a Wyatt Data Services Company, *Middle Management Report, 1983/1984* (Fort Lee, NJ: 1983), p. 364.
[18]It is possible that an employee meeting all executive requirements could be excluded from minimum wage, overtime, and recordkeeping requirements established by the FLSA as amended.
[19]Ibid., pp. 1–2. The "shortcut" or, as it is sometimes called, the "upset" provision states that if an employee is paid at least $250 per week and spends more than 50 percent of his or her time on duties relating specifically to the exemption category (i.e., executive, administrative, or professional), the individual is automatically exempt from overtime requirements. (In fact, because of recent court decisions, the 50 percent requirement is arguable; however, the need to supervise employees working a total of 80 hours per week is essential.)
[20]U.S. Department of Labor, Employment Standards Administration, *Defining the Terms "Executive," "Administrative," "Professional," and "Outside Salesman"* (W.H. Publication 1281, Regulation 541.115 Washington, DC: Government Printing Office, 1975).

The Wage and Hour Division interprets the term *administrator* as follows:

(a) The employee's duty must be either:
 (1) Responsible office or nonmanual work directly related to the management policies or general business operations of his employer or his employer's customers; or
 (2) Responsible work that is directly related to academic instruction or training carried on in the administration of a school system or educational establishment.
(b) The employee must customarily and regularly exercise discretion and independent judgment, as distinguished from using skills and following procedures, and must have the authority to make important decisions; and
(c) The employee must:
 (1) Regularly assist a proprietor or a bona fide executive or administrative employee;
 (2) Perform work under only general supervision along specialized or technical lines requiring special training, experience, or knowledge; or
 (3) Execute special assignments only under general supervision; and
(d) The employee must not spend more than 20 percent of the time worked in the work week (less than 40 percent if employed by a retail or service establishment) on nonexempt work—that is, work not directly and closely related to the administrative duties; and
(e) The employee must be paid on a salary or fee basis at a rate of not less than $155 per week. In the case of academic administrative personnel, the salary requirement for exemption must be at least $155 or alternately, a salary which is at least equal to the entrance salary for teachers in the school system or educational establishment or institution by which he or she is employed;
(f) If the employee receives a salary of $250 per week, the "short-cut" test applies.[21]

The exception in item (f) is called an upset or high-salary proviso.

The Bureau of Labor Statistics views the administrator as being more of a staff specialist. Administrators normally function in areas such as personnel, accounting, finance, law, medicine, research and development, and planning.

The DOL has its own special definition for sales personnel who are exempt from overtime requirements. An *outside salesman* is defined by DOL as an employee who is:

(a) employed for the purpose of and who is customarily and regularly engaged away from his employer's place of business;
(b) selling tangible or intangible items such as goods, insurance, stocks, bonds, real estate, or
(c) obtaining orders or contracts for services or use of facilities such as advertising, repairs, etc. (sales of these services are performed away from the employer's establishment);

---

[21]U.S. Department of Labor, *Executive, Administrative, Professional,* 1973, pp. 3–4.

(d) not working in activities other than those described above; does not exceed 20 percent of the hours worked in the workweek by nonexempt employees of the employer.

There is no salary test for outside salespersons.[22]

The Wage and Hour Division interprets the term *professional* as follows:

(a) Primary duty consists of the performance of work requiring knowledge of an advanced type in a field of science or learning customarily obtained by a prolonged course of specialized instruction and study, or work that is original and creative in character in a recognized field of artistic endeavor and the result of which depends primarily on the invention, imagination, or talent of the employee; *and*

(b) Work requires the consistent exercise of discretion and judgment; *and*

(c) Work is predominately intellectual and varied in character and is such that the output produced or the result accomplished cannot be standardized in relation to a given period of time; *and*

(d) No more than 20 percent of the hours worked in the workweek are devoted to activities other than those described in tests (a), (b), and (c) above; *and*

(e) Must be compensated at a rate not less than $170/week ($8,840 per year), exclusive of board, lodging, or other facilities.

The streamlined test for professional employees provides that regardless of other considerations, a professional employee paid at least $250 per week ($13,000 per year), exclusive of board, lodging, or other facilities, may be "exempt" if he or she meets tests (a) *and* (b) as listed previously.[23]

Until recent times, the establishment of a professional exemption for employees in computer-related occupations has been extremely difficult. A 1990 amendment to the FLSA directed the DOL to issue a regulation that would allow certain computer-related occupations to qualify for exemption under Section 13(9)(1) of the FLSA.[24]

The exemption for professional employees was expanded by the Department of Labor in 1992 to include highly skilled computer-related workers. In general, these employees will qualify for the white-collar exemption test if their primary duties involve:

- The application of systems analysis techniques and procedures, to include consultations with users to determine hardware and software specifications;
- The design of computer systems based on and related to user specifications;
- The creation or modification of computer programs based on or related to system design specifications;
- The creation or modification of computer programs related to machine operating systems; or
- A combination of the above duties, where the performance of those duties requires the same level of skill.

---

[22]U.S. Department of Labor, *Executive, Administrative, Professional*, p. 9.
[23]U.S. Department of Labor, *Executive, Administrative, Professional*, pp. 5–8.
[24]Public Law 101–583, enacted November 15, 1990.

To qualify for the exemption for highly skilled employees in computer-related fields, however, the employee also must be paid:

- At least $170 on a salary basis each week and meet the primary duty requirements of the general test (see above);
- At least $250 on a salary basis each week and meet the primary duty requirements of the simplified test (see above); or
- At least $27.63 an hour if they are paid on an hourly basis. (Note: Previously, highly skilled computer-related workers were exempt from overtime if their hourly rate of pay was more than 6.5 times the minimum wage. However, the Small Business Job Protection Act of 1996 has changed the threshold to $27.63 per hour, regardless of the minimum wage.)

In addition to the exemptions just identified, workers in the following categories may also be exempted from wage and hour provisions of the FLSA:

1. Employees of seasonal amusement or recreational establishments or camps
2. Independent contractors
3. Casual babysitters and companions to the disabled
4. Volunteers who work without pay
5. Retail and service establishment employees if sales are made primarily within the state (except for laundries, dry cleaners, hospitals, nursing homes, and schools)

Regular and Temporary (Contingent) Employees

Another approach to grouping employees that is especially important for compensation purposes is the identification of regular and temporary (contingent) employees and, within these groups, the further subclassification of full-time and part-time employees. One principal way to separate regular and temporary employees is on the basis of hours worked per week and weeks worked per year.

Regular Employees   Any person hired for a specific job who is expected to work on a continuing basis and to meet certain minimum performance and time-on-job requirements is a regular employee.

Typically, regular employees are expected to work between 35 and 40 hours per week. Although most employees are expected to work a 40-hour workweek, it is not uncommon to find office workers and second-shift (4:00 P.M. to 12:00 midnight) and third-shift (12:00 midnight to 8:00 A.M.) workers working 35 to 37½ hours and being paid for 40 hours.

Temporary Employees   Any person hired for a special project, or on an as-needed basis, or for seasonal work, or for any kind of work of a transitory or casual nature is considered a temporary employee. (Although a temporary employee may typically be one who works six months or less in a year, it is not unusual to find employees who have temporary status in an organization but have been employed for a number of years.)

Full-Time Employees   A full-time worker is an employee who works the number of hours per week and the number of weeks per year typically required of jobholders in the specific work unit. A typical full-time employee works between 35 and 40 hours per week, 52 weeks per year. (A full-time employee may have either regular or temporary status.)

Part-Time Employees   A part-time employee is typically any person working on a continuing basis who works less than a full-time employee but who performs similar or identical work assignments. In some organizations, there may be a specific hour cutoff that differentiates the full- and part-time employees. A part-time employee may be anyone working less than 35 hours, 30 hours, or 20 hours per week. (A part-time employee may have either regular or temporary status.)

Regular part-time employees may be defined as those working in a long-term position (of six months or more duration) and working more than a prescribed number of hours per year (i.e., 780). Temporary part-time employees, on the other hand, would work less than 780 hours per year. Temporary part-time employees can further be defined as any employees occupying short-term positions (of six months or less duration) and working less than 15 hours per week.

Temporary Employment Agencies   Many organizations use an intermediary organization to hire their temporary workers. Those agencies hire workers and then, upon request, send them to the clients. The clients are responsible for assigning the temporary specific work and determining the actual amount of time on the job. The hiring agency pays the worker and then bills the client for the work performed. Temporary employees are frequently found performing clerical and manual labor. A growing number of temporary workers are being used in the security guard, nursing (health care), and computer-related fields.

Compensation systems are designed to meet the demands of regular full-time employees. The plans normally vary for part-time and temporary employees. Because compensation plans for those employee groups may vary significantly, it is important that their hours be closely monitored. The term *contingent employee* is frequently used to describe a worker who is not a member of the regular full-time workforce.

PAY RELATIONSHIPS: A FAIRNESS ISSUE

At a time when many American workers are losing their jobs or occasionally being asked to take reductions in pay and benefits, the pay and benefits packages provided to executives continue to be the envy of the world. Beginning in the early 1980s, when reports on the pay and bonuses of top U.S. executives became "front page" issues in April, May, and June of each year, various views have been expressed about their pay. Kevin Murphy, an associate professor at Harvard Business School, stated that a previously held view that corporate executives are overpaid is wrong. His research of the compensation policies of almost 1,200 large corporations over a 10-year period showed that pay of top executives and corporate performance strongly and positively correlate. He stated: "On average, compensation policies encourage executives to act on behalf of their stockholders and to put in the best managerial performance they can."[25] Another professor, Peter F. Drucker, took a contrary view: "Resentment over top management

---

[25]Kevin J. Murphy, "Top Executives Are Worth Every Nickel They Get," *Harvard Business Review,* March–April 1986, pp. 125–133; Kevin J. Murphy, "Executive Compensation in Corporate America: 1992" in *Executive Compensation of Corporate America, 92* (Washington, DC: United Shareholders Association, 1992), pp. 3–6; Michael C. Jensen and Kevin J. Murphy, "CEO Incentives—It's Not How Much You Pay, But How," *Harvard Business Review,* May–June 1990, pp. 138–153; Andrew R. Brownstein and Morris J. Panner, "Who Should Set CEO Pay? The Press? Congress? Shareholders?" *Harvard Business Review,* May–June 1992, pp. 28–35, 38.

compensation is by no means confined to unions and rank-and-file employees. It extends to professionals and managers."[26]

In 1991, an executive compensation consultant turned college professor wrote a widely publicized book that grabbed the attention of an already disgruntled American public. The book, *In Search of Excess: The Overcompensation of American Executives,* became a rallying point for individuals who were severely disturbed regarding the compensation of many top executives in the United States.[27] There is a further discussion of executive compensation in chapter 16.

Pay Equity

For most employees, the job rate of pay is an essential issue. Fairness in pay is evaluated by asking "How well does my pay compare with that of other members of the work unit and the organization?" Comparisons are also made with friends or family members. In the past years when economic conditions worsened, it appeared that one group of workers—top executives—were immune from the economic stress at the marketplace. Although pay for many employees leveled, declined, or even disappeared, top executives saw their pay equal, if not surpass, the pay received by top entertainers. Organizational employees recognize that their top executives should be the highest-paid members of the organization, but there must be some reasonable, equitable relationship among the pay of all employees (including the chief executive officer—CEO).

By 1996, the issue of ever-increasing CEO pay was becoming a national political, social, and economic issue. *Business Week*, in its annual report on CEO pay, noted that average CEO pay increased by 18 percent in 1995 to $1,653,670. Where long-term compensation such as stock options were included, the average CEO compensation rose to $3,746,392, an annual increase of 30 percent. Much of the increase in CEO compensation was related to an increase in corporate profits. In the five-year period from 1990 to 1995, corporate profits rose 75 percent. CEO pay, meanwhile, rose by 92 percent.[28]

During this same period, the rate of pay for the great majority of workers was stagnating or, at best, increasing relative to cost of living, which in the mid-1990s was very stable. Some researchers noted that although CEOs' salaries and bonuses soared in 1995, overall U.S. wages and benefits climbed by 29 percent and the pay of nonunion salaried employees grew by 42 percent. This 10-year period of continuing increases in CEO compensation has been titled "The Decade of Greed." By 1996, many influential organizations and individuals were calling for efforts to restrict such compensation practices.[29]

Most employees realize that certain jobs pay better than other jobs. Certain organizations pay higher than other organizations, and working in certain geographic locations results in higher pay than working elsewhere. These conditions are recognized and usually accepted without hostility. In fact, the strength and value of a market-based economy is that each individual has the opportunity (albeit, sometimes quite limited) to make changes within the market to improve his or her job and earnings opportunities.

---

[26]Peter F. Drucker, "Reform Executive Pay or Congress Will," *The Wall Street Journal,* April 24, 1984, p. 34.
[27]Graef S. Crystal, *In Search of Excess: The Overcompensation of American Executives* (New York: W.W. Norton & Co., 1991).
[28]"Special Report: How High Can CEO Pay Go," *Business Week*, April 22, 1996, pp. 100–102.
[29]Joann S. Lublin, "The Great Divide," *The Wall Street Journal*, April 11, 1996, p. R1; Jill Smolowe, "Reap As Ye Shall Sow," *Time*, February 5, 1996, p. 45; Joe Spiers, "The Myth of Corporate Greed," *Fortune*, April 15, 1996, pp. 67, 68.

Top executive pay of the 1980s and 1990s appears to be a return to a Just Wage Economic Theory. "We, the chief executives, have reached this exalted position because we are superior (by birthright, or whatever means) and we deserve a rate of pay that recognizes our superiority." Top executive pay is, in reality, a prime example of the weakness in a market-based pay system.

Pay Ratios

Before making any decisions regarding the appropriateness of executive pay, it is useful to look at pay as a coordinated system that recognizes the contributions of all employees in an orderly and organized manner. There must be some desirable relationship among the pay/total compensation of all employees from the newly hired file clerk to the long-tenured CEO. Looking at the compensation and pay practices in foreign countries, Mark Green and Bonnie Tenneriello, in their report on executive pay, note that the ratio from the lowest-paid to the highest-paid worker in Japan was at that time 5 to 1.[30] (A University of Michigan study noted a 7 to 1 ratio between a top executive in a Japanese automobile manufacturing firm and an assembly-line, blue-collar worker.[31]) Whatever the actual ratio, the difference between the pay of lower-level employees and top executives is much smaller in Japan than in the United States. Little research is available relating pay levels of the average worker with the pay received by top executives in foreign countries to enable us to make these comparisons with a variety of foreign countries.

What is known, however, is that the United States has a strong middle-class orientation, and central to this middle-class orientation is the concept of fairness (see chapter 1 for further discussion of wealth, earnings, and middle class in the United States). Although very few people have negative views regarding the opportunity to become wealthy, there are strong views regarding injustice. From a job perspective, these injustices relate to the pay/compensation received by certain employees or groups of employees. The last part of this book focuses on ways and means of recognizing individual contributions and rewarding more handsomely those who make the greater contributions. But the question that remains unanswered is this: How much better should those at the top be rewarded than those in the trenches who do their jobs and help make the "good times" possible?

CEOs receive about three to four times as much salary and short-term bonuses as the lowest-paid senior manager (see Table 4–9). Then, starting from the bottom and moving up through the organizational hierarchy, the lowest-paid worker today in many organizations receives about $6.00 per hour. The median hourly rate for all union workers is around $15.05 per hour, and the highest paid of the operating managers earns in the lower $100,000 range per year. The lowest-paid senior managers have base salaries comparable to those received by the highest-paid operating managers. Organizing this pay data among various levels in the organizational hierarchy provides the ratios shown in Table 4–9.

For rewards to have positive motivational value, they must be perceived as fair by kind and amount. Organizations must make every effort to ensure a high degree of

---

[30]Mark Green and Bonnie Tenneriello, "Executive Merit Pay," *The New York Times,* April 25, 1984.
[31]*The American and Japanese Auto Industries in Transition: Report of the Joint U.S.–Japan Automotive Study* (Ann Arbor, MI: Center for Japanese Studies, University of Michigan, 1984), chapter 12.

TABLE 4–9   Rates of Pay and Ratio Comparisons of CEOs to Other Workers

Worker by Group	Hourly Rate of Pay ($)	Ratio Comparison with CEO
[a]Low-paid operative employee	$ 6.50	104.4:1
[b]Average 1995 earnings of all private-sector production workers	12.99	52.3:1
[c]Average 1995 earnings of all manufacturing-sector employees	13.78	49.3:1
[d]Average earnings of all manufacturing workers who are members of unions	15.15	44.8:1
[e]Average rate of pay of first-level (supervisory) manager	18.75	36.2:1
[f]Average rate of pay for middle manager	32.31	21.0:1
[g]Average rate of pay for upper mid-level manager (plant manager)	43.27	15.7:1
[h]Rate of pay for top manufacturing executive	149.86	4.5:1
[i]Rate of pay for CEO	678.89	1.0:1

[a]Rate of pay below which many individuals through the United States will not accept employment (author).
[b]*Employment and Earnings,* Washington, DC, Bureau of Labor Statistics, Table B-15, p. 101, January 1999.
[c]Ibid., Table 43, p. 222, January 1999.
[d]Ibid., Table 43, p. 213, January 1999.
[e]Watson Wyatt Data Services, Rochelle Park, NJ: Watson Wyatt Worldwide, 1998/99. *Supervisory Management Compensation,* p. 847. Total Cash Compensation for Supervisor of Floor Assembly, Level 2 (of 3 levels)—$39,000 ÷ 2080 = $18.75.
[f]Ibid., *Middle Management Compensation,* p. 1056, Median Total Cash Compensation for Plant Superintendent, All Organizations—$67,200 ÷ 2080 = $32.31.
[g]Ibid., *Middle Management Compensation,* p. 1044. Median Total Cash Compensation, All Organizations for Plant Manager—$90,000 ÷ 2080 = 43.27.
[h]Ibid., *Top Management Compensation,* p. 573. Median Total Cash Compensation for Top Manufacturing/ Production Executive—$311,700 ÷ 2080 = $149.86.
[i]Ibid., *Top Management Compensation,* p. 58. Median Total Cash Compensation for Sales of $5 Billion and Over for Chief Executive Officers—$1,412,100 ÷ 2080 = 678.89.

order and fairness regarding organizationally provided rewards. Regarding base pay relationships, the following recommendations have been made:

top–bottom ratio: 15 to 1 in small organizations
                     25 to 1 in large enterprises[32]

Another possible approach for viewing pay and short-term incentive relationships is through the size of a business. The size of the business, as measured by sales, affects the entire pay structure of an organization. It has not been unusual to find the following pay ratios between highest- to lowest-paid employees:

under $25 million	10:1 to 20:1
$25 to $100 million	12:1 to 25:1
$100 to $250 million	15:1 to 35:1
$250 to $500 million	20:1 to 40:1

[32]Green and Tenneriello, "Executive Merit Pay."

$500 million to $1 billion	25:1 to 45:1
$1 to $3 billion	25:1 to 50:1
$3 to $6 billion	25:1 to 55:1
over $6 billion	25:1 to 60:1

Table 4–10 combines pay data from various sources to analyze current relationships of pay in U.S. organizations. This analysis indicates that the ratios between various groups of employees and the top executives in the United States vary significantly.

Relating Pay to the Strategy and Tactics of the Organization

A major topic of the 1990s relating to the performance of top U.S. managers involved their skill deficiencies in planning and implementing long-term strategies. An issue related to this possible serious weakness is that current pay and compensation practices reward tactical planning and achievement of short-term goals. The large difference between the lowest to highest paid, such as the 75 to 1 and greater ratios, indicates an almost obsessive demand by the highly paid for immediate returns on their investments

---

TABLE 4–10 Current U.S. Pay Relationships

Company	Salary and Bonus of Highest-Paid Executive[a]	Industrial Worker Group	December 1998 Average Earnings of Workers[b] Hourly	December 1998 Average Earnings of Workers[b] Annualized	Ratio of Highest-Paid Executive to Industrial Worker	Ratio of Highest-Paid Executive and Average Earnings of All Goods-Producing Workers in Total Private Sector December 1998 $12.99/hr or $27,019/yr[b]
Ford Motor	12,500,000	Motor vehicle and car bodies	21.02	43,722	285.9:1	462.6:1
Philip Morris	5,000,000	Cigarettes	24.04	50,003	100.0:1	185.1:1
Chevron	2,460,000	Petroleum refining	23.55	48,984	50.2:1	91.0:1
Union Pacific	800,000	Class 1 railroads	17.76	36,941	21.7:1	29.6:1
Anheuser-Busch	2,857,800	Malt beverages	23.77	49,442	57.8:1	105.8:1
USX	2,417,900	Blast furnaces and steel mills	19.81	41,205	58.7:1	89.5:1
Reynolds Metals	1,329,600	Metal cans	17.96	37,357	35.6:1	49.2:1
PPG Ind.	1,735,000	Flat glass	17.72	36,858	47.1:1	64.2:1
Owens-Illinois	1,251,400	Glass containers	16.56	34,445	36.3:1	46.3:1

Source: [a]"Executive Pay," *The Wall Street Journal,* April 8, 1999, pp. R12–R15 (all except Ford Motor); Jeffrey Ball, "Ford Motor Awards Ex-CEO Trotman $10 Million Bonus," *The Wall Street Journal,* April 19, 1999, p. B9.

[b]U.S. Department of Labor, Bureau of Labor Statistics, *Employment and Earnings,* March 1999 (Washington, DC: U.S. Government Printing Office, 1999), Table B-15.

and contributions. This in no way implies that these same individuals are not also recipients of bountiful long-term incentive awards (see chapter 16). However, the strategic-tactical compensation issues concern not only the absolute sizes of these short- and long-term awards, but the relationship between these two major parts of the compensation package.

In the future, it is quite possible that the fixed short-term and long-term compensation packages for all employees will shrink (possibly not on an absolute basis, but most likely on a purchasing power basis), but the variable (incentive) short- and long-term parts of the compensation package will increase. As more interest develops in the relationship between successful performance and employee compensation, increasing attention will focus on the pay relationships (ratios) among the various employee groups.

Summary

Organizations evolve through a series of decisions that include:

1. Establishing a philosophy that may or may not be in writing.
2. Identifying a mission that becomes the company's overall, long-term purpose.
3. Developing a policy that states a broad guideline for action.
4. Formulating organizational strategy.
5. Determining objectives and goals that delineate specific organizational requirements.
6. Defining work unit activities.
7. Grouping tasks into jobs.

After grouping tasks into jobs and jobs into an organizational hierarchy, different rates of pay and compensation packages are provided to incumbents in these various jobs. Currently, as in the past, pay and compensation for most employees have had a significant relationship to immediate and short-term results. As organizations begin to modify their focus from an almost completely short-term view to one that integrates short-term tactical operations with longer-term strategic considerations, pay and compensation will change to respond to and support the achievement of short-term goals and long-term objectives.

Review Questions

1. Discuss the work relationships among such organizational groups as the board of directors, executives, senior managers, and operating managers.
2. Describe the kinds of responsibilities, knowledge, and skills required of employees in the basic groups of an organization (managers, administrators, professionals, paraprofessionals, technicians, skilled trades, clerical, unskilled).
3. Discuss what is meant by an exempt employee and the various exemption criteria established for identifying this group of workers.
4. Among the many occupations identified in this chapter, which will be most influenced by the change from a manufacturing to a service economy?
5. Distinguish between the philosophy of the organization and the mission of the organization.
6. What major groups of employees comprise the line structure of an organization?

CHAPTER 5

Legislation and Compensation

Learning Objectives

In this chapter you will learn about:

1. The influence of wage and hour legislation on employment practices.

2. Pension reform legislation and the impact of ERISA on the pension plans of many organizations.

3. The effects of legislation on health care benefits.

4. The impact of tax treatment legislation on employee spendable income and employer profits.

5. Antidiscrimination legislation and how it affects employment practices.

Compensation Strategy

Ensure that the compensation system of the organization complies with government regulations and advances the well-being of society.

Since the dawn of civilization there have been rules and laws to control human behavior. Early written records document laws that regulated hours worked, compensation, and taxation. For thousands of years, work and compensation-related laws were fairly simple. From very early times, farmers had to donate a certain percentage of crops and animals to a ruler or to charity to take care of the less well-off, or contribute to show appreciation to the gods for the fertility of their land and livestock.

The work hours of early farmers and craftworkers were controlled by hours of daylight, variations in weather, and climate. As more workers became involved in crafts and the production of buildings, goods, and services, government and religious leaders recognized the need to regulate working hours. Regulated time off from work allowed for both the replenishment of physical energy and the nourishment of social and spiritual needs. To sustain these needs, early societies established sacred or holy days, as well as a weekly day of rest.

Even though leaders in Egypt and other early civilizations provided special food, housing, and entertainment for the artisans who built and decorated their magnificent buildings and other structures, the laws of nature and religion continued to be primary in regulating work and the rewards gained from work for most members of society well into the Middle Ages.

By the fourteenth century, the rising commercial revolution and the final disintegration of medieval society in Europe introduced change and disorder into the world of work. No longer were earnings set by custom and tradition. By the fourteenth and fifteenth centuries, European workers were negotiating wages, and the early craft guilds (forerunners of the modern unions) were major forces in setting wage rates. As socially controlled "just price" wage rates began to crumble, rulers began to assign specific wage rates for specific occupations to block escalation of wage demands.[1]

By the sixteenth century, widespread trade and competition for the consumer's money provided an impetus for the rise of the cottage industry. Working in their own homes, families produced goods required by commercial traders at prices lower than those demanded by the urban guilds. Competition for supplying the goods and services resulted in a decline in the prices paid to nonfarm workers of this period.

With the decline in the price of labor and increases in the cost of food and shelter, sixteenth-century workers in England experienced a decline in their standard of living. Commercial workers who had given up their share of the food and the shelter available in the agricultural community for the wages available in a commercial society were unemployed and destitute in many cases. In attempting to improve the plight of the nonfarm worker, the English Parliament passed a minimum wage act in 1562.[2]

In the seventeenth and eighteenth centuries the cottage industry that had been centered in homes in rural areas moved into the homes of workers in the towns and cities. The individuals responsible for giving out work to these home workers set rates of pay for pieces produced. Because of the decentralization of activities and the lack of any mechanism for wage standardization, the piece rates set by business enterprises for cottage industry work were extremely low.

The last half of the eighteenth century witnessed the birth of the Industrial Revolution and the invention of the steam engine and other technologies that, in turn, led to the development of factories for spinning and weaving fabrics independent of water as a source of power. During this period, major changes occurred in the way masses of people earned their livelihood through work. Within a hundred years after the beginning of the Industrial Revolution, working conditions had become so bad that, by the latter part of the nineteenth century, the term *sweated* was applied to conditions under which many English workers toiled. Sweating applied to "(1) a rate of wage inadequate

---

[1]Barbara Nachtrieb Armstrong, *Insuring the Essentials* (New York: Macmillan, 1932), pp. 17–19. Just price theory was first proposed by Plato and Aristotle 300 years before Christ. They suggested that a person is foreordained to occupy the same status in life as his or her parents. This theory resurfaced in the Middle Ages when the Catholic Church, under pressure from wealthy noblemen and landholders, established just wage schedules for skilled artisans, who were in short supply and demanding higher pay. The Church recognized the artisans' birthright and right to more pay by placing them in a higher social group than other workers of that time. See discussion on economic theory, appendix 3A.

[2]Ibid., p. 14.

to the necessities of the workers or disproportionate to the work done; (2) excessive hours of labor; and (3) unsanitary state of houses in which work is carried on."[3]

By the nineteenth century, efforts were under way in the industrialized nations, including the United States, to establish laws to regulate hours worked and improve working conditions. The twentieth century witnessed a veritable explosion of legislation that either mandated or regulated employment practices, and a significant portion of these legislative actions related to compensation received for work performed. From early efforts to regulate hours worked and establish minimum wages, legislation began to encompass almost every part of employee compensation.

The Great Depression of the 1930s led the U.S. Congress to pass legislation that would provide income to large numbers of people when they became too old or physically incapable of working. It also provided income to families of deceased workers. Unemployment insurance became available to workers who lost their jobs through no fault of their own. By the 1960s, legislation forbade employers from making compensation-related decisions that would discriminate against an individual because of race, gender, age, national origin, religion, or handicap status.

Since the 1970s, even more job and economic security has been granted to workers with the passage of laws to protect an employee's right to severance pay, unemployment insurance, earned pension, and receipt of certain kinds of health care. These continuing legislated mandates are sending a loud, clear message to employers that employees must be treated fairly. People are not commodities that can be bought in the market and disposed of at will. Once an employer makes the decision to hire an individual, a commitment is made to that individual's welfare and usually to that of his or her dependents not only for the period of employment, but for possibly a period extending beyond the death of the employee.

The coming decades will witness expansion of legislation that influences employer-provided compensation. This legislation may include mandated health care for all employees and retirees, day care for dependent children, and expanded severance payments for employees of terminated operations or businesses. Regulated practices regarding pensions, health care, and even incentive awards, promotions, and terminations will become more restrictive. The design of compensation plans for members at all levels in an organization will continue to be influenced by tax legislation. Determining what payments are taxable, what payments can be used as a tax-recognized expense, what payments can receive tax-deferred treatment, and what payments escape taxation is important to employer and employee alike.

The remainder of this chapter reviews the legislative, administrative, and judicial processes and some of the critical areas currently addressed by legislation.

THE LEGISLATIVE PROCESS

The ripening of democratic processes and increasing industrialization have led to the enactment of a wide variety of legislation. But no law covers all administrative details; nor can it relate precisely to all situations. For this reason, various federal, state, and local government departments and agencies have been established and empowered to de-

---

[3]Ibid., pp. 34–35.

velop and execute policies, regulations, and practices for the enforcement and administration of federal, state, and local government legislation. After the passage of legislation and the development of administrative and enforcement policies and regulations, disagreements may occur between the enforcement bodies and concerned individuals and organizations. Disputes related to the constitutionality of federal legislation and the propriety of administrative policies and regulations are resolved through the federal court system—the Supreme Court of the United States, the U.S. Court of Appeals, the U.S. district courts, and the U.S. tax courts. A similar process relates to laws passed by local and state governments. In these cases, disputes would normally begin in some local or state court, and move eventually through a state supreme court to the U.S. Supreme Court. The following list provides a brief description of the federal court system.

> *Supreme Court of the United States*   Adjudicates all cases in law and equity arising under the Constitution, the laws of the United States, and treaties made.
>
> *U.S. Court of Appeals*   Reviews almost all final decisions of federal district courts and federal administrative bodies.
>
> *U.S. District Court*   Hears and decides cases as related to federal jurisdiction.
>
> *U.S. Tax Court*   Tries and adjudicates controversies involving deficiencies or overpayments in income, estate, gift, and personal holding company surtaxes.

When the U.S. Supreme Court resolves disputes with which Congress disagrees, Congress then has the opportunity to write new legislation to remedy social issues. For example, in 1976, in the case of *Gilbert* v. *General Electric,* the Supreme Court found that pregnancy was not a disability and was not to be a concern for sex discrimination. By 1978, the U.S. Congress had enacted the Pregnancy Discrimination Act, which included pregnancy as a disability. A later section of this chapter focuses on antidiscrimination legislation and provides an example of how the interpretation develops through case law based on court decisions.

WAGE AND HOUR LEGISLATION

Demands for improvement in working conditions, fewer hours of work a week and shorter working weeks, and improved pay were made early in the nineteenth century. A major breakthrough occurred in the United States in 1840 when President Martin Van Buren issued an executive order that established the 10-hour day for workers on government contracts.[4] At this time, a 13-hour day and a 6-day workweek were the norm. From 1840 until 1866, the 12-hour workday was accepted practice for industrial workers.

Ira Steward, a Boston machinist, provided a philosophical base for an 8-hour day when he stated that wages were determined by worker habits and that because wages depended on wants, the surplus provided by the advancing technology through the establishment of an 8-hour day should result in increased wages for workers.[5] Following the Civil War, 8-hour leagues were established throughout the United States extolling the benefits of the 8-hour day. Some states passed 8-hour laws, and the federal

---

[4]Ray Marshall, "The Influence of Legislation on Hours," in Clyde E. Dankert, Floyd C. Mann, and Herbert R. Northrop, eds., *Hours of Work* (New York: Harper & Row, 1965), pp. 36–53.
[5]Ibid., p. 43.

government passed an 8-hour law for federal employees. However, all these statutes were weak and provided for only minimal enforcement.[6]

Although many groups continued to champion an 8-hour day, the 12-hour day was still an integral part of the life pattern of many workers in the United States into the 1920s. Efforts toward shortening the workweek did, however, result in a reduction of the length of an average workday to 9.5 hours by 1890 (see Table 5–1).

By the latter part of the nineteenth century, reformers seeking to improve unsafe working conditions, reduce long hours, and raise low pay had some success with laws that restricted hours to be worked. In 1896 the province of Victoria in Australia enacted the first minimum wage law in a modern industrial state. New Zealand and England soon followed with minimum wage legislation covering workers in certain industries. In 1912 Massachusetts passed the first minimum wage legislation in the United States. The Massachusetts law was enacted to protect women and children. Although the earnings received by male industrial workers were extremely low, payments received by women and children were even lower. By 1923, 14 more states had passed minimum wage laws aimed at protecting women and children.[7]

These wage and hour laws signaled a major shift in the way employers compensated employees. Until relatively recent times, most employers followed the Iron Law of Wages theory formulated by economist David Ricardo in 1817. This theory stated that "The *natural price* of labour is that price which is necessary to enable the labourers, one with another, to subsist and to perpetuate their race without increase or diminuation."[8] The U.S. Supreme Court, however, did not look favorably upon these legislative changes. A New York State law that had barred employees in bakeries from working more than 60 hours a week was ruled unconstitutional in a 1905 decision in *Lochner* v. *New York.* The ruling was based on the law's unconstitutional interference with the workers' "liberty of contract" (the right of an employee to sell his or her services)—a right derived from the due process clause of the Fifth Amendment. By 1908, however, in *Muller* v. *Oregon,* the Supreme Court unanimously upheld Oregon legislation that limited women to 10-hour workdays. Justification for this decision, as different from *Lochner*, was that the Supreme Court considered the Oregon legislation to be protective in nature and not involved in "liberty of contract."

A major influence on all kinds of hours worked and minimum wage legislation occurred in 1913 when Henry Ford initiated the conveyor assembly line and introduced

TABLE 5–1 Average Weekly Hours for American Nonagricultural Workers													
1850	*1860*	*1870*	*1880*	*1890*	*1900*	*1910*	*1920*	*1930*	*1940*	*1980*	*1990*	*1995*	*1998*
65.7	63.3	60.0	58.8	57.1	55.9	50.3	45.5	43.2	41.1	35.3	34.5	34.4	34.6

Source: J. Frederic Dewhurst et al., *America's Needs and Resources* (New York: Twentieth Century Fund, 1955), p. 1073; 1980 statistics in U.S. Department of Labor, Bureau of Labor Statistics, *Employment and Earnings,* December 1991 (Washington, DC: Government Printing Office, 1991), p. 87; 1995 data from *Employment and Earnings,* January 1996, Table B-8, p. 63; 1998 data from *Employment and Earnings,* January 1999, Table B-8, p. 60.

---

[6]Ibid., pp. 44–45.
[7]Armstrong, *Insuring the Essentials,* pp. 42–65.
[8]David Ricardo, *On the Principles of Political Economy and Taxation,* 3rd ed. (London: John Murray, 1821), p. 93.

the 8-hour day and a $5 per day standard wage. At this time, employees in the iron and steel industry were still working approximately 60 hours per week. In 1923, "liberty of contract" resurfaced in a Supreme Court ruling in *Adkins* v. *Children's Hospital.* This ruling nullified an act of Congress that fixed minimum wages for women and children in the District of Columbia. The battle between "liberty of contract" and employee protection continued until the 1930s. By that time, almost every state had enacted legislation regulating working conditions, hours worked, and minimum wages for women and children. In 1937 the Supreme Court, in *West Coast Hotel* v. *Parrish,* narrowed the scope of "liberty of contract" in sustaining a State of Washington law that established minimum wages for women only. Then, in 1938, Congress passed the Fair Labor Standards Act (FLSA). Through the years, this act and its amendments have been the most powerful wage and hour legislation of the land.

In 1996, the president signed a bill that increased the minimum wage to $4.75 per hour effective October 1, 1996, with an increase to $5.15 per hour on September 1, 1997. Those in favor of increasing the minimum wage argue that to be viable and provide even the semblance of a living wage, the minimum wage should be at least 50 percent of the average national wage, which by 1998 was $12.77 per hour for an American worker.[9]

In the late 1990s, proponents for a $1.00 per hour increase in federal minimum wage made the following points in support of such an increase.

1. Unemployment is near record lows; jobholders are at an all-time high.
2. There is minimal inflation.
3. An increase would not lead to economic problems.
4. An increase would promote upward mobility.
5. An increase would lead to better training of lower-level workers.

Thirty-nine cities have passed living wage laws requiring organizations doing business with the city governments to pay their workers a wage that is considerably higher than the federal minimum wage. In some cases, this living wage is as much as $8.00 per hour.

Those arguing against an increase in the minimum wage note that between 1980 and 1987, 12 million jobs were created. Even though many of these are low-paying jobs, they provide work with pay opportunities for millions of young people. A 1987 study conducted by the Bureau of Labor Statistics (BLS) identified 5.1 million workers out of 96.9 million employed workers earning $3.35 per hour or less. This included 3.3 million who usually work part time. Of this group, 37 percent were teenagers and an additional 34 percent were 20 to 24 years old. Overall, part-time workers were nearly six times as likely as full-time workers to be paid the then existing minimum wage of $3.35 per hour or less.[10] From studies made of the teenage entrant into the labor market, low-paying jobs become stepping stones to higher-paying jobs. Opponents of minimum wage increases state that if the minimum wage increases, there is a good chance that these job opportunities will cease to exist.[11] In addition, opponents state that increases in minimum wage lead to a rise in inflation.

---

[9]U.S. Department of Labor, Bureau of Labor Statistics, *Employment and Earnings* (Washington, DC: U.S. Government Printing Office, January 1999), Table B-2, p. 44.

[10]Earl F. Mellor, "Workers at the Minimum Wage or Less: Who They Are and the Jobs They Hold," *Monthly Labor Review,* July 1987, pp. 34–38.

[11]Bradley R. Schiller, "Training Keeps the Job Machine Running," *The Wall Street Journal,* June 24, 1987, p. 26.

Those opposed to raising the minimum wage feel that not only will entrants into the labor markets suffer because of fewer available jobs, but those who benefit most are those at the higher end of the wage scale, who are already among the highest-paid industrial workers in the world. It is felt that these workers will demand even further increases resulting in their employers being placed in an even more noncompetitive position.

A description of the major pieces of wage and hour legislation follows.

1926: Railway Labor Act   This act grants railway and airline employees the right to bargain collectively with their employers on questions of wages, hours, and conditions of work. When a majority of workers vote to have a union, all employees must pay union dues. Right to work laws do not apply to this act.

1931: The Davis-Bacon Act   The first national legislation on minimum wages came with this act, which required construction contractors and their subcontractors receiving federal funds in excess of $2,000 to pay at least the prevailing wages in their area. The secretary of labor was granted the authority to determine the prevailing wages— the minimum wage that must be paid for work on covered government projects or purchases. (It has been common practice for the secretary of labor to review existing relevant union contracts and use the negotiated wage rates as the "prevailing wages" for a specific locale, but recent rulings permit the secretary of labor more latitude in establishing prevailing wages. Often, only 30 percent of workers in the locale have been used as the representative sample for determining the "prevailing wage.") Amendments to the act provided for employee benefits and required contractors or subcontractors to make necessary payments for these benefits.

1933: National Industrial Recovery Act (NIRA)   The federal government's next step toward enacting a national minimum wage law was the passage of the National Industrial Recovery Act. This attempt to establish a national minimum wage, as had been the case with previous state efforts, was foiled by the U.S. Supreme Court in 1935, which ruled that the law was unconstitutional.

1935: National Labor Relations Act   This act provides employees with the right to bargain collectively for wages, benefits, and working conditions.

1936: Walsh-Healy Public Contracts Act   The federal government again moved into minimum wage regulations with this act. The act requires the payment of the prevailing wage as established by the secretary of labor in all government-let contract work exceeding $10,000, and also requires that time and a half be paid for work exceeding eight hours a day and 40 hours a week. The *Defense Authorization* bill of 1986 excepted federal contractors from overtime pay requirements after eight hours of work a day. They now must only pay time and a half for hours worked in excess of 40 in a week.

1938: Fair Labor Standards Act (FLSA)   This legislation enabled the federal government to become deeply involved in regulating minimum wages for all employees engaged in interstate or foreign commerce or in the production of goods for such commerce, and for all employees in certain enterprises. In addition, this act established overtime wage requirements and defined specific exempt occupations. (Chapter 4 discusses these exempt occupations.) From 1938 until the present time, amendments to the act have enlarged the number of work groups covered by the law and have steadily increased the minimum wage. This act, as amended, not only sets a floor or base wage for most employees, but also allows the minimum wage to act as an index for wage increases received by practically all workers. The act requires employers in covered enterprises to pay time and a half the regular rate received by nonexempt employees for all hours worked in excess of 40 hours a week. (By the 1990s, unions began exerting pressure to raise the overtime premium to double time for hours worked over 40 per week.) Employers must maintain and keep for two years records of time worked for all nonexempt employees. These files must be readily available for examination by U.S. Department of Labor officials. The employer has some discretion in defining a workweek, but it must be fixed and be within a regularly recurring period of 168 hours, for example, from midnight Tuesday until midnight of the following Tuesday. Some provisions, however, allow businesses to operate under a 336-hour work period or 80-hour pay period. In an 80-hour pay period, a business may give compensatory time off at the rate of 1½ hours off for each hour worked in excess of eight within the same timecard period.

The minimum wage began at 25¢ an hour, and by 1997 had reached $5.15 an hour. This act also established a ceiling over a working week in which any hours worked over the ceiling must be paid at the rate of time and a half. In 1938 the ceiling was 44 hours, in 1939 it was lowered to 42, and by 1940 it had dropped to the 40-hour ceiling that is still in effect. In 1982, 61.3 million workers were covered by the minimum wage requirements of the FLSA. Table 5–2 lists the changes in minimum wages between 1938 and 1997.

Provisions of the FLSA permit payment of subminimum wages for the following groups, if approved by the wage-hour administrator:

1. Learner in semiskilled occupations.
2. Apprentices in skilled occupations.
3. Messengers in firms primarily engaged in delivering letters and messages.
4. Handicapped persons, including those employed in a sheltered workshop.
5. Students in retail or service establishments, in agriculture, or in institutions of higher education.
6. Employees who receive over $30 per month in tips (up to 40 percent of the minimum wage requirement may be covered by tips).

In addition to the executive, administrative, professional, and salesperson exemptions discussed in chapter 4, the FLSA also contains provisions that exempt the

TABLE 5–2 Changes in Minimum Wage, 1938–1997

1938	1939	1945	1950	1956	1962	1964	1967	1968	1974
0.25	0.30	0.40	0.75	1.00	1.15	1.25	1.40	1.60	2.00

1975	1976	1978	1979	1980	1981	1990	1991	1996	1997
2.10	2.30	2.65	2.90	3.10	3.35	3.80	4.25	4.75	5.15

following employees from its overtime requirements (although specific qualifications must be met):

Certain highly paid commission employees of retail or service establishments.

Auto, truck, trailer, farm implement, boat, or aircraft salesworkers.*

Partsmen and mechanics servicing autos, trucks, or farm implements.*

Employees of railroad and air carriers, taxi drivers, certain employees of motor carriers, seamen of U.S. vessels, and local delivery employees paid on approved trip rate plans.

Announcers, news editors, and chief engineers of certain metropolitan broadcasting stations.

Domestic service workers residing in the employer's residence.

Employees of motion picture theaters and farm workers.

The child labor provisions of the FLSA are as follows:

1. Minimum hiring age is 14 to 16, depending on the kind of work to be performed and whether or not the employer is the child's parent.
2. Employees must be 18 to work in hazardous occupations.

Information on the Fair Labor Standards Act and its amendments and on the maintenance of records necessary to comply with the act is available from the U.S. Department of Labor, Employment Standards Administration, Wage and Hour Division, Washington, DC, or its nearest regional office. This department is responsible for the administration and enforcement of the act. The Bureau of National Affairs, Inc. provides looseleaf materials that describe the law in detail, its interpretation, and the impact various court rulings have had on the enforcement of the act.

State Laws on Minimum Wages   Over the years, most states have passed their own minimum wage legislation. These laws cover employees who are exempt from FLSA regulations. In 1999 eight states, the District of Columbia, Guam, and the Virgin Islands had a minimum wage higher than the federal requirement. The highest minimum wage that had been adopted at that time was $6.50 per hour in Oregon. It is important to understand that when state labor laws are more rigorous than federal laws, they supersede the federal statutes.

1947: Portal-to-Portal Act   This act exempts employers from calculating time in transit to the work site as part of hours worked for calculating pay and overtime rates. For some jobs there is considerable variation in the time of arrival at the employer's premises and arrival at the work site (e.g., it may take a miner one hour or even more to arrive at the excavation site after entering the external entrance to the mines). This exemption only holds when make-ready time is not counted as work hours.

1965: Service Contract Act   The Service Contract Act ensures that service workers on federal contracts of $2,500 or more receive wages and benefits equivalent to those

---

*These two groups must be employed by nonmanufacturing establishments primarily engaged in selling these items to ultimate purchasers.

prevailing in the area where work is performed but no less than federal minimum wage. It provides additional coverage beyond the Davis-Bacon and Walsh-Healy Acts.

The government requires the use of surveys to identify the prevailing wage in an area (see chapter 10, "Surveying Market Pay and Compensation Practices"). In 1982, the federal government provided regulations to define prevailing wages in an area: (1) the wages paid to a majority of area employees in the job classification, or (2) a wage calculated under a weighted average formula, if the majority of area employees do not work at a single rate.[12] In the mid-1990s, there was considerable discussion in Congress to modify prevailing wage legislation, but no changes were made.

EMPLOYEE PENSION AND WELFARE (BENEFITS) LEGISLATION

Throughout the twentieth century, federal and state governments were increasingly involved in providing protection for workers who suffered an earnings loss owing to circumstances beyond their control. Initial efforts focused on providing income to employees who were unable to work because of job-related illnesses or accidents. Passage of the Social Security Act in 1935 guaranteed some amount of income to workers reaching retirement age and to workers who became unemployed through no fault of their own. This legislation also provided income protection for dependents of covered workers. These early employee welfare laws mandated specific benefits and coverage for individuals and groups specifically covered by the legislation.

Then, during the late 1960s and into the 1970s, a number of pension plans of U.S. businesses became insolvent, and many workers employed by those businesses as well as retired workers found their pension plans in jeopardy or, in some cases, worthless. Senator Jacob Javits of New York, a leader in pension plan reform, pointed out that private U.S. pension plans were based on "three dangerously obsolete assumptions":

1. An employee will stay with one company most of his working career.
2. The company can and should use the plan as a "club" to keep the employees.
3. The company will stay in business forever in substantially the same form as when it installed the plan.[13]

Because of employer defaults on pension promises, Congress passed the Employee Retirement Income Security Act of 1974 (ERISA). This act provides broad regulations concerning employer-offered retirement plans. It does not mandate the offering of pension plans by employers, but those who do offer them must comply with regulations established by ERISA. At the present time, about 50 percent of the nonfarm American workforce receives some form of retirement protection from employers through private pensions, deferred profit sharing, or thrift/savings plans. In recent years, these private retirement protection programs have come under increasing federal regulation (pensions and long-term security plans are discussed in detail in chapter 15).

---

[12]*Federal Register,* May 27, 1982 (47 FR 23644).
[13]"Compensation Currents: Pension Debate Under Way," *Compensation Review,* third quarter 1971, pp. 2–3.

Changes and Potential Changes in Benefits Legislation

As in the development of wage and hour legislation, state governments continue to take the lead in the development of employee benefits legislation. In 1987, the U.S. Supreme Court upheld a California law that requires employers to provide unpaid pregnancy leave and to reinstate jobs to women workers at the conclusion of their pregnancy leave. In 1993, the Family and Medical Leave Act was signed into law. This federal law entitles employees to 12 weeks of unpaid leave during any 12-month period to care for (1) the employee's newborn child; (2) a child placed with the employee for adoption or foster care; (3) employee's spouse, child, or parent with serious health condition; and (4) employee's serious health condition that prevents performance of his or her job functions. This law applies to employers with 50 or more employees. The employee must have been with the employer 12 months and have at least 1,250 hours of service during the 12-month period before the leave.

At the same time some states are granting employees additional compensation rights, Congress continues to wrestle with a broad array of benefits that could be mandated. These new benefits include:

1. Minimum level of employer-provided health care benefits for all employees. By requiring minimum health care benefits, it is calculated that an additional 24 million workers and their dependents who currently have minimal to no protection will be covered. The proposed law provides for a minimum package of physician, hospital, prenatal, and well-baby coverage. In 1988, Massachusetts became the second state (after Hawaii) to require most employers to provide health care for their employees. The Massachusetts legislation levies a tax of up to approximately $1,700 per year for each worker without health insurance; the state provides the insurance. Massachusetts claims this law makes the state "a laboratory for the nation" in providing universal health care.

2. Catastrophic illness legislation expanding Medicare to cover 365 days of hospital care and limiting out-of-pocket expenses to $2,000. This package also includes extended nursing home and long-term home and outpatient care coverage. This program would be paid for by increasing Medicare premiums. In 1999 the Medicare Part B monthly premium was $45.50.

3. Risk pool legislation to allow states to tax self-insured health plans to establish safe risk pools for employees not currently covered by employer-provided health insurance and to cover hard to insure people, including early retirees with existing health problems. (This legislation would cover the one in eight employees who has no employer-provided medical insurance.)

One fact that appears to be common to all these new approaches to *mandated* benefits is to place the cost burden firmly on the employer. These newly mandated benefits may appear as amendments to existing laws, sections or amendments to tax laws, or special new pieces of legislation. Tax legislation of the 1970s and 1980s frequently included sections that restricted benefits by imposing desired or undesirable tax requirements on certain kinds of benefits with specific features. A description of employee pension and welfare benefits legislation follows.

1911: Workers' Compensation   As the United States moved into an industrial economy at the close of the nineteenth century, the increase of industrial accidents and personal injury suits caused by rapid industrialization underscored the inadequate protection provided to workers injured on the job. This led to the enactment in 1911 of the first enduring workers' compensation laws. Today, workers' compensation covers over 85 million American workers.

Each of the 50 states currently has its own workers' compensation laws and administrative agencies. Although the provisions of the laws vary among the states, they do have six common objectives:

1. To provide sure, prompt, and reasonable income and medical benefits to victims of work-related accidents, or income benefits to their dependents, regardless of fault.
2. To provide a single remedy and reduce court delays, costs, and work loads arising out of personal injury litigation.
3. To relieve public and private charities of financial drains incident to uncompensated industrial accidents.
4. To eliminate payment of fees to lawyers and witnesses as well as time-consuming trials and appeals.
5. To encourage maximum employer interest in safety and rehabilitation through an appropriate experience-rating mechanism.
6. To promote frank study of causes of accidents (rather than concealment of fault), and thereby to reduce preventable accidents and human suffering.[14]

Most states require all employers to carry workers' compensation insurance with private, state-approved insurance companies. Normally, each state has some form of minimum provision regarding the size of the business before insurance coverage is compulsory. In states in which coverage is not compulsory, employers may elect not to carry such insurance, but they are then liable to employee lawsuits under punitive conditions.

Some states have their own insurance programs. When this is the case, employers may have to insure with the state, or they may have the option of using the programs of private insurance companies. Most states also permit self-insurance. Usually, only large companies take advantage of this option because they can spread the risk over a large number of employees. These self-insurers will normally develop a protective service similar to that established by an insurance company. During the 1980s and into the 1990s, employer costs for workers' compensation increased significantly. Some small business employers were forced out of business because of premium increases.

1935: The Social Security Act   This act was established to provide American workers with protection from total economic destitution in the event of termination of employment beyond their control. Employers and employees contribute equally to the benefits provided by this act, as amended. Self-employed persons must pay out of their own pockets an established amount to gain Social Security protection. This tax is withheld from the employee's paycheck and is called FICA (Federal Insurance Contribution Act) withholding. This government-imposed tax has escalated rapidly in recent years and will continue to increase in the coming decade. Table 5–3 lists existing Social Security tax rates, wage bases, and maximum payments. Three avenues are open to employers for minimizing this tax burden: First, they may reduce the total size of the

---

[14]*Analysis of Workers' Compensation Laws,* 1980 ed. (Washington, DC: U.S. Chamber of Commerce, January 1980), p. vii.

workforce; second, they may reduce the amount of employee turnover; and, third, they may permit employees to reduce taxable income by funneling pretax dollars into payments for medical insurance premiums, medical reimbursement plans, dependent and child care costs, and so on. Under present regulations, employers must pay for each employee up to the established total contribution. This payment is mandatory even if an earlier employer has already made contributions toward this amount. However, with the increased size of the wage base, the second option has become less important.

Although Social Security is basically a retirement program, it also established the Federal Old-Age, Survivors, Disability, and Health Insurance System. By 1999 Social Security covered over 90 million workers and provided benefits to over 44 million retired or disabled workers and their dependents. In addition, the original law established the federal and state unemployment compensation system. Amendments to this act also provide for Medicaid and Medicare programs. Because of the concern over the economic stability of the Social Security system, Congress in 1983 enacted the Social Security Reform Bill, which made significant changes in the Social Security program.

TABLE 5-3 Existing Social Security Tax Rates, Wage Bases, and Maximum Payments for Employers and Employees

Year	Tax Rate[a]		Wage Base[b]		Maximum Tax
1979	6.13		$22,900		$1,403.77
1980	6.13		25,900		1,587.67
1981	6.65		29,700		1,975.05
1982	6.70		32,400		1,975.05
1983	6.70		35,700		2,170.80
Employee-1984	6.70		37,800		2,391.90
Employer-1984	7.00		37,800		2,532.60
1985	7.05		39,600		2,646.00
1986	7.15		42,000		2,791.80
1987	7.15		43,800		3,003.00
1988	7.51		45,000		3,131.70
1989	7.51		48,000		3,379.50
1990	7.65		51,300		3,604.80
1991	6.20	1.45	53,400	125,000	3,924.45
1992	6.20	1.45	55,500	130,200	5,123.30
1993	6.20	1.45	57,500	135,000	5,328.90
1994	6.20	1.45	60,600	–	–
1995	6.20	1.45	61,200	–	–
1996	6.20	1.45	62,700	–	–
1997	6.20	1.45	65,400	–	–
1998	6.20	1.45	68,400	–	–
1999	6.20	1.45	72,600	–	–

[a] The tax rate is divided into two components: (1) the Social Security wage rate and (2) the Medicare wage rate. In 1991 and 1992, the tax rate of $7.65 consisted of $6.20 for Social Security and $1.45 for Medicare.

[b] Beginning in 1991, the Social Security wage base and Medicare wage base became different. By 1999, the Social Security wage base increased to $72,600. Total salary is now taxed for Medicare.

Unemployment Insurance (UI)   Title IX of the Social Security Act of 1935 imposed a federal payroll tax on employers. Because all states that established a state unemployment compensation plan would be given credit for almost all of the tax paid by the employers, by 1937 all states had unemployment compensation laws. When workers become unemployed through no fault of their own, the state provides them with certain weekly benefits—weekly benefits amount (WBA). Each state (as well as the District of Columbia, Puerto Rico, and the Virgin Islands) has its own unemployment insurance (UI) laws that define the terms and benefits of its unemployment program. Although these programs are legislated and administered by the states, they follow federal guidelines prepared by the Employment and Training Administration, Unemployment Insurance Service, U.S. Department of Labor (USDOL, ETA/UIS).

Federal law requires each employer (except certain nonprofits and governmental agencies) to pay an annual federal UI tax on the first $7,000 earned by each employee at a "gross" tax rate of 6.2 percent. Employers in states conforming with federal UI standards are allowed to take a 5.4 percent credit for state UI taxes paid. The 5.4 percent credit is allowed even if the individual employer has paid state UI taxes at a rate less than 5.4 percent. As a result of this credit, the "net" effective federal tax rate is 0.8 percent and the annual per employee federal UI tax is $56.00.

In addition to this flat-rated federal UI tax, employers also pay an experience-rated state UI tax. Within broad federal standards—each state must have a taxable wage base at least equal to the federal taxable wage base and must have a minimum maximum tax rate of 5.4 percent—each state is allowed to determine its own taxing provisions. For 1998, 12 states had a $7,000 taxable wage base, whereas 21 states exceeded $10,000. Alaska and Hawaii had taxable wage bases of $24,400 and $26,400, respectively. For 1998, maximum UI tax rates ranged from 5.4 percent in 18 states to 12.2 percent in Pennsylvania. Minimum tax rates ranged from 0.0 percent in Florida, Kansas, Missouri, North Carolina, Oklahoma, South Dakota, and Virginia to 2.6 percent in New York.

Employer-paid federal UI taxes are used for two purposes: to pay for the administration of the federal-state UI program and to establish a reserve from which a state can borrow when its UI trust fund is depleted.

Employer-paid state UI taxes are used exclusively for the payment of regular UI benefits. The various states are allowed to establish benefit schedules, benefit duration (usually a maximum of 26 weeks), and benefit eligibility and qualification.[15]

When a state depletes its trust fund, it borrows monies to pay benefits from the Federal Trust Fund. This is an interest-bearing loan that if not repaid on time causes employers in that state to lose a portion of the 5.4 percent credit for federal UI tax purposes. As of December 31, 1998, no state had an outstanding Federal Trust Fund loan.

During the recession of the early 1980s, 23 state trust funds had become insolvent.[16] At that time, various states had passed legislation requiring employers to contribute additional money to the state UI fund. Some states required a flat contribution of $1.00 per $7,000 of salary (Pennsylvania), whereas other states required payment of a payroll surtax ranging from $12 to $77 per worker. During the recession of the early

---

[15]Much of the unemployment insurance (UI) information presented in this section was developed and authored by Mr. Ronald L. Adler, President, Laurdan Associates, Inc., Potomac, MD 20854.

[16]William J. Gaines, *Unemployment Insurance: Issues Relating to Reserve Adequacy and Trust Fund Solvency* (Washington, DC: U.S. General Accounting Office, December 14, 1987), p. 2.

1990s, Maryland initially instituted a surtax of 1.7 percent, which was added to all employers' experience-based tax rate. With the continuing drain on the UI reserve fund, a second surcharge of 0.5 percent was added. This meant that employers enjoying a minimum tax rate of 0.1 percent in Maryland had their UI tax rate increased to 2.3 percent, an increase of 2200 percent.

As stated previously, each state establishes minimum and maximum amounts of WBA, the total number of weeks that an unemployed person may receive such benefits, the qualifying relationship between past earnings and benefits received, and the waiting period after termination of employment before receipt of the first benefit payment. The actual amount of WBA is determined by a formula established by each state. The formula usually considers (1) total wages paid to a claimant during a base period, (2) weeks of wages in the base period, and (3) claimant's number of employers (if claimant had more than one employer). In 1998, an unemployed person in Maryland could receive a WBA ranging from a low of $25 (minimum qualifying wage of $900) to a maximum of $250 (minimum qualifying wage of $9,000).

Because of the economic crisis of the 1970s, Congress enacted the Federal-State Extended Unemployment Compensation Act of 1970, which made available 13 weeks of extended benefits (EB) during periods of "high" unemployment. Then, on December 31, 1974, the Federal Supplemental Compensation (FSC) program was created through the Emergency Unemployment Compensation Act of 1974, and the program was further extended through the Emergency Unemployment Compensation Extension Act of 1977. Depending on the state's unemployment rate, this program provided an additional 8 to 16 weeks of benefits to those who have exhausted both their regular (UI) and extended benefits (EB). These laws provide for special unemployment benefits programs relating to local as well as national conditions. For example, some jobless benefits were extended beyond the normal 16-week period to as much as 65 weeks and include those individuals who in the past had not been covered by unemployment benefits.

From 1991 to 1993, during a period of a sagging economy, emergency UI benefits legislation was enacted that provided an additional 20 to 26 weeks of unemployment benefits to the regular program. In 1991, an additional 13 to 20 weeks of emergency UI benefits were added to the standard 26 weeks of regular benefits. Then, in 1992, an additional 13 weeks of emergency unemployment benefits were added for the unemployed in qualifying states. Each state must qualify for unemployment benefits that extend the standard unemployment period. Similar to past qualification requirements, qualification depends on the rate of unemployment in each state. In 1991, 37 states qualified for 39 weeks of unemployment and 13 states qualified for 46 weeks, with the 1992 amendment adding 13 weeks of UI. The additional 13 weeks program expired July 4, 1992.

Then, in July 1992, the Unemployment Compensation Amendment of 1992 was signed by the president. This legislation extended the emergency benefits program until March 6, 1993. Workers who exhausted their regular unemployment insurance benefits received up to 26 additional weeks of benefits in states where the adjusted insured unemployment rate was at least 5 percent, or the total unemployment rate was at least 9 percent. Workers in all other states received up to 20 weeks of additional benefits. As of June 21, 1992, workers in 15 states were eligible for 26 additional weeks of UI benefits. The 1993 emergency benefits extension legislation had the same requirements, with workers in six states being eligible for 26 weeks of jobless pay and unemployed workers in all other states receiving 20 additional weeks.

Beginning March 7, 1993, states had the option of using a Total Unemployment Rate (TUR) trigger for the permanent EB program. The TUR includes all of the unemployed workers in a state, whereas the existing system, the Insured Unemployment Rate (IUR), counts only those jobless workers receiving UI payments. Under TUR, extended benefits would be paid when (1) the state's seasonally adjusted total unemployment rate for the most recent three months is at least 6.5 percent and (2) that rate is at least 110 percent of the state average TUR in the corresponding three-month period in either of the two preceding years. (The 6.5 percent trigger is one percentage point above the 5.5 percent considered to be full employment.)

States triggering on to the EB program under either trigger would provide 13 weeks of benefits. (This is the same number of weeks of benefits provided in the current extended benefits program.) In addition, seven more weeks would be available in states where the TUR is at least 8 percent and is 110 percent of the state's TUR for the same three months in either of the two preceding years.[17] The Rescissions Act of 1995 eliminated the federal EB program. The various states that continue to have extended benefits provisions in their laws will pay EB if their state programs trigger "on."

Unemployment compensation in the United States took a new form with the introduction of a *short-time compensation plan*. Although short-time compensation programs have been used by several European nations since the 1920s, the United States did not implement this type of program until 1978, when the state of California adopted its Work Sharing Unemployment Insurance program (WSUI). The program works this way: Employers forced to cut production during a downturn in business reduce the number of hours worked by all affected employees instead of laying off a certain number of workers. Employees who have their hours reduced can then apply to the state for unemployment compensation assistance to make up the difference between their normal pay and the reduced pay. The unemployment assistance is provided on a pro rata basis. A person who works three days instead of the normal five days is eligible to receive two-fifths or 40 percent of the maximum benefits available to the worker for a given week of unemployment benefits.

1959: Welfare and Pension Plan Disclosure Act   This act grants the U.S. Department of Labor review and regulatory influence over private pension plans. As amended, it applies to welfare and pension plans covering more than 25 participants in industries affecting commerce. Welfare plans are those providing medical, surgery, or hospital benefits or care and benefits in the event of sickness, accident, disability, death, or unemployment (not including benefits provided under workers' compensation). The term *pension plan* covers profit-sharing plans providing benefits upon retirement.

1973: The Health Maintenance Organization (HMO) Act   This act requires employers who are subject to the Fair Labor Standards Act and who have 25 or more employees to whom they are now providing health insurance to offer an HMO option if it is available in the area in which the employees reside. HMOs are health care organizations that provide medical care at a fixed monthly fee.

Over the past decade, Congress has worked on various forms of national health insurance legislation, but up to this time nothing has been enacted. However, the federal

---

[17]"Conference Agreement on 'Unemployment Compensation Amendments of 1992' (HR5260), Reached by House-Senate Conferees July 2, 1992," Bureau of National Affairs, Inc. (Washington, DC: July 6, 1992), p. F1.

government will probably continue to play a large role in financing health care services. Federal intervention in this area will further extend government influence over programs related to health care. There is an extended discussion of health care benefits in chapter 17.

1974: Trade Act   The Trade Act was passed to assist employers and employees who have been hurt by foreign competition. For workers who have lost their jobs or have had their hours cut because of import competition, the act provides retraining and relocation assistance and a cash allowance equal to the amount of the weekly unemployment benefits for which the worker is eligible. No benefit is paid until the worker has exhausted all other jobless benefits. In 1986 Congress extended the Trade Adjustment Assistance Program, providing up to 52 weeks of payments for eligible workers participating in job search or retraining programs.

1974: Employee Retirement Income Security Act   To protect pension plans from failures and obsolete assumptions, leading political figures and government officials introduced several proposals for reforming private pension plans. Their efforts resulted in the Employee Retirement Income Security Act of 1974 (commonly known as ERISA or the Pension Reform Law). This law establishes fiduciary responsibilities, reporting and disclosure, employee participation and coverage, vesting, funding, limitations on benefits, lump-sum distributions, plan termination insurance, and other requirements.

ERISA also established the Pension Benefits Guaranty Corporation (PBGC). By the end of 1976, more than 10,000 corporate pension plans covering more than 350,000 employees had been terminated because of the additional demands placed on employers by ERISA.[18]

The Pension Benefit Guaranty Corporation (PBGC) administers single-employer and multiemployer insurance plans to ensure that covered employees receive their basic pension benefits. The corporation provides insurance protection for employer liability upon termination of a pension plan. Currently, PBGC covers about 44,000 defined benefit, single-employer retirement plans with over 42 million participants. Since its start, over 1,000 terminated plans have been accepted by PBGC. All single employers who provide ERISA-approved, defined benefit pension plans currently pay an annual insurance premium that can vary between $19.00 and $72.00 per participant. The maximum premium paid is established by a formula relating to the unfunded vested benefits of the employer. This premium provides PBGC with funds to meet obligations to retirees in plans in which fundings are insufficient to meet promised payments. The PBGC maximum guaranteed annual benefit for a plan terminating in 1999 was $36,163.68.

A voluntary portability program permits the tax-free transfer of vested pension benefits. The PBGC also administers this program. Employees may place their benefits in this clearinghouse. If the former employer releases the vested rights when the employee leaves the business, the right may then be transferred to the next employer's qualified plan without tax consequences. It is also possible to maintain the funds in PBGC until the employee retires, at which time the funds are either paid out to the retiree or used to purchase an annuity from an insurance company.

---

[18]Eugene J. Keogh, "Why Does the Corporation Need to Know About Private Retirement Plans?" 1977 Regional Conference Proceedings, Scottsdale, AZ, American Compensation Association, and Charles N. Stabler, "A Closer Look: The New Pension Law May Cut Profits Less Than First Thought," *The Wall Street Journal,* October 1, 1974, pp. 1, 18.

1980: Multiemployer Pension Plan Amendment Act   Further efforts to improve the operation and financial viability of private pension plans occurred with the passage of an amendment to ERISA—the Multiemployer Pension Plan Amendment Act of 1980. Generally, multiemployer pension plans are established and maintained through collective bargaining between employee representatives and more than one employer. According to the PBGC, in 1980 multiemployer plans accounted for only 2 percent of the approximately 106,000 defined benefits plans.

A major problem with multiemployer pension funds is the possibility that an employer member may withdraw from the pension fund. Because few multiemployer pension plans are fully funded, the withdrawal of any employer member, whether voluntary (buyout) or involuntary (bankruptcy), shifts increased liability to all remaining members.

The Multiemployer Pension Plan Amendment Act broadened the legal definition of a defined benefits plan, putting virtually all multiemployer pension plans into the defined benefits category. The major changes made by the act include:

1. Increased employer liability for unfunded benefits
2. Reduced benefit guarantees
3. Faster amortization of unpaid past costs
4. New requirements aimed at improving the financial condition of financially distressed plans

1984: Retirement Equity Act (REA)   This act was designed to eliminate discrimination in pensions provided to women. It recognizes that women have more gaps in their employment history and reduces allowed penalties that can be imposed under ERISA. The act provides for sharing of pensions as common property in the event of divorce.

1988: Worker Adjustment and Retraining Notification Act of 1988   This act requires employers with 100 or more employees to provide a 60-day notice of plant closings and layoffs. This is the first piece of federal legislation to assist employees being laid off or terminated. There is further discussion of severance pay opportunities in chapter 17.

1993: Family and Medical Leave Act   (See discussion on pp. 102 and 121.)

1996: Health Insurance Portability and Accountability Act of 1996   In 1996, the president signed a health insurance bill that guaranteed that (1) workers who change jobs will be eligible for insurance coverage in the new job; (2) workers cannot be denied coverage by their employer's insurer for more than one year because of a preexisting health condition; and (3) individuals who have been covered in a group plan for at least 18 months will have access to individual insurance coverage.

TAX TREATMENT LEGISLATION

The federal income tax program is a major source of revenue for the federal government. Individuals, corporations, estates, and trusts may be required to pay income taxes. A philosophical issue underlying income tax legislation is that it should promote equality and yet enhance equity. The equality issue underlies various tax schedules/rates, or progressiveness, involved in designing income tax programs. The progressiveness issue addresses the fact that those who can afford to pay taxes should shoulder the greatest burden, but at the same time, tax designers do not want legislation to block individual initiative.

After Congress passes tax legislation, the Internal Revenue Service (IRS) of the Treasury Department has the responsibility for implementing the letter and intent of these laws. IRS policies and regulations can be very effective in determining the kinds and features of compensation plans an organization offers to its employees and the manner in which it funds and operates these plans.

When meeting IRS qualification requirements, employers can deduct contributions to a plan as business-related costs, and the employee does not have to declare the employer-made payment as earned income until actual receipt of the contribution (and any gains the contribution may have earned). Over the past 20 years, however, income tax legislation has significantly restricted the offering of these tax-preferred benefits. Chapters 15, 16, and 17 contain in-depth discussions of how various laws affect the use and design of long-term incentives and a wide variety of benefits. Following is a description of tax treatment legislation.

1861: Tax Revenue Act   This act was the first income tax legislation and was passed to assist in financing the Civil War. It imposed tax at the rate of 3 percent on income in excess of $800.

1872:   The income tax act was repealed.

1894:   A tax was imposed on personal income derived from various services but was ruled unconstitutional by the Supreme Court.

1909:   Congress approved a corporate income tax in the form of a special excise tax. The rate was 1 percent of a corporation's net income above $5,000.

1913:   The Sixteenth Amendment to the Constitution was passed, granting Congress the right to levy and collect taxes on income from whatever source.

1913: Income Tax Law   This law imposed a 1 percent tax on personal income between $3,000 and $20,000. A surtax of 1 to 6 percent was imposed on income over $20,000.

1917:   Income tax credits were allowed for dependents and deductions were allowed for charitable contributions.

1918: Revenue Act   This act permitted corporations to deduct as an expense "reasonable" levels of compensation.

1921:   Tax exemptions were granted to profit-sharing and bonus plans.

1922:   Separate capital gains tax rate was established. Initial capital gains rate was 12.5 percent on assets held more than two years.

1934: Revenue Act   This act required corporations subject to federal income tax regulations to submit the names and salary amounts of all executives who earned more than $15,000 a year.

1938: Tax Revenue Act   The salary disclosure figure established in 1934 was raised to $75,000.

1939: Internal Revenue Code   Existing tax laws were codified, making it possible to amend existing laws and eliminating the requirement to rewrite them.

1944:   Standard deductions were adopted.

1948:   Exemptions were allowed for blindness and old age. Split-income joint returns began for married couples.

1950: Tax Revenue Act   This act established rules for the favorable tax treatment of what were termed *restricted stock options.*

1954: Internal Revenue Code   This code repealed the Internal Revenue Code of 1939 and established present tax laws. It modified requirements for restricted stock options.

1962: Self-Employment Individual Tax Retirement Act   This act allows individuals to contribute up to 15 percent of their self-employment income to a retirement plan. The maximum amount to be contributed is $7,500. The Tax Equity and Fiscal Responsibility Act of 1982 raised the contribution to 25 percent and the maximum amount of contribution to $30,000.

1964: Revenue Act   In this act, restricted stock options were replaced with qualified stock options. It lowered maximum marginal tax rates to 70 percent.

1969: Tax Reform Act   This legislation reduced the maximum income tax rate on earned income to 50 percent, raised the maximum tax rate on capital gains to 35 percent, introduced a 10 percent minimum tax on preference income, and established provisions for taxing income set aside for retirement purposes.

1975: Tax Reduction Act   The Tax Reduction Act Employee Stock Ownership Plan was introduced. The act allows corporations to claim 11 percent investment tax credit if an extra 1 percent is contributed to an employee stock ownership plan. This act raised investment tax credit from 7 percent to 10 percent.

1976: Tax Reform Act   This act eliminated qualified stock option plans as of May 20, 1981, and sanctioned group legal plans, liberalized tax treatment of deferred payments, increased minimum tax on preference income to 15 percent, and increased the holding period for capital gains. It also redefined legal, tax-exempt benefits received by employees. The changes in tax exemption relate to (1) the elimination of sick pay as a tax-deductible, employer-sponsored disability benefit; (2) the elimination of tax-deductible, employer-paid attendance to more than two foreign conventions in one taxable year and limitations on travel and subsistence rates to these conventions; and (3) the ability to offer prepaid legal services that are tax deductible to the employer and nontaxable to the employee.

1978: Revenue Act   This act lowered the capital gains maximum tax to 28 percent, continued favored treatment of deferred income, reduced the impact of minimum tax, introduced a second alternative maximum tax, and prohibited discrimination in favor of highly compensated employees relative to certain benefits. Provisions of this act also affect various types of benefits employers provide to their employees. The major benefits-related provisions are:

1. Benefit options selected in a cafeteria-flexible benefits plan need not be included in gross income.
2. A payroll reduction plan can be established that is more flexible and has greater tax advantages than an IRA. (This is the basis for the 401[k] plans that are described in greater detail in chapter 15.)

1981: Economic Recovery Tax Act (ERTA)   The passage of this act reduced individual tax rates by 5 percent on October 1, 1981; 10 percent on July 1, 1982; and 10 percent on July 1, 1983. It reduced maximum tax rates on all income to 50 percent, which in turn reduced the maximum capital gains tax rate to 20 percent from 28 percent as of June 10, 1981. Starting in 1984, individual tax rates were "indexed," which automatically adjusted personal income tax brackets to changes in the consumer price index. It excluded from taxation the first $75,000 of income for Americans employed abroad and housing expenses for these employees in excess of $6,059, a threshold based on a formula tied to the salaries of federal workers. It extended current prohibition against IRS regulations on taxation of fringe benefits to December 31, 1983, and included a provision for recipients of stock options to pay tax at capital gains rate on the difference between the option price and the actual price of the stock at the time of the sale. Options must be exercised in the sequence in which they were made available; the employer is not permitted to deduct the option cost as a business expense.

1982: Tax Equity and Fiscal Responsibility Act (TEFRA)   Provisions of this act established a single, consolidated, alternative minimum tax that replaced minimum add-on tax and alternative minimum tax provisions and reduced qualified retirement benefits for highly paid employees by limiting defined benefits to the lesser of average three-year-high compensation or $90,000, and defined contribution to the lesser of 25 percent of compensation or $30,000. Other restrictions were also placed on qualified retirement benefits. The act placed strict requirements on top-heavy plans (any plan maintained by a corporate or noncorporate endeavor under which more than 60 percent of the accrued benefits of a defined benefits plan are provided for key employees). It liberalized Keogh plan requirements for the self-employed; changed various rules affecting employee and survivor benefits; modified Social Security "integration" rules for defined contribution plans; and established new requirements for group term life insurance.

1984: Deficit Reduction Act (DEFRA)   This act, also known as the Tax Reduction Act of 1984, contains provisions that regulate such common employee benefits as (1) group term life insurance, (2) welfare benefit plans, (3) cafeteria plans, (4) qualified retirement plans, (5) defined contribution and defined benefits plans, and (6) PAYSOPs and ESOPs. The act established tests for identifying key or highly compensated employees. It imposes a nondeductible excise tax on employers that provide disqualified benefits through a welfare plan. DEFRA restricts employer deductible contributions and accumulation of tax-free reserves under welfare benefit plans.

1985: Consolidated Omnibus Reconciliation Act (COBRA)   This act enables employees and their families to continue temporarily (up to 36 months) their health insurance coverage that they would otherwise lose because of employment termination or other qualifying events. Health benefits are separated into core (medical) and noncore (dental and vision) benefits for selection purposes. Qualifying individuals must pay all or part of the applicable premium on selected benefits. Certain employers may impose the 2 percent surcharge for administrative purposes.

The act also increased termination insurance annually per plan participant from $2.80 to $8.50 for employers with defined benefits plans and made it more difficult and more expensive for companies to terminate underfunded pension plans.

1986: Omnibus Budget Reconciliation Act (OMBRA)   This act amends health care continuation provisions of COBRA and makes changes that affect pension plans. Retirees and dependents who lose or have a substantial reduction of their employer-provided health insurance either one year before or after their employer files for Chapter 11 bankruptcy can elect to continue coverage if they pay up to 102 percent of applicable premiums. A retiree can remain in the plan until death; surviving spouse and dependents can remain in the plan for up to three years.

This act requires qualified defined benefit pension plans to continue accruals at an unreduced rate for employees who work after normal retirement age. Defined benefit plans must give service credit for time worked after normal retirement age.

Defined contribution plans cannot suspend or reduce contributions to an employee's account because the employee has reached normal retirement age. Pay-related plans must grant credit for pay received after normal retirement age.

A defined benefit plan is allowed to continue to recognize limits on years of service credits or on benefit amounts. The plan makes special provisions for employees hired at age 62 or older. The plan also eliminates the 3 percent trigger in CPI before Social Security recipients are eligible for a COLA increase.

1986: Tax Reform Act (TRA 86)   This act made extensive changes in the tax laws including reducing tax brackets, covering all tax rates for individuals, and taxing capital gains at the same rate as ordinary income. It also reduced corporate income tax rates and eliminates corporate investment tax credits. The tax affects a wide range of benefits. It establishes tests that limit the deferrals highly compensated employees can make to a 401(k) plan. TRA 86 encourages employers to provide retirement benefits for rank-and-file employees by tests it establishes for qualifying a plan. It makes major changes in vesting requirements and integration of qualified retirement plans and Social Security. The act limits benefits to be paid by a qualified plan and continues federal government support of ESOPs. Changes in capital gains tax laws reduced the value of incentive stock options (ISOs). The act restricts the value of corporate-owned life insurance (COLI) by eliminating the opportunity to deduct interest payments on loans on life insurance policies totaling $50,000 or more for a single employee.

In this act, the top individual tax rate was reduced from 50 percent to 33 percent, and the top capital gains tax rate was increased from 20 percent to 33 percent. The top corporate tax rate was reduced from 48 percent to 34 percent with passive losses disallowed and investment tax credits eliminated.

1987: Omnibus Budget Reconciliation Act   A number of provisions of this act affect defined benefits pension plans. The act increases PBGC premiums from $8.50 to $16.00 per participant in single-employer plans and introduces a variable component at a rate of $6 per participant per $1,000 of unfunded vested benefits with a maximum variable premium of $34. Some of the other provisions affect timing of employer contribution to a plan and interest rates and actuarial assumption to determine current liabilities of unfunded plans and required contributions. Plans mandating employee contributions must credit these contributions at an interest rate equal to 120 percent of midterm federal interest rates (mandated interest rate was 5 percent).

1988: Technical and Miscellaneous Revenue Act of 1988 (TAMRA)   This act changed the tax treatment of refunds of earnings attributable to deferrals that exceed 401(k) and 403(b) tax-sheltered annual dollar limits. It also required the IRS to issue additional Table I rates for individuals over age 64. IRS-provided

Table I rates establish imputed income taxation under IRC Section 79 for employees covered under employer-sponsored term life insurance.

1989: Omnibus Budget Reconciliation Act of 1989 (OBRA 89) This act prohibits nonparticipating Medicare physicians from charging more than 115 percent in excess of Medicare's prevailing charge. This is called the "limiting charge." It increased medical payments for family and internal medicine practitioners relative to surgeons, radiologists, and other procedural specialists.

1990: Omnibus Budget Reconciliation Act of 1990 (OBRA 90) This act affects executive compensation planning by (1) increasing maximum marginal income tax rates from 28 percent to 31 percent; (2) reducing allowable itemized deductions to 3 percent of a taxpayer's adjusted gross income (AGI) in excess of $100,000; and (3) phasing out personal exemptions for single taxpayers whose AGI is greater than $100,000 and heads of household whose AGI is greater than $125,000. This act raises the tax base for the Medicare portion of Social Security to $125,000 and makes the earnings of outside directors subject to Social Security taxes. It also permits employers to transfer some amount of the excess in overfunded qualified pension plan trusts to pay the organization's portion of certain retiree and survivor health care benefits.

1993: Omnibus Budget Reconciliation Act of 1993 (OBRA 93) This act, for income tax purposes, generally prohibits publicly traded companies from deducting the pay of more than $1 million to each of its top five officers as a business expense unless that pay is based on performance criteria approved by outside directors and shareholders.

1997: Taxpayer Relief Act of 1997 (TRA 97) This act reduced the top rate on capital gains from 28 percent to 20 percent for assets held at least 12 months. It continued a 28 percent midterm capital gains tax rate for assets held for more than one year but less than 18 months. It also made more than 800 changes to the tax code. For homeowners, it granted tax-free profits up to $500,000 for a home used as a residence for two of the five years preceding the sale. Beginning in 1998, the law created the Roth IRA. Individuals can contribute up to $2,000 per year ($4,000 for a couple). The contributions are not tax deductible but earnings accumulate tax free. The law also established specifications for converting an existing IRA to a Roth IRA. Education IRAs were also established by this act.

1998: The Internal Revenue Service Restructuring and Reform Act of 1998 This act corrected many of the technical errors contained in TRA 97. The new provisions of the act reduced the required holding period for long-term capital gains tax treatment from 18 months to 12 months. The gains on most assets are taxed at 20 percent (10 percent for individuals in the lowest tax brackets). The act also made a number of revisions regarding the operation of a Roth IRA and an Education IRA.

ANTIDISCRIMINATION IN EMPLOYMENT LEGISLATION

From the founding of the United States and beginning with the first 10 amendments to the Constitution—the Bill of Rights—all who reside in the United States are guaranteed certain rights under law. However, it was not until the 1930s, with the enactment of a broad spectrum of federal laws, that the human resources and compensation programs of all kinds of organizations began to feel the strong influence of government intervention. With each new law, opportunities for organizational initiatives and management prerogatives became less.

Of all the different kinds of legislation enacted in the past 70 years, laws barring discrimination in employment practices have placed the most pressure on human resources and compensation professionals. Antidiscrimination legislation has forced organizations to review how much employees are to be paid, how they are paid, the kinds and quantity of benefits they receive, and the incentives to be offered. In addition, these laws affect the recruitment, selection, and hiring of new employees; the classification of jobs; the appraisal of performance; and the training, transfer, promotion, termination, and retirement of all employees. A listing and description of antidiscrimination legislation follows.

1866, 1870, 1871: Civil Rights Acts   The Thirteenth Amendment to the Constitution of the United States abolished slavery, whereas the Fourteenth Amendment gave the right to vote to former slaves and forbade any state to deny them equal protection under the law. These amendments were supported by the Civil Rights Acts of 1866, 1870, and 1871. The primary thrusts of these acts were (1) to provide equal rights under the law, (2) to ensure property rights, (3) to prohibit state laws from depriving a person of rights, and (4) to prohibit conspiracies to interfere with civil rights.

Section 1 of the Civil Rights Act of 1866 and the provisions of the Civil Rights Acts of 1870 and 1871 have been codified as Title 42, Chapter 21, sections 1981–1983 of the U.S. Code.

Section 1981, Title 42, U.S. Code, precludes job discrimination on the basis of race. A discrimination suit filed under section 1981 does not require that administrative remedies be exhausted, as does Title VII of the Civil Rights Act of 1964. Section 1981 also provides for recovery of compensatory or punitive damages, and the only existing statute of limitations to filing a claim is the statute in the state in which the action is brought. This section does not require an employer to be engaged in interstate commerce.

1963: Equal Pay Act   The Equal Pay Act (EPA), which is the first federal antidiscrimination law relating directly to women, is an amendment to the Fair Labor Standards Act (FLSA). It applies to all employees and employers covered by the FLSA, including executives, administrators, professionals, and outside salespersons.

This act specifically prohibits employers from paying unequal wages for equal work on jobs the performance of which requires equal skill, effort, and responsibility, and which are performed under similar working conditions.

The U.S. Supreme Court has ruled that substantially different or dissimilar working conditions relate primarily to two subfactors—*surroundings* and *hazards*. *Surroundings* measure such conditions as the frequency of exposure to and intensity of toxic chemicals or fumes encountered on the job. *Hazards* take in the physical environment and its impact on the increased chance of an accident and the possible severity of an injury from such an accident (falling off a high platform or working near moving parts).

Under the Equal Pay Act, employers can establish different wage rates on the basis of (1) a seniority system, (2) a merit system, (3) a system that measures earnings by quantity or quality of production, and (4) a differential based on any factor other than sex. (These conditions are often referred to as the four affirmative defenses of the Equal Pay Act.) Shift differentials are also permissible under the Equal Pay Act. All these exemptions must apply equally to men and women. Because of merit system exemptions from equal pay, a number of court rulings have defined what are or are not acceptable performance appraisal programs.

Prior to passage of the EPA, a major issue that had to be resolved concerned the words *equal* and *comparable*. In final arguments just prior to passage, the legislation required *equal* pay for *comparable* work. After considerable debate, it was decided that the word *comparable* would invite too broad an interpretation of the act, and the word *equal* was substituted.

Congress clearly recognized the difference between the words *equal* and *comparable* for identifying differences among jobs. During World War II, the National War Labor Board established regulations requiring equal pay for comparable work. This regulation gave the War Labor Board the authority to make wage determination decisions. It assisted in further establishing job evaluation as a tool of human resources management. (Job evaluation is discussed in detail in chapters 8 and 9.) In 1963, to prohibit the U.S. Department of Labor and federal judges from determining whether or not jobs were comparable and from making pay determination decisions, Congress rejected a comparable worth standard in favor of an equal pay standard. *Equal* (not comparable) *pay* for *equal work* (not worth) became the law of the land.

When applying various tests of equality, federal enforcement officials review the whole job. It is possible to see if jobs are the same or closely related only by analyzing job content and the kinds of activities required in the performance of the job and the amount of time devoted to these activities. Jobs requiring equal skill, effort, and responsibility are seldom identical in every respect. In determining job comparability, it is necessary to consider degrees of difference in skill, effort, and responsibility involved in job performance. Because the EPA is an amendment to the FLSA, the U.S. Department of Labor was given responsibility for its enforcement. However, on July 1, 1979, responsibility was transferred to the Equal Employment Opportunity Commission (EEOC).

1964: Civil Rights Act—Title VII   Title VII of the Civil Rights Act, also known as the Equal Employment Opportunity Act of 1964, as amended, continues to have an impact on the hiring, training, compensation, promotion, and termination practices of organizations. The act established the Equal Employment Opportunity Commission (EEOC) to enforce requirements of Title VII. EEOC is responsible for investigating charges by an employee that the employer has been guilty of unlawful employment practices. Such practices include failure to hire, failure to provide employment opportunities, or failure to promote any individual because of the individual's race, color, religion, sex, or national origin.

Bennett Amendment   Within months after the passage of the EPA, Congress passed the Civil Rights Act. Just before passage, the Bennett Amendment [Section 703(h)] was added to ensure that the EPA would continue to provide the basic laws regarding pay practices. The Bennett Amendment states simply that an employer cannot be charged with violation of Title VII with regard to discrimination in pay unless that employer is also violating the EPA.

Early arguments over the Bennett Amendment concerned whether or not Title VII incorporated both the equal pay for equal work standards, and the four affirmative defenses of the EPA: (1) seniority, (2) merit, (3) quality or quantity of work, and (4) any condition other than sex (existing labor market rates, experience, training, or any other business necessities), or only the four affirmative defenses. If only the four defenses were incorporated, it would be unnecessary to establish unequal pay for equal work before proving a Title VII violation. Moreover, if only the four affirmative defenses were incorporated, how then should the fourth affirmative defense in particular—"a differential based on any factor other than sex"—be interpreted?

Within the decade following the passage of the EPA, women's rights groups recognized that minimal changes in pay practices related to women were occurring because of a strict interpretation of the EPA by the federal court. To obtain judicial support for decreasing the disparity between the pay received by women workers and that received by men workers, *comparable worth* became their battle cry. A basic tenet underlying comparable worth is that workers in jobs held predominantly by women are paid less than workers in jobs held predominantly by men, and the jobs, though different, are of equal or comparable worth to the employer. This difference is a discriminatory action.

The issue underlying comparable worth is how valid and accurate comparisons can be made between unlike jobs. Such comparisons are the purpose of job evaluation and underlie the problem job evaluation experts have faced since becoming involved in this area in the nineteenth century. Whether or not an organization uses some kind of a systematic, orderly, and rational process to measure the worth of unlike jobs for pay practices, *jobholders are paid differently, and different jobs are recognized as having different degrees of worth to the organization.*

After smoldering for over half a century, this issue began attracting public interest by the mid-1970s. The fundamental problem is that when women dominate an occupational field, the rates of pay for jobs within those occupations appear to be unfairly depressed when compared with the pay men receive in jobs in which they are the dominant incumbents within the occupational field.[19]

This problem gave birth to the cries of "job segregation" and "pay discrimination." Women's rights groups and government agencies responsible for eliminating employment discrimination practices—principally, the EEOC and the Office of Federal Contract Compliance Programs (OFCCP)—began taking an extremely active role in resolving the apparent disparity between rates of pay for men and women in segregated occupations. (*Segregated* occupations are those occupations in which at least 70 and possibly 80 percent of the incumbents are of one sex.) The basis for this argument is that women have never been considered the primary wage earner for the family and, thus, it has been assumed that they do not have to be paid as much as men when performing comparable work.

In the late 1960s and throughout the 1970s, these organizations focused attention primarily on employment practices that led to "systemic discrimination" and its resulting "disparate impact." The early EEOC and OFCCP actions in the area of systemic

---

[19]Those interested in obtaining an in-depth overview of the comparable worth issue may wish to read these two articles in the *University of Michigan Journal of Law Reform:* Ruth C. Blumrosen, "Wage Discrimination, Job Segregation and Title VII of the Civil Rights Act of 1964" (Spring 1978), and Bruce A. Nelson et al., "Wage Discrimination and the 'Comparable Worth' Theory in Perspective" (Winter 1980).

discrimination centered on selection criteria for initial hiring decisions and for use in making promotion decisions.

Efforts in these areas have helped women and minorities move into a wider range of jobs and better-paying jobs. With each passing year, however, women working in what are considered traditional female kinds of work have witnessed little improvement in their wage rates compared with the pay men receive for doing traditional male kinds of work. In fact, government pay statistics indicated that the disparity between earnings for women and men, rather than shrinking, increased in the 1960s and 1970s. During the 1980s, the difference began to narrow. By 1999, women were earning approximately 77¢ for each $1 earned by men.[20]

1964: Executive Order 11141 This order prohibits federal contractors from discriminating against employees on the basis of age.

1965, 1967: Executive Order 11246 (1965), as Amended by Executive Order 11375 (1967) These orders ban discrimination because of race, color, religion, sex, or national origin by any employer with a government contract of more than $10,000. The orders are enforced by the Labor Department's Office of Federal Contract Compliance Programs (OFCCP). OFCCP regulations require affirmative action programs of all employers with 50 or more employees and government contracts of $50,000.

1967: Age Discrimination in Employment Act This act prohibits discrimination in hiring individuals between 40 and 65 years of age. It covers employers with 20 or more employees, labor organizations with 20 or more members in an industry involved in interstate commerce, employment agencies, and public employers.

1972: Equal Employment Opportunity Act This act empowered the Equal Employment Opportunity Commission to prevent any person from engaging in any unlawful employment practice as described in Title VII of the Civil Rights Act of 1964. It also empowered the commission to investigate unlawful employment practices on the part of state government, government agencies, and political subdivisions.

1973: Rehabilitation Act The act prohibits employers performing under a federal contract or subcontracts exceeding $2,500 from discriminating against handicapped persons. Handicapped persons are those having physical or mental impairments that substantially limit one or more major life activities. This act further requires private contractors with federal contracts of $50,000 or more or those hiring 50 or more employees to develop a written affirmative action plan. The goal of such a plan is to take affirmative action to employ and advance qualified handicapped individuals.

1974: Vietnam Era Veterans Readjustment Act This act protects the rights of employees to return to their former jobs after engaging in military service. The employee must have made application for reemployment within 90 days after discharge or not more than one year if hospitalization continues after discharge.

An employee qualified to perform the duties of a previously held position must be returned to that position or to a position of like seniority, status, and pay and must be

---

[20]*Employment and Earnings* (Washington, DC: USDOL Bureau of Labor Statistics, January 1999), Table D-20, p. 159.

entitled to participate in all benefits offered by the employer that would have been gained by the employee if the employee had been on furlough or leave of absence.

1978: Age Discrimination in Employment Act Amendments   The Mandatory Retirement Age amendment to the Age Discrimination in Employment Act covers most employees. Beginning January 1, 1979, it prohibits forced retirement of any employee under 70 years of age. College professors and top business executives are exempt from this law, as are employees who have certain bona fide occupational qualifications. The law does not preclude the discharge or layoff of older employees because of unsatisfactory performance. However, an organization must be able to substantiate that such actions are based on job performance. (Performance implications of this act are discussed in greater detail in chapter 13.) The law also requires certain revisions in pensions and profit-sharing plans and in medical and life insurance plans. Differences are allowed if based on a bona fide seniority system or a bona fide benefit plan.

1978: Pregnancy Discrimination Act   Congress enacted the Pregnancy Discrimination Act as a result of its unwillingness to accept the ruling of the Supreme Court in the case of *Gilbert* v. *General Electric,* 13 FEP Cases 1657 (1976). In this case, EEOC and Gilbert contended that General Electric had an insurance disability plan that excluded pregnancy-related disabilities and that this was a violation of the Civil Rights Act. The Supreme Court, meanwhile, ruled that discrimination on the basis of pregnancy was not sex discrimination, but discrimination based on the person's condition, and that no existing law prohibited discrimination against someone on the basis of the condition of the individual. This act is an amendment to the Civil Rights Act of 1964. It prohibits employers from excluding from employment opportunities (disability insurance, medical benefits, leave, accrual of seniority, etc.) any applicant or employee because of pregnancy or related conditions. Disability by, or contributed to, any of these conditions shall be treated the same as disabilities caused by or contributed to by any other medical condition.

This law was further broadened in the case of *Newport News Shipbuilding and Drydock Co.* v. *EEOC,* 29 FEP Cases 200 (1982), in which the court ruled that the employer unlawfully discriminated against its male employees on the basis of sex by limiting pregnancy-related benefits to employees' wives, while affording more extensive insurance coverage to employees' spouses for all other medical conditions requiring hospitalization. Male employees were thus treated less favorably than female employees because the husbands of female employees received hospitalization coverage for all conditions and the wives of male employees received the same coverage except for pregnancy-related conditions.

1986: Age Discrimination in Employment Amendments   These amendments to the Age Discrimination in Employment Act abolish mandatory retirement at any age by removing the upper limit (age 70) on the protected age group. Exempted are firefighters and law-enforcement officers. States and their political subdivisions can establish a mandatory retirement age under certain circumstances for these occupations. An executive exemption permits mandatory retirement at age 65 of a bona fide executive—those in a high policy-making position for the two-year period before retirement—if the retirement income attributable to employer contributions (from a defined contribution and a defined benefits plan) is $44,000 a year or more.

1990: Americans with Disabilities Act (ADA)   This act gives civil rights protection to individuals with disabilities similar to those provided to individuals on the basis of race, sex, national origin, age, and religion. It guarantees equal opportunities to qualified disabled individuals with regard to employment, public accommodations, transportation, telecommunications, and state and local government service. On July 26, 1992, employers with 25 or more employees had to comply with employment provisions of the act. As of July 26, 1994, employers with 15 or more employees were required to comply with the employment provisions. Employment provisions include hiring practices, layoff, leave, termination, advancement, compensation, training, and all other employment-related activities.

The ADA defines an "individual with a disability" as a person who has a physical or mental impairment that substantially limits one or more major life activities. ADA covers (1) mental retardation, (2) paraplegia, (3) schizophrenia, (4) cerebral palsy, (5) epilepsy, (6) diabetes, (7) muscular dystrophy, (8) multiple sclerosis, (9) cancer, (10) HIV, and (11) visual, speech, and hearing impairments. Each one of these disabilities must be considered as a unique case and when making workplace accommodations employers must not place disabled individuals within one group or even broad subgroupings. A qualified individual with a disability is a person who meets legitimate skill, experience, education, or other requirements of an employment position that he or she holds or seeks and can perform the "essential functions" of the position with or without reasonable accommodation. A job description that completely and accurately defines job activities can be considered as evidence, although not necessarily conclusive evidence, of the essential functions of the job (see chapters 6 and 7 for discussion of job content).

Reasonable accommodation is any modification or adjustment to a job or the work environment that will enable a qualified applicant or employee with a disability to perform essential job functions. Reasonable accommodation can include making existing facilities used by employees readily accessible and usable by an individual with a disability; restructuring a job; modifying work schedules; acquiring or modifying equipment; providing qualified readers or interpreters; or appropriately modifying examinations, training, or other programs. Decisions related to appropriate accommodations must be based on the particular facts of each case. An employer is not required to make an accommodation if it would impose an "undue hardship" on the operation of the employer's business. "Undue hardship" is defined as an "action requiring significant difficulty or expense" when considered in light of a number of factors. These factors include the nature and cost of accommodation in relation to size, resources, nature, and structure of the employer's operation. When a facility making the accommodation is part of a larger organization, the structure and overall resources of the larger organization would be considered, as well as the financial and administrative relationship of the facility to the larger organization. In general, larger employers would be expected to make accommodations requiring greater effort or expense than would be required of a smaller employer.

Complaints regarding employment provisions of the ADA can be filed with the Equal Employment Opportunity Commission or designated state human rights agencies.

1990: Older Workers Benefit Protection Act (OWBPA)   This amendment to ADA placed additional restrictions on the benefits practices of employers. Older employees can be required to pay more for health care insurance than youthful employees. This situation can occur when older workers collectively do not make proportionately larger contributions than younger workers. Employers can also legally reduce life insurance coverage of older workers if the cost of providing the insurance is significantly greater than the cost of life insurance for younger workers. OWBPA does not require employers to provide equal or more benefits to older workers when the costs to do so are greater than for younger workers—equal benefits or equal cost principle.

1991: Civil Rights Act (CRA)   Once a complaining party can show an employment practice has disparate impact (by showing a numerical disparity in selection or other employment actions), the employer will have to justify the challenged practice by showing that the practice was required by "business necessity." The CRA defines "business necessity" as "job-related for the position in question and consistent with business necessity." Such employment practices as performance appraisals, supervisory ratings, and interviews must be shown to be job related to the position in question and consistent with business necessity.

1993: Family and Medical Leave Act of 1993 (FMLA)   This act provides employees with job protection in cases of family emergency. See the discussion in the section "Changes and Potential Changes in Benefits Legislation" earlier in this chapter on page 102.

Linking Employment Discrimination and Pay Discrimination

In the early years following the passage of the EPA and Title VII, enforcement of Title VII had the most severe impact on organizations. Because Title VII has a broader scope than the EPA, more organizational employment-related practices can be reviewed, tested, and litigated under Title VII.

An immediate effect of Title VII on organizations was that they had to begin developing records and procedures that define employment standards on the basis of job requirements. They also had to begin identifying working conditions and the manner in which a job is performed. These requirements brought a strong and renewed interest in job analysis (see chapters 6 and 7) and the realization that it must be accurate and complete.

Establishing BFOQs and Disparate Impact   Employers have the right to insist that a prospective applicant meet job qualifications, but the qualifications must be well defined and relate directly to success in job performance. Only bona fide occupational qualifications (BFOQs) can be used to discriminate among applicants. This holds true for promotional opportunities, but organizations must permit freedom of movement or access to higher-rated jobs to all employees.

The concept and use of BFOQs became part of accepted employment practices after the Supreme Court ruling in *Griggs* v. *Duke Power Company,* 3 FEP Cases 175 (1972). In this landmark case, the disparate impact theory of discrimination was established. *Disparate impact* occurs when personnel policies and practices that seem neutral have an adverse impact on protected groups. When disparate impact has occurred, proof of intent is not required; intent will be inferred and a *prima facie* case proved if certain facts are established by the plaintiff. (In a *prima facie* case, the plaintiff can request a court to accept a claim with a minimal amount of facts.) Facts can be established through the use of statistical analysis. After establishing a *prima facie* case, the burden of proof shifts to the defendant. In the *Griggs* case, the central issue was that an educational restriction on an employment decision is useless unless it can be proved that there exists a BFOQ between the test and actual job performance. The burden of proof is on the employer to show nondiscrimination in any employment decision related to discrimination. Here, the impact of an employer's actions becomes even more important than the intent of such actions.

In the case of *Wards Cove Packing Co.* v. *Atonio et al.,* 109 S.Ct. 2115 (1989), the U.S. Supreme Court placed the burden of persuasion (proof) in disparate impact cases on the plaintiff. In this case, the court upheld the employment practices of the defendant, stating that the plaintiffs failed to show that the defendant's employment practices, although neutral and fair, had a disparate impact on women and minorities. This action of the court limited the remedies for sexual, racial, and religious discrimination.

Affirmative Action   Organizations found guilty of discrimination in past hiring or promotional practices have been subject to attorney's fees and court costs in addition to extensive award payments to parties whose rights have been violated. The awards have covered a broad gamut of activities that range from back pay for as much as seven years, to immediate promotional opportunities, to adjustments in profit-sharing and pension plans. Normally, the award is based on what the claimant would have received, according to his or her seniority with the company, had the discriminatory practices not existed.

In addition to these punitive actions, organizations are agreeing to remedial action to remove vestiges of past discrimination. These actions often result in the setting of numerical goals and timetables to remedy present effects of past discriminatory practices. To achieve these goals and timetables, organizations are implementing affirmative action programs—results-oriented programs that specifically spell out hiring and promotion goals designed to increase minority and female employment in job classifications in which members of these groups are currently underutilized. Job classifications identified for affirmative action are (1) officials and administrators, (2) professionals, (3) technicians, (4) protective service workers, (5) paraprofessionals, (6) office and clerical workers, (7) skilled craftworkers, and (8) service maintenance workers.

Opportunities for advancement—for greater use of the potential available within each individual—have been the focal point of much of the effort of the affirmative action programs. Any such program committed to eliminating discriminatory promotional practices must have current and valid job requirements, including up-to-date job descriptions and specifications as well as work standards and procedures. Concurrent with the development of this type of job information program, an inventory of the education, the experience, and the skills (EES) of each employee must be developed.

The personnel EES inventory must then be divided into race, gender, and possibly age groups. These inventories can then be related to each job or classification category, indicating available EES qualification and potential areas of discriminatory practices in which there are indications of significant underutilization or a concentration of minorities and females. (*Underutilization* refers to having fewer minority members or women in a particular job category than would reasonably be expected by their presence in the relevant labor market, job categories, classifications, or grade levels.)

By matching available EES with the EES necessary for advanced jobs or classes, the business is able to identify training and development requirements. By laying such an affirmative action foundation, it can then develop goals and timetables that will improve the use of minorities and females.

Training and development programs that focus on improving upward mobility for employees must not only have well-designed job description, classification, and grading programs but also well-ordered job progressions that relate to lateral transfers and vertical promotions.

WAGE AND PRICE CONTROL LEGISLATION

Wage and price controls have been instituted during times of low levels of unemployment to reduce the chances for rapid inflation. Normally, low levels of unemployment bring higher wage rates and a higher total national income, which in turn mean increased demands for goods and services. These demands cause the prices for the goods and services to escalate, and the result is a national economic condition called inflation.

Since the early days of World War II, the federal government has looked at ways to maintain a stable economic environment. Over the past 55 years, legislation has been passed three times to stabilize the economy by controlling wages and prices. Currently, the Council of Economic Advisors reports directly to the president on policies for stabilizing the economy.

Over the years, various courses of action have been recommended to limit the ravages of inflation and improve economic conditions. They include:

1. Across-the-board wage freezes.
2. Tying compensation increases to overall productivity increases.
3. Providing employers with formulas to determine their own compliance with pay standards.

It has been found that wage and price controls cannot be enforced indefinitely, and that with the lifting of such controls, wages and prices may rise rapidly. When a government implements a wage and price control program, large amounts of bureaucratic regulations and reviews must be promulgated. The costs and effects of these bureaucratic procedures may frequently be more costly to the economy than it would be to let inflation run its course.

Wage controls restrict an organization in designing its own unique compensation system. Although wage controls have restrictive elements, they need not be straitjackets. Operating within a wage control system, compensation managers must know the legal requirements thoroughly. With this knowledge, they will almost always be able to develop procedures that will stimulate performance by providing special payments to those who make unusual or exceptional contributions.

By providing identical pay increases to all employees (the 5.5 percent guidelines of the wage and price controls that resulted from the Economic Stabilization Act of 1970 and that became a commonly accepted standard for annual increases for large numbers of American workers), compensation specialists abdicated their responsibility to recognize contributions of the high-performing employee. Blanket increases of 5.5 percent had a harmful effect on performance and in many cases caused pay to become a "demotivator." In effect, the standard 5.5 percent increase came to be expected by all workers and eventually had no relationship to improved performance or increased productivity of the business. This led to an increase in inflation, which wage and price controls were designed to limit.

However, innovative compensation managers operating within the legal requirements of the controls found ways to distribute pay increases to the most deserving employees, and thereby to enhance the motivational value of compensation. For example, one opportunity afforded to a business under the 5.5 percent guidelines was that the business was not required to give a specific raise to an individual employee. Instead, the total raises for all employees could not exceed 5.5 percent of the total wage package of the prior year. Dividing pay increases by a method other than an equal proportion among all employees requires some form of objective performance standards and methods for measuring employee performance against these standards. The division of a lump sum among individual employees requires the innovative talents of skilled compensation designers and wise operating managers. The following three acts were passed to enhance economic stability.

1942: Wage Stabilization Act   With the passage of this act, wages were frozen for the remainder of World War II at the level that prevailed on September 15, 1942. The government established "going rates" for key occupations and then permitted pay increases up to the minimum of a "going rate" bracket. Benefits could be instituted only if employers could show that they were customary in the area. (This act stimulated employers to use benefits such as paid holidays and vacations in the compensation package.)

1950: Defense Production Act   Wage increases were restricted during the Korean conflict.

1970: Economic Stabilization Act   The president was granted the authority to impose wage and price controls. In 1971, President Richard M. Nixon used this law to impose wage and price controls similar to those enforced during World War II.

LEGISLATION AFFECTING PUBLIC EMPLOYEES

Because public employees work for governments and because of the nature of their work, certain pieces of legislation have been enacted especially for their benefit and also for the benefit of the public.

Public-sector employees, like their counterparts in the private sector, had to fight for their rights and for protection under the law. Some states still prohibit nonfederal public-sector employees from organizing. A major difference between unionized federal employees and private-sector workers is that federal employees do not have the right to strike but must use arbitration and mediation to reconcile employment issues typically related to the bargaining process.

Over the years, state and local government employees have received many of the same rights and benefits provided to federal employees. A list and description of legislation affecting public employees follows.

In 1883, the Pendleton Act established the Civil Service to eliminate the corruption and inefficiencies of the "spoils system"—the placement and rotation of employees in government jobs who were loyal to the political party in power. A major provision of the Pendleton Act was the establishment of a listing of government jobs that would be filled through competitive examination.

1912: Lloyd-LaFollette Act   This act stated that employees could only be terminated through just cause.

1920: Civil Service Retirement Act   Pensions for employees were established.

1923: The Classification Act   This legislation established a system of testing, classification, and pay.

1944: The Veteran's Preference Act   Veterans were given certain preferences in the hiring of workers for federal jobs.

1945: The Federal Employees Pay Act   A 40-hour workweek and overtime were established.

1951: Annual Sick Leave Act   A schedule for vacations, holidays, and leaves was introduced.

1969: Executive Order 11491   Federal employees were permitted to engage in collective bargaining, except for those in the (1) postal service, (2) military, (3) Tennessee Valley Authority, and (4) agencies concerned with internal security, foreign intelligence, and foreign affairs.

1970: Federal Pay Comparability Act of 1970   An analysis of comparability of pay between federal employees and private-sector workers was implemented.

1978: The Civil Service Reform Act of 1978   This act established the Senior Executive Service (SES) (GS16 to Executive Level IV). It requires that accountability of senior executives be fixed and that individual performance be linked to organizational performance. It provides for bonuses for SES employees and merit increases for middle managers (GS13–15) and requires that the performance of federal employees be reviewed in a systematic and objective manner.

1990: Federal Employees Pay Comparability Act of 1990   The setting of pay for federal white-collar employees from a national to locality basis was established by this act. This act requires the expansion of the BLS Area Wage Surveys to higher-level professional and administrative occupations. See discussion of BLS surveys in chapter 10.

Summary

In the latter part of the nineteenth century, governments began to influence the compensation practices of organizations. Since then, minimum wages, hours worked, retirement plans, unemployment insurance, and workers' compensation for employees disabled as a result of work-related accident or illness have all been influenced by legislation. In the 1930s, the U.S. government became actively involved in and significantly influenced the compensation behavior of organizations. Then, in the 1970s, legislation aimed at reducing if not eliminating unjust and unethical discrimination changed the way organizations managed their personnel and, in particular, their compensation systems. The antidiscrimination legislation of the 1960s and 1970s focused specifically on improving employment opportunities for individuals regardless of gender, race, age, national origin, or practically any kind of physical handicap. Pay systems and opportunities for employment and advancement came under close scrutiny by government agencies and the federal courts.

Legislation influences all aspects of organizational life. These influences have an impact on practically every aspect of compensation system design. Legislation requires compensation policy makers and compensation system designers to follow certain well-defined procedures and limit kinds and amounts of compensation components that may be made available to employees. The influence of legislation is felt not only in the design of compensation systems but in the way employees perceive and value the worth of compensation components. Taxes and their influence on net income have an impact on broader numbers of employees each year.

Review Questions

1. Discuss the evolution of minimum wage and hour legislation.
2. How does the Fair Labor Standards Act affect the wage structure of most organizations?
3. What is the major purpose of the Equal Pay Act and what does it require of organizations?
4. In what way does Title VII of the Civil Rights Act of 1964 affect the compensation system of an organization?
5. What is the current relationship between the state and federal governments in the areas of workers' compensation, and unemployment compensation?
6. Discuss the reasons underlying pension reform legislation and the impact of ERISA on the pension plans of many organizations.
7. Describe how income tax legislation influences compensation system design and employee workplace behavior.

PART II

Microeconomic Compensation Concepts

The content of the chapters in the second part of the book explains the methods and processes used to establish the base pay system of an organization. Although there are truly hundreds of compensation components, the single most important component to the great majority of employees is their base pay. As discussed in chapter 1, almost all workers in the United States base their lifestyles on their job-related earnings, which consist primarily of base pay and base pay-related add-ons (e.g., overtime). The exceptions are those in the poverty class who depend on government assistance and the ultrarich who enjoy significant income derived from interest, dividends, and capital gains.

Chapters 6 through 12 explain how organizations determine the base pay for workers in all kinds of jobs. There is a definite relationship among job requirements, employee-required knowledge and skills, and employer-provided pay. The process that moves from (1) analyzing jobs, to (2) ensuring accurate and complete description of job activities, to (3) ranking jobs by a worth mechanism, to (4) collecting and comparing pay practices of similar kinds of organizations for comparable jobs, to (5) linking base pay of all jobs of the organization is the intended output of chapters 6 through 12.

In recent years, there has been considerable discussion as to whether or not jobs continue to exist in the knowledge-based world. Many employees have work assignments that are very dynamic and the activities they perform can vary significantly from day to day. Some consultants and academicians state that *narrowly defined jobs* restrict the work opportunities of employees and are the direct cause of work dissatisfaction. Also, the move toward teams and the concomitant enlargement of work area assignments reduce the need for jobs in contemporary society.

The last chapter in this part analyzes the work of the team members and the setting of base pay in a team-based environment. Whatever the name given to define the work of an employee, all of the processes or functions described in part II are applicable within any organizational setting.

CHAPTER

Job Analysis

Learning Objectives

In this chapter you will learn about:

1. The uses an organization can make of job analysis.

2. The importance of gaining employee acceptance and cooperation before beginning a job analysis program.

3. Information available in an organization to assist in designing and developing a job analysis program.

4. The roles of the job analyst, the incumbent, and the immediate supervisor in conducting a job analysis.

5. The procedures used for collecting job information.

Compensation Strategy

Determine the kinds and levels of knowledge and skills and the number of qualified employees required to achieve organizational objectives and promote organizational success and profitability.

The word *job* has been under fire because it implies restrictive work opportunities for the involved employee. The use of the word *job* does not restrict the work opportunities of the jobholder. Jobs can be as broad and flexible as an organization wishes them to be. At this time, no better word or term has been proposed to substitute and better define the work activities of employees. For this reason, the word *job* continues to be the focus of discussion in the remaining chapters of this book.

Possibly the most misunderstood, undervalued, and poorly implemented management process is job analysis. *Job analysis* involves the identification and description of what is happening on the job. This process uses a number of methods and instruments for collecting and refining job data into job facts that will be used for a variety of useful organizational purposes. The successful completion of the job analysis process is usually labor-intensive, consuming large amounts of time of the incumbent, the incumbent's

supervisor, and job analysts or subject matter experts. It demands a far greater understanding of human behaviors, job requirements, and writing skills than one might think.

Whatever time demands job analysis places on the personnel of an organization to
differentiate the compensation it provides to employees on the basis of job content, job
specifications, working conditions, and employee job performance, the organization
must be able accurately and precisely to identify the required tasks, the knowledge and
the skills necessary for performing them, and the conditions under which they must be
performed. This kind of analysis enables an organization to establish a sound compensation system, using criteria that measure and differentiate job and performance requirements accurately so that all employees receive fair and just treatment.

In the past two decades federal legislation against discriminatory practices by race,
gender, national origin, disability, or age has placed extreme burdens on most employers. Because they must demonstrate the validity (most likely, content validity) of their
recruitment, testing, hiring, compensation, training, transfer, promotion, termination,
and disciplinary practices, the need for accurate and valid job-related data becomes
critical. (There are extensive definitions of the various kinds of validity in chapter 13.)

According to federal government guidelines, practically any method or procedure
used for making a personnel-related decision is considered a test. Thus, in the broadest sense, the compensation system itself can be considered a test. Tests must be valid;
that is, there must be a high degree of association or correlation between the data produced by testing procedures and instruments and the behaviors they describe or predict. The Equal Employment Opportunity Guidelines on Employment Selection
Procedures, Section 1604.7(c), further clarifies this point:

> Evidence of a test's validity should consist of empirical data demonstrating
> that the test is predictive of or significantly correlated with important ele-
> ments of work behavior which comprise or are relevant to the job or jobs for
> which candidates are being evaluated.

For compensation purposes, the establishment of valid pay practices that provide
both equal and equitable treatment to all employees begins with the collection and the
analysis of job content and specification data and information.

An organization may start a job analysis program for many reasons. The decision
may be the result of a demand by employees or union representatives for a change in
job descriptions and the assignment of jobs to pay grades, or for the development of a
classification system that reflects more accurately the work they perform, or for real-
location of job activities in conjunction with an organizational restructuring or redesign
of the organization and its jobs. Legislative mandates for developing nondiscriminatory
employment standards or the need to restructure jobs to eliminate artificial employment barriers can also prod employers into such action.[1] Good management practices
also dictate a periodic review and revision of existing personnel practices. Whatever the

---

[1]Artificial employment barriers arise when employment standards and their related job duties, as expressed
in some institutionalized process or instrument, are essentially unrelated to the primary content of the job,
or when the employment standards of the job call for the employee to have skills to perform duties significantly above the normal level of duties actually required on that job. This results in the screening out of qualified candidates.

reason, an ideal spot to begin is to look at what is happening in the workplace through an analysis of the job.

PRELIMINARY CONSIDERATIONS

The activities involved in collecting, analyzing, and recording job data must not be taken lightly. Before undertaking this costly operation, it is wise to consider two important factors: (1) What kind of support can be expected from senior management? (2) What kind of cooperation can be expected from all employees?

Senior Management Support

Does senior management understand what is involved in performing a job analysis? Have time and cost considerations been fully explored? Are they understood and approved? Have the implications of the kinds of changes that may be recommended because of the analysis been considered? To gain increased output, reduced costs, and improved worker satisfaction, will senior management support the restructuring of certain jobs, the elimination of others, and the upgrading or reclassification of still others? Will they be willing to spend money or even support recommendations for technological changes? Such questions must be discussed before starting a job analysis program. In fact, these questions must be answered to avert a potential court action claiming *intentional discrimination* when management fails to fulfill implied or actual promises that will result in compensation-related changes that should or could have been made.

This approach helps to reduce the shock these demands cause to senior management. In fact, when management faces a deluge of demands, it frequently reacts by doing nothing. If this could possibly be the result of the project, it may be wise *not* to start a job analysis program.

Workforce Cooperation

Have past job analysis programs resulted in no action, or possibly worse, actions contrary to the job security or best interests of employees in all kinds of jobs at all levels? Because of past actions, the workforce may demonstrate attitudes to a new analysis that range from apathy to hostility. Certainly, this will influence the success of any analysis program. The means of overcoming such behaviors must be considered either before or during the design of the program.

The success of a job analysis program hinges on the quality and quantity of data collected. Meeting quality and quantity requirements depends to a large degree on the cooperation and involvement of all jobholders. All members of the organization must support the program and become involved in all its phases—planning, collecting data, analyzing data, and making necessary changes as identified by the program.

PLANNING A JOB ANALYSIS PROGRAM

Formulating the job analysis program and developing a budget require that those involved in analysis activities give intense thought to what must be done. In developing an action plan, specific activities and methodologies will be identified. In addition, forces that may promote or block success must be recognized. Timetables are developed, personnel recruited and selected, and data collection methods defined. Attention to detail and wise reviews at this time will assist in resolving the operational problems that are quite likely to occur.

Frequently, employees assigned to a job analysis project have had minimal experience or training in such basic but critical areas as interviewing and editing. Some job analyst training may be required. The attitudes of employees at all levels must be understood. Although cooperation facilitates the completion of a job analysis program, the demonstration of this vital human quality will vary significantly. If it is possible to identify those who may be uncooperative, actions can be taken to minimize their resistance and possibly turn a negative feeling into a positive one. The following four planning steps are helpful in performing a successful job analysis:

1. Determine the organizational use of job content and other related data.
2. Learn about the structure, operations, and jobs of the organization.
3. Identify and select methods for collecting job content data and other related facts.
4. Schedule the necessary and logical work steps.

Step One: Determine the Organizational Use of Job Content and Other Related Data

The scope of the job analysis program relates directly to the future use of its outputs. Because there are so many potential users of job analysis output data and information, a review of the wide variety of uses of the data provides an excellent starting point to identify what must be accomplished. Major users and uses of job analysis are as follows.

Employment   From recruiting to final selection, the employment function makes extended use of job analysis data. Recruiting, interviewing, and job posting require the best available description of the job. An accurate and complete job description—a basic output of job analysis—assists an applicant to make a more informed decision regarding the desirability of the job and certainly assists recruiters and interviewers in matching applicants with requirements. A truly representative sample of activities (tasks or behaviors) assists in developing valid selection instruments for testing job applicants.

Training   Having job-required knowledge, skills, and abilities available assists a trainer in developing programs that provide instruction for improving and expanding employee competencies. Job analysis is a primary source of job knowledge and skill requirements.

Organization Design and Staffing   A review of job descriptions is invaluable to those responsible for redesigning jobs or even restructuring a work unit or an organization. This review assists in identifying where levels of management can be eliminated, where jobs can be combined, and where technology can improve efficiency.

Compensation   From the establishment of base pay, to pay for dangerous and distressing assignments, to incentive pay plans, basic information lies with the job, and job analysis provides critically needed data.

Performance Review   Although the subject of performance review and measurement can be considered part of both the employment (promotion to new jobs) and compensation (additional pay for performance) functions, it is sufficiently important to be considered on its own merits. Performance dimensions and related performance standards based on job activities and behaviors have their foundation in the outputs of job analysis.

Safety and Health   Job analysis also considers the requirements of the Occupational Safety and Health Act of 1970 (OSHA). The location of potential sources of occupational hazards and initial insights into procedures for eliminating them should be an essential part of the analysis program. Employee safety and health are no longer simply concerned with working in dangerous areas or under distressing conditions. Stressful conditions that could lead to severe emotional problems must also be considered. These environmental conditions can be identified in the performance of a job analysis.

Affirmative Action Planning   Clearly identifying the knowledge, skills, responsibilities, and duties of each job makes it possible to select, train, and develop applicants for both entry-level and promotional opportunities without consideration of race, gender, age, or national origin.

Hiring the Handicapped   With the passage of ADA, organizations must hire, place, and advance individuals with "evenhanded" treatment. Employers must not use any selection criteria that "screen out" or tend to "screen out" qualified personnel with disabilities or any class of persons with disabilities. To overcome charges of disparate impact, the employer must be able to show that the job presents insurmountable barriers to the individual with disabilities. To establish insurmountable barriers, the employer must be able to identify physical and mental requirements and essential job functions that present these barriers and also be able to show reasons of business necessity for not hiring an individual with disabilities. An employer must treat each kind of disability separately to overcome any charge of disparate treatment. (Chapters 5 and 7 include additional discussions of ADA issues.)

Step Two: Learn about the Structure, Operations, and Jobs of the Organization

Selecting methods and procedures for securing job data and information requires a broad understanding of the operations of the organization. Numerous in-house sources are available in organizations for providing job-related information. Some of these are the organization mission statement, organization and work unit objectives and goals, and existing job descriptions. Three general sources of information that can provide valuable assistance toward understanding the jobs of the organization prior to the actual collection of job facts are organization charts, process charts, and any procedures manuals.

Organization Chart   A typical organization chart describes the relationship among the various functions and activities of the organization by showing the individuals, the groups, or the departments responsible for performing these functions. Most charts differentiate pictorially between line functions (producing the products of the organization) and staff functions (furnishing expert advice to the line functions). Figure 6–1 is a basic organization chart. Organization charts should be developed for each work unit to be reviewed. When charts do not exist, one of the first steps in preparing for the job

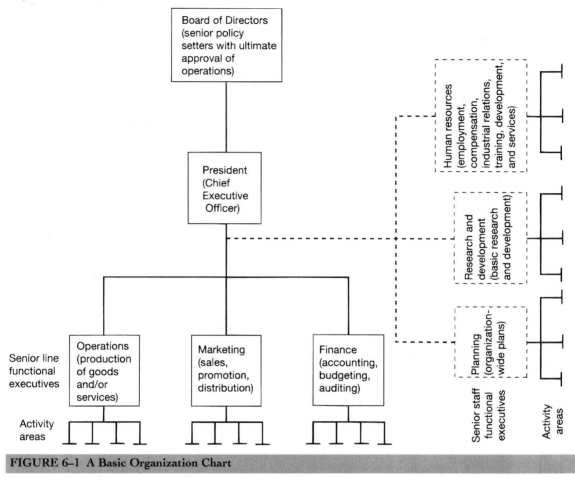

FIGURE 6–1 A Basic Organization Chart

analysis program should be the development of appropriate and useful organization charts.

The organization chart in Figure 6–1 emphasizes the difference between the line functions (solid-line relationships) and the staff functions (dotted-line relationships). The number of levels following a functional box indicates reporting levels relative to designated areas of authority. This picture of the hierarchy of an organization provides an excellent introduction to the functions and activities of an organization and their interrelationships.

A word of warning: Existing organization charts are often obsolete and may not reflect the operations of the organization. In this case, updating is necessary. The updating process, as well as the actual construction of a chart, is not only a valuable exercise in becoming familiar with the organization but also the first indicator of missing, needed, overlapping, or superfluous jobs. Visualizing the organization makes it easier to understand the characteristics and the value of each job.

It may be useful to develop a list of job titles and names of incumbents to support each organization chart. This outline can then be used as a checklist for identifying who did or did not complete questionnaires or for scheduling interviews and observations. The completion of a position table in each appropriate work unit assists in this identification process (see Figure 6–2).

Process Chart   A process chart provides a more detailed understanding of the job or the flow of work than that obtained from a review of the organization chart. A simple process chart may indicate the flow of inputs and outputs to the job under study (see Figure 6–3). Or it could take the form of a flow of activities necessary to prepare a particular output—for example, the steps leading to the filling of a customer's order (see Figure 6–4).

Procedures Manuals   Although many organizations may not have formal procedures for jobs, incumbents, on their own initiative or at the request of immediate supervisors, often develop lists that describe step-by-step what they do. These lists usually identify inputs and outputs of the job, including forms or computer printouts used in performing job assignments. The description of job tasks may not need to be as detailed as some job procedures, but the procedures can be extremely helpful for identifying and assisting in developing task statements.

FIGURE 6–2 Position Table

DIVISION: _____   DEPARTMENT: _____

FUNCTIONAL TITLE	NAME	GRADE	# FULL-TIME EMP.			
			EXEMPT		NONEX.	
			APP	CURR	APP	CURR

EXEMPT				
NONEXEMPT				
PART-TIME				
TOTAL	(APP)		(CURR)	

HUMAN RESOURCES DEPARTMENT _____
(Date)

DIVISION HEAD _____
(Date)

(APP = Approved)

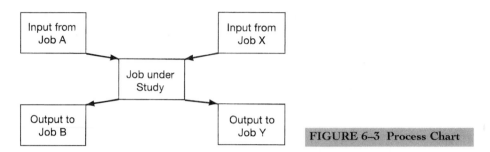

FIGURE 6–3 Process Chart

Step Three: Identify and Select Methods for Collecting Job Content Data and Other Related Facts

Once there is an understanding of the basic reasons for the existence of the job, it is necessary to learn more about its specific tasks or duties. Methods for collecting, analyzing, and recording job activity information are (1) interviews with workers or groups of workers performing the job or with the manager supervising them, or even with a subject matter expert (SME) who may not be an incumbent; (2) observation of the work being performed; (3) completion of questionnaires by workers performing the jobs or by the manager supervising them, or with SMEs; (4) completion of logs or diaries by employees indicating each activity as it is performed over a period of time; or (5) any combination of these. Job analysis data and information can also be obtained through various kinds of checklists of job tasks, behaviors, knowledge, skills, or any job-related requirements or specifications that assist in identifying job similarities and differences. These checklists are produced by a number of commercial and research organizations.

Interview The interview method involves analyzing the job by interviewing either the worker performing the job or the immediate supervisor, or an SME, or possibly all three. The interview is a face-to-face situation. Depending on such conditions as noise,

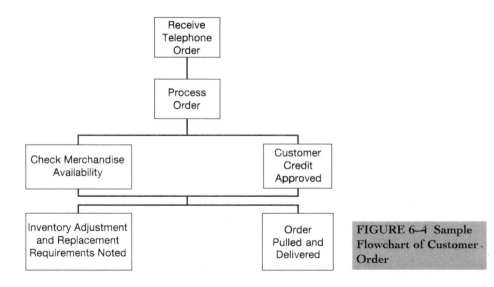

FIGURE 6–4 Sample Flowchart of Customer Order

weather, safety, accessibility, secrecy, privacy, or management desires, the workplace is the first choice for the interview site. A typical job analysis interview takes about one hour. However, for a fairly simple job where the incumbent has good communication skills, the interview could be completed in 30 minutes or less, whereas a review of a difficult or complex job may require more than two hours. Given the availability of interviewers and sufficient time to conduct the interview, this method may be the most effective single approach.

Questionnaire   The questionnaire may be the least costly method of collecting data. A well-designed questionnaire is the most efficient way to collect a wide array of job data in a short period. However, there is the danger that a respondent will not complete the questionnaire, complete it inaccurately, or take an excessively long time to return it. A questionnaire may be inappropriate for groups that have minimal reading or writing skills. Even when performing an interview, it may be helpful to have the person initially complete a questionnaire to assist in organizing his or her thoughts about the job. It is not unusual for a questionnaire to require from one to four hours for completion.

Observation   In the observation method, the analyst actually observes the jobholder performing the job and records what is seen. To analyze the job fully, however, the analyst must observe the complete work cycle. This may be difficult in many jobs because some activities in the job cycle occur at infrequent or irregular intervals. Observation also may require the analyst to take excessive notes of all data pertinent to the job and to its environment to develop a complete description of the job. When actually observing, the analyst should select a vantage point that will provide a clear view of the work being performed and, at the same time, not interfere with those under observation. Like the interview, observing a job could take anywhere from 30 minutes to an hour or more.

Diary/Log   The diary/log normally is a less structured approach than the basic job analysis questionnaire format, although it can contain specific topical questions. The employee is usually asked to record daily activities or tasks; this exercise requires considerable effort and diligence on the part of the employee. Most people are not sufficiently self-disciplined to detail such activities, and it is sometimes difficult for them to outline accomplishments in clear, concise, and simple language.

At the end of the day, it is necessary to review the diary/log and, from memory, compare it with the activities of the day. The diary/log should also contain sections for recording activities performed at infrequent or irregular intervals (weekly, monthly, quarterly). Actually, a diary/log is ideal for this particular purpose. It is also especially useful when working with professionals or on jobs that require a high degree of technical or scientific knowledge.

The lightweight portable tape recorder is a valuable aid in this method. It permits the jobholder to describe work activities vocally and almost at the time of occurrence. The analyst can transcribe the tape later.

Combination   Any combination of the preceding four methods may provide better results than one used by itself. Sometimes the interview, questionnaire, and observation can be combined. This approach requires the incumbent to complete the questionnaire. After reviewing it, the analyst returns to the work site, interviews the employee, and observes the job being performed. By then the analyst should have a good working knowledge of the job and be able to ask a variety of questions to obtain in-depth data about the job that can be used to describe accurately the work required and performed. In fact, observation combines well with any of the methods. The on-site observation of the job is immensely valuable to any analyst. Another alternative is to use a personal interview to collect job content data from one incumbent in a multiple-incumbent job, develop a definition of the job, and send it to all incumbents in that job for review and analysis. The next step would be to conduct a group interview to obtain a consensus on identified job activities.

Step Four: Schedule the Necessary and Logical Work Steps

A time and cost schedule of necessary and logical work steps assists in obtaining job data in conformity with desired results. The development of a job analysis budget is an ideal starting point. Forecasting financial requirements for such a project is especially valuable in preparing a coordinated program that achieves its goals. The planning steps discussed earlier provide some of the basic data necessary for the development of such a schedule.

With knowledge of the intended use of the job analysis and a review of the criteria for the selection of particular data-collecting instruments, it is possible to consider the human resources necessary to implement the program. The number of involved individuals; their skill, education, and experience; and the time necessary to perform the assignment are the primary cost factors.

Developing a budget involves identifying and forecasting the significant events in a job analysis program, as follows:

1. Determining the intended uses of the job analysis. Will it be used for a wide variety of personnel and management-related functions (recruiting, selection, performance appraisal), or only for compensation purposes?
2. Deciding on the kind(s) of instrument(s) that will be used to obtain relevant data and information.
3. Identifying the jobs to be studied.
4. Appraising the knowledge of employees and their trust and willingness to assist in:
   a. Designing and developing data-collecting instruments
   b. Collecting data
   c. Presenting data in a form valuable for future use
5. Identifying job analysis activities and required times. Depending on responses to steps 1 through 4, some of these activities may not be implemented:
   a. Job analysis program presented and explained to employee (may use mass meeting, written communications, visual communications using a VCR, supervisor-held staff meeting). *30 minutes (incumbent's and presenter's time)*
   b. Incumbents complete questionnaire. *30–120 minutes; 45 minutes average (incumbent's time)*
   c. Supervisor of incumbent reviews completed questionnaire for completeness and accuracy. *10–30 minutes; 15 minutes average (supervisor's time)*
   d. Analyst scans completed questionnaire (quick overview to group all questionnaires together where employees appear to be doing similar work). *5–15 minutes; 10 minutes average (analyst's time)*

e. Analyst reviews questionnaire(s) and writes first draft of job description. *45–120 minutes; 75 minutes average (analyst's time)*

f. Analyst performs desk or bench audit (clarifying unresolved issues, adding missing data). *30–90 minutes; 45 minutes average (analyst's and incumbent's time)*

g. Analyst revises job description based on on-site interview and observation. *15–45 minutes; 30 minutes average (analyst's time)*

h. Incumbent and immediate supervisor review edited job description and make final changes. *10–30 minutes; 15 minutes average (incumbent's and supervisor's time)*

GAINING EMPLOYEE ACCEPTANCE AND COOPERATION

Before the start of any job analysis, the persons responsible for the jobs should know what the goals of the analysis are, who is involved, and what will happen. A wide variety of media are available to communicate this information, including meetings, bulletin boards, company newspapers, electronic networking, or special memos. The following brief memo exemplifies a useful introduction to the program:

Compensation and Your Job

We at Olympia realize that all employees have a vital interest in and concern with their pay and the policies and procedures used by the company in determining pay practices. To develop a fair compensation program, we have set forth these three objectives.

(1) All employees must understand the responsibilities and duties of their jobs.

(2) There must be complete agreement between employees and their supervisors as to these responsibilities and duties.

(3) All employees must receive fair rewards for the knowledge necessary to solve work-related problems, to make decisions, and to accept other responsibilities required for the successful performance of their jobs.

To reach these objectives, it is necessary to analyze a variety of jobs throughout Olympia. You can help to improve our knowledge of your job by cooperating fully with the individual assigned to analyze it. If your job is selected, you will receive complete information on your role in this project at the time of analysis.

Thank you.

To help the analyst gain acceptance in the workplace, the manager in the particular job area should introduce the analyst to the workplace supervisor and the incumbent and request one of them to take the analyst on a tour of the work area. Positive acceptance depends on the worker's trust in the motives of the analyst. A major factor in determining trust is the past treatment the worker has received from the organization. An analyst may have to overcome distrust and bitterness directed against the organization because of real or imagined betrayals. When jobs are being analyzed in a union shop, it is also necessary to explain the study to appropriate union officials.

Other Methods   The relatively low costs of the camcorder and VCR and the skills of the many people who can operate this equipment make it possible for almost all organizations to develop a tape that could introduce a job analysis program to employees. The completed tape can then be reviewed by an employee or group of employees with a readily available VCR at a convenient time.

The tape can include an introduction by a senior member of management as to the organizational use of the job analysis data and how the job analysis will benefit all employees. It could then include a discussion of the job analysis collection methodologies and instruments with examples of individuals completing a questionnaire or participating in an interview. The tape could discuss what the employee can expect and what he or she should do to prepare for the data collection. It could also discuss the role of the employee in reviewing data that have been edited and finalized by the job analyst and approved by the immediate supervisor.

COLLECTING AND DESCRIBING JOB DATA

In most cases, each job, like its jobholder, is unique, and the requirements and content of each unique job must be documented accurately and precisely. To accomplish this, a proper combination of the most descriptive words is essential. An existing barrier is that many of the words and terms common to the field of job analysis are often used interchangeably and inconsistently and are poorly defined. This situation has led to considerable misunderstanding, which is a problem not only for the newcomer trying to develop skills in this area, but also for experienced practitioners, consultants, and researchers. To establish a sound basis for understanding the processes and methods developed in this chapter, the following commonly used words are defined:

Activity: A word with broad general meaning that includes any kind of action, movement, or behavior required of an incumbent in performing job assignments. The word *activity* is often used as a generic in lieu of the following words: *function, element, task, duty, responsibility,* and *behavior.*

Major Activity or Responsibility: A term that relates to an important or critical area of the job. Major activity statements are statements that, taken together, describe the general nature of the job. They organize the job into distinct categories. They provide the top of a funnel classification scheme that moves from major activities to tasks to procedures. (The word *responsibility* is used in lieu of *major activity* when identifying the "major activities" in a job description.)

Function: The natural or proper action an individual, work unit, or mechanism performs.

Element: The smallest step into which it is practical to subdivide any work activity without analyzing separate motions and mental processes. Elements are the individual activity units of identifiable and definable physical and intellectual work that produce an output.

Task: A coordinated series of work activity elements used to produce an identifiable and definable output that can be independently consumed or used.

Duty: One or more tasks performed in carrying out a job responsibility. (The words *responsibility* and *duty* are used to identify the activities in a job description.)

Behavior: The actions an individual takes under certain circumstances. *Behavior* may be used as a generic term to describe a set of interacting activities.

Essential Job Function: An ADA-related term that is equivalent to an activity as previously defined, or possibly equivalent to a responsibility or a duty. It is an activity that the individual who holds the position must be able to perform unaided or with the assistance of a reasonable accommodation. (See further discussion of essential job function in the section titled "Activity-Worth Dimensions and Rating Scales" in chapter 7.)

Competency: A combination of knowledge, skill, behaviors, and attitudes demonstrated by an employee in the performance of job assignments. Some compensation professionals even include results achieved as part of employee competency. (This term is a recent addition to compensation management and, at this time, no one definition has been accepted.)

There are definitional problems related not only to these words but to practically every word used in defining what a person does. The same word has different meanings to people in different situations. Conversely, different words have common meanings to individuals in different situations. For example, Eskimos have over 50 words to describe snow. To ensure common understanding of the words and terms used in describing a job, the job analysis process should follow accepted rules in sentence (phrase) structure and in defining words and terms.

The computer revolution is now on the verge of making dramatic changes in the way job analysis is performed and in the many administrative activities required to conduct it successfully. Before discussing in detail the stages and steps of job analysis, a brief digression into the computer's influence in this field is vital.

The Computer and Job Analysis

A major problem facing anyone involved in job analysis is the amount of time it takes for incumbents to provide job content data, for immediate supervisors to review the data, for analyst and SME to review, revise, edit, and write job data, and for administrative personnel in all kinds of jobs to enter, type, and produce final copy. Today, computer-based word processing provides the capacity to simplify the editing and revision of job description statements. Task statements entered and stored in computer databases make it possible for all participants in the process to review and select well-written statements without the drudgery of having to find the best words or terms for writing the task statements that define a job. Computer-inventoried task statements include stored lists of related knowledge, skills, and abilities and, potentially, performance standards. The last part of this chapter and appendix 6A provide information on currently available job analysis methodologies that have strong computer orientation.

The Internet and Job Analysis   The Internet and other electronic media have opened a completely new dimension for the job analyst. Many bulletin boards have been developed to share and retrieve information. Websites such as Skillsnet offer a forum for people to provide information and to seek answers to problems they are having when conducting job analysis and identifying related training opportunities.

Many of the sources of occupational analysis information, such as the U.S. Departments of Education and Labor, V-TECS, major universities, and other organizations, have constructed Internet World Wide Web pages and offer job analysts the opportunity to search for relevant information. This information can be ordered, downloaded, or forwarded to various users. This permits simultaneous job analysis interviews in many locations and permits job analysts to "chat" on-line to share experiences, information, and to plan future strategies.

This new dimension allows the job analyst to streamline traditional methods that required on-site visits, extensive analysis, and time-consuming recordkeeping. Today, on-site visits can be minimized as Web pages can be constructed to collect and disseminate information within a single company or various branches of a single company in many geographical locations, as well as several related companies that are collaborating on job analysis to reduce costs.

The e-mail link of the Internet allows timely communications with single memoranda distributed simultaneously to multiple sites. These memoranda can outline the information required and where it should be faxed. Faxes connected to computers can receive this information and then format it into a consistent format for the completion of job analysis reports.[2]

Developing a Data Collection Instrument

Thousands of different kinds of job analysis questionnaires have been developed for collecting content data. It is not unusual for a questionnaire to be 15 pages in length, which often is threatening enough to cause the incumbent to put the form back on the pile of "things to do," delaying as long as possible any effort to complete the document. Some employees have a difficult time putting their thoughts and ideas into written form; others with the skill just do not like to write; still others feel they do not have the time to spend on this unimportant "personnel" activity. For these and other reasons, incumbent responses to a questionnaire leave much to be desired.

It is unlikely that anyone involved in job data collection is completely satisfied with a particular instrument. Professionals seeking to improve the questionnaire process have taken a number of different courses of action. One approach is to divide the data collection process into at least two major parts. Part 1 involves the collection of task data only; part 2 requires the incumbent to review task data as edited and developed by the job analyst and complete a specifications questionnaire. The second questionnaire collects knowledge and skill data, job environment data, and other necessary job-related data.

Collecting Job Activity Data

In the great majority of cases, the best source of job activity data is the incumbent. For this reason, the logical place to begin the data collection process is with this individual. Whether the incumbent is to complete a questionnaire or provide oral responses in an interview, instruction must be given to ensure that he or she provides complete and accurate data and that comparable data about different jobs are obtained from all employees. The forms in Figures 6–5 through 6–8 can be used as a questionnaire or as a structured outline to be followed and completed by the analyst-interviewer.

---

[2]This discussion of the Internet was written by Chris Olson of the Vocational Technical Education Consortium of States (V-TECS) in a letter to the author dated June 7, 1996.

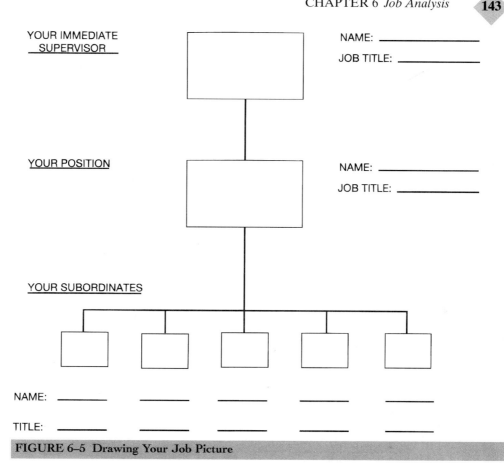

FIGURE 6–5 Drawing Your Job Picture

Figure 6–5, Drawing Your Job Picture, is a mini-organization chart. It is a good starting point for data collection because it requires the incumbent to think of his or her job as it relates to other jobs in the organization. (The analyst will be surprised to find that quite often the incumbent does not know the identity of his or her immediate supervisor.) After completing the mini-organization chart, the incumbent is requested to think about his or her job. Figure 6–6 is an example of the cover sheet of a task-driven questionnaire. The barrier to overcome here is in having the incumbent think about the activities of the job relative to three to five (and possibly more) major categories of work, as in Figure 6–7. Once an employee identifies these major work activity areas, it is much easier to obtain a more complete and accurate list of tasks or, as in Figure 6–8, duty statements. Many people have a difficult time thinking in abstract terms about the work they do. If, however, they can be directed into identifying several major categories of work, it will be much easier for them to describe what they do within each major category.

Figure 6–7, the Responsibility Identification Form, provides the incumbent (or, for that matter, an interviewer) with some structure for identifying and describing major work activities. After completing this form, the incumbent or interviewer can move to

PART I: RESPONSIBILITY AND DUTY IDENTIFICATION

Instructions: We now want to find out exactly what you do in your job. What are all the activities you perform on your job? By completing this job analysis questionnaire, you will help us to update or write a job description for your job. We will be using two terms to help describe your job: (1) RESPONSIBILITIES and (2) Duties.

(1) *RESPONSIBILITIES:*	The major job activities you perform that make up your *whole* job.
(2) *Duties:*	The specific, more detailed activities you perform when accomplishing each responsibility.

Look at the following EXAMPLES:

JOB: *Secretary I*

RESPONSIBILITY   1.0 *Acts as a receptionist.*

Duties
- 1.1 Answers telephone, relaying information or transferring calls to appropriate individuals to meet their demands.
- 1.2 Greets visitors, answering their questions and/or directing them to appropriate individual to meet their demands.

RESPONSIBILITY   2.0 *Performs various administrative activities.*

Duties
- 2.1 Schedules appointments to effectively use manager's time.
- 2.2 Composes routine correspondence to reduce workload of manager.
- 2.3 Makes travel arrangements to ensure travel efficiency and comfort.
- 2.4 Reserves meeting rooms as necessary to ensure their availability.
- 2.5 Notifies participants of scheduled date and time of meetings to facilitate attendance.

We would now like you to do the following:

1. Think of the major things you do in the performance of your job. On the next page (Figure 6–7), list these major activities or, as we call them, RESPONSIBILITIES. Please begin each RESPONSIBILITY with the verb that best exemplifies the action you must take in performing this specific assignment. Each verb should be stated in third person, present tense. (As a general rule, most jobs can be described with 3 to 7 responsibility statements.)

2. On the top of the following page (Figure 6–8), list one of the RESPONSIBILITIES you identified on the preceding page. Now think of the more detailed activities you must perform in order to accomplish this RESPONSIBILITY. We call these statements Duties. (Normally, 3 to 10 duties will fully describe a responsibility.)

3. Continue by listing another RESPONSIBILITY on the next page. Then, following the same procedure, list all of the duties you perform in accomplishing this RESPONSIBILITY. Continue this process until each RESPONSIBILITY you previously listed and all appropriate duties have been identified and listed.

4. After you have written all your RESPONSIBILITIES and Duties, review each RESPONSIBILITY and think about its overall importance in terms of your whole job. Then rank-order your RESPONSIBILITY statements according to importance. Write a "1" in the space to the left of the RESPONSIBILITY that is the *most important* thing you do. Write a "2" before the second most important thing you do. Continue ranking all of your RESPONSIBILITIES until you have a number written to the left of each. (The statement with the *highest* number is the one you consider to be least important.)

continued

FIGURE 6–6 Cover Sheet of a Job Analysis Questionnaire

5. The final step in analyzing the duties of your job is to identify those that are *essential* (with an *E*) or *nonessential* (with an *N*) to the performance of your job. An *essential* (E) activity/duty is one you must be able to perform with or without the assistance of a reasonable accommodation (facility readily accessible to individuals with disabilities, part-time or modified work schedules, special equipment or devices, modified examinations and training materials, and qualified readers and interpreters). A *nonessential* (N) activity/duty is one where you could expect readily available assistance from other employees.

6. If at any time you need to give us additional information, please continue your response on the back of the page.

FIGURE 6–7 Responsibility Identification Form

DEPARTMENT _____ ORG. # _____   EMPLOYEE'S NAME _____

JOB TITLE _____   DATE _____

RESPONSIBILITY IDENTIFICATION FORM

Rank Order	WHAT IS DONE? (Action Verb)	TO WHAT IS IT DONE? (Object)	MODIFYING WORDS OR PHRASE (if appropriate)
	RESPONSIBILITY # 1		
	RESPONSIBILITY # 2		
	RESPONSIBILITY # 3		
	RESPONSIBILITY # 4		

Name of Employee _____ Date _____

Job Title _____ Division _____

**Make sure responsibilities are rank-ordered according to importance
***Circle appropriate E (essential) or N (nonessential) for each duty

RANK
ORDER
_____

RESPONSIBILITY # _____

_____

DUTIES:

E—N   _____   1. _____

_____

E—N   _____   2. _____

_____

E N   _____   3. _____

_____

E—N   _____   4. _____

_____

E—N   _____   5. _____

_____

E—N   _____   6. _____

_____

E—N   _____   7. _____

_____

E—N   _____   8. _____

_____

E—N   _____   9. _____

_____

E—N   _____   10. _____

_____

FIGURE 6–8 Duty Identification Form

Figure 6–8, the Duty Identification Form. One responsibility from Figure 6–7 is transferred to the top of Figure 6–8 (in the location titled Responsibility # _____).

In completing the responsibility and duty identification forms, the incumbent and interviewer (if the forms are used in an interview) must realize that this is an "iterative" process. In this context, iterative means that, in the assignment of duties within a responsibility, a statement previously described as a responsibility may appear as a duty. In this case, the responsibility is eliminated. Also, in developing a list of duties, the incumbent may identify an activity that, in retrospect, is truly a responsibility and should be so listed. When this happens, it is necessary to return to the Responsibility Identification Form and add the newly identified responsibility. After completing the Responsibility Identification Form and all necessary Duty Identification Forms (one form for each responsibility), the incumbent should review the list to determine whether a duty or possibly a responsibility is missing.

Defining a Job Activity or Task   Like many other job analysis-related efforts, writing activity statements appears to be a fairly simple assignment. It is far from simple, however; it is a demanding and difficult challenge that faces all those involved in describing work content.

First and foremost, those responsible for writing job activity statements must describe precisely what they mean. Because of the many crucial organizational- and employee-related programs that are rooted in job content, effort and discipline are required.

The data collection and description phase obtains details about the job. Processing job data into activity statements requires the writer first to think, "What do I want to say?" and, second, "How do I say what I want to say?" Because of the need for brevity and clarity, the suggested syntax of *action verb + object + why and how descriptive information* becomes the "control tower" syntax that establishes a measure of conciseness for those writing activity statements.

action verb (word) + object of the verb
+ words or terms that further describe action taken = the activity

The "control tower" approach exerts a degree of discipline in writing style. When the sentence begins with the action verb, third person, present tense, the resulting direct and vigorous writing style permits the verb to pull the rest of the words in the statement and make it truly action oriented. In reality, the subject of the sentence is the job title. For example, in the job description of a *payroll clerk,* an activity statement reads: "Records daily hours worked." The full form of this statement would be "*Payroll clerk* records daily hours worked." (It is certainly acceptable to use first person, present tense. In that case, the subject of the activity statement is "I [the incumbent] do this or that.")

Certain requirements apply to the writing of all kinds of activity statements. These requirements may be met by taking the actions implied by the following questions:

1. *Is the verb selected the most descriptive verb possible?*   If there is any question, continue to search for a better, more appropriate verb. Searching for and selecting the most appropriate verb is very important and time consuming. The action word glossary at the back of the book provides definitions for over 400 verbs commonly used to describe what workers do.

2. *Does the statement require the use of more than one verb?*   If it does, check to see whether or not it is possible to find one verb that conveys the meaning or action transmitted by the compound verbs. When using compound verbs, be sure that they fit together into a natural, commonly occurring sequence of actions. If this is not the case, separate the verbs into two or more statements.

3. *Does the statement involve a sequential relationship of verb + object, verb + object, verb + object, and so on, plus other modifying information?*   In this case, is it possible to use one verb and object that have a comprehensive meaning and that can combine with some common *why* and *how* modifiers? As in point 2, if this series of verbs and objects does not fit into a common and sequential series of actions, it is preferable to separate the verbs + objects into separate statements.

4. *Does the statement consist of a single verb + object with compound modifiers?*   If it does, it may be useful to divide the single statement into two or more statements, each with its own modifying words or phrases.

Selecting the most appropriate/applicable verb to describe the action taken is the secret in writing an accurate activity statement. In most cases, more than one verb can be used to open the sentence. Because many verbs have more than one meaning, care and attention should be given to the selection of the most suitable verb. For example, in clerical assignments related to working with forms, the verb *handles* frequently appears in the activity statement. Does *handle* mean review the data on the form for accuracy, enter data on the form, transcribe data to other forms, or transfer the form to other individuals? Or, possibly even more important, does it mean that the incumbent is reviewing what is on the form and making decisions and taking actions in response to those data?

Verb selection requires an effort to identify the word that best describes the activity. This kind of effort will be invaluable in reducing vagueness or ambiguity in a major product of the job analysis—the job description. The right verb will tell the reader exactly what is happening on the job. The right verb—the most appropriate verb—must be one the person performing the job and those reviewing the job recognize and understand. In other words, a commonly used word will, in most cases, be the best word.

Adding to the confusion is the subjectivity problem, which has its roots in the meanings of the action verbs. Verbs are words; words are not nearly as precise and uniformly understood as numbers. A certain amount of ambiguity or vagueness is present in many verbs. Verbs may have a variety of meanings as to level or degree of action. These differences in meaning can easily result in significant variations in interpretation of the work to be performed and the expected outcome.

Also, beware of jargon—that is, words used by specific occupational groups. Those outside the field may be unable to recognize the intended meaning of the verb and, thus, may wrongly interpret the description. Jargon may be used as long as the words are widely and clearly understood.

The final, edited copy of accurate and precise major activity and task statements cannot be left to amateurs—not even incumbents or immediate supervisors. Many managers, even human resources specialists, make the mistake of requesting the incumbent or an immediate supervisor to write a description of the job under study and then expect to receive an acceptable final draft. The writing of clear, precise, and concise activity statements requires the efforts of highly skilled professionals.

Attention must also focus on the use of every word in the activity statement. When selecting words, be consistent in their use. Establish a meaning for a word and stick to it. Try to avoid ambiguous words. Use quantitative words when possible ("makes 20 customer contacts daily," not "makes *many* customer contacts daily"). Avoid making conclusions ("performs work requiring the lifting of 94-pound bags of concrete," instead of "performs strenuous work").

Editing Job Activity Data

After concluding the interview or upon receipt of the completed questionnaire, the analyst is ready to develop a first draft of the responsibility and duty statements. Figures 6–9 and 6–10 are examples of Responsibility and Duty Identification Forms completed by an accounting clerk. These responses are quite good, but there are some changes and improvements the analyst can make when reviewing and editing the responsibility and duty statements. The following guides are useful in editing incumbent-provided data into responsibilities and duties that define the job:

1. Are there sufficient responsibilities to cover all major areas of the job?
2. Do the identified duties fit within the assigned responsibility?
3. Does it appear that there may be missing duties?
4. Are the responsibility and duty statements too vague or too specific?
5. Is there an excessive number of responsibility statements (more than 7) and duty statements (more than 10)?
6. Is it possible to combine responsibility or duty statements, or should any responsibility or duty statement be further subdivided?

FIGURE 6–9 Responsibility Identification Form Completed by an Accounting Clerk

RESPONSIBILITY IDENTIFICATION FORM		
WHAT IS DONE ? (Action Verb)	TO WHAT IS IT DONE? (Object)	ADDITIONAL DESCRIPTION (Modifiers)
RESP. # 1 Calculates	payroll costs	for Human Resources Department
RESP. # 2 Maintains	records	for Finance Department
RESP. # 3 Answers	telephone	

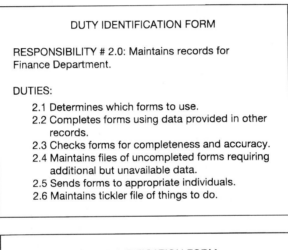

DUTY IDENTIFICATION FORM

RESPONSIBILITY # 1.0: Calculates payroll for Human Resources Department.

DUTIES:
    1.1 Computes employee straight-time pay.
    1.2 Checks employee attendance and work hours.
    1.3 Calculates employee overtime pay.
    1.4 Computes holiday pay.
    1.5 Calculates travel allowances.
    1.6 Calculates employee payroll deductions.
    1.7 Reconciles payroll errors and discrepancies.

DUTY IDENTIFICATION FORM

RESPONSIBILITY # 2.0: Maintains records for Finance Department.

DUTIES:
    2.1 Determines which forms to use.
    2.2 Completes forms using data provided in other records.
    2.3 Checks forms for completeness and accuracy.
    2.4 Maintains files of uncompleted forms requiring additional but unavailable data.
    2.5 Sends forms to appropriate individuals.
    2.6 Maintains tickler file of things to do.

DUTY IDENTIFICATION FORM

RESPONSIBILITY # 3.0: Answers telephone.

DUTIES:
    3.1 Answers questions regarding data and forms.
    3.2 Transfers callers to appropriate individuals.
    3.3 Places calls to collect data.
    3.4 Answers questions about work performed or in programs.

FIGURE 6–10 Duty Identification Forms Completed by an Accounting Clerk

7. Review the action verbs. Are they appropriate? Is one verb used too often? Could it be replaced with a more descriptive verb? Remember, the verbs actually draw a job picture. The more and better the verbs used to define work activities, the more descriptive the definition. The challenge to any writer of responsibility and duty statements is not only to use the most descriptive action verb possible, but to start

each duty statement with a verb that is different from the verb used to originate the responsibility statement. Using the same verb in the duty statement and in the responsibility statement is like defining a word with the same word.

Some of these questions may not be answerable without returning and asking more specific and detailed questions of the incumbent or higher levels of management. Frequently, the incumbent and even the immediate supervisor are so close to the job that they fail to recognize everything that is going on or they assume that others recognize activities being performed, when in reality they are undetected.

Clarifying Deviations   Before completing a first draft job definition, it may be necessary to clarify issues arising from the completed Responsibility and Duty Identification Forms. In the review process, the analyst may sense, from having reviewed other completed questionnaires or from learning work unit operations, that an activity is missing or that an activity is poorly described. In this case, the analyst must verify the problem areas with someone—normally the incumbent or that individual's supervisor—to get a more accurate description of the job. A form requiring verification should be so noted. One procedure is to place a "V" at the top of the completed form, indicating the need to review and verify that particular job.

It is not unusual to find employees who have had insufficient instruction or training and who are doing things they should not be doing. However, deviations between what the employee is doing and *should be* doing do not necessarily arise from faulty effort or work knowledge. There may be valid reasons for deviations. For example, the employee may have developed unique improvements and found a better way of doing the job, or some of the tasks may have been assigned permanently or temporarily to another employee. Other reasons may involve different production requirements, the availability of equipment, revised or new technology, or the array of knowledge among members of the work group. Thus, a complete analysis may require more detailed information.

These deviations may arise because past job descriptions included obsolete duties that continue to be considered part of the job or duties of minimal importance. Maintaining such inaccuracies may ensure an unwarranted high pay for the incumbent or may assist managers in building "empires" by making jobs appear to be more important than they actually are. Unwarranted or unimportant duties also assist in the development of artificial employment barriers.

Because the job analysis touches so many areas fundamental to effective and efficient working relationships, both the worker performing the job and the immediate supervisor must have the opportunity to review the analyst's editing efforts. This review provides an excellent opportunity to determine if the edited copy is (1) factually correct, (2) easily understood, and (3) complete. The report may also require a review by others performing the same job.

This review procedure is a major step in gaining employee acceptance of the entire compensation program. Involvement at this stage provides employees with the opportunity to gain some insight into the way the organization views their jobs and vice versa. It also enables the employees to take a good look at themselves in their jobs and to inform the organization about their contributions and the work they actually perform.

Editing the Accounting Clerk's Responsibilities and Duties   After reviewing the responsibility and duty statements provided by the accounting clerk (see Figures 6–9 and 6–10), the job analyst developed the following first-draft job definition (listing of job responsibilities and duties):

Accounting Clerk—Job Definition

1.0 Maintains payroll records for Personnel Department.
E   1.1 Checks employees' attendance and work hours.
E   1.2 Computes employee straight-time pay, overtime pay, and holiday pay.
E   1.3 Calculates travel allowances.
E   1.4 Calculates employee payroll deductions.
E   1.5 Reconciles payroll errors and discrepancies.
2.0 Processes various forms and records for Finance Department.
E   2.1 Determines which forms to use.
E   2.2 Completes forms using data available in other documents.
E   2.3 Checks forms for completeness and accuracy.
E   2.4 Maintains file for incomplete forms requiring unavailable but necessary data.
E   2.5 Distributes forms to appropriate individuals.
E   2.6 Maintains tickler file of things to do.
3.0 Communicates with others by telephone.
E   3.1 Responds to questions regarding data on various forms.
E   3.2 Transfers calls to appropriate individual.
E   3.3 Places calls to collect data.
E   3.4 Answers questions about work performed or in progress.

Edited Changes: Responsibility 1.0—replaced verb *Calculates* with verb *Maintains*. Wish to use verb *calculates* in duty statement. More precise than *maintains*. Combined duties 1.1, 1.3, and 1.4 into one duty, 1.2. All duties require similar skills and same general kind of knowledge.

Responsibility 2.0—replaced verb *Maintains* with verb *Processes*. Wish to vary verbs in Responsibilities 1.0 and 2.0. Replaced verb *Sends* in duty 2.5 with verb *Distributes*—matter of choice.

Responsibility 3.0—replaced verb *Answers* with verb *Communicates*. The employee does more than *Answer* phone in this responsibility. Need broader, more general action verb. Also used verb *Answer* as action verb in duties 3.1 and 3.4. Replaced verb *Answers* in 3.1 with verb *Responds*.

With the editing of the job definition, step 2 in the data collection process is now ready to begin.

Collecting Job Specification Data

The job specification portion of the questionnaire is now delivered to the incumbent. (Even when an incumbent was interviewed and did not personally complete the responsibility and duty portion of the questionnaire, he or she could be sent the specification section for completion.) Figure 6–11 is an example of a Job Specification Questionnaire.

PART II. KNOWLEDGE AND SKILLS:

1. Please review the enclosed reviewed and edited list of responsibility and duty statements that describe your job. If you find any statements, either responsibilities or duties, missing, please place them on a separate sheet of paper and clip it to the enclosed list. Also, in your review, if you find any statements that do not adequately describe what you do, please revise the statement on the enclosed list.

2. Next, review each duty within the first responsibility statement and, thinking of the knowledge and skills you must have to perform each duty, list them below. Continue this knowledge and skill identification procedure for each additional responsibility and its related duties. (Example of knowledge for a clerk could be, "Knowledge of payroll procedures." A skill could be, "Able to add, subtract, multiply, and divide.")

3. Review your knowledge list, thinking about how you acquired each one (that is, where you learned it). In the column labeled "How Knowledge Acquired," write a number using the code below that describes how you acquired each knowledge.

   1 = In grammar school   6 = In specialized training sessions
   2 = In high school   7 = Through experience on the current job
   3 = In junior (2-year) college   8 = Through experience gained on other jobs
   4 = In college   9 = Other
   5 = In graduate school

4. After you have completed Instruction #3, write an asterisk (*) to the left of the knowledge and skills that you think a person should have *before* being hired for your job.

Responsibility #	Knowledge	How Knowledge Acquired	Skills
1	_____	_____	_____
	_____	_____	_____
	_____	_____	_____
	_____	_____	_____
2	_____	_____	_____
	_____	_____	_____
	_____	_____	_____
	_____	_____	_____

(To adapt this questionnaire to meet your needs, be sure to provide sufficient numbers and space for other responsibilities.)

PART III. EDUCATION AND EXPERIENCE REQUIREMENTS/LICENSES/CERTIFICATION/REGISTRATION:

1. If you were hiring someone to replace you in your present position, what is the *lowest* educational level you would require them to have?
   _____ completion of a high school education
   _____ graduation from a technical or junior (2-year) college
   _____ graduation from a 4-year college or university
   _____ possession of a master's degree or equivalent
   _____ other (specify)

2. If you were hiring someone to replace you in your present position, how many years of experience would you require them to have? (i.e., minimum experience requirement)

continued

FIGURE 6–11 Job Specification Questionnaire

3. What licenses, certifications, or registrations *are legally required* to perform your job? Please list:

4. Are you required to either participate or attend any additional training in order to maintain your licensures, certifications, or registrations? If yes, please list them below:

5. Are there any other jobs an applicant should have performed before entering this job? If yes, please list the job titles below:

PART IV. MISCELLANEOUS:

1. What specific laws or ordinances do you use or follow in your work? (Laws or ordinances that you must have knowledge of and use as a reference to perform your job.)

2. Describe the physical demands of your job. (Examples: work is generally sedentary; requires long periods of standing or walking; recurring bending or stooping; constant lifting of items weighing 60 pounds or more.)

3. Describe any working conditions that cause you to feel stress when performing your job activities. (Examples: must frequently meet critical deadlines with little advance notice; workload is extremely heavy allowing no time to relax; employees in department on each other's back; minimal to no cooperation or support.)

4. Describe the normal and usual conditions of your work. (Example: work is performed in an office; in a very noisy place; around much dust, dirt, grease, etc.; around smoke, fumes, irritating chemicals or toxic conditions; outdoors; on call 24 hours a day.)

5. Please list below the number of the *most difficult* responsibility you perform. (The one that is hardest for you.) Why is this responsibility difficult?

PART V. ADDITIONAL INFORMATION:

1. Are there any job activities that you are *not* performing now that you should be? If so, please list them below.

2. Are there any job activities you are now performing that you should *not* be? If so, please list them below.

3. Is there any additional information that you would like to tell us about your job that you feel we should know?

IF YOU HAVE ANY PROBLEMS COMPLETING THIS FORM, PLEASE CONTACT:

CERTIFICATION

I certify that the above information is accurate and complete.

SIGNATURE OF EMPLOYEE _____ DATE _____

REVIEWING AND REVISING JOB FACTS

After receiving the reviewed first draft of the job definition and the completed Job Specification Questionnaire, the analyst is ready to review these documents with appropriate individuals. The immediate supervisor will normally be the most appropriate authority. In some organizations, however, the reviewing authority may be one, two, or more levels higher in the managerial hierarchy.

A major goal of this review is to identify any variance between what is happening versus what should be happening. Any data-collecting process may be potentially weak if it collects and describes only what is happening and omits what *should be* happening. To overcome this weakness and to discover what should be happening on a particular job, the analyst must review the job with a supervisor who fully understands the requirements and the outputs of the job.

The identification of what should be happening gives the analyst deeper insights into the job. The analyst can become aware of whether or not the job is being performed in harmony with the mission of the organization or work unit or in conformance with desired standards. Knowing what should be done allows the analyst to recognize when an incumbent is "puffing up" the job and even to identify cases when an employee is understating requirements. In any case, using the results of the review, the analyst can make any necessary changes in the job definition.

The analyst must realize that it is not unusual for an incumbent and a supervisor to have different views as to what the incumbent should be doing. One of the most crucial benefits of the analysis process is to stimulate supervisor–subordinate communications. It is at the review stage, if not earlier in the process, that any misunderstandings are reconciled.

DESIGNING A CUSTOM-MADE JOB ANALYSIS QUESTIONNAIRE

The sample Job Analysis Questionnaire presented in Figures 6–5, 6–6, 6–7, 6–8, and 6–11 is only one possible format. As mentioned earlier, questionnaires can have several different formats. The particular design of the questionnaire depends on the organization and situation. Answering the following two questions can be most helpful in designing any job analysis questionnaire: (1) What kinds and quantities of job data do I want to collect? (2) What collection process(es) will work best in our organization? The following discussion provides some guidelines and examples for designing a questionnaire.

Guidelines for Designing a Questionnaire

The development of a good questionnaire should follow these two suggestions: (1) Insert only those response requests that are absolutely necessary; and (2) indicate that all answers should be as brief as possible. In addition, a good questionnaire must be neat, with topical areas grouped in a logical sequence that relates to the natural flow of work. This type of format assists the respondents in analyzing their jobs by enabling them to identify and clarify significant activities and describe the qualifications and conditions related to job performance.

A pressing issue that faces each designer of a questionnaire, and one that no text can settle, is the degree of structure to be used; that is, to what extent should the questions be open-ended (responses provided in narrative form) and to what extent should the questionnaire consist of a highly structured checklist? Each approach has strong and weak points and, as in most cases when such issues arise, the answer is that a mixture of both is best.

A narrative approach permits the incumbent to describe the job as it is currently being performed. The questionnaire designer may not take into consideration things that happen on the job and may inadvertently omit items that would be valuable data if they were identified. The open-ended questionnaire requires incumbents to think about their jobs and, from this intellectual exercise, more fully appreciate and understand the whys and whats of the job.

On the other hand, an open-ended questionnaire takes time to complete and audit. Open-ended questionnaires require a certain amount of writing skill to be completed successfully, and many workers do not have these necessary writing skills. In fact, those with good writing skills can verbally upgrade a job by describing it in terms that make it appear to be more important and complex than it actually is. Individuals with minimal or no basic writing skills may describe the job in insufficient detail, with the result that the content and the value of the job may be underestimated.

The structured checklist or closed-response questionnaire takes more time to develop initially because all the vital areas in which questions should be asked have to be identified. A checklist allows a respondent to select among a number of alternative responses. A properly designed set of checklist statements provides a broad spectrum of possible responses, which enhances the probability that the respondent will find the right descriptions that relate to the job under study. A checklist approach often requires a set of questions that determines a magnitude of difference among particular activities of the job. It is often difficult to compose a checklist that reflects important differences in a work activity or work requirement. In turn, it is easy for an incumbent to check a response that, in reality, is inappropriate for the level of the job. However, a well-designed checklist minimizes differences in analyst interpretation. By having only specific, well-defined responses available to the respondent, different analysts cannot make different interpretations of specific responses to the same questions.

Checklist questions also have disadvantages. Employees are unlikely to formulate responses that do not appear as alternative responses for a specific job feature. What may be more harmful is that employees may interpret the alternative responses in a context other than that intended. And, of course, some employees will select responses that they feel will place their jobs in the most favorable light, not necessarily ones that most closely relate to their particular jobs. An example of a checklist used to identify two factors related to the work environment—physical conditions and personal contacts—follows.

Physical Conditions. Please check the objectionable conditions under which you must perform your job and check whether the condition exists rarely, occasionally, or frequently.

		Rarely	Occasionally	Frequently
(a) _____	Dust	_____	_____	_____
(b) _____	Dirt	_____	_____	_____

(c) _____	Heat	_____	_____	_____
(d) _____	Cold	_____	_____	_____
(e) _____	Fumes	_____	_____	_____
(f) _____	Odors	_____	_____	_____
(g) _____	Noise	_____	_____	_____
(h) _____	Vibration	_____	_____	_____
(i) _____	Wetness	_____	_____	_____
(j) _____	Humidity	_____	_____	_____
(k) _____	Others	_____	_____	_____

Personal Contacts. Please check items that best describe the nature of the people with whom you have contact:

(a) _____	Skeptical	(e) _____	Emotionally unstable
(b) _____	Uncooperative	(f) _____	Frightened
(c) _____	Hostile	(g) _____	Confused
(d) _____	Normally courteous	(h) _____	Mentally retarded

A checklist approach requires closer auditing on the part of the analyst. When auditing checklist items, a first step is to compare the checked items with provided duty (task) statements. Does the level of work activities support the item checked? If the answer is negative or doubtful, the analyst must return to the incumbent to find out why the specific item was checked.

Second in importance is the need to identify necessary knowledge and skills. The start of knowledge and skill identification begins with a complete and accurate description of job content. (Differences in the rates of pay for most jobs are influenced more by these two factors than any other job variable.) Like job content information, the best source of job-required knowledge and skills is the incumbent. Just as job content information collected from incumbents may be inaccurate, the knowledge and skill information provided by incumbents may be inaccurate or incomplete. To be confident that a complete and accurate listing of knowledge and skills has been obtained, the incumbent's list should be compared with some kind of information provided by other incumbents, higher levels of management, and other subject matter experts involved in job requirements (such as job test design and selection professionals).

Knowledge required may include, for example, knowledge of (1) organization operating practices, (2) basic filing procedures, (3) gasoline engine mechanics, or (4) complex electronic systems. Typical skills required of incumbents are skill in (1) communicating with others, (2) operating a keyboard or PC, (3) setting work priorities, and (4) meeting deadlines under pressure. It must be noted that practically any skill can be described as an ability, and vice versa. When job analysis is undertaken for test design and selection, ability identification is of paramount interest. Tests are designed primarily to identify acquired abilities.

At this stage in the personnel process, it is possible to identify what an employee *can* do, but not necessarily what that person *will* do when performing a job assignment. Those involved in defining job requirements for determining job worth, however, begin making the transition from abilities to skills (skills being demonstrated abilities). The final step in transition from abilities to skills occurs with performance appraisal. Here, the abilities possessed are not significant; all that is important is what the individual did while performing the job assignment—the skills the incumbent demonstrated.

An optional approach for obtaining knowledge and skill information is to follow the request for task information with this instruction:

> Please list the knowledge and the skills required in the performance of the tasks you just listed.

GUIDELINES FOR CONDUCTING A JOB ANALYSIS INTERVIEW

The interview depends on the interviewee's willingness and ability to provide the necessary information. When both the interviewer (the analyst) and the interviewee are interested enough to prepare for the interview, the likelihood of success is enhanced. There is always the possibility that the authority vested in the interviewer may frighten the interviewee, who may then hide the truth about a job by exaggerating its importance. This situation is just as dangerous as trying to learn the truth from a stubborn, uninterested employee who is unwilling to provide relevant and valid data.

After good background preparation and a proper introduction to the interviewee, the interview begins. Empathy is an important attribute of any analyst. (*Empathy* is the ability to see something through another's eyes. It requires understanding, not sympathy.) The analyst must recognize each jobholder as an important person and a unique individual. Interviewing should not be taken lightly, for this intrusion into the territory of the jobholder provides a basis for the development of mistrust and hostility. The analyst must always assume that the job is vital to the organization and that the performance of each jobholder is a necessary and valuable contribution. Any other attitude conveys negative thoughts to the interviewee and blocks success.

A personal interview often assists or allows an incumbent to express views and ideas that would never be stated in writing or that might not be recognized during a limited observation. Granting an employee an opportunity to state some deeply felt views or opinions concerning the job is important not only for gaining job information, but also for allowing the employee to vent feelings that may cause considerable anxiety and hostility. At times, these views should be revealed to persons who have appropriate decision-making authority. At other times, it may be necessary only to listen.

Here are some suggestions for accomplishing a successful interview:

1. When only a select group or small number of incumbents are to be interviewed, ask the supervisor responsible for the job to select as an interviewee the individual who knows most about the job. (The supervisor should be careful not to select a self-serving flatterer. Another danger here is that the worker singled out by the manager may feel that social interactions with the work group are jeopardized. In that case, why not let the work group make the selection?)

2. Establish immediate rapport with the interviewee, introduce yourself, know the incumbent's name, speak in easily understood language, briefly review the purpose of the interview, and explain how the selection was made and what opportunity the incumbent will have to review the final report for accuracy and validity. Do not exhibit impatience if the interviewee is nervous or ill at ease.

3. When possible, use structured outlines to obtain job information. Forms that may be of great help when requesting job information could be similar to those described in Figures 6–7 and 6–8. It may be helpful to give the interviewee a copy of the form to be completed and explain what is meant by a responsibility and duty and how you would like to have the task information presented. In most cases, the employee will soon recognize what is desired and will provide the information by using a verb and an object and stating the effect of the action and even the work aids used.

4. If possible, confine questions to one area at a time when asking more than one question. Always focus the discussion on what the incumbent does and the processes and technologies, including work aids, materials, devices, tools, machines, and so on required in the work activities. Differentiate between what the incumbent does and what the equipment produces. If the interviewee begins to stray from the subject, summarize the data collected to that point and then return to the subject.

     Give the incumbent sufficient time to ask additional questions to stimulate thought about infrequent assignments. At this point, it may be a good idea to give the interviewee an opportunity to complain. In this manner, the interviewer may discover hidden job issues. Always close the interview on a friendly note and express appreciation for the time and the effort spent on the interview.

5. After completing the interview, verify the job data. Normally, the interviewee's immediate supervisor is the best person to ask about accuracy. The supervisor will probably be able to interpret the interviewee's comments or clarify certain hazy terms or phrases.

At times it may be appropriate to interview a group of incumbents. This situation normally arises when a significant number of employees are performing similar, if not identical, work, or when the work is closely related in complexity from one level to the next. For group interviewing, the interviewer must be able to interact with a group of people in situations in which diverse and conflicting views may arise. A well-conducted group interview session should spark different points of view and thus lead to an accurate and complete description of job activities. Chapter 12 includes a discussion of a group/team interview in which the analysis process is used to identify the work activities of all team members.

The normal approach for conducting a group interview is to include the immediate supervisor(s) of those involved. There may be times, however, when the workers prefer to speak to the interviewer privately. When this occurs, the analyst is wise to review the situation with the supervisor(s) before conducting the interview. Although the supervisor(s) need not be present, he or she must be kept informed of everything that transpires.

Another kind of group interview is to convene a panel of subject matter experts. The group of experts may be selected employees who are highly skilled and have extended experience on the job; or they may be supervisors or others who have knowledge of the job. This kind of panel could be used in designing a new job for which the experts are aware of the proposed inputs and expected outputs.

OTHER JOB ANALYSIS METHODOLOGIES

Over the years, many large organizations and consulting firms have developed job analysis methodologies designed to improve the quality of collected data; to lower the costs involved in the collection, analysis, and summarization processes; and to make job content data more applicable to objective analysis.

Various agencies within the federal government have been prime movers in developing better ways of collecting and analyzing content data. Among the major contributions that relate to federal government efforts are the U.S. Department of Labor (DOL) Methodology, Functional Job Analysis (FJA), Job Information Matrix System (JIMS), the Job Element Method, and CODAP. Each of these methods uses a somewhat different approach to capture content data.

In addition to the federal government, universities such as Purdue (source of PAQ and PMPQ) and many private-sector consulting firms have contributed and continue to contribute applications designed to improve the job analysis process. (Appendix 6A provides a description of some of the better-known job analysis methodologies.)

Summary

Job analysis is the first step in designing and implementing a compensation system. The objective in completing a job analysis is to identify the content of the job, the knowledge and skills necessary to perform the job successfully, and the conditions under which the job is performed.

Five procedures are available for collecting job information: the interview, the questionnaire, observation, the diary/log, and any combination of these. Whatever method is used, job content must be clearly and concisely identified through the use of activity statements.

The process of gathering job facts can be labor-intensive and quite expensive. Setting aside for a moment the time human resources and compensation specialists must spend on job analysis, consider the time required of higher-level managers, immediate supervisors, and the employees involved in gathering useful and complete data. The time human resources specialists (job analysts) spend in reviewing completed questionnaires or in actually interviewing or observing incumbents can quickly mount into scores of hours for just one job.

If time and cost issues are not of sufficient concern, another worry is that the results of many job analysis programs are soon out of date, and there appears to be no way to maintain the program and keep it current. As more and more job activity data are stored in computer-based word processors, with access to the stored data available to all employees, the costs of maintenance will be reduced dramatically.

On the other hand, few people would deny that there is a need for useful and current job content and specification data. A vital link in the communication program of any organization is the information that tells all concerned parties what is included in each job. These activities provide a solid foundation for setting procedures when necessary, and, above all, for establishing standards that inform each employee just what is acceptable performance.

Review Questions

1. Why is it necessary to perform a job analysis?
2. How do organizations use job analysis data and information?
3. Describe an orderly and systematic procedure for developing a job analysis program.

4. Describe various methods for generating job analysis data and information, giving examples of where each method would best fit the requirements of the situation.

5. With the advent of word processing and computing capabilities, organizations can develop their own major activity and task inventories. What is the role of job analysis in this process?

Appendix 6A
Other Job Analysis Methodologies

DOL METHODOLOGY

In 1934, the U.S. Employment Services (USES) began a study to identify, through job analysis, the common denominator of jobs, regardless of industry. The USES and, currently, the Employment and Training Administration of the U.S. Department of Labor (DOL) have been involved in developing a methodology for analyzing and classifying job content. Through the research and training efforts of the USES and the DOL, many government agencies (federal, state, and local) and private-sector businesses have received training in the DOL methodology, or a variation of it.

The DOL methodology first classifies job analysis into two major categories: (1) *work performed* and (2) *worker traits* or *characteristics.* Work performed is further subdivided into (1) worker functions, (2) work fields, and (3) materials, products, subject matter, and services. Worker traits have five subheadings: (1) training time, (2) aptitudes, (3) temperament, (4) interests, and (5) physical demands and environmental conditions. A brief description of the three subdivisions of work performed follows.

1. The *worker functions* describe what the worker does in relation to *data, people,* and *things.* To describe the varying complexities of data, people, and things, the DOL has developed a scale of values for each category. The highest combination of activities that describes the three areas of worker functions identifies the relative importance of the job. The 24 identifying activities of the worker function areas are shown in Table 6A–1. Normally, each successive function reading down each column in Table 6A–1 includes or involves all functions that follow.

2. The *work fields* are the specific methods used to carry out technological or socioeconomic requirements of the job. The DOL identifies 99 categories for further classifying these fields. This section contains methods verbs and machines, tools, equipment, and work aids. Methods verbs are commonly used to describe actions taken in performing work. (The action word glossary in this book is a direct descendent of these methods verbs.) The machines, tools, equipment, and work aids section provides examples of instruments, devices, and processes used to carry out the action described by the specific methods verb.

3. The *materials, products, subject material, and services* identify material worked on, final product produced, knowledge dealt with, and services rendered.[3]

---

[3]U.S. Department of Labor, Manpower Administration, *Handbook for Analyzing Jobs* (Washington, DC: U.S. Government Printing Office, 1972). This book includes a complete description of the DOL methodology. It is a valuable reference for anyone involved in compensation management and is essential for anyone involved in the use of DOL methodology.

TABLE 6A–1 DOL Worker Functions

Data	People	Things
0 Synthesizing	0 Mentoring	0 Setting Up
1 Coordinating	1 Negotiating	1 Precision Working
2 Analyzing	2 Instructing	2 Operating-Controlling
3 Compiling	3 Supervising	3 Driving-Operating
4 Computing	4 Diverting	4 Manipulating
5 Copying	5 Persuading	5 Tending
6 Comparing	6 Speaking-Signaling	6 Feeding-Offbearing
	7 Serving	7 Handling
	8 Taking Instruction and Helping	

FUNCTIONAL JOB ANALYSIS (FJA)

Sidney A. Fine, a long-time professional in the Occupational Analysis Section (OAS) of the United States Employment Service and later a private consultant, has added to the DOL methodology through his Functional Job Analysis (FJA).[4] This spin-off of the DOL methodology stresses the area of worker functions (data, people, and things) and makes some modifications to the 24 DOL activities used to scale the three major worker functions. The changes are descriptive of work performed in the human services field. In addition, Fine has reversed the numerical coding so that Level One now represents the least complex relationship (more in line with typical classification numbering systems).

The FJA method also uses a number of additional scales to identify job requirements further. These scales include (1) Scale of Worker Instructions, which identifies levels of discretion available and exercised by employees, and (2) Scales of Educational Development (also used in the DOL methodology), which include a Reasoning Development Scale, a Mathematical Development Scale, and a Language Development Scale.[5]

Fine also claimed that the FJA overcomes one of the major failings inherent in the DOL methodology—failure to relate work performed to the purposes, goals, and objectives of the organization. Fine stated that the FJA incorporates the goals and objectives of the organization into the task statements structured around worker functions and through a "systems approach" to the full articulation of goals and objectives.[6]

Fine further claims that the FJA is not only useful for analyzing job requirements but also for providing criteria for evaluating the worth of a job because it distinguishes between functional, adaptive, and specific content skill requirements of each job. Fi-

---

[4]Sidney A. Fine and Wretha W. Wiley, *An Introduction to Functional Job Analysis: A Scaling of Selected Tasks from the Social Welfare Field, Methods for Manpower Analysis No. 4* (Kalamazoo, MI: W. E. Upjohn Institute for Employment Research, 1971).

[5]Sidney A. Fine, *Functional Job Analysis Scales: A Desk Aid, Methods for Manpower Analysis, No. 7* (Kalamazoo, MI: W. E. Upjohn Institute for Employment Research, 1973).

[6]Sidney A. Fine, Ann M. Holt, and Maret F. Hutchinson, *Functional Job Analysis: How to Standardize Task Statements, Methods for Manpower Analysis, No. 9* (Kalamazoo, MI: W. E. Upjohn Institute for Employment Research, 1974).

nally, by specifying and defining expected functional performance, it develops criteria useful for appraising the performance of a particular worker.

JOB INFORMATION MATRIX SYSTEM (JIMS)

The Job Information Matrix System (JIMS) was developed by Dale Yoder and C. Harold Stone under a contract with the U.S. Department of Labor.[7] JIMS uses five categories to form a standard approach for gathering and recording job information:

1. What the worker *does*.
2. What the worker *uses*.
3. What *knowledge* the worker must have.
4. The worker's *responsibilities*.
5. The *working conditions* of the job.

JOB ELEMENT METHOD

The Job Element Method was developed by Dr. Ernest Primoff of the U.S. Civil Service Commission to establish selection standards and to validate selection tests for federal government jobs.[8] Primoff's job elements are the various kinds of knowledge, skills, abilities, and personal characteristics that can be used to determine job success. The method requires, first, that a job analyst and a panel of experts identify job tasks. Second, the panel identifies the abilities, knowledges, skills, and other personal characteristics necessary to perform the job. Here, the job tasks are transformed into job elements. For an employee in a fast-food restaurant, a task may be, "Cooks hamburgers." The job element would be, "Can cook hamburgers." Each job element is measured using the following four dimensions:

1. Barely acceptable worker.
2. To pick out superior worker.
3. Trouble likely if not considered.
4. Practicality. Demanding this element, we can fill.

The job experts (panel member, incumbent, supervisor) then use a three-point rating scale to measure the four dimensions of job performance for each identified job element. The rating scale includes the following interval scores: 0, a "none" type of rating; 1, a "some" kind of rating; and 2, an "all" or important kind of rating. After doing the rating, an "item index" is computed by multiplying these values.

STRUCTURED AND SCORED JOB ANALYSIS

The term *structured job analysis* has been applied to various kinds of questionnaires, the output of which can be used to describe a job. At times, these inventories are referred to as *worker-oriented inventories* and *job-oriented inventories*. Worker-oriented

---

[7]U.S. Department of Labor, Manpower Administration, *Task Analysis Inventories* (Washington, DC: U.S. Government Printing Office, 1973).
[8]Ernest S. Primoff, "How to Prepare and Conduct Job-Element Examinations" (Washington, DC: U.S. Civil Service Commission, Personnel Research and Development Center, 1975).

inventories describe worker characteristics common to jobs regardless of industry. They describe *how* people do their work, or the behaviors required to perform the job, whereas job-oriented inventories describe *what* is done. These two approaches differ in the methods used to collect and identify job facts, but both are useful in developing profiles of jobs. Some of the specific inventories developed over the last three decades are PAQ, PMPQ, OAI, CODAP, and JAQ.

PAQ

The Position Analysis Questionnaire (PAQ) was developed by three industrial psychologists at Purdue University.[9] (The lead researcher in PAQ, Dr. Ernest J. McCormick, had a federal government background in job analysis going back to the early 1940s, when the federal government methodologies were being developed.) The PAQ is called a worker-oriented task inventory because 187 of the 194 elements that make up the PAQ are considered to be behaviors demonstrated by workers performing a wide variety of jobs. As a result of its design, PAQ does not provide actual job behaviors as they are but rather as they should be. The elements of the PAQ are relatively abstract, and some incumbents may have difficulty in understanding them.

The PAQ consists of 194 elements that are grouped within six major divisions and 28 sections. The six major divisions are (1) information input, (2) mental processes, (3) work output, (4) relationships with other persons, (5) job context, and (6) other job characteristics. Figure 6A–1 lists the divisions within PAQ. The PAQ includes a list of 68 work-relevant human attributes that match against the 187 PAQ elements. These attributes relate to all kinds of work. They are further divided into 41 of an aptitude nature and 27 of an interest or temperament nature.

Employees familiar with a particular job complete the PAQ instrument, rating each of the 194 job elements against certain identified scales. For example, the section *Job Demands* (job elements 169–182) is described by a job element (#169), "specified workplace (on continuous assembly line, etc.)." The respondent would rate this element in terms of how important it is to the total job. The possible responses are: N—Does Not Apply; 1—Very Minor; 2—Low; 3—Average; 4—High; and 5—Extreme.

Over the years, large numbers of respondents in a wide variety of jobs have completed the PAQ instrument. A statistical procedure called factor analysis has been used to analyze and evaluate the scores of each of the 194 job elements and each of the 32 PAQ dimensions. (PAQ also makes use of the statistical tool multiple linear regression for predicting job worth.) The score a job receives on the PAQ dimension provides a job profile. This profile is then compared with standard profiles of known job families (groupings of jobs having comparable responsibility and duty assignments and similar knowledge demands but varying in magnitude of scope, intensity, importance, or skill levels), and the job is assigned to the appropriate family.

---

[9]Ernest J. McCormick, Paul R. Jeanneret, and Robert C. Mecham, "A Study of Job Characteristics and Job Dimensions as Based on the Position Analysis Questionnaire (PAQ)," *Journal of Applied Psychology,* August 1972, pp. 347–368.

1.0 Information Input
    1.1 Sources of Job Information (1–19)
    1.2 Sensory and Perceptual Processes (20–27)
    1.3 Estimation Activities (28–35)
2.0 Mental Processes
    2.1 Decision Making, Reasoning, and Planning/Scheduling (36–38)
    2.2 Information Processing Activities (39–44)
    2.3 Use of Learned Information (45–49)
3.0 Work Output
    3.1 Uses of Devices and Equipment (50–77)
    3.2 Manual Activities (78–84)
    3.3 Activities of the Entire Body (85–86)
    3.4 Level of Physical Exertion (87)
    3.5 Body Positions/Postures (88–92)
    3.6 Manipulation/Coordination Activities (93–98)
4.0 Relationship With Other Persons
    4.1 Communications (99–109)
    4.2 Miscellaneous Interpersonal Relationships (110–111)
    4.3 Amount of Job-Required Personal Contact (112)
    4.4 Types of Job-Required Personal Contacts (113–127)
    4.5 Supervision and Coordination (128–134)
5.0 Job Context
    5.1 Physical Working Conditions (135–143)
    5.2 Physical Hazards (144–147)
    5.3 Personal and Social Aspects (148–153)
6.0 Other Job Characteristics
    6.1 Apparel Worn (154–159)
    6.2 Licensing (160)
    6.3 Work Schedule (161–168)
    6.4 Job Demands (169–182)
    6.5 Responsibility (183–185)
    6.6 Job Structure (186)
    6.7 Criticality of Position (187)
    6.8 Pay/Income (188–194)

FIGURE 6A–1 PAQ Divisions

Six major divisions of PAQ and associated 28 sections. (Numbers following each section are the PAQ job element numbers in that section.)

Ernest J. McCormick, Paul R. Jeanneret, and Robert C. Mecham, *Position Analysis Questionnaire* (West LaFayette, IN: Purdue Research Foundation, 1969).

This ability to group jobs by common characteristics and reflect differences in relative value makes PAQ useful in identifying applicable tests for selecting candidates for jobs and for evaluating job worth.

The basic assumptions made by the designers of the PAQ are as follows:

1. Job requirements are the same for a given kind of work activity.
2. Job elements that are useful for describing job activities may be reliably identified and rated as they exist within the job under study.
3. Human work has an order or structure, and work-ordered job elements make it possible to determine statistically the nature of that structure.

PMPQ

The PAQ researchers at Purdue next developed a Professional and Managerial Position Questionnaire (PMPQ) that is also a structured and scored job analysis questionnaire. It is used in analyzing the jobs of executives, managers, staff personnel, supervisors, scientists, engineers, practicing professional personnel, technicians, teachers, and so on.

Section I of the PMPQ investigates job functions—(1) planning/scheduling, (2) processing of information and ideas, (3) exercising judgment, (4) communicating, (5) interpersonal activities and relationships, and (6) technical activities. Section II requests personal information on (1) personal development and (2) personal qualities, and Section III requests miscellaneous information about the job. The major dimensions used to measure these items are (1) part of the job, (2) complexity, (3) impact, and (4) responsibility. The questionnaire uses primarily a 1 to 9 scale, and a 0 to signify "does not apply."

OAI

The Occupational Analysis Inventory (OAI), developed by J. William Cunningham and his associates, is a variation of the PAQ. It consists of 622 work elements separated into five groups: (1) information received, (2) mental activities, (3) work behaviors, (4) work goals, and (5) work context. The OAI differs from the PAQ in that it contains not only worker-oriented tasks such as information received, mental activities, and work behaviors, but also job-oriented tasks, including output indicators such as work goals. Most of the 622 work elements are rated by the following three scales: (1) significance to the job, (2) extent of occurrence, and (3) applicability. There are special rating dimensions and scales for some elements.[10]

CODAP

For over four decades, the Air Training Command of the United States Air Force has been developing task inventories for Air Force specialties. This program is called the Comprehensive Occupation Data Analysis Programs (CODAP). In these programs, task inventories have been developed for approximately 216 out of the 240 Air Force specialties.[11] (An Air Force specialty is very similar to an occupation.) The 240 specialties cover thousands of different kinds of jobs. CODAP could be considered a job-oriented task inventory. An example of a typical task listed in a CODAP inventory is the computer systems specialty, "Change or align paper in printer." A respondent would first check whether or not this task is currently being performed, then rate the task on the "average time spent" scale that ranges from 1 (very small amount) to 9 (very large amount). This particular inventory lists 577 task statements.

---

[10]J. W. Cunningham, T. C. Tuttle, J. R. Floyd, and J. A. Bates, *Occupational Analysis Inventory* (Raleigh, NC: North Carolina State University, Center for Occupational Education, 1970).
[11]Raymond E. Christal, "The United States Air Force Occupational Research Project, AFHRL-TR7375," Occupational Research Division, Lackland Air Force Base, TX, January 1974.

JAQ

The Job Analysis Questionnaire is a proprietary job-oriented task inventory (different from the generic JAQ as described in this chapter) that provides specific job task, job environment, and job knowledge information. In a project for Northern States Power, Jerry Newman and Frank Krzytofiak identified 598 task items, 30 job environment items, and 130 job knowledge items. Analysis of the responses to the 598 task items yielded 60 underlying factors that were relevant to and useful for developing profiles of job content of 1,700 exempt positions.[12] The JAQ involved a detailed investigation of the technical aspects of the job and, by investigating this dimension, came close to describing the jobs as they existed in the organization under study.

Other Inventory Programs

Many other organizations have been working on inventories. The Vocational-Technical Education Consortium of States (V-TECS), a unit of The Southern Association of Colleges and Schools, has been working for over 25 years to develop task listings that will assist vocational education schools in designing educational programs that provide the knowledge and skills their students will require to successfully perform assignments when they go to work. Over the years, V-TECS has developed more than 125 inventories that they call catalogs. Each catalog consists of one or more job titles listed in the *Dictionary of Occupational Titles.*

Other organizations and associations have generated inventories for data processing jobs, jobs in the clerical-secretarial field, and for police officers and firefighters. The Tennessee Valley Authority (TVA) has developed task inventories for almost all of its jobs. Much of the work in this area has not been widely communicated, but dozens of occupational inventories have already been developed and put to some use. The expanded use of computer-based task inventories will bring more attention to this area in the coming years.

---

[12]Jerry Newman and Frank Krzytofiak, "Quantified Job Analysis: A Tool for Improving Human Resource Management Decision Making," paper presented at the Academy of Management, Orlando, Florida, August 15, 1977.

CHAPTER

Job Description

Learning Objectives

In this chapter you will learn about:

1. The purpose and organizational use of a job description.

2. The major parts of a basic job description.

3. Responsibility and duty statements and how to write them.

4. The usefulness of job descriptions in complying with various pieces of government legislation.

5. The differences among a job description, a position description, and a class description.

6. The usefulness of task inventories in writing job descriptions.

7. Using the computer to develop, write, and update job descriptions within acceptable cost limits.

Compensation Strategy

Design jobs that (1) support a desired organizational structure that in turn ensures organizational effectiveness; (2) are compatible with organizational culture and philosophy; and (3) permit each jobholder to recognize the relationship between job activities and the common purpose of the organization.

Possibly no area of human resources (HR) management has received more adverse publicity than the job description. As mentioned in the earlier discussion on job analysis, many experts and HR managers claim that the job description is an anachronism, a relic of the old industrial engineering world and not only unnecessary but also a barrier to improved worker performance and organizational productivity.

In recent years, a number of organizations have stopped using job descriptions. However, it does appear that there is a renewed interest in them. Because this author is a strong believer in the value of a job description, this chapter goes into detail on what it is and what it will do.

One of the most important outputs of job analysis is the job description. The job description comes in a wide variety of forms, but whatever the form, it attempts to provide what its title states—statements of facts that describe the job. In some organizations, the completed job analysis questionnaire acts as the job description. In most cases, however, job analysis data are reviewed, edited, and then formatted into the job description. A major controversy surrounding job descriptions centers on whether they are accurate and complete and whether they are of any value. In some cases, the job description is a basic component of the organizational communication system; at other times, it is nothing more than a worthless piece of paper. Although there has been considerable argument concerning the value of the job description, many organizations continue to exert much effort and spend much money developing this multipurpose personnel and management tool.

A second major current issue related to job descriptions is whether the description should consist of broad, generic activity statements that cover a number of employees doing different kinds, even different levels of work, or if it should narrowly and precisely describe the work of one jobholder, or, more broadly, if it should describe the work of more than one incumbent where all involved employees do the same or very similar work activities.

Before learning how to write a job description, it is crucial to understand the meanings and differences of the following six words:

Position: Work consisting of responsibilities and duties assignable to one employee (there are as many positions as there are employees; in fact, there can be more positions than employees when there are unfilled positions). Example: Mary Jones, Secretary, Purchasing Department.

Job: Work consisting of responsibilities and duties that are sufficiently alike to justify being covered by a single job analysis/job description. A job may be assignable to one or more employees. Example: Secretary, Purchasing Department.

Class: A group of jobs sufficiently similar as to kinds of subject matter; education and experience requirements; levels of difficulty, complexity, and responsibility; and qualification requirements of the work. Example: Secretary II.

Class-series: A grouping of job classes having similar job content but differing in degree of difficulty, complexity, and responsibility; level of skill; knowledge; and qualification requirements. The jobs within a class-series can form a career ladder. Example: Secretarial Series (I to IV).

Family: Two or more class-series within an organization that have related or common work content. Example: Administration Occupation (Secretarial-Clerical).

Occupation: A grouping of jobs or job classes within a number of different organizations that have similar skill, effort, and responsibility requirements. Example: Administration Occupation (Secretarial-Clerical).

BROAD, GENERIC JOB (CLASS) DESCRIPTIONS VERSUS NARROW, SPECIFIC JOB (POSITION) DESCRIPTIONS

In recent years, a number of major organizations have proudly claimed an advance in their human resources (HR) management practices by eliminating a hundred or more job titles/descriptions and replacing them with 5 or 10 job titles/descriptions. A reason frequently given for this effort is to eliminate the need to define what one or a few employees do by defining the work of relatively large numbers of employees. These broad, generic job descriptions could better be called class descriptions. These descriptions identify all or at least the "major" tasks performed by all or a major group of employees in a work unit or section of the organization. All of the identified tasks are not performed by any one employee.

A major reason for developing such a class/job description is to permit management more flexibility in assigning work to a specific employee or to a group or team of employees. The issue revolves around the "that isn't in my job description" syndrome. This most often occurs in a unionized situation or in a large, highly structured organization, where employees will perform only those activities/tasks identified in their job descriptions.

If a supervisor wishes to reassign or assign some special or temporary activities to a subordinate, the supervisor may often be required to obtain time-consuming special permission to make such assignments or write a revised job description and possibly have the job reclassified (reevaluated) to see if it should be assigned to a different pay grade (receive a different rate of pay). To escape this kind of problem, many organizations include the statement, "Performs other duties as assigned" as the last activity in a job description.

The broad, generic job description does not diminish the need to perform job analysis. It just means that a basic output of a job analysis—the position or job description—that completely and accurately describes what a worker does has not been produced. This, in turn, means that the description of what each employee does takes a more informal rather than a formal route. The replacement of job/position descriptions with job/class descriptions could be a dangerous and foolish HR-management activity.

A JOB CONTRACT

An organization that provides the employee with an accurate and current job description is in reality giving the employee a deed to the job. Like a true deed, the job description acts as a contract—it conveys employee rights to the job, but at the same time it establishes obligations to maintain those rights. The deed/job description works in two ways: It protects the employee by letting him or her know what is expected, and it protects the employer by letting the employee know what must be done. Like a deed, to be a valid and useful contractual instrument, it must be accurate and complete. It must describe the job as it is. A job description differs from a normal contract in that jobs change, and when jobs change, their descriptions must change.

A critical problem facing most organizations is the need to establish an environment in which employees trust management. Possibly, no single effort will enhance employee trust more than granting employees a sense of ownership in their jobs. Job ownership starts with the job description. Recognizing what must be done and coming to an agreement with the immediate supervisor regarding job activities go a long way toward enhancing job security and trust, which in turn promote the commitment and involvement of each employee. Before delving into the design and development of a job description, it is helpful to look at other potential uses.

PLANNING, OPERATIONS, AND CONTROL

The job description is one of the few tools available to managers in performing the three basic functions of management—planning, operations, and control. The job description is basic to operational planning (the planning of day-to-day activities), and it also serves as a direct link to the area of strategic or long-range planning. From an operations point of view, the most important single part of a job description is that which describes the activities and the requirements of the job as it exists today. Although seldom mentioned, the control elements of job descriptions are vital. When used as one of the basic elements for setting performance standards (expected results), the job description becomes a valuable tool of control—an instrument with immense feedback value.

Planning

The job description can be valuable in a number of planning activities. These include (1) organization design, (2) staffing levels, (3) career ladders and career pathing, (4) job design, and (5) pay system design.

Organization Design   The job description supplements other descriptive instruments such as organization charts, work unit function statements, and input-output charts by providing more complete information regarding organizational relationships and outputs. It becomes useful when decisions must be made about centralization or decentralization; or about some form of functional, geographic, or product dispersion; or about reengineering, downsizing, or restructuring.

Staffing Levels   The review of the job definition section (responsibilities and duties) assists in pinpointing potentially unneeded positions (overlapping or redundant activities) and missing activities. Although the job description does not identify workload requirements, a comparison of job description data with workload requirements can be useful for determining staffing levels.

Career Ladders and Career Pathing   The identification of responsibilities and duties requiring a common body of knowledge, skills, and other requirements can be used in establishing classes, class-series, and families of jobs for designing career development programs. By recognizing job-specific knowledge and skills, it is possible to develop career ladder programs and to identify bridging jobs for career pathing opportunities to other career ladders.

Job Design   The development of teams and the rotation of individuals among a number of jobs or workstations makes it essential that there be clear and understood explanations of what must be done at each job or workstation. It also helps in reallocating activities among various employees, ensuring that activities are performed and making jobs more interesting and vital to incumbents.

Pay System Design   The job description is a basic tool in determining or documenting internal job worth decisions. It provides job data for comparison with jobs in other organizations when capturing market data. The combination of internally equitable and externally competitive data then becomes the basic inputs for designing a pay structure.

Operations

The job description is a useful document for individuals who have various responsibilities in the day-to-day operation of the organization. These activities include (1) recruiting and screening, (2) test design, (3) hiring and placement, (4) orientation, (5) developing procedures, and (6) training and development.

Recruiting and Screening   The job description provides individuals responsible for recruiting and screening with a clear picture of the job, its requirements, and the demands it places on an employee. It also provides a preview for the job applicant.

Test Design   Those involved in designing tests that will be used for identifying the most suitable candidates for the job must be certain that they can relate test items to job requirements. Being able to relate knowledge, skill, and ability requirements to job description duties assists in designing tests and significantly enhances their probable validity, legality, and acceptability to job applicants.

Hiring and Placement   Final selection and placement are normally the joint responsibilities of HR specialists and the job candidate's immediate supervisor. When the HR specialist has total responsibility, however, the knowledge, responsibilities and duties, and physical working requirements spelled out in the job description are usually relied on heavily in matching the candidate's qualifications with the job requirements.

Orientation   Possibly the most important predictor of job success is the new employee's first impression of the job. Using the job description as an introduction to the job assists in setting forth its requirements and helps the new jobholder to understand more fully what the organization expects and how the job fits into the overall structure of the organization.

Developing Procedures   For many jobs, it is necessary to develop specific procedures that describe the step-by-step actions an employee must take in performing job assignments. The duties within the job description provide a starting point for the development of procedures.

Training and Development   It is seldom possible for an organization to fill a vacancy without providing some degree of training to new jobholders. Possibly even more important, however, is the fact that as the job and its description change, training and development must keep pace.

Control

Recognition of individual contributions is increasing in importance. Over 70 percent of all workers are employed in service industry jobs, which, like their manufacturing counterparts of a hundred years ago, are now being scrutinized to identify possible ways of measuring performance objectively. Control systems must be implemented to ensure compliance with legal requirements and, when necessary, to meet union demands.

Performance Standards   Almost all employees want to know how well they are doing. To be effective, a performance measurement must be able to identify demonstrated behaviors and compare actual with expected or desired results. Well-written duty statements provide the basis for setting performance standards. These standards inform an employee of the minimal acceptable level of performance and can also identify levels of performance ranging up to excellent or superior.

Legal Requirements   Changes in legislation, as well as changing emphasis in enforcement patterns, have placed new stress on the importance of the job description. The Fair Labor Standards Act requires most organizations to support their determinations of exempt and nonexempt employees. Job descriptions provide primary support for such decisions. The Equal Pay Act requires equal pay for employees performing work in similar occupations requiring equal skill, equal effort, and equal responsibility under similar working conditions. The Americans with Disabilities Act (ADA) requires employers within certain identified limits to make jobs doable for employees who have disabilities. The job description relates jobs to proper occupational groups and identifies the skills, the effort, and the responsibilities needed to perform the job. In addition, it provides useful information on what can and cannot be done in job and workplace design and redesign to permit job performance by a disabled person.

A quality job description provides a sound base for determining the comparable worth of jobs and for establishing employment and performance standards for each job. It helps an organization to eliminate artificial employment barriers and to meet standards required by Title VII of the Civil Rights Act. The job description should identify working conditions that endanger the health of the incumbent. The specification of safety and health considerations is a vital part of a job description and assists in compliance with the Occupational Safety and Health Act.

Collective Bargaining   A key labor principle is "equal pay for equal work." Many union demands focus on the elimination of varied pay rates for similar work or the distortion or imbalance of the pay structure among comparable organizations. The job description provides a starting point for standardization. Although unions want uniform rates, organizations must defend themselves by recognizing and identifying which jobs are similar and protecting those pay levels that truly discriminate among jobs that require different levels of knowledge and responsibilities and among employees who provide different contributions.

ELEMENTS OF THE JOB DESCRIPTION

Although the following discussion focuses on the writing of a job description, the identical activities may be used for writing a position description.

The job description describes the assignments a person is hired to perform. To perform these assignments, the incumbent must have certain knowledge and skills, ranging from pushing a broom to influencing hostile individuals to accept a distasteful concept, to creating a new technology, to inventing a new product. In addition, job assignments are performed under a wide variety of conditions. The unique physical, intellectual, and emotional demands must also be recognized and described as precisely as possible. Although there is no universal form, most job descriptions contain at least five sections: (1) identification; (2) summary; (3) definition; (4) accountabilities; and (5) specifications. In many cases, the identification, summary, and definition sections are placed on one side of the page (see Figure 7–1) and the accountabilities and specifications on the opposite side (see Figure 7–2). When a job specification section is not included in the job description, or when the specification section does not adequately describe the minimum education and experience qualifications required by the job, there must be an employment standards section (which normally follows the accountabilities section). (Compensable factors, as described through the substantiating data in the sample job specification—see Figure 7–2—are discussed in detail in chapter 8.)

All job descriptions in an organization should follow the same format, and those responsible for writing them should receive similar instructions and follow identical guidelines so that the job descriptions provide a balanced and fair picture of the jobs of the organization.

Job Identification

The identification section of the job description takes the following form:

Job Title	Status Job Code
Date	Plant/Division
Written by	Department/Section
Approved by	Grade Points
Title of Immediate Supervisor	Pay Range

Job Title   The most critical part of the identification process is specifying a title for the job. A title that correctly and precisely identifies the job is of value (1) for the jobholder's information and self-esteem, (2) for purposes of job relationships, and (3) for comparison with similar jobs in other organizations.

The title indicates to anyone reviewing the description, and specifically to the jobholder, the particular field of activity of the job, its relationship to that field, and its

Lead Programmer-Analyst
Job Title

April 10, 1999
Date

Arthur Allen
Written by

Juanita Montgomery
Approved by

Programming and Analysis Supervisor
Title of Immediate Supervisor

Exempt
Status

007.167
Job code

Olympia, Inc.—Main Office
Plant/Division

Data Processing—Information Systems
Department/Section

17   1960
Grade   Points

36,099–54,148
Pay Range

Summary

Under direction. Performs studies, develops, and maintains program concerned with employee benefits, focusing specifically on life, medical and hospitalization, accident and disability, and retirement insurance for all divisions of Olympia.

Responsibilities and Duties

1.0 Serves as a lead member of the employee benefits team of programmers.
    1.1 Updates, modifies, and designs new applications in such areas as enrollment, premium costs, premium collections.
    1.2 Maintains existing programs constituting employee health and retirement benefits program for employees of Olympia.
    1.3 Develops reports on the status of existing program for which responsible.
2.0 Recommends needed redesign studies.
    2.1 Reviews proposed changes in legislation.
    2.2 Consults with user representatives on proposed changes in existing benefits programs, constraints, and potentially relevant developments.
    2.3 Discusses with other programmers and software specialists use of most suitable application programming technology.
    2.4 Identifies impact of program changes on existing computer programs.
    2.5 Advises supervisor of changes to be made in applicable software.
3.0 Carries out study projects.
    3.1 Investigates feasibility of alternate design approaches with a view to determining best solution within constraints set by available resources and future demands.
    3.2 Explores desirability of various possible outputs, considering both EDP and non-EDP costs, benefits, and trade-offs.
    3.3 Identifies types and designation of inputs needed, system interrelationships, processing logic involved.
    3.4 Develops programming specifications.
    3.5 Informs supervisor of progress, unusual problems, and resources required.
4.0 Designs internal program structure of files and records.
    4.1 Determines detailed sequences of actions in program logic, reviewing operations.
    4.2 Codes, tests, debugs, and documents programs.
    4.3 Writes and maintains computer operator instructions for assigned programs.
    4.4 Monitors existing programs to ensure operation as required.
    4.5 Responds to problems by diagnosing and correcting errors of logic and coding.
5.0 Coordinates efforts of other DP professionals.
    5.1 Assigns and schedules work as required.
    5.2 Reviews the work of other DP professionals.
    5.3 Interprets user requirements for other DP professionals.
    5.4 Assists other DP professionals to obtain full user cooperation.

All identified duties are essential.

FIGURE 7–1 Sample Job Description

Accountabilities

1. Completion of projects on assigned schedule.
2. Development of programs that best use resources of organization.
3. Prompt recognition of program defects or shortcomings.

Specifications

Factor	Substantiating Data	Level	Points
Knowledge Required	Knowledge of operation and capabilities of computers of Olympia. Detailed knowledge of processes and rules governing programming to carry out assignments. Knowledge of relevant employer and employee benefits program of Olympia.	6	950
Supervisory Controls	Assigned responsibility for development and operation of several programs. Consults with supervisor on target dates, unanticipated problems and conflicts that arise with other work units of Olympia. Projects reviewed in terms of effectiveness in meeting requirements.	3	275
Guidelines	Published subject matter procedures, programming standards; modification of existing documentation frequently required. Judgment required in gathering information and developing programs that meet system and client demands.	3	275
Complexity	Wide variety of programs requiring changes to meet exceptions and new technology, changes in benefit designs; must anticipate future changes.	4	225
Scope and Effect	Formulate project recommendations; analyze technical problems; establish specifications.	3	150
Personal Contacts	Representatives of users in other work units, other programmers, and computer operations personnel.	2	25
Purpose of Contacts	Determine program and system requirements; monitor production to correct errors; answer questions; relay instructions; assist other programmers in solving their problems.	2	50
Physical Demands	Work is sedentary. Some travel to office of clients.	1	5
Work Environment	Work is performed in typical office setting.	1	5
	Total points		1,960

FIGURE 7–2 Accountabilities and Specifications Sections of a Job Description

The factors, levels, and points in this example come from the Factor Evaluation System (FES), which is discussed in detail in chapter 9.

professional standing. However, caution should be used in selecting a title that tends to *inflate* job importance or value. This could lead to higher expectations of pay among incumbents, inappropriate (higher) job matches when performing market surveys, and even assist managers in developing dysfunctional empires.

The title should lend some prestige to the job and should contribute to the personal satisfaction of the jobholder. Every effort must be made to establish a legitimate and realistic title that provides the maximum possible amount of dignity and status to the incumbent. The title should not allude to gender or age requirements. The title is the first step in defining the job and establishing a ranking order with other jobs. It is valuable as an outline to department, division, or functional groupings, a guide for promotions or transfers, and an indicator of training and development requirements.

The job title is especially important when one is attempting to compare the job with similar jobs in other organizations, a process critical in developing pay surveys and in recruiting employees. For this reason, every effort should be made to use titles commonly found in the marketplace. It is possible to use a double title with the generic (common) title first, followed by the organizational identifier, such as Executive Secretary–Finance; Senior Clerk–Accounting.

Like the job description, job titles must be kept current. Jobs with similar duties and similar requirements should have the same title. The *Dictionary of Occupational Titles* (DOT) is extremely valuable for this purpose.[1]

Job Status   The job status section of a job description permits quick and easy identification of the exempt or nonexempt status of the job relative to its compliance with the Fair Labor Standards Act.

Job Code   The job code permits easy and rapid referencing of all jobs. It may consist of letters or numbers in any combination. Each code must have sufficient characters to identify all the jobs in the organization. The code can be a four-character alphanumeric code (B 735) or even a six-digit numeric code (007.167), as used by the U.S. Department of Labor, Employment and Training Administration in the DOT.[2] Any other suitable combination of numbers or letters will serve, but brevity is vital.

The DOT is a valuable guide for developing job descriptions. It not only provides job titles and an excellent method for coding jobs, but it describes work performed, worker requirements, clues for relating applicants and requirements, and training and methods of entry for specific types of work. The two volumes of the DOT provide a fundamental guide for job comparison purposes.

---

[1]U.S. Department of Labor, Employment & Training Administration, *Dictionary of Occupational Titles*, 4th ed. (Washington, DC: Government Printing Office, 1977).

[2]The *Dictionary of Occupational Titles* actually supplies a nine-digit code, but the final three-digit suffix is seldom used. The complete DOT code takes this appearance: 007.167.018. The 018 suffix identifies additional specialty job titles when the DOT provides only one principal title and job description. In the case of Computer Programmer, for example, if programming activities were specialized by types of data such as machine programming data, business data, scientific research data, and so on, the suffix code could be used to identify computer programming.

A brief review of the manner in which the DOT uses its six-character code will aid any organization that develops its own code or that uses the DOT code. An example follows:

007.167

007	—The first three digits signify occupational group arrangement.
0	—Professional, technical, and managerial occupations.
00	—Occupations in architecture and engineering.
007	—Mechanical engineering.
.167	—The second three digits represent worker trait arrangement: respectively, data, people, and things; .167 specifically relates to engineering, scientific, and technical operations.
.1	—Coordinating data.
.16	—Speaking-signaling to people.
.167	—Handling things. (The final three digits relate to worker functions. The section on the DOL methodology in the appendix to chapter 6 describes in detail these worker functions and what these numbers relate to.)

Date   The date on the job description refers to the date that it was actually written. (Next to the title, the date is the most important job identification detail. It is frequently critical to know when the description was written.)

Written by   This is the person who writes the job description.

Approved by   This space is for the signature and the title of the person who approves the job description.

Plant/Division and Department/Section   This space provides for the precise location of the job.

Grade   This space is for the grade of the job if there is such a category.

Points   If a point job evaluation system is used, this space provides for the number of points assigned a job.

Title of Immediate Supervisor   This space is self-explanatory.

Pay Range   This space provides for the specific pay or pay range of a job. Many organizations do not use the plant/division and department/section, grade/level, points, and pay range elements because they consider them unnecessary or because rapid changes or variations would require frequent revisions of the job description. It must be remembered that the benefits gained from a current, valid job description are worth the updating costs. In the near future many organizations will have their job descriptions on word processors. Changes can then be made quickly and easily and a hard copy produced automatically.

Like most planning tools, job descriptions require constant review and reevaluation, which is a costly process. In a world of rapid change, updating is a necessity; but there never seems to be enough time to do it. Furthermore, an obsolete job description may not only be worthless, it may be harmful because it describes a job inaccurately.

Job Summary

The job summary is normally a word picture of the job that delineates its general characteristics, listing only major functions or activities (Figure 7–1). Through precise ordering and careful selection of words, it indicates clearly and specifically what the jobholder must do. This section of the job description provides enough information to identify and differentiate the major functions and activities of the job from those of others. It is especially valuable to the individual who wants a quick overview of the job. The summary is often used in job matching when participating in a pay survey.

An invaluable aid in writing job summaries is the DOT, which contains general descriptions of over 20,000 jobs. The statements used to describe a job in the DOT are sufficiently universal to be transferable. In writing a job summary, however, the analyst must be sure that the phrases selected from the DOT match the responsibilities and duties of the job being described.

Although job summaries often include code words for describing various aspects of the job ("under close supervision," "general supervision," "considerable," "unusual"), care should be taken in the use of these words. As organizations grow and more and different employees take on the responsibility of collecting and analyzing job data and writing job descriptions, it becomes difficult to achieve total understanding of the meaning of such code words, especially among employees who have some of their job activities defined by these words. Additionally, these words may give supervisors and even incumbents an opportunity to try to gain unwarranted higher ratings of jobs under review. Using behavioral examples to anchor or further describe code words minimizes misinterpretation.

When such words are used, however, they should be defined as precisely as possible and their definitions made available to all employees. The following code words for Kind and Frequency of Direction Received in the Performance of a Job are often found in the summary section of a job description. In fact, these terms are often the first words used in the summary section.

Under Immediate Direction: Within this job, the incumbent normally performs the duty assignment after receiving detailed instructions as to methods, procedures, and desired end results. These detailed instructions normally allow little room for deviation. The immediate supervisor may, at times, provide close and constant review while work is under way and when the assignment is completed.

Under General Direction: Within this job, the incumbent normally performs the duty assignment after receiving general instructions as to methods, procedures, and desired end results. The incumbent has some opportunity for discretion when making selections among a few, easily identifiable choices. The assignment is usually reviewed upon completion.

Under Direction: Within this job, the incumbent normally performs the duty assignment according to his or her own judgment, requesting supervisory assistance only when necessary. The assignment is frequently reviewed upon completion.

Under Administrative Direction: Within this job, the incumbent normally performs the duty assignment within broad parameters defined by general organizational requirements and accepted practices. Total end results determine effectiveness of job performance.

Under Guidelines Set by Policy: Within this job, the incumbent normally performs the duty assignment at his or her discretion and is limited only by policies set by administrative or legislative authority. Total end results determine effectiveness of job performance.

The Job Definition—Responsibilities and Duties

Responsibilities identify the primary reasons for the existence of the job. These are the major or broad categories of work activities that, in total, define the scope of the work assignments. A responsibility is of sufficient importance that *not* carrying out the duties within it or performing them below a minimally established standard will critically affect the required results and demand remedial actions by management. Unacceptable performance of a responsibility may result in one or more of the following:

1. Removal from current job that could include lateral transfer, demotion, or even termination
2. Prohibition of receipt of performance-based rewards
3. Provision of training and other developmental services

With the establishment of responsibilities, the job becomes subdivided into specific categories or component parts, as illustrated in Figure 7–3. In this example, the job has four responsibilities. It is at this stage of the process that the art and skill required for writing quickly become apparent. As the job summary becomes further enlarged through the responsibility statements, the problem of detail and specificity arises. Responsibility statements may have far more detail than a job summary paragraph, but the question is what amount of detail. The scope and specificity of the responsibility statement will vary according to the scope and complexity of the job.

After developing a list of responsibility statements, the job description writer must then review the total package and answer these questions:

1. Do these statements adequately describe the purpose of the job?
2. Are any responsibilities missing?
3. Can any responsibilities be omitted?
4. Can two or more responsibilities be combined and made into a more useful statement?
5. Is it possible to clarify or improve the statements?

After the responsibility statements are completed, each statement should be analyzed separately, and a list of duties should be developed for each responsibility. The classification process is continuous, from the broad and relatively vague to the narrow and precise. Duties further describe a responsibility. The job pie and its major slices of responsibilities are further divided into duties (Figure 7–4).

FIGURE 7–3
Responsibilities of a Job

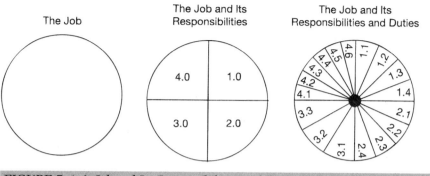

FIGURE 7–4 A Job and Its Responsibilities and Duties

The duties explain in more detail what actually occurs in the performance of a responsibility. Typically, duties describe not only *what* is done, but *why* and *how* it is done and, thus, provide more individuality and uniqueness to the job description. They establish the foundation for performance standards and, when necessary, the procedures to be followed in performing them. Each responsibility and its assigned duties become a module of work, or a responsibility module.

Now a question arises. Is there a specific limit to the number of responsibility and duty statements? The answer is *yes*. Over the years, researchers in a wide variety of disciplines have recognized some common constraints to human activity that probably have their foundation in the design of the human brain. In this case, the research relates to the magic number 7. Whether it is 7 ± 2, or 7 ± 4, depending on scope and complexity, most jobs will require from three to seven—possibly (though infrequently) as many as nine to eleven—responsibility modules to describe them completely.

Job Analysis–Provided Job Content Data   The information used in writing responsibility and duty statements normally comes from the job analysis process (see chapter 6). In making the transition from job analysis–provided data to responsibility and duty statements, the analyst/description writer must develop a broad understanding of reasons for the job's existence and the demands and the requirements placed on the jobholder. Many kinds of job analysis questionnaires simply require that the respondent list all tasks performed on the job. When these kinds of job content data are used to write responsibility and duty statements, the analyst must review the task statements and (1) select from three to seven statements that describe the major activities of the job, or (2) write relatively broad activity statements that can be used as umbrella statements that describe major functional areas of work requirements. Knowledge and skill requirements are usually quite valuable in identifying a major activity area. Normally, different functional areas will require different kinds or levels of knowledge and skills and may also be performed in different locations. The time of performance may also aid in establishing major job activities. A review of the task statements may identify certain tasks that can be used as major job activity statements. Sometimes, the combination of two or more tasks may be required to identify a major activity; at other times, a responsibility statement must be synthesized to act as an umbrella statement for a number of directly related task statements.

After the responsibility statements are developed, the analyst returns to the task statements in the job analysis and selects those that further describe or amplify the responsibility statement. The responsibility and duty statement list is complete when the analyst can review the task list developed in the job analysis and identify the presence of each task within the responsibility and duty statements. Not every task statement has to be used, however. Quite often, one task statement can be used to represent a number of tasks identified by the jobholder, or one statement can be synthesized to represent a number of task statements. For example, a clerk-typist in a finance department may have identified job tasks as "(1) records expenses incurred by the marketing department; (2) records expenses incurred by the research and development department; (3) records expenses incurred by the warehouse department; (4) records expenses incurred by the manufacturing department." One statement, such as "Records expenses as incurred by all departments," may be sufficient.

If major activity and related task statements have had to be prepared for the initial job analysis, then the writing of job descriptions becomes a much simpler assignment. Now the analyst is mainly involved in review and editing efforts, as major activity and task statements (as defined in the job analysis) are translated into responsibility and duty statements for job description purposes. Thus, the analyst is relieved of creating umbrella statements and of assigning the correct tasks to each statement.

Ranking Responsibility and Duty Statements   After identifying the responsibilities and the duties of a job, the next step is to place them in some kind of order so that the reader can obtain a clear and concise picture of the content of the job. Two possible ways of structuring responsibility and duty statements are (1) to list and sequence by occurrence, and (2) to list by order of importance relative to overall successful performance of the job.

For jobs that have a routine order of occurrence of work activities, the best way to structure the responsibility and duty statements is to list the responsibility that normally occurs first, then to follow it with the second responsibility, and so forth, with the final responsibility possibly occurring only at a random or irregular interval. The same procedure can be used for listing the duties within each responsibility.

Jobs in which the activities do not occur in any natural order but which must meet specific demands as they arise may follow the "importance" approach for structuring.

Task measurement dimensions and scales have been developed that are useful for making inferences concerning the relative importance of job tasks. The information available from such scaling and measurement procedures can be used to identify the most important to the least important responsibility and also the relative importance of the duties that further describe each responsibility. Using the same approach as described in ordering responsibilities, duties can be listed by importance. When reviewing the responsibilities and duties of a job description written in this manner, the reader immediately recognizes the key or crucial activities.

A major point emphasized in this chapter is that the closer the written description of an employee's job reflects what the employee actually does, the better off are both employee and organization. Standardized, ready-made job descriptions are of little value, other than for providing insights into the typical or common activities performed by incumbents in jobs or classes of jobs.

If the work of an employee is in some manner unique, then the uniquely different aspects of the work must be identified. The activity analysis and description process described so far in this chapter are not by any means unusual. One point that may differ from or add to the normal practice, however, is the listing of responsibilities and their applicable duties by order of importance within the definition section. This procedure not only provides an opportunity for employee involvement, but it also centers on the unique qualities or features of each job.

Ranking responsibilities and duties by importance must involve incumbents and others who are familiar with the work being performed. The involvement of these individuals permits those most knowledgeable about job content requirements to have a voice in the final product, which is a listing and ordering of the responsibility and duty statements.

A current and complete job definition that includes rank-ordered responsibility and duty statements becomes a key supervisor-incumbent communication tool. It assists in ensuring that:

1. The incumbent knows what he or she is supposed to be doing.
2. The incumbent is able to set priorities recognizing the relative importance of each activity.
3. The supervisor feels confident that the incumbent understands what has to be done and why it has to be done.
4. The incumbent recognizes how his or her contribution leads to the success of the work unit.
5. The incumbent recognizes the limits within which he or she can perform (must do this; can't do that).

This kind of interaction and agreement will minimize, if not eliminate, such unacceptable statements as, "I didn't know I was supposed to do that," or "Why didn't you tell me you were doing this?" or "You never told me this was more important than *that*," or "Why didn't you do that?"

Incumbent involvement in establishing a rank-ordered job definition may begin with the following approach. A draft of the ordered and edited responsibility and duty statements is returned to each incumbent. The following cover letter is sent with the draft of the job definition:

Through your past efforts in providing activity information, we have been able to develop this set of job responsibilities and duties. The responsibilities are the major activities you perform on your job. They are listed as 1.0, 2.0, etc. The duties are the subresponsibilities or activities that amplify or further describe the activities you perform in completing an assigned responsibility. They are identified by the numbers .1, .2, .3, etc.

Please review this list of responsibilities and duties. Are there any activities you perform that have not been included in this list that you believe should be included? Please list these missing activities in their most appropriate location. Next, review the list for any activities that are not performed by you or that are so inconsequential that they should not be listed. Strike through these unnecessary activity statements. Now, review the responsibility statements and place a *1.0* by the statement you think is most critical for overall successful job performance. Then, place a *2.0* by the second most important responsibility statement and complete this numbering process for all the responsibility statements in your job. The same process must be followed in ordering the duty statements within each responsibility. This input enables you to inform us as to how you view the relative importance of the things you do.

Review this list of activities with care. They not only assist management in determining the overall worth of your job to the organization, but they also provide the basis for establishing the standards of performance you will be expected to meet.

At this early stage of the pay-setting process, employee participation is sought and used. The incumbent not only provides activity information but also has a voice in the various stages of the review to ensure that the transformation from an unstructured list of activities results in an accurate and understandable description and ordering of responsibility and duty statements.

Activity-Worth Dimensions and Rating Scales   In addition to the pragmatic, empirical knowledge of the incumbent and supervisor in rank-ordering responsibilities and duties, it is also possible to use activity-worth dimensions and ratings scales. Here, the computer and database management come into focus. Using activity-worth dimensions can be done rapidly and at minimal cost when incumbents, also supervisors and subject matter experts (SMEs), have the opportunity to interact directly in the rating process through the use of a terminal. The ratings resulting from the use of the activity-worth dimensions can be used in conjunction with the pragmatic approach for the final ordering of responsibilities and duties.

The following activity-worth dimensions may be used for this purpose; frequency, duration, criticality/consequence of error, extent necessary upon entry to the job, relationship to overall successful job performance, importance, complexity, and difficulty. An additional dimension that must now be considered is "essential" as in essential job function as stated within the ADA.

Like other parts of the description process, the measurement of job activities appears to be simple but in fact is not. The measurement of an activity by each scale is open to individual bias. What may be difficult for one individual may not be so for another. This also holds true for *complexity. Importance* may relate more to a specific situation than to a general statement that is overall job related. *Criticality* is certainly environmentally related. Everything done in performing a job is important or critical. It is not easy to differentiate among activities as to whether *a* is more important or complex than *b*.

The issues related to ADA strongly influence the need to confront and adequately define such dimensions as complexity, importance, criticality, and, now, what is essential.

In order to be protected under ADA, a disabled individual must be able to perform the essential functions of the job, with or without reasonable accommodation. Although the ADA does not define essential job functions, it does permit, if not require, the employer to determine what functions are necessary to the performance of the job.

The issues related to ADA and essential job functions are somewhat similar to earlier civil rights legislation. In the 1960s, federal legislation and court rulings included the term *job related*. To this day, a precise definition of *job relatedness* does not exist. A major contribution to the dilemma concerning the meaning of *job related* is the lack of precise definition of such terms as *job activity, task, duty, responsibility, function,* and even *job behavior.* Lack of uniformity or understanding related to these words and terms is compounded by the addition to the words and terms of adjectives such as *major* and *minor* or *critical* and *noncritical.* With ADA, attention now focuses on the term *essential job function(s).* What is meant by (1) a *job function* and (2) an *essential job function*? Court rulings and possibly future legislation will shed light on this issue. However, to ensure compliance with ADA, compensation professionals now must develop their own definition, using currently available and credible definitions as their foundation, and build job descriptions that recognize essential job functions.

The job analysis–job description process frequently requires incumbents, immediate supervisors, even SMEs to identify critical job activities. Using some measurement code, these individuals must rate "how critical" the activity is to overall successful job performance. The addition of *essential* to the rating dimensions may, at first glance, appear to be semantically similar, if not identical, to *critical.* However, recognizing the ADA brief description of essential job function, an important difference does appear. Even though a job activity (function) may be critical, it is possible that the jobholder can receive support in performing the activity and, at times, possibly transfer the activity to another employee.

When the employee must perform the specific job activity (function) unaided or with the assistance of a reasonable accommodation, the designation *essential* should be affixed. Therefore, the determination of criticality should be addressed separately but in association with the determination of essential. It could, therefore, be concluded that some job functions may be critical without being essential, but that usually all essential job functions are critical.

An underlying concept here is that all jobs are important or they should not exist. Conversely, all job activities are critical or they should be eliminated. Information commonly requested is the percentage of *time* spent on an activity. This again appears to be a rational, simple request. However, many activities require various amounts of time to complete under different situations. Many conditions external to the control of the incumbent determine how much time a specific activity requires of an employee. In addition, an activity requiring, on the average, far less time than another may be much more critical to overall successful performance.

This brief list of the negative aspects of activity measurement does not mean that ordering or measurement is unnecessary. It simply means that measurement is a difficult and complex chore. Here again, the analyst's artistry comes into play. It may be that the ordering of activities requires the use of all activity measurement dimensions and that ratings should be completed by all individuals who perform or are intimately knowledgeable about the job—normally the incumbent and his or her immediate supervisor.

After the activity-worth dimensions are identified, scales must be designed. The basic design features of a scale are the number of intervals to be used and the description provided for each interval that assists raters in making the most accurate inferences about responsibility and duty statements and the level of the specific dimension under review. The number of intervals within a scale used to measure each dimension may vary according to individual choice and values. The greater the number of intervals, the larger the possible variation in final rating scores. The fewer the intervals, the greater the likelihood of a smaller dispersion of scores. The other side of this coin focuses on how precisely differences can be noted with any accuracy by a rater. There may be some who argue that only a three-interval scale can be used with any reliability, whereas others may opt for a scale with nine or even 99 intervals. The following examples of activity-worth dimensions and rating scales use different numbers of intervals and descriptions for each interval.

A *stanine* ("standard nine") or nine-interval rating scale for frequency and duration could take the following form:

1. *Frequency:* How often is this activity typically performed on the job?
   1 = At least once a year.
   2 = At least once each six months.
   3 = At least once each quarter.
   4 = At least once each two months.
   5 = At least once a month.
   6 = At least once each two weeks.
   7 = At least once a week.
   8 = At least twice a week.
   9 = Daily.

2. *Duration:* Time spent in performing the activity.
   1 = Less than 30 minutes.
   2 = 31 minutes to 1 hour.
   3 = Over 1 hour to 2 hours.
   4 = Over 2 hours to 4 hours
   5 = Over 4 hours to 8 hours.
   6 = Over 8 hours to 16 hours.
   7 = Over 16 hours to 32 hours.
   8 = Over 32 hours to 40 hours.
   9 = More than 40 hours.

In the Comprehensive Occupation Data Analysis Programs (CODAP) of the U.S. Air Force (described in the appendix to chapter 6), the primary dimension used to measure tasks is Time Spent on Present Job. Incumbents completing a CODAP job inventory respond to the following nine-interval scale for each task they perform:

1. Very small amount
2. Much below average
3. Below average
4. Slightly below average
5. About average
6. Slightly above average
7. Above average
8. Much above average
9. Very large amount

Incumbent responses to this scale are transformed into percentage of time spent on each task through the use of a *normalizing process* (see chapter 8). Over the years, job analysts have asked incumbents to provide percentage of time spent on each task (duty). This percentage of time statistic is then used as a proxy for importance.

Using the activity-worth dimensions and rating scales or the results negotiated between supervisor and incumbents, the analyst lists the responsibility and duty statements in sequential order of importance. The first responsibility listed is the most important; the second listed, the second most important; and so on. The duties listed under a specific responsibility also follow an ordering by importance or worth. The actual value assigned to a responsibility or duty through the use of activity-worth dimensions and rating scales provides a quantitative basis for determining the relative order of the responsibility and duty statements.

Describing Jobs of Different Levels of Complexity   The level of complexity of responsibility and duty statements varies with the level of the job in the organization. The responsibility and duty statements for an office messenger, a janitor, or a data entry operator will be formulated in very precise terms. On the other hand, responsibilities and duties of jobs higher in the organizational hierarchy will be defined in more general terms. Because of the change in the level of the responsibility and duty statements, the same approximate number of statements can be used to describe the job of the president or the job of an entry-level file clerk. Figure 7–5 is an example of a job definition for a top executive of an organization. Figure 7–6 is a job definition for a first-line manager. A review of the two job definitions reveals that:

1. The higher the level of the job, the more complex the job requirements and associated incumbent activities.
2. The more complex the requirements and activities, the more difficult it is to describe them in clear, unambiguous terms.
3. The more complex the activities, the more difficult it is to identify relevant activities that are observable and measurable in quantitative terms, although qualitative measurements are certainly possible and applicable.

FIGURE 7–5 Responsibilities and Duties of the Job of an Executive

1.0 Commits unit to new courses of action.
   1.1 Allocates resources to individuals and projects having the greatest impact on the achievement of organizational goals.
   1.2 Directs activities of unit to adapt to changing environmental conditions.
   1.3 Recognizes disturbance issues, redirecting efforts to minimize resulting ill-effects.
   1.4 Negotiates issues having a negative impact on organizational performance.
2.0 Monitors, collects, and transmits information for work unit.
   2.1 Scans environment, interrogates liaison contacts, and receives unsolicited information.
   2.2 Disseminates privileged information among subordinates.
   2.3 Passes information between subordinates not having readily accessible communication channels.
   2.4 Sends information to people outside the organization for subordinates.
3.0 Maintains interpersonal relationships with individuals both external and internal to the organization.
   3.1 Directs efforts of immediate subordinate/own staff personnel.
   3.2 Encourages all employees to coordinate efforts in order to meet group, unit, and organizational goals.
   3.3 Acts as a liaison with individuals outside the vertical chain of command.
   3.4 Performs assignments of a ceremonial nature.

Paraphrased from Henry Mintzberg, "The Manager's Job: Folklore and Fact," *Harvard Business Review,* July–August 1975, pp. 49–61.

1.0 Plans and schedules work assignments.
    1.1 Establishes and reviews group and individual goals.
    1.2 Sets workplace methods and procedures.
    1.3 Schedules daily work assignments.
    1.4 Coordinates work activities with related work group.
    1.5 Ensures that subordinates have necessary equipment and material.
    1.6 Establishes and maintains records and reporting systems.
2.0 Monitors performance to ensure acceptable levels and quality of output.
    2.1 Observes employee performance at work site.
    2.2 Compares individual performance to group norms.
    2.3 Compares actual performance with present performance standards.
    2.4 Conducts specified number of quality inspections.
    2.5 Investigates accident and damage claims.
    2.6 Resolves grievances and informal problems.
3.0 Develops employees to maximize performance potential.
    3.1 Reviews records to identify low performers.
    3.2 Instructs employees on preferred procedures.
    3.3 Schedules formal training programs.
    3.4 Detects through observation unsafe work practices.
    3.5 Inspects equipment for safe working conditions.
    3.6 Appraises employee performance.
    3.7 Provides training to correct knowledge- and skill-related deficiencies.
4.0 Schedules employees to ensure work coverage within guidelines prescribed by government legislation, corporate policy, and union contract.
    4.1 Assigns hourly tours to provide appropriate job coverage.
    4.2 Develops weekly work schedule to ensure 8 hours per day and 40 hours per week workload.
    4.3 Establishes holiday and vacation schedules.
    4.4 Rotates work to allow for equal distribution of various types of work assignments.

FIGURE 7–6 Responsibilities and Duties of the Job of a First-Line Manager

4. The higher the level of the job, the greater the likelihood that the way identified job activities are performed will vary significantly among incumbents.
5. As jobs increase in importance, the cognitive and affective domains become more important, and the psychomotor domains become less important. (Cognitive domain refers to intellectual pursuits characterized by thinking, reasoning, and understanding skills; affective domain refers to feelings and emotional pursuits characterized by interests, attitudes, openness to change, and appreciation of differences; and psychomotor domain refers to physical pursuits characterized by motor skills involving synchronized and coordinated movement of hands, arms, legs, torso, head, and eyes.)

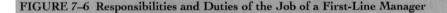

The complexity issue also affects the development of skill-based pay, knowledge-based pay, and competency-based pay as being promoted for establishing pay systems within team-based organizations. This discussion of complexity has a direct relationship to discussions of team-based pay in chapter 12.

Other Definition Issues   As mentioned earlier, some organizations conclude the list of responsibility and duty statements with the sentence, "Performs other duties as assigned." This builds in an area of flexibility. This sentence is, however, a potential area for entrapment. It is specifically included to give supervisors flexibility in detailing work assignments. This statement should *not* be on any individual's job description.

The basic reason for this statement is so critical to organizational success that it should be included within organizational policy, and each new employee should be told upon hiring that a supervisor has the right to make any assignment to any employee as long as the assignment is within the employee's knowledge and skill base, permits performance in an adequate manner, will not cause the employee any physical or emotional harm, and is not illegal. Also, employees should be told that when they are assigned new or temporary tasks and these tasks continue for a prescribed period (e.g., 30 days), they should notify appropriate individuals to have these tasks placed on their job descriptions. It is imperative that each supervisor has the right to make assignments to any subordinate employee to "get the job done." At the same time, each employee has the right to be protected from abusive, discriminatory treatment by a supervisor when the supervisor treats a particular employee unfairly by assigning that individual additional difficult, demeaning, hazardous, or dirty tasks and does not assign those kinds of tasks to other individuals. A major theme of a job description is to provide a base for understood and accepted fair treatment.

It is unnecessary to start an activity statement with the words *responsible for.* The activity statements in a job description are responsibility statements and the term *responsible for* is superfluous. Although the format of activity statements may take either an outline or paragraph form, this text promotes the use of an outline. The outline form requires that each statement stand on its own merit and facilitates a reader's quick review. The paragraph form too often permits a statement to hide behind a series of commas, semicolons, or periods in the paragraph and remain unrecognized.

Accountabilities

The accountabilities section of a job description briefly describes the major results achieved in the satisfactory performance of the job responsibilities and duties. It acts as a guide for the goal-setting process that integrates job requirements with jobholder contributions.

Job Specifications

The section on job specifications provides information to determine the worth of a job. This section identifies the knowledge and skill demands made on the incumbent and the physical and emotional conditions under which the incumbent must work. The design of the job specification section and the information it provides relate to the kind of job evaluation plan used by the organization. Normally, job specifications are part of the job descriptions when an organization uses a compensable factor-based job evaluation plan (see chapter 8). In this case, the job specification provides substantiating data that assist in identifying the level or degree of the compensable factor as it relates to the job being described. The sample job specification section described in Figure 7–2 relates to the compensable factors used in the Factor Evaluation System (FES) (see chapters 8 and 9).

When writing managerial job descriptions, the specification section may include such items as:

1. Number of employees directly supervised.
2. Number of employees within area of accountability (indirectly supervised).
3. Annual dollar amount of payroll of employees within area of accountability.
4. Size of budget of area of accountability.
5. Whether job/position is at the "officer" level.

Employment Standards

When a job description does not include a specification section, or if the specification section does not adequately identify *employment standards* or *job qualifications,* then an *employment standards* section should follow the accountabilities section. Employment standards relate to (1) levels of education, which may include actual description of language and mathematical skills required and reasoning skills needed to comply with the job performance (see Vol. 2 of DOL *Dictionary of Occupational Titles* [DOT] for detailed description of Reasoning, Language, and Mathematical requirements by occupation); (2) levels of experience, which may be further divided into general and specialized categories; (3) abilities and skills; (4) physical standards, which may include actual lifting or pressure exerted (by pounds) in the performance of the job; and (5) certification or licensure requirements. Even when a specification section is part of a job description, it may be worthwhile to include an employment standards section to spell out minimum qualification requirements for the job for selection procedures. Volume 2 of the DOT also lists human attributes required in the performance of different kinds of jobs. In turn, these attributes can be related to specific responsibility modules or even job duties.

Writing a brief but accurate job description that is useful for a variety of management functions is an art. Success in writing it depends primarily on the availability of sufficient data. The various tools and techniques of a properly performed job analysis can provide such data. Success also depends on the knowledge of the writer. A combination of the job analysis data and the writer's own knowledge can produce a job description that becomes a valuable information tool.

Many of the guides and the outlines presented in this chapter can help writers of job descriptions to develop their own procedures and skills. The approaches given here need not be considered inflexible. They are meant to be an outline from which each individual can develop the procedures that best satisfy the requirements of a particular organization, assignment, or individual aptitude.

OTHER KINDS OF INFORMATION USED IN DESCRIBING JOBS

Although it does not often appear, a section entitled Conditions of Employment may be added to a job description.

Conditions of Employment

Specific information can be requested by using each responsibility as a center of focus; or review of information already collected might be used to identify and describe

(1) the environmental conditions within which the responsibility is performed; (2) reasonable accommodation to ensure compliance with ADA; and (3) the knowledge, skills, and abilities required of an incumbent to perform the responsibility at minimally acceptable levels (entry into the job); and proficient levels (fully qualified incumbent).

Environmental Conditions　　This area is often classified as *working conditions*. In the past, it normally centered on the physical demands and hazards encountered when performing job assignments. Today, additional factors have been added that describe intellectual and emotional demands.

In reviewing conditions that may have a detrimental effect on the jobholder, the analyst must be aware of and able to identify accurately the kinds and degree of physical, intellectual, and emotional conditions that may, in some manner, endanger the health of the employee. Unusual working conditions such as extreme temperatures, excessive dust, dampness, toxic elements, heights, and depths have been recognized for many years. Today, attention also focuses on stressful conditions that may result in anxiety, frustration, fear, alienation, and hostility. Failure to recognize the existence of these conditions could result in a far from adequate understanding of workplace conditions.

Reasonable Accommodations　　In order to comply with ADA, organizations must take an even more careful and intense look at conditions of employment. Compliance with ADA demands that employers make reasonable accommodations for jobholders.

Reasonable accommodation has been defined as accommodation that includes the making of facilities readily accessible to individuals with disabilities, providing part-time or modified work schedules, acquiring equipment or devices, modifying examinations and training materials, and providing qualified readers and interpreters. Possibly the most difficult assignment facing an employer attempting to comply with ADA is in making reasonable accommodations for individuals with disabilities. The problem of contention focuses on the word *reasonable*. Since the writing of the U.S. Constitution over 200 years ago, "reasonable doubt" has been a legal phrase to protect a defendant. Over the years, courts have wrestled with ways of defining reasonable doubt and, in most legal cases, courts have favored as brief and sparse a definition as possible. In the coming years, the definition of "reasonable accommodation" will most likely follow the same course as that provided to "reasonable doubt."

This in no way relieves the employer from taking all necessary actions to provide accommodations that permit individuals with disabilities to perform job assignments. Accommodations can be as simple as providing additional space for a wheelchair or separating heavy, bulky packages into smaller, lighter packages that individuals with certain physical impairments or limitations can process. Far more complex accommodations permit not only blind and deaf individuals to perform job assignments but also individuals with learning disabilities that restrict their knowledge level to that acquired through an elementary school education (seventh grade or less).

What "reasonable accommodation" means to an employer is that the job must be carefully analyzed. What must the jobholder do? What kind of assistance can the jobholder be expected to receive from coworkers, supervisors, providers of inputs to the job, and recipients of job outputs? Time demands, variability of inputs and outputs, opportunities to modify inputs and outputs, technology currently on hand, and technology that can be obtained from knowledge and skills required from the first moment on the job to those that are essential but can be learned over a period of time to permit job proficiency must all be considered when discussing accommodation, let alone reasonable accommodation.

An important point to be made at this time and stressed throughout this book is that each job is unique. Even in jobs in which the sets of activities to be performed are identical, a wide variety of environmental conditions, incumbent characteristics and qualities, coworker characteristics and qualities, and client demands change those appearing to be identical jobs into jobs that are similar but not identical. Reasonable accommodations will make an employer look at each job situation and then make well-thought-out decisions and take the necessary and possible actions that permit reasonable accommodations for individuals with disabilities.

After an employer has analyzed the job, identified and defined job requirements, and searched for opportunities to reasonably accommodate individuals with disabilities, he or she then has the right to recognize hardships made on the organization. *Undue hardships* are actions that would require significant difficulties or expenses. To date, when courts have ruled on undue hardship, they have recognized the nature and cost of accommodations, the overall financial resources of the employer, and the kinds of operations of the employer. Undue hardship will be different for different employers and Congress intended for courts to take a flexible approach when ruling on undue hardship. The more complete the processes for identifying physical and mental job requirements, essential job functions, and reasonable accommodations, the more successful employers will be in establishing an undue hardship defense to an ADA-based charge.

Knowledge, Skills, and Abilities (KSAs)   Knowledge, skills, and abilities may be defined as follows:

> **Knowledge:** Prerequisites for thinking and action required to perform assignments necessary to produce acceptable output.
>
> **Skill:** Demonstrated level of proficiency of an ability.
>
> **Ability:** A natural talent or acquired proficiency required in the performance of work assignments.

Although KSA information is typically collected for establishing minimum job qualifications and developing minimum hiring requirements, this kind of information can be developed to identify requirements normally expected of a fully proficient employee. It also assists in test design and validation. To acquire this kind of information, the analyst may have to return to the supervisor or discuss the KSA requirements with other personnel specialists. Individuals responsible for the design of testing and selection instruments or those involved in recruiting and hiring may be an excellent source of information. Questions relating to KSAs can also be directed to an incumbent.

It often appears that jobs are becoming simpler; the opposite is actually the case. Not only are work requirements becoming more demanding, but the relationship between employee performance and organizational productivity is also increasing in complexity. Computer-assisted machines are replacing humans where there is an emphasis on repetitive physical labor and repetitive intellectual demands. Software that directs these machines accommodates a certain amount of flexibility in assignments and can quickly react to changes in input data. Human labor, however, is required to operate and repair these sophisticated machines.

Many positions in contemporary organizations require the incumbent to act as an interface between different groups of computer-driven machines. In this high-technology world, the workforce is called on to perform less physical work, but the speed and number of interactions and the accuracy demanded in every phase of operations require workers to have significantly higher levels of knowledge and skills and a broader understanding of the reasons or causes of the interactions that influence their assignments. Workers have less time to make decisions, must consider more alternatives in the decision-making process, and frequently have less control over what they do than workers did prior to the computer revolution. This has resulted in emotional and intellectual stress, which is replacing physical stress at the workplace.

Comparing Conditions of Employment

The environmental conditions, ADA requirements, and KSA identification processes are performed for each responsibility and for its assigned duties. This permits the use of one of the first of many checks and balances that must be built into the writing of job definitions. If the duties truly fit within an identified responsibility, they should be performed under similar environmental conditions and require similar KSAs. After the environmental conditions and KSAs for each responsibility have been developed, each duty assigned to a responsibility should be compared to the conditions of employment established for that responsibility. If they match, this is further evidence that the assigned duties support the specific responsibility. If a duty does not match:

1. The conditions of employment may not have been adequately described and require further clarification.
2. The duty does not fit within its assigned responsibility.
   a. If this occurs, the first action is to see whether or not the duty would fit better under another responsibility.
   b. If this is not a satisfactory solution, the next alternative is either to develop the duty as a new responsibility and identify its own conditions of employment or to use the duty as a basis for establishing a new responsibility.
   c. At this stage, it may be useful to review the initial task analysis to see whether or not certain tasks can be identified as duties that further describe this additional responsibility.

OTHER WAYS OF DESCRIBING JOB FACTS

Although the job description is the instrument most commonly used to identify and describe the work of an employee, two other kinds of communication media are also used—the position description and the class (description) specification.

Position Description

Some organizations use the generic word *position* to describe the work performed by top managers. The counterpart word used for all other employees is *job*. In this book, however, the words *position* and *job* are not applied in this way. Here, a position description has to do with the work done by a specific individual. A position and job description could be identical; this could also *not* be true. Position descriptions become very important when the measurement and rating of employee performance become an issue. Because performance is not easy to measure (see chapter 13), it is important to start the appraisal process with a position description.

The position description can follow the format suggested for the job description. The title of the position, however, may be more specific than the job title and may be what is commonly called a working title. Another possible difference involves ranking the responsibility and duty statements within the definition section. It is certainly preferable to rank responsibility and duty statements for job descriptions; this practice is critical, however, in the writing of position descriptions. For example, by ranking the statements in the position definition section, it is possible to delineate the differences in the work of two file clerks, or two executive secretaries, or two computer operators. The kinds of work performed can vary by shift (work turn), geographic location, or functional area of responsibility (clerk in marketing or clerk in manufacturing).

Two individuals who perform in what has been identified as the same job may not necessarily consider the ordering of the responsibilities and duties to be the same. This provides documentation supporting the concept that the work done by two employees is seldom identical. The great majority of positions cannot be made uniform; they cannot be completely standardized.

Once again, the computer and its word processing capabilities become valuable. With word processing capabilities, incumbent and supervisor can quickly and easily re-order responsibility and duty statements (in addition to adding, deleting, or changing specific responsibility and duty statements), and the computer can provide an instant hard copy of the new position definition. In this way, incumbent and supervisor will be working from a current and accurate "contract."

Another contribution computer/word processing capabilities can offer is that, in moving from an occupation task statement to job duties and responsibilities to position activity statements, it is possible not only to use the provided verb and object, but also to add modifying words or phrases that make the position description unique.

Class (Description) Specifications

Class specifications are the written descriptions of the major activities and features of jobs included within a class (Figure 7–7). A class is a group of jobs that have sufficiently similar responsibilities and duties, have the same entrance requirements, receive the same amount of pay, and can be referred to by the same class title although they may have different job titles (class title—Senior Clerk; job titles—Chief Payroll Clerk, Market Analyst Clerk, Senior Production Control Clerk).

A typical format for a class specification consists of:

1. Encompassing class title
2. Brief description of the basic purpose of the class
3. Sample of duties performed by jobs in the class (the class specification will normally include at least 50 percent of the duties performed by any job included within the specific class)
4. Minimum qualifications in terms of education, experience, skill, or ability

The class specification (description) is a rather broad or general description of the work assigned to an individual. A class specification frequently includes the word *may*—*may* do this or *may* do that—because it may describe the work done by em-

---

*Senior Clerk**

Purpose of Class:
Under general direction. Performs advanced and complex clerical duties. Requires some skill in typing. Operates all kinds of basic computer equipment and standard office duplication equipment. Trains new hires and lower-level clerks on work procedures and may provide direction as to the timing and the correct performance of assignments to lower-level employees. Must be thoroughly familiar with department operating procedures and be skilled in reviewing, analyzing, and reconciling data of a complex nature from a variety of sources.

Examples of Duties:
1. Maintains various records and files.
2. Compiles data periodically and prepares reports, informative fact sheets, etc.
3. Operates various office machines such as computer, calculator, keypunch, duplicating equipment.
4. May type letters and reports.
5. May post and maintain various records and program data.
6. May handle payroll, purchase orders, and payment of bills.
7. May perform high volume of detailed work.
8. May make arrangements for travel, meetings, conferences, or other miscellaneous office functions.
9. May make detailed counts for inventory purposes.
10. Acts as receptionist; answers telephone and personal inquiries either firsthand or through referral; refers visitors and secures and transmits routine information.
11. Assists the public by checking routine records and files for requested information.

Minimum Qualifications:
Knowledge of grammar, spelling, and arithmetic.
Knowledge of office information and data processing, storing and retrieving practices and procedures, and use of standard office equipment.
Skill in typing reports and memoranda.
Skill in directing work of other clerks.
Skill in communicating to employees in other work units and to other people outside the organization.
Ability to understand and carry out oral and written instructions.
Ability to work with minimal supervision and little verification.

*This class is part of a class-series that could include clerk, associate clerk, senior clerk, and lead clerk (could also be Clerk I, Clerk II, Clerk III, and Clerk IV).

FIGURE 7–7 Sample Class Specification

ployees in a variety of settings. On the other hand, a job description is more specific. It describes variations in the work done by employees in performing similar kinds of assignments. The position description, which is more narrow in scope than the other two descriptions, describes the work of a specific employee.

Standing Operating Procedures

The description of work, although considerably more limited, continues with standing operating procedures. Standing operating procedures describe step-by-step how an employee performs a specific assignment. For example, a duty of an office receptionist may state: "answers telephone." The standing operating procedures for answering a telephone in this particular organization may state:

1. When answering incoming calls, say "Good morning! Good afternoon! Olympia."
2. The caller will identify the staff person with whom he or she wishes to speak or the specific topic or issue to be discussed and may not give his or her name. Do not ask "Who is calling?" but simply say "One moment please," and put the caller on hold.
3. Locate the staff member or the appropriate individual to respond to the call and dial his or her intercom number and speak directly into the phone, saying, "Mr._____, line 07 please," and release the intercom. If you have to speak to the individual first, then say, "Mr._____, intercom 1, please." (Mr._____ will then depress intercom 1 and speak to you before answering the phone.)

This kind of a step-by-step description may be required not only when an employee is performing an assignment in accordance with organizational specifications, but even more important, when he or she is interacting with various kinds of machines, especially the computer.

Performance Standards

The final step in the process of describing work requirements occurs with the setting of performance standards. A performance standard describes the results that should exist upon the completion of a specific assignment or activity. Performance standards provide answers to such questions as *how much, how thorough, how well,* and *by when.* (Performance standards are discussed in more detail in chapter 13.) Figure 7–8 is a pictorial representation of the identification process that moves from a very general to a very precise description of job activities, resulting in an output measured by performance standards.

REVISING JOB DESCRIPTIONS

Jobs change, people change, so job descriptions must change. As in almost every aspect of job description writing, there is disagreement as to the timing, amount of change, and locus of responsibility relative to the revision of job descriptions.

The first rule in writing a job description is that it must describe the job as it is. However, in many cases, once an individual accepts and is assigned to a job, the job begins to change. Each individual has unique qualities. The strengths and weaknesses, knowledge and skills, areas of interest and energy levels of the incumbent change the job. Sometimes these changes are imperceptible; sometimes they are dramatic. Sometimes changes made to the job by the incumbent are unacceptable to the organization. At other times, the jobholder both enriches and enlarges the job, making both incumbent and job more valuable to the organization.

A major reason for disillusion regarding job descriptions is that they do not describe the job as it is. Frequently, the reason may be that the job was not described adequately or acceptably to begin with. At other times, it is because job changes have not been recognized. A problem that continues to affect the adequacy of job descriptions is administrative in nature—trained individuals who have job analysis–job description writing skills are unavailable, and there are not enough clerical-secretarial support per-

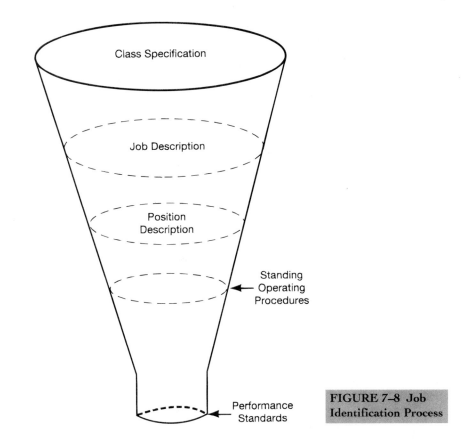

FIGURE 7–8 Job Identification Process

sonnel to type revised job descriptions and maintain proper files. These issues are currently being addressed by the introduction of the computer into the domain of job description writing and maintenance.

Incumbent Responsibility

The person who should be given primary responsibility for maintaining the job description must be the incumbent. Even with computer support, it is not necessary to revise a job description with each new assignment. However, once an assignment becomes a permanent part of the job, actions should be taken to include the assignment within the existing job definition and other applicable sections of the job description.

If the job description is recognized as a document that affects job-worth rating and is also part of the incumbent's performance review process, these become two motivators for ensuring the completeness and correctness of the job description. If job-worth rating is the only reason for updating the job description, there is always the possibility that an incumbent (even the supervisor) may "puff up" the job and make it appear more valuable than it actually is. However, by making the job description part of the performance appraisal process (see chapter 13), the employee may not want to be held accountable and measurable for something that he or she does not do.

Monitoring and Auditing Job Descriptions

Incumbent inputs to the revision of a job description should be on an as-needed basis. However, formal systems should be in place to review jobs to ensure that the descriptions are accurate and complete. The individual with major *monitoring* responsibilities is the immediate supervisor.

All jobs should be reviewed at least once a year. An ideal review date is 60 days before the annual performance review (if an organization formally measures and rates employee performance). If an organization does not measure and rate performance formally, then reviews should occur at a specified time each year. The monitoring supervisor can interview the incumbent with the sole purpose of reviewing and revising the existing job description. Two weeks before the interview, the incumbent should be asked to review the current job description and make any necessary revisions, additions, or deletions and be ready to explain these changes to the immediate supervisor during the scheduled interview.

If an organization has an active job description monitoring system in use, it may be necessary to *audit* the jobs of the organization once every three to five years. Auditing responsibility lies in the human resources department, or possibly with an outside third party. This process may require the completion of a job analysis questionnaire by the incumbent and interviews with selected jobholders.

Other times for reviewing jobs and revising descriptions are:

1. When assigning a new incumbent to the job
2. When major changes are made in the product or outputs provided by a work unit or individual
3. With the introduction of new technology, equipment, methods, or procedures to the workplace
4. With the reorganization of the work unit
5. With the implementation of a new pay system
6. When a new responsibility (a major work activity area) is added to the job

The job description must never be considered a straitjacket or a top limit as to what can be done by the jobholder. Within agreed-to limits, the employee should be permitted to use his or her own innovative talents to perform job assignments in the most productive manner.

USING THE COMPUTER

This chapter and the preceding one have alluded to the costs involved in collecting and analyzing job content data and in writing job descriptions. A solution to the cost problem is now available. The answer to these costs is to use word processing and computing technologies for describing job content. New developments in mini- and micro-computers are now having a significant impact in this area.

To use the data storage, retrieval, and rapid printouts of accessed and manipulated data, human resource/compensation specialists who want to make use of these automated office services will have to take certain actions. The strength of any computer application depends on the quality of the data stored in the database, the capacity of the database, and the ability to manipulate and coordinate data.

Technological improvements and the reduction in costs of scanning equipment will significantly enhance the development and use of task inventories. Scanning equipment will enable organizations to review inputs from many sources and in various forms and place desired data on a disk for further word processing, thereby eliminating the need for massive manual data input requirements.

The major purpose of job analysis is to develop useful descriptions of job facts. The marriage of job analyst and job description writers to computing technology begins with the establishment of job content databases, which can take the form of task and major activity inventories.

Developing Task Inventories

Task data are collected in the same way as the data needed to write a job description, except that now task statements are collected under occupational headings. Each organization or its analyst(s) has the opportunity to broaden or narrow the scope of a specific occupation. In other words, a broad occupational heading such as *office administration* can be subdivided into more narrow occupational groups, such as (1) clerical, (2) typist-stenographer, (3) word processor, (4) secretary, or (5) administrative assistant. A secretary task inventory could be further subdivided into specific inventories related to such specialties as legal, medical, or engineering.

Narrow groupings make it easier and quicker for an incumbent to review the appropriate inventory. However, the more narrow the inventory, the more time specialists will have to spend developing it. Using the task statements provided by the respondents through the questionnaire, interview, or some other means, the analyst develops an edited list of *occupation-oriented* task statements. This is accomplished by first reviewing and combining the output from the analysis of jobs that would normally be found in the same occupation. To compile a well-written and complete master list of occupational tasks requires a combination of knowledge of the jobs under study and editing skills. Information presented in chapter 6 and in this chapter is also helpful in assisting those responsible for writing and developing task inventories.

When analyzing and possibly rephrasing task statements provided by incumbents and supervisors for use in a task inventory, the "inventory developer" must make certain that the inventory:

1. Does not have more than one statement describing the same or almost the same action
2. Has sufficient statements to reduce the chances for a deficiency (failure to have sufficient statements to describe adequately a specific position or job within the occupation)
3. Does not include a task that could lead to contamination (providing information on things that do not occur in positions or jobs in the occupation)
4. Avoids describing tasks in a manner that causes distortion (using words or terms that make the task appear to be more or less important than it is within an applicable position or job)

To ensure common understanding, action verbs must be defined both from a broad organizational context and from the view of the occupation being described. It is critical that the incumbent, supervisors, and any other individual reviewing inventories of tasks or position/job definitions that contain responsibilities and duties have a common interpretation of the meaning of the key word—the action verb. To accomplish this goal, an action verb glossary can be developed that precisely describes the meaning of the verb as used in the context of a specific occupation or family of jobs.

The occupational action verb glossaries can then be combined into an organizational glossary that will be available for all parties involved in writing or reviewing tasks statements and position/job definitions. When the occupational glossaries are combined into a single glossary for the organization, some verbs will have a number of different meanings. Unless these different occupational meanings are recognized, action verbs can cause severe misunderstanding. The following steps can be taken to develop an action word glossary:

1. Group all task listings by occupation.
2. Develop a complete list of all action verbs used in statements that describe all jobs within each occupation.
3. Use a dictionary and other appropriate glossaries to define verbs.
4. Review verb definitions with individuals who are capable of stating whether or not the definitions are adequate and fully understood and whether or not possible revisions or additions would improve their descriptive qualities within the occupational setting.

Although much effort goes into the writing of task inventories, changes will occur, and they must be recognized and described. Modifications, additions, or deletions to task inventories occur because of changes in technology, organizational demands, and raw material inputs.

With the final editing of the occupational statements and action word glossary, a significant amount of the time-consuming development work is over. In the future, as jobs change, new task statements can be added as necessary, or existing statements can be removed, revised, or modified when more descriptive verbs, objects, and other modifiers are identified. Action word glossaries can also be updated and refined. Also, with computer capabilities any changes or deletions in a task inventory can be stored and easily accessed from a readily available file. This eliminates the chance of losing information that may be valuable at some future time (e.g., "What did we do then when we did that?").

Developing Major Activity Inventories

As discussed in chapter 6, much work has already been done in the development of task inventories. The solid foundation established by the U.S. Air Force with CODAP and many spinoffs, including the work by V-TECS, has enlarged the scope of task inventory development.

The subject of major activity inventories, however, is another problem. In most cases, minimal thought and effort have gone into this crucial part of job description/definition writing. CODAP groups tasks under such functional headings as Management, Inspecting and Evaluating, and Performing Automated Data System Functions. This mixed bag of nouns, adjectives, and modifying phrases is inadequate. The responsibility (the job-specific counterpart of the major activity) should be described in the same way as the duty (task counterpart): verb + object + modifier.

In developing the major activity statements, the analyst/writer must review the task inventories or already completed job definitions and develop useful umbrella statements. These statements will use verbs that have broader, more general meanings than will the task statements. For example, good verbs for management-related major activity statements could be *directs, supervises, coordinates,* and *organizes and expedites.* Within the context of managerial jobs, these verbs could be defined as follows:

Directs: Manages the quality, quantity, and timeliness of work flow

Supervises: Oversees and inspects general human resource development and recognition activities

Coordinates: Interacts with other managers and professionals to achieve effective and efficient operations

Organizes and expedites: Arranges work activities in an acceptable and progressive manner

An example of how major activity statements could be designed using these verbs and the kinds of task statements that could be attached to the umbrella statement follows.

1.0 Directs activities of unit.
   1.1 Reviews incoming work and work distribution.
   1.2 Checks attendance, making reassignments as necessary.
   1.3 Requests temporary and permanent additions to staff, recognizing workload, turnover, absenteeism, and employees in training.
   1.4 Spot checks each production area twice daily.
   1.5 Discusses production problems daily with managers to resolve operational problems and to implement necessary changes.
2.0 Supervises staff.
   2.1 Counsels employees on acceptable workplace behaviors and performance-related problems.
   2.2 Organizes nonwork-related information programs for staff with Human Resources.
   2.3 Interviews and recommends job applicants for hiring.
   2.4 Trains and ensures the training of the staff.
3.0 Coordinates operations with other managers.
   3.1 Informs human resources of openings and other staff requirements.
   3.2 Discusses personnel-related problems with staff—workers' compensation, leave of absence, termination and discipline, and other unique situations.
   3.3 Discusses problems with senior managers, directors, and managers of other departments.
   3.4 Recommends changes in operations and procedures to other managers and to senior management.
4.0 Organizes and expedites work flow.
   4.1 Recognizes opportunities for improving departmental performance through system changes.
   4.2 Documents system change requests.
   4.3 Reviews system change specifications developed by analyst and potential effects of recommended changes.
   4.4 Reviews test output to ensure adequacy and correctness of system changes.

The development of major activity statements may be a more difficult assignment than the development of task statements. With task statements, the analyst has the assistance of subject matter experts—notably, the incumbent. In major activity development, the analyst may be alone. As already mentioned, the best recommendation is to review existing job definitions in which responsibilities have already been defined. If these are not available, the next suggestion is to review inventories and identify areas in which tasks can be grouped together. Another suggestion is to review Figures 6–6 and 6–7 and use the approach described for collecting responsibility statement data. Whatever method is used, through attention to detail and good editing practices, major activity inventories can be developed.

Linking Inventories to the Computer

The development of computer-based inventories may appear to be unduly time-consuming and quite costly. Before accepting this assumption, however, and dismissing this stage as an unnecessary part of the job analysis–job description process, it may be helpful to review how computer-based data processing can provide accurate and comprehensive data that can be stored and processed for availability at some later time. The computer-stored data may consist of:

1. A list of all occupations and position or job titles currently assigned to each occupation
2. A complete list of occupation-oriented task and major activity inventories
3. Action word glossaries for each occupation that precisely define what the verb means when used in the context of that occupation
4. An action word glossary for the entire organization that identifies different meanings for the same word when used in a variety of organizational settings
5. Activity-worth dimensions and rating scales that permit easy access and operation by all involved in activity-worth measurement

This information can then be placed on disks, tapes, or other word processing or computer-applicable data storage devices. The information can be recalled by anyone with access to a video display terminal (VDT). For example, an incumbent sitting at a VDT with a four-section or more split screen can review an inventory on one section of the split screen, make selections from the inventory, and maintain the selected statements on another section of the screen. In a third section, the user can concurrently review major activity inventories and assign selected task inventory statements to the appropriate major activity.

The selections made by the incumbent can be stored and grouped, and, upon receipt of specific instructions, the printer can provide a hard copy of the results. Both supervisor and incumbent can review the document and make necessary changes. They can both search for missing activities, either major activities or tasks, or possibly restate the activity in a manner that improves the description of the position. They can then review the hard copy, make any changes they think necessary, and if they require the help of a human resource specialist, can request such aid through the computer terminal or other communication device. This entire process will take supervisor and incumbent out of the activity-writing business. They will, however, make modifications, additions, or deletions to the generic statements as necessary. Through their on-line connection to job analysts or inventory development specialists, they will be able to identify where changes must be made not only in their specific positions, but also in the computerized inventories and glossaries. Constant updating of position descriptions and occupational inventories and glossaries will eliminate the need for massive job analysis programs when current position/job descriptions and occupational inventories are out of date. Instead of reinventing the wheel—writing new job descriptions—job analysts can be constantly reviewing the process and searching for better or more appropriate ways of defining jobs, by first developing generic task inventories and, second, through slight modifications if necessary, operationalizing these generic statements to fit a specific position or job.

Task inventories may be developed that permit supervisor and incumbent to add *why* and *how* (or other appropriate modifier) information to the basic verb and object. When the supervisor and incumbent add *why* and *how* information to the basic *what* and *to what* terms that are universally applicable (generic) to the occupation, the task statement becomes truly unique, providing the descriptive material necessary for a position description. Once again, supervisor and incumbent jointly review these inputs. They discuss differences in requirements or possibly differences in perception. This process leads to a much improved mutual understanding of what the job is and what the job is *not*. The computer-based process eliminates the drudgery (for most people) of thinking, reviewing, and attempting to describe what the individual does.

This process involves greater startup costs but significantly lower maintenance charges than most current approaches. The approach used by most organizations today requires substantially lower startup costs, but maintenance is a constant drain, and the result of such reactive behavior is job content identification and description that are far from adequate. The tedious, costly job analysis overhaul and the concern with out-of-date, obsolete job descriptions may shortly become part of the past, sad history of human resources management. Here, with computer-based inventories, is an excellent application of the "do it right the first time" concept.

Currently Available Job Description Writing Software

A few software firms already have commercial products available for producing job descriptions. Knowledge Point of Petaluma, California, markets job description writing software that meets the following critical user criteria: (1) has clear documentation and easy to use programs; (2) is IBM PC compatible with a less than 5 megabyte database; (3) permits title and key word search; (4) produces job descriptions in more than one format (i.e., short format for recruiting, long format for compensation); (5) allows use of a single database; and (6) is available at a low cost.

Knowledge Point's description writing software now contains a library of more than 2,500 jobs that includes job summaries and duties. This software package also permits the development of individualized and comprehensive job descriptions through an interactive question and answer process.

Summary

The job description is a tool used to help managers to meet legal requirements and to aid in industrial relations and collective bargaining procedures. In addition, the job description is also used in the following human resources and compensation management functions: recruitment, screening, hiring, placement, orientation, training and development, pay grade and pay structure design, executing compensation surveys, and completing performance appraisals.

The elements of a job description include job title, job summary, a list of responsibilities and duties, accountabilities, and job employment standards. The job responsibilities and duties list becomes the definition of the job—the work assignments and purpose of the job as derived from job analysis information. Rank-ordering the responsibilities and duties helps employees and supervisors to communicate with each other in establishing and prioritizing *what* is to be done and *why,* and *how* the job fits into the scope of the work unit. Activity-worth dimensions and rating scales are tools that aid in rank-ordering the responsibilities and duties, using dimensions such as complexity, time spent on the activity, and its importance.

The chapter includes a discussion of the specifications and requirements that constitute the job standards section of a job description. These standards include environmental or work conditions and the knowledge, skills, and abilities necessary to do the job. Finally, there is a detailed description on how to develop inventories that can be stored in a computer. Then employees with access to a terminal can quickly and easily write and update their own job descriptions.

Review Questions

1. Some experts in the field have expressed the opinion that job descriptions are unnecessary and a waste of time. Describe your opinion of the value of job descriptions and present reasons to support your opinion.
2. Describe some of the ways in which an organization can utilize a job description.
3. Why are current laws requiring organizations to take a renewed look at their job descriptions?
4. Describe the major sections of a job description. What purpose does each section serve?
5. What is the *Dictionary of Occupational Titles*? How does it help the person responsible for writing a job description?
6. How does the glossary of action words assist in the writing of a job description?

CHAPTER

Job Evaluation

8

Learning Objectives

In this chapter you will learn about:

1. The methodologies available for establishing the worth or value of jobs.

2. The reasons for implementing a job evaluation program.

3. The advantages and disadvantages of whole job ranking.

4. The strengths and weaknesses of market pricing.

5. Compensable factors and how they are used.

6. Different kinds of point-factor job evaluation methods and their value to organizations.

7. The influence of federal government legislation on job evaluation.

Compensation Strategy

Determine relative worth of all jobs to ensure fair and equitable pay treatment for all employees.

P roper and acceptable performance of different kinds of jobs requires different kinds and amounts of employee knowledge and skills, which vary significantly among individuals. In the course of their lives, many individuals acquire various kinds and levels of knowledge that organizations value. Additionally, through education, experience, training, and natural predisposition, some individuals are able to demonstrate different and greater skills than others. The worth to the organization of the individually acquired and job-required knowledge and skills is identified through job rates of pay.

Successful completion of certain kinds of job responsibilities also make significantly greater demands on the physical, emotional, and intellectual well-being of employees. These job-related differences must be recognized in as orderly and objective a manner as possible to ensure equitable relationships between rates of pay provided by the organization and employee contributions. Developing different rates of pay can be a systematic and orderly process, or it can be one that is reactive to the particular influence or pressures of the moment.

The steps in a systematic process may be so tightly integrated that movement from one step to the next is almost unrecognizable. In other cases, the steps are carefully defined and delineated. The mechanism presented in this and the following chapters delineates each phase of the pay-setting process. The three major phases are (1) identifying a hierarchy of jobs by worth, using some kind of a job evaluation methodology; (2) investigating the marketplace to identify what other organizations are paying workers in comparable jobs (chapter 10); and (3) combining job-worth data and market data in some unique manner that results in an organizational pay structure (chapter 11).

JOB REQUIREMENTS AND PAY

It became apparent by the 1880s that the productivity of workers in mills, factories, and many related industries was far from satisfactory and that means had to be developed to improve output. One area that received early attention was employee pay. In the last half of the nineteenth century, the development of the huge steel mills, the railroads, and all of the inputs to steelmaking, fabrication, and transportation manufacturing, with the concomitant wide variety of jobs associated with these operations, emphasized the need for orderly, logical, and progressive pay plans. The last quarter of the century witnessed the establishment of modern pay programs.

In the early 1880s, Frederick W. Taylor's search for ways to improve the productivity of the Midvale Steel Company led to a formal and systematic study of assigning pay to jobs. The results of this study became known as *job evaluation*. From this start, job evaluation slowly became part of the administrative function of many businesses, and during the 1920s job evaluation began to achieve fairly widespread acceptance in business, industry, and government. However, by the 1990s, a number of academicians and human resources professionals claimed that job evaluation, as described in this chapter, was no longer necessary. They claimed that job evaluation was a relic of the industrial engineering era.

Historically, job evaluation has encompassed all the tools and techniques described in chapters 6–12, but, in an attempt to give a more precise meaning to job evaluation, this text views it as *that part of the process in which the organization finally decides the relative internal worth relationships of jobs*. (Worth normally relates to the importance of the job or its contribution to the overall attainment of the goals and objectives of the organization.)

The combination of the dynamic nature of work in a high-technology society and the unceasing demands of employees on the reward systems of organizations establishes the need for job evaluation. The following are among the more important reasons for implementing a job evaluation program:

1. To establish an orderly, rational, systematic structure of jobs based on their worth to the organization.
2. To justify an existing pay rate structure or to develop one that provides for internal equity (consistent and ethical treatment).

3. To assist in setting pay rates that are comparable with similar jobs in other organizations. This enables the organization to compete in the marketplace for the best available talent and also allows employees to compare the pay they receive with that received by employees doing similar work in other organizations—to be externally competitive.

4. To provide a rational basis for negotiating pay rates when bargaining collectively with a recognized union.

5. To identify a ladder of progression or direction for future movement to all employees interested in improving their compensation opportunities.

6. To comply with equal pay legislation and regulations determining pay differences according to job content.

7. To develop a base for a merit or pay-for-performance program.

JOB EVALUATION ISSUES

Most professionals and scholars define job evaluation similarly. Eugene J. Benge, a pioneer in this area, defined it as "a method which helps to establish a justified rank order of jobs . . . it is only one of the starting points for establishing the relative differentiation of wage rates."[1] George T. Milkovich and Jerry M. Newman, contemporary scholars, define job evaluation as "a systematic procedure designed to aid in establishing pay differentials among jobs within a single employer."[2]

Controversy over job evaluation occurs when an organization must decide: (1) Which one of many methods should be used? (2) Should more than one method be used? (3) Does job evaluation accomplish what it purports to accomplish? (4) Is job evaluation useful in minimizing or eliminating unjust, even illegal, pay practices? (5) Possibly more damaging, does it promote or cover up unjust and illegal pay practices? Individuals and organizations with their own personal agendas frequently promote one job evaluation method over another. In recent years, labels have been attached to certain job evaluation methods to make some more or less appealing than others. Two such labels are "policy capturing" and "a priori." Scholars promoting the "white hat" policy-capturing job evaluation methods base their claims on the use of objective and scientifically pure statistical procedures (multiple linear regression) to identify and weight compensable factors (regression model independent variables) that, in turn, produce bias-free dependent variable data—the pay or possible pay grade for a job.

Job evaluation methods not using regression analysis have been given a "black hat" label of "a priori," meaning that these methods are based on hypothesis and theory—conjecture, but without use of scientific investigation or empirical application. The fact is that no job evaluation method has been designed or operates in a bias-free environment and few useful methods operate for any period of time without having a strong empirical and pragmatic foundation. Surveys indicate that approximately 90 percent of all job evaluation methods are either point-factor or market pricing. Tables 8–1 and 8–2 provide some information on job evaluation practices.

---

[1]Eugene J. Benge, *Job Evaluation and Merit Rating* (Deep River, CT: National Foremen's Institute, 1941).
[2]George T. Milkovich and Jerry M. Newman, *Compensation,* 3rd ed. (Plano, TX: Business Publications, Inc., 1990), p. 103.

TABLE 8–1 Job Evaluation Methodologies by Major Employee Groups (percentage of responding organizations using a specified method)[a]

Job Evaluation Method	Middle Management Report	Supervisory Management Report	Professional and Scientific Personnel Report	Office Personnel Report	Technician and Skilled Trades Personnel Report
Point factor	41.0%	40.8%	44.1%	51.4%	54.8%
Ranking	28.2	26.3	26.4	24.0	26.7
Market pricing	68.8	69.8	64.9	57.0	69.4
Factor comparison	8.3	9.6	8.7	7.5	8.4
Other	8.4	5.9	5.5	4.3	4.5

[a] Totals add to more than 100 percent as some responding organizations use two, three, or four methods.
Source: Wyatt Data Services/ECS, 1991/92 reports as identified in column headings.

TABLE 8–2 Job Evaluation Methods Used by State Governments

Kind	Total[a]	0 <5	5 <10	10 <20	20+
Point factor	25	12	8	4	1
Grading	14	0	1	4	9
Ranking	7	0	1	1	5
Factor comparison	4	0	1	1	2
Other	14	1	6	5	2

[a] Some states use more than one method (different methods for different groups of employees).
Source: U.S. General Accounting Office, *Pay Equity Status of State Activities* (Gaithersburg, MD: General Accounting Office, 1986), p. 9.

THE INTRAOCCUPATIONAL AND INTEROCCUPATIONAL METHOD OF JOB CLASSIFICATION

While Taylor was designing pay plans to improve productivity in the private sector, E. O. Griffenhagen was charting a similar route in the public sector. His work led to the establishment of a classification plan that was adopted by the City of Chicago in 1901.[3] Griffenhagen's work has become known as the intraoccupational and interoccupational (I & I) method of job classification.

---

[3]Charles W. Lytle, *Job Evaluation Methods,* 2nd ed. (New York: Ronald Press, 1954), p. 127.

Basic steps in the I & I method are these:

1. Identify major occupations or families of occupations in the organization.
2. Place each class of jobs within its respective occupation (see definition of *position, jobs, job class, class-series, occupation,* and *family* in chapter 7).
3. Rank all classes within the occupation. This provides a vertical array of job classes with the highest-ranked class at the top of the vertical array. (The ranking procedure is discussed in the next section.)
4. Select classes within each vertical array in which the responsibilities, duties, and qualifications (worker specifications) are clearly recognized and understood. These well-identified and understood classes become benchmark or key job classes. (There is an extensive discussion of benchmark jobs in chapter 9.)
5. Array benchmark or key classes in different occupations.
6. Place benchmark or key classes from different occupations that can be considered to have *comparable* responsibilities, duties, and qualifications on the same horizontal level. (Again, the ranking process described later is used for the comparability analysis.)

Table 8–3 is an example of an I & I comparison chart.

TABLE 8–3   An Intraoccupational and Interoccupational Comparison Chart

Clerical—classes of jobs concerned with making, classifying, and filing records, including a wide variety of verbal communications. (DOT Codes 201., 209.)	*Nursing*—jobs concerned with administering nursing care to the ill or aged. (DOT Codes 075., 079.)	*Public safety*—classes of jobs concerned with protecting the public, maintaining law and order, detecting and preventing crime, directing and controlling motor traffic, and investigating and apprehending suspects in criminal cases. (DOT Code 375.)
		Police Chief[a]
Executive Secretary[a]	Director Nursing Service	
Special Occupation Secretary[a]	Head Nurse[a]	
Stenographer	Special Duty Nurse[a]	Desk Officer
Secretary[a]		
		Commanding Officer[a]
	General Duty Nurse[a]	Detective
	Licensed Practical Nurse	Police Officer[a]
Clerk-Typist		
File Clerk[a]	Nurse's Aide[a]	

[a] Key classes.

Using I & I in a Contemporary Organization

Although the I & I method of job evaluation is still useful, it has limited value in classifying jobs in a contemporary organization. During the hundred years since Griffenhagen developed his "whole class" methodology, job assignments and associated knowledge and skill requirements have continued to vary. Assigning various positions and jobs to a class and then using some form of generic class description (specification) to describe activities that "may" be performed on a specific job or class is inadequate. In developing a modern pay plan, it is critical to recognize and understand what each incumbent is doing. Sometimes, fine differences between positions/jobs may result in different pay treatment, and sometimes the differences may be so inconsequential that no differences in pay should be awarded. However, the differences in job requirements must be recognized by the employer and employees must be informed why changes or no changes in pay treatment in comparison with other jobs are made.

Using inter- and intraoccupational ranking of all jobs (and ranking of all jobs within work units or departments) is an extremely powerful review exercise capable of identifying where jobs have been inappropriately ranked.

WHOLE JOB RANKING

The comparison of jobs or classes of jobs as in the I & I method requires those doing the comparing to consider the whole job and to establish an order by determining the overall worth of jobs or classes as they compare with one another.

When determining the worth of one job or class versus another, the evaluator uses job-worth ideas and concepts stored in his or her brain. These ideas are, in reality, *constructs*—theoretical notions or ideas developed to explain and organize some aspects of existing knowledge. In whole job ranking, these constructs are never defined, weighted, or provided with any kind of a measurement scale in written form, which can lead to serious evaluator errors caused by previously developed stereotypes.

The easiest kind of job ranking occurs when comparing jobs in the same occupation or in the same organizational unit. When evaluators are intimately familiar with all jobs being ranked, they may only have to direct their decision-making processes to a job title. In cases in which there is less familiarity with job content and requirements, the documentation may range from a brief summary of activities to a completed job analysis questionnaire or job description. These documents can provide varying levels of data concerning the responsibilities, duties, and accountabilities of the job, minimum qualifications for selection, and normal or typical environmental conditions within which an incumbent performs job activities.

However, when jobs are to be compared among various units of an organization or in different occupational groups, ranking and recognizing comparability on a horizontal level (interoccupational or even interorganizational) are extremely difficult assignments. Few persons are wise and impartial enough and have the understanding and the knowledge to sift through (1) the objectives of the organization, (2) the activities and goals of various jobs or classes, (3) the contributions these dissimilar jobs or classes make to the achievement of the objectives of the organization, (4) the various responsibilities and duties of the jobs within these groups compared to jobs in other classes, and (5) the value of the jobs in achieving both group and organizational objectives.

Slotting

By developing comparability among key jobs or classes at the highest, the center, and the lowest end of the hierarchy of value, a framework of adjoining ladders is provided within which to *slot* other job classes. *Slotting* is a commonly used term to describe ranking of nonbenchmark or nonkey jobs. In essence, slotting is a ranking process in which the job is compared with an existing scale and placed in the appropriate slot. Slotting is typically an intuitive process, and its accuracy depends on the knowledge and skill of the individual doing the slotting. If the process is to be more formal, the paired-comparison procedures described in appendix 8A could be used.

Advantages and Disadvantages

Whole job ranking is the quickest to perform of all job evaluation methods. When evaluators know the jobs with which they are working, the whole job ranking method can produce accurate results. One problem with this method in a modern organization in which communication of employee-related issues is vital is the lack of substantiating data to justify the final results. There is nothing for the jobholders to discuss with the evaluators except the results, and it is difficult for anyone simply to accept "This is the way it is because I said so."

Another major disadvantage of the ranking system, and probably the most important, is that it provides no yardstick for measuring the relative value of jobs. Therefore, it is not too helpful in developing a scale of pay rates based on the relative value of all jobs. It also provides little assistance in comparing jobs in different or geographically dispersed units when there is no basis for equating jobs that differ by kind of subject matter or kind of work but that have similar levels of difficulty, responsibility, and qualification requirements.

In addition, the ranking method is quite inflexible. It does not readily identify changes in job content, which could lead to internal equity inconsistencies; nor does it recognize shifts in labor market demands. Finally, there is always the danger that when evaluators are familiar with both the job and the jobholder, the behavior and the personality of the employee may unduly influence the evaluator's estimate of job worth. An existing pay rate may cause a similar type of bias. Ranking, however, is always valuable as a first step in job evaluation or as a tool for teaching anyone the basic concepts of evaluation. It certainly fosters a basic understanding of the evaluation process.

A number of paired-comparison procedures are invaluable for job-ranking purposes. These include the deck-of-cards, the stub selection, the paired-comparison ranking table, and the alternation ranking procedures. These procedures are described in appendix 8A.

POSITION (JOB) CLASSIFICATION — PREDETERMINED GRADING APPROACH

In 1919, a joint congressional commission working on reclassification of salaries in the federal government appointed Ismar Baruch, an examiner of the Civil Service Commission, to investigate the classification of jobs on the basis of duties. As a result of his findings, Congress passed the Classification Act of 1923. By 1933, Baruch had been appointed chief of the newly established Personnel Classification Division of the Civil Service Commission. At that time, he was given the authority to classify federal positions on the basis of job analysis. His work also included the use of predetermined pay grades.[4] A pay grade is a defined area that establishes a specific rate of pay or a range of pay for all jobs that meet certain specifications.

A major contribution of Baruch's efforts in developing pay grades was to overcome the weakness of the I & I methodology in relating job rankings to differences in rates of pay. By having well-documented pay grades that fit together in a logical and orderly manner, many of the issues related to assigning a rate of pay to a particular incumbent or job were resolved.

Developing a Class Standard/Pay Grade Narrative

The first step in developing a predetermined pay grade approach is to identify and describe benchmark or key jobs that would normally be paid at the highest and lowest levels of pay and sufficient jobs between these two points to establish an orderly scale of pay relationships. Job content requirements and features common to benchmark or key jobs receiving approximately the same rate of pay are identified. This job content and common features are used to formulate narrative classification standards that describe the kind of work found at each pay grade with examples from jobs assigned to the pay grade.

Pay grade classification standards specify in broad terms the kinds and levels of responsibilities assigned to jobs in each grade, the difficulty of work performed, and the qualifications (knowledge, experience, skill) required of incumbents. Positions are analyzed and evaluated in terms of these measures and are placed (or classified) into grades. Narratives of class standards can be quite long and complex, especially when numerous details are required to differentiate among the many jobs to be assigned to the various pay grades. The pay grade classification standard must have sufficient detail so that the nonbenchmark job descriptions can be compared with the grade narratives and the jobs then placed in the appropriate grades.

Broadbanding

In the last decade of the twentieth century, a variation in pay grade development was given the title of *broadbanding*. Very simply, broadbanding groups a number of progressively higher-paying grades into one "broader" pay grade band. This reduces the need to more precisely define and measure job differences and promotes the paying of jobs with varying required knowledge and skills the same rate of pay. Whereas the first 75 years of the twentieth century witnessed attention on identifying and paying for minimal differences in kinds and levels of knowledge and skills, the broadbanding decade focused efforts on valuing somewhat dissimilar jobs similarly for pay purposes. Broadbanding will be further discussed in chapters 11 and 12. Also, see discussion of Decision Band Method of Job Evaluation later in this chapter (appendix 8B).

---

[4]Committee on Position-Classification and Pay Plans in the Public Service, *Position-Classification in the Public Service* (Chicago: Civil Service Assembly of the United States and Canada, 1941). This report is frequently referred to as the Baruch Report.

Assigning a Position/Job to a Pay Grade

No matter how lengthy and comprehensive the pay grade narratives, the placement of a specific position (the work of one employee) into a pay grade can be quite difficult. One problem is the accurate and complete description of the position. As discussed in chapters 6 and 7, job analysis and description are not easy assignments, and many actions can be taken in the process to either over- or underemphasize job content and employee specifications, leading to the assignment of a position to an inappropriate pay grade. Another major issue that frequently arises is that some duties of a position or job relate to a lower pay grade in the structure (hierarchy), a majority of duties to another grade, and a smaller number of duties to yet a higher grade. The question that then arises is to which pay grade the position or job should be assigned. These kinds of concerns have been a driving force for those promoting the use of broadbands.

Classification in the Federal Government

The Classification Act established five job evaluation (or pay) services.[5] The two principal services were the Professional (P) Service, consisting of professionals and engineers, with eight pay grades, and the Clerical, Administrative, and Financial (CAF) Service with 10 pay grades. From the start, the connecting grades between the two services were P1 and CAF5. P1 included recent college graduates with a bachelor's degree, and CAF5 included senior clerks and secretaries with three years of progressively more responsible experience.

In 1949, these two services were combined into the 18-grade General Schedule (GS) with GS 1 to 10 being comparable to the previous CAF 1 to 10, and GS 5, 7, 9, 11 to 15 being comparable to the eight grades in the P Service. Currently, the pay of over 1 million federal employees is controlled by the GS. The two grades with the largest number of incumbents are GS 5 and GS 11. These pay grades include approximately 25 percent of all GS employees. GS 5 continues to be the link between various occupational groups. Employees in this grade can be senior secretaries or clerks, fully qualified technicians, or entry-level professionals.

The federal government now has a single gradeless structure called the Senior Executive Service (SES) that has replaced the supergrades GS 16 to 18.

Over half a million blue-collar workers are classified under the Federal Wage Schedule (FWS). FWS uses the whole job evaluation method; rates of pay for each grade are determined with respect to the going wages in 187 local wage areas. The GS moved from a national wage schedule to locality pay in 1995. (See discussion of locality pay for federal employees in chapters 5 and 10.)

Some federal employees have their pay determined by rank-in-person pay plans rather than rank-in-job plans. Rank-in-person plans include military personnel, foreign service personnel with the State Department, and physicians in the Medicine and Surgery Systems of the Department of Veterans Affairs. Rank-in-person plans relate specifically to the qualifications of the individual (what he or she knows and can do) rather than to the requirements of the job occupied by the individual (rank-in-job).

---

[5]See Paul A. Katz, "Specific Job Evaluation Systems: White-Collar Jobs in the Federal Civil Service," in *Handbook of Wage and Salary Administration,* 2nd ed., ed. Milton L. Rock (New York: McGraw-Hill, 1984), pp. 14-1–14-10.

A MARKET PRICING APPROACH

By the 1940s, some researchers and a number of compensation professionals studying the various kinds of job evaluation methods came to the conclusion that no matter what kind of evaluation methodology was used, organizations very quickly had to recognize the realities of the marketplace. These organizations had to offer competitive rates of pay if they wished to attract and retain competent employees. With this view, methods were developed to recognize market wage rates. There are two basic market pricing approaches for determining pay rates: (1) the pure market pricing method and (2) the market pricing guide line method.

Pure Market Pricing Method

The pure market pricing approach uses the labor market to set the worth of jobs. In this method, the organization first develops narratives that describe job activities and incumbent requirements. These narratives (ranging from a brief title to an extensive job description) are communicated (by phone, in person, through the mail) to other organizations having employees who perform similar work assignments in the same labor markets. These organizations are asked to match the jobs that are comparable to the ones in the narratives and provide the pay rates for these matching jobs. When using a pure market pricing method, an organization allows the market to dictate the pay of the job and, thus, its relative worth.

A number of important issues are involved in market pricing:

1. It is difficult to establish the true identity and meaning of a job through narratives that describe the job to representatives of other organizations without understanding the environmental context of the job in the organization that is requesting pay data.
2. Total reward and compensation practices vary dramatically among organizations; and although it is a significant compensation component, pay is still only one component. Using market pay data may lead as easily to overpayments as to underpayments. (External competitiveness replaces requirements for assessing internal equity.)
3. Pay survey data are susceptible to a wide variety of errors, from simple transcription errors to the matching of jobs that are supposed to be comparable but actually have different responsibilities and duties.
4. An organization may relate to more than one labor market in filling the various jobs of its workforce, and it must collect data from organizations in the appropriate markets. The broader the geographic area covered by a labor market, the more difficult it is to obtain a representative sample of pay data.
5. Many competitors in the labor market will not provide pay data, or they may provide it in a form that is of minimal value for decision-making purposes. There is always the possibility that the pay data provided are not accurate and do not validly describe the pay practices of the organization.
6. Pure market pricing does not provide a solid foundation for slotting jobs for which market data are unavailable. The slotting of nonmarket-priced jobs becomes an exercise that is both difficult to do and to explain (defend).

Of all job evaluation methodologies, pure market pricing is the least costly. By focusing on the market and emphasizing the need to recognize supply and demand, it is relatively easy to explain, and its basic simplicity makes it judicially defensible.

Market Pricing Guide Line Method

Recognizing the weaknesses in the pure market pricing approach, Richard C. Smyth and Matthew J. Murphy developed the guide line method for market pricing. Their method permits the influences of internal equity to interact with existing market rates when an evaluator is determining rates of pay for the jobs of an organization.

The Smyth-Murphy guide line method consists of the following key elements: (1) a guide line scale, (2) a job description containing scope data (data that identify and define job importance—the definition, accountability, and specification sections of a job description as presented in chapter 7 provide scope data), (3) market pricing, and (4) a horizontal guide line display.[6]

The Guide Line Scale

The *guide line scale* is a standard scale of salary ranges, including a series of salary grades and a minimum, midpoint, and maximum rate of pay for each. Smyth and Murphy contend that a 5 percent difference in midpoints between grades is ideal. This difference permits the development of a larger number of grades that in turn provide the compensation manager with the flexibility of moving a job up or down one or two grades without creating major feelings of inequity. It also permits greater opportunity for more precise distinctions between jobs. Depending on the variety and the number of jobs to be allocated within the pay structure, the number of grades could range from 30 to 70. Further discussion of midpoint-to-midpoint differences in design of pay structures is found in chapter 11.

Job Scope Data   Realistic job descriptions should include *scope data*. This kind of job description helps to identify benchmark or key jobs—those for which it is possible to determine what other marketplace competitive employers are paying for directly comparable jobs.

Market Pricing   The third step is to conduct a compensation survey to accomplish *market pricing*. Smyth and Murphy found that normally 40 to 60 percent of the jobs in an organization are benchmark jobs. By relating the midpoint of the pay grade that is closest to the average salary paid by other employers, each benchmark job can be assigned to a pay grade that relates the benchmark job to the amount other employers pay for a comparable job. At this point, the members of the organization who are responsible for evaluating the job can exercise their own judgment if there is a difference of opinion about the placement of the job on the guide line scale. When differences arise over the actual payment to be allocated to a benchmark job, evaluators normally are permitted to adjust that job up or down one pay grade. An adjustment of two grades is sometimes permitted. After the ranking has been completed, all

---

[6]Richard C. Smyth and Matthew J. Murphy, *The Guide Line Method of Job Evaluation* (Rhinebeck, NY: Smyth & Murphy Associates, Inc., n.d.).

nonbenchmark jobs are slotted among those already identified and located on the vertical guide line scale.

Horizontal Guide Line Displays The fourth step is to develop *horizontal guide line displays* that relate jobs in various departments or plants where each job evaluation group conducted the third step independently of the others. This process relates two or more vertical guide line displays, ensuring internal equity within the pay structure.

THE MATURITY CURVE METHOD

At approximately the same time pioneering professionals were designing and developing structured approaches to pay plans in industrial and government settings, comparable efforts were underway in the scientific world. Similar to the previously described market-pricing approaches, this 1920s invention, which became known as the Maturity Curve Method, makes direct use of market-acquired pay data.

In 1926, the American Physical Society analyzed the pay of physicists. Its study identified a close correlation between the salaries received by physicists and their ages. In the early 1930s, a salary administration plan was established for engineers in the Esso research laboratories in New Jersey that related their pay to years since receipt of their baccalaureate degrees.[7]

In the early 1950s, with an increase in the demand for engineers, management at Bell Laboratories in New Jersey recognized that they had to devise a simpler, less subjective method of salary administration. Their efforts led to the use of the Esso research laboratory-developed "experience curves." The experience curves evolved into the maturity curves, which quickly spread from Bell Laboratories to a number of engineering and scientific research organizations throughout the United States.

Maturity curves are used principally to establish rates of pay for scientists and engineers engaged in technical work at the professional level. Large research and development organizations hiring hundreds of scientists and engineers find it difficult to use detailed job analysis to determine the relative worth of jobs. In addition, because the professional has a dramatic influence over the job, the requirements of the job frequently take a secondary role to the knowledge, skill, and dedication of the incumbent. These pay determination processes can provide a solid foundation for establishing rates of pay for the continuing expansion of knowledge-based jobs into the twenty-first century.

The maturity curves, as developed at the Bell Laboratories (now part of Lucent Technologies), use number of years of applicable experience since receiving the BS degree as the *x*-axis dimension and *rates of pay (dollars)* as the *y*-axis dimension. The theory behind the use of the *number of years since degree* factor is that professional employees normally must have certain qualifications before they are hired and a certain amount of experience before they become proficient in their professions. Thus, maturity best reflects the market worth of these points.

With the maturity curve method, a series of curves is developed to provide differing levels of worth or value for individuals with the same years since receiving their degree. Each curve provides a value or worth scale for different years of experience. The

---

[7]Historical information on the development of the maturity curves was acquired through personal correspondence with Richard C. Fremon, retired salary administrator of Bell Laboratories. He was responsible for the implementation of maturity curves at the Bell Laboratories in the early 1950s.

distribution of rates of pay within any one interval originating on the horizontal axis (specific age or years since BS degree) would indicate a level of performance. A curve is formed by connecting the same distribution point in each interval. (Actually, the dimension *years since degree* is a proxy for the compensable factor experience, or knowledge, or skill, or responsibility, depending on the specific definition of the compensable factor. See discussion of compensable factors in the next section.)

Maturity curves frequently resemble learning curves in that in the early years the curve rises rapidly; then it flattens out and may even bend slightly downward in its latter stages. This movement indicates the obsolescence of scientific and engineering knowledge acquired during the bachelor's program and the need for continuing education. This drop may also be interpreted to mean that engineers and scientists who have spent 20 to 25 years or more in their field receive reductions in pay. The decline in pay almost never occurs for any particular individual. A better answer for this downward bend may be that the higher-paid engineers and scientists in that particular time measurement have moved out of the field (into private consulting or a management job), and the group whose pay is being identified in the later stages of the curve is different from the one in the earlier stage. In fact, some firms "ventilate" their series of curves, pulling the curves apart and making it impossible for any curve to actually show a decline in pay at any time. A maturity curve is a snapshot of the marketplace at a fixed time; it does not predict a pay path for any one individual. An additional discussion and models of maturity curves appear in chapter 18.

THE DEVELOPMENT AND USE OF COMPENSABLE FACTORS

By the 1920s, it became evident that the occupation and classification approaches developed by Griffenhagen and Baruch were inadequate to satisfy the continuing demands for more precise methods of differentiating pay in many private-sector organizations. A measurement methodology—intelligence tests—provided seeds for thought. World War I had proven that selection devices using some form of intelligence testing could be useful in measuring the aptitude of recruits and placing them in the most suitable jobs for a rapidly expanding military. Recognizing what had been learned in the development of constructs for measuring individual aptitudes provided an excellent foundation for developing well-defined criteria for measuring job differences that could then be used to determine differences in pay for different kinds of jobs. Pioneers responsible for relating the concept of constructs as used in measuring intelligence to the development of constructs used for measuring and defining job differences and job worth were Eugene J. Benge,[8] Merrill Lott,[9] A. W. Bass, Jr.,[10] and Edward N. Hay.[11] Constructs used to measure job differences and job worth have been given the title *compensable factors*—factors used to determine differences in job rates of pay.

---

[8]Benge, *Job Evaluation and Merit Rating.*
[9]Merrill R. Lott, *Wage Scales and Job Evaluation: Scientific Determination of Wage Rates on the Basis of Services Rendered* (New York: Ronald Press, 1926), pp. 46–59.
[10]A. W. Bass, Jr., "Evaluating Shop Jobs by the Point System," *The Iron Age,* September 10, 1936, pp. 42–44, 47, 123.
[11]Edward N. Hay, "Characteristics of Factor Comparison Job Evaluation," *Personnel,* May 1946, pp. 370–375.

Compensable Factors—A Definition

Compensable factors are paid-for, measurable qualities, features, requirements, or constructs that are common to many different kinds of jobs. Because these factors normally do not represent identifiable job activities, specific observable behaviors, or measurable outputs, they are synthetic in design. *Synthetic,* in this context, means that these factors are a composition or combination of qualities, features, or requirements of a job that, taken together, form a coherent whole. This coherent whole is a complete or almost complete description of the factors that identify the reasons for and determine the amount of money to be paid to an incumbent to perform a specific job. These factors are qualities intrinsic to the job and must be addressed in an acceptable manner if the job is to be performed satisfactorily. In addition to being quantifiable, compensable factors should be relatively easy to describe and document, and those involved in using compensable factors to measure job worth should consistently arrive at similar results.

In the 1920s, Benge identified five compensable factors—mental requirements, skill requirements, physical requirements, responsibility, and working conditions—as the factors most often used for developing base wage differences. At this same time, Lott proposed the use of 15 factors, and Bass contended that only three—skill, responsibility, and working conditions—were necessary. Hay later countered with know-how, mental activity, and accountability. The factors developed by these pioneers have become known as *universal compensable factors*—universal because they can be used to measure differences among a wide variety of jobs. From these efforts and those of other early compensation specialists, representatives of three major electrical equipment manufacturers—Western Electric, General Electric, and Westinghouse—developed a job evaluation plan for their own use and for the use of members of their trade association, the National Electrical Manufacturers Association (NEMA). This plan used four *universal compensable factors—skill, effort, responsibility,* and *job conditions.* In the late 1930s, the National Metal Trades Association, now known as NMTA Associates, accepted the NEMA plan for use by its members. This plan, with minor modifications, is still one of the most commonly used job evaluation methods and is probably responsible for more spinoffs than any other plan.[12]

Possibly the most significant use of universal factors developed with the Equal Pay Act of 1963 (EPA), which identifies four tests for measuring substantially equal work, the performance of which requires *equal skill, equal effort,* and *equal responsibility* when performed under *similar working conditions.* With the enactment of this law, it has become increasingly important for an organization to develop and use pay practices that can be not only substantiated and justified to its workforce but also defended in court.

In many ways, arguments and discussions over the identification and acceptance of universal compensable factors came to an end with the passage of the EPA. The universal compensable factors of *skill, effort, responsibility,* and *working conditions* have the federal government's stamp of approval. However, a major problem continues to

---

[12]American Association of Industrial Management, *Job Rating Manual (Shop)* (Melrose Park, PA: AAIM, 1969).

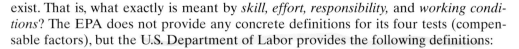

exist. That is, what exactly is meant by *skill, effort, responsibility,* and *working conditions*? The EPA does not provide any concrete definitions for its four tests (compensable factors), but the U.S. Department of Labor provides the following definitions:

> **Skill:** The experience, training, education, and ability required to perform a job under consideration—not with the skills an employee may possess.

> **Effort:** The measurement of the physical or mental exertion needed for performance of a job.

> **Responsibility:** The extent to which an employer depends on the employee to perform the job as expected, with emphasis on the importance of job obligation.

> **Working conditions:** The physical surroundings and hazards of a job, including dimensions such as inside versus outside work, excessive heat or cold, fumes and other factors relating to poor ventilation.

The Abstract Nature of a Universal Compensable Factor

If these four compensable factors are to be the universal constructs for determining job worth or predicting rates of pay, they must be abstract or general. The broader the job universe covered by a compensable factor, the more abstract it must be. The more abstract the factor, the more difficult it is to describe it with words and terms that provide similar meaning to those having different vested interests in job evaluation. (Vested interests result in differences in perception that in turn result in differences in interpretation. The necessity for using abstract terms only aggravates this critical situation.)

Universal factors must cover all common job elements. It is essential that the universal factors for any job evaluation plan do not omit any job elements. Failure to cover certain job elements could lead to the underevaluation of certain jobs. Since the introduction of compensable factor-based job evaluation methods, much controversy has been directed toward the suitability and validity of compensable factors. Do these factors truly describe job worth? Are job evaluation plans using compensable factors guilty of *contamination* (containing factors that do not provide a universally appropriate worth to measured jobs), *deficiencies* (failures to include factors that should be recognized when measuring job worth), and *distortion* (inadequate weighting of compensable factors or the levels or degrees used for further describing a factor)? The development and description of compensable factors is basically an artistic endeavor. It does require the use of experts who understand world of work requirements and who are able to formulate their ideas into logical, rational, and orderly processes. Job evaluation then requires people who have an open mind who wish to perform in a knowledgeable and fair manner the analysis and evaluation of jobs.

Over the years, various terms have been used to identify similar if not identical universal compensable factors. Table 8–4 lists commonly used universal compensable factors.

Skill

Skill, mental and skill requirements, knowledge, know-how, or whatever term(s) a particular system uses, relate to the same universal factor. The following definitions for this

TABLE 8–4 Groups of Commonly Used Universal Factors

Bass	Benge	NEMA-NMTA	FES[a]	Hay and Purves	Equal Pay Act
Skill	Mental requirements	Skill	Knowledge required by the position	Know-how	Skill
Responsibility	Skill requirements	Effort	Supervisory controls	Problem solving	Effort
Working conditions	Physical requirements	Responsibility	Guidelines	Accountability	Responsibility
	Responsibility	Job conditions	Complexity		Working conditions
	Working conditions		Scope and effect		
			Personal contacts		
			Purpose of contacts		
			Physical demands		
			Work environment		

[a] FES—Factor Evaluation System developed by the U.S. government in the mid-1970s.

universal factor as listed in Table 8–4 provide some idea of the semantic or definitional problem.

Skill (Bass): The knowledge of a subject combined with mastery of its techniques. Such skill, however, must presuppose a certain inherent intelligence.

Mental requirements (Benge): Either the possession of and/or the active application of inherent mental traits, plus acquired general education and/or acquired specialized knowledge.

Skill (Benge): Acquired facility in muscular coordination and/or acquired specific job knowledge (experience).

Skill (NMTA-AAIM): Defined only by listing its subfactors: *education, experience, initiative,* and *ingenuity.*

Knowledge (FES): The nature and the extent of information or facts that the worker must understand to do acceptable work and the nature and the extent of the skills needed to apply these knowledges.

Know-how (Hay and Purves): Includes every kind of knowledge or skill required for satisfactory performance of the job. Specifically, it includes every skill gained through experience and all kinds of required education or special training.

Working Conditions

An entirely different set of issues relates to the universal factor *working conditions* (job conditions, work environment, etc.). This factor is primarily context based—it covers the situations or conditions within which the job must be performed. The knowledge, skill, responsibility, mental effort, complexity, and guide lines factors are content based; the performance of job duties in a proficient manner requires an incumbent to have specific levels of knowledge and skill, or intelligence. In the blue-collar industrial (manufacturing) world, where a significant portion of currently used job evaluation technologies evolved, the physical demands placed on a worker and the environmental situation—extreme heat, cold, and dampness, or working in locations where accidents could lead to severe disabilities, even death—required recognition in determining the worth of a job, especially if the worth value led to the assignment of a rate of pay.

By the 1970s, another workplace context issue—stress—emerged. Stress had always existed but had seldom been directly recognized in the pay determination process. In the commonly recognized working conditions factor, it is relatively easy to observe and measure temperatures different from the normal or expected. Dangerous working conditions such as moving machinery, extreme heights and depths, and working in a mine or with nuclear radiation are relatively easy to describe and, at times, readily measurable. Stress, on the other hand, frequently has an individual or highly personalized relationship. Confusion and noise that to one individual are stressful could be energizing and enjoyable to another. A leisurely pace of work could be stressful to one person and relaxing to another. Working with "people" problems could be satisfying to one individual but cause migraine headaches in another. In a knowledge-oriented service economy the issue of stress will become an increasingly critical problem facing human resources management, including those involved in establishing job rates of pay.

Premium Pay in Lieu of Working Conditions

Because the job context issue is related to the working conditions factor, many organizations have not included such a factor when evaluating their jobs. Even when this kind of a factor is used, it frequently receives such a low weight that it has little influence on the pay of an employee. A possible better answer to the working conditions problem may be through the use of premium pay for those working under dangerous and distressing (D&D) conditions. Hay Management Consultants provides an Additional Compensable Elements (ACEs) analysis form (see Table 8–5) to assist clients in addressing working conditions issues.

After the organization identifies and defines what it considers to be D&D conditions, it can then assign a premium to anyone involved in the situation. The premium could be (1) a percentage of the employee's base rate of pay, (2) a flat amount provided to anyone who must perform assignments under D&D conditions, or (3) it could vary according to the percentage of time an individual works under those conditions. If the premium varies according to a percentage of involved time factor, it can relate to a *same* rate for all involved employees or differ according to some fixed base—like a percentage of the employee's base rate of pay.

When a D&D premium recognizes the amount of time a person is involved under such conditions, it could use the following formulas: Those working more than 75 percent of the time will receive 100 percent of their earned premium; from 25 to 75 percent, 50 percent; less than 25 percent, none. Such programs would be similar to the hazardous duty pay used by the military. The job analysis should provide enough data to identify the jobs that must be performed under D&D conditions.

Definitions—From the Abstract to the Specific

Because most compensable factor job evaluation methods are designed to cover many different kinds and levels of jobs, the factor description and classification scheme normally consists of two or more further redefinitions of the primary or universal

TABLE 8-5 Additional Compensable Elements

HayGroup

Additional Compensable Elements

DEFINITIONS: Relatively enduring characteristics of jobs which may justify differential compensation. ACES usually derive from the physical, temporal or perceptual conditions under which work must be done (context). ACES do not represent reactions to individual performance variation within the same job, but are measured as the job is expected to be performed by a qualified incumbent. It is assumed that all appropriate action necessary to eliminate or minimize undesirable conditions has been taken: what remains is unavoidable.

☐ **ELEMENTS OR CONDITIONS:** May be common to many organizations or may reflect unusual characteristics of the local client organization. The most commonly measured elements include the following, but others may be addressed to reflect local conditions. Always relevant for each element are variables of intensity, duration and frequency. Common elements include: **Physical Effort, Environment, Hazards, Sensory Attention.**

☐ **MEASUREMENT:** All scales are the same length and measure the range from none to extreme of the element. Each element scale may be weighted differently. The sum total of all scales constitutes 100% of elements measured. The client should determine scale weighting in the space provided below each scale.

PHYSICAL EFFORT			ENVIRONMENT			HAZARDS			SENSORY ATTENTION			OTHER		
Occasional, intermittent or constant handling of light, medium or heavy weight materials in normal to difficult work positions or unusual circumstances which results in physical exertion.			Occasional, intermittent or constant exposure to objectionable or noxious conditions such as dirt, dust, fumes/gases, extreme temperatures or wide fluctuations in temperature, moisture, odors, noise which results in physical discomfort.			Occasional, intermittent or constant exposure to mechanical, electrical, chemical, biological, or physical factors which involve risks of accident, personal injury, health impairment or death.			Occasional, intermittent or constant requirements for concentrated levels of sensory attention, including seeing, hearing, smelling, tasting, touching which may vary in intensity, duration or frequency.			**Definition**		
A. Very Light/Minimal Physical effort normally found in clerical work. Although largely sedentary, work requires lifting and carrying small objects and tools. Occasional walking or standing.	0 0 1		**A. Good/Minimal** Regular exposure to favorable conditions such as those found in a normal office setting.	0 0 1		**A. Safe/Minimal** General office or equivalent conditions result in little or no exposure to injury or accident.	0 0 1		**A. Minimal** Normal levels of sensory attention, with only occasional requirements for concentration or focused attention.	0 0 1		**A. Minimal**	0 0 1	
B. Light/Moderate Frequent handling of light objects/materials and use of light hand tools. Standing and walking most of the time and/or need to perform work with hands or arms in largely the same position.	2 3 4		**B. Fair/Moderate** Occasional exposure to objectionable conditions or variations such as those found in variable weather conditions or light industrial settings.	2 3 4		**B. Marginal/Moderate** Occasional exposure to hazards or risk of injury which are generally protected against or predictable.	2 3 4		**3. Moderate** Intermittent periods of concentration and focused attention of low intensity and short duration.	2 3 4		**B. Moderate**	2 3 4	
C. Moderate/Considerable Continuous handling of light or medium weight objects/materials and use of medium weight tools. Climbing and working from ladders or while in awkward positions.	5 6 7		**C. Unfavorable/Considerable** Regular exposure to unfavorable conditions such as all weather conditions, confined, noisy, or dirty locations.	5 6 7		**C. Dangerous/Considerable** Regular exposure to conditions which are unpredictable/uncertain and which result in risk of personal injury.	5 6 7		**C. Considerable** Regular periods of concentration and focused sensory attention of medium intensity and longer duration.	5 6 7		**C. Considerable**	5 6 7	
D. Strenuous/Extreme Continuous handling of heavy objects and materials. May involve use of heavy tools, or require strenuous application, in awkward positions.	8 9 10		**D. Disagreeable/Extreme** Continuous exposure to very disagreeable surroundings such as those found in extreme weather conditions, very confined, noisy, or dirty settings.	8 9 10		**D. Hazardous/Extreme** Continuous exposure to life threatening conditions or accidents which are difficult to identify or protect against.	8 9 10		**B. Extreme** Continuous concentration and focused sensory attention of high intensity, and long duration.	8 9 10		**D. Extreme**	8 9 10	

PHYSICAL EFFORT = _____ ENVIRONMENT = _____ HAZARDS = _____ SENSORY ATTENTION = _____ OTHER = _____

ACES, WEIGHT (TOTAL = 100%)

compensable factor. This redefinition-classification process moves from the general or most abstract to the specific.

To facilitate the use of compensable factors within a job evaluation method, it is common practice to classify the factors into three major categories: (1) universal factors, (2) subfactors, and (3) degrees or levels.

Universal compensable factors are the general, relatively abstract, and complex qualities and features that relate to all kinds of jobs. To make these abstract universal factors easier to understand relative to the kinds of work employees do while performing their job assignments, a subset of factors is used to further describe each universal factor. These are frequently called *subfactors*. Subfactors are statements that define the specific attributes of a particular job more precisely. (Many compensable factor job evaluation methods, however, do not use subfactors.) The second subset of a factor definition involves the development of *degrees* or *levels*. These degrees or levels provide a yardstick, or measurement scale, that assists in identifying the specific amount of the factor required in the performance of the job.

Subfactors

Although there are at least four widely accepted and used universal compensable factors, there are hundreds of subfactors that provide for more precise measurement of job differences. By the early 1950s, Richard H. Leukart and Jay L. Otis had identified over 100 subfactors for the four universal factors (skill, effort, responsibility, and working conditions) that could be used to evaluate factory and clerical jobs.[13]

Whether or not a hundred or more subfactors are necessary to measure job differences in the service world of knowledge-directed jobs, it is necessary to make certain that the subfactors relate to the kinds of work performed in the organization. In this manner, managers, workers, even lawyers and judges will be able to recognize a relationship between the compensable factors and the operations of the organization. For example, the subfactors under the universal factor *working conditions* do not always directly or adequately relate to the growing problem of psychological stress in today's world, where the computer influences the lives of so many workers and requires the use of extensive knowledge and skills with extremely short response times and minimal opportunity for periods of relaxation. From a definitional perspective, each organization that uses compensable factors to evaluate jobs must provide its own operational definition for the factors it uses.

It must be recognized that the major inputs to the development of compensable factors came from industrial settings. Today, factory production, construction, and other physical jobs provide employment for less than 30 percent of the workforce. Most workers today are processing data and transforming them into decision-making information. This means that far better efforts must be made in the identification and description of the more specific, job-related subfactors. Even with the abstract universal compensable factors, use and implementation problems exist. Table 8–6 provides the narratives that describe the subfactors within the universal compensable factor *knowledge–skill–know-how* of four different job evaluation methods. Because subjectivity and relativity issues

---

[13]Jay L. Otis and Richard H. Leukart, *Job Evaluation: A Basis for Sound Wage Administration,* 2nd ed. (Englewood Cliffs, NJ: Prentice-Hall, 1954).

TABLE 8–6 Factor and Subfactor Definitions

Skill (Bass) Subfactors described through the use of the following terms:

1. Intelligence or mental requirements
2. Knowledge required
3. Motor or manual skill
4. Learning time

Skill (NMTA-AAIM)

1. *Education.* The basic trades training of knowledge or "scholastic contact" essential as background or training preliminary to learning the job duties. The job knowledge or background may have been acquired either by formal education or by training on jobs of lesser degree or by any combination of these approaches.
2. *Experience.* The time it would take a "normal" person working under "normal" supervision to learn to apply the assigned education effectively in the performance of the job, assuming that each element was supplied about as rapidly as the individual could absorb it.
3. *Initiative and ingenuity.* The independent action, the use of judgment, the making of decisions, and the amount of resourcefulness and planning the job requires as determined by the complexity of duties performed.

Know-how (Hay-Purves)

1. *Practical procedures, specialized knowledge, and scientific disciplines.* Practical specialized, technical, professional, or administrative knowledge.
2. *Managerial.* Human skills in evaluating, motivating, organizing, or developing people, singly or in groups.
3. *Human relations.* Degree of human relations.

Knowledge Required by the Position (Factor Evaluation System)

Nature and extent of information or facts that the workers must understand to do acceptable work (steps, procedures, practices, rules, policies, theories, principles, and concepts) and the nature and the extent of the skills needed to apply these types of knowledges. To be used as a basis for selecting a level under this factor, a given type of knowledge must be required and applied.

---

are important in compensation management, concerned parties must have a similar and clear understanding of the issues, and this requires careful use of words and terms. Minimizing and eliminating verbal misunderstandings are a vital part of the job of any compensation specialist.

Although there can be a problem of semantics in any area that must be defined, the major problem related to subfactors is not one of definition but of overlap. Just as failure to identify and define a universal factor can lead to serious *underevaluation,* the use of more than one factor to identify identical or even fairly similar elements of a job can lead to *overevaluation.* It is easy for the compensation manager to fall into the overlap or overevaluation trap.

The first step in eliminating the danger of overlap is to keep the universal factors fundamental and to be as general as possible in defining them. Then, as the subfactors develop that further define the universal factors, it is important to be as precise as possible. Finally, after identifying all subfactors, each one must be reviewed with all the others (including those that identify other universal factors) to be sure they are not stating the same thing.

Organization-Specific Factors

With the increasing popularity and use of teams within organizations, a major addition to job evaluation technology has been the development of skill- and knowledge-based pay plans. These job evaluation plans focus on the work-related skill and knowledge possessed by the individual and not necessarily on the skill and knowledge required of the work performed at a specific point in time. Chapter 12 includes an in-depth discussion of skill- and knowledge-based plans. The major difference between the team-based pay (job evaluation) plans now being designed and used in some organizations in the United States and the more traditional compensable factor-based job evaluation plans is that these newly designed plans are more organization specific, whereas the plans discussed in this chapter are universal in nature and designed for a wide variety of organizations.

Degrees (Levels)

The final stage in the process for determining job differences occurs with the development of degrees or levels. The abstract universal compensable factors provided a setting for the more precise subfactors. With the degrees attached to each subfactor, quantitative differences can be developed for different levels of the subfactor. Thus, the degrees provide a measurement scale for rating each subfactor (or universal factor when no subfactors are used). Through the use of degrees, it is possible to develop an orderly approach for measuring each job relative to every other job in the organization. The grouping of the specific degrees from the available subfactors furnishes a unique worth profile for each job.

For this reason, degrees are frequently called *profile statements.* Because they are unique, it may be necessary to use more than one word or even a small group of words to define them. A pragmatic approach available to the specialist responsible for defining degrees consists of describing the simplest requirement or the minimum acceptable standard for that factor, moving to the most complex or highest possible requirement, and then, in succeeding stages, working up and down the ladder of importance. (The discussion of rating scale development later in this chapter describes in greater detail how to establish a set of degrees or profile statements.)

At the definition stage, such nebulous modifying terms as *minimal, slight, moderate, average, considerable, broad,* or *extensive* often become part of the profile statement and part of the semantics problem. These terms are most valuable in developing a series of profile statements that provide an orderly scale of importance or levels of magnitude. To overcome some of the semantic or definitional problems, however, it is important to clarify these nebulous modifiers by combining them with concrete examples of activities, specific operations, compensable qualities or features, or behavioral terms applicable to the activities being performed in the jobs. Joining the commonly used modifier with a specific activity phrase promotes common understanding and blocks wide and varied interpretation. For example, instead of saying, "Job requires considerable physical demands," say, "Job requires considerable stooping, bending, lifting, and walking in filling order trays."

When degrees or levels are used to define a subfactor, the two major areas to consider are (1) the number of degrees necessary and (2) the methods necessary to describe differences adequately. The series of degrees or profile statements must develop an observable scale of differences or levels of magnitude that define the subfactor in terms of increasing importance, complexity, or difficulty. It is important that there be no more degrees, or profile statements, than absolutely necessary, but enough should be used to describe adequately the complete range of differences.

Weighting Compensable Factors

Sooner or later anyone involved in the evaluation process must come to grips with its primary purpose: the establishment of an internally equitable ordering of all jobs. It is for this reason that the entire compensable factor process has been described in such detail. By identifying and defining each factor, it is easier to compare each one relative to all the others, and easier to rank and rate each job. When reviewing the objectives of the organization, it may be that some factors are more important than others. When this occurs, weighting each factor by its importance in the scheme of organizational philosophy, policy, and objectives is necessary. The weighting or comparison process must be as exact as possible, even though it consists of subjective judgments made by experts in the field.

A number of extremely sophisticated statistical procedures are available for analyzing large numbers of individual decisions and for identifying differences in the value or in the weights of compensable factors. The weighting of the nine FES factors required the use of more than 60 rater panels involving hundreds of job specialists. These rater panels rank-ordered hundreds of jobs relative to the FES compensable factors. The rank-order data were transformed into arc sine scale values, which eventually were transformed into point scores for each factor. Today, a number of job evaluation plans use multiple linear regression to establish weights for their compensable factors.

The Normalizing Procedure   A mathematical procedure called *normalizing* provides a simple approach to weighting a set of compensable factors. In this approach, a group of job experts or a job evaluation committee first reviews the compensable factors and then establishes a rank order for the factors. (A paired-comparison procedure is extremely useful for this purpose.)

After the factors are ranked, the highest-rated factor is assigned a value of 100 percent. Then a value is assigned the next highest factor as a percentage of its importance as compared to the 100 percent factor. This relative comparison process is repeated for each remaining factor. In this procedure, each factor is always compared with the highest-rated factor.

For example, Olympia Service Center rank-ordered the four compensable factors in its job evaluation plan as shown in Table 8–7. In the next step, all values in column 2 are added; they total 290. Then the values in column 2 are divided by the total of column 2. This value is the normalized weight of each factor. The same procedure can be used for weighting the subfactors within a factor.

Determining the Number of Points for the Method   A point-factor job evaluation method may have a unique total number of points assigned to each factor and to each degree or level of a factor. The total number of points used in a particular method is more or less a matter of individual choice. For example, the FES method has 4,480

TABLE 8–7 The Normalizing Process

Column 1	Column 2		Column 3
Order of Ranking	*Percentage of Highest-Rated Factor*		*Weight of Each Factor*
(1) Knowledge and its application	100	$\dfrac{100}{290} =$	34.5
(2) Problem solving	70	$\dfrac{70}{290} =$	24.1
(3) Communication	60	$\dfrac{60}{290} =$	20.7
(4) Work environment	$\dfrac{60}{290}$	$\dfrac{60}{290} =$	$\dfrac{20.7}{100.0}$

points; the three basic factors in the Hay Associates method, successor to the Hay-Purves method, normally require the use of 6,480 points. The number of Hay points used in a particular application depends on the kind, size, and character of the organization. The NMTA Associates plan, successor to the NEMA-NMTA plan, has 825 points. A job evaluation plan developed by the Glass Container Manufacturers Institute in negotiation with the Glass Bottle Blowers Association (a union) has a maximum total of 24.2 points. The method selected must provide a sufficient number of points so that a significant difference in points can be awarded to jobs that are of different worth and so that the points can then be related to a money value that accurately indicates the difference in worth of the jobs of the organization.

One pragmatic approach available for determining the number of points is to inspect the range of pay from the lowest to the highest. If the base salary of all members is to be determined through the use of a single scale or pay structure and a single job evaluation plan, a sufficient number of points to differentiate among all jobs from the lowest to the highest must be designed into the system. If there is more than one scale or structure—for example, one for exempt (managerial, administrative, and professional) employees and one for nonexempt (operative) employees—then this problem becomes less important.

For example, if an organization decided to use one method to evaluate all its jobs, the following process would be helpful in determining the number of points required. The president currently receives an annual salary of $210,000, and the lowest-paid workers earn $6.75 an hour, or $14,040 based on a 40-hour, 52-week work year. A rough measure of the total points necessary is obtained by dividing the highest salary by the lowest. In this case, $210,000/$14,040 = 15. There must be a sufficient point spread within the degrees to permit the most important job to receive an evaluation of approximately 15 times greater than the least important job. This is true only if all jobs are related on a single linear pay scale.

When using a linear relationship and a single pay scale and when the difference in pay or expected pay between the highest and lowest jobs is a factor of 15, the point spread from the minimum to the maximum among the degrees should be at least a factor of between 18 to 20. The reason for this is that the very lowest job may not receive the minimum rating in every factor. It is also unlikely that the highest-paid job would receive the maximum number of degree points for every rating factor.

When a point-factor job evaluation method is used, the number of points assigned to the factor indicate the weight of the factor. In turn, when degrees to profile the factor or subfactor are developed, the number of points assigned to the factor is also the number of points assigned to the highest degree of the factor. In most cases, the lowest degree is assigned a certain number of points, although in some cases, the lowest degree has no points.

In FES, the maximum total number of points assignable to a job is 4,480, whereas the minimum total number of points assignable to a job is 190. The difference is a factor of 4,480/190 = 23+. The difference in pay earned in 1999 by the lowest-paid GS-1 and the highest-paid GS-15 was

$$\frac{\$97,201}{\$13,362} = 7.3$$

or approximately a factor of 7. The point spread developed within FES should be more than sufficient to differentiate jobs in the 15 GS pay grades.

Observable/Perceptible Differences   When developing factor weights and measurement scales for determining job point-score differences, the final result is an established hierarchy of jobs with different rates or ranges of pay for each job. Because pay is an extremely important concern to most employees, many will review their rates of pay with others doing similar work, with coworkers, even with friends and associates. And because pay has both absolute (the purchasing value of pay received) and relative (comparison with others) values, the development of weights and scale values must recognize perceptual (relative) considerations. Some of the most interesting work into observable or perceptible differences was conducted in the early nineteenth century by Ernst H. Weber (1795–1878).[14] His efforts became known as Weber's Law, which states: "The increase of stimulus necessary to produce an increase of sensation in any sense is not an absolute quantity but depends on the proportion which the increase bears to the immediate preceding stimulus."

More simply stated, the small perceptible difference in two objects is not absolutely the same, but it remains relatively the same. That is, it remains the same fraction (percentage) of the preceding stimulus. For example, if one can distinguish between 16 and 17 ounces, one should be able to distinguish between 32 and 34 ounces but not necessarily between 32 and 33.

$$\frac{17-16}{16} = \frac{1}{16} = C_1 \qquad \frac{34-32}{32} = \frac{2}{32} = C_1 \qquad \frac{33-32}{32} = \frac{1}{32} \neq C_1$$

The addition in only the first two cases is one-sixteenth of the preceding stimulus.

In the 1940s, Edward N. Hay tested Weber's Law in a series of studies of just observable differences and noted that a 15 percent or approximately one-seventh difference in the importance of one level of a factor as compared with the level of the

---

[14]*Encyclopaedia Britannica,* Micropaedia, vol. 10, 15th ed. (Chicago: Encyclopaedia Britannica, 1974), p. 593.

preceding factor was discernible by trained raters at least 75 percent of the time.[15] This 15 percent difference provided a valuable criterion, index, or rule of thumb for a variety of uses when developing a scale or a grouping in which just observable magnitudes of difference are an important issue. In review, it appears that there should be at least a 15 percent difference between any two levels of a factor in the compensation area before the recognition value is significant.

When the 15 percent index is used, it appears that 7 degrees should be adequate for defining the magnitudes of difference of a subfactor. Although in the study of degrees the number 7 may not be an absolute, it can probably be used as a good midpoint, with a range of 5 to 9 degrees providing adequate descriptions for any subfactor. That is:

$$1/5 = 20\% \quad 1/7 = 14.3\% \quad 1/9 = 11.1\%$$

Because job evaluation involves concept identification, research into specific spans of attention and short-term memory may also be of value when attempting to solve magnitudes of difference problems. Possibly some of the most interesting research in this area has been done by George A. Miller of Harvard.[16] Miller investigated how individuals learn to identify specific dimensions and to select the correct dimension when facing a specific stimulus. Many of the decisions job evaluation personnel must make relate to their involvement in complex situations in which they must make observations within a short time. To be effective under such conditions, these individuals must learn to classify stimuli. Most people can learn to respond almost perfectly to a reasonable number of previously learned and classified stimuli. In his research, Miller recognized that there are severe limits to the capacity of short-term memory. He concluded that short-term memory is used primarily for identifying lists of unconnected events. (In the world of the job evaluator, these unconnected events are the activities—job requirements—related to the establishment of job worth.) Short-term memory not only uses few items for measurement but also operates on a "push-down" principle for retrieving information stored in the brain (last-in, first-out is an example of the push-down principle).

Miller theorized that most people can work concurrently with five to nine items of information (e.g., criteria, dimensions, factors, variables) when making decisions. The more different items with which an individual works concurrently and the more input information required for analysis and discrimination purposes, the greater the likelihood of errors. Over the years, Miller and other researchers have noted that individual short-term perceptual and memory abilities normally permit discrimination of about seven variables. The great majority of people can work with five variables. Using less than five may unduly restrict an individual's ability to discriminate, and the result will not be as precise as it could be. On the other hand, few people can use more than nine variables. The writings of both Hay and Miller indicate that a fairly restricted number of distinctive job features or qualities should be used in the identification, the observation, and the measurement of job worth. The works of Weber, Hay, and Miller can be most useful and helpful in understanding the development of teams and team-based pay as discussed in chapter 12.

[15]Edward N. Hay, "The Application of Weber's Law to Job Evaluation Estimates," *Journal of Applied Psychology,* 34, 1950, pp. 102–104.
[16]George A. Miller, "The Magical Number Seven Plus or Minus Two: Some Limits on Our Capacity for Processing Information," *The Psychological Review,* March 1956, pp. 81–97.

When points are assigned to degrees, Weber's Law may be quite helpful. If it is felt that there is a just observable difference between each degree, the highest number of points for the factor can be assigned to the highest degree. Dividing this value by 1.15 (1 for the initial value and 0.15 for the Weber-Hay 15 percent difference) will give the next value of the next highest degree. Succeeding values should continue to be divided by 1.15 until a value is obtained for all degrees.

Because of the way a degree is described, it is sometimes possible to determine a just observable difference above and below a degree statement. In this case, each degree could have a +, 0, – score. If this were the case and the 15 percent difference approach were used, a score would be assigned to each step in the scoring process. A third approach would be to have a half step between each verbally identified degree (1, 1½, 2, 2½ . . .). This approach permits evaluators to make a selection midway between two identified and defined degrees.

WEIGHTING AND RATING OF COMPENSABLE FACTORS

The reason for the development of compensable factors is to be able to measure job differences. To facilitate the measurement process, pioneers in the development of compensable factors developed rating scales. Reviewing the work of Lott, Benge, the designers of the NEMA plan, and Hay and Purves will assist in acquiring an understanding of how these scales developed.

Lott's Point Method

Lott recognized that the 15 compensable factors he identified for measuring job differences were not of equal importance or value. To recognize differences in values among these factors, he first weighted each factor through the normalizing process. After determining the weights of each factor, he used benchmark jobs to establish a 10-point interval scale. The scale development process used the following five steps:[17]

Step 1. Identify and define the factors useful in describing the fundamental elements of the general nature of all jobs under study.

Step 2. Weight the factors and assign a specific value to each factor. (In the Lott method, the total value of all weighted factors equals 100 and the value of each of his 15 factors is some percentage of 100—again see normalizing approach to weighting.)

Step 3. Identify a sufficient number of benchmark jobs to cover the entire range of difficulty or importance of all factors.

Step 4. Using each factor, assign a value of from 1 to 10 to each benchmark job. The job demanding the greatest possible degree of a factor receives a 10 and the job demanding little or no amount of a factor receives a 1. Values between 1 and 10 are assigned to other jobs using the same procedure.

Step 5. Multiply weighted factor value (step 2) by the benchmark job value (step 4). This provides a weighted point score for each factor for each benchmark job.

---

[17]Lott, *Wage Scales and Job Evaluation.*

After using benchmark jobs to develop rating scales for all factors, all nonbenchmark jobs are rated factor by factor. The factor points assigned to the benchmark job that most closely compares with the nonbenchmark job are the points assigned to the nonbenchmark job for that factor. The total points assigned for the nonbenchmark job are the total points for all factors. Once again, the use of a paired-comparison procedure is invaluable.

Benge's Factor Comparison Method

Following closely in the footsteps of Lott, Eugene J. Benge and his associates developed the factor comparison method for the Philadelphia Rapid Transit Company in 1926. This method uses a series of rankings and slottings to determine both the relative value and absolute worth of a job.[18]

Instead of using a point scale like Lott's, Benge's plan develops a wage rate scale for each universal factor. After assigning a wage rate to each benchmark job, it is possible to develop a wage rate or monetary scale for each of Benge's five universal factors. By establishing a monetary scale for each universal factor, all other jobs in the organization can be evaluated. (This scaling method gave rise to the other name for this evaluation process—the weighted-in-money method.) Summing the monetary value of all factors for a particular job establishes its pay rate.

Benge's factor comparison method of job evaluation can be performed in eight steps:

1. Jobs to be evaluated are ranked. This step assists in developing a better understanding of the values and contributions of each job.
2. From information provided through a market survey, a going rate of pay is assigned to each benchmark job.
3. Using the five compensable factors identified by Benge (skill, mental demands, physical demands, responsibility, and working conditions), each rater privately ranks each benchmark job by each factor, with the lowest number—one—indicating the job receiving the highest level of value for that factor.
4. The job evaluation committee as a whole reviews ratings of each member and comes to a final, agreed-upon ranking. If members cannot agree to the ranking of a particular job—if consensus cannot be reached, it may be necessary to eliminate that job as a benchmark job.
5. Each committee member now assigns a monetary value to each factor with the sum of the monetary values for factors equal to the market or going rate of pay for the job.
6. In a step similar to step 4, the job evaluation committee members reach an agreement on the monetary value of each factor for each job. The final value is not a mathematically derived average value but rather a "meeting of the minds" average.
7. Using the money values for each factor, the committee develops a monetary scale for each factor. All of the remaining jobs of the organization are compared with the factor scale and, through a slotting process, assigned a specific value for each

---

[18]Benge, *Job Evaluation and Merit Rating.*

factor. The sum of the monetary values assigned to each job for all factors then becomes the pay for the job.

8. As a final check, the committee develops a final benchmark job ranking schedule that compares job ranking, money ranking, and monetary value by each factor for each benchmark job.

The greatest weakness in Benge's method is the difficulty in allocating a specific portion of a rate of pay for a job to each compensable factor. If this allocation process is in itself not difficult enough, changes in relative rates of pay among benchmark jobs may cause additional problems.

Over the 25 years following Benge's invention, a number of modified factor comparison plans were developed. To overcome the weakness inherent in using wage rates for benchmark jobs to establish measurement scales for each compensable factor, William D. Turner developed the "per cent method of job evaluation."[19] Instead of a scale of values based on the wages of benchmark jobs, Turner used percentages for measurement purposes. The per cent method starts in the same way as Benge's factor comparison. After ranking the recommended 12 benchmark jobs within the same five compensable factors identified by Benge, Turner used a number of mathematical procedures to convert two independent sets of judgments into two comparable sets of factor rating scales. Through the use of F values (expressed as percentages of factor column totals) and J values (ratings expressed as percentages of their job row totals), Turner described a process of determining relative factors within jobs that are also comparable between jobs.

Hay's Profile Method

Another major contributor to the factor comparison method was Edward N. Hay. In 1938, Hay used the factor comparison approach to determine the worth of managerial and professional jobs in a bank, The Pennsylvania Company. The method developed by Hay used three factors to evaluate job content: *skill, mental effort,* and *responsibility.* These factors were subsequently modified to Know-How (KH), Problem Solving (PS), and Accountability (AC).

The three Hay factors used no preestablished rating scales. Hay required evaluators to make a comparative measurement of the KH requirement in each job. He used his modification of Weber's Law to assign percentage differences for KH to each job. Through the use of Weber's Law, Hay developed a measurement scale of geometric step values that could be assigned to a hierarchy of KH ratings. This approach resulted in step values currently used in the Hay Guide Charts.

When comparing two jobs to determine differences in a compensable factor, Hay stated that if you cannot see any difference, there is none; they are, therefore, the same. If, after thorough study of the job, you *think* there is a just noticeable difference, there is a one-step or 15 percent difference. If, after considered study, there is clearly a difference—the difference is quite evident—there is a two-step or 33 percent difference (two 15 percent intervals). If the difference is noticeable without even having to study the job, the magnitude of difference is probably three steps (50 percent) or more. When

---

[19]William D. Turner, "The Per Cent Method of Job Evaluation," *Personnel,* May 1948, pp. 476–492, and "The Mathematical Basis of the Per Cent Method of Job Evaluation," *Personnel,* September 1948, pp. 154–160.

determinations must be made among jobs in which a magnitude of difference is greater than 50 percent, it is best to compare a chain of jobs in which the differences between any two jobs are not more than three steps. It is difficult to "sense" accurately differences of more than 50 percent. Using this method for establishing differences in KH requirements, Hay could (1) develop a hierarchical ranking of jobs by levels of KH and (2) assign a value to each level through the use of his Weber-based measurement scale.

Hay Guide Charts   More than 4,000 organizations throughout the world use the Guide Chart-Profile Method, which is commonly known as the Hay Plan. This method is popular for evaluating executive, managerial, and professional positions, but it is also widely used in evaluating nonexempt, clerical, blue-collar, and technician jobs. In recent years, Hay has modified its plan to accommodate customer demands.

In addition to the KH, PS, and AC Guide Charts (see chapter 9), Hay provides an ACEs chart (see Table 8–5) for an organization wishing to recognize working or other environmental conditions relating to job context. Hay recommends to its clients that job content measurement be treated separately from ACEs measurement and pay. The ACEs values should not be included in the total KH, PS, and AC point scores.

The Hay Guide Charts have both standardized and customized features. The geometric measurement scales use the same values with each step, reflecting the 15 percent (or one-step) perceptible difference in values developed by Hay. The customized portion of the Guide Charts relates to the number of rows and columns of each Guide Chart; that is, depending on the character and size of a client, the Know-How Guide Chart could include all or a limited number of the depth and breadth of Knowledge levels and the Managerial Know-How levels (see chapter 9). The Accountability Guide Chart can also be expanded or reduced, depending on the size and character of the client organization.

The Know-How (KH) Guide Chart includes three subfactors: the row elements that describe the depth and breadth of job knowledge required to perform job assignments. The management breadth column element describes the requirement for planning, organizing, review, and control to integrate diversified functional elements. Within each column element is the third know-how element—Human Relations Skill. Each of the three elements is defined in the upper left-hand column of the KH Guide Chart. The levels of the first two elements are defined in their respective rows and columns. The levels of the Human Relations Skills are defined at the bottom of the Guide Chart. Each level of each element has an alphanumeric header that is used to code a rating.

The second compensable factor, Problem Solving, includes two subfactors. The row element includes levels of the Thinking Environment, and the column element includes levels of the Thinking Challenge. The third factor, Accountability, also has three subfactors. The row element is Freedom to Act. The column element measures the magnitude of the impact of the job on end results. Inside the level of the Magnitude column element is the third element, Job Impact on End Results.

The NEMA Method

The NEMA method was a major breakthrough in the development of a rather simple and useful job evaluation method. The NEMA method used universal compensable factors, and each universal compensable factor had a set of subfactors. Each subfactor was then assigned a rating scale. Each interval in the rating scale was given a narrative descriptor to assist evaluators in making an appropriate inference from job requirements to the correct interval in the rating scale. As mentioned earlier in this chapter, the NEMA method gave birth to hundreds, if not thousands, of job evaluation plans based on the compensable factor-subfactor rating scale. Table 8–8 is an example of a typical NEMA plan containing the four universal compensable factors with their respective subfactors and assigned degrees.

Factor Evaluation System (FES)

In 1977, after more than five years of research that involved approximately 4,000 jobs, 26 federal agencies, and 256 field installations, the U.S. Civil Service Commission (CSC), now known as the Office of Personnel Management (OPM), developed a nine-factor job evaluation method known as the Factor Evaluation System (FES). This method has proven to be capable of accurately measuring the worth of more than 1 million nonsupervisory General Schedule (GS) positions. The FES differs from the previously developed point-factor methods such as those of the NMTA and the NEMA and their many offshoots in that it contains three stages of descriptive data, not simply a defined set of universal compensable factors, subfactors, and degrees. The three stages of FES are (1) primary standards, (2) factor-level descriptions for the series (occupational standards), and (3) benchmark jobs that cover the full range of pay for the jobs in each occupation or series.[20]

TABLE 8–8 A NEMA-Type Plan

Factors	First Degree	Second Degree	Third Degree	Fourth Degree	Fifth Degree
Skill					
1. Education	14	28	42	56	70
2. Experience	22	44	66	88	110
3. Initiative and Ingenuity	14	28	42	56	70
Effort					
4. Physical Demand	10	20	30	40	50
5. Mental or Visual Demand	5	10	15	20	25
Responsibility					
6. Equipment or Process	5	10	15	20	25
7. Material or Product	5	10	15	20	25
8. Safety of Others	5	10	15	20	25
9. Work of Others	5		15		25
Job Conditions					
10. Working Conditions	10	20	30	40	50
11. Unavoidable Hazards	5	10	15	20	25

---

[20]U.S. Civil Service Commission, *Instructions for the Factor Evaluation System* (Washington, DC: Government Printing Office, May 1977).

The primary standards are similar to many other compensable factor plans. Table 8–9 lists the nine FES compensable factors and their weights and levels.

After establishing the primary standards, the next step in the FES is to develop factor-level descriptions for the series. (This is the application of the primary standards to a specific occupation or to groups of closely related occupations.) By further defining the factors in terms of the work/job content of jobs in a specific occupation, it is easier to relate a specific level of a factor to a particular job. This, in turn, makes it easier to reach a consensus during the evaluation process.

Multiple Regression-Based Job Evaluation[21]

Although multiple regression has been used in the job evaluation process since the 1950s, the developers of PAQ recognized in the 1970s that, by combining certain items in their scored 194-item questionnaire with multiple regression, the PAQ could be used to predict rates of pay. By the 1980s a number of consulting firms were promoting their own particular method. Many of the methods included most if not all of the following 12 steps:

1. Identify and define set of generic (universal) compensable factors and subfactors that would be useful in determining job worth in a typical client organization.
2. Review client requirements. Present examples of compensable factors. Obtain client input as to acceptability of presented compensable factors. Identify compensable

TABLE 8–9 Factor Evaluation System Factors, Weights, and Levels

Factor	Points for Factor	Value of Factor as Percentage of Total (weight of factor)	Number of Levels	Points for Each Level
Knowledge required by the position	1,850	41.3%	9	50, 200, 350, 550, 750, 950, 1,250, 1,550, 1,850
Supervisory control	650	14.5%	5	25, 125, 275, 450, 650
Guidelines	650	14.5%	5	25, 125, 275, 450, 650
Complexity	450	10.0%	6	25, 75, 150, 225, 325, 450
Scope and effect	450	10.0%	6	25, 75, 150, 225, 325, 450
Personal contact	110	2.5%	4	10, 25, 60, 110
Purpose of contact	220	4.9%	4	20, 50, 120, 220
Physical demand	50	1.1%	3	5, 20, 50
Work environment	50	1.1%	3	5, 20, 50
Total	4,480	99.9%		

---

[21]Appendix 8B provides an in-depth discussion on how to perform a regression analysis. Courtesy of Theresa Mee, Compensation Consulting Division, Watson Wyatt Worldwide, Atlanta, GA.

factors not included in the generic listing required for determining worth of jobs in client organization.

3. Develop structured and scored questionnaire using rating scales (in this case, statements or items that request either a yes-no response or a specific selection among a choice of items) for each compensable factor or subfactor.

4. Review questionnaire with client for acceptability of all factors, subfactors, and rating scales.

5. Incumbents in selected benchmark jobs complete questionnaires.

6. Supervisors review incumbent responses for accuracy and completeness.

7. Incumbents' demographic data and responses to questionnaires entered into the computer.

8. Perform a multiple regression analysis of the data. The dependent variable data can be the pay grade for the job, midpoint rate of pay, or possibly the highest rate of pay for the job. The multiple linear regression model first requires the preparation of scatter diagrams for the paired observations of the dependent variable (pay grade) and each independent variable (compensable factor or subfactor). If the relationships prove to be curvilinear, it may be possible to transform the independent variable data to a linear form through the use of logarithms, or possibly by squaring the value or taking the square root of the value. If transformation to a linear relationship is not possible, the independent variable should be dropped from the model.

9. After ensuring the linearity of all independent variables, run the model to generate weights for each independent variable.

10. Review first "best fit" model with client. Check to see if incumbents who answered questionnaires provided a true sample of the universe of jobs in the organization. Also check to see if the variables included in the model are those that should be included. Check weights to see if they are appropriate. (Cross-validation can be used for determining the most appropriate factor weights.)

11. Make any identified changes and rerun the model to obtain appropriate weights. (This exercise will be repeated as many times as necessary until the consultant and client feel that a truly "best fit" model has been developed.)

12. Employees in nonbenchmark jobs complete questionnaires. Data entered into the computer and developed regression model predict value of dependent variable (i.e., midpoint rate of pay, pay grade, possibly highest rate of pay).

JOB EVALUATION AND COMPARABLE WORTH

In 1963, prior to the passage of the Equal Pay Act (EPA), representatives of Corning Glass, participating with other members of American industries, testified before the House and Senate subcommittees on the value of job evaluation. Industry feared that if the four standards of the EPA—skill, effort, responsibility, and working conditions—were not better defined, the secretary of labor would be cast in the position of second-guessing the validity of a company's evaluation system. They urged that the bill be amended to include an exception for job evaluation systems, or otherwise to incorporate the language of job evaluation into the bill, but not simply to use the standards without further amplification and definition.

At these hearings, the Corning representatives provided the following testimony on job evaluation:

1. Job evaluation is an accepted and tested method of attaining equity in a pay relationship.
2. A great part of industry is committed to job evaluation by past practice and by contractual agreement as the basis for wage administration.
3. "Skill" alone, as a criterion, fails to recognize other aspects of the job situation that affect job worth.[22]

This testimony was used a decade later by Corning in its role as defendant in the early and very important court case on the EPA—*Corning Glass Works* v. *Brennan.*

By the mid-1970s, proponents of comparable worth recognized that a potential tool for proving discrimination was job evaluation. One of the early proponents of comparable worth defined this issue as "the application of a single, bias-free point-factor job evaluation system within a given establishment, across job families, both to rank order jobs and to set salaries."[23] Recognizing the problems they could now have with EPA and Title VII, companies modified their approach to the acceptance of job evaluation. The Equal Employment Advisory Council (EEAC) commissioned a group of scholars to identify the inherent weaknesses and failures of job evaluation.[24]

The work of these scholars resulted in a book that discussed issues related to comparable worth and focused attention specifically on job evaluation. One of the authors, George Hildebrand, states that "no 'value-free' system of job evaluation has yet been shown to exist . . . comparable worth involves sheer rhetoric alone . . ."[25] Donald P. Schwab, a scholar specifically commissioned by the EEAC to review job evaluation, goes into significant detail in discussing the differences between the conventional description of job evaluation and what it actually accomplishes. He states that job evaluation does not arrange "jobs in a hierarchy determined by worth through job content. Specifically as practiced, job evaluation is used by organizations to establish wage rates for non-key jobs (where the market is difficult to assess) from variables (called compensable factors) that are related to key job wage rates (where market forces can be more readily determined)."[26] Schwab further states that "job evaluation identifies and differentially weights compensable factors to maximize the relationship between them and the wages for key jobs which are assumed to reflect the market. Thus, the actual criterion of job evaluation is not worth in a job content sense, but market wages."[27] A point emphasized by Schwab and other contributors to the book is that the "market" is a true source of pay data and that nothing should be done to circumvent or destroy the influence of the "market" on pay decisions. (See chapter 10 for discussion of market influences on pay-setting processes.)

---

[22]See First Session (1963) of the Senate and the House Hearings on Equal Pay Act of 1963.

[23]Helen Remick, "Major Issues in *a Priori* Applications," in *Comparable Worth and Wage Discrimination,* ed. Helen Remick (Philadelphia: Temple University Press, 1984), p. 99.

[24]E. Robert Livernash, ed., *Comparable Worth: Issues and Alternatives* (Washington, DC: Equal Employment Advisory Council, 1980).

[25]Ibid., p. 83.

[26]Ibid., pp. 62, 63.

[27]Ibid., p. 63.

Schwab further states, ". . . While the notion of comparable worth is consistent with job evaluation, as theoretically prescribed, it is not consistent with practice. Comparable worth is based on the premise that worth can be defined and measured, something which job evaluation does not in fact do. As practiced, job evaluation chooses and weights factors to conform to a wage distribution which is assumed to be appropriate, i.e., reflects the market."[28] Schwab defends this position by stating that several procedures are commonly employed to increase the correspondence between job evaluation scores and existing wage distributions: "First, the sample may be changed through the addition, or more likely, deletion of key jobs. Second, factors may be added or deleted. Third, jobs may be reevaluated and, finally, the *a priori* weighting system may be changed."[29] He further states that the weights given the factors do not determine the actual significance of the factors in influencing relative job standing. Actual weights depend on the variability of the distribution of factor scores, not absolute values.

What Schwab states is neither correct nor incorrect. If an organization is establishing a new job evaluation method or is significantly modifying an existing one, each of the four steps mentioned by Schwab may be used. However, in thousands of other applications, an existing method may be used and the only step consistently followed is the reevaluation of jobs. This reevaluation occurs in all point-factor job evaluation programs. One of the strengths of any point-factor job evaluation method is the opportunity to review, from a variety of perspectives, the ratings given any job and, above all, the rating of a job factor by factor. A good job evaluation plan requires the review of a number of subject matter experts who know the jobs being rated and are familiar with the evaluation method.

Schwab's effort to destroy the credibility of job evaluation is, in many ways, a red herring. His presentation takes the point-factor methodology out of context as to its use in tens of thousands of applications throughout the world. A number of preformulated job evaluation plans are available, and when implemented properly, they can do precisely what they claim to do—*establish a job-worth hierarchy.*

What Schwab and other authors of the EEAC book failed to recognize is that there is a far more common and broader understanding of job worth and job-worth–related pay than they are willing to admit. Certainly, rates of pay for jobs vary by industry and locality, and the ordering of some jobs by market rates of pay vary, but these variations are more an industry and locality phenomenon whereas, for most jobs, there is consistent understanding regarding job worth and job rates of pay.

Job evaluation is not an end in itself; it is but one part of the pay and total compensation determination process. For job evaluation to be an effective tool in the pay determination process, these four steps must be followed:

1. The unique requirements and content of each job must be identified, documented, and understood.
2. Individuals involved in job evaluation must be familiar with the job under review to make the critical and potentially hazardous inferential leap from job content and requirements to a level or degree of a specific factor.

---

[28]Ibid., p. 68.
[29]Ibid., p. 67.

3. Pay structures must be developed that reflect organizational pay policy and a desired relationship with identified markets. (In developing pay policy, all other components of the compensation reward system, and even the noncompensation reward system, must be recognized.)

4. Jobs assigned to a specific location (pay grade) in a pay structure in which the rate of pay reflects market demands but does not relate to job-worth value require specific recognition and treatment (establishing market-driven rates of pay for exotic jobs).

In a variety of rulings, the courts have recognized job evaluation as only part of the pay determination process. For example, in the case *American Nurses Association* v. *State of Illinois,* 37 FEP cases 705 (1985), job evaluation was identified as a useful diagnostic tool. The Court further stated that the law does not require an employer to implement whatever pay changes a particular study suggests without regard to economic considerations, the labor market, bargaining demands, or the possibility that some other study might produce different results.

The National Academy of Sciences and Comparable Worth

To further clarify issues related to comparable worth such as how pay decisions are to be made and what technologies are to be used in making these decisions, the Equal Employment Opportunity Commission (EEOC) in 1976 commissioned the National Academy of Sciences (NAS), an independent research institute, to investigate whether appropriate job measurement procedures exist or can be developed. The results of the findings of NAS were documented in *Job Evaluation: An Analytic Review,* and unofficial guidelines were published in 1979. Of particular interest to those involved in job evaluation and comparable worth were the five unofficial guidelines established by NAS.

1. Each enterprise that uses job evaluation procedures should use a single job evaluation system for all its employees.
2. The employer should make explicit the criteria of worth for jobs in the enterprise—that is, there should be an explicit and open policy about what attributes of jobs are regarded by the enterprise as deserving compensation.
3. When factor-based job evaluation procedures are used, the choice of measured factors should adequately present the criteria of job worth enunciated in conformity to point 2.
   a. The employer should make explicit the basis for the choice of factors and the relationship of the measured factors to the concept of job worth held by the enterprise. The employer should take care to ensure that the factors identified account thoroughly for all the compensable features of jobs.
   b. Specifically, the employer should ensure that the choice of measured factors is equally appropriate for the evaluation of all jobs and is not biased in favor of or against jobs held mainly by particular race or sex groups.
   c. If use of a job evaluation system results in jobs held mainly by women or minorities scoring lower on the average than jobs held mainly by white males, it is the obligation of the employer to demonstrate that the choice of measured factors is justified by business necessity—specifically, that the measured factors validly measure the criteria of job worth held by the enterprise and that no

other measurable factors are available that would be equally valid but less discriminatory.

4. In point-factor systems, the range of scores for each factor should represent the full range of variability of the job feature being measured and the division of the full range into levels should be accurately specified.

   a. Factor scores should be chosen to represent the full range of variability of the feature of the job being evaluated.

   b. The specification of the available levels of a factor must be justified in terms of the firm's definition of job worth (point 2) and must be accurately described. In particular, factor-level descriptions should be written as concretely as possible, with careful specification of equivalencies for different types of jobs.

5. In point-factor systems the factor weights must be chosen in a bias-free way.

   a. Because jobs held mainly by women tend on the average to pay less than jobs held mainly by men, the use of existing wages to derive factor weights is unacceptable unless the employer can show that such weights are unbiased with respect to sex.

   b. The specification of factor weights by the employer to reflect the relative importance of job factors to the enterprise imposes an obligation on the employer to ensure that the chosen weights do not have an adverse impact on women or minority workers or, if they do, that they are justified by business necessity.

The final report on the NAS study on job measurement published in *Women, Work, and Wages: Equal Pay for Jobs of Equal Value* noted that these unofficial guidelines were not made official.[30] The entire issue of relating job evaluation to comparable worth remains unresolved.

Summary

A number of methodologies are available for establishing the worth or value of jobs. The term *job evaluation* is used to identify various methodologies that provide a hierarchy or ordering of jobs according to some concept of value or worth to the employer. Two general ways of classifying job evaluation methods are those that investigate the job as a whole or those that investigate the job from a variety of components. These components are frequently labeled compensable factors. Major kinds of whole job evaluation methods are ranking and position classification-predetermined grading. Major methods using compensable factors are point-factor, factor comparison, and multiple regression–based methods.

A goal of any job evaluation method is to minimize subjectivity and promote objectivity. The more complex job methodologies such as the point-factor method and the multiple regression methods have been designed to improve the inference-making process of relating job facts (elements) to levels or degrees of compensable factors in a point-factor plan or weights of a variable in a multiple regression method.

---

[30]Donald J. Treiman and Heidi I. Hartman, eds., *Women, Work, and Wages: Equal Pay for Jobs of Equal Value* (Washington, DC: National Academy Press, 1981).

Review Questions

1. What is meant by internal equity? What is the relationship between internal equity and job evaluation?
2. What is a benchmark or key job? Why are these kinds of jobs so critical in various job evaluation methodologies?
3. What are some of the strengths and limitations in the use of ranking for job evaluation purposes?
4. What must be done to develop a predetermined grading or position classification method?
5. How does the Smyth-Murphy method of market pricing differ from a pure market-pricing approach to establishing job worth?
6. Define a compensable factor and give a few examples.
7. Which piece of legislation gave the federal government stamp of approval to a compensable factor job evaluation? Name the factors identified in this legislation.
8. What are used as scales or "yardsticks" for measuring job differences and worth in point-factor job evaluation methods?
9. Describe how the normalizing process is used in developing compensable factor weights.
10. Discuss the design features of one of the first point-factor job evaluation methods that continues to be widely used today.

Appendix 8A
Paired-Comparison Procedures

The Deck-of-Cards Procedure

One of the simplest yet most effective of the paired-comparison procedures used for ranking a group of items is the deck-of-cards procedure. In this procedure, the rater

1. Places each name or item (job title) to be compared on a separate card and into a pile.
2. Chooses two cards from the pile, compares them, and selects the best.
3. Holds the best in his or her hand and discards the loser into a new pile.
4. Selects another card from the first pile, compares it with card in hand, chooses the best, and discards the loser in the new pile.
5. Continues with this step, until the original pile has been depleted.
6. Places the card in his or her hand in a second new pile. This is the top selection.
7. Repeats all steps, using the first new pile as the replacement for the original pile for the eventual second choice.
8. Continues the process until all remaining names have been placed in the pile with his or her first choice. This gives the ranking for the group.

An additional step that may be included in this process to exclude rating bias is to perform the entire process a second time. Beginning with Step 2, the rater identifies the lowest or least important item and then builds to the highest by always returning to the pile that item rated higher. This reversal process should provide the same order of rank. Any discrepancy becomes an area for further investigation.

The Stub Selection Procedure

The stub selection procedure attempts to overcome two basic weaknesses of other paired-comparison procedures: (1) the inability of the human brain to store and compare a large variety of items (in fact, it is difficult for most brains to compare more than five items at one time), and (2) the "halo effect" (i.e., once an item is judged to be superior to a number of items, it begins to carry an inborn superiority over items that follow). In the stub selection procedure, the name or item on each stub represents the name or item to be compared. In this case, the name or item circled represents a specific choice. The rater

1. Cuts out the stubs
2. Circles the selected item or name on each stub (the circled item is considered a vote)
3. Makes a pile for each circled item
4. Counts the stubs in each pile upon completion of all comparisons

The pile with the largest number of stubs is the highest-ranking item, the next largest number is second, and so on. The lowest-ranking item is the one that received the fewest votes.

1 2			
1 3	2 3		
1 4	2 4	3 4	
1 5	2 5	3 5	4 5

If ties are permitted and a rater wishes to recognize a tie, each item is circled, the stub is cut in half, and each half of the stub is placed in the appropriate pile. In case of a tie, half a point is granted to each item.

The Paired-Comparison Ranking Table

An adaptation of the stub selection procedure is to develop a matrix in which all the items to be compared are listed in both the rows and the columns of a table known as a paired-comparison ranking table. In the boxes formed by the intersection of the rows and columns, the appraiser places an X where the item in the row is more important or valuable (or some other characteristic) than the item in the column. The item receiving the highest score (i.e., number of Xs) is the most important or valuable, or possesses some characteristic considered to be of more worth than the item in the column. Table 8A–1 gives an example of a paired-comparison ranking table when different jobs are being compared.

If ranking procedures permit ties, a symbol such as O may be used to indicate a tie. When ties are allowed, a half point is granted to each item for that item's total score.

TABLE 8A–1 Paired-Comparison Ranking Table

Columns / Rows	Messenger	*Data Proc. Mgr.*	*Data Entry Opr.*	*Exec. Sec.*	*Computer Opr.*	*Sys. Anal.*	*Control Clk.*	*Programmer*	*File Clk.*	*Asst. Dir.*	*Total*
Messenger	—										0
Data processing manager	X	—	X	X	X	X	X	X	X	X	9
Data entry operator	X		—						X		2
Executive secretary	X		X	—	X		X	X	X		6
Computer operator	X		X		—		X		X		4
Systems analyst	X		X	X	X	—	X	X	X		7
Control clerk	X		X				—		X		3
Programmer	X		X		X		X	—	X		5
File clerk	X								—		1
Assistant director	X		X	X	X	X	X	X	X		8

Place X in box where item in row is more important than item in column.

When a number of individuals are independently performing a ranking of all jobs, the individual rankings must be added and then an average ranking determined by dividing the sum by the number of raters.

The Alternation Ranking Procedure

Another available paired-comparison technique is alternation ranking. Here, the rater has a list of all jobs to be ranked. The first selection is the job the rater considers to be of highest worth. The name of this job is placed on the first line of a sheet of paper that has numbered lines—one for each job to be ranked. The rater then strikes the ranked job from the list. The second selection is the job considered to be of lowest worth. The name of this job is placed at the bottom of the list and is also crossed out on the original list. The third job ranked is the highest remaining in the original list; fourth is the lowest-rated remaining job, which is placed on the rank-ordered list and stricken from the original list. This process continues until all jobs are ranked.

An alternation ranking list with 20 jobs to be ranked follows:

1 Highest-rated job	first
2 Next highest-rated job	third
3 Next highest-rated job	fifth
•	
• etc.	
•	
18 Next lowest-rated job	sixth
19 Next lowest-rated job	fourth
20 Lowest-rated job	second

As in any paired-comparison technique, if the rating is to be accurate, the rater must know the factors or characteristics to be rated and the job being rated.

Paired comparison is unwieldy when one is comparing large numbers of items, as shown by the following formula. This formula determines the number of comparisons to be made for a given number of comparison items:

$$\frac{N(N-1)}{2} \text{ where } N = \text{the number of comparison items}$$

For example:

$$\text{comparing 7 factors } \frac{7(7-1)}{2} = 21 \text{ comparisons}$$

$$\text{comparing 15 jobs } \frac{15(15-1)}{2} = 105 \text{ comparisons}$$

In this example, the approximate doubling of the number of factors to be compared (from 7 to 15) increases the number of comparisons to be made by a multiple of five.

Appendix 8B
Other Job Evaluation Methods

The following examples provide different designs for job evaluation methods. Each method provides a somewhat unique approach to compensable factors. The first three methods use a single factor. They are (1) Time-Span of Discretion, (2) the Decision Band Method, and (3) the Problem-Solving Method. A fourth method uses benchmarks and guide charts that, in turn, use different compensable factors for different occupational groups. A fifth method uses a set of core factors and various secondary factors for different jobs.

Time-Span of Discretion (TSD) Method

Elliot Jaques initially proposed a different way to evaluate job worth in the 1950s, contending that the differences in responsibility required in the performance of jobs establish the differences in job worth. He further contends that the responsibility in a work role can be measured by determining "the longest period of time which can elapse in a role before the manager can be sure that his subordinate has not been exercising marginally substandard discretion continuously in balancing the pace and the quality of his work."[31]

Jaques maintains that the time-span of discretion jobholders have in the performance of their work is the basic factor in determining pay, stating that commonly held social norms provide an "unconscious awareness" among all employees that differ-

---

[31]Elliot Jaques, *Time-Span Handbook* (London: Heinemann Educational Books, 1964), p. 10.

ences in pay should relate directly to differences in time-span of discretion.[32] He further states that to define this span it is necessary to determine the following:

1. Whether it is a single- or multiple-task job (the time-span of a multiple-task job is that time required to perform the longest task).
2. The quality and quantity standards used as a basis for determining substandard performances of discretion.
3. The normal length of time between the time a subordinate starts a task and the time his or her superior checks his or her performance.

Although Jaques maintains that the use of this one universal factor makes it possible to reduce conflict over wage inequities, the results of a series of studies conducted in the 1960s and 1970s fail to support his position.[33] TSD has had almost no use in the United States, but it may be one additional technique available to compensation managers to assist them in developing equitable levels of pay in their organizations. A possible important contribution of Jaques is that TSD can be extremely useful in defining and measuring the worth of knowledge-based jobs.

Decision Band Method of Job Evaluation

T. T. Paterson and T. M. Husband proposed the use of the Decision Band Method™ (DBM) for evaluating jobs. They claim that DBM overcomes the purely subjective measures that are inherent weaknesses in previously developed methods of job evaluation. Paterson and Husband state that this weakness is especially apparent when organizations try to compare unlike jobs. From their research, they found that all jobs differ according to the kinds of decisions that are made in performing them.[34]

The basic concept underlying DBM is that the value of a job to an enterprise is directly related to the decision-making requirements of that job. All jobs—line or staff, supervisory or nonsupervisory, union or nonunion—require the incumbent to make decisions of some kind. Because decision making is common and the level of decision making is measurable in all positions, Paterson and Husband contend that it is the primary—if not the only—factor by which the importance of jobs can be equitably compared. Because this method of job evaluation uses one principal or key factor, it has also been called *broadbanding*. DBM includes six decision bands that span every kind of decision that can be made in an organization. The bands form a continuum, each band building on the one before.

Abbreviated definitions of the six bands are listed at the top of the next page.

---

[32]Elliot Jaques, *Equitable Payment* (New York: Wiley, 1961), p. 17.

[33]A few of the studies conducted analyzing Jaques's time span theory are discussed in Thomas Atchison and Wendell French, "Pay Systems for Scientists and Engineers," *Industrial Relations,* October 1967, pp. 44–56; Paul S. Goodman, "An Empirical Examination of Elliot Jaques' Concept of Time Span," *Human Relations,* May 1967, pp. 155–170; Michael E. Gordon, "An Evaluation of Jaques' Studies of Pay in the Light of Current Compensation Research," *Personnel Psychology,* Winter 1969, pp. 369–389; Jerry L. Gray (ed.), *The Glacier Project: Concepts and Critiques* (New York: Crane and Russek, 1976); Don Hellriegel and Wendell French, "A Critique of Jaques' Equitable Payment System," *Industrial Relations,* May 1969, pp. 269–279; George T. Milkovich and Keith Campbell, "A Study of Jaques' Norms of Equitable Payment," *Industrial Relations,* October 1972, pp. 267–271.

[34]T. T. Paterson and T. M. Husband, "Decision-Making Responsibility: Yardsticks for Job Evaluation," *Compensation Review,* Second Quarter 1970, pp. 21–31.

Band	Kind of Decision	Definition of Decision
F	Policy	Decisions on the mission, directions, and overal goals of the organization, subject to few constraints other than those imposed by law or economic conditions
E	Programming	Decisions about strategic plans or to acheive the goals established at Band F, within the constraints and limits established at Band F.
D	Interpretive	Decisions on the use of recources allocated to the job and translating programs decided at Band E into operational plans and schedules.
C	Process	Decisions concerned with the selection of a specific process for accomplishing the work determined at Band D.
B	Operational	Decisions on carrying out the operations of the selected process.
A	Defined	Decisions that primarily are concerned with the manner and speed of performing the elements of operation.

Essentially, implementation of DBM involves three basic phases: job analysis, job grading, and pay structure determination.

Job analysis, as discussed in chapter 6, involves gathering information concerning job tasks. After gathering task information, it is possible to determine the nature and frequency of the decisions an employee has to make when carrying out the tasks and to prepare position descriptions. Under DBM, only the intrinsic work content (i.e., the tasks performed) is considered. In DBM, factors unrelated to the work itself are considered to be discriminatory and, therefore, are not used to determine the value of the job. In this way, the relative value of a job can be more readily determined regardless of its level in the enterprise and the type of employee assigned to it.

After the tasks have been identified, the first step requires that each task be banded relative to the kind or level of decision made by the incumbent in the performance of that task. The band assigned to the highest-rated task is the final band rating given to the job. The second step divides jobs in each band into two grades (with the exception of Band A). The employees in the upper-graded jobs (designated *M* in the following model) manage other jobs that have been assigned to the same band. The employees in the lower-graded jobs (designated *NM* in the model) *do not* manage other jobs in the same band. The third step includes a further distribution of the banded and graded jobs into subgrades (with the exception of the upper portion of Band F). Normally, the upper grade of each band can be divided into two subgrades, and each of the lower grades of each band can be divided into three subgrades. With the upper grade of Band F having only one grade, and the lower grade of Band F having three subgrades, the subdivision makes it possible to convert DBM evaluated jobs, typically, into 27 pay grades. Depending upon the organization in which DBM is implemented, the number of pay grades may be somewhat higher or lower than 27, which permits further flexibility within the system. Or, an organization may not wish to use all 27 pay grades, leaving some vacant.

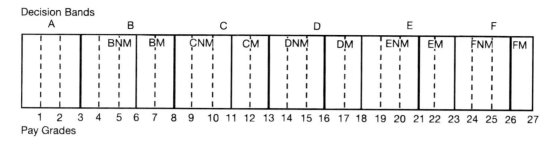

The distribution of jobs into subgrades is based on the relative complexity of the highest-banded tasks of a job. The overall criteria used to determine complexity are:

1. The number of decisions at the highest band and grade.
2. The frequency of decisions at the highest band and grade.
3. The diversity of the preceding decisions.

These additional criteria for determining job worth are also considered compensable factors in the DBM method.

The third and final phase of DBM involves pay structure determination. In this phase, the organization compares its existing pay curve with an external pay curve derived from market-generated survey data. By analyzing this information, decisions are made concerning pay structure policy, pay inequities, and contingency payments for unique situations. Two of the unique situations that may warrant contingency payments are working conditions and labor market conditions. Working conditions should be treated separately for several reasons:

- An employee may do the same work under variable conditions—sometimes unpleasant, sometimes not.
- Different employees may do the same work—some always under unpleasant conditions, others always under pleasant conditions.
- Employees react to conditions differently. What one employee finds unpleasant, for example, monotonous work or tasks involving strenuous effort, may not be objectionable to another.

When payments for working conditions are not built into the basic pay scales, improvements in conditions can be reflected by changing the amount of contingency payments. (See prior discussion of distressing and dangerous conditions in this chapter.)

Labor market conditions reflect changes in supply and demand for different skills and knowledge and they rarely remain static. Because of this, pay increases dictated by labor market conditions should also be treated separately from basic pay. If labor market conditions change and the shortage of a particular kind of skill no longer exists, any contingency payments for the former market shortage can be adjusted with relatively little difficulty. If, as is often the case with other job evaluation methods, extra pay during a labor shortage is built into the basic pay structure, it can distort the equitable pay relationships and create dissension with other employees in the enterprise. In addition, if the labor market condition disappears, this becomes an unjustified built-in pay differential.

DBM provides a foundation for those interested in understanding and using the broadbanding concept currently being promoted for organizational pay structure design.

Problem-Solving Compensable Factor Method

A. W. Charles proposes problem solving as a single universal factor useful in evaluating all jobs in an organization, from the lowest to the highest.[35]

The Charles approach uses ordinal rather than cardinal relationships in performing job-to-job comparisons based on problem-solving complexity. Ordinal numbers (first, second, third, etc.) provide a specific or absolute position in a series; cardinal numbers (1, 2, 3, etc.) permit numerical scoring and the establishment of percentage differences in comparing job worth. The Charles method results in a ranking of jobs through the use of a factor rather than the use of the whole job.

The first step in the problem-solving compensable factor method is to develop a two-dimensional matrix that lists all the jobs to be compared in both the rows and columns. In the squares formed by the intersection of the row and column, if the job in the row has greater problem-solving responsibilities than the job in the column, a plus sign is placed in the square. The job accumulating the most plus signs has the largest amount of problem-solving responsibility and is, thus, the most important job in the matrix.

The following steps in the process involve joining together the matrices that describe the problem-solving responsibilities of the various departments of the organization. An analysis of the multidepartment matrix then establishes the order of importance of all jobs in the organization.

Charles contends that multicompensable factor plans are not truly universal in scope and that the use of cardinal point values establishes a scale of values that further compounds the error by assuming that the quantities to be measured are meaningful. Charles's method claims to correct these basic job evaluation errors.

Benchmark Guide Chart Method

The Benchmark Guide Chart Method of job evaluation attracted attention when the U.S. Civil Service Commission's Job Evaluation and Pay Review Task Force introduced the Factor Ranking/Benchmark Method in the mid-1970s.[36] Although this method was never implemented within the federal government, it laid the groundwork for the Factor Evaluation System (FES), which is discussed in depth in chapter 9.

This method is a composite of a number of previously discussed factor methods. It requires (1) identifying and describing the relevant compensable factors, (2) weighting and assigning points to factors, and (3) placing two or more factors on one guide chart (similar to the Hay Guide Charts) for use in the point rating of jobs being evaluated.

Like any compensable factor job evaluation method, the key to successful implementation and administration of the Benchmark Guide Chart Method is the collection

---

[35]A. W. Charles, "Installing Single-Factor Job Evaluation," *Compensation Review,* First Quarter 1971, pp. 9–17.
[36]Philip M. Oliver, "Modernizing a State Job Evaluation and Pay Plan," *Public Personnel Management,* May–June 1976, pp. 168–173.

of sufficient valid job content and job requirement data and information to write descriptions that are current and understandable, and that have an orderly format. The next step is to develop benchmark job or class descriptions that identify areas of work content and requirements, including information that permits accurate comparisons with identified, defined, and weighted factors.

There are two approaches available for those interested in using a Benchmark Guide Chart Method. One involves the use of *general factor* guide charts, and the second uses *occupational factor* guide charts.

Factor guide charts are similar to the guide charts used in the Hay Plan. The factors, subfactors, and degrees are defined in terms broad enough to cover a wide range of jobs and can be used by organizations that vary widely in size and geographic location and that provide diverse outputs.

Occupational guide charts are similar to factor guide charts, but the factors relate to a specific occupation. The job content and the requirements of the jobs that make up a specific occupation provide the information for preparing an occupational guide chart. Occupational guide charts are, in reality, a refinement or added step of the factor guide chart method.

The Benchmark Guide Chart Method includes the following occupational guide charts:

1. Professional, Administrative, and Technological occupations (PAT)
2. Supervisory and Management occupations (SAM)
3. Clerical Personnel, Office Machine Operators, and Technicians (COMOT)
4. Protective Occupations/Law Enforcement (POLE)
5. Trades and Crafts occupations (TAC)
6. Executive, Scientific, and Medical occupations (ESM)

The guide charts for each of these six broad groups use different sets of factors to evaluate jobs in each occupational group, and the weights of the factors differ from one occupation and group to another. To ensure consistent and fair relationships among jobs in these diverse occupations, factor guide charts must be developed before preparing occupational guide charts. The factor guide charts provide general definitions of the compensable factors and set limits for degree definitions and the assignment of point values to ensure acceptable interoccupational alignments.

Job Evaluation Methods with Core and Secondary Factors

Some organizations now use job evaluation plans with a core set of factors and another group of factors (secondary factors). The core factors are used for evaluating all jobs in the organization, whereas the second set of factors is used for evaluating the worth of management, professional, and administrative jobs. In essence, this approach states that certain jobs receive 0 points with respect to certain factors, that is, job requirements do not have any relevance regarding the specific factor. This approach permits an organization to use one job evaluation method for an entire organization; this approach facilitates the development of one pay structure.

A "core" job evaluation plan developed by Bernard Ingster for SmithKline Beckman Corp. has three universal factors: (1) knowledge, (2) complexity, and (3) responsibility. Each of these three universal factors is further defined by subfactors or, as they are called in this plan, "aspects." The aspect places particular emphasis on each factor. The factors and their aspects are

Knowledge (K)

K1 Specialized/professional knowledge

K2 Knowledge of SmithKline Beckman

K3 Knowledge of influencing others

K4 Enterprise knowledge

K5 Knowledge of supervisory techniques

Complexity (C)

C1 Characteristics of problem

C2 Independent thinking

C3 Nature of planning

C4 Creativity requirements

Responsibility (R)

R1 Staff support

   or

R2 Impact on market status

   or

R3 Line leadership, together with

R4 Stewardship/physical assets

The aspects (subfactors) that are evident in the content of every job are K1, K2, C1, C2, and R1 or R2, or R3 and R4 (only one of three possible "R" aspects is used for measuring any one job). On the basis of job content, decisions are made to use none, one, or more than one of the optional or secondary aspects for evaluation purposes. This use of core and secondary factors can be further modified by having different sets of secondary factors for jobs in particular occupations or functional areas of the organization.

This approach to job evaluation is not new. Early job evaluation plans often included factors in which the first level or degree of the factor was "does not appear to be or is not an aspect of the job," and received zero points. At times, a first or base level or degree would be assigned an extremely low point value. This degree was frequently termed a *warm body score*. The score was so low as to be meaningless and would relate only to a minimum or base wage.

The "core" plan developed by Ingster provides a set of base factors that acts as the trunk of the evaluation plan; other factors branch from the trunk and recognize more complex, difficult, and important kinds of responsibilities and contributions that relate only to certain jobs.

Appendix 8C[37]
Using Multiple Regression Analysis
in Questionnaire-Based Job Evaluation

In the 1980s, the use of computer-assisted job evaluation became more popular, affordable, and easy to use. As a result, companies could afford to use more sophisticated methodologies for developing job evaluation models. One such approach is the use of multiple regression to develop a relationship between job content and market pay levels.

Multiple regression analysis is a statistical technique that analyzes the relationship between two or more variables and uses the information gained from this analysis to estimate the value of the *dependent* variable for given levels of the *independent* variables. Thus, through multiple regression, it is possible to estimate the job value (dependent variable) for given levels of the job factors (independent variables).

Historically, the multiple regression approach to job evaluation arose out of the need to blend market competitiveness with internal job worth in a systematic fashion. Thus, the methodology centers around two major processes: the definition of a market-based hierarchy of a representative sample of benchmark jobs, and the development of a closed-ended questionnaire that captures information about multidimensional job factors.

Definition of the Market-Based Hierarchy of Benchmark Jobs

The multiple regression model is developed using a sample of benchmark jobs that are arranged into a hierarchy according to market value. Based on its position in the hierarchy, each job is assigned a value, which may be represented by salary amount, points, or a job grade. This value is then used in the multiple regression analysis as the dependent variable.

Development of the Closed-Ended Questionnaire

To standardize job information and make it easy to analyze, a closed-ended job questionnaire is used. The questionnaire captures information about job factors that are important to the organization. In most cases, the factors contain core information about key factors such as decision making, job knowledge, supervisory responsibility, and so on. However, because the data are intended to be computerized, this approach allows the use of many more factors (typically, between 30 and 50) than are typically found in point-factor systems, so that organizations can include factors that are of special interest to them but may not be found in typical point-factor systems. Examples of such factors include customer service, team participation, or use of different types of equipment.

---

[37]This appendix was written by Theresa Mee of the Atlanta office of Wyatt's Compensation Consulting Division.

Closed-ended questions, in which responses can be numbered and entered into a computer file, are used to make the data easy to analyze using computers. Examples of closed-ended questions follow:

- (check the box)

  Education
  ***What is the minimum formal education level* necessary *to do your job?* This may or may not be the same as your own education level.**

  1. ☐ Less than High School
  2. ☐ High School/GED
  3. ☐ Vocational School Diploma
  4. ☐ Technical Diploma or Associate's Degree
  5. ☐ Bachelor's Degree
  6. ☐ Master's Degree
  7. ☐ Doctorate Degree (Ph.D., J.D., Ed.D.)

- (circle a number—menu of items)

PREPARING WRITTEN COMMUNICATIONS	Not Applicable	Infrequently	Monthly	Weekly	Daily/ Shift
16. Writing articles/press releases/newsletters	1	2	3	4	5
17. Writing contracts	1	2	3	4	5
18. Writing documentation	1	2	3	4	5
19. Writing internal memoranda	1	2	3	4	5
20. Writing letters/fax messages	1	2	3	4	5
21. Writing procedures, technical material, or manuals	1	2	3	4	5
22. Writing reports/ proposals/catalogs	1	2	3	4	5
23. Translating foreign language (written documents)	1	2	3	4	5

- (number of employees supervised)

  Total Reports
  ***If you are a supervisor, or group leader, how many employees do you supervise?* Count all employees that report directly to you and/or report to you through other supervisory levels.**
  Enter a number for each type of employee. If not applicable, enter zero (0).

  1. _____ Number of employees that are exempt (not paid overtime).
  2. _____ Number of employees *eligible* for overtime pay.
  3. _____ Number of temporary employees.

Because the questionnaires are quite detailed, many companies arrange for employees to provide the initial information, with review by supervisors and Human Resources. However, other data collection methods have been used, including completion of the questionnaire by supervisors, by teams of employees, or by job analysts.

Questionnaire responses for the jobs in the benchmark sample are used to build the job evaluation model. Each question is used as an independent variable in the multiple regression analysis.

Developing the Multiple Regression Model

A data set is developed, consisting of the questionnaire responses for the benchmark jobs (independent variables) and the benchmark job values (dependent variable). The first step is to maximize the predictive relationship of each independent variable (questionnaire responses for each question) to the dependent variable (job value). The questionnaire data may be "transformed" to result in a better fit. Possible transformations include:

- Rescaling the question (for example, changing the scale from 1–2–3–4 to 1.5–2–2.5–4.5)
- Taking the log of the response
- Squaring the response
- Combining the responses to more than one question (by addition, multiplication, etc.)

The appropriate transformation is determined through analysis of the data pattern for each question, using scatter plots (as follows) or other statistical methods.

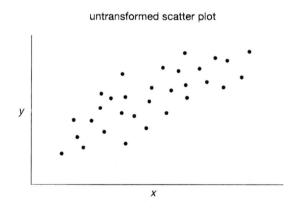

untransformed scatter plot

Next, using standard statistical procedures for multiple regression, the "best fit" relationship of all independent variables to the dependent variable is developed. The result is an equation describing the line of best fit: one which results in the smallest average difference in the actual value of the dependent variable and the predicted value described by the line. Chapter 11 contains an expanded discussion of a line of best fit or trend line.

transformed scatter plot

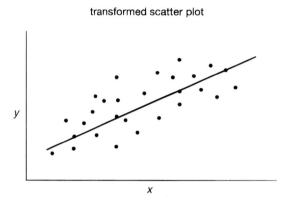

The equation is in the form:

$$Y = a + b_1X_1 + b_2X_2 + b_3X_3 + \ldots + b_NX_N$$

where Y is the job value, X_N is the question response for question N, a is a constant, and b_N is the slope or weight assigned through the multiple regression process to question N.

The quality of the equation's fit to the data is measured by the following statistics:

- Standard error: measures the difference in predicted versus actual values; it is measured in the same units as the dependent variable (i.e., job grade, points).
- R^2 (coefficient of determination): measures the amount of variation in the dependent variable that is explained by the independent variables.

A model that adequately "fits" the data will typically have an R^2 greater than .90. The magnitude of the standard error will vary according to the units in which the dependent variable is measured. For example, if the job grade is used for the dependent variable, it would be desirable to have a standard error of less than .80 grades.

Usually, the multiple regression equation uncovers outlier points, or points with large variations between the actual value and predicted value. For these outlier points, data are examined (both questionnaire data and job value data) for correctness and revised if necessary. Then the process is repeated, resulting in a new multiple regression equation.

Once the regression analysis has been completed, the multiple regression equation can be used to estimate a job value for any combination of questionnaire responses within the range of the model. The range of the model is determined by the range of the data on which the model is developed. Therefore, for example, job values higher than the highest benchmark job value, or lower than the lowest benchmark job value, cannot be predicted with reliability.

The multiple regression equation is typically programmed into computer software to allow for easy evaluation of nonbenchmark jobs, based on their questionnaire responses.

Advantages/Disadvantages of Multiple Regression–Based Job Evaluation

Advantages of using multiple regression–based job evaluation include:

- Allows one system for entire organization
- Can tailor factors to organization's values
- Uses objective/uniform standards of measurement
- Efficient to use on an ongoing basis
- Statistically reliable
- Effectively blends market value, internal equity, and organization's compensation philosophy

There are also certain disadvantages to using multiple regression for job evaluation. The method is, in general, quite time consuming to develop the initial model as well as more expensive than market pricing or standard point-factor systems. In addition, changing or adjusting the model can require extensive analysis of all data, including selection of benchmarks, benchmark ranking, and questionnaire data. Multiple regression models are also more difficult to explain to managers and employees.

For these reasons, multiple regression–based job evaluation is probably most suited to medium to large organizations that are mature, or growing at a manageable rate. This method is not well-suited for smaller organizations, organizations undergoing rapid change, or where the job market fluctuates significantly from year to year.

CHAPTER

Job Evaluation

Two Point-Factor Methods

Learning Objectives

In this chapter you will learn about:

1. The operation of a job evaluation committee.

2. The FES and the Hay methods of job evaluation.

3. Evaluating jobs using FES and Hay.

4. The differences and similarities between FES and Hay.

5. How the factor-comparison process improves the accuracy of point-factor job evaluation methodology.

Compensation Strategy

Evaluate job content using a process that is understood by all employees and recognized as fair and just.

This chapter focuses on the application of two point-factor methods of job evaluation—the Factor Evaluation System (FES) and the Hay Method.

The FES and the Hay Method developed from the compensable factor work done in the 1920s and 1930s, as described in chapter 8. Although the FES method is a creation of the mid-1970s and the Hay Method dates from the early 1950s, the FES is presented first because it is a method that more closely resembles the work of Lott, Bass, and the NEMA developers. The Hay Guide Charts are somewhat more complex. A thorough knowledge of the operation of FES facilitates a quicker and more solid understanding of the Hay Method.

Both methods have common problems. Similar to all other point-factor job evaluation methods, a particular point-factor rating for many jobs is open to differences in interpretation and argument. The underlying problems common to all point-factor job evaluation methods relate to the abstract nature of definitions (factors and rating scales) and to the issues related to inference making between job facts and a specific point score of a factor.

Minimizing subjectivity in the inference-making process of relating job facts (elements) to levels or degrees of compensable factors has been an unending struggle for designers of point-valued compensable factor job evaluation methodologies. The more that is known about the responsibilities and duties of a job, its environmental requirements, and the associated knowledge and skills demanded of the jobholder, the more accurate the inferences between these job requirements and the degree or level of a compensable factor. This, of course, assumes that the integrity and fairness of the rater are above reproach.

Chapter 8 focused on the description and semantics problems related to the identification and description of universal compensable factors, subfactors, and degrees. The more abstract each of these components is, the more difficult it is for an evaluator to understand what the compensable factor is all about. This, in turn, leads to the increased probability of making inference errors when attempting to match a possibly inadequately described and understood job with a poorly or abstractly defined compensable factor. This chapter provides insights into how these kinds of inference-making errors can be limited or reduced.

COMBINING POINT-FACTOR AND FACTOR-COMPARISON METHODS

The following sections of this chapter focus on the evaluation of a job using FES and the Hay Method. The presentations are made for instructional purposes only. *No* point-factor job evaluation instructions can be followed literally. After evaluating a range of jobs within any organizational setting, the unique organizational interpretation of the levels of the factor and organizational job requirements become at least as critical as what may be written in a guidebook.

A critical check of the results of a point-factor job evaluation involves the use of factor comparison. Possibly one of the most powerful approaches available for job evaluation is to combine a point-factor method with the factor-comparison method. As those who actually perform job evaluation assignments or act as job evaluation committee members become familiar with the factors and assign specific levels or degrees of a factor to various jobs, they begin to establish their own interpretation of how a level or degree of each factor relates to the kinds of work performed within their organization.

If point-factor job evaluation begins with a rating of key or benchmark jobs, evaluation scores for jobs rated from the lowest to the highest are established. The results of these ratings provide a matrix with the jobs listed on the rows and the factors listed in the columns. At the intersection of rows and columns are the points assigned to the job, with total points being the last column. All jobs are listed in order of total points in ascending order.

The first check is to be sure the factor points assigned to each job make sense relative to all other evaluated jobs. Here, the comparison now moves from a point-factor to a factor-comparison process. Combining point-factor with factor-comparison methods allows the organization to state what the degrees or levels of the factors mean relative to its jobs. Employees and present and future evaluators no longer have only abstract statements to relate to the worth of jobs but can now compare the knowledge, skill, responsibility, and working conditions in certain jobs with the same factors in evaluated jobs. This is no longer an abstract, academic process, but rather a real activity that entails comparing the familiar work requirements for jobs already evaluated with those being evaluated.

The eventual success or failure of any point-factor job evaluation plan is the ability of the plan to develop a hierarchy of job ratings that is accepted by both management and the involved employees. This means that in operationalizing within an organizational setting, almost all point-factor job evaluation plans become unique.

To overcome problems related to abstract terminology and inference-making errors, the implementation of point-factor job evaluation requires the use of more than one individual who is knowledgeable of the jobs to be evaluated and of the method used for evaluation. Eugene Benge, a pioneer in the use of compensable factor methods, based much of his work on the use of job evaluation committees in which knowledgeable people of goodwill worked together in a cooperative mode to provide satisfactory and accurate rankings and ratings.

JOB EVALUATION COMMITTEE

Essential to all job evaluation processes is the need for expert judgment. The success of any job evaluation program depends on the quality of the decisions made by those responsible for designing the program and making it work. In turn, the quality of the decision depends directly on the quality and the quantity of available data and information. This process cannot be appreciated and understood without some knowledge of the concepts connected with the terms *data, knowledge, information, judgment,* and *decision.*

Data denotes unevaluated facts. They are presumed to be valid.

Knowledge equates to familiarity, awareness, or understanding gained through experience or study. Knowledge combines job-related data and previously acquired data stored in the brain.

Information is the measure of the net value obtained from the process of matching the elements of a present problem with appropriate elements of data. In this sense, information is a process that occurs within a human brain when a problem and the data for its solution are brought into productive union.[1]

Judgment is the process of forming an opinion involving the interaction of the intellectual and emotional components of the brain requiring the comparison or evaluation of pieces of information.

Decision is the selection among optional choices for intended actions.

[1]Adrian M. McDonough, *Information, Economics, and Management Systems* (New York: McGraw-Hill, 1963), pp. 75–76.

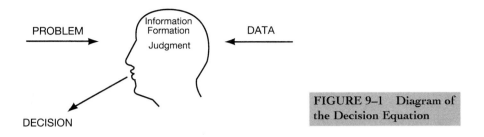

FIGURE 9–1   Diagram of the Decision Equation

The decision equations take the following form (see also Figure 9–1):

$$data + knowledge = information$$
$$information + judgment = decision$$
$$(decision + luck = success)$$

The quality of the outputs of any job evaluation process using point-scored compensable factors relates directly to the quality of decisions made by those doing the ratings. Each individual has his or her own unique perception of any problem or issue. Valuing the worth of a job provides an excellent example of critical problems that relate to differences in individual perceptions and opinions. When an issue as critical as an employee's rate of pay is on the line, inappropriate or misguided perceptions must be recognized and appropriate judgments made. Even though one individual may be extremely knowledgeable about a specific job, it is unlikely that this same person can be an expert on all jobs being evaluated. Making the difficult leap from job facts (or, possibly, fables) to the appropriate compensable factor level to rate a job is no easy assignment. Very seldom, and especially in the white-collar or knowledge-oriented jobs of today, is one job exactly like another. Frequently, jobs with the same title have subtle and, sometimes, not so subtle differences that go unrecognized by even the "job evaluation expert."

Accuracy in evaluations requires the knowledge and skill of more than one individual. Job evaluation committees are groups of two or more individuals who work together to assign a rating to the jobs of the organization. Because it is unlikely that any one individual is intimately familiar with all jobs to be evaluated, the documentation processes described in chapters 6 and 7 are invaluable aids for providing sufficient and necessary data to acquire a good understanding of job content, the requirements of the job, and the environment within which it must be performed. Basic data for the job evaluation process are (1) the job description, together with any necessary supporting documents (e.g., the job analysis questionnaire, organization charts, procedures manuals, manning tables) and (2) work performed in the development of the evaluation method (such as the study that goes into the identification, definition, and weighting of compensable factors). It must also be recognized that a job evaluation committee can operate strictly from orally provided data and previously acquired data stored in the brain of each committee member.

Roles of the Job Evaluation Committee

A job evaluation committee may have three roles—(1) rank and rate jobs, (2) select a job evaluation method, and (3) choose benchmark jobs. The primary role of a job evaluation committee is to rank and rate the jobs of the organization. Because the job-worth ratings have critical influence on the base pay of jobs, psychological pressure becomes more intense as the committee reaches the final stages of ranking and rating all jobs. Recognizing that job evaluation is neither simple nor objectively pure, individual biases and self-enhancement, even survival, are issues that cloud the evaluation process.

A second role that may be played by the job evaluation committee is the selection of a *job evaluation method*. Although not a common requirement, there are times when the first assignment of a committee is the selection of the job evaluation method. When the committee has this responsibility, it is not only the committee's first assignment, it is also the one that is most important and difficult.

When the committee is responsible for this decision, its members must become knowledgeable about the various kinds of job evaluation methods to be reviewed, their features, and their strengths and weaknesses, as well as how a particular method best meets the requirements set forth by the organization. It is highly recommended that the compensation staff specialists develop a completed staff work presentation in which the pros and cons of each evaluation method and its specific features are offered to the committee. The compensation department staff may even make recommendations after presenting the benefits and the costs connected with each. It is then the responsibility of the committee to review the staff work and make a final recommendation. The committee may become involved in the actual evaluation process, but normally this is too time consuming and such details are left to the staff of the compensation department and selected lower-level managers. It is strongly recommended that mid- to upper-level managers be used as members of a committee to select the job evaluation method. If an organization has a union, it may be wise to have a top local union official included as a member. When a special group of managers is chosen to select only the job evaluation method, and other managers are involved in the more time-consuming effort of evaluating jobs, two different job evaluation committees are formed.

Job evaluation committees can also be used to identify and select benchmark jobs. The careful selection of a limited number of jobs that adequately describe a wide span of responsibilities, duties, and work requirements enhances the success of any job evaluation program. These well-known jobs, called *benchmark* or *key* jobs, represent jobs that are common throughout the industry or in the general locale under study and have responsibilities and duties that are well recognized and understood. These jobs may also contain large numbers of incumbents for whom there is a relatively stable supply and demand. The benchmark jobs should represent both the entire pay structure and the major kinds of work performed in the organization. Because these jobs may represent only a small number of all jobs in the organization, they may furnish only a limited amount of data, but their commonality and acceptance provide a basis for sound understanding and agreement of the tasks and human requirements necessary for the achievement of organizational goals. Job evaluation based on selected benchmark jobs may provide a more valuable database than one using masses of data obtained from hundreds of jobs. Normally, 15 to 50 benchmark jobs are enough. (However, when using a market-pricing type of job evaluation method, it may be useful to identify as many as 70 percent of the jobs as benchmark jobs.) If at some stage it is necessary to drop two or three, it will not be critical. The major factor influencing the number of benchmark jobs is the different kinds of work that need to be represented at each interval in the pay structure. (The number of benchmark jobs required relates directly to the number of pay grades to be used in the design of a pay structure. This is the subject of chapter 11.)

Before selecting benchmark jobs, the compensation department must screen all jobs and select those that meet benchmark job requirements. The potential benchmark jobs presented to the evaluation committee should require a wide variety of technological and interpersonal skills, as well as rates of pay ranging from lowest to highest. For job evaluation purposes, either a complete, well-written job description or an accurate and complete job analysis questionnaire must be available. When completed questionnaires are used for job evaluation purposes and the questionnaires are completed by incumbents and not subject matter experts, it is essential that the incumbent-completed questionnaires be reviewed and approved by the incumbents' immediate supervisors. Although a well-written job description may be a preferable job evaluation resource document, it is quite likely that completed questionnaires are more widely used.

Size and Composition

A committee may range from three to ten members, with the smaller end of the range usually preferable. Although more than one set of eyes is needed to review, analyze, and rate a variety of jobs, large committees (in excess of five) may prove to be cumbersome and unwieldy and may consume excessive amounts of time with little or no additional insights to the job or accuracies in ratings. However, when job evaluation committee members work as ambassadors of a specific work unit, carrying job-related information back to the committee and then carrying job-worth information back to the work unit, a committee of from seven to nine members may be preferable.

At times, committees of senior managers are formed as a basic education device to assist them in learning and understanding exactly what the job evaluation methodology is capable of providing. It may be useful to have a committee of senior managers review the work of an operating job evaluation committee and provide an official, high-level stamp of approval. As previously mentioned, if the committee is to select the job evaluation methodology, senior managers should populate this committee. However, involving higher-level members in the evaluation of all jobs may be extremely dysfunctional. Job evaluation takes time; it can become arduous, even boring work for some individuals, especially those who think they could be spending their time much more productively working at their own desks. However, if the job evaluation study includes *all* jobs in the organization, then a select group of top managers should be involved in the evaluation of senior management jobs. Normally, a committee of three to five qualified individuals can provide all the insights and knowledge necessary to fairly and accurately evaluate the jobs of an organization.

A job evaluation committee may consist of one to three permanent members (at least one a representative of the human resources/compensation department) and rotating members representing the unit whose jobs are being evaluated. The permanent member provides a common interpretation of the meanings of the compensable factors and rating scales and inferences between the job facts and the evaluation factors, whereas a unit-job specialist acts as a subject matter expert providing additional insights into the jobs being evaluated.

Training Job Evaluation Committee Members

Job evaluation is neither simple nor precise. It is a problem-solving, decision-making process that requires the subjective judgment of some of the best minds in the organization. Because of varying interests and dissimilar backgrounds, views will quite often differ and, thus, contribute to the complexity of the activities of the job evaluation committee. At times there will be excessive discussion and debate. These discussions can lead to a waste of valuable time. To improve the efficiency and effectiveness of a job evaluation committee, time should be spent in training all individuals who will, at some time, participate in committee activities. A well-designed training program should have at least the following two behavioral or learning objectives for each committee member:

1. Skill in looking for and seeing the same things when reviewing instruments that provide job data, for example, completed job analysis questionnaires, job descriptions, manning tables, career ladders, and so on.
2. An understanding and an acceptance of the procedures used in the job evaluation plan in order to reach agreement on the relative value of all jobs.

A variety of training techniques and aids is available for achieving these twin goals. A first step could be to provide all members of the committee with a completed job analysis questionnaire of a well-known, simple job and have them develop a job description. After writing the job description, they could then analyze each step, its meaning and use. A review and a critique of their work would help all members to gain a better understanding of the process.

The next step would be an explanation of the selected job evaluation method. Then the committee as a group would evaluate the described job. After being introduced to the job evaluation method, the committee members would take a set of jobs in one department and rank each one individually using some form of a paired-comparison procedure. After each member has ranked the jobs individually, all rankings would be compared and there would be a discussion as to the reasons involved in the job ranking. Next, using the selected job evaluation method, the committee members would independently rate the set of selected jobs. Each individual then would discuss and justify his or her ratings and, finally, the committee would come to an agreement on a final rating for each job.

The training program has one fundamental goal—to develop the judgment of all committee members so that they will be able to recognize what is important in a job, its relative difficulty, the scope and criticality of its responsibilities and duties, and the level of performance required of a fully proficient employee.

Each committee member should receive a job evaluation manual developed by those responsible for the design of the job evaluation program. This manual is useful both as an introduction to the process and as a guide in the problem-solving, decision-making activities required of the committee members.

The manual should contain a brief description of the compensation policies of the organization. For example:

> The management of Olympia, Inc. wishes to provide equitable pay to every member. For this reason, it must recognize the contributions made by all jobs, the demands each job places on a jobholder, and the relationship of all jobs in order to develop a fair division of the funds available for pay purposes among all its members.

If one of the tasks of the committee is to select an evaluation method, then the manual should contain a brief description of each method with a list of the advantages and the disadvantages of each. Members should review the methods before a joint training and discussion session. The actual selection meeting follows the training session, and at this time the compensation specialist can still answer any questions of unanswered doubts about any of the methods.

USING FES TO DETERMINE JOB WORTH

In 1977, after more than five years of research that involved approximately 4,000 jobs, 26 federal agencies, and 256 field installations, the U.S. Civil Service Commission (CSC), now known as the Office of Personnel Management (OPM), developed a nine-factor job evaluation method known as the Factor Evaluation System (FES). This method has proven to be capable of accurately measuring the worth of more than 1 million nonsupervisory General Schedule (GS) positions. The FES differs from the previously developed point-factor methods such as those of the NMTA and the NEMA and their many offshoots in that it contains three stages of descriptive data, not simply a defined set of universal compensable factors, subfactors, and degrees. The three stages of FES are (1) primary standards, (2) factor-level descriptions for the series (occupational standards), and (3) benchmark jobs that cover the full range of pay for the jobs in each occupation or series.[2]

The primary standards are similar to many other compensable factor plans. Table 9–1 lists the nine FES compensable factors and their weights and levels. Table 9–2 is the 1999 pay schedule for GS (General Schedule) federal employees. Figure 9–2 is a complete description of the nine factors and their assigned levels. (See Table 11–10 for the 27 grade pay schedule based on FES points developed and used by the author.)

TABLE 9–1 Factor Description Table

Factor	Points for Factor	Value of Factor as Percentage of Total (weight of factor)	Number of Levels	Points for Each Level
Knowledge required by the position	1,850	41.3%	9	50, 200, 350, 550, 750, 950, 1,250, 1,550, 1,850
Supervisory control	650	14.5%	5	25, 125, 275, 450, 650
Guidelines	650	14.5%	5	25, 125, 275, 450, 650
Complexity	450	10.0%	6	25, 75, 150, 225, 325, 450
Scope and effect	450	10.0%	6	25, 75, 150, 225, 325, 450
Personal contact	110	2.5%	4	10, 25, 60, 110
Purpose of contact	220	4.9%	4	20, 50, 120, 220
Physical demand	50	1.1%	3	5, 20, 50
Work environment	50	1.1%	3	5, 20, 50
Total	4,480	99.9%		

[2]U.S. Civil Service Commission, *Instructions for the Factor Evaluation System* (Washington, DC: Government Printing Office, May 1977).

TABLE 9–2   U.S. Office of Personnel Management, 1999 General Schedule[a] (not including locality rates of pay) Effective January 1999

FES Points	Grade	Annual Rates for Steps (in dollars)									
		1	2	3	4	5	6	7	8	9	10
190–250	1	13,362	13,807	14,252	14,694	15,140	15,401	15,838	16,281	16,299	16,718
250–450	2	15,023	15,380	15,878	16,299	16,482	16,967	17,452	17,937	18,422	18,907
455–650	3	16,392	16,938	17,484	18,030	18,576	19,122	19,668	20,214	20,760	21,306
655–850	4	18,401	19,014	19,627	20,240	20,853	21,466	22,079	22,692	23,305	23,918
855–1,100	5	20,588	21,274	21,960	22,646	23,332	24,018	24,704	25,390	26,076	26,762
1,105–1,350	6	22,948	23,713	24,478	25,243	26,008	26,773	27,538	28,303	29,068	29,833
1,355–1,600	7	25,501	26,351	27,201	28,051	28,901	29,751	30,601	31,451	32,301	33,151
1,605–1,850	8	28,242	29,183	30,124	31,065	32,006	32,947	33,888	34,829	35,770	36,711
1,855–2,100	9	31,195	32,235	33,275	34,315	35,355	36,395	37,435	38,475	39,515	40,555
2,105–2,350	10	34,353	35,498	36,643	37,788	38,933	40,078	41,223	42,368	43,513	44,658
2,355–2,750	11	37,744	39,002	40,260	41,518	42,776	44,034	45,292	46,550	47,808	49,066
2,755–3,150	12	45,236	46,744	48,252	49,760	51,268	52,776	54,284	55,792	57,300	58,808
3,155–3,600	13	53,793	55,586	57,379	59,172	60,965	62,758	64,551	66,344	68,137	69,930
3,605–4,050	14	63,567	65,686	67,805	69,924	72,043	74,162	76,281	78,400	80,519	82,638
4,050–4,480	15	74,773	77,265	79,757	82,249	84,741	87,233	89,725	92,217	94,709	97,201

[a]Incorporating a 3.10% general increase.

After establishing the primary standards, the next step in the FES is to develop factor-level descriptions for the series. (This is the application of the primary standards to a specific occupation or to groups of closely related occupations.) By further defining the factors in terms of the work/job content of jobs in a specific occupation, it is easier to relate a specific level of a factor to a particular job. This, in turn, makes it easier to reach a consensus during the evaluation process.

At this time, more than 60 occupational standards have been developed. However, many of the occupational standards include jobs with large numbers of incumbents and jobs that are found in all kinds of public- and private-sector organizations, that is, secretary series, clerk series, computer personnel series, accounting series. Figure 9–3 describes the compensable factor *Complexity* for the secretary series (GS-318). Note that each level in the secretary series is described in terms of the kind of work a secretary performs, whereas in the Primary Series, the descriptions of each level are more general because they must relate to literally thousands of jobs in over 400 occupations. It must also be noted that the compensable factor *Complexity* for the secretary series has only three levels. This is a result of a review of all kinds of secretarial jobs and the finding that no secretarial job has greater than a third level of complexity. Each occupation series includes only the levels of the factors applicable to that specific series. This kind of "bobtailing" or including only those levels (degrees) of a factor that relate to jobs in the occupation reduces the opportunity for argument and hastens the evaluation process.

CHAPTER 9 *Job Evaluation* **265**

FACTOR 1. KNOWLEDGE REQUIRED BY THE POSITION

Factor 1 measures the nature and extent of information or facts which the workers must understand to do acceptable work (e.g., steps, procedures, practices, rules, policies, theories, principles, and concepts) and the nature and extent of the skills needed to apply those knowledges. To be used as a basis for selecting a level under this factor, a knowledge must be required and applied.

Level 1–1 *50 points*

Knowledge of simple, routine, or repetitive tasks or operations which typically includes following step-by-step instructions and requires little or no previous training or experience;

OR

Skill to operate simple equipment or equipment which operates repetitively, requiring little or no previous training or experience;

OR

Equivalent knowledge and skill.

Level 1–2 *200 points*

Knowledge of basic or commonly-used rules, procedures, or operations which typically requires some previous training or experience;

OR

Basic skill to operate equipment requiring some previous training or experience, such as keyboard equipment;

OR

Equivalent knowledge and skill.

Level 1–3 *350 points*

Knowledge of a body of standardized rules, procedures or operations requiring considerable training and experience to perform the full range of standard clerical assignments and resolve recurring problems;

OR

Skill, acquired through considerable training and experience, to operate and adjust varied equipment for purposes such as performing numerous standardized tests or operations;

OR

Equivalent knowledge and skill.

Level 1–4 *550 points*

Knowledge of an extensive body of rules, procedures or operations requiring extended training and experience to perform a wide variety of interrelated or nonstandard procedural assignments and resolve a wide range of problems;

OR

Practical knowledge of standard procedures in a technical field, requiring extended training or experience, to perform such work as adapting equipment when this requires considering the functioning characteristics of equipment; interpreting results of tests based on previous experience and observations (rather than directly reading instruments or other measures); or extracting information

continued

FIGURE 9–2 FES Primary Standards and Assigned Levels

from various sources when this requires considering the applicability of information and the characteristics and quality of the sources;

OR

Equivalent knowledge and skill.

Level 1–5 750 points

Knowledge (such as would be acquired through a pertinent baccalaureate educational program or its equivalent in experience, training, or independent study) of basic principles, concepts, and methodology of a professional or administrative occupation, and skill in applying this knowledge in carrying out elementary assignments, operations, or procedures;

OR

In addition to the practical knowledge of standard procedures in Level 1–4, practical knowledge of technical methods to perform assignments such as carrying out limited projects which involves use of specialized complicated techniques;

OR

Equivalent knowledge and skill.

Level 1–0 950 points

Knowledge of the principles, concepts, and methodology of a professional or administrative occupation as described at Level 1–5 which has been either: (a) supplemented by skill gained through job experience to permit independent performance of recurring assignments, or (b) supplemented by expanded professional or administrative knowledge gained through relevant graduate study or experience, which has provided skill in carrying out assignments, operations, and procedures in the occupation which are significantly more difficult and complex than those covered by Level 1–5;

OR

Practical knowledge of a wide range of technical methods, principles, and practices similar to a narrow area of a professional field, and skill in applying this knowledge to such assignments as the design and planning of difficult, but well-precedented projects;

OR

Equivalent knowledge and skill.

Level 1–7 1250 points

Knowledge of a wide range of concepts, principles, and practices in a professional or administrative occupation, such as would be gained through extended graduate study or experience, and skill in applying this knowledge to difficult and complex work assignments;

OR

A comprehensive, intensive, practical knowledge of a technical field and skill in applying this knowledge to the development of new methods, approaches, or procedures;

OR

Equivalent knowledge and skill.

Level 1–8 1550 points

Mastery of a professional or administrative field to:

—Apply experimental theories and new developments to problems not susceptible to treatment by accepted methods;

continued

OR

—Make decisions or recommendations significantly changing, interpreting, or developing important public policies or programs;

OR

Equivalent skill and knowledge.

Level 1–9   *1850 points*

Mastery of a professional field to generate and develop new hypotheses and theories;

OR

Equivalent knowledge and skill.

FACTOR 2. SUPERVISORY CONTROLS

"Supervisory Controls" covers the nature and extent of direct or indirect controls exercised by the supervisor, the employee's responsibility, and the review of completed work. Controls are exercised by the supervisor in the way assignments are made, instructions are given to the employee, priorities and deadlines are set, and objectives and boundaries are defined. Responsibility of the employee depends upon the extent to which the employee is expected to develop the sequence and timing of various aspects of the work, to modify or recommend modification of instructions, and to participate in establishing priorities and defining objectives. The degree of review of completed work depends upon the nature and extent of the review, e.g., close and detailed review of each phase of the assignment; detailed review of the finished assignment; spot-check of finished work for accuracy; or review only for adherence to policy.

Level 2–1   *25 points*

For both one-of-a-kind and repetitive tasks the supervisor makes specific assignments that are accompanied by clear, detailed, and specific instructions.

The employee works as instructed and consults with the supervisor as needed on all matters not specifically covered in the original instructions or guidelines.

For all positions the work is closely controlled. For some positions, the control is through the structured nature of the work itself; for others, it may be controlled by the circumstances in which it is performed. In some situations, the supervisor maintains control through review of the work which may include checking progress or reviewing completed work for accuracy, adequacy, and adherence to instructions and established procedures.

Level 2–2   *125 points*

The supervisor provides continuing or individual assignments by indicating generally what is to be done, limitations, quality and quantity expected, deadlines, and priority of assignments. The supervisor provides additional, specific instructions for new, difficult, or unusual assignments including suggested work methods or advice on source material available.

The employee uses initiative in carrying out recurring assignments independently without specific instruction, but refers deviations, problems, and unfamiliar situations not covered by instructions to the supervisor for decision or help.

The supervisor assures that finished work and methods used are technically accurate and in compliance with instructions or established procedures. Review of the work increases with more difficult assignments if the employee has not previously performed similar assignments.

Level 2–3   *275 points*

The supervisor makes assignments by defining objectives, priorities, and deadlines; and assists employee with unusual situations which do not have clear precedents.

continued

The employee plans and carries out the successive steps and handles problems and deviations in the work assignment in accordance with instructions, policies, previous training, or accepted practices in the occupation.

Completed work is usually evaluated for technical soundness, appropriateness, and conformity to policy and requirements. The methods used in arriving at the end results are not usually reviewed in detail.

Level 2–4   *450 points*

The supervisor sets the overall objectives and resources available. The employee and supervisor, in consultation, develop the deadlines, projects, and work to be done.

At this level, the employee, having developed expertise in the line of work, is responsible for planning and carrying out the assignment; resolving most of the conflicts which arise; coordinating the work with others as necessary; and interpreting policy on own initiative in terms of established objectives. In some assignments, the employee also determines the approach to be taken and the methodology to be used. The employee keeps the supervisor informed of progress, potentially controversial matters, or far-reaching implications.

Completed work is reviewed only from an overall standpoint in terms of feasibility, compatibility with other work, or effectiveness in meeting requirements or expected results.

Level 2–5   *650 points*

The supervisor provides administrative direction with assignments in terms of broadly defined missions or functions.

The employee has responsibility for planning, designing, and carrying out programs, projects, studies, or other work independently.

Results of the work are considered as technically authoritative and are normally accepted without significant change. If the work should be reviewed, the review concerns such matters as fulfillment of program objectives, effect of advice and influence of the overall program, or the contribution to the advancement of technology. Recommendations for new projects and alteration of objectives are usually evaluated for such considerations as availability of funds and other resources, broad program goals or national priorities.

FACTOR 3. GUIDELINES

This factor covers the nature of guidelines and the judgment needed to apply them. Guides used in General Schedule occupations include, for example: desk manuals, established procedures and policies, traditional practices, and reference materials such as dictionaries, style manuals, engineering handbooks, the pharmacopoeia, and the Federal Personnel Manual.

Individual jobs in different occupations vary in the specificity, applicability and availability of the guidelines for performance of assignments. Consequently, the constraints and judgmental demands placed upon employees also vary. For example, the existence of specific instructions, procedures, and policies may limit the opportunity of the employee to make or recommend decisions or actions. However, in the absence of procedures or under broadly stated objectives, employees in some occupations may use considerable judgment in researching literature and developing new methods.

Guidelines should not be confused with the knowledges described under Factor 1, Knowledge Required by the Position. Guidelines either provide reference data or impose certain constraints on the use of knowledges. For example, in the field of medical technology, for a particular diagnosis there may be three or four standardized tests set forth in a technical manual. A medical technologist is expected to know these diagnostic tests. However, in a given laboratory the policy may be to use only one of the tests; or the policy may state specifically under what conditions one or the other of these tests may be used.

continued

Level 3–1   *25 points*

Specific, detailed guidelines covering all important aspects of the assignment are provided to the employee.

The employee works in strict adherence to the guidelines; deviations must be authorized by the supervisor.

Level 3–2   *125 points*

Procedures for doing the work have been established and a number of specific guidelines are available.

The number and similarity of guidelines and work situations requires the employee to use judgment in locating and selecting the most appropriate guidelines, references, and procedures for application and in making minor deviations to adapt the guidelines in specific cases. At this level, the employee may also determine which of several established alternatives to use. Situations to which the existing guidelines cannot be applied or significant proposed deviations from the guidelines are referred to the supervisor.

Level 3–3   *275 points*

Guidelines are available, but are not completely applicable to the work or have gaps in specificity.

The employee uses judgment in interpreting and adapting guidelines such as agency policies, regulations, precedents, and work directions for application to specific cases or problems. The employee analyzes results and recommends changes.

Level 3–4   *450 points*

Administrative policies and precedents are applicable but are stated in general terms. Guidelines for performing the work are scarce or of limited use.

The employee uses initiative and resourcefulness in deviating from traditional methods or researching trends and patterns to develop new methods, criteria, or proposed new policies.

Level 3–5   *650 points*

Guidelines are broadly stated and nonspecific, e.g., broad policy statements and basic legislation which require extensive interpretation.

The employee must use judgment and ingenuity in interpreting the intent of the guides that do exist and in developing applications to specific areas of work. Frequently, the employee is recognized as a technical authority in the development and interpretation of guidelines.

FACTOR 4. COMPLEXITY

This factor covers the nature, number, variety, and intricacy of tasks, steps, processes, or methods in the work performed; the difficulty in identifying what needs to be done; and the difficulty and originality involved in performing the work.

Level 4–1   *25 points*

The work consists of tasks that are clear-cut and directly related.

There is little or no choice to be made in deciding what needs to be done.

Actions to be taken or responses to be made are readily discernible. The work is quickly mastered.

Level 4–2   *75 points*

The work consists of duties that involve related steps, processes, or methods.

The decision regarding what needs to be done involves various choices requiring the employee to recognize the existence of and differences among a few easily recognizable situations.

continued

Actions to be taken or responses to be made differ in such things as the source of information, the kind of transactions or entries, or other differences of a factual nature.

Level 4–3   *150 points*

The work includes various duties involving different and unrelated processes and methods.

The decision regarding what needs to be done depends upon the analysis of the subject, phase, or issues involved in each assignment, and the chosen course of action may have to be selected from many alternatives.

The work involves conditions and elements that must be identified and analyzed to discern inter-relationships.

Level 4–4   *225 points*

The work typically includes varied duties requiring many different and unrelated processes and methods such as those relating to well-established aspects of an administrative or professional field.

Decisions regarding what needs to be done include the assessment of unusual circumstances, variations in approach, and incomplete or conflicting data.

The work requires making many decisions concerning such things as the interpreting of considerable data, planning of the work, or refining the methods and techniques to be used.

Level 4–5   *325 points*

The work includes varied duties requiring many different and unrelated processes and methods applied to a broad range of activities or substantial depth of analysis, typically for an administrative or professional field.

Decisions regarding what needs to be done include major areas of uncertainty in approach, methodology, or interpretation and evaluation processes resulting from such elements as continuing changes in program, technological developments, unknown phenomena, or conflicting requirements.

The work requires originating new techniques, establishing criteria, or developing new information.

Level 4–6   *450 points*

The work consists of broad functions and processes of an administrative or professional field. Assignments are characterized by breadth and intensity of effort and involve several phases being pursued concurrently or sequentially with the support of others within or outside of the organization.

Decisions regarding what needs to be done include largely undefined issues and elements, requiring extensive probing and analysis to determine the nature and scope of the problems.

The work requires continuing efforts to establish concepts, theories, or programs, or to resolve unyielding problems.

FACTOR 5. SCOPE AND EFFECT

Scope and Effect covers the relationship between the nature of the work, i.e., the purpose, breadth, and depth of the assignment, and the effect of work products or services both within and outside the organization.

In General Schedule occupations, effect measures such things as whether the work output facilitates the work of others, provides timely services of a personal nature, or impacts on the adequacy of research conclusions. The concept of effect alone does not provide sufficient information to properly understand and evaluate the impact of the position. The scope of the work completes the picture, allowing consistent evaluations. Only the effect of properly performed work is to be considered.

continued

Level 5–1   *25 points*

The work involves the performance of specific, routine operations that include a few separate tasks or procedures.

The work product or service is required to facilitate the work of others; however, it has little impact beyond the immediate organizational unit or beyond the timely provision of limited services to others.

Level 5–2   *75 points*

The work involves the execution of specific rules, regulations, or procedures and typically comprises a complete segment of an assignment or project of broader scope.

The work product or service affects the accuracy, reliability, or acceptability of further processes or services.

Level 5–3   *150 points*

The work involves treating a variety of conventional problems, questions, or situations in conformance with established criteria.

The work product or service affects the design or operation of systems, programs, or equipment; the adequacy of such activities as field investigations, testing operations, or research conclusions, or the social, physical, and economic well being of persons.

Level 5–4   *225 points*

The work involves establishing criteria; formulating projects; assessing program effectiveness; or investigating or analyzing a variety of unusual conditions, problems, or questions.

The work product or service affects a wide range of agency activities, major activities of industrial concerns, or the operation of other agencies.

Level 5–5   *325 points*

The work involves isolating and defining unknown conditions, resolving critical problems, or developing new theories.

The work product or service affects the work of other experts, the development of major aspects of administrative or scientific programs or missions, or the well-being of substential numbers of people.

Level 5–6   *450 points*

The work involves planning, developing, and carrying out vital administrative or scientific programs.

The programs are essential to the missions of the agency or affect large numbers of people on a long-term or continuing basis.

FACTOR 6. PERSONAL CONTACTS

This factor includes face-to-face contacts and telephone and radio dialogue with persons not in the supervisory chain. (NOTE: Personal contacts with supervisors are covered under Factor 2, Supervisory Controls.) Levels described under this factor are based on what is required to make the initial contact, the difficulty of communicating with those contacted, and the setting in which the contact takes place (e.g., the degree to which the employee and those contacted recognize their relative roles and authorities).

Above the lowest level, points should be credited under this factor only for contacts which are essential for successful performance of the work and which have a demonstrable impact on the difficulty and responsibility of the work performed.

continued

The relationship of Factors 6 and 7 presumes that the same contacts will be evaluated for both factors. Therefore, use the personal contacts which serve as the basis for the level selected for Factor 7 as the basis for selecting a level for Factor 6.

Level 6–1   *10 points*

The personal contacts are with employees within the immediate organization, office, project, or work unit, and in related or support units;

AND/OR

The contacts are with members of the general public in very highly structured situations (e.g., the purpose of the contact and the question of with whom to deal are relatively clear). Typical of contacts at this level are purchases of admission tickets at a ticket window.

Level 6–2   *25 points*

The personal contacts are with employees in the same agency, but outside the immediate organization. People contacted generally are engaged in different functions, missions, and kinds of work, e.g., representatives from various levels within the agency such as headquarters, regional, district, or field offices or other operating offices in the immediate installations;

AND/OR

The contacts are with members of the general public, as individuals or groups, in a moderately structured setting (e.g., the contacts are generally established on a routine basis, usually at the employee's work place; the exact purpose of the contact may be unclear at first to one or more of the parties; and one or more of the parties may be uninformed concerning the role and authority of other participants). Typical of contacts at this level are those with persons seeking airline reservations or with job applicants at a job information center.

Level 6–3   *60 points*

The personal contacts are with individuals or groups from outside the employing agency in a moderately unstructured setting (e.g., the contacts are not established on routine basis; the purpose and extent of each contact is different and the role and authority of each party is identified and developed during the course of the contact). Typical of contacts at this level are those with persons in their capacities as attorneys; contractors; or representatives of professional organizations, the news media, or public action groups.

Level 6–4   *110 points*

The personal contacts are with high-ranking officials from outside the employing agency at national or international levels in highly unstructured settings (e.g., contacts are characterized by problems such as: the officials may be relatively inaccessible; arrangements may have to be made for accompanying staff members; appointments may have to be made well in advance; each party may be very unclear as to the role and authority of the other; and each contact may be conducted under different ground rules). Typical of contacts at this level are those with members of Congress, leading representatives of foreign governments, presidents of large national or international firms, nationally recognized representatives of the news media, presidents of national unions, state governors, or mayors of large cities.

FACTOR 7. PURPOSE OF CONTACTS

In General Schedule occupations, purpose of personal contacts ranges from factual exchanges of information to situations involving significant or controversial issues and differing viewpoints, goals, or objectives. The personal contacts which serve as the basis for the level selected for this factor must be the same as the contacts which are the basis for the level selected for Factor 6.

Level 7–1   *20 points*

The purpose is to obtain, clarify, or give facts or information regardless of the nature of those facts, i.e., the facts or information may range from easily understood to highly technical.

continued

Level 7–2   *50 points*

The purpose is to plan, coordinate, or advise on work efforts or to resolve operating problems by influencing or motivating individuals or groups who are working toward mutual goals and who have basically cooperative attitudes.

Level 7–3   *120 points*

The purpose is to influence, motivate, interrogate, or control persons or groups. At this level the persons contacted may be fearful, skeptical, uncooperative, or dangerous. Therefore, the employee must be skillful in approaching the individual or group in order to obtain the desired effect, such as, gaining compliance with established policies and regulations by persuasion or negotiation, or gaining information by establishing rapport with a suspicious informant.

Level 7–4   *220 points*

The purpose is to justify, defend, negotiate, or settle matters involving significant or controversial issues. Work at this level usually involves active participation in conferences, meetings, hearings, or presentations involving problems or issues of considerable consequence or importance. The persons contacted typically have diverse viewpoints, goals, or objectives requiring the employee to achieve a common understanding of the problem and a satisfactory solution by convincing them, arriving at a compromise, or developing suitable alternatives.

FACTOR 8. PHYSICAL DEMANDS

The "Physical Demands" factor covers the requirements and physical demands placed on the employee by the work assignment. This includes physical characteristics and abilities (e.g., specific agility and dexterity requirements) and the physical exertion involved in the work (e.g., climbing, lifting, pushing, balancing, stooping, kneeling, crouching, crawling, or reaching). To some extent the frequency or intensity of physical exertion must also be considered, e.g., a job requiring prolonged standing involves more physical exertion than a job requiring intermittent standing.

NOTE: Regulations governing pay for irregular or intermittent duty involving unusual physical hardship or hazard are in Chapter 550, Federal Personnel Manual.

Level 8–1   *5 points*

The work is sedentary. Typically, the employee may sit comfortably to do the work. However, there may be some walking; standing; bending; carrying of light items such as papers, books, small parts; driving an automobile, etc. No special physical demands are required to perform the work.

Level 8–2   *20 points*

The work requires some physical exertion such as long periods of standing; walking over rough, uneven, or rocky surfaces; recurring bending, crouching, stooping, stretching, reaching, or similar activities; recurring lifting of moderately heavy items such as typewriters and record boxes. The work may require specific, but common, physical characteristics and abilities such as above-average agility and dexterity.

Level 8–3   *50 points*

The work requires considerable and strenuous physical exertion such as frequent climbing of tall ladders, lifting heavy objects over 50 pounds, crouching or crawling in restricted areas, and defending oneself or others against physical attack.

FACTOR 9. WORK ENVIRONMENT

The "Work Environment" factor considers the risks and discomforts in the employee's physical surroundings or the nature of the work assigned and the safety regulations required. Although the use of safety precautions can practically eliminate a certain danger or discomfort, such situations, typically place additional demands upon the employee in carrying out safety regulations and techniques.

continued

NOTE: Regulations governing pay for irregular or intermittent duty involving unusual physical hardship or hazard are in Chapter 550, Federal Personnel Manual.

Level 9–1   *5 points*

The work environment involves everyday risks or discomforts which require normal safety precautions typical of such places as offices, meeting and training rooms, libraries, and residences or commercial vehicles, e.g., use of safe work practices with office equipment, avoidance of trips and falls, observance of fire regulations and traffic signals, etc. The work area is adequately lighted, heated, and ventilated.

Level 9–2   *20 points*

The work involves moderate risks or discomforts which require special safety precautions, e.g., working around moving parts, carts, or machines; with contagious diseases or irritant chemicals; etc. Employees may be required to use protective clothing or gear such as masks, gowns, coats, boots, goggles, gloves, or shields.

Level 9–3   *50 points*

The work environment involves high risks with exposure to potentially dangerous situations or unusual environmental stress which require a range of safety and other precautions, e.g., working at great heights under extreme outdoor weather conditions, subject to possible physical attack or mob conditions, or similar situations where conditions cannot be controlled.

Source: U.S. Civil Service Commission (currently U.S. Office of Personnel Management, Office of Classification), *Factor Evaluation Standards and Primary Levels* (Washington, DC: U.S. Government Printing Office, 1997).

Evaluating Jobs Using FES

This section presents the material as if a new job evaluation method were being implemented. Although the focus is on FES, what occurs at each step in the process is applicable to most point-factor job evaluation methods.

Step One—Introduce FES   In this first step, the evaluator becomes familiar with the nine factors and recognizes which aspect of the job can be associated with each specific factor. At this initial step, the evaluator also learns to differentiate the factors.

Step Two—Review Job Facts   Now the evaluator becomes as familiar as possible with job content, job specifications or requirements, the expected performance level of a fully qualified incumbent, the fit of the job within the assigned work unit and organization, and the environmental factors that influence incumbent performance.

Step Three—Rate Factor 1—Knowledge Required by the Position   This begins the actual rating process. This is not only the first step but possibly the most important step. In FES, *knowledge* receives a 41 percent weighting. (Note: In Table 9–1, the highest-level point score available for *knowledge* is 1,850 points, which is 41.3 percent of the total available FES points of 4,480.) This factor has the most significant influence on the final rating of the job and also on the pay received by a jobholder. Most job evaluation plans heavily weight the knowledge, know-how, or skill factor. Some plans, like FES and Hay, provide certain patterns (discussed later in this chapter) that restrict or at least "red flag" other factor ratings relative to the selected rating of the knowledge, know-how, skill factor. In this factor, even when not specified, the reviewer must make inferences from job duties regarding the level of education and the amount of prior job-related experience and training demanded of an incumbent. A major problem currently facing

FACTOR 4. COMPLEXITY

This factor covers the nature, number, variety, and intricacy of tasks, steps, processes, or methods in the work performed; the difficulty in identifying what needs to be done; and the difficulty and originality involved in performing the work.

Level 4–1   *25 points*

The work consists of a few clear-cut tasks. The secretary typically provides typing or stenographic services, maintains simple office files, sorts mail into a few categories, and refers phone calls and visitors to staff members.

There is little choice in deciding what needs to be done or when it should be done. Work is performed either as it arrives or in an order set by someone else.

Actions to be taken are readily discernible (e.g., phone calls are simply referred to the requested staff member); otherwise, the secretary requests assistance.

Level 4–2   *75 points*

The work consists of duties that involve various related steps, processes, or methods. In addition to duties as varied as those described at level 4–1, secretaries at this level perform a full range of procedural duties in support of the office, including such duties as requisitioning supplies, printing, or maintenance service; filling out various travel forms for staff members; arranging for meeting rooms; and preparing scheduled reports from information readily available in the files.

Decisions regarding what needs to be done involve various choices requiring the secretary to recognize the existence of and differences among clearly recognizable situations.

Actions to be taken or responses to be made differ in such things as the sources of information, the kind of transactions or entries, or other readily verifiable differences. Decisions at this level are based on a knowledge of the procedural requirements of the work coupled with an awareness of the specific functions and staff assignments of the office.

Level 4–3   *150 points*

The work includes various duties involving different and unrelated processes and methods. For example, in addition to duties described at levels 4–1 and 4–2, the secretary performs a number of duties comparable to the following:

—prepare one-of-a-kind reports from information in various documents when this requires reading correspondence and reports to identify relevant items, and when decisions are based on a familiarity with the issues involved and the relationships between the various types of information; and

—set up conferences requiring the planning and arranging of travel and hotel accommodations for conference participants when this is based on a knowledge of the schedules and commitments of the participants.

Decisions regarding what needs to be done, and how to accomplish them, are based on the secretary's knowledge of the duties, priorities, commitments, policies, and program goals of the supervisor and staff, and involve analysis of the subject, phase, or issues involved in each assignment. The chosen courses are selected from many alternatives.

FIGURE 9–3   Complexity Factor, Secretary Series (GS-318)

many organizations is the need to meet pay demands of jobholders in the Information Technology domain. A possible solution to this problem is to recognize fully the knowledge requirements of these jobs. It has not been unusual for job evaluators to underrate the knowledge requirements of these jobs, which causes them to be underpaid.

Step Four—Rate Factor 2—Supervisory Controls   The rating of this factor requires the evaluator to recognize direct and indirect controls exercised by the supervisor (read introductory section to Supervisory Controls in Figure 9–2). The important issue to recognize here is that the supervisor does not have to be directly behind the employee to maintain close controls. The kind of work and the structured nature of the work establish the degree of controls exercised by a supervisor. A supervisor may not actually observe an employee for weeks, even months; yet in some manner, perhaps by checking finished work, the supervisor can exercise strict to loose controls.

Step Five—Rate Factor 3—Guidelines   Confusion can arise in differentiating the rating of this factor from Factor 2, Supervisory Controls. The important issue here is the amount of judgment the incumbent is permitted to use in performing job assignments. Here, procedures, standing orders, policy manuals, and other kinds of reference material establish the guidelines within which the job is performed and the amount of judgment required of the employee. The guidelines factor does not rate the knowledge required, but rather the constraints imposed on the use of knowledge.

Step Six—Rate Factor 4—Complexity   This factor recognizes the nature, number, variety, and intricacies of the interactions required in getting the job done. Difficulty of assignments and originality in work performed are recognized and valued.

Step Seven—Rate Factor 5—Scope and Effect   The purpose, breadth, and scope of work are recognized by Factor 5. In addition, the factor recognizes the impact the job has on the work of others. A question that must be answered is: How does the assignment of this job affect the work output of others or the delivery of quality services?

Step Eight—Rate Factor 6—Personal Contacts   This factor recognizes with whom the incumbent must interact in performing job assignments and the degree of structure relative to these contacts.

Step Nine—Rate Factor 7—Purpose of Contacts   Now the evaluator identifies the reasons for the contact that were rated in Factor 6. In this factor the complexity of the situation and the reasons for the contacts must be explained.

Step Ten—Rate Factor 8—Physical Demands   This factor recognizes the frequency and intensity of various kinds of physical demands placed on an incumbent in performing job assignments.

Step Eleven—Rate Factor 9—Work Environment   This factor recognizes unpleasantness, discomfort, and risks encountered by an incumbent on the job.

Step Twelve—Rating a Set of Benchmark Jobs   Steps Two through Eleven are repeated for a set of benchmark jobs. As mentioned earlier in this chapter, the benchmark jobs cover the full range of jobs (from lowest- to highest-paid and in different occupational settings—check the discussion of Griffenhagen's intra- and interoccupational classification in chapter 8). The major reason for rating a set of benchmark jobs is to establish an accepted interpretation between kinds and levels of job facts and a specific factor rating. In fact, after a sufficient number of jobs has been evaluated at different levels and in different occupations, the jobs themselves become factor-level benchmarks (see the discussion of Benge's factor-comparison method in chapter 8).

The factor-comparison component of point-factor job evaluation is discussed in detail later in this section, but what must be recognized now is that the benchmark jobs carry with them an organizational-related meaning to a specific level (degree) of a factor. It is always possible for anyone to argue about the assignment of a particular level of a factor relative to a specific job (again, the problems related to ambiguity and inference making). However, the argument becomes much more difficult to prove when the arguer is asked to compare the job and factors in question with already accepted ratings of benchmark jobs. The rebuttal takes this route: "John, do you believe the job of secretary in the Purchasing Department is more complex than the librarian job in the computer center?" Once well-recognized and understood jobs are evaluated and their evaluations have been accepted, they then supplement the rating material provided in the primary standards, series standards, or the FES-provided benchmark jobs. This factor-comparison addition holds true and is useful for any point-factor job evaluation methodology.

Evaluating the Job of Lead Programmer-Analyst

A job description for a lead programmer-analyst at Olympia, Inc., is provided in Figure 7–1. Figure 9–4, Factor Evaluation System Position Evaluation Statement, is a form completed by an evaluator following Steps Three through Eleven developed in the preceding section.

Step One Become familiar with the nine FES factors and the levels within each factor.

Step Two Review job description of lead programmer-analyst.

Step Three—Rate Factor 1—Knowledge Required by the Position When involved in a point-factor evaluation process, an evaluator must become skilled in the "field artillery" method of pinpointing a target. In the process of centering on a target, those who control the sighting of the gun will often find that, after firing the projectile, it is either short or long of the target. The firing officer then goes back and forth over the target until the exact directions are provided and the target is hit.

In ranging in on the most appropriate knowledge level for the lead programmer-analyst, an evaluator can quickly skim over levels 1 through 4, recognizing that they are inadequate or inappropriate. At level 5, the knowledge level begins to make sense. The incumbent must have knowledge of a discipline that is of a professional level and he or she is involved in performing projects requiring the use of specialized, complicated techniques.

Moving on to level 6, an evaluator also is able to make comparisons between statements in level 6 and job requirements. The incumbent must have thorough knowledge of languages used for applications programming, be familiar with embedded computer systems' programming specifications, be able to predict the influence that new applications will have on applications already in the system, and certainly be familiar with user requirements.

Level 7 is also a possibility for the job, but there is a good likelihood that an incumbent would not have to have knowledge of a wide range of concepts, principles, and practices as described at this level.

After a review of level 8, the evaluator notes that there is no relationship between the job and level 8. Now the evaluator must make adjustments between levels 5

FACTOR EVALUATION SYSTEM
POSITION EVALUATION STATEMENT

TITLE: Lead Programmer-Analyst

DEPARTMENT: Data Processing-Information Systems

EVALUATION FACTORS	LEVEL / POINTS	ASSIGNED	COMMENTS*
1. Knowledge Required by the Position	6	950	Could be a *Level 7;* need to know more about required knowledge
2. Supervisory Controls	3	275	Could be a *Level 4;* discuss supervision given with supervisor
3. Guidelines	3	275	Solid *Level 3*
4. Complexity	4	225	Possible light *Level 4* but appears to be 4 because of complex features, changing applications
5. Scope and Effect	3	150	Heavy *Level 3*, but stayed with 3. Did not think incumbent developed criteria or formulated projects
6. Personal Contacts	2	25	Looks like Solid *Level 6–2*. Could be 6–3 if makes contacts with benefits professionals outside organization
7. Purpose of Contacts	2	50	Solid *Level 7–2*. Strictly an exchange of information related to dept.
8. Physical Demands	1	5	Principally sedentary. May involve some walking
9. Work Environment	1	5	Work performed in an office setting
SUMMARY — TOTAL POINTS		1,960	* (As appropriate, audit findings or other considerations not previously documented that affect final evaluation.)

FIGURE 9–4 Factor Evaluation System Position Evaluation Statement

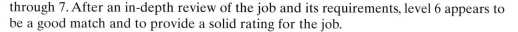

through 7. After an in-depth review of the job and its requirements, level 6 appears to be a good match and to provide a solid rating for the job.

Step Four—Rate Factor 2—Supervisory Controls   In a review of the five levels of Supervisory Controls, the "bracketing" approach focuses on levels 2, 3, and 4. In this job, the supervisor assigns a particular project and is available for consultation when difficult problems arise. Programming specifications and project directions define the results to be achieved and deadlines that must be met. The employee plans his or her own assignments and makes necessary day-to-day decisions, resolving problems in accordance with established practices. The employee provides written and oral reports at specific times and upon completion of the project. Completed work is reviewed and rated for timeliness and adequate accomplishment of specifications and compatibility with other programs. Because the employee is on his or her own, using knowledge gained through prior training, a level 2 was rejected. Because the job does not require interpreting policy and establishing objectives and other high-level controls as described in level 4, it also was rejected. It appears that there is a strong match between job requirements and level 3.

Step Five—Rate Factor 3—Guidelines   After quickly rejecting level 1, level 2 appears to describe the guidelines and judgment used by the incumbent. Moving on, level 3 also has some applicability because this lead programmer-analyst must work where there are gaps in specificity and must use judgment in interpreting and adapting guidelines.

Level 4 discusses initiative and resourcefulness in deviating from traditional methods and in developing new methods and criteria. Level 5 does not apply. The evaluator must make a decision between levels 2 and 3. The incumbent must meet programming specifications and department standards. This individual must use some judgment in interpreting guidelines and in developing logic. A careful review of the job requirements and levels 2 and 3 results in a selection of level 3.

Step Six—Rate Factor 4—Complexity   Moving through the six levels of complexity, level 1 is quickly eliminated. Level 2 is also eliminated after reading such statements as "related steps, processes . . ." and "requiring the employee to recognize the existence of differences among a few easily recognizable situations." Level 3 may be appropriate—the work does involve different and unrelated processes—that is, writing application programs, reviewing requirements with users, explaining software and hardware constraints to users, ensuring that new applications interface properly with existing applications, and so on. Level 4 appears to be appropriate. The work does involve different and unrelated processes. It requires the interpretation of considerable data. Level 4 is a possibility. Level 5 identifies a degree of complexity beyond that found in the job.

Returning to levels 3 and 4, the evaluator selects a level 4. This level was selected because each project required different programming applications and configurations. Each new application must integrate with programs currently in use. The incumbent must be able to advise users on significant aspects of application design and programming specifications. This individual must also explain user requirements to other Information Systems personnel.

Step Seven—Rate Factor 5—Scope and Effect   Once again, level 1 is quickly eliminated. Level 2 may be appropriate because the work involves the execution of specific rules and regulations and affects the reliability of other services. Level 3 also appears to be a possible match. The work treats conventional problems and affects the operation of systems, programs, and so on. At level 4, concepts appear that do not relate to the job being evaluated. The work at this level does not involve the establishment of criteria or the formulation of projects. Once again, the choice is between levels 2 and 3. Because the work of the incumbent affects all employees and influences a number of different internal units and external organizations such as insurance companies and various government agencies, level 3 was selected rather than level 2.

Step Eight—Rate Factor 6—Personal Contacts   A review of the four levels of this factor quickly eliminates level 1, but level 2 looks like a good choice. The incumbent works with individuals in the Information Systems department and with personnel specialists, possibly finance and accounting personnel, and also various providers of insurance and other benefits. The settings are rather structured. Level 3 may be a possibility—the contacts are made in a moderately unstructured setting. Level 4 is not appropriate.

Level 2 was selected rather than level 3, recognizing that even when the incumbent meets with other people in a moderately unstructured setting, both parties know rather precisely why they are meeting and what facts they wish to exchange.

Step Nine—Rate Factor 7—Purpose of Contacts   A review of the four levels of this factor focuses on level 2. Although many contacts of this job relate to obtaining, clarifying, or giving facts (level 1), the employee must also plan, coordinate, and advise on work efforts to resolve operating problems, making level 2 a better choice. Level 3 was rejected because the employee is not required to work with skeptical, uncooperative individuals in a dangerous situation.

Step Ten—Rate Factor 8—Physical Demands   A scan of the three levels of this factor takes the evaluator back to level 1. The job is primarily sedentary in nature.

Step Eleven—Rate Factor 9—Work Environment   With most of the work of this job performed in an office setting, a review of the three levels of this factor also results in the selection of level 1.

After each individual committee member completes the rating as described in Steps 3 through 11, the committee as a whole reviews the individual evaluations factor by factor and comes to an agreement on a selected factor level. Here, each person defends his or her rating, explaining why a specific level was selected. If individual committee members cannot adequately respond to questions pertinent to the selection of a specific level of a factor, calls are made to the incumbent, the supervisor, or to other subject matter job experts to answer any questions. It may even be necessary for the committee or a selected member to revisit the job and collect the necessary job data. This example may begin to provide some view as to the amount of time consumed in evaluating jobs. It is impossible to overstate the importance of multiple and consensus judgment in the job evaluation process. A certain amount of subjectivity may always be found in any form of job evaluation. The committee process—the use of the intellect of committed and knowledgeable individuals seeking the most accurate rating—will minimize the negative aspects of subjectivity.

FES Quality Check and Patterns

In the early 1980s, Paul Krumsiek and Thelma Nixon analyzed 506 FES evaluated benchmark jobs within the U.S. Customs Services. From an analysis of their review, this author has developed an FES Knowledge Level Convention (see Figure 9–5). Using the data from the report by Krumsiek and Nixon, a percentage relationship was developed between the rating level of knowledge and the occurrence of the rating levels of all the other eight factors. There is no surprise that there is a direct relationship between the selected level of the knowledge factor and levels selected of all other factors. It is highly unlikely that a job requiring a low level of knowledge (e.g., level 1 or 2, possibly 3) would require an incumbent to work in an unstructured setting receiving minimal supervision or that the job would be as complex or broad in scope or have as critical an influence on the success of the organization as a job requiring a higher-level of knowledge. Conversely, a job requiring a higher-level of knowledge would not be simple in nature, would not require close supervision, and would have major impact on the performance of the organization. As discussed previously in chapter 8, the knowledge or skill requirements of a job drive the evaluation rating, whereas other compensable factors provide additional information to "fine tune" the final rating.

Because the percentages provided in Figure 9–5 come from a study of a major agency of the federal government, the percentage relationship may not relate exactly to another government or even to a private-sector organization. However, this convention provides a pattern of relationships that permits a quick review of all ratings. When a rating falls outside the range provided in the FES convention, it should be an immediate warning that either the factor should be reevaluated or possibly that an inappropriate knowledge level was selected. Again, because the convention comes from the work in only one federal agency, it should be used only as a guide. For example, a study in a particular organization may find a job receives a knowledge level rating of 5 and a guidelines rating of 4. The convention says this level of guidelines should not occur. After close review, however, it may be that in this organization the job under study requires the incumbent to deviate from traditional methods and use resources, initiative, and judgment based on experience, resulting in a level higher than that normally expected to occur.

"Sore Thumbing" the Ratings

After all jobs have been evaluated, printouts (this phase of the evaluation process makes excellent use of readily available software spreadsheet programs) can be developed that rank all jobs from the highest- to the lowest-rated point score that includes the points (or levels) assigned to each factor. This analysis can be done in many ways. (Once again, computer technology can be extremely helpful. By entering a job code, job title, and evaluation score for each factor into a database, desired combinations can be quickly reproduced and changes can easily be made with regard to any factor rating.)

High to low job evaluation spreadsheets can be developed for all jobs in the organization, or all jobs in a specific unit, or location, or by such major job groupings as (1) all managers, (2) all professionals, (3) all technicians, (4) all administrative support (including clerical), (5) all exempt, and (6) all nonexempt. Reviewing ratings using these kinds of spreadsheets assists in identifying factor ratings that don't make sense. This analysis is often called *sore thumbing* because an inappropriate rating stands out like a sore thumb when doing this kind of factor-comparison analysis. Figure 9–6 is a factor-comparison spreadsheet for the Information Systems Division within Olympia, Inc.

Knowledge Level Selected	Factor Level Selected	Other FES Factors							
		2 Super	3 Guide	4 Compl	5 Scpef	6 Perco	7 Purco	8 Phyde	9 Woren
		Percentage of time factor level selected with given knowledge level							
1	1	70	100	100	100	75	100	85	75
	2	30	—	—	—	25	—	15	25
	Dominant Level	1	1	1	1	1	1	1	1
2	1	15	70	70	100	80	100	70	65
	2	85	30	30		20		30	35
	Dominant Level	2	1	1	1	1	1	1	1
3	1	7	4	—	—	11	41	41	63
	2	67	92	63	97	86	52	52	26
	3	26	4	37	3	3	7	7	11
	Dominant Level	2	2	2	2	2	2	2	1
4	1	—	—	—	—	10	25	65	65
	2	40	75	20	60	75	75	33	33
	3	60	25	80	40	15	—	2	2
	Dominant Level	3	2	3	2	2	2	1	1
5	1	—	—	—	—	15	25	67	70
	2	20	30	15	50	70	75	33	30
	3	65	70	70	50	15			
	4	15	—	15	—	—			
	Dominant Level(s)	3	3	3	2/3	2	2	1	1
6	1	—	—	—	—	—	—	100	100
	2	—	—	—	50	60	100	—	—
	3	50	100	50	50	40	—	—	—
	4	50	—	50	—	—	—	—	—
	Dominant Level(s)	3/4	3	3/4	2/3	2	2	1	1
7	1	—	—	—	—	—	2	3	43
	2	—	—	—	—	25	40	60	49
	3	28	85	2	85	73	58	37	8
	4	72	15	92	15	2	—	—	—
	5	—	—	6	—	—	—	—	—
	Dominant Level	4	3	4	3	3	3	2	2
8	1	—	—	—	—	—	—	75	75
	2	—	—	—	—	—	—	20	20
	3	—	—	—	—	85	75	5	5
	4	35	50	—	30	15	25	—	—
	5	65	50	85	60	—	—	—	—
	6	—	—	15	10	—	—	—	—
	Dominant Level(s)	5	4/5	5	5	3	3	1	1
9	1	—	—	—	—	—	—	100	100
	3	—	—	—	—	25	—	—	—
	4	—	—	—	—	75	100	—	—
	5	100	100	—	20	—	—	—	—
	6	—	—	100	80	—	—	—	—
	Dominant Level	5	5	6	6	4	4	1	1

FIGURE 9–5   FES Knowledge-Level Conventions

Job Description Title	Factor 1	Factor 2	Factor 3	Factor 4	Factor 5	Factor 6	Factor 7	Factor 8	Factor 9	Total Points
Senior Systems Programmer	8 / 1,550	5 / 650	5 / 650	5 / 325	5 / 325	3 / 60	4 / 220	1 / 5	1 / 5	3,790
Senior Programmer-Analyst	7 / 1,250	4 / 450	4 / 450	5 / 325	4 / 225	3 / 60	2 / 50	1 / 5	1 / 5	2,820
Systems Programmer	7 / 1,250	4 / 450	3 / 275	4 / 225	3 / 150	3 / 60	2 / 50	1 / 5	1 / 5	2,470
Lead Programmer-Analyst	6 / 950	3 / 275	3 / 275	4 / 225	3 / 150	2 / 25	2 / 50	1 / 5	1 / 5	1,960
Senior Programmer	6 / 950	3 / 275	3 / 275	3 / 150	3 / 150	2 / 25	1 / 20	1 / 5	1 / 5	1,855
Programmer Analyst	6 / 950	2 / 125	3 / 275	3 / 150	2 / 75	2 / 25	1 / 20	1 / 5	1 / 5	1,630
Associate Programmer	5 / 750	2 / 125	2 / 125	2 / 75	2 / 75	1 / 10	1 / 20	1 / 5	1 / 5	1,190
Secretary	3 / 350	3 / 275	2 / 125	2 / 75	2 / 75	2 / 25	2 / 50	1 / 5	1 / 5	985
Senior Computer Operator	3 / 350	2 / 125	2 / 125	3 / 150	2 / 75	2 / 25	1 / 20	2 / 20	1 / 5	895
Programmer (Trainee)	3 / 350	2 / 125	2 / 125	3 / 150	2 / 75	1 / 10	1 / 20	1 / 5	1 / 5	865
Senior Computer Clerk	3 / 350	2 / 125	2 / 125	2 / 75	2 / 75	2 / 75	1 / 20	2 / 20	1 / 5	820
Associate Computer Operator	2 / 200	2 / 125	2 / 125	2 / 75	2 / 75	2 / 25	1 / 20	2 / 20	1 / 5	670
Associate Computer Clerk	2 / 200	2 / 125	1 / 25	2 / 75	2 / 75	1 / 10	1 / 20	2 / 20	1 / 5	555
Data Entry Clerk	2 / 200	2 / 125	1 / 25	2 / 75	2 / 75	1 / 10	1 / 20	2 / 20	1 / 5	555
Computer Clerk	2 / 200	2 / 125	1 / 25	1 / 25	1 / 25	1 / 10	1 / 20	2 / 20	1 / 5	455

FIGURE 9–6   Factor Comparison Spreadsheet

USING THE HAY PLAN TO DETERMINE JOB WORTH[3]

In the early 1950s, Edward N. Hay and Dale Purves developed a Guide Chart-Profile Method for evaluating jobs that is one of the more popular methods used today. By 1992, the Hay Group had 9,000 clients worldwide and provided services to 470 of the U.S. Fortune 1,000 businesses. The Hay Method is particularly popular for evaluating executive, managerial, and professional positions, but it is also widely used in evaluating nonexempt clerical, blue-collar, and technician jobs.

The Hay Guide Charts evolved from the late 1930s and 1940s factor-comparison work of Ned Hay (see Hay discussion in chapter 8). In attempting to improve a client's understanding of the Hay factor-comparison method using the 15 percent just perceptible difference (see Weber's Law in chapter 8), it became clear to Hay and Purves that a methodology had to be developed, both to guide the logic of the evaluation process and also to provide an "audit trail" or "footprint" so that management could reconstruct and confirm the logic and come to a similar conclusion or, if disagreeing, provide a rational basis for their disagreement. The results of their efforts were the three Hay Guide Charts.

Although the following explanation centers on the point-factor part of the Hay job evaluation process, it must be recognized that Hay consultants continue to use the factor-comparison methodology to develop an "envisioned profile" of a range of benchmark jobs. The factor-comparison results are also used after measuring the job to compare the measurement-derived profile with the envisioned profile for quality assurance purposes.

The Hay Plan or the Hay Guide Chart-Profile Method uses the following three universal factors to evaluate all jobs: (1) Know-How (KH), (2) Problem Solving (PS), and (3) Accountability (AC). If an organization wishes to recognize working or other environmental conditions relating to job context, Hay provides an ACEs chart (see Working Conditions and ACEs chart in chapter 8) to identify such job-related issues. Hay recommends to its clients that job content measurement be treated separately from ACEs measurement and pay. The ACEs values should not be included in the total KH, PS, and AC point scores. Each Guide Chart defines a factor in detail in terms of two or three elements. Ned Hay, the principal architect of the Hay Method, coined the term *Guide Chart* because it guides the evaluator's decision about the relative amount of a particular factor that is present in the job being evaluated.

The descriptions that form the rows and the columns of the Guide Chart provide a measure of the level of difficulty, or importance, of each factor. When comparing the factor requirements of a specific job to the Guide Chart standards, the intersection of the most appropriate row and column descriptor provides a point value.

The KH and AC Guide Charts provide actual point scores. The PS Guide Chart, however, provides a percentage. The percentage value identifies the amount of know-how used in solving problems. The problem-solving point score is determined by multiplying the problem-solving percentage by the point score previously determined for the

---

[3]Major conceptual and writing contributions to this section were provided by Norman Lange, VP of Job Measurement Practices, Hay Management Consultants.

know-how factor. However, in the Hay methodology, a table is used to calculate the PS points (this determination is discussed in detail later in this section—see Figure 9–11A).

The Hay Guide Charts have both standardized and customized features. The geometric measurement scales use the same values with each step, reflecting the 15 percent (or one-step) perceptible difference in values developed by Hay (see Weber's Law in chapter 8). The customized portion of the Guide Charts relates to the number of rows and columns of each Guide Chart; that is, depending on the character and size of a client, the Know-How Guide Chart could include all or a limited number of the depth and breadth of Knowledge levels (L to J) and the Managerial Know-How levels (T to IV). The Accountability Guide Chart can also be expanded or reduced, depending on the size and character of the client organization. The Guide Charts could be likened to a ruler with uniform gradations to indicate fractions of an inch. Some rulers are six inches long; some are three feet long. The larger the object being measured, the longer the ruler.

The Know-How (KH) Guide Chart (see Figure 9–7) includes three elements (the elements within a Guide Chart could be considered as subfactors for the particular universal factor). The three elements included within the KH Guide Chart are the row elements that describe the depth and breadth of job knowledge required to perform job assignments. The management breadth column element describes the requirement for planning, organizing, review, and control to integrate diversified functional elements. Within each column element is the third Know-How element—Human Relations Skill.

Each of the three elements are defined in the upper left-hand column of Figure 9–7, the Know-How Guide Chart. The levels of the first two elements are defined in their respective rows and columns. The levels of the Human Relations Skills are defined at the bottom of the Guide Chart. Each level of each element has an alphanumeric header that is used to code a rating.

The second compensable factor, Problem Solving, includes two elements. The row element includes levels of the Thinking Environment, and the column element includes levels of the Thinking Challenge. The two elements and their respective levels are defined on the Problem-Solving Guide Chart (Figure 9–8). The levels of each of the elements have an alphanumeric header and title (e.g., A. Strict Routine, and so on) followed by a brief definition.

The third factor, Accountability (for end results) (see Figure 9–9), also has three elements. The row element is Freedom to Act. The column element measures the magnitude of the impact of the job on end results. Inside the level of the Magnitude column element is the third element, Job Impact on End Results.

The Freedom to Act and Magnitude elements are described on the bottom of Figure 9–9. The levels within each of these two elements are further described in their appropriate rows and columns. The Job Impact element and its levels are described on the top of Figure 9–9. The Magnitude values are adjusted annually through the use of an Accountability Magnitude Index (AMI) rating. This AMI is calculated annually by Hay and is similar to the Bureau of Labor Statistics Consumer Price Index. The AMI for 1999 was 5.0.

In the following section, the lead programmer-analyst job previously evaluated using FES is evaluated using the Hay Plan. The section includes a discussion of Hay profiling procedures and other Hay quality checks that assist all involved parties to (1) develop consistent interpretations of the Hay Guide Charts and (2) recognize

FIGURE 9–7 Know-How Guide Chart

| HUMAN RELATIONS SKILLS ⇒ | 1 Basic Courtesy, tact, and effectiveness in dealing with others in everyday working relationships, including contacts to request or provide information. | 2 Important Alternative or combined skills in dealing with and/or influencing people, and causing understanding or actions of others, are important to achieving objectives. | 3 Critical Alternative or combined skills in understanding, influencing, and causing commitments to (as well as understanding and acceptance of) actions by others are important in the highest degree. |

MANAGERIAL KNOW-HOW ⇒

KNOW-HOW ⇩	T. Task Performance of one or more tasks that are highly specific as to objective and content, with limited awareness of surrounding circumstances and events.			I. Minimal Performance or supervision of an activity or activities that are specific as to objectives and content, with general awareness of related activities			II. Related Operational or conceptual integration or coordination of activities that are relatively homogeneous in nature and objective.			III. Diverse Operational or conceptual integration of activities that are diverse in nature and objectives in an important managed area.			IV. Broad Integration of major functions in an operating complex.		
SPECIALIZED KNOW-HOW	1	2	3	1	2	3	1	2	3	1	2	3	1	2	3
L Limited Basic instructions and simple work routines to carry out manual tasks	29	33	38	38	43	50	50	57	66	66	76	87	87	100	115
	33	38	43	43	50	57	57	66	76	76	87	100	100	115	132
	38	43	50	50	57	66	66	76	87	87	100	115	115	132	152
A Primary Basic literacy and numeracy plus work indoctrination for performance of repetitive operational or clerical routines, which may involve use of common tools and standard single purpose machines.	38	43	50	50	57	66	66	76	87	87	100	115	115	132	152
	43	50	57	57	66	76	76	87	100	100	115	132	132	152	175
	50	57	66	66	76	87	87	100	115	115	132	152	152	175	200
B Elementary Vocational Familiarization with uninvolved, standardized work routines and/or use of equipment and complex or multi-purpose machines.	50	57	66	66	76	87	87	100	115	115	132	152	152	175	200
	57	66	76	76	87	100	100	115	132	132	152	175	175	200	230
	66	76	87	87	100	115	115	132	152	152	175	200	200	230	264
C Vocational Procedural or systematic proficiency, which may involve a facility in the use of specialized equipment.	66	76	87	87	100	115	115	132	152	152	175	200	200	230	264
	76	87	100	100	115	132	132	152	175	175	200	230	230	264	304
	87	100	115	115	132	152	152	175	200	200	230	264	264	304	350
D Advanced Vocational Some specialized (generally non-theoretical) skill(s), acquired on or off the job, giving additional breadth or depth to a generally single function.	87	100	115	115	132	152	152	175	200	200	230	264	264	304	350
	100	115	132	132	152	175	175	200	230	230	264	304	304	350	400
	115	132	152	152	175	200	200	230	264	264	304	350	350	400	460
E Basic Specialized Sufficiency in a technique which requires a grasp either of involved practices and precedents, or of scientific theory and principles, or both.	115	132	152	152	175	200	200	230	264	264	304	350	350	400	460
	132	152	175	175	200	230	230	264	304	304	350	400	400	460	528
	152	175	200	200	230	264	264	304	350	350	400	460	460	528	608
F Seasoned Specialized Proficiency gained through wide exposure in a technique that combines a broad understanding either of involved practices and precedents, or of scientific theory and principles, or both.	152	175	200	200	230	264	264	304	350	350	400	460	460	528	608
	175	200	230	230	264	304	304	350	400	400	460	528	528	608	700
	200	230	264	264	304	350	350	400	460	460	528	608	608	700	800
G Specialized Mastery Determinative mastery of techniques, practices, and theories gained through wide seasoning and/or special development.	200	230	264	264	304	350	350	400	460	460	528	608	608	700	800
	230	264	304	304	350	400	400	460	528	528	608	700	700	800	920
	264	304	350	350	400	460	460	528	608	608	700	800	800	920	1056

Know-How is the sum total of every kind of skill, however acquired, necessary for acceptable position performance. This sum total, which comprises the overall "fund of knowledge" has three dimensions . . . the requirements for:

⇒DEPTH AND BREADTH OF SPECIALIZED KNOWLEDGE, ranging from basic knowledge of the most simple work routines to unique and authoritative knowledge within learned disciplines. A position may require some knowledge about a lot of things (diversity) or a lot of knowledge about a few things. The total Know-How is the combination of breadth and depth. This concept makes practical the comparison and weighing of the total Know-How content of different positions in terms of: How much knowledge about how many things?

⇒KNOW-HOW OF HARMONIZING AND INTEGRATING the diversified functions involved in managerial situations (operating, supporting, and administrative). This know-How may be exercised consultatively as well as executively and involves, in some combination, the areas of organizing, planning, executing, controlling, and evaluating.

⇒HUMAN RELATIONS SKILLS consisting of active, practicing, person-to-person skills in the area of human relationships.

These Guide Charts® have been produced specifically to illustrate use of this proprietary methodology. They may not be reproduced without Hay permission. Copyright 1996 Hay Group Inc.

FIGURE 9-8 Problem-Solving Guide Chart

PROBLEM SOLVING

THINKING CHALLENGE ⇒

THINKING ENVIRONMENT ⇓

PROBLEM SOLVING	1 Repetitive — Identical situations requiring solution by simple choices of learned things.	2 Patterned — Similar situations requiring solution by discriminating choices of learned things that generally follow well defined patterns.	3 Interpolative — Differing situations requiring searches for solutions or new applications within areas of learned things.	4 Adaptive — Variable situations requiring analytical, interpretive, evaluative, and/or constructive thinking.	5 Uncharted — Novel or nonrecurring pathfinding situations requiring the development of imaginative approaches and new concepts.
A Strict Routine — Simple rules and detailed instructions.	10% / 12%	14% / 16%	19% / 22%	25% / 29%	33% / 38%
B Routine — Established routines and standing instructions.	12% / 14%	16% / 19%	22% / 25%	29% / 33%	38% / 43%
C Semi-Routine — Somewhat diversified procedures and precedents.	14% / 16%	19% / 22%	25% / 29%	33% / 38%	43% / 50%
D Standardized — Substantially diversified procedures and specialized standards.	16% / 19%	22% / 25%	29% / 33%	38% / 43%	50% / 57%
E Clearly Defined — Clearly defined policies and principles.	19% / 22%	25% / 29%	33% / 38%	43% / 50%	57% / 66%
F Broadly Defined — Broad policies and specific objectives.	22% / 25%	29% / 33%	38% / 43%	50% / 57%	66% / 76%
G Generally Defined — General policies and ultimate goals.	25% / 29%	33% / 38%	43% / 50%	57% / 66%	76% / 87%
H Abstractly Defined — General laws of nature or science, business philosophy, and cultural standards.	29% / 33%	38% / 43%	50% / 57%	66% / 76%	87%

Problem-Solving is the original "self-starting" thinking required by the work for analyzing, evaluating, creating, reasoning, arriving at, and making conclusions. To the extent that thinking is circumscribed by standards, covered by precedents, or referred to others, Problem Solving is diminished, and the emphasis correspondingly is on Know-How.

⇒ MEASURING PROBLEM SOLVING. Problem solving measures the intensity of the mental process which employs Know-How to 1) identify, 2) define, and 3) resolve a problem. "You think with what you know." This is true even of the most creative work. The raw material of any thinking is knowledge of facts, principles, and means; ideas are put together from something already there. Therefore, Problem Solving is treated as a percentage utilization of Know-How.

⇒ THINKING ENVIRONMENT describes the degree of freedom permitted to initiate the thinking process as a result of external conditions (laws of nature, science, business, etc.), as well as internal conditions of the organization (goals, objectives, policies, procedures, practices).

⇒ THINKING CHALLENGE describes the situational nature of mental effort required to come to conclusions, make decisions, provide answers, or discover new things.

These Guide Charts® have been produced specifically to illustrate use of this proprietary methodology. They may not be reproduced without Hay permission. Copyright 1996 Hay Group, Inc.

FIGURE 9–9 Accountability Guide Chart

	IMPACT:
QUANTIFIABLE ⇒	Informational, recording, or other incidental services for use by others.
	Interpretive, advisory, or facilitating services for use by others.
	Participating in control with others (except own subordinates and superiors).
	Control of end results, where shared accountability of others is secondary.
NON-QUANTIFIABLE ⇒	Incidental support services with very indirect effects on the work unit.
	Services or sub-tasks that indirectly support others in the work unit.
	Tasks (e.g. analysis or production) that directly affect the work unit's results.
	Leadership in key services or production tasks of the work unit.

A ANCILLARY | C CONTRIBUTORY | S SHARED | P PRIMARY

FREEDOM TO ACT ⇓	N Non-Quantifiable				1 Very Small — Base Yr. = NQ - $100M (X AMI =)				2 Small — Base Yr. = $100M - $1MM (X AMI =)				3 Medium — Base Yr. = $1MM - $10MM (X AMI =)				4 Medium-Large — Base Yr. = $10MM - $100MM (X AMI =)			
	A	C	S	P	A	C	S	P	A	C	S	P	A	C	S	P	A	C	S	P
L Limited — Explicit instructions covering simple tasks.	5	7	9	12	7	9	12	16	9	12	16	22	12	16	22	29	16	22	29	38
	6	8	10	14	8	10	14	19	10	14	19	25	14	19	25	33	19	25	33	43
	7	9	12	16	9	12	16	22	12	16	22	29	16	22	29	38	22	29	38	50
A Prescribed — Prescribed instructions covering assigned tasks and/or immediate supervision.	8	10	14	19	10	14	19	25	14	19	25	33	19	25	33	43	25	33	43	57
	9	12	16	22	12	16	22	29	16	22	29	38	22	29	38	50	29	38	50	66
	10	14	19	25	14	19	25	33	19	25	33	43	25	33	43	57	33	43	57	76
B Controlled — Instructions and established work routines and/or close supervision.	12	16	22	29	16	22	29	38	22	29	38	50	29	38	50	66	38	50	66	87
	14	19	25	33	19	25	33	43	25	33	43	57	33	43	57	76	43	57	76	100
	16	22	29	38	22	29	38	50	29	38	50	66	38	50	66	87	50	66	87	115
C Standardized — Standardized practices and procedures and/or general work instructions, and/or supervision of progress and results apply wholly or in part.	19	25	33	43	25	33	43	57	33	43	57	76	43	57	76	100	57	76	100	132
	22	29	38	50	29	38	50	66	38	50	66	87	50	66	87	115	66	87	115	152
	25	33	43	57	33	43	57	76	43	57	76	100	57	76	100	132	76	100	132	175
D Regulated — Practices and procedures set by precedents or well defined policies and/or supervisory review apply wholly or in part.	29	38	50	66	38	50	66	87	50	66	87	115	66	87	115	152	87	115	152	200
	33	43	57	76	43	57	76	100	57	76	100	132	76	100	132	175	100	132	175	230
	38	50	66	87	50	66	87	115	66	87	115	152	87	115	152	200	115	152	200	264
E Clearly Directed — Broad practices and procedures set by functional precedents and policies, specific operational plans, and/or managerial direction apply due to nature or size.	43	57	76	100	57	76	100	132	76	100	132	175	100	132	175	230	132	175	230	304
	50	66	87	115	66	87	115	152	87	115	152	200	115	152	200	264	152	200	264	350
	57	76	100	132	76	100	132	175	100	132	175	230	132	175	230	304	175	230	304	400
F Generally Directed — Functional policies and goals and/or general direction apply due to nature and significant size.	66	87	115	152	87	115	152	200	115	152	200	264	152	200	264	350	200	264	350	460
	76	100	132	175	100	132	175	230	132	175	230	304	175	230	304	400	230	304	400	528
	87	115	152	200	115	152	200	264	152	200	264	350	200	264	350	460	264	350	460	608
G Guided — Broad policies and/or general guidance apply due to major size and complexity.	100	132	175	230	132	175	230	304	175	230	304	400	230	304	400	528	304	400	528	700
	115	152	200	264	152	200	264	350	200	264	350	460	264	350	460	608	350	460	608	800
	132	175	230	304	175	230	304	400	230	304	400	528	304	400	528	700	400	528	700	920
H Strategically Guided — Very broad guidance is inherent due to high independent effects on overall results.	152	200	264	350	200	264	350	460	264	350	460	608	350	460	608	800	460	608	800	1056
	175	230	304	400	230	304	400	528	304	400	528	700	400	528	700	920	528	700	920	1216
	200	264	350	460	264	350	460	608	350	460	608	800	460	608	800	1056	608	800	1056	1400

Accountability is the answerability for actions and for their consequences. It is the measured effect of the job or position on end results. It has three dimensions in the following order of importance:

⇒ FREEDOM TO ACT. The degree of control and guidance for work. This is a function of the organizational framework, the personal and policy direction, and the flows, processes, and systems, that are established in the organization.

⇒ IMPACT ON END RESULTS. The principle nature of the job or position's influence on end results, which ranges from very direct control to very indirect support.

⇒ MAGNITUDE. A broad categorization of how much of the organization is affected by a job or position's basic purpose. The relationship may be indicated in quantitative terms (such as annualized dollars stated in constant dollars, 1965 base year), or by other aspects of size. (Non-quantifiable indicates relationships that cannot be determined clearly or are too small to be perceived as significant.) AMI: Established for 1995$=4.60 Forecast for 1996$=4.70

These Guide Charts® have been produced specifically to illustrate use of this proprietary methodology. They may not be reproduced without Hay permission. Copyright 1996 Hay Group, Inc.

differences in interpretation of the Guide Charts among different organizations or different groups of jobs or units within an organization (i.e., strictly undervalued or loosely overvalued jobs based on normal or usual evaluation of comparable jobs by Hay and its clients).

Evaluating the Job of Lead Programmer-Analyst

This is the same job that was evaluated earlier using FES. The job description appears in Figure 7–1. Figure 9–10, Hay Position Evaluation Statement, is a form the evaluator completed when using the three Hay Guide Charts to rate the job.

FIGURE 9–10 Hay Position Evaluation Statement

TITLE: ____Lead Programmer-Analyst_____

DEPARTMENT: ____Data Processing - Information Systems_____

EVALUATION FACTORS		LEVEL	POINTS ASSIGNED	COMMENTS
1. KNOW-HOW:				Predominantly a basic technical specialized skill but requires some seasoned technical skill—requires considerable human relations skill when interacting with users and other technicians and professionals.
	Training Skills	E (line 3)	230	
	Managerial Know-How	I		
	Human Relations Skill	2		
2. PROBLEM SOLVING:				Thinking environment restricted by established and understood procedures and precedents. "Adaptive" selected over "interpolative" because of innovative thinking required to produce output.
	Thinking Environment	D	87	
	Thinking Challenge	4 (38)		
3. ACCOUNTABILITY:				This job has well-defined procedures and the incumbent must conform to recognized precedents and well-defined policy. This job was slotted into a "2" row recognizing the incumbent makes a contributory "C" impact on a programming budget that ranges between $1 and $2 million.
	Freedom to Act	D (line 1)	76	
	Magnitude	2		
	Impact	C		
S U M M A R Y	TOTAL POINTS		393	

Step One—Introduce the Hay Guide Charts   In this step, the evaluator becomes familiar with the Hay Guide Charts. If a factor-comparison approach for profiling the benchmark jobs was performed initially, the evaluator is familiar with the three factors. If the factor-comparison step was skipped, then the evaluator must become familiar with both the factors and the Guide Charts. Developing a familiarity with the Guide Charts requires an analysis of the elements and their respective levels in each Guide Chart.

Step Two—Review Job Facts   Now, through reading the job description, the evaluator becomes as familiar as possible with job content, job specifications or requirements, the expected performance level of a fully qualified incumbent, the fit of the job within the assigned work unit and organization, and the environmental factors that influence incumbent performance.

Step Three—Using the Minus (–) or Plus (+) in Level Selection[4]   When using the Guide Charts, it must be recognized that for each level of the KH and AC elements there are three point choices and for each PS element there are two point choices. When analyzing the level within each element and making inferences between the job content of the element and its respective level, the evaluator selects the most appropriate level. When making the selection, the novice evaluator can take a – or + approach to the selected level. Selection of the mid-value in a cell indicates that there is a strong or good fit between the description of the level and the job content. A – indicates a possible better fit between the selected level and the preceding level, and a + indicates that the choice was between the selected level and the succeeding level. A final choice is not made until all elements within each factor are rated. After reviewing the selected levels within each element and their associated pluses and minuses, the evaluator makes the final factor selection.

Step Four—Rating Specialized and Technical Know-How   The same bracketing approach used to quickly center on the appropriate levels of the FES factors is used with the Hay Guide Charts. Note: When making any kind of measurement in a form that requires an analysis of rows (x-axis) and columns (y-axis), always enter first through the rows—remember, in paired coordinates (x, y), the x precedes the y. Thus, when determining the proper row or level for the lead programmer-analyst, the evaluator can quickly descend through the rows (levels) of the Know-How Guide Chart (see Figure 9–7) until reaching level E. A quick analysis here tells the evaluator that level E may be appropriate, but it appears to fail to fully recognize the breadth and depth of knowledge required of the job. Continuing through to level F, another possible appropriate description of the required knowledge is provided. Taking the next step to level G, the evaluator quickly realizes this mastery level is inappropriate.

The bracketing approach now focuses on E and F, and it is here that some additional major differences between FES and Hay appear. (Remember, in FES the evaluator is not permitted to interpolate between two levels of a factor. The Hay Plan does permit a form of interpolation. It is here that the evaluator may use the – or + approach previously described in Step 3.) After reviewing the two levels in question, the evalu-

---

[4]In the United States, Hay does not recommend the use of the plus or minus approach because it may become too mechanistic. However, the Hay overseas offices, particularly in Europe, are very strong believers in the plus or minus practice.

ator selects what appears to be the most appropriate level. In the programmer-analyst example, the evaluator determines that the job is an E (possibly an E⁺) rather than an F (possibly an F⁻). In the next section, Recognizing PS, AC, and KH relationships, there is further discussion as to the reasons for selecting the third line at a lower level or the first line at the next highest level.

Step Five—Rating Breadth of Managerial Know-How   For this element, managing involves planning, organizing, integration, coordination, and control activities of others. This element of Know-How may be exercised consultatively as well as executively. A review of the job description reveals no direct managerial responsibilities for the lead programmer-analyst, although this individual does operate as a team leader and coordinates the work of other programming professionals and on a consulting basis performs some management functions such as planning and organizing. For these reasons, the Column I or minimal managerial breadth is selected.

Step Six—Rating Human Relations Skills   Following the initial column selection (in this case I), it is then noted that there are three additional columns inside each management Know-How element. These three inside columns relate to human relations skills, which are described at the bottom of the Know-How Guide Chart.

After reviewing the job description, it is evident that the incumbent must possess and use some human relations skills. The incumbent interacts with clients (users) and other data processing personnel. These meetings require information interchanges, coordination of activities, and the providing of technical consulting services. A comparison of job description data and the three levels of human relations skills at the bottom of the Know-How Guide Chart results in the selection of the important or level 2 rating. Once again, the description of level 2 appears to be a close match with job content, giving this job a 2 rating.

The rating of EI2 forms a cell or box of the three step values. The evaluator must make a selection among these three values. A careful reexamination of the E⁺I and 2 rating results in the elimination of the low value in the box (175). However, the choice between the middle value in the box and the high value in the box required considerable review. Because of the strong leaning toward the F level leading to the E⁺ rating, the value of 230 was the final choice. EI2 = 230.

| 175 |
| 200 |
| 230 |

Step Seven—Rating the Thinking Environment   An analysis of the Problem-Solving Guide Chart (Figure 9–8) reveals that the rows A through H are grouped under the title Thinking Environment and the columns 1 through 5 are grouped under the title Thinking Challenge. The Thinking Environment ranges from one that is very rigorously controlled to one that is quite abstract. Row or level A relates to jobs that are extremely routine and thinking is constrained—"Don't think—follow the procedures." At level H, the incumbent's thinking is controlled only by laws of society, nature, and overall organizational policies and mission.

In descending through the levels A to H, the evaluator makes a stop at level D, then continues to F, realizing that it is most likely inappropriate. The bracketing process quickly narrows the choice to D and E. A careful reading of the levels D and E results in elimination of E. The evaluator recognizes that the programmer-analyst's thinking is guided by flowcharts, the standards to be met by the system rather than policies and principles. From this analysis, D⁺ is the selected level.

Step Eight—Rating the Thinking Challenge   The column element allows for the measurement of the complexity in job assignments. This job is professional in nature and requires evaluation, analysis, and constructive thinking in solving complex problems.

The evaluator now enters the Problem-Solving columns—the Thinking Challenge element—and selects the most appropriate column (level). A scan of the column definitions quickly moves the evaluator to column 3. Column 4 may also be an appropriate response, but column 5 is quickly eliminated. After a careful review of columns 3 and 4, the adaptive (4) column (level) is selected. Because the programmer-analyst must do constructive thinking, the *adaptive* level is selected because of the in-depth analysis of user requirements and ways to meet the user needs. A careful review indicates a strong relationship between the adaptive description and job content, resulting in a 4 choice. The D$^+$4 rating initially places the evaluator at the 38 percent value. The evaluator then tests both the D$^+$ and 4 selections to see if the 43 percent selection would be more appropriate. Upon more careful review of the D and E levels of the Thinking Environment and the 3 and 4 levels within the Thinking Challenge, the 38 percent choice is made. Because the row choice was a solid D and the column choices were between 3 and 4, the upper left-hand value was the selected percentage value. Thus, PS = D4 (38).

Because the problem solving rating score is given as a value of know-how, the problem-solving percentage—in this case, 38 percent—must be multiplied times the know-how score—in this case, 230—to obtain the know-how rating score of 87 points. Figure 9–11A is a copy of the PS Conversion Table. To use this table, an evaluator enters through the row titled "PS %" (in the lead programmer-analyst example, 38 percent) and moves across to the appropriate KH point score, which, in this case, is 230. The value at the row and column intersection is 87.

In determining PS points, the evaluator must always use the Hay PS Conversion Table to determine the appropriate point score. Actual multiplication of PS percentage times KH point score may, at times, provide a PS score that varies from the table by one or two points. The table PS score maintains the Hay 15 percent step difference and uses the standard scale value.

Step Nine—Rating Freedom to Act   The last of the major Guide Charts is the factor *Accountability*. Accountability has three elements. The row element is Freedom to Act. The major column element is Magnitude, and the columns have an inner element titled Job Impact on End Results. In the lead programmer-analyst example, a scan of the Freedom to Act rows (levels) centers on D and E. The evaluator must now determine if the incumbent is regulated by precedents and well-defined policy, or if the incumbent is subject to broad practices and is covered by functional precedents. Also, are the "what" and "by when" of the assignments specifically prescribed with reviews coming at the end of a day or a week? Or, does the supervisor simply identify desired end results and completion dates with the incumbent being granted considerable latitude regarding the "how to's"? It was found that definite results are expected from the work of the incumbent and that the job is subject to certain kinds of procedures and precedents. For these reasons, there is a strong case for a D-level selection.

Step Ten—Rating Magnitude   After making the row (level) decision, the next decision is to select an appropriate column for Magnitude. The levels of Magnitude may be defined by a dollar value or a size indicator (i.e., Minimal, Very Small, Small . . .), or both. The size magnitudes on the Accountability Guide Chart are used to determine

FIGURE 9–11A PS Percentage Conversion Table

POINT CONVERSION TABLE

Read the Problem-Solving Points at the Intersection of the Know-How Points Column and the PS% Row in This Table

KH PTS. PS%	29	33	38	43	50	57	66	76	87	100	115	132	152	175	200	230	264	304	350	400	460	528	608	700	800	920	1,056	1,216	1,400
87%	25	29	33	38	43	50	57	66	76	87	100	115	132	152	175	200	230	264	304	350	400	460	528	608	700	800	920	1056	1216
76%	22	25	29	33	38	43	50	57	66	76	87	100	115	132	152	175	200	230	264	304	350	400	460	528	608	700	800	920	1056
66%	19	22	25	29	33	38	43	50	57	66	76	87	100	115	132	152	175	200	230	264	304	350	400	460	528	608	700	800	920
57%	16	19	22	25	29	33	38	43	50	57	66	76	87	100	115	132	152	175	200	230	264	304	350	400	460	528	608	700	800
50%	14	16	19	22	25	29	33	38	43	50	57	66	76	87	100	115	132	152	175	200	230	264	304	350	400	460	528	608	700
43%	12	14	16	19	22	25	29	33	38	43	50	57	66	76	87	100	115	132	152	175	200	230	264	304	350	400	460	528	608
38%	10	12	14	16	19	22	25	29	33	38	43	50	57	66	76	87	100	115	132	152	175	200	230	264	304	350	400	460	528
33%	9	10	12	14	16	19	22	25	29	33	38	43	50	57	66	76	87	100	115	132	152	175	200	230	264	304	350	400	460
29%	8	9	10	12	14	16	19	22	25	29	33	38	43	50	57	66	76	87	100	115	132	152	175	200	230	264	304	350	400
25%	7	8	9	10	12	14	16	19	22	25	29	33	38	43	50	57	66	76	87	100	115	132	152	175	200	230	264	304	350
22%	6	7	8	9	10	12	14	16	19	22	25	29	33	38	43	50	57	66	76	87	100	115	132	152	175	200	230	264	304
19%	5	6	7	8	9	10	12	14	16	19	22	25	29	33	38	43	50	57	66	76	87	100	115	132	152	175	200	230	264
16%	5	5	6	7	8	9	10	12	14	16	19	22	25	29	33	38	43	50	57	66	76	87	100	115	132	152	175	200	230
14%	4	4	5	6	7	8	9	10	12	14	16	19	22	25	29	33	38	43	50	57	66	76	87	100	115	132	152	175	200
12%	3	4	5	5	6	7	8	9	10	12	14	16	19	22	25	29	33	38	43	50	57	66	76	87	100	115	132	152	175
10%	3	3	4	5	5	6	7	8	9	10	12	14	16	19	22	25	29	33	38	43	50	57	66	76	87	100	115	132	152

FIGURE 9–11B Characteristic Hay Profiles (Percentage of KH-PS-AC)

PROFILES: FACTOR POINTS AS A PERCENTAGE OF TOTAL POINTS

The CHARACTERISTIC is the number of step differences between Problem Solving and Accountability and the direction of the difference. The PROFILE is KH, PS, and AC Points respectively as a % of Total Points. Read the PROFILE at the intersection of the CHARACTERISTIC Column and the Problem-Solving % Row. Each total is 100%.

PS%	Accountability Higher Than Problem Solving				AC = PS	Problem Solving Higher Than Accountability			
	A4	A3	A2	A1	LEVEL	P1	P2	P3	P4
87%	29 26 45	32 27 41	33 29 38	35 30 35	36 32 32	38 33 29	40 34 26	41 36 23	42 37 21
76%	32 25 43	34 26 40	36 28 36	38 29 33	40 30 30	42 31 27	43 32 25	44 34 22	45 35 20
66%	36 23 41	36 24 38	40 26 34	42 27 31	44 28 28	45 29 26	46 31 23	47 32 21	49 32 19
57%	39 22 39	41 23 36	43 25 32	45 26 29	46 27 27	48 28 24	49 29 22	51 30 19	53 30 17
50%	42 21 37	44 22 34	46 23 31	48 24 28	50 25 25	52 26 22	53 27 20	55 27 18	56 28 16
43%	45 20 35	47 21 32	49 22 29	52 22 26	54 23 23	55 24 21	56 25 19	58 25 17	59 26 15
38%	49 19 32	51 19 30	53 20 27	55 21 24	56 22 22	59 22 19	60 23 17	62 23 15	62 24 14
33%	53 17 30	55 18 27	56 19 25	59 19 22	60 20 20	62 20 18	63 21 16	65 21 14	66 22 12
29%	56 16 28	58 17 25	60 17 23	62 18 20	64 18 18	65 19 16	66 19 15	68 19 13	69 20 11
25%	59 15 26	62 15 23	63 16 21	65 16 19	66 17 17	68 17 15	70 17 13	70 18 12	72 18 10
22%	62 14 24	65 14 21	66 15 19	68 15 17	70 15 15	72 15 13	72 16 12	74 16 10	75 16 9
19%	66 12 22	68 13 19	70 13 17	72 13 15	72 14 14	74 14 12	75 14 11	76 15 9	77 15 8
16%	69 11 20	70 12 18	72 12 16	74 12 14	76 12 12	76 13 11	77 13 10	79 13 8	80 13 7
14%	72 10 18	74 10 16	76 10 14	76 11 13	78 11 11	79 11 10	80 11 9	81 12 7	82 12 6
12%	75 9 16	76 9 15	77 10 13	79 10 11	80 10 10	81 10 9	82 10 8	83 11 6	84 11 5
10%	77 8 15	79 8 13	80 9 11	81 9 10	82 9 9	83 9 8	84 9 7	85 10 5	86 9 5

These STEP VALUES, each 16% greater than the next lower, may be used in full expansions of the Guide Charts. The listing is also convenient to count the distance between PS and AC when using the Profiles Table.

7,360	3,680	1,840	920	460	230	115	57	29	14	7
6,400	3,200	1,600	800	400	200	100	50	25	12	6
5,600	2,800	1,400	700	350	175	87	43	22	10	5
4,864	2,432	1,216	608	304	152	76	38	19	9	4
4,224	2,112	1,056	528	264	132	66	33	16	8	3

CALCULATION AIDS

how much of the organization is affected by the jobholder's actions. In the case of the lead programmer-analyst, a dollar measure could be the department's budget upon which the incumbent has some impact. The column descriptors use both adjective and dollar values. The dollars used in the Magnitude column are indexed to a base year (1965), and are called "constraint dollars." Current dollar measures such as budget or sales revenues are compared to the base year using the AMI index. For example, the 1999 AMI was 5.0. In 1999, all dollar values were increased by a magnitude of 5.0. In the case of the lead programmer-analyst, the extent to which this job directly affects company operations could be from indeterminate to in excess of $500,000. The work of the lead programmer-analyst could have an impact on the cost of benefits to the organization and the value of benefits to the employees. For this reason, column 2 (small—$420,000 to $4,200,000) was selected, resulting in a 2⁻ selection.

Step Eleven—Rating Job Impact on End Results   The final selection is the Job Impact on End Results element. The columns of the Job Impact element are A (ancillary), C (contributory), S (shared), and P (primary). A review of the definitions in the upper right-hand corner of the Accountability Guide Chart (Figure 9–9) focuses the evaluator's attention on the C (contributory) column. The job is fundamentally a staff job providing services for users or clients.

The D2C evaluation of AC places the evaluator in the following step value box or cell:

66
76
87

Following a reexamination of the D2C rating, the evaluator eliminates the high and low values in the box and selects the middle value of 76 points. D2C = 76. The final rating of the job of lead programmer-analyst is:

Know-How   = EI2   = 230
Problem Solving = D4 (38) = 87
Accountability   = D2C   = 76
                            ———
                            393

Job Evaluation Quality Checks and Patterns

The Hay Guide Chart-Profile Method of Job Evaluation provides a number of quality control checks to assure that reasonable and rational job evaluations result from the application of the process. Among the more powerful quality control procedures are:

1. Profiling—Recognizing the Characteristic Shapes of Jobs.
2. Reviewing and Comparing Job Profiles within Functions and Hierarchies.
3. Sore Thumbing Job Scores, Level Elements, and Profile Patterns.

Profiling—Recognizing the Characteristic Shapes of Jobs   KH and PS job evaluations are closely linked in the Guide Charts and were originally measured on a common Guide Chart. Job evaluation patterns demonstrate that as KH requirements for jobs increase, more and more of that know-how should be utilized in thinking—to analyze, evaluate, and think constructively or make correct decisions under more complex and difficult situations. A job with relatively low know-how and relatively high problem solving is unusual and would warrant review of the evaluation. The opposite is also true.

Figure 9–12 demonstrates the pattern of problem-solving percentages an evaluator tends to select. The shaded area of the chart suggests that as jobs require more freedom to think, higher percentages of problem solving are usually required to make decisions, develop solutions, and so on.

Returning to the lead programmer-analyst example, a KH depth and breadth level of E was selected. If, then, either an E or D level of PS is selected, the evaluator will most likely make a Thinking Challenge level selection of between column 2 and column 4.

After application of the Guide Charts to the evaluations of thousands of jobs, Hay has evolved general conclusions regarding the patterns of PS-AC relationships. This characteristic relationship for different kinds and levels of jobs provides an important check on each evaluation as it is completed.

The Hay step values provide the opportunity to describe jobs based on their PS and AC relationship. Although every job has some amount of both PS and AC, some jobs require a higher proportion of one factor than the other. Jobs high in PS emphasize thinking. They require the incumbent to develop plans, do analysis, and make recommendations. These individuals are both problem solvers and opportunity finders. On the other hand, jobs with higher AC than PS are action jobs. The jobholder is responsible for committing resources and is held accountable for achieving end results. This person is the decision maker. Jobs that have a greater proportion of AC than PS are called DO jobs. Those having more PS than AC are called *THINK* jobs. When PS equals AC, it is a *LEVEL* job.

Reviewing the job of the lead programmer-analyst reveals that the PS evaluation number (87) is greater than the AC number (76). Next, in order to determine the profile of the job, the evaluator must determine the number of steps difference between the PS and AC scores. Figure 9–11B shows a profile table and a step value scale on the left-hand side. Locating the number 87 on the step value scale, the evaluator counts down one value to arrive at number 76. The % PS/KH column in Figure 9–11B is then searched until the 38% PS number given to the lead programmer-analyst job is reached. Reading horizontally to the right half of the table, the 1 down column with a profile of 59 22 19 is reached. The job is 59 percent Know-How, 22 percent Problem Solving, and 19 percent Accountability. Another way to view this profile is that for each dollar paid to the lead programmer-analyst, 59 cents is for Know-How, 22 cents for Problem Solving, and 19 cents for Accountability.

Reviewing and Comparing Job Profiles within Functions and Hierarchies   A basic Hay quality control check is to compare the profile predicted prior to the start of the evaluation with the profile calculated following job measurement through the use of the Guide Charts. This check is usually done immediately after the job has been evaluated and, when differences occur, a reexamination of each factor may be required.

Following the completion of a project or a major section of the organization, a profile table is completed on all evaluated jobs. Figure 9–13 is an example of a Job Evaluation Summary Sheet for Information Systems jobs. The three right-hand KH, PS, and AC columns provide an example of the proportional relationship among jobs. In descending from the highest-rated professional (or managerial) job, the KH percentage usually increases and the AC percentage usually decreases. This tells the evaluator that, normally, as job worth increases, problem-solving and accountability requirements increase, whereas the proportional amount of knowledge required of the jobholder

FIGURE 9–12   Hay Guide Chart for Evaluating Problem Solving

HAY GUIDE CHART FOR EVALUATING

PROBLEM-SOLVING

COPYRIGHT 1964

PROBLEM SOLVING HAS 2 DIMENSIONS:
- Freedom to Think
- • Thinking Challenge

	•• THINKING CHALLENGE				
	1. REPETITIVE	2. PATTERNED	3. INTERPOLATIVE	4. ADAPTIVE	5. CREATIVE
A. STRICT ROUTINE:					
B. ROUTINE:					
C. SEMI-ROUTINE:					
D. STANDARDIZED:					
E. CLEARLY DEFINED:					
F. BROADLY DEFINED:					
G. GENERALLY DEFINED:					
H. ABSTRACTLY DEFINED:					

ENVIRONMENT (Freedom to Think)

| | POINTS | | | | | | PERCENT | | |
Job Title	KH		PS		AC		Total Points	KH	PS	AC
Systems Consultant	FI2	304	E4(50)	152	E2C	115	571	53	27	20
Senior Systems Analyst	FI2	264	D4(43)	115	D3C	100	479	55	24	21
Programmer-Analyst III (Lead)	EI2	230	D4(38)	87	D2C	76	393	59	22	19
Systems Programmer	EI1	200	D4(38)	76	C2C	66	342	59	22	19
Programmer-Analyst II	EI1	200	D3(33)	66	C2C	57	323	62	20	18
Programmer III	EI1	175	D3(33)	57	D1C	57	289	60	20	20
Programmer-Analyst I	EI1	175	D3(33)	57	D1C	50	282	62	20	18
Programmer II	DI1	152	D3(29)	43	C1C	43	238	64	18	18
Secretary	DI2	132	C3(29)	38	C1C	43	213	62	18	20
Programmer I (Trainee)	DI1	132	C3(25)	33	C1C	33	198	66	17	17
Computer Operator II	DI1	115	C2(22)	25	B1C	29	169	68	15	17
Computer Clerk III	CI1	100	C2(22)	22	B1A	22	144	70	15	15
Computer Operator I	CI1	100	C2(19)	19	B1A	22	141	73	12	15
Data Entry Operator	CI1	87	B2(16)	14	B1A	16	117	74	12	14
Computer Clerk I	BI1	87	B2(16)	14	A1A	14	115	76	12	12

FIGURE 9–13 Job Evaluation Summary Sheet for Information Systems Department of Delphi Inc.

declines. This *does not* mean that the knowledge and skill requirements of a higher-level job are less than those of a lower-level job. It simply means that jobs of higher worth are normally those jobs that have the highest problem-solving and accountability requirements. Or, in basic management terms, jobs at higher levels in an organization require an incumbent to accept significantly higher levels of responsibility. Higher-level jobs are also normally more complex, requiring incumbents to have greater problem-solving skills. It must be recognized that profiling focuses on relative relationships. As jobs increase in value and, normally, receive higher rates of pay, the accountability portion of the jobs increases relatively, whereas the know-how or knowledge portion of the jobs decreases. Figure 9–14 provides a profile of a Clerical, Professional, and Managerial job in the Information Systems Department. Note that as the KH profile percentage decreases from the Clerical to the Management job, the KH point score increases with each succeeding higher-level job.

When a job profile does not follow these usual patterns, it suggests either an unusual job or a possible mistake in the evaluation. This indicates the necessity for additional review of the job and reevaluation to determine (1) if a mistake was made and (2) which element(s) of the factor(s) were evaluated incorrectly.

Profile patterns are also indicators of job rank within an organization. Accountability percentages above 38 percent usually connote top management; up to 27 percent,

PROFILES CHECK EVALUATION JUDGMENT

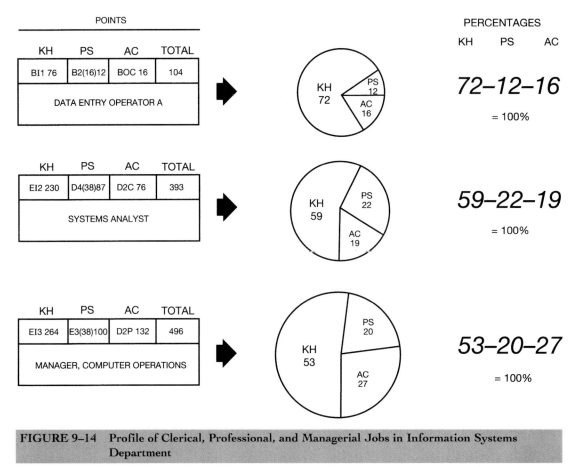

FIGURE 9–14 Profile of Clerical, Professional, and Managerial Jobs in Information Systems Department

Hay Management Consultants.

first-level operating managers; below 18 percent, entry-level professionals and most clerical positions. The following are four examples of typical management profiles from highest- to lowest-rated management positions.

General Manager	41	23	36
Plant Manager	44	22	34
Operations Manager	56	19	25
Office Manager	60	17	23

Sore Thumbing Job Scores, Level Elements, and Profile Patterns This process arrays the job evaluations in total point rank order, beginning with the highest evaluated job. All job evaluation routings are also shown and a review of the array will quickly identify jobs that fall out of the pattern. As job size is reduced, so should Depth of KH, Management KH, Thinking Environment, and so on. Jobs that fall out of the pattern are then reviewed and reevaluated, which may result in a change in the factor rating, or in no change, which suggests a possible job design or organizational problem.

Job Measurement Quality Assurance (JMQA)

Hay maintains a staff of senior job evaluation specialists who provide quality assurance and guidance to consultants and clients throughout the installation of a Guide Chart-Profile Method job evaluation project. Their activities include (1) determination of the degree of customizing required of the Guide Charts because of client value systems, size, or organizational characteristics; or (2) change in the weightings of compensable factors. Additionally, quality assurance procedures include benchmark selection, review of applicable Hay evaluation standards, models and norms, and setting the upper limit on the evaluation scales through evaluation of the highest-ranked executive position.

After the completion of the benchmark evaluation phase, benchmark evaluations are reviewed by Hay senior job evaluation specialists to:

1. Convert or normalize the customized chart evaluation scale to standard Hay points for salary survey comparisons within the Hay survey data bank.
2. Detect evaluation bias by the client among functional areas by position level, and so on, and apply a correction factor before accepting client compensation data into the Hay data bank.
3. Determine job evaluation anomalies or problems that indicate an unacceptable level or percentage of evaluation variance from normal patterns.

This tests the reliability of the client's evaluations.

The product of the JMQA is a factor that is used to convert client evaluation points to Hay points and represents an average or trend. Its application is to compare salary structures of two client organizations but is not used to compare specific job scores between two client organizations.

Compu Guide

In 1986, Hay introduced a new service—Compu Guide—to its clients. Compu Guide uses a knowledge compensable factor and a second chart called Grade Classification, which corresponds to both the Problem-Solving and Accountability Guide Charts. Compu Guide is designed to be an adjunct approach to the Guide Chart methodology.

Compu Guide users are usually companies that want Hay Access® (measured job content compensation data) but are unwilling to go through the time and expense associated with a traditional Guide Chart installation. Compu Guide works in this manner:

1. Client and Hay consultant select a comprehensive group of benchmark jobs.
2. Benchmark jobs are evaluated using the three traditional Hay Guide Charts.
3. Benchmark jobs are correlated by the Hay JMQA group.
4. Compu Guide Charts are developed for the client.

COMPARING FES AND HAY

In 1981, the Merit System of the State of Georgia implemented a project to investigate the possibility of developing a valid, viable, and measurable link among the following three functional areas of human resources management: (1) selection, (2) job evaluation, and (3) performance appraisal.[5] As part of this project, an in-depth comparison was made between FES and Hay as to the comparability of results in evaluating a set of jobs. In this study, comprehensive task lists were developed for the Computer Operator, Programmer-Analyst, and Systems Programmer series within the Georgia state government.

Project members who were involved in the evaluation processes received training from professionals familiar with FES and Hay. After completing their evaluation, a Pearson product moment correlation coefficient of +.93 was obtained by correlating total points assigned by each job evaluation plan to the job-classes. From their efforts, it was concluded that both FES and Hay provided very similar results for the jobs reviewed.

Comparing the Hay and FES Profiles of the Lead Programmer-Analyst

To compare Hay and FES, the first step is to organize a set of factors of one plan in a configuration similar to the other plan. In performing their comparison, the State of Georgia Merit System personnel designed the configuration described in Figure 9–15 with some modifications by this author. (In their initial study, the Merit System personnel left FES Factor 6—Personal Contacts—unmatched. This author, however, feels that Personal Contacts is an integral part of the Human Relations element of the Know-How factor of Hay.)

After combining the FES factors to match the three Hay Guide Chart factors, it is possible through a normalizing process to develop a job profile comparable to that accomplished in the Hay methodology. The total point score for the job being evaluated is used as the denominator. However, because there was not a comparable match for all FES factors (factors 8 and 9), the total FES point scores for the normalizing process were determined by subtracting the points of the assigned factors 8 and 9 from the total points assigned to the job-class. In the State of Georgia Merit System study, Physical Demands (factor 8) and Work Environment (factor 9) never provided a combined contribution of more than 5 percent of the total points assigned to any job. The average percentage contribution was 1.7 percent. In the lead programmer-analyst job, factors 8 and 9 provided only one half of 1 percent ($\frac{10}{1,960}$) of the total point score.

Using the FES configuration provided in Figure 9–15, the following profile can be developed for the job of the lead programmer-analyst.

Hay Guide Chart Factor	Comparable FES Factors	Lead Programmer-Analyst Assigned Factor-Level Points	Percentage of Total
Know-How	$\dfrac{1+6+7}{\text{Total Points}-(8+9)}=$	$\dfrac{950+25+50}{1,960-(5+5)}=\dfrac{1,025}{1,950}=$	52.6
Problem Solving	$\dfrac{3+4}{\text{Total Points}-(8+9)}=$	$\dfrac{275+225}{1,960-(5+5)}=\dfrac{500}{1,950}=$	25.6
Accountability	$\dfrac{2+5}{\text{Total Points}-(8+9)}=$	$\dfrac{275+150}{1,960-(5+5)}=\dfrac{425}{1,950}=$	21.8

$$\text{Hay Profile} = 59.0 - 22.0 - 19.0$$
$$\text{FES Profile} = 52.6 - 25.6 - 21.8$$

---

[5]Developing Integrated Job Content-Based Standards for a Human Resources System, IPA Grant No. 796A08.

HAY EVALUATION SYSTEM	FACTOR EVALUATION SYSTEM
Know-How Element 1. Practical, Specialized and Technical Depth: A continuum that goes from basic education (primary and secondary) plus work experience to specialized technical and professional skills built on postsecondary education to mastery, which is widely recognized as single in kind or excellence.	*FES Factor 1. Knowledge Required by the Position:* The nature and kind of skills needed and how these knowledges and skills are used in doing the work—that is, how much of a particular kind of knowledge is needed to to a particular task.
Know-How Element 2. Breadth of Management: The degree of integrating and harmonizing the diversified functions involved in managerial situations.	No comparable FES Factor.
Know-How Element 3. Human Relations: The active, practicing person-to-person skills in the area of human relationships.	*FES Factor 6. Personal Contacts:* People and conditions under which contacts are made (except supervisor).
Know-How Element 3. Human Relations: The active, practicing person-to-person skills in the area of human relationships.	*FES Factor 7. Purpose of Contacts:* Reasons for contacts in Factor 6 below; skill needed to accomplish work through person-to-person activities.
Problem-Solving Element 1. Thinking Environment: The degree to which thinking is guided or circumscribed (i.e., the limits on approaches to use in solving problems).	*FES Factor 3. Guidelines:* The nature of guidelines for performing the work and the judgment needed to apply the guidelines or develop new guides.
Problem-Solving Element 2. Thinking Challenge: The challenge presented by the thinking to be done to solve problems in a given thinking environment.	*FES Factor 4. Complexity:* The nature of the assignment, the difficulty in identifying what needs to be done, and the difficulty and originality involved in performing the work.
Accountability Element 1. Freedom to Act: The controls over action, supervisory, procedural, and thinking environment.	*FES Factor 2. Supervisory Controls:* How the work is assigned, the employee's responsibility for carrying out the work, and how the work is reviewed.
Accountability Element 2. Impact: The job impact on end results.	*FES Factor 5. Scope and Effect:* Purpose of the work and impact of the work product or service.
Accountability Element 3. Magnitude: The general accountability of the area(s) most clearly or primarily affected by the job (on an annual basis).	No comparable FES Factor.
The Three Hay Guide Charts do not contain elements comparable to FES Factors 8 and 9; however, Hay does provide its clients with ACEs (see description of ACEs in chapter 8 within discussion of Dangerous and Distressing Working Conditions). Although ACEs do not influence the profile of a job, they do provide a logical and rational foundation for determining additional pay for such conditions.	*FES Factor 8. Physical Demands:* The nature, frequency, and intensity of physical activity. *FES Factor 9. Work Environment:* The risks and discomforts imposed by physical surroundings and the safety precautions necessary to avoid accidents or discomfort.

FIGURE 9–15   Comparable Factors of the Hay Plan and the Factor Evaluation System

Both profiles provide a similar relationship and tell a comparable story. In this case, the FES method makes a slightly stronger "pitch" for both the problem-solving and accountability requirements of the job and slightly downplays the *relative* importance of the Know-How or Knowledge factor. In both cases, the profile analysis informs the evaluator that the job has strong problem-solving requirements and the incumbent must be a person who is able and willing to be accountable for activities that influence the successful operations of the organization.

Summary

Most well-designed point-factor job evaluation methods will produce similar hierarchical results or internal equity relationships. Point-factor job evaluations depend on the evaluators' knowledge of the jobs to be evaluated and their skill in the use of the job evaluation methodology. Point-factor evaluation ratings can be manipulated by incumbents, supervisors of jobs being rated, or the raters themselves. Evaluation methods such as the Hay Guide Charts and FES have conventions that assist raters in recognizing similarities and differences among jobs. The ultimate strength and test of point-factor ratings occur when all job ratings by organization, by work unit, or by occupation are compared factor by factor. The factor-comparison process is made readily available through the use of spreadsheet software programs.

Job or class titles provide little to no substantive information about the content of a job and the context or situations within which it is performed. The more detailed the available job content information, the more accurate the possible selection of the degree or level rating of each factor. There are many who believe that job evaluation is some form of witchcraft or black magic. There are others who contend that point-factor job evaluation is only credible when the weight of the factors and the points assigned to each level or degree are faithful and accurate representations of market practices. Extended use and experience with sound job content–based point-factor job evaluation reveal that far from being black magic, the point-factor process provides a sound logic base for knowledgeable individuals of goodwill to establish an internal worth hierarchy for jobs.

There is a certain truth to the view that point-factor job evaluation methods replicate market relationships. There is a strong historical base for paying jobs according to knowledge and skill requirements and working conditions, and many jobs in all kinds and sizes of organizations relate to these compensable factors. However, there are jobs occupied by women and minorities and new exotic jobs that fail to follow conventional market knowledge, skill, and working conditions requirements, and it is with regard to these jobs that the development of internally equitable hierarchies becomes critical in developing such pay systems. Most point-factor job evaluation methods are not designed to provide precise dollar values to all jobs of an organization. They do, however, permit and promote the grouping of jobs that have similar or comparable job requirements.

Review Questions

1. What is the role of the job evaluation committee in job evaluation?
2. Who should be included in a job evaluation committee? What credentials should they have? How many members should be included within a job evaluation committee?

3. What is so unique about the Hay Guide Chart method of job evaluation?
4. How does FES differ from other point-factor job evaluation methodologies?
5. Give examples of bobtailing in both FES and the Hay Guide Charts.
6. Why is it so important to develop a correct and accurate rating for the factor Knowledge in FES and Know-How in Hay?
7. A job is found to be an "up" job upon completion of a Hay Guide Chart evaluation. What does this mean?
8. What is the relationship between PS and KH in the Hay method?
9. How do raters use the bracketing process when evaluating a job using a point-factor method?
10. When analyzing a group of jobs evaluated by a point-factor method, how does sore thumbing occur?

CHAPTER 10

Surveying Market Pay and Compensation Practices

Learning Objectives

In this chapter you will learn about:

1. The major problems that restrict the gathering and analysis of pay survey data.

2. The importance of conducting pay surveys.

3. Preparing to conduct a survey.

4. Various kinds of survey methods.

5. Designing a survey.

6. Analyzing survey data.

7. Organizations that provide third-party surveys.

Compensation Strategy

Recognize what competitors for comparable jobholders are paying in relevant labor markets to permit organizations to attract and keep competent employees.

In the United States, there is something apparently "magical and absolutely truthful" when one party says to another: "This is the market rate for this job." After all, the United States is the paragon of the capitalist, free enterprise system. Free enterprise is driven by market forces. Thus, when someone wishes to justify a rate of pay and does an analysis of the market (telephone call to a "knowledgeable" source) to come up with a "market" rate of pay, all other pieces of pay-related data become, in reality, practically worthless. In the market-driven U.S. economy, the so-called untainted, impossible-to-manipulate market provides accurate and untarnished data. At least, this is the impression people who want to justify specific pay actions wish to promote.

Just as skill, effort, responsibility, and working conditions have historically been used to differentiate rates of pay among major job groupings, surveys have been used to determine a specific rate of pay for a particular incumbent/jobholder. Also, because there are so many problems in defining the factors of skill, effort, responsibility, and working conditions, and even more critical issues related to developing scales for measuring differences within these factors, it is difficult to perform job evaluations—job-worth exercises—in an objective manner. Because factor-based job evaluation methods have potentially strong roots in subjectivity, using the "objective" market for determining rates of pay is much more palatable, more acceptable, and actually easier and less costly. Before investigating opportunities, methods, and procedures available for collecting market-related pay data, a review of the problems related to the collection of accurate and comprehensive data may assist in obtaining a better fix on the accuracy and objectivity of market-provided pay data.

CRITICAL PAY SURVEY PROBLEMS

Some major problems that restrict the gathering and analysis of data useful for making pay decisions that relate to competitive market conditions are these:

1. Obtaining a proper job match
2. Collecting useful pay data
3. Ensuring an acceptable sample of organizations and jobs
4. Relating data to organizational pay policies
5. Integrating market pay data with internally generated job-worth data and pay structure design data
6. Recognizing the goals of pay survey data designers and implementers
7. Analyzing and making inferences from collected pay data
8. Recognizing pay as but one component of the total compensation or even total reward system of the organization
9. Using third-party data versus performing a survey

Obtaining a Proper Job Match   Possibly the most critical deficiency or opportunity for error in a survey is in matching the pay of different jobs. In many organizations, jobs are poorly defined and described. If immediate supervisors do not know precisely what their subordinates are doing, how can the human resources department or some other group properly and completely describe the job so that survey participants can identify the job in their organization that relates to the survey job for which there is a request for pay data?

In today's world, a secretary is not a secretary. No one is sure what a Secretary I is. A computer terminal operator can be anyone doing work that requires the input of data following simple instructions, or it can be someone who analyzes all kinds of computer-provided reports, identifies problems, and develops solutions the computer is incapable of developing. Job matching is a critical problem in conducting a useful and valid pay survey. In moving from a manufacturing economy in which jobs have been fairly well defined to a service economy in which jobs have historically been poorly defined, and in which jobs with similar titles have significantly different duties, accurate job matching becomes both more difficult and more important.

Collecting Useful Pay Data   The kinds of pay data collected in a pay survey range from incorrect and harmful, to worthless, to extremely useful. For participants in a survey, providing pay data is often a time-consuming, futile assignment with no discernible benefits. Often, those who actually complete the pay survey questionnaires are some of the least experienced, lowest-paid members of the human resources/compensation or payroll departments, and may not even understand the kinds of data being requested.

A pay survey questionnaire may provide nothing more than a job title—secretary—and ask for nothing more than minimum and maximum rates of pay for that title. The provider of data may give the minimum or maximum of the pay grade (range) to which the job is assigned if the organization has a graded pay structure. And yet the organization may actually pay employees under the minimum and over the maximum. On the other hand, the provider may give the actual highest and lowest rates of pay currently earned by any jobholder or even review pay records and give the actual lowest and highest rates paid to any employee during the past year, even though these employees may no longer be in the jobs.

The survey may request average pay data and the respondent may provide an average of all the rates of pay of all incumbents or the midpoint of the pay grade. The provider of pay data may give some sort of a gross earnings figure that includes overtime pay and other differentials and premiums, even though the survey requested base pay data. (The individual completing the survey may not understand the meaning of base pay.) Because a survey may clearly state the kinds of pay data desired, that does not mean that those responding to the survey will understand the instructions and provide the specific requested data.

Ensuring an Acceptable Sample of Organizations and Jobs   For an organization of any size (say, over 100 members), it is unlikely survey questionnaire data will be provided for every job. Once again, the old standby, benchmark jobs, comes into play. In the surveying business, other benchmarks may include organizations that are major competitors in specific job markets. Frequently, no one organization is a competitor for all jobs. Some organizations may be competitors in the labor trades occupations; others may be competitors in the administrative support/clerical field; still others, competitors in the information systems/data processing area, and so on. This means that different organizations must be surveyed in order to capture pay data on different kinds of jobs.

In addition to major labor market competitors, it is critical to know what other firms providing similar goods and services are paying employees doing comparable work. These competitors are often called *product competitors.* Because most U.S. businesses thrive or die in the product market, labor (pay) costs are critical to the selling price of output and to profitability of the firm. Organizations must know something of competitive labor costs when establishing their own base pay or actual rates of pay for their jobs. When making statistical inferences from a sample of a universe, certain requirements regarding sample size must be adhered to, or at least the possibility of an improper relationship between the sample and the universe must be recognized.

Relating Data to Organizational Pay Policies   Pay surveys should be additional and valuable inputs to the pay policies of an organization. Pay data should be the "tail of the dog," but not the "tail that wags the dog." To be truly useful and to be used properly, the pay policy should be well defined. Embedded within a pay policy should be an understanding of what pay surveys can do and what they cannot do. Also, if significant demands are to be placed on pay survey data, the costs involved in acquiring valid and reliable data must be understood and accepted.

Many organizational policymakers still look at compensation and human resources staff and their practices and tools as somewhat less than competent. By focusing attention on survey data, executives feel it is possible to eliminate or at least minimize the influence of dubious methods, if not "black magic" practices (job analysis, job descriptions, job evaluation) of the human resources department in setting pay rates. Top policymakers and executives have faith in the "market," and what the market pays is far more impressive than the subjective outputs of the human resources department.

Integrating Market Pay Data with Internally Generated Job-Worth and Pay Structure Design Data   Those involved in the collection and analysis of pay survey data must understand how the market data they provide will be used. Understanding how market data will be used then helps in designing an organization's own pay survey or the purchase and use of surveys conducted by other organizations—third-party surveys.

Recognizing the Goals of Survey Designers and Implementers   Just as the data requested may not be the data received, the designers and operators of a pay survey may have their own "hidden agenda." These individuals design a survey to provide certain kinds of data that they, in turn, can manipulate to justify a predetermined position. The hidden agenda may be to show that employees of an organization are extremely low paid and to justify certain increases to a naive or poorly informed constituency or pay review and approval board. Satisfying hidden agenda goals for a surveying organization may succeed. However, other organizations using some form of summary of the collected pay data may find it controversial, and also that it can be used by parties within another organization having their own hidden agenda to make unacceptable, even improper claims.

Analyzing and Making Inferences from Collected Pay Data   Are the pay survey implementers picking up average data and using it as actual pay data? Are those responsible for analyzing and summarizing the data eliminating what they consider to be outliers—the lowest and highest 10 percent of rates collected?

In the analysis and inference-making process, the old adage, "Figures don't lie, but liars figure," becomes ever so true and apparent. A major goal of most pay surveys is to predict accurately the so-called market rate of pay. Typically, this market rate of pay is the median or average rate of pay for the jobs for which pay data have been collected. It is amazing how easily pay surveys can develop a median or average rate of pay by collecting only minimum and maximum rates of pay, forgetting the fact that these minimum and maximum rates can mean almost anything and, more often, *nothing.*

Recognizing Pay as One Component of the Total Compensation or Total Reward System of the Organization   Although this book focuses on pay systems and recognizes the importance of pay in the physical, emotional, and intellectual well-being of employees, pay, although important, is only one component of the reward system. However, when pay surveys are conducted (even when data on other pay-related and benefits components are also collected), pay data are frequently reviewed in isolation from other compensation/reward components. Sometimes, in the eyes of compensation policymakers, they become the surrogate for the total compensation, even total reward, package. How well can an organization use even median or average data from a well-designed, well-conducted survey in isolation from other compensation/reward data?

"With great difficulty" is the answer. Many assumptions are made, and when anyone assumes anything, problems may result. A major issue here is that there is no way for a user of pay data to even obtain an average cost of the benefits packages or the innate values of the reward systems of the particular organizations. A logical assumption to make is that "the benefits and rewards programs of the participants are like ours." Or, possibly, a conscious decision is made that "our benefits and rewards packages are so much stronger (or weaker) than those provided by the participating organizations."

If the entire issue of benefits, which now cost employers, on an average, 35 to 40 percent of base pay, is not ambiguous and confusing enough, how are such imponderables as relationships among employees, relationships between managers and subordinates, and feelings of security of future employment with the employer added into the total reward formula to generate data regarding the critical dependent variable—employee willingness to be contributing, high-performing participants? Once again, the only statistic widely available is base pay. How accurate that statistic may be is questionable, yet because of availability, that is where attention is focused and how decisions are made.

Using Third-Party Data versus Performing a Survey   A well-designed, professionally conducted annual survey can easily cost an organization $25,000 per year, and if it goes into any depth, it can rise above $50,000 in cost. Very few organizations are willing to spend this kind of money to collect pay data. The least expensive approach is to participate in other organizations' pay surveys and use the summaries that are usually sent to participants. Here, the cost is the time of an employee to complete the survey questionnaires. Many organizations do not have the opportunity to participate in useful surveys and must depend on surveys the organization conducts or purchase third-party surveys. The subject of third-party surveys is explored later in this chapter. It must be noted now that the quality of data provided in third-party surveys varies greatly.

Major considerations other than cost when selecting third-party surveys are determination of (1) the jobs or groups of jobs for which pay data are needed; (2) organizations by geographic location, product, and size by some dollar criterion and number of employees needed to obtain useful data for comparability purposes; and (3) use of surveys for identifying trends to make pay structure adjustments. The wide diversity of jobs and various comparing organizations make practically all organizations users of some kind of third-party survey, and normally more than one. Now the issues arise as to which survey to choose, determining exactly what the data mean, and how to use the data.

DETERMINING THE NEED FOR A SURVEY

Employers must be aware of how their reward system compares with others competing for workers in the same geographic areas and in the same industry or with specific knowledge and skills, but they may be making the comparison on only one part of the total rewards being provided.

The pay/compensation survey is one of the most helpful tools available to the compensation manager. The data it provides enable an organization to compete in relevant labor markets. It is primarily a planning tool. Like all such tools, it demands valuable time both from within the organization and from those outside who contribute their data inputs.

Units and interested individuals within the organization often conduct their own surveys to compare their pay with that of similar jobs in other organizations. This practice often results in piecemeal, inaccurate data, and leads to job dissatisfaction and declining productivity. If for no other reasons, an organization should formalize the process to ensure that compensation data and information are as correct and valid as possible to provide a sound basis for developing a pay structure that is competitive with external markets and meets established pay policy criteria.

A survey enables the organization to learn what other organizations pay their employees in general and what rate or range of rates they pay for specific classes of jobs. Although the pay of an individual job is in many ways an internal matter relating to individual requirements and contributions, the going rate—or market rate—that is paid by other organizations in a specified area for a comparable job influences the pay structure of practically every other organization in that area. The very term *going rate* implies that there is a standard rate for a job in a community. Normally, this is not so. It is more likely that a variety of rates exists, and the survey process makes it possible to identify this range and a central tendency figure—a mean, median, or mode—for each job. The going rates in a certain labor market also reflect kinds of industries, sizes of organizations, supply and demand of labor, financial strength and profitability of organizations, union demands, cost of living or other related standard-of-living factors, and the unique requirements and reward features of organizations competing in the identified markets.

Why Conduct a Survey?

A good place to start in developing a survey is to answer these two questions: (1) Is it necessary to conduct a survey? (2) If so, why? Some of the factors discussed next will help provide the answers.

Factor 1: Hiring and Retaining Competent Employees   The success of an organization depends on skilled employees who see in their jobs the opportunity to promote their own self-interest as well as the interests of the organization. Contributing employees are those who help solve organizational problems and, thus, help to improve output and reduce waste. Motivated, well-trained people are required. Turnover, absenteeism, and uncaring, uninvolved attitudes destroy the efficiency of any organization. To survive, let alone grow, an organization must constantly search for the best applicants and strive to keep those it has already hired and trained.

The survey enables the organization to know what rates of pay the market demands and to direct its efforts toward maintaining and even improving upon these market participation rates.

Factor 2: Promoting Worker Productivity   People work for rewards—that is, the carrots. Some rewards come from the job itself (the satisfaction and achievement derived from expending innovative effort), whereas others satisfy off-the-job needs. A reward package that tells workers their jobs are important and that they have done a good job goes a long way toward promoting positive, productive efforts.

Practically all workers measure their pay in both absolute and relative terms. The absolutes concern the ability of earned income to buy desired goods and services. In relative terms, workers compare their pay with that of coworkers, close friends, associates, and relatives from their geographical community or community of interests. If workers are to see their pay as being fair, it must satisfy their absolute requirements and it also must appear to be fair in comparison with the pay of their associates. A primary means for an organization to maintain pay credibility and promote a feeling of fairness among employees is to use surveys.

Factor 3: Developing an Adequate and Acceptable Pay Structure   Equal pay for equal work, equal pay for comparable worth, and pay that rewards individual contributions can and should be more than organizational platitudes. In developing a pay structure, an organization must recognize equivalent levels of knowledge and application of that knowledge in the responsibilities and the duties of the job. The organization must also provide incentives for effort and must encourage development of each employee. It must (1) review rates of pay of those competing in the labor market, (2) have a good idea of how other organizations provide for lateral transfers and vertical promotions, and (3) recognize total compensation opportunities and their relationship to the pay structure. By focusing on these three areas of concern, an organization can determine if it actually needs survey data. Recognizing that the collection and the analysis for survey data are costly, this judgment must always be made before conducting a survey. Do the benefits outweigh the costs? At this stage, it may be possible to identify and use a third-party survey developed by some public or private organization that will supply enough data for decision-making purposes.

No matter whether the decision is made to implement a new compensation survey, to cooperate with an existing one, or to use one or more third-party surveys, compensation managers should be aware of the factors relating to the scope, the method, and the procedures involved. The development of such knowledge permits compensation managers to determine not only whether a survey is needed, but also what kind should be used; when, where, and how it will be used; who will use it; and who will be involved.

Factor 4: Recognizing Pay Trends in the Marketplace   Possibly the greatest value of a survey is that it informs the user of what is happening in the marketplace. Above all, it identifies trends. After trends are recognized, the next step is to identify detailed information about specific changes in pay practices that may have occurred. Because it is important to be able to identify trends or recognize precedents, the methods used to collect and report compensation data must be consistent. Consistency also involves a rather stable group of survey participants—or when using third-party surveys, the same survey each year. But even when using third-party surveys, the user is at the mercy of the producers of the survey. The user must be able to recognize whether the survey collects data from the same sources or significantly similar sources each time.

Factor 5: Defending Pay Practices in a Court of Law   All employers must recognize the critical relationship between the importance employees place on their pay and the litigious nature of the American society. If an employee is to bring a lawsuit against an employer, there is significant likelihood that all or part of the lawsuit will consist of allegations of unfair or discriminatory pay practices. An employee can use such acts as Title VII, the Equal Pay Act, age discrimination in employment, the Americans with Disabilities Act, or simply breach of contract as a legal basis for a lawsuit. In these kinds of lawsuits over the past two decades, one of the best defenses available to an employer is that its pay practices are based on "market" considerations. Invoking the market claim has almost been enough to defend a pay discrimination case. However, as plaintiff attorneys and judges become more sophisticated in the acquisition and application of market pay data, employers will have to go to greater lengths in explaining (1) how they obtained the data; (2) how the raw data were summarized, analyzed, and interpreted; (3) the comparability of survey participants' jobs and jobs in their organizations; (4) how the organization used the data in making pay policy and pay structure decisions; and (5) how the organization used market data in determining the pay of most if not all jobs in the organization, not merely those involved in the lawsuit.

There is no doubt that courts will continue to accept "market practices or conditions" as legal or legitimate approaches for setting pay. It is quite likely that managers will have to defend pay-setting practices with the same rigor as they have been required to defend hiring and promotion practices. If an organization uses pay survey data only as a general guide to assess the adequacy of the pay structure (recognizing trends in the marketplace) or to identify changes in rates of pay for select jobs, it may then be very difficult to defend a position that market data were used directly to establish the rates of pay for all jobs or even jobs involved in a lawsuit.

Scope of Survey

Once a decision has been made about the need for a survey, the next step is to determine its scope. The answers to a series of questions provide a start. Such questions as the following are helpful:

1. With what jobs is the organization having the greatest trouble hiring and retaining employees?
2. Where is worker dissatisfaction centered?
3. Where do quality and productivity problems appear to be most serious?
4. Where does it appear that market rates outweigh internal rate relationships?
5. Where is market competition for particular skills or exotic talents most fierce?[1]

A wise procedure for developing answers is to begin with a broad overview of the organizational structure. Through a series of refinements, it is possible to pinpoint those areas requiring survey data. A review could take the following form:

1. Do the problem areas exist only within certain functions or work units (accounting, data processing), do they include only exempt (managerial/administrative or professional) categories, or are they in the nonexempt area?
2. Within these functional, or exempt or nonexempt categories, do the problems center among middle-management jobs, particular professional jobs, certain clerical jobs, and so on?
3. Is it possible to define these jobs further by responsibility areas or by particular knowledge requirements (such as environmental planners), or by particular job classifications (such as computer programmers)?
4. Is it possible to reduce or eliminate the need for a specific skill area through an organizational training program?

---

[1]Exotic jobs are relatively new or different jobs in which demand far exceeds the supply of qualified applicants. This creates a special situation in which pay offerings are considerably higher than those normally justified through conventional evaluation or pay structuring processes. These jobs may have a temporary or short-term worth that is unusually high.

Having determined internal requirements, the survey designer's next step is to decide where to look for the needed data. Direction is provided by the following questions:

1. Is the local labor market the dominant source of supply for the jobs requiring survey data?
2. Are these managerial or professional jobs in which the labor market encompasses specific regions or the entire nation? Or are they possibly international in scope?
3. Are these jobs found only in industries providing specific kinds of goods and services?

After reviewing these questions, the next step is to identify organizations that hire from the specified labor markets. It must be decided whether it is important to include only those organizations in comparable industries (by size and product), or if the survey is to be made for a public-sector organization, whether it is necessary to survey private employers. The issue is to obtain a true picture of the compensation offered by *all* organizations competing in the labor market. A survey that limits respondents to a kind or a size of industry or to a sector of the economy (public or private), or to a portion of the actual labor market will result in biased data that may lead to invalid or unrealistic decisions.

As the variety of organizations responding to a survey broadens, the need for different kinds of compensation data and for different statistical methods for analyzing these data increases. A major problem in any survey is comparability. It is highly unlikely that any two jobs in two different organizations are identical. The forces in each organization influence each job, and impart certain unique characteristics. This uniqueness results in different compensation patterns. Even when jobs have the same titles or when their responsibilities, duties, or specifications are described in the same way, they probably are not identical. These comparison problems again stress the fact that compensation management is an art best performed by those who understand its fine differences and use all available tools and techniques to identify them. The survey is a tool of the artist. There are certain quasi-scientific procedures that will assist in developing a valid and useful picture of the compensation labor market, but, ultimately, success depends on the skill of the surveyor.

PREPARING FOR THE SURVEY

Significant amounts of time must be spent in developing a survey, having respondents (participating organizations) complete it, and analyzing the data collected. These time requirements emphasize the need to request no more data than absolutely necessary and to lighten the burden on the participants by designing a format that is easily understood, simple to follow, and easy to complete.

Answering the following questions concerning major areas is helpful in determining the extent of the survey requirements.

Development, Implementation, and Analysis

1. Is skilled talent available to develop and implement the survey?
2. Is skilled talent available to compile and analyze data?

3. If the answers to (1) and (2) are No, where is talent available, or can unskilled employees be trained to perform necessary activities?
4. Who should be selected for these activities (based on individual knowledge, skills, and interests)?
5. What technical and interpersonal skills are necessary?
6. Are computer software packages and hardware available for inputting, summarizing, and analyzing data and for producing desired output?
7. When will the survey data be collected?

Classification of Job or Occupation

1. Is the pay problem unique to a small number of jobs or to one occupational group?
2. Is the job unique or exotic?
3. Which jobs are benchmark or key jobs?

Pay Structure

1. If the organization has multiple pay plans, will the survey relate to all pay structures or only to specific pay structures?
2. Is the pay structure of the organization so unique that pay data from other organizations will be of little value?
3. Do other organizations face similar pay issues?

Identification of the Labor Market

1. Has the labor market been properly identified?
2. Does the organization compete in a variety of labor markets (local or regional for lower-level jobs and interregional or national for more specialized occupations or professions)?
3. Are demographic variables important considerations (rural or urban, population of community)?

Influence of Competing Organizations

1. Do those organizations hiring the largest number of employees or the largest number of employees for a specific job or occupational group dominate the labor market?
2. Is there a relationship between the dollar volume of business and the leadership roles in the setting of pay rates?
3. Is there a relationship between similarity of output (good or service) or kind of organization (public or private, profit or nonprofit)?

Selection of Respondents

1. Which organizations appear to have significant influence on applicants seeking employment?
2. Which organizations have lost their employees to the organization conducting the survey?
3. Which organizations require incumbents to perform jobs having similar job content and that, in turn, require similar incumbent knowledge and skills?
4. Which organizations have enough jobs similar to those identified in the survey to make their responses valuable?

Cooperation of Respondents

1. Have mutual needs been identified and stressed?
2. Will introductory telephone calls or even personal visits be necessary, or will a letter or e-mail requesting participation be sufficient?
3. Are introductions available from associations, friends, or managers in either the survey-producing or participating organization?
4. Will respondents' participating efforts be rewarded (promise of delivery of a well-developed summary of the surveys; a formal presentation of summarized data to all participants)?

Kinds of Data to Be Collected

1. Are only base pay data desired?
2. Is it necessary to analyze job fit—where proper match is made?
3. Should organizational demographic data be requested?
4. Is there a need for various kinds of pay policy data?
5. Should data be collected on other compensation components (compensation policy, incentive plans, benefits, services, perquisites)?
6. If the answer to (5) is Yes, how much detail should be requested?

Maintenance of Confidentiality

1. Will concern regarding secrecy prohibit participants from responding to the survey or possibly provide invalid or meaningless data?
2. What procedures will best ensure confidentiality of respondents' data?

The issue of confidentiality received widespread attention when the International Union of Electrical Workers sued General Electric Company (GE) for unfair labor practices before the National Labor Relations Board (NLRB). In this case, the company had provided the union with wage survey information in connection with grievances but had not identified which rates came from which companies. The NLRB required GE to furnish the union with such data, but in the future will not require that GE reveal the identity of the companies furnishing data for a survey if such data have not been disclosed to it; this action protects third-party survey organizations and promotes the use of third-party surveys.

Compliance with Legislative Mandates

1. Will there be any conflict between legal statutes and survey operations and results?

In the 1980s and 1990s, a number of lawsuits occurred that emphasized the need for compensation professionals to become aware of potential violations of legislative mandates. The issue of confidentiality, as just discussed regarding a potential NLRB issue, moved further into the legislative arena with a number of legal actions brought against The Boston Survey Group. The Boston Survey Group, a 34-member association, produced a compensation survey of a variety of clerical jobs in the Boston area. A major member of the group whose HR/Compensation Staff provided professional work on the production of the survey was the Boston Federal Reserve Bank.

In 1982 the 9 to 5 Organization for Women Office Workers in Boston filed a lawsuit against The Board of Governors of the Federal Reserve System (551 F.Supp. 1006

1982). The 9 to 5 Organization wanted copies of certain records the board had obtained from The Boston Survey Group (the vehicle used by the Boston Federal Reserve Board and other participating members for conducting their annual compensation surveys). The board refused, saying that it had a commitment to keep the records confidential and was protected under the Section (b)(4) exemption of the Freedom of Information Act (FOIA). A U.S. district court ruled that the records in the board's possession were not confidential within the meaning of the exemption in Section (b)(4) because it did not impair the board's ability to obtain information necessary to conduct its business.

In addition to the U.S. district court, the Office of the Attorney General of the State of Massachusetts investigated the operations of The Boston Survey Group. In particular, its attention focused on the survey's identification of each participating organization by company name and how survey results were reported by industry group. In a consent decree between The Boston Survey Group and the Office of the Attorney General of the State of Massachusetts, the following survey procedures were agreed to:

- Survey data will no longer be identified by company names.
- Only aggregated information will be reported; salaries of individual employees will not be published.
- No survey data will be published on a per industry basis.
- No survey data will be reported if fewer than 10 people are in a job.
- Members may choose to allow their employees to see the aggregated survey results for their own jobs.

In 1994, another attack on survey practices was adjudicated in a U.S. district court in the district of Utah. In this case, the Utah Society for Healthcare Human Resources Administration, the Utah Hospital Association, and eight hospitals were accused of keeping entry-level wages for registered nurses in the Salt Lake City area artificially low by exchanging wage and budget information and proposed starting pay offers to entry-level nurses. These actions were considered violations of the Sherman Antitrust Act because they interfered with competitive prices and artificially held down wages.

The agreement reached in the case stipulated that no health care facility in Utah can

1. Design, develop, or conduct a wage survey.
2. Respond to a written request for wage survey data from a third party unless the response is only in written form and the third party provides assurance that the survey will be conducted with particular safeguards. Any data must be sufficiently aggregated to prevent identification of source and only historic data can be obtained.
3. The survey (a) may not identify facilities that participated in the survey; (b) may not disseminate entry-level rates for a particular job; and (c) may only disseminate average rates of pay for entry-level jobs.

The legal problems faced by The Boston Survey Group and the Utah Society for Healthcare Human Resources Administration underscore the importance of compliance with existing legal requirements and the need for designers and implementers of compensation surveys to carefully review all aspects of survey design, implementation, and final disclosure to ensure that legal requirements are met.[2]

---

[2]*District of Utah U.S. District Court* v. *Utah Society for Healthcare Human Resources Administration, et al., Federal Register* 59, no. 58 (March 25, 1994): 14203, Microfiche.

Data Collection Techniques

After making the decision to perform a survey, the next step is to decide how to collect the survey data. If the survey is informal and relates to one or a small number of jobs, the telephone is both the simplest and most widely used approach for gathering data. Other increasingly complex techniques include the questionnaire, the face-to-face interview, and group conferences.

Telephone   Telephone surveys are useful for collecting data on a relatively small number of easily identified and quickly recognized jobs. Telephone contact can be made quickly with compensation specialists in comparable organizations throughout a particular region or even on a nationwide basis. These contacts can provide data for immediate or emergency use. The telephone technique is also useful for clarifying issues, checking discrepancies, or obtaining data overlooked by other collection methods. One drawback is that it places a great burden on respondents because it requires their immediate time and attention, which may be in demand elsewhere. Because of this type of imposition, the telephone survey should be as concise as possible and, when possible, scheduling of the call should be prearranged.

Mailed Questionnaire   The mailed questionnaire is the most common technique for collecting formal survey data. It not only permits respondents to complete it at their discretion, but it allows time for careful thought and deliberation in job matching. The questionnaire is useful for collecting data on 100 jobs or on 10 jobs. However, time is money, and time as well as the costs incurred in preparing, producing, distributing, completing, and analyzing questionnaires requires that no more data be requested than absolutely necessary.

When using a mailed questionnaire, do not expect more than a 50 percent response before the third or fourth week. A telephone follow-up after the second and fourth weeks may speed up the process and may also stimulate some responses that otherwise would never occur.

Face-to-Face Interview   Probably the best technique for collecting data is the completion of a questionnaire during a face-to-face interview. A well-trained interviewer who knows every aspect of the survey intimately and is especially conversant with the functions of the jobs included in the survey is invaluable for collecting valid and reliable data.

In the job matching process, the interviewer may review relevant organizational records (job descriptions, pay structures, organization charts) and possibly even observe a job in action. The interviewer may personally record pay data from payroll or other records provided by the selected respondents. This process relieves the respondents of much of the clerical work and the necessity for making subjective judgments from limited descriptive data.

As in any successful interview, the interviewer must have the confidence and the cooperation of the interviewee. Once an interviewer has developed such interpersonal relations, it is always easier to return for a follow-up assignment or to obtain additional or special data over the telephone or through the mail or e-mail.

Conference   Although the conference is one of the least used techniques for collecting compensation data, it has certain strengths. If a group of specialists has common data requirements and if location is not a problem, this technique may be ideal.

Prior to the meeting, one individual must prepare an agenda detailing its purpose, the kind of compensation data to be reviewed, and the jobs (with their descriptions) to be matched. When attendees have done their homework and come well prepared, the quality and the quantity of data developed in a fairly short time can be remarkably good.

The conference technique also promotes closer understanding among those responsible for compensation management, a greater awareness of business similarities and differences, and an increased willingness to cooperate when interaction and data flow are vital.

IDENTIFYING SURVEY METHODS

After deciding on the techniques to be used for collecting survey data, the next problem is to determine the best method for identifying benchmark jobs or classes of jobs, or even occupations for which data are to be requested.

Job Matching

Job matching, the most commonly used survey method, requires respondents to match benchmark jobs with similar jobs in their organizations through comparison with identification data supplied by the survey. Benchmark jobs used for compensation surveys are highly visible jobs that are common to a variety of organizations and normally employ many workers.

The identification data may simply take the form of a job title, and the survey may request respondents to identify similar jobs in their organization, listing rates of pay, pay range, and number of employees in those jobs. It is logical to assume that the more identification data made available to the respondents the better the match, but then the quality-quantity data problem arises. What is meant by *sufficient* data? What should the data provide? What are the benefits and costs? It is expensive to provide data because of the initial research and preparation costs and the printing and mailing costs. If the respondents are overwhelmed by the physical size of the survey, there is a good chance they will not respond. Too much data are often more damaging than too little. One of the best solutions is the *thumbnail sketch,* or job summary, which is a brief recap of a job description that provides information concerning general and specific responsibilities or duties and other remarks or notations that will assist in differentiating the job under review from others that may to some degree have similar requirements or titles.[3]

Success with a job matching survey requires careful selection and definition of jobs to be used for comparison purposes. The guidelines in the following list are helpful. The job should:

1. Be widespread.
2. Be precisely defined and have a title that has a fairly uniform meaning and is not easily misconstrued.

---

[3]The bulletins of the Bureau of Labor Statistics that describe compensation practices throughout the nation normally have Occupational Descriptions in their appendixes that are typical examples of these thumbnail sketches. The Bureau of Labor Statistics is an invaluable source of compensation data. Anyone involved in this area should first check the wide variety of bulletins, reports, and so on that it makes available to the public, usually free or at a minimal cost. A basic guide for anyone involved in surveys is the U.S. Department of Labor, *BLS Handbook of Methods for Surveys and Studies,* Bulletin 1711 (Washington, DC: Government Printing Office, 1971).

3. Be performed in a rather similar manner by most organizations.
4. Be an elementary job of a class when it is part of a class-series. When possible, however, all skill levels within a class-series should be used. This limits the tendency to identify several different jobs as one, and minimizes development of a bimodal or even trimodal distribution.
5. Be commonly used in a collective bargaining situation.

Even when these guidelines are followed carefully, however, the data may not necessarily be valid and reliable. Certain problems can form a barrier to the success of any job matching survey. For example, the job defined in the survey may have unique responsibilities and duties, thus providing poor matching prospects. Or the manner of defining jobs for constructing a job or class-series may vary to such a degree among the respondents' organizations that it is almost impossible to arrange pay rates for a series from one or even two jobs within the series.

To further facilitate the matching process, the respondent can identify how closely each survey job fits the comparable job in his or her organization. This can be accomplished by including a "job fit scale" in the pay reporting section (see Figure 10–1). The scale could have five intervals: (1) poor fit, (2) slight fit, (3) moderate fit, (4) considerable fit, and (5) identical fit. Such data will assist those responsible for compiling and summarizing the survey data to make a final decision as to whether or not to include the data or whether modifications need to be made in the design of the survey.

If space and costs are not a significant problem, but fit is an important issue, instead of providing job summaries for matching purposes, job definitions (see chapter 7) can be used. The job fit scale can be applied to each duty and can provide much more complete job matching information. This approach certainly requires more time of the respondent and in survey analysis. For certain kinds of surveys—for example, higher-level management and exotic professional jobs—this may be the best approach for establishing comparability in survey jobs.

In most cases, the job matching method requires from 15 to 50 benchmark jobs, with 30 as a good average. The survey situation is the final determinant; a large organization may require a larger number. Rates of pay and pay ranges from 15 jobs covering the spectrum of the pay structure, including various classes, occupations, or families, normally provide sufficient reference points to check or assist in developing a valid and workable pay structure.

The ideal condition for conducting a job matching survey exists when each organization uses the same compensable factors and evaluation plan to identify and weight each job. This is seldom the case, but it is helpful to know the standards or procedures used by the respondents for evaluating their jobs.

Class Matching

The identical procedures and problems used for job matching apply to matching classes of jobs because a class of jobs is nothing more than a grouping of comparable jobs. The surveys conducted by the Bureau of Labor Statistics (BLS) are of the class matching nature. In these procedures, Roman numerals or letters of the alphabet identify the class-series hierarchy. When using letters, the A class is most advanced; however, when using Roman numerals, the highest number is most advanced.

COMPENSATION SURVEY PACKAGE
1. Letter of Transmittal

Dear _____:

In accordance with our telephone conversation, I am enclosing a survey questionnaire with a self-addressed, stamped envelope. Thank you for agreeing to participate.

The survey has three sections: Organizational Policy, Employee Benefits, and Job Data. Answers to the *policy* section will assist us in relating compensation differences among the participating organizations. Because of their ever-expanding importance and cost, *employee benefits* have become increasingly important to many organizations. The *job data* section is the heart of the survey. If you have any doubt about the similarity of the job you match with the one we describe, please feel free to comment in the margin beside the matching job. Or, if you wish, send us a copy of your parallel job description and we will do the matching.

To ensure anonymity of your response, we will not list organizations by name or make any grouping where it is possible to combine such data as number of organization, size of organization, or number of employees so that identification of a specific organization is possible.* We have coded each survey only to allow us to check with you concerning any missing data or where it appears that the data may have been incorrectly transcribed by transposing numbers or placing a number in the wrong column.

After compilation and analysis of the surveys, each participating organization will receive a summary. If you need further information or clarification of summary data, please call me.

Sincerely yours,

Compensation Manager
OLYMPIA, INC.

....

*A Bit of Information for the Surveyor:

A National Labor Relations Board ruling required a company to provide the following information to its bargaining union:
>   (1) Area wage rates,
>   (2) Companies surveyed,
>   (3) Identification of which rates came from a particular company.

However, the NLRB does not require an organization to disclose the identity of the companies if it is not furnished such information. In essence, this protects companies using survey data provided by outside parties. ("Total Disclosure of Wage Data," *Compensation Review,* Third Quarter 1971, pp. 5–6.)

continued

FIGURE 10–1 Compensation Survey Package

COMPENSATION SURVEY PACKAGE (Cont.)
2. The Survey
Organizational Policy

Staff and Hours

Number of employees? _____

How many hours per week do your employees normally work? _____

How much time allotted for lunch? _____

How many breaks? _____ How much time allotted for them? _____

Do you have a 4-day workweek? YES _____ NO _____

Do any of your employees work on shifts? YES _____ NO _____

If YES, answer below

Shift	Shift Hours	% Premium Pay
Evening (2nd)	_____	_____
Late Night (3rd)	_____	_____
Other	_____	_____

Do you have any form of Flexitime (allowing employees to choose working hours)?

YES _____ NO _____ If YES, please describe

_____

_____

Salary Payment Policies

If your standard number of hours worked per week is less than 40, do you pay overtime for hours in excess of the normal workweek but less than 40? YES _____ NO _____

If certain groups within the organization have less than a 40-hour workweek, please list them.

Group	Hours
_____	_____
_____	_____
_____	_____

What is the overtime rate for individuals required to work on regularly scheduled holidays?

1½ times normal pay _____ 2 times normal pay _____ Other _____

Have you paid a bonus or made a supplemental salary payment at any time within the past 12 months?

YES _____ NO _____ If YES, Date of last one _____

Approximate % of Salary _____

Please identify occupational groups receiving bonuses.

_____

_____

Have you granted any general across-the-board adjustments in salary within the past 24 months?

YES _____ NO _____ If YES

Date	Approximate % Adjustment
1._____	_____
2._____	_____

continued

COMPENSATION SURVEY PACKAGE (Cont.)

Are they linked to the Bureau of Labor Statistics Consumer Price Index?

YES _____ NO _____ If linked to any other price index, please indicate _____

Starting Salaries—High School Graduates

What is your average starting salary for a high school graduate with *no* work experience who cannot type or take shorthand? $ _____

What is your average starting salary for a high school graduate with *no* work experience who can type 50–60 words per minute accurately? $ _____

What is your average starting salary for a high school graduate with *no* experience who can type 50–60 words per minute and take shorthand 80–90 wpm? $ _____

Starting Salaries—Community College-Technical School Graduates

What is your average starting salary for a technical school graduate who has a usable technical skill? $ _____

What is your average starting salary for a community college graduate with an Associate Degree pursuing a *nontechnical* occupation in your firm? $ _____

Starting Salaries—College Graduates

What is your average starting salary for a college graduate with a Bachelor's degree in Business Administration, Accounting, Finance, Economics, Management, etc., pursuing a *nontechnical* occupation in your firm? $_____

What is your average starting salary for a college student with a Bachelor's degree in Engineering, Mathematics, Statistics, etc., pursuing a *technical* occupation in your firm?

$_____

Employment Policies

Do you pay employment agency fees for noncollege graduates? YES _____ NO _____

If YES: Do you pay fee at time of employment? YES _____ NO _____

If NO: When? _____

Do you require that aptitude tests be passed prior to employment? YES _____ NO _____

Employee Benefits

Paid Vacations

What paid vacations are allowed?

Years Service (Inclusive)	Weeks of Vacations Allowed Nonexempt	Exempt	Executive
0–1	_____	_____	_____
1–4	_____	_____	_____
5–9	_____	_____	_____
10–15	_____	_____	_____
Others	_____	_____	_____

Can unused vacation time be carried over to the following year? YES _____ NO _____

If YES: how many days? _____

continued

COMPENSATION SURVEY PACKAGE (Cont.)

Paid Holidays

How many paid holidays do you grant? _____

Christmas Day	_____	Independence Day	_____
New Year's Day	_____	Labor Day	_____
Presidents' Day	_____	Columbus Day	_____
Martin Luther King, Jr. Day	_____	Veteran's Day	_____
Good Friday	_____	Thanksgiving Day	_____
Memorial Day	_____	Employee's Birthday	_____

Sick Leave

Do you have an official sick leave plan? YES _____ NO _____

How many days of sick leave do you grant per year? _____

Do you have a waiting period before an employee is eligible for sick leave?

YES _____ NO _____

Do you have a lifetime maximum number of sick leave days an employee can take?

YES _____ NO _____

Do you have a plan that permits the employee to convert sick leave to other uses?

YES _____ NO _____

If YES, check the applicable conversion:

Cash_____   Carryover to future years _____

Vacation_____   Credit at retirement_____

Other Leaves

Do you grant leave with pay for any of the following reasons?

Reason	Number of Days	Reason	Number of Days
Jury Duty	_____	Death in Family	_____
Marriage	_____	Dental Appointment	_____
Graduation Exercises	_____	Other	_____
Family Illness	_____		

Thrift Plan or 401(k) Matching Plan

Do you have a thrift or 401(k) plan? YES _____ NO _____

How much does the employer contribute per $1.00 of employee contribution? (please circle appropriate amount)

$0.25, $0.50, $0.75, $1.00, other (if other, list amount) _____

Credit Union

Do you offer a credit union? YES _____ NO _____

What interest do you pay on savings? _____

What interest do you charge on loans? _____

Insurance Benefits

Do you have a group hospitalization and/or surgical plan? YES _____ NO _____

If YES: What percentage is paid by employer? _____ %

continued

COMPENSATION SURVEY PACKAGE (Cont.)

What is the monthly cost to employee? Single Plan $ _____

Family Plan $ _____

Is there a major medical addition to the regular insurance plan? YES _____ NO _____

If YES, what is the one-time illness maximum? $ _____

What is the lifetime illness maximum? $ _____

At what amount of "out-of-pocket" employer cost per illness does the major medical plan assume full responsibility? $ _____

Do you have a group dental plan? YES _____ NO _____

If YES, what percentage is paid by employer? _____ %

Do you have a group life insurance plan? YES _____ NO _____

If YES, is it contributory? YES _____ NO _____

If YES, what percentage does the employer pay? _____ %

Is amount of insurance made available a percentage of annual salary? YES _____ NO _____

If YES, what amount of insurance is made available as a multiple of annual salary? (please circle appropriate figure)

   1.5, 2.5, 3.5, other (if other, list) _____

Is there a base to your insurance plan? YES _____ NO _____

If YES, what is the base? $ _____

Is there a cap to your insurance plan? YES _____ NO _____

If YES, what is the cap? $_____

Pension Plan

Do you have a pension plan? YES _____ NO _____

Does it include all employees? YES _____ NO _____

   If NO: Which groups are excluded? _____

_____   _____

Is it integrated with Social Security? YES _____ NO _____

How do you determine average salary for pension purposes? (please circle your method)

   Salary of final 3 yrs., 5 yrs., 10 yrs., career average, other (if other, please describe)

_____

Is it a defined benefit plan? YES _____ NO _____

If YES, what formula do you use for determining final pension benefits?

_____

Is it a defined contribution plan? YES _____ NO _____

If YES, how do you determine contributions?

_____

continued

COMPENSATION SURVEY PACKAGE (Cont.)

Which ERISA vesting plan are you using?

_____

What is your normal retirement age? (please circle appropriate number)
  55, 60, 62, 65, other (if other, please state) _____

Do you have an early retirement eligibility? YES _____ NO _____

If YES, how do you determine (please circle appropriate method)
  Age, Service, Age and service, other (if other, please describe) _____
_____

Have you provided a pension plan supplement for retirees in the past five years?
YES _____ NO _____

Do you provide death benefits for retirees? YES _____ NO _____

Do the retirees contribute to the death benefit premiums? YES _____ NO _____

General

  Do you provide a cafeteria service for your employees? YES _____ NO _____

  If YES, do you subsidize the operation? YES _____ NO _____

  If YES, % subsidization _____ %

  Do you provide parking for all employees or subsidize parking fees? YES _____ NO _____

  If subsidized, approximate cost per employee: $ _____

  Do you have a labor union among your nonclerical employees? YES _____ NO _____

  Do you have a labor union among your clerical employees? YES _____ NO _____

  Do you have an educational reimbursement plan? YES _____ NO _____

  If YES, for what programs (circle appropriate programs)
    High School, Undergraduate, Graduate, Vocational

  If YES, what percentage of tuition do you reimburse? (circle appropriate amount)
    50%, 75%, 100%, other (if other, please list) _____%

  Do you provide day care facilities? YES _____ NO _____

Merit Review Plan

  Do you have a merit rating plan for executives? YES _____ NO _____

  Briefly describe: _____
_____

  Do you have a merit rating plan for nonexecutives? YES _____ NO _____

  Briefly describe: _____
_____

continued

COMPENSATION SURVEY PACKAGE (Cont.)

Job Data

Our Job Title _____   Other Possible Titles _____

Job Code   _____   _____

Thumbnail Job Description:

Special Notes: This section of the form must be completed by the surveying organization prior to the printing of the form. (See text material on *Job Data*, for example.)

....

PLEASE COMPLETE THIS FORM FOR YOUR COMPARABLE JOB:

                                                                    Degree of Fit

Job Title:_____   1   2   3   4   5[a]

Job Code: _____   (circle the appropriate number)

Minimum Pay: _____ (or entry-level hiring rate)

Maximum Pay: _____ (or maximum longevity rate)

Please indicate on each line the number of employees receiving the particular rate of pay and indicate the rate under the applicable column.

NUMBER OF EMPLOYEES	DOLLARS				AVERAGE YEARS ON THIS JOB
	PER HOUR	PER WEEK	PER MONTH	PER YEAR	

[a]1 = poor fit   4 = considerable fit
2 = slight fit   5 = identical fit
3 = moderate fit

Occupational Survey Method

The occupational survey method has been developed to overcome many of the inadequacies and the weaknesses of the job or class comparison methods.[4] This method begins by identifying certain basic occupational groups—accounting, manufacturing, human resources, purchasing, and so forth—and then identifying certain class-series within the occupational groups. For example, purchasing could include procurement, procurement expediting, and the like. A thumbnail sketch and a code number are used to describe and identify each occupation. Each organization responding to the survey is requested to list by class title and hierarchy (A, B, C or I, II, III) the classes it has within each specific occupation. The respondent is also requested to list for each class the minimum and the maximum, as well as the average rate of pay and the number of employees in that class.

Proponents of the occupational method credit it with the following advantages:

1. It does not require the respondent to match specific jobs.
2. It is easier for the respondent to report objective data.
3. It provides pay data on a greater number of jobs.
4. It simplifies summarization and an analysis of raw data.[5]

There is no doubt that this method, when properly used, results in broader samplings of occupational hierarchies than those achieved through job matching. It is debatable, however, whether it is that much easier for an organization to respond to this method and whether it provides a more stable base for updating and revision. Like any survey method, its true strength depends on its design, execution, and analysis.

Job Evaluation Method

The job evaluation method requires that all parties participating in the survey use the same general method for evaluating jobs. This method compares job content (as measured by points or grades) with pay in dollars. The comparison produces a series of curves that identify minimum, midpoint, and maximum pay for jobs of comparable content, as measured by points or grade level.

The job evaluation method minimizes job comparability error, but the surveyor must recognize the possibility that some organizations may use different point systems for evaluating similar jobs and that the importance of job content may be interpreted differently even when identical compensable factor information is used. If the survey is to produce valid and relevant data, the unit making the survey must be aware of any differences in the manner or the method used by the respondents for identifying and evaluating the worth of their jobs.

The Hay Group, an international management and compensation consulting firm, produces a number of these kinds of surveys annually for its thousands of clients.[6] The Job Measurement Quality Assurance unit provides a comparability mechanism that permits all Hay clients to compare their pay behaviors with those of other Hay clients.

---

[4]Morton Adelby, "Wage and Salary Surveys: The Occupational Approach," *Personnel,* November–December 1960, pp. 36–44.
[5]Ibid., pp. 43–44.
[6]Milton L. Rock, ed., *Handbook of Wage and Salary Administration,* 2nd ed. (New York: McGraw-Hill, 1984), chap. 40, pp. 40/1–40/8.

A variation of the job evaluation method is to request the responding organization to provide pay data and job descriptions for selected jobs. The surveying organization then evaluates the jobs using its own system. This procedure provides the surveying organization with two job point figures derived in an identical manner and one pay amount. All that remains is to solve for the other pay figure—that is, the appropriate pay that the surveying company should provide, given the quality of respondent data.

Where the job evaluation plan is not common among the survey participants, a system of job leveling is often used by a third-party surveyor. This method is found in the SIRS survey conducted by Organization Resources Counselors, Inc. (ORC).

In SIRS, benchmark jobs are generically described. Then survey participants use a detailed leveling chart to classify the jobs into one of four to six levels according to the kind of job and the responsibilities and skill levels required. Separate leveling charts are used for supervisory, professional, and administrative jobs.

In addition to this job evaluation system, groups of participants organized by industry meet to discuss job matching and, finally, SIRS staff members visit each participant annually to review the job matches.

Like other organizations that perform compensation and pay surveys, SIRS asks each respondent to do a job matching with its benchmark descriptions. In this process, the responding organization compares its jobs with each benchmark included in the survey. A typical matching request would be (1) a close match; (2) respondent's job is less complex than survey-provided job; or (3) respondent's job is more complex than the survey respondent's job. Table 10–1 is a salary survey report produced by ORC.

Broad Classification Method

Two major broad classification methods, the maturity curve and the frequency distribution, are also useful in collecting pay rate data for relatively homogeneous professions. The various broad classification methods provide easily understood guides for grouping pay levels. These methods help the respondent provide desired and accurate data and the surveyor to develop useful summaries. (See discussions of maturity curves in chapters 8 and 17.)

DESIGNING THE SURVEY

With the completion of the various predesign steps, the time arrives to develop the actual survey. Figure 10–1 is a survey package developed by the compensation manager of Olympia, Inc. It includes:

1. Letter of transmittal
2. The survey
3. Summary sheet

Letter of Transmittal

The letter of transmittal is an official letter explaining the survey and requesting the addressee to participate. It should be brief, informative, and interesting enough to attract attention and achieve intended results. The letter should contain information about the purpose of the survey, its value to the addressee, the classes of jobs to be cov-

TABLE 10–1 ORC Compenation Information Services Salary Information Retrieval System Nonsupervisory Exempt Benchmarks—Global Summary for Company X001—Alpha Technologies

			Selected Market		
	Total Cos	*Total Inc*	*Wtd Avg Base Salary*	*Average Mid/Ctl*	*Wtd Avg Total Cash*
A020–Auditing					
Level 1	5	–	–	37,061	–
Level 2	8	19	38,563	42,530	39,265
Level 3	9	18	52,185	50,741	52,745
Level 4	4	7	65,402	67,227	65,402
A022–Auditing–EDP					
Level 2	1	1	39,026	42,145	39,026
Level 3	1	20	58,186	48,785	58,386
Level 4	1	14	69,511	56,475	70,973
A040–Budgeting					
Level 1	1	2	30,876	31,380	30,876
Level 2	4	9	35,872	38,455	36,220
Level 3	3	11	48,489	48,032	48,489
Level 4	1	–	–	50,640	–
A060–Accounting-Cost Analysis					
Level 1	8	9	30,480	33,096	31,722
Level 2	10	19	36,575	40,988	37,176
Level 3	7	27	45,298	47,963	47,227
Level 4	3	–	–	54,379	–
A070–Program Cost Scheduling and Control					
Level 1	3	16	30,759	32,617	30,759
Level 2	2	37	36,266	38,210	36,266
Level 3	3	29	41,941	44,054	41,941
Level 4	2	7	52,981	53,855	52,981
A080–Financial Analysis					
Level 1	9	22	33,926	36,198	34,623
Level 2	14	577	36,338	41,873	37,333
Level 3	15	475	47,179	50,742	48,628
Level 4	10	185	57,998	60,227	59,703
Level 5	2	12	78,077	79,950	80,162
A100–Accounting-General					
Level 1	11	188	30,282	32,042	30,703
Level 2	12	106	38,234	38,553	38,840
Level 3	10	66	45,267	45,601	46,377
Level 4	3	10	56,791	55,320	56,791

		Computer Industry					All Industries Combined		
Total Cos	Total Inc	Wtd Avg Base Salary	Average Mid/Ctl	Wtd Avg Total Cash	Total Cos	Total Inc	Wtd Avg Base Salary	Average Mid/Ctl	Wtd Avg Total Cash
4	2	37,708	38,819	42,117	68	149	30,864	35,215	31,327
6	13	42,945	45,001	45,018	150	538	38,995	42,841	39,624
7	18	55,650	53,642	56,953	162	664	49,580	52,109	51,068
4	8	62,884	67,010	64,538	64	323	57,287	62,126	59,018
–	–	–	–	–	21	25	43,441	48,251	44,079
1	2	63,000	62,566	63,000	48	110	54,140	54,162	54,957
–	–	–	–	–	12	33	65,489	63,886	67,702
–	–	–	–	–	68	222	31,800	36,725	32,054
4	6	40,372	40,880	40,894	143	850	39,711	43,299	40,064
5	12	54,743	61,767	55,302	147	1,148	48,656	53,402	49,244
–	–	–	–	–	56	508	56,345	61,912	57,098
4	1	29,288	34,667	29,288	83	116	33,401	37,036	33,923
8	10	35,914	40,284	36,073	166	451	40,436	43,967	41,156
6	6	50,854	49,115	50,854	142	548	49,240	52,641	50,008
3	–	–	55,343	–	35	227	61,315	62,295	62,551
–	–	–	–	–	48	393	29,482	33,629	29,504
–	–	–	–	–	64	740	37,632	40,640	37,735
–	–	–	–	–	63	1,270	46,887	48,386	46,971
–	–	–	–	–	47	981	57,496	55,854	57,700
8	38	34,220	38,944	34,554	128	435	32,789	36,894	33,384
15	63	42,541	44,180	43,532	236	1,738	39,671	44,414	40,515
16	124	49,989	53,559	50,298	253	2,483	50,245	53,695	51,352
7	85	62,543	62,182	62,809	119	1,261	57,631	62,918	59,138
2	12	78,076	79,950	80,162	24	94	72,813	76,080	75,299
12	55	29,491	34,834	29,544	274	1,624	32,217	35,276	32,574
13	102	37,702	41,533	37,908	338	2,156	38,538	41,972	39,085
9	52	43,313	47,134	43,351	236	1,533	47,540	49,906	48,583
2	11	55,183	53,880	55,183	59	353	56,736	58,469	58,696

ered, the manner in which the survey will be conducted, assurances of confidentiality, and methods or procedures for completing it. This letter of transmittal is often preceded by a short letter or phone call requesting participation. This request may be directed to the head of the responding organization. Approval and commitment by the top executive of the responding organization may be most valuable.

The Survey

The survey instrument should be clear and precise, with the questions phrased in such a way that they will not be misunderstood. The respondent should be able to answer with a check, one or two words, or a number. The survey should require minimum research on the part of the respondent. The format as well as the questions should make sense and should project a sense of importance to the respondent. If the questionnaire is fairly extensive and goes to a wide variety of participants, it may be worthwhile to eliminate sections that are not applicable to certain participants on their particular surveys.

The survey in Figure 10–1 consists of three sections: Organizational Policy, Employee Benefits, and Job and Pay Data. Each section serves a useful and different purpose, but together they provide an in-depth picture of the compensation system of that organization. Figure 10–2 is an outline of a summary sheet of pay data to be included in the final report of a compensation survey.

Organizational Policy   The first section on organizational policy provides an insight into the framework that sets the limits of the compensation program of the organization. This permits the surveyor, or those responsible for compiling and analyzing data, to allow for differences that affect the pay scale.

Employee Benefits   With employee benefits costing, at a minimum, 25 percent of base pay and in some cases more than 50 percent, it is vital for those analyzing and using compensation data to have a grasp of the benefits packages of the participating organizations. See chapter 17 for an extensive discussion of employee benefits.

Job Data   The job data section may be expanded to include as many jobs or classes as necessary to accomplish the mission of the survey. A typical job description in the matching process may take this form:

Title—Stock Clerk   Other Titles—Stock Attendant
Code—233.387   Supply Clerk
                                                Stockroom Clerk

Thumbnail sketch:
Assists in the operation of the stockroom by filling all stock requisitions; receives and inspects incoming supplies and notes defects and shortages. Replenishes shelves or bins with needed items. Wraps supplies and makes all necessary preparation for mailing.

Note: Has no supervisory responsibility; along with senior clerk, accountable for stock.

Job data may be provided in a separate section in which the jobs are listed by some kind of code number followed by a description.

COMPENSATION SURVEY PACKAGE

PAY SUMMARY SHEET FOR EACH JOB IN THE SURVEY

Job Title _____   Job Code _____

Job Summary:

Reporting Data

    Number of firms   _____

    Number of employees   _____

    Average pay reported   _____

Actual Pay Data

    Number of firms reporting   _____

    Lowest reported pay rate   _____

    First quartile pay rate   _____

    Median pay rate   _____

    Third quartile pay rate   _____

    Highest reported pay rate   _____

Range Data Reported

    Number of firms reporting   _____

    Lowest reported pay range   _____

    Median reported minimum range   _____

    Median reported of the median
      of the ranges   _____

    Median reported maximum range   _____

    Highest reported pay range   _____

Ranking of Reported Pay

    Pay shown below is rank-ordered from low to high. If the first value begins at "0," the list is in deciles. If the first value begins at "1," the figures are actual pay. (Deciles were used when more than 25 individual pay rates were reported.)

0 _____				
1 _____	6 _____	11 _____	16 _____	21 _____
2 _____	7 _____	12 _____	17 _____	22 _____
3 _____	8 _____	13 _____	18 _____	23 _____
4 _____	9 _____	14 _____	19 _____	24 _____
5 _____	10 _____	15 _____	20 _____	25 _____

FIGURE 10–2   Compensation Survey Report

Actual Pay Data   Many surveys collect average pay data. Such data include number of employees; average pay; and the minimum, midpoint, and maximum of the pay range for the particular job. This procedure is basically unacceptable for current compensation decision-making purposes. The survey should collect *actual* pay data for each person in each surveyed job. These kind of data make it possible to identify *actual* pay practices and develop a true picture of what the array of pay data for a job actually looks like.

Compensation managers now recognize that pay for a job is not normally distributed and that a mean value may be inadequate or may not provide an accurate statistic for making decisions. Pay data for most jobs relate to a nonparametric distribution rather than to a normal distribution. A nonparametric distribution is one in which the mean, the mode, and the median are not the same. Because such distribution is usually the case, median, percentile, decile, and quartile data are more valuable than average data. The only way a survey can generate the more valuable data is for the initial collection instrument to capture actual, individual pay rates. (The mean and median are discussed later in this chapter.)

In the past, it was difficult for respondents to provide such data because of the payroll systems in use. Today, however, with well-designed computerized payroll systems and printouts of the current pay for each employee, actual pay data for each employee are available.

A major hurdle the surveyor still must overcome is to demonstrate to the respondents why it is to their advantage to spend the time to provide pay data for each incumbent on each job in the survey. A first and most important step in overcoming this barrier is to explain to the respondent why survey data based on individual pay rates will be critical for making good compensation decisions.

Permission to Include Name of Company   To ensure maximum value of the survey to all respondents, the survey summary and analysis should include a list of all participating organizations. At the outset, the surveyor must request permission from participants to include the names of their organizations. It is vital for those using or reviewing the compensation data for decision purposes to know the names of the organizations that provided the data. Without written permission, however, the use of a participant's name may lead to legal action. All the surveyor must do is include with the survey a brief form letter stating that the participating organization permits its name to be included in a list of participants and that the list will not in any way reveal confidential data and information. A member of the participating organization signs the letter and returns it with the completed survey.

Keeping a Record of Provided Data   Two copies of a survey should be sent to each participant—one copy to be completed and returned to the surveying organization and a duplicate copy to be completed for the respondent's own files. A file copy is essential when comparing organization-provided data with summarized data and is also helpful in completing future surveys. If two copies are not sent, the respondent should be requested to make a copy for its file purposes.

Compensation Survey Report   Figure 10–2 is an example of a pay summary sheet for the final report on the results of the survey. A summary sheet should be completed for each job. In the final report, it is preferable to keep occupational groups of jobs together and to separate the exempt categories from the nonexempt. At the discretion of the surveyor, the final report may include a recap of employee benefits.

Date Data Were Collected   The date the data were collected must be identified in any kind of a survey report. Users must know when data were collected so that they will be able to reconcile survey-provided data. This is important when users of third-party surveys compare data from a number of different surveys. Users should age data. One approach is to age data to January 1 of the coming year.

A simple adjustment/aging procedure may take this form:

Job	Survey Pay Data	Date of Survey	Adjustment to Desired Date	Adjusted Market Value
___	_____	_____	_____	_____
___	_____	_____	_____	_____
___	_____	_____	_____	_____

PERFORMING A STATISTICAL ANALYSIS OF THE DATA

The entire survey process is subject to statistical validation. However, it is seldom possible or even necessary to survey the entire labor market. Instead, the sampling method can be used for obtaining pay data.

Statistical Sampling

Statistical sampling is a study of relationships that exist among selected items that form a specific group and are representative of the entire group. The group from which the sample is drawn is called the *universe* or *population,* and the sample itself is known as the *sample universe* or *sample population.* The objective of statistical sampling is to provide data that accurately describe the parent population or universe.

Those involved in pay surveys will find that, among the various sampling techniques, either *random sampling* or *stratified random sampling* will be adequate for their purpose.

Random Sampling   The random sampling technique uses a variety of statistical methods that may include the development of an array of data and the use of a table of random numbers. A random sample is selected from the universe, without regard for any type of preselection (i.e., each unit of the universe has an equal and independent chance for selection).

Stratified Random Sampling   In stratified random sampling, the universe is first divided into various strata or segments. Segmentation may be by kind of business, by size of organization (number of employees, dollar volume, etc.), by geographic area, or some other characteristic. Then, after stratification has been completed, stratified random sampling follows the same selection procedures as those used in random sampling. That is, a random sample is conducted within the strata.

Both sampling techniques make it possible to collect valid pay data that provide an adequate basis for comparing entire pay structures or the rates of pay of specific jobs, classes, or occupational groups.

Weighting   An integral part of the stratified random sampling technique is the *weighting* of collected data. It is possible that the data from one organization are more important than the data from another. If this is the case, weighting is important. For example, in stratifying the universe, one organization is selected from each of two strata. Then, if one stratum contains 60 percent of all jobs and the second stratum contains only 40 percent of the jobs, when the total universe is analyzed, the data received from the organization representing the first sample receives 50 percent more weight than the other and the development of any measurement statistic from the data is influenced proportionally:

$$60\% - 40\% = 20\% \quad \frac{20\%}{40\%} = 50\%$$

A major weighting issue that often faces the compensation manager revolves around the location of the labor market. As a rule of thumb, data from outside the labor market as well as that representing a limited part of the local market (approximately 15 to 20 percent) are not weighted. Normally, weighting occurs only when the data represent a deep and broad cross section of the local labor market.

Another factor to be aware of when weighting data relative to specific jobs is that employers hiring the largest number of employees are not necessarily the ones hiring the largest number of employees for a specific job. It may also be necessary to eliminate data from organizations that report only one or two incumbents. These jobholders may perform assignments not normally required or detailed in the job description. This holds especially true when using a nonweighted approach to data manipulation.

The entire purpose of sampling and weighting is to minimize the effect of developing a biased sample—one that does not accurately represent its universe or parent population. A review of a statistics or sampling text may be necessary if these mathematical issues arise. The *BLS Handbook of Methods* (BLS Bulletin 1711), Chapter 13, pages 131–133, contains a brief but useful discussion of the sampling and weighting procedures used by the BLS.

No doubt, the more closely one adheres to proper sampling methods, the better the quality of survey data, but this does not preclude the old standby—*trial and error.* Furthermore, it is not always easy to define the labor market. Its definition may be one of individual or organizational perception. Even if one accurately defines the market and identifies those organizations that make up the market universe, there is nothing to guarantee that faithful following of proper sampling methods will produce desired results. For these and other reasons, sampling frequently results in a trial-and-error operation. In itself, this is not bad. If each trial is objective, it becomes possible to reduce the margin of error and to improve the value of the survey.

Measuring Statistics

A wide variety of yardsticks enables compensation managers to compare the various elements of the pay structures in their organizations with those in others. The two most used measures of central tendency are the *mean* (average) and the *median* (the middle value in an array of all values received). The mean value can be identified in a number of different ways. Some of the different ways of identifying the mean or average value are through (1) a weighted average, (2) a modified weighted average, (3) a raw or unweighted average, and (4) a trimmed mean.

In working with average pay information, compensation specialists may at times wish to use weighted averages or modified weighted averages rather than raw or unweighted averages. Although not too useful a statistic, the data that many surveys provide result in a *raw* or *unweighted average*. When organizations provide only average pay data for jobs and then these data are summed and divided by the number of averages included within the sum, the result is an unweighted average. A *weighted pay average* recognizes the number of employees receiving a specific rate of pay from each unit (organization) providing pay data. An example of developing unweighted and weighted average data occurred when RICH Compensation Consultants collected and summarized pay data for the job of senior clerk-typist (see Table 10–2).

Because Olympia employs almost 50 percent of the senior clerk-typists in this survey and those organizations with higher rates of pay are not that much higher than Olympia, the weighted average ($15,200) is somewhat less than the unweighted average ($15,477).

A *modified weighted average* reduces the influence of an unusual population. RICH Compensation Consultants conducted a pay survey and collected the pay data shown in Table 10–3 on data entry operators. When modified weighted averages are

TABLE 10–2 Unweighted and Weighted Average Pay Data

Business	Senior Clerk-Typists	Annual Pay Rate	Total Annual Pay
Olympia	14	$14,938	$209,138
Alpha	3	15,708	47,124
Omega	5	16,786	83,930
Delta	8	14,476	115,808
	30	$61,908	$456,000
raw or unweighted average		$\dfrac{\$61,908}{4}$ =	$ 15,477
weighted average		$\dfrac{\$456,000}{30}$ =	$ 15,200

TABLE 10–3 Modified Weighted Average Pay Data

Business	Data Entry Operators	Hourly Rate of Pay	Total Hourly Pay
Omega	14	$ 7.00	$ 98.00
Alpha	9	7.45	67.05
Olympia	50	9.15	457.50
Delta	16	7.95	127.20
Gamma	6	8.40	50.40
	95	$39.95	$800.15

used for pay data, the influence of an employer with an extremely large number of employees in a particular job is reduced, as shown in the following steps:

Step 1: Determine average number of employees per company.

$$\frac{95}{5} = 19$$

Step 2: Identify the excess of difference in population between the population of the highly influencing organization and the average population. In this example, Olympia is the employer with the highly influencing population:

$$50 - 19 = 31$$

Step 3: Reduce the influence of the organization having the large population to some arbitrary figure. A frequently used arbitrary value is 10 percent of the excess population plus the average population:

$$10\% \times 31 = 3 + 19 = 22$$

Step 4: Develop a modified weighted average (Olympia as the influencing organization is the only organization to have its population modified):

Omega	14	×	7.00 =	$ 98.00
Alpha	9	×	7.45 =	67.05
Olympia	22	×	9.15 =	201.30
Delta	16	×	7.95 =	127.20
Gamma	6	×	8.40 =	50.40
	5	67	39.95	$543.95

modified weighted average $= \dfrac{\$543.95}{67} = \$8.12$

weighted average $= \dfrac{\$800.15}{95} = \$8.42$

raw or unweighted average $= \dfrac{\$39.95}{5} = \$7.99$

By reducing the influence of Olympia in the survey, the modified average value is approximately 3.7 percent less than the weighted average, and the raw or unweighted average is approximately 5.4 percent less than the weighted average.

The term *trimmed mean* is often used to identify the average value of an array in which extreme values are eliminated at either end of the array. In this case, the median and trimmed mean will be similar, if not identical.

In addition to measures of central tendency, a range of values is important. The range values may be the average low and average high value of all data received, or they may simply be the lowest and highest value received. The range is frequently divided into tenths (deciles), quarters (quartiles), or thirds. For pay comparison purposes, many feel the interquartile (the middle 50 percent) range to be the best indicator of the span of the range (see Figure 10–3). Using the interquartile range eliminates the effect of widely divergent values at either end of the pay spectrum.

In compiling pay data, most surveys allow for differences when a standard workweek is less than 40 hours. For example, a conversion factor is normally applied to the

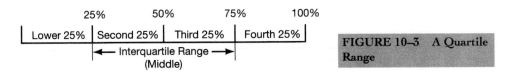

FIGURE 10–3 A Quartile Range

	Hourly	*Weekly*	*Monthly*	*Annually*
TABLE 10–4 Converting Pay Rates from One Time Period to Another				
Hourly		× by 40	× by 174	× by 2,088[a]
Weekly	+ by 40		× by 4.35	× by 52.2[a]
Monthly	+ by 174	+ by 4.35		× by 12
Annually	+ by 2,088[a]	+ by 52.2	+ by 12	

[a] Most years include one extra working day, and for that reason work hours in one year are 2,088 and the number of workweeks in a year are 52.2 (a leap year may include two extra working days).

pay of employees who work only a 35-hour week and receive time and a half (or some other premium) for hours worked in excess of 35. If the employee receives an additional straight-time pay for hours worked between 35 and 40, no conversion factor is normally applied.

When requesting pay rate data, the surveyor should try to identify the time period that most frequently applies to the pay of the jobs in the survey or the practices of responding organizations. The most often used pay rate time periods are hourly, weekly, monthly, and annually. Table 10–4 is helpful in converting pay rates from one time period to another.

Finally, an analysis for accuracy assists in improving the quality of the survey. Recording errors are not only possible but probable, although most of them can be eliminated by careful checking.

USING THIRD-PARTY SURVEYS

Sooner or later, almost all organizations will use third-party surveys. Other than some form of "quick and dirty" survey, most organizations do not have the resources to collect all the kinds of data needed for pay policy purposes. A major factor determining which survey is to be used is cost. Third-party surveys can range in cost from free to in excess of $100,000. However, most third-party surveys range from $50 to $1,000. Although at first glance these costs may not seem excessive, it is possible to spend thousands of dollars to acquire all needed and desired data. Surveys can be placed into four price categories: (1) 0–$200, (2) $201–$2,500; (3) $2,501–$20,000; and (4) $20,001–$150,000, or more.

Free to $200 Some good surveys, including the BLS surveys, are in this price range. These surveys may require significant amounts of interpretation as to comparability with jobs in the user organization and as to kinds of organizations providing the data. Frequently, providers of data are not identified. In many of the low-cost surveys, only average, minimum, and maximum rates of pay are provided. Often, the so-called average rate of pay is nothing more than a derived midpoint figure between minimum and maximum.

Some low-cost surveys may not relate to the specific labor markets of interest to the user. At times, the data are old or the user does not know when the data were collected or how the raw data were transformed into the report data.

$201 to $2,500 Many of the professionally developed third-party surveys are in this price range. These surveys can relate to specific industries, with the industries further grouped by some kind of size statistics—sales, number of employees, profitability, ROI. At the high end of this range, surveys designed with designated comparison groups (DCG) or clusters begin to appear. Here, the purchaser has an opportunity to identify a selected "cut" of the survey participants by kind of industry, size, and so on.

$2,501 to $20,000 These surveys are principally cluster types. Now the user has the opportunity to purchase a customized survey rather than simply selecting participants and positions from an existing database. The purchaser can obtain responses to a broad range of specific compensation-related questions. The client can receive measured job matches and other data relating to company performance and size characteristics. Matching organizations can be selected by zip code of location and kind of industry and other size characteristics. Many of the major compensation consulting firms provide this kind of service.

$20,001 to $150,000 or More Surveys in this price range provide clients with industry or other relevant market-pricing modules. Through the use of multiple regression or other appropriate statistical methods, jobs can be priced relative to industry practices. A wide variety of variables can be recognized, and the data provided to the client can be extremely precise. Various internal measurements are performed inside the client organization, and then matching data are collected from the organizations that comprise the relevant market to obtain desired results.

Major trade associations frequently commission professional third-party surveying organizations to perform high-quality surveys of their members. A wide variety of data is available to all participants. In some cases, firm-specific data are made available but require approval of the firm providing the data. These kinds of surveys can range in cost from five to seven figures.

SOURCES OF THIRD-PARTY DATA

Each passing year finds new sources of survey data. Today, thousands of organizations annually collect data on jobs in various industries, on kinds of work performed, and even on specific occupations. This section includes a description of the surveys provided by six major conductors of surveys: the U.S. Department of Labor, Bureau of Labor Statistics (BLS); Watson Wyatt Data Services/ECS; The Hay Group; Economic Research Institute (ERI); William M. Mercer, Inc.; and Organization Resources Counselors, Inc. (ORC).

Bureau of Labor Statistics (BLS) Surveys

Occupational Compensation Survey Program (OCSP) The Service Contract Act of 1965 requires federal contractors to pay their employees locally prevailing wages and benefits. OCSP conducts area wage and benefit surveys used by the Employment Standards Administration of the U.S. Department of Labor to administer the act. Then the Federal Employees Pay Comparability Act of 1990 changed the way the pay of white-collar federal government workers is set and adjusted. Beginning in 1994, this law requires adjustments in the pay of white-collar federal workers based on pay levels of nonfederal workers in their locality. OCSP survey results are used by the president's pay agent (the secretary of labor and the directors of the U.S. Office of Personnel Management and the U.S. Office of Management and Budget) in determining local pay adjustments under the act. To meet the act's requirements, the bureau's White-Collar Pay and Area Wage Survey programs were integrated into the OCSP. This new program resulted in (1) expanding the survey's industrial coverage to include all private nonfarm establishments (except households) employing 50 workers or more and to state and local governments and (2) adding more professional, administrative, technical, and protective service occupations to the surveys.

The OCSP includes compensation data for approximately 168 areas. These areas are organized into 32 larger areas and the "remaining others." The larger areas collect data on 44 occupations: 4 professional, 9 administrative, 4 technical, 8 clerical, 3 protective service, 8 maintenance and toolroom, and 8 material movement and custodial occupations, whereas the "others" have data collected on 28 occupations.

Occupational data are published by skill level and include mean, median, and quartile earnings; distribution of employees by earnings intervals and average weekly hours (for white-collar occupations). When possible, survey results are tabulated separately for private industry and state and local government and establishments employing 500 workers or more.

Employee Benefits Surveys   In addition to OCSP, BLS established a broad-based annual survey of employee benefits plans in private industry in 1979. As employer costs for employee benefits approached 30 percent of total compensation costs, the federal government recognized the obsolescence of the term *fringe benefits* coined in the 1940s and began focusing attention on "total compensation comparability." The survey currently covers private industry and state and local government workers, and provides separate data for major employment groups.

Other Data Provided by BLS   The BLS also provides a wide variety of pay data that are of value to compensation professionals. The *BLS Measures of Compensation, Bulletin 2239,* February 1986, describes data collected by the BLS and provides guidance regarding the appropriate uses and limitations of these data.

Two other publications of the BLS are (1) *Compensation and Working Conditions (CWC)* and (2) *Employment and Earnings (EE)*. These publications provide measures that compensation professionals find extremely useful. They are

1. *Indexes*—show change in employer costs for total compensation, including the change in wages, salaries, and employee benefits.
2. *Cost levels*—means, medians, and middle ranges of wages paid to specific occupations.
3. *Benefit incidence and provisions*—the number and percentage of employees offered and covered by selected benefits with details of specific benefit plans.

Watson Wyatt Data Services/ECS   A wholly owned subsidiary of Watson Wyatt Worldwide, Watson Wyatt Data Services (WWDS/ECS), which is a major international compensation, actuarial, and benefits consulting firm, furnishes a broad array of executive, managerial, professional, and clerical compensation data in the following reports: Board of Directors Compensation Policies and Practices; Top Management (over 80 executive positions in more than 25 industry categories and up to 14 employee-sized groups); Middle Management (over 141 middle-management positions analyzed in over 100 industry categories); Supervisory Management (111 jobs reported for 15 state groups, 40 states, and some 200 metropolitan areas); Professional and Scientific Personnel (data on more than 134 professional and scientific positions in 15 state groups, 40 states, and some 200 metropolitan areas); Technician and Skilled Trades Personnel (over 106 jobs for over 200 geographic subsets for the nation; Office Personnel (125 nonexempt office positions reported nationally in 200 metropolitan areas in almost every state and 16 state groups); Sales and Marketing Personnel (detailed salary data on over 35 sales and marketing management positions, sales support, and marketing positions in four levels of skill and responsibility from entry to supervisor with a wide variety of compensation data reported nationally and for 5 regions).

Special reports include executive perquisites, executive capital accumulation programs, annual incentives and other alternative reward programs, workforce efficiency and human resources personnel compensation, and a report on Information Technology Personnel compensation.

In addition to the U.S. surveys, WWDS produces an international series of salary surveys covering expatriate compensation and compensation practices in Canada, 17 European and Middle East countries, and 14 countries in Asia and the Pacific.

The Hay Group

The Hay Group, a management consulting organization and parent company of the Hay Guide Chart-Profile Method of Job Evaluation, produces a wide variety of surveys that cover all kinds of jobs at all levels in all major industrial sectors. The surveys conducted annually by Hay include Executive Compensation Comparison (cash compensation for management, professional, and technical positions), Engineering Compensation Comparison (professionals in engineering positions in major companies), Sales Compensation Comparison (includes incentive plan features and expense reimbursements), EDP Compensation Comparison (professionals in data processing), Hay Compensation Comparisons (cash compensation for management, professional, and technical positions), Community Wage and Salary Surveys (200 standard nonexempt office and plant jobs in over 100 metropolitan areas), Standard Reports (prepared for a wide variety of industries, providing a view of the compensation practices of each participant), and Hay Benefits Report (summary of all kinds of benefits, perquisites, and personnel practices).

Economic Research Institute (ERI)

The ERI of Redmond, Washington, provides a number of extremely useful compensation reports. There are wage and salary differentials and cost-of-living and employment demographics, using data compiled from over 298 cities and 2,750 wage and salary and cost-of-living data sources. Their data are available on diskettes for the personal computer. The *Relocation Assessor* diskette provides cost-of-living comparisons and reports for any of 4,000 U.S. and Canadian cities and/or 1,400 international locations. These data can be useful to both compensation and management professionals and to employees considering a relocation offer or temporary assignment.

The *Geographic Assessor* diskette calculates wage and salary differentials for more than 4,000 North American cities. It also summarizes Relocation Assessor rental data for comparison purposes. It is useful for assessing branch location salary competitiveness and equity. The *Salary Assessor* reports median salary and range data with descriptions for more than 3,000 positions. It also profiles benchmark listings for jobs in 2,000 industries and contrasts cost-of-living competitive pay for any job in multiple geographic locations.

The *Consultants Assessor* includes full Salary Assessor job descriptions, executive compensation data, and demographic data that can assist with Americans with Disabilities Act (ADA) compliance and glass ceiling and reasonable compensation analysis. The *Benefit Assessor* produces health/welfare benefit discrimination tests, Consolidated Omnibus Reconciliation Act of 1985 (COBRA) letters, cost analyses, and state alliance rates. It is designed to assist in controlling benefit costs.

William M. Mercer, Inc.

William M. Mercer, Inc., a worldwide consulting organization, provides human resources services in such areas as compensation, employee benefits, communications, and asset planning. It conducts 10 national surveys, including (1) Compensation Planning Surveys that provide information on annual actual and projected pay increase budgets and structure adjustments, actual payouts of management incentive plans, and information on nontraditional pay practices; (2) geographic salary differentials for lower-level exempt and nonexempt jobs for over 250 cities; (3) executive jobs; (4) 91 executive, finance, accounting, and legal positions; (5) 53 human resources jobs sponsored by the Society for Human Resource Management (SHRM); (6) 116 data processing jobs; (7) 82 software executive, management, middle-management, professional, and technical jobs for the Information Technology Association of America; (8) 61 materials and logistics management jobs; (9) 60 levels of physicians' jobs in a variety of specialty areas; and (10) 93 hospital and hospital systems jobs.

Organization Resources Counselors, Inc.

Organization Resources Counselors, Inc. (ORC) is an international management consulting firm that is a major provider of compensation data services. ORC produces a number of major surveys, with their largest and possibly most widely used being the Salary Information Retrieval Systems (SIRS)—a computerized system for the exchange of compensation data. SIRS is a semiannual benchmark survey in which almost 600 companies participate. It covers exempt entry-level to upper-middle-management positions in more than 275 occupations. SIRS also includes compensation pay data on more than 25 nonexempt clerical, technical, production, and maintenance jobs. Participants can select companies with which they want to exchange data according to criteria such as company size, location, sales, type of industry, and/or product. ORC staff members perform on-site validation of job matches.

ORC also conducts many regional and national surveys for associations and employer groups. Each survey is designed to meet client requirements. Overall, more than 2,000 major U.S. employers participate in ORC-conducted surveys.

In recent years, ORC has become very active in international compensation. It provides clients with expatriate information that recognizes differences in income tax and other taxes and differences in housing costs and expenditure costs between the home country and host country. These kinds of data permit employers to compute an estimated gross salary that allows the transferee to maintain an equivalent standard of living in a host country. ORC provides extensive compensation-related data for 35 countries.

Professional, Trade, and Industrial Associations

Most professionals belong to national associations that represent their particular career fields, and provide a variety of services to members. One highly desired and commonly provided service is an annual compensation survey of members and a summary of data in some association publication. Over the years, the quality of these surveys has improved, and interest in the results has steadily increased. Similar to the professional associations are trade and industrial associations. They represent organizations providing comparable kinds of goods and services. These trade and industrial associations also perform compensation surveys for their members and provide them with the results. Most members of these associations pay attention to the results of the surveys, and it is quite likely that the results significantly influence their pay practices.

Others

A large number of other organizations also perform wage surveys. Among these are many national consulting firms, and in each metropolitan area, a variety of local organizations. National publication firms such as the Bureau of National Affairs (BNA) and Simon & Schuster's Division of the Bureau of Business Practice produces "Compensation and Benefits Manager's Report" that includes a section on the setting of pay levels and where to get pay surveys and how to use them. The American Management Association's bimonthly publication, *Compensation and Benefits Review,* contains a wide range of valuable articles in the field of compensation, and a review of current survey activities.

Summary

The compensation survey facilitates an understanding of the competitive forces in the marketplace regarding pay practices. Recognizing and relating to compensation trends is useful to organizations in hiring and retaining competent employees, in promoting worker productivity, and in developing an adequate and acceptable pay structure. Steps in conducting a compensation survey include deciding on the data needs of the organization, deciding where the data will come from, determining the survey method, and determining the information collection method. Survey data may be gathered through matching benchmark jobs or classes, or by using the occupational survey method, the job evaluation method, or broad classification methods. The chapter then provides a detailed description and examples on how to design and conduct a pay/compensation survey. The data may be collected by telephone, mailed questionnaire, face-to-face interviews, or conference.

The chapter discusses statistical tools available for evaluating and validating collected information and provides a detailed example of a compensation survey data collection instrument. The chapter concludes with a discussion of a few major third-party services available for conducting a survey.

Possibly the greatest value of a survey is that it informs the user of what is happening in the marketplace. Above all, it identifies trends. After trends are recognized, the next step is to identify detailed information about specific changes that may have occurred. Because it is important to be able to identify trends or recognize precedents, the methods used to collect and report compensation data must be consistent. Consistency also involves a rather stable group of survey participants.

Review Questions

1. Identify some of the major reasons for conducting a compensation survey.
2. Explain why an organization must relate to a variety of labor markets when conducting a compensation survey.
3. What is meant by the scope of the survey? Describe some of the factors that affect the scope of a survey.
4. What are thumbnail sketches? How are they used in a compensation survey?
5. Describe various methods available for collecting compensation survey data. Describe cases in which each method would be most effective.

Designing a Base Pay Structure

11

Learning Objectives

In this chapter you will learn about:

1. The design characteristics of a pay structure.

2. A pay policy line and how to develop it.

3. The design of pay grades and their relationship to internal worth and market value.

4. The use of pay grades for different employee groups.

5. The need for more than one pay structure in some organizations.

Compensation Strategy

Develop a clear link between work required, performance demonstrated, and pay provided to each employee.

Decisions that provide guidelines for the compensation manager to follow in developing a pay structure are made at the higher levels of the organization. These policy decisions include guidelines concerning:

1. Minimum and maximum levels of pay (taking into consideration ability and willingness to pay, concern for profitability, government regulations, union influences, and market pressures).

2. The general relationships among levels of pay (between nonexempt and exempt, senior management and operating management, operatives and supervisors).

3. Whether or not the pay structure should lead the market, lag the market, or lead-lag the market.

4. The division of the total compensation dollar (i.e., what portion goes into base pay, what portion into benefits, what portion into merit pay, and what portion into pay-for-performance programs).

Additionally, senior management decides how much money to allot for the total compensation package—that is, how much will go into pay increases for the next year, who will recommend them, and generally how they will be determined. In other words, will they be based on seniority, on merit, or on cost-of-living adjustments? If they are based on merit, what performance standards will be used and who will make the determination? Last, but not least, decisions made at this level determine the extent to which compensation policies are detailed and communicated throughout the organization. At this point, the issue of openness or secrecy in the communication of compensation information becomes one of the most important issues facing this level of management. This chapter centers on the design of the pay structure. (Pay administration is covered in chapter 18.)

Although decisions made at the top seldom determine specific employee pay rates, they do set guidelines for compensation managers. From guidelines, these managers must consider the issues and make acceptable and workable determinations concerning the following:

1. What is the lowest rate of pay that can be offered for a job that will entice the quality of employees the organization desires to have as its members?
2. What is the rate of pay that must be offered to incumbents to ensure that they remain with the organization?
3. Does the organization want to recognize seniority and meritorious performance through the base pay schedule?
4. Is it wise or necessary to offer more than one rate of pay to employees performing either identical or similar kinds of work?
5. What is considered to be a sufficient difference in base rates of pay among jobs in a class-series that require varying levels of knowledge, skills, responsibilities, and duties?
6. Does the organization wish to recognize dangerous and distressing working conditions within the base pay schedule?
7. Should there be a difference in changes in base pay progression opportunities among jobs of varying worth?
8. Do employees have a significant opportunity to progress to higher-level jobs? If so, what should be the relationship between promotion to a higher job and changes in base pay?
9. Will policies and regulations permit incumbents to earn rates of pay higher than established maximums and lower than established minimums? What would be the reasons for allowing such deviations?
10. How will the pay structure accommodate across-the-board, cost-of-living, or other adjustments not related to employee tenure, performance, or responsibility and duty changes?

PAY STRUCTURE ARCHITECTURE

Previous chapters provided information on how to develop data to facilitate the equitable ordering of jobs into natural groups based on comparable responsibility, knowledge, and skill requirements. The establishment of an internally fair relationship among jobs is as important to each jobholder as it is to management. Management must be able to substantiate its reasons for the placement of jobs in a specific order. For this reason, strong recommendations have been made in this text to provide in-depth job analysis, develop useful job descriptions that are current, and implement an evaluation plan that provides a basis for establishing a systematic ordering of jobs.

Chapter 10 focuses specifically on the use of the compensation survey to generate data regarding the pay comparable jobs are receiving in relevant geographic and industry labor markets. Valid data, interpreted properly, enable decision makers to relate the pay received by their employees to that provided by other competing organizations. Acquiring external data assists in establishing a competitive pay posture that permits the organization to hire and retain reliable, competent employees.

With the generation of internal and external pay data and information, managers are now ready to design a pay structure. To do so, they must (1) determine a trend or pay policy line, (2) decide on the need for one or more pay structures, (3) display job data, (4) establish the characteristics of the pay structure (number, width, and height of pay grades and the overlap among them), and (5) lock overlapping pay structures (when using more than one).

These five technical features determine to a large degree the unique compensation characteristics of the organization. Above all, they tell employees how the organization values its jobs; what job and compensation advancement opportunities are available; and how competitive the pay practices are with those of other organizations.

Determining a Pay Policy Line

Each organization must develop its own pay policy line, which is a trend line or line of best fit that best represents the middle pay value of jobs that have been evaluated or classified to have particular worth. A line of best fit produces a trend line by minimizing the sum of the squares of the vertical deviations around the line. A line of best fit can be a straight or curved line. In either case, it is one that best represents the middle pay value (the central tendency) of all jobs or the benchmark jobs used to establish a pay policy line.

A useful or practical first step in developing a pay policy line is to establish the lowest and highest rates of pay for the organization. With the identification of these two rates of pay, the next step is to draw a line connecting them (see Figure 11–1a). The line connecting the lowest-offered to highest-offered rates of pay could be the pay policy line for the organization, or it could be at least a first approximation of a pay policy line. Another simple procedure for establishing a pay policy line is to obtain the market rate or going rate of pay for the lowest-paid and highest-paid jobs. Connecting these two points can also provide a first approximation for a pay policy line (Figure 11–1b).

The procedure most organizations normally follow in establishing a pay policy or trend line is to identify the market rates for various benchmark jobs that cover the entire pay spectrum from lowest to highest rates of pay. By plotting on a chart the pay rate information obtained through surveys, a scatter diagram or scatter plot can be developed (Figure 11–1c).

Scatter Diagram/Scatter Plot   A compensation scatter diagram plots the points or dots on a chart where each point represents a job. Plotted job data provide a convenient way to see an entire array of relationships and identify natural groupings of jobs.

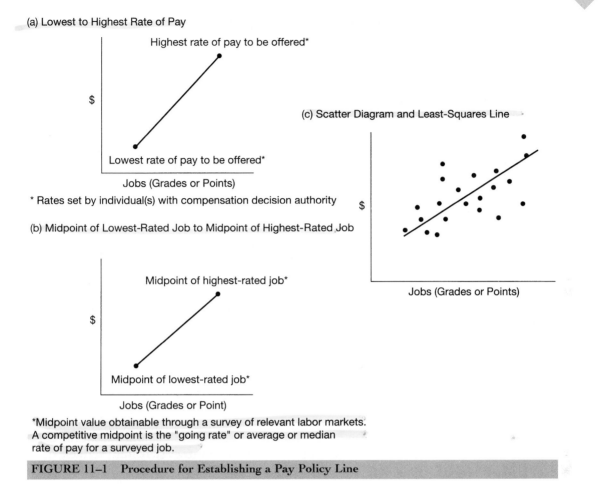

(a) Lowest to Highest Rate of Pay

Highest rate of pay to be offered*

$

Lowest rate of pay to be offered*

Jobs (Grades or Points)

* Rates set by individual(s) with compensation decision authority

(b) Midpoint of Lowest-Rated Job to Midpoint of Highest-Rated Job

Midpoint of highest-rated job*

$

Midpoint of lowest-rated job*

Jobs (Grades or Point)

(c) Scatter Diagram and Least-Squares Line

$

Jobs (Grades or Points)

*Midpoint value obtainable through a survey of relevant labor markets.
A competitive midpoint is the "going rate" or average or median
rate of pay for a surveyed job.

FIGURE 11–1   Procedure for Establishing a Pay Policy Line

The paired coordinates for locating each point are the evaluated score for the job and its actual pay.

A scatter diagram uses job points, an assigned pay grade, or some other job-worth indicator as a scale for the horizontal axis (the *x*-axis or abscissa) and the dollar value of the job as the scale for the vertical axis (the *y*-axis or ordinate). The *x, y* values for a specific point are called an ordered pair. (In plotting pay survey data, the *x*-coordinate will normally be the points assigned to the job used for matching purposes.) In cases in which point scores are not available for surveyed jobs, the current rate of pay for the jobs in the organization conducting the survey could be used as the points for the *x*-coordinates. The *y*-coordinate will be the dollar value surveyed organizations indicated they pay for each job. Each plotted point or dot on the graph represents one job.

Different procedures are available for developing a trend line from a scatter diagram. These range from the very simple line-of-sight or freehand procedure to the two-point straight-line method to the fairly complex least-squares procedure or regression analysis, all of which use different statistical procedures. (Appendix 11A describes the least-squares procedure.)

The *line-of-sight (freehand) procedure* is a simple way to determine the trend line. In most cases, this procedure provides an acceptable first approach to what the trend line will look like. Using this approach requires the data analyst to perceive visually (to eyeball) a line that cuts through the center of the points on the scatter diagram and that minimizes the vertical differences among points in the same vertical plane.

The *two-point procedure* is also very simple and involves drawing a line that connects the lowest and highest values. When this procedure is used, the lowest and highest points may actually be aberrations—illogical or unacceptable pay data—and should have been eliminated from consideration. An arithmetic procedure that minimizes the likelihood of such an error is to array the pay data and divide them into two groups having the same number of values, selecting the median (middle) value of the lower group as one point and the median value of the top group for the other point. Both the line-of-sight and the two-point procedures require nothing more than a pencil and straightedge (ruler) for drawing the line. If a curved line is more suitable for providing a line of best fit, a piece of string can be used in drawing it. Another two-point procedure that is useful when plotting many jobs is to locate the central point of a cluster of low-paying jobs and the central point of a cluster of high-paying jobs and then connect these two points.

The *least-squares method* is a statistical procedure that produces a trend line by minimizing the sum of the squares of the vertical deviations around the line. In a least-squares linear regression, the line goes through the $\bar{x}, \bar{y}$ points—the mean values for all x and y values (see appendix 11A).

With the accessibility of modern calculators and computer programs, mathematical calculation problems are of secondary importance. Because of these technological advancements, the least-squares method is a practical alternative for developing a line of minimum deviations.

Computer programs using multivariate (regression) analysis will permit the computer terminal operator to input x (job evaluation score) and y (pay rate) variable data. The computer, through a stored algorithm, analyzes the data and develops a visual display of a line of best fit.[1]

In using any procedure, it is essential to analyze visually the line and the location of the points above and below it before accepting it as a line of best fit. After an initial pay policy line is set, it may be possible to eliminate some of these outlying points—outliers. They cannot be eliminated, however, without an analysis of why they developed and whether it is permissible to eliminate them. For example, when technological changes have simplified the job but the job has never been reevaluated and the jobholders' rates of pay have not been reduced in line with the job requirements, it is possible, even necessary, to disregard these data points when developing a pay policy line. This principle also applies in cases in which, strictly because of seniority increases, individuals are receiving rates of pay out of line with job requirements.

Many organizations use the pay policy line to set midpoint values for all their jobs. Pay policy lines are useful when plotting survey data and comparing them with the in-

---

[1]An *algorithm* is a prescribed set of well-defined rules or procedures for the solution of a problem in a finite number of steps.

ternal pay structure. From the pay policy line, organizations establish the minimum and maximum pay levels, the relationship between pay grades, and the range of a pay grade.

The Need for More Than One Pay Structure

Whether more than one pay structure is needed must be established early by those responsible for structure design. There are a number of logical and rational considerations for having multiple pay structures that focus on the forces that influence the actual pay of the various occupational groups comprising most organizations. It is not unusual for large organizations to have at least three pay structure lines—one for blue-collar manual labor, craft, and trade workers; another for nonexempt white-collar salaried workers; and a third for managerial, administrative, and professional exempt employees. Some organizations have a fourth pay structure for their highly paid executives.

In relating the actual pay provided to a specific job or class, a number of issues must be resolved:

1. What does the organization consider to be the appropriate value of each job as it relates to all others?
2. What historical influences alter internally fair relationships?
3. How will the organization relate its pay policy to labor markets or externally competitive demands?
4. To what degree do negotiated collective bargaining contracts influence pay considerations (directly for the unionized organization, indirectly for many that are not unionized)?

To some degree, occupational groups such as clerical workers; unskilled, semi-skilled, and skilled craft and trade workers; technicians; paraprofessionals; professionals; administrators; and managers require different pay treatments. The establishment of different pay treatments may require different pay structure design. A brief review of the forces that influence the pay of each of these groups assists in clarifying some of the related issues.

Clerical Workers   In the past, unions have had little impact on the pay of this occupation. Pay received normally relates to local labor market rates. Because large numbers of these workers are women, this group may be significantly influenced by the comparable worth issue and rising union pressures.

Unskilled and Semiskilled Workers   This group is related to local labor markets; it may also be a highly unionized labor force. Local, regional, and even national labor contracts strongly influence rates of pay of jobs in these occupational groups.

Skilled Craft and Trade Workers   These are highly mobile and frequently unionized groups influenced by regional and national pay schedules and differentials.

Technicians and Paraprofessionals   These are normally nonunionized groups influenced principally by local and regional pay practices.

Professionals and Administrators   These are highly mobile groups whose rates of pay relate to disciplines or functional areas of responsibility. The widespread use of pay surveys for these groups influences regional and national pay scales to such an extent that the data become a major force in setting their pay.

Managers   The pay of this occupational group varies dramatically among its levels. The pay of lower-level operating managers is closely related to the pay received by the upper levels of operative employees. The pay of executives is related to such business and industry factors as sales volume, profit, return on investment, number of employees in the organization, and so on. The pay of top- and upper-level operating managers is influenced directly by the pay received by the executives of their respective organizations and certain individual and organizational-related performance criteria. The pay of senior managers and executives, however, may be influenced more by how other organizations in similar kinds of work are paying this group of top officials. Their pay is then modified by organizational operating characteristics such as profitability or size as measured by sales volume (or a proxy for sales appropriate to that industry) or number of employees. The availability and the extensive use of surveys have a strong influence on the pay of managers at all levels and in all organizational settings.

A quick analysis of a scatter diagram may provide a first indicator of the need for more than one pay structure. If there appear to be disjointed groupings or distinct breaks in the rates of pay of various jobs, as shown by the scatter diagram, the pay structure designer may decide that more than one trend line will be required for setting up a workable system. A major reason for using multiple pay structures is that rates of pay for more advanced jobs increase geometrically rather than linearly.

Displaying Job Data

The use of multiple pay structures may at first glance appear to be the answer to meeting the pay demands of various occupational groups. However, it may only open a Pandora's box to issues of inequity and unacceptability.

Even when there is an apparent need for more than one trend line or pay policy line that would then lead to more than one pay structure, there is a statistical procedure for avoiding multiple structures. This procedure allows pay data to be presented by means of some form of curvilinear relationship rather than a relationship that relates to a straight line. Figure 11–2 describes various mathematical procedures for developing trend or pay policy lines.

When the pay of the jobs in an organization uses an arithmetic progression and takes the form of a straight line, the pay policy line can be described by the equation $y = a + bx$. Figure 11–2a describes three trend or pay policy lines. However, when pay rates vary by some constant rate of increase—a geometric progression—it is possible to use an exponential curve for the trend line, which can be described by the formula $y = ab^x$ (see Figure 11–2b). The use of a geometric progression develops a pay scale that turns upward on the right-hand side, providing higher levels of pay for the higher levels or grades within one continuous pay structure. The rate of pay received proportionate to the scored value of the job is greater for those receiving higher point scores than it is for those receiving lower point scores. This helps to avoid the disruptive effects of a multiple-structure pay system.

Both the straight and curved line approaches for displaying job data normally use a grid that has an arithmetic (linear) scale for both the horizontal (x) axis and the vertical (y) axis. An arithmetic scale is one in which equal distances represent equal *amounts* of whatever value is being displayed.

(a) Three disconnected linear pay structures where $y = a + bx$

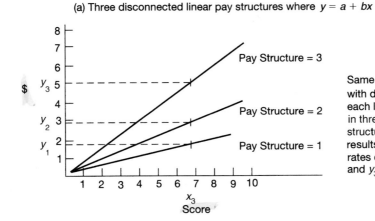

Same point score x_1 with different slope for each line—b resulting in three different pay structures that in turn results in three different rates of pay—y_1, y_2, and y_3

(b) A curvilinear pay structure where $y = ab^x$

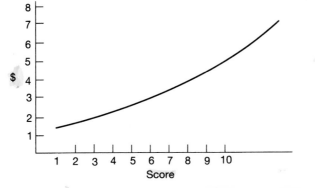

Curvilinear relationship turning upward to the right results in higher rates of pay at upper grades for comparable absolute increases in point score

(c) Curvilinear pay structure on semilogarithmic plotting paper

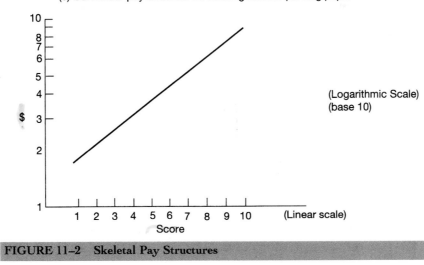

(Logarithmic Scale)
(base 10)

(Linear scale)

FIGURE 11–2   Skeletal Pay Structures

Another approach for displaying job data uses a logarithmic scale or grid for one or both axes. A logarithm is the exponent to which a base is raised to produce a certain value. A common base is 10. To raise the base 10 to 100, the exponent is 2 and is stated in this manner: $\log_{10} 100 = 2$. Frequently, relative considerations are more important or meaningful than absolutes in making compensation comparisons. Logarithms are invaluable for displaying such relationships graphically.

Many job data displays use a logarithmic scale on the vertical axis and a linear scale on the horizontal axis. This type of grid is called a *semilog display*. Some job data displays require the use of logarithmic scales on both the horizontal and vertical axes, a type of display called a *log-log grid*. Equal distances on logarithmic scales represent equal *ratios*. Figure 11–2c describes a *semilog grid*.

Logarithmic scales must begin with a positive value (any value). In using a scale for a pay structure, it is preferable to select an initial value that relates closely to the minimum pay value of the structure. This could be an hourly figure or a weekly, monthly, or annual rate. For example, when using the pay scale to identify hourly wage rates, if no rate is below $5 an hour, it is ideal to use $5 as the initial value.

A single logarithmic cycle accommodates a tenfold increase; two cycles, a hundredfold increase. It is unlikely that a need would ever arise for more than three cycles when constructing a semilogarithmic (semilog) presentation of a pay structure. (A complete description of logarithms can be found in an applied statistics text.)

Figure 11–3 provides logarithmic equivalents for a linear scale. The logarithmic values are used to identify the linear scale values on the vertical axis when developing a

FIGURE 11–3 Two-Cycle Semilog Grid

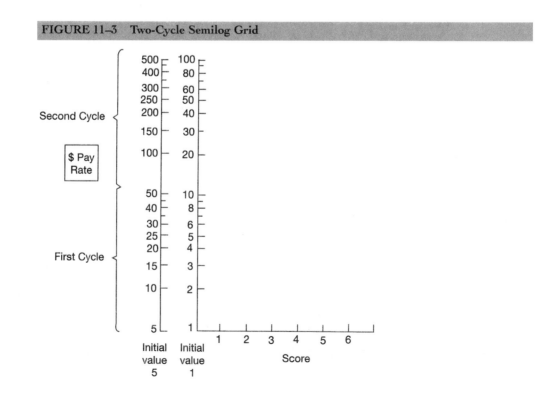

semilog presentation of a pay structure. A semilog grid is useful when there is an extreme variation in the data to be displayed on one of the axes. If the data of the variables to be displayed on both axes vary widely, then a log-log grid is useful.

Data that have a geometric relationship and appear as a curved line on a linear grid appear as a straight line on semilog or log-log grids because logarithmic scales represent geometric relationships—that is, equal ratios, not equal amounts as described with arithmetic or linear scales.

Care in the Use of Numbers   Compensation managers have to be very careful about the way they interpret and use pay data. Although the old adage says "Figures don't lie," the misuse and misinterpretation of figures can result in poor decisions. A major interpretation issue is the use of average or central tendency values and the way these should be calculated.

Two values of central tendency most used in analyzing pay relationships are the *mean* and the *median*. When the market value or going rate of a job is being determined, the average value or mean is frequently the value selected. Should it be selected? The first thing to consider is that the pay for a particular job is hardly ever normally distributed—that is, it is rare that the mean, the median, and the mode are identical values. When the mean, median, and mode are identical, the distribution is said to be normal or bell-shaped—it is also called a parametric distribution. A nonparametric distribution is one in which the mode, median, and mean are of different values. Figure 11–4 describes two kinds of nonparametric distributions. In Figure 11–4a, the value of the median is less than that of the mean. Figure 11–4b describes a distribution in which the value of the median is greater than that of the mean. (Moving from left to right, the *x*-axis indicates increasing rates of pay. The *y*-axis indicates the number of times [frequency] a specific rate of pay occurs.)

FIGURE 11–4   Nonparametric Distributions

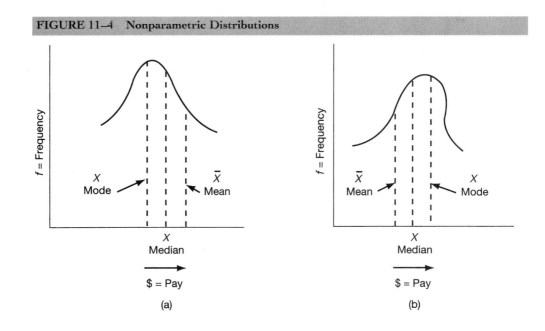

Figure 11–4a describes a common situation in which the median is frequently 3 to 4 percent less than the mean.[2] This occurs because the lower rates of pay for most jobs have fairly precise lower limits. The lower limit can relate to minimum wage, union-negotiated rates of pay, historical relationships, and rates of pay that represent the lowest amount for which someone with necessary qualifications will work. The rates of pay stretch out to the right because of seniority, pay-for-performance, widely varying pay practices and pay policies, and possibly unidentified, even unrecognized, additional responsibilities and duties performed by some employees (job mismatch). Although the median may be a better predictor of the middle rate of pay for a particular job, in 1995 the U.S. DOL took the position that the only acceptable statistic for establishing a prevailing wage or a market measure of central tendency is the arithmetic mean.

The (b) model describes situations in organizations with highly structured pay policies and a senior workforce (a number of employees at or near the top of the pay schedule and a wide distribution of rates of pay from the new hires to the highly paid senior employees).

Because the pay relationships depicted in Figure 11–4a are more common than those found in 11–4b, it may be more useful for organizations to use a median statistic as an indicator of a middle rate of pay rather than the mean.

There are times, however, when the mean rather than the median is a better statistic to use as a value of central tendency and vice versa. The mean is superior when (1) using small samples in which the dispersion of rates of pay is within rational bounds and (2) computing year-to-year changes. The median is superior when (1) a sample has widely varying values and does not approximate a normal distribution, and (2) the compensation manager wishes to identify a "typical" pay rate. On the one hand, the mean provides the rate of average pay; on the other, the median provides the rate of pay for the jobholder in the middle of the pay distribution. In most cases, the median value is what the decision maker is looking for.

If an organization wishes to set its pay policy line around the rate of pay received by the middle jobholder and then uses the mean as the value for setting pay practices, it may be overpaying by 3 to 4 percent. For example, if Olympia's pay policy states that the rate of pay for employees should be 5 percent higher than the market and that the market is to be a middle rate of pay, and if it then uses mean values to determine a pay policy or trend line, it could be paying almost 10 percent over what the middle jobholder is receiving in the labor market. Managers using pay information in this manner are thus responsible for furthering the inflation of wage payments, leading to a noncompetitive position for their organizations.

There may be times when a distribution of rates of pay for benchmark jobs or jobs under review have neither a parametric distribution nor a nonparametric distribution. Rather, the data (see Figure 11–5) may take a bimodal (a), multimodal (b), or possibly a rectangular (c) form. When the pay data for a job take these forms, the data need to be checked. The problem may be with the job—it may have been poorly described and, thus, the matches may be poor, or it may have been incorrectly evaluated in the first

---

[2] In an analysis of 80,000 pay rates, Robert J. Greene, former director of the A. S. Hansen, Inc. *Annual Weber Survey on Data Processing Positions,* found that in 68 out of the 70 data processing jobs the median value was 3 to 4 percent lower than the mean value. An analysis of Bureau of Labor Statistics data produces similar results.

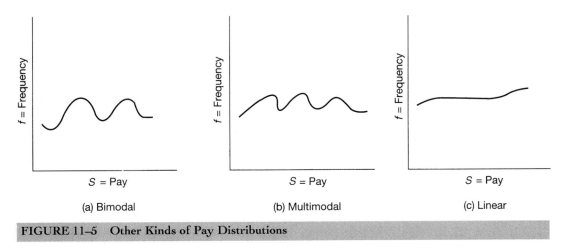

FIGURE 11-5   Other Kinds of Pay Distributions

place. Or the problem may be that other organizations pay a different rate for that spe-cific job. In any case, it would be wise to discard such a job for any kind of a pay struc-ture design purpose.

Identifying Lowest and Highest Rates of Pay

In identifying the lowest and highest rates of pay, many organizations first consider the legal issue. What are the minimum standards prescribed by the federal government through regulations set under the Fair Labor Standards Act of 1938 as amended (Wage and Hour Law)? In some cases, the Davis-Bacon Act (1931) and the Walsh-Healey Pub-lic Contract Act (1936) may also influence the lower end of the pay scale or set a floor for base pay. When states set even more rigorous minimum requirements than those set by the federal government, state laws preempt federal regulations. Organizations that must bargain collectively will normally have their lowest rates of pay set through nego-tiations with representative unions. Even when an organization is nonunion, collectively bargained wage rates have a significant influence on practices to be followed by nonunionized organizations.

Another major consideration is the general influence a particular geographic area or industry labor market has on wage rates. Where employment is high and insufficient numbers of people are seeking entry-level jobs or specific kinds of jobs, minimum wage rates must be high enough to attract job seekers who are able and willing to perform job assignments. A floor set too high, however, may force all following rates also to be set high, and may create excessive labor costs, which may in turn limit competitiveness and profitability.[3] On the other hand, if the level is too low, the number of suitable ap-plicants will be inadequate and, thus, the pay structure may be disproportionately lower than necessary to meet hiring, retention, and performance requirements. A main reason for the pay survey is to assist in solving this basic pay structure problem. The factors that

---

[3]The increase of the base minimum or floor pay of an organization will normally have a ripple effect on all or a significant number of its jobs. The effect occurs when the increase at the bottom end of a pay structure in turn increases the rates of pay of the higher-paid jobs.

influence pay decisions were identified by Richard A. Lester and John Dunlop (see discussion of economic theories in the appendix to chapter 3).

The upper limit or highest rates of pay are a more subjective consideration in which senior policymakers determine what they believe to be an acceptable rate of pay for jobs considered to be of highest worth to the organization. The chief executive of the organization usually earns the highest rate of pay, which establishes the maximum or ceiling rate. At the chief executive level, it is more difficult to relate the contributions the incumbent makes to the success of the job than it is at lower levels. At the top levels of most organizations, the job is designed to fit the knowledge, skill, and even style of the executive. For this reason, the performance of the chief executive officer significantly influences job pay. The higher the job level, the more difficult it is to set reasonable pay with mathematical precision.

Although not always the case, there is frequently a reverse progression through the managerial ranks, in which pay for a less senior job bears a direct relationship to that of the job directly above it. In effect, what happens is that the government, the union, or the labor market sets the minimum level, and the organization, its performance, and chief executive pay set maximum levels. In other words, labor markets set minimum pay levels and product markets determine maximum levels. In the public sector and in nonprofit organizations, however, maximum pay may be set by legislation for the most senior elected or appointed official.

Identifying the lowest and highest rate of pay is a basic step in establishing a pay policy line. After identification, the next step is to establish what management expects to be the average or central tendency value paid to the lowest-rated job and the average pay rate of the highest-rated job. These highest and lowest average values should be the midpoint of the pay for those jobs assigned this rate when there is a range of pay available for each category. When there is only one rate of pay assigned to a job or group of jobs, normally the average or midpoint value is the single rate. The midpoint value is normally the market or going rate for that job or a very close approximation.

One of the first statistics of value in pay structure design is the r_{h-l} ratio. This statistic identifies the ratio between the highest and lowest midpoint pay rates expected.

After reviewing pay information, the compensation management team at Olympia decided that the lowest midpoint pay range expected for the nonsupervisory clerical trades and crafts structure would be $12,480 a year, and the highest midpoint would be $37,440 a year.

$$r_{h-l} = \frac{\text{highest expected midpoint pay rate}}{\text{lowest expected midpoint pay rate}} = \frac{37,440}{12,480} = 3.0000$$

Determining Progression from Lowest to Highest Pay Rate

The basic design criterion that determines pay differences in moving through a pay structure is the midpoint-to-midpoint difference. Midpoint-to-midpoint pay difference is the percentage change in the middle value (again, pay policy or market rate of pay for a job) from one adjacent pay grade to the next. Midpoint-to-midpoint pay progressions range from as low as 3 percent to as high as 20 to 25 percent, possibly higher in some cases. (Normally, low midpoint-to-midpoint differences are found in pay structures of lower-paid, unskilled, semiskilled, and clerical employees, whereas high midpoint-to-midpoint differences are found in the pay structures of the executives and the senior managers of an organization.)

Common midpoint-to-midpoint differences are these:

Major Groups	Differences		
	Low	Average	High
Nonexempt	3–4.5	6–7.5	8–10
Exempt	6–8	8–10	12–15
Senior management	10	15–25	30–50

When applicable or appropriate midpoint-to-midpoint differences are being determined, the following issues should be considered:

1. The smaller the difference between midpoints, the more pay rates available to assign to a specific job because there will be many more grades available within the pay structure. That is, a 3 percent midpoint-to-midpoint difference may result in 50 or more pay grades, whereas a 20 percent difference may result in five or six pay grades.
2. The more pay rates available, the greater the opportunity for assigning different rates of pay to jobs with minor differences in responsibilities and duties and required knowledge and skills.
3. The greater the difference between pay rates, the easier it is for jobholders to perceive differences in worth between jobs. (See Weber's Law on just perceptible differences, chapter 8.)
4. A small difference between midpoints may force an organization to have more than one pay structure.

Rates of differences between midpoints are not the only consideration in this phase of the design of the pay structure. Designers must also consider the uniformity of change between midpoints. Should all midpoints increase at the same rate of differences, or should they vary as jobs move toward the higher end of the pay structure? A uniform approach is always easier to justify and substantiate, but in using a single pay structure, it may be necessary to increase the difference between midpoints in moving from the low to the high end of the structure. For those jobs at the lower end of the pay structure, a 6 to 7.5 percent difference between midpoints may be appropriate; at the top end, the distance between midpoints may vary from 15 to 25 percent, while 8 to 10 percent may be appropriate in the middle of the structure.

The compensation manager must be aware by this time that there are no firm rules for setting specific quantitative guidelines for developing a pay structure—only acceptable indicators. When determining the difference between midpoints, all the previously mentioned issues once again come into play. The possibility of having a constant percentage throughout the structure or the need to change midpoint differences depends on organizational requirements. Those organizations using a standard difference between midpoints will normally use a value ranging between 5 and 10 percent.

358

There are those who feel that a 5 percent difference between midpoints is ideal because it allows for a greater number of grades within a set pay structure. The greater number of grades then permits greater opportunity for placement of jobs in different grades. These same proponents of the 5 percent difference also state that there can be a 5 percent judgmental error in any job evaluation. The opportunity to move a job up or down a pay grade permits adjustment for such errors.[4] In recent years, a number of compensation professionals, consultants, and academics have promoted the use of fewer pay grades, stating that it is impractical, unwise, and too bureaucratic to define job differences, job worth, and job pay as precisely as those who promote the use of many pay grades with 5 to 7 percent midpoint-to-midpoint differences. This new alternative to pay structure design is called broadbanding and is discussed in detail at the end of this section.

Setting the Midpoint   The factor that most influences the midpoint value is probably the going rate or market value of the job. The midpoint may also come from internal data of what has normally been considered a standard rate for the job. Once the midpoint rate is set for an entry-level job (or one near entry level), the adjoining midpoint rates may be set by multiplying (if above) or dividing (if below) by the particular rate. For example, Olympia decides that there should be a 15 percent difference between midpoints. An identified lower-grade midpoint is $6.00 an hour; the next highest midpoint is $6.00 an hour × 1.15, or $6.90 an hour.

Developing Pay Grades

After identifying midpoint or market rates for the jobs of an organization and determining acceptable percentage progression between midpoints, the compensation designer is ready to develop pay grades. *Pay grades* are nothing more than convenient groupings of a wide variety of jobs or classes similar in work difficulty and complexity requirements but possibly having nothing else in common. Grades provide a connecting link between the evaluation and classification processes and the assignment of pay to a particular job or class. A pay grade may provide for a single rate, or it may allow for a range of pay within a certain grade.

Pay grades are an integral part of the pay structure. The top or maximum rate of pay of a pay grade states that this is the most that work produced by a job(s) in this grade is worth to the organization. The bottom, on the other hand, places a minimal value on the contributions of the assigned job(s). The distance between the minimum and maximum recognizes the range of performance and experience of incumbents in the assigned job(s). Most pay grade systems have certain common or general characteristics:

1. Each grade provides for a range of pay, although there are single-rate pay grade structures that, as the title implies, provide for only one rate of pay within the grade.
2. Within a pay grade range there is a minimum, a midpoint (this normally is the pay within a single rate structure), and a maximum pay.
3. The range from the minimum to the maximum within a single pay grade may vary from 20 to 100 percent. The most common range is from 30 to 50 percent.

---

[4]Richard C. Smyth and Matthew J. Murphy, *The Guide Line Method of Job Evaluation* (Rhinebeck, NY: Smyth & Murphy Associates, Inc.).

4. The number of steps within a grade may also vary. Grades having steps will normally have from 3 to 10 steps, with 6 to 7 in-grade steps being most common.

5. There is a direct relationship between the rate of increase per step and the number of steps within a grade. The federal government General Schedule (GS) has 10 steps for most grades, with a percentage increase between steps of approximately 3.33 percent or 30 percent within the grade—the spread from minimum to maximum rate of pay (see Table 9–2).

6. The midpoint of each pay grade is normally a constant percentage greater than the one preceding it. This percentage normally varies from 5 to 10 percent.

7. Adjoining pay grades normally overlap. If there is a 30 percent range within a pay grade and there is a 10 percent difference between midpoints, there will be a 67 percent overlap.

8. The requirements of the organization will provide answers to the correct number of grades, the number of steps within grades, and the rates of progression within and between grades. The four principal considerations that have a strong impact in this area are as follows:

   a. Identifying the number of different kinds of jobs in the organization that should receive different rates of pay.

   b. Determining the number of pay structures used by the organization. If the organization uses only one structure for both exempt and nonexempt employees, it will probably have more grades than if it uses more than one structure.

   c. Using steps within grades to recognize seniority or longevity. Many organizations use the steps between the minimum and midpoint to recognize seniority pay increases.

   d. Using steps to recognize merit increases. Some organizations use steps between midpoint and maximum to recognize merit increases.

The General Schedule (GS) grade system of the federal government has the following general characteristics (see Table 9–2 for 1999 GS pay schedule):

1. Grades: 15
2. Steps within grades: 10
3. Percentage increase from minimum to maximum within each grade: varies from 25 to 30 percent.
4. Differences between the fifth steps of adjoining pay grades range from a low of 8.9 percent to a high of 19.9 percent. (There is an 8.9 percent difference between steps 5 of grades 1 and 2; there is a 19.9 percent difference between steps 5 of grades 11 and 12.)

The number of pay grades to be included within a pay structure varies with the circumstances—there is no right number. Therefore, compensation system designers and managers all face the same answer—it all depends. It all depends on the demands of the organization: What is acceptable to top management? What do employees perceive as fair? What is administratively practical? What best recognizes differences in job worth, employee behavior, and the opportunity to maintain a logical and rational control over wage payments? Too many grades require extremely fine distinctions among jobs. The work of Weber and Hay suggests that truly fine differentiations between jobs or classes probably cannot be made. On the other hand, too few grades can result in failure or inability to recognize significant differences in difficulty, responsibility, or knowledge requirements among jobs and classes.

The following numbers of pay grades are found in pay plans/pay structures for the following major groups of employees:

Major Groups	Number of Pay Grades
Nonexempt	Up to 12–16
Exempt	Up to 10–15
Senior management	Up to 8–10

Some organizations use market surveys and guide charts to establish job rates of pay that have 70 to 80 and possibly more pay grades. Some behavioral scientists today are promoting the idea of using as few as four to six grades. (See discussion of broadbanding later in this chapter.)

The issues to be considered and the results of using a large number of pay grades versus the use of a very small number are as follows:

1. Is there to be only one pay structure and will it include all jobs from the lowest entry-level job requiring minimum education, experience, and skill to that of the chief executive officer demanding a large amount of knowledge and skills to cope with the responsibilities of the job? If so, even a small organization with, say, 500 employees would probably require 18 to 30 pay grades.
2. Is it desirable to have a small variation between pay grades—somewhere between 3 to 5 percent? If this is the case and the organization is using only one pay structure, then it would not be unusual to find 50 to 75 pay grades being used. By having a small variation in pay grades, a mistake made in assigning a job to a pay grade that is one or even two grades too high or too low relative to job worth would hardly be noted. More grades also allow for the assignment of jobs with different evaluations to different pay grades. If the number of pay grades is large, the overlap between pay grades will be large—in the vicinity of 75 to 90 percent.
3. A small number of pay grades will normally result in less overlap between them. It will also require the assignment of more jobs to the same grade. Having fewer grades permits a greater spread, allowing increased recognition of growth of job knowledge through seniority and merit in-grade pay increases. The larger the range in a pay grade, the greater the opportunity to vary the pay of employees who perform in a different manner while doing the same job or equivalent kinds of work.

Single-Rate Pay Grade   It is possible for a pay grade to be one point in the pay structure. In the case of a single-rate pay grade, the rate is usually the "average" rate in the marketplace (the competitive midpoint or the amount a competent, fully trained employee would expect to receive for that job) or, in a collective bargaining situation, the agreed-to wage rate. Depending on its pay policy and competitive posture, an organization with a single-rate pay structure can certainly raise or lower the rate it pays for a job in comparison with the going or market rate, except where the wage rate is set by collective bargaining.

Organizations with only single-rate pay grades frequently use the terms *flat rate* or *standard rate* to describe their pay structures. A flat rate structure appears most often in organizations in which pay rate negotiations between management and unions are common practice, in small organizations, or in industries using skilled craftworkers. The single-rate structure provides no opportunity for progression within the grade, although this weakness is partly overcome by having closely related classes of jobs with closely associated rates of pay. Even with single-rate pay grades, many employers pay new hires at a rate significantly lower than that paid to the fully tenured employee. Attaining full rate may take the new hire anywhere from three months to three years.

Two-Tier Wage Plan   A major concession in a number of union contracts negotiated between 1982 and 1986 was the addition of a two-tier wage agreement. Two-tier wage plans permit employers to pay new hires a rate of pay lower than that received by current employees. Although many two tiers start new employees at rates of pay 20 to 30 percent less than current employees, some call for starting wages that grant new employees half or even less than half of what current employees receive. In some two-tier plans, new hires will never attain the rate of pay of the more senior employees (their plan is called a permanent two tier). Others, however, permit the new employees to reach the rate of the more senior employees in anywhere from three to five to ten years. (These plans are called temporary two tiers.) Although examples of two-tier contracts go back to the 1950s, what is different in the concessions of the 1980s is that relatively financially sound organizations requested and received the two-tier opportunity. In a 1983 contract signed between Boeing and the International Association of Machinists, current workers received a 6 percent pay hike, whereas the pay rates for new hires was reduced by as much as 41 percent.

Multiple-Point Pay Structure   Although not common, some organizations that use point-factor job evaluation plans establish a rate of pay for every possible point score a job can receive. That is, add all of the minimum points for each factor, the sum of which provides the score for the lowest rate of pay; then add all the maximum points for each factor, which provides the score for the highest possible rate of pay. Then, depending on the point distribution for the degrees or levels of all factors, a complete array of all possible sum values any job could receive is established. This array is then placed between the already established lowest and highest scores. A value is assigned for each additional point.

Through a simple multiplication and addition process, all other possible point scores receive a specific rate of pay. The next step is to establish a range for each point score. The calculated rate of pay is the midpoint of the range, and the organization then establishes a range around that rate of pay. Each point score is a grade with its own unique range. This approach requires considerable confidence in the ability of the job evaluation plan to recognize precise differences among jobs.

Range or Spread Dimension   The height (or *y*-axis dimension) of a pay grade is its *spread.* When establishing a spread within a pay grade, the first question is what the spread or height of the pay grade should be. Like most other compensation questions of this nature, there is no right or wrong answer.

The *range* or *spread of the range* of a pay grade is the difference between the upper and lower limits of the grade. The range may be expressed in absolute dollar amounts or as a percentage. When expressed as a percentage, the range is the

$$\frac{\text{maximum dollar} - \text{minimum dollar}}{\text{minimum dollar}} \times 100 = \%$$

Pay grade spread, like midpoint progression, can vary widely depending on pay policy and business practices. In many cases, the spread from the midpoint to the maximum pay rate of a grade and the spread from the midpoint to the minimum pay rate of a grade are uniform throughout the structure. The major reason for uniformity is ease in explaining and justifying a basic fairness in the structure design.

However, many compensation professionals believe that the spread of the grades should increase progressively. At entry levels, a typical spread is ±10 percent on either side of the midpoint. At the middle levels of management, the spread may reach ±20 percent. The reasons for a narrow pay spread at entry level and a broader spread at the professional and managerial levels are based on several philosophical considerations. Management frequently considers entry-level jobholders as transients. In a relatively short period of time, these jobholders will have the opportunity to progress to higher-level jobs. There is also the feeling that lower-level jobs can be mastered quickly, that they make a limited contribution to the success of the organization, and that holders of lower-level jobs have relatively little influence in changing the nature of the job. For these reasons, movement below or above the going rate should be more or less restricted.

The philosophy connected with upper-level jobs is that it takes jobholders extended periods of time to become fully competent performers. The persons holding these jobs are in most cases career personnel; and these jobs are critical to the success of the organization. Upper-level jobholders have a greater influence on the success of job activities, and they can stretch their jobs by making them more valuable through individual contributions. For these reasons, the spread of the pay grade is much higher than at lower levels. Here are some common ranges:

Major Groups	Spread of the Range (%)
Nonexempt: Laborer and trades	Up to 30
Nonexempt: Clerical, technical, paraprofessional	25–40
Exempt: First-level management, administrative, professional	40–60
Exempt: Middle and senior management	50–100

Pay Grade Width Procedures for establishing a pay grade width (*x*-axis dimension) are not as specific or precise as those related to the spread or height of the pay grade (the *y*-axis). When using a point-factor plan, points often are the *x*-axis values. However, arbitrary decisions must be made regarding the range of points for identifying the left and right parameters of the pay grade. Often, when using a job evaluation method, the points are distributed equally for each pay grade. At times, the width or *x*-axis values are simply pay grade numbers, and in this case the *x* dimensions are sufficient to provide a useful geometric representation. The width dimensions are usually identical for each pay grade.

Determining Pay Grade Minimum and Maximum Rates of Pay   Most organizations set the minimum and maximum rates of pay for grades in relation to demands they wish to make on their pay systems. The spread of the pay range provides an opportunity to differentiate the pay received by the newly hired person, the probationary employee, the competent performer, and the excellent performer. The pay grade range also provides opportunity to recognize extended and faithful service.

The most practical method of establishing lower and upper limits for a pay grade is first to establish a midpoint line at a competitive level and then to determine what percentage of spread is required on either side of the midpoint to accomplish objectives that may be attained through a well-designed pay grade.

Internal Design Considerations   With the establishment of minimum, midpoint, and maximum rates of pay, the next step is to determine if the grade itself is to have a more detailed internal structure. Many pay grades have steps within each grade. Organizations use in-grade step pay increases for a number of reasons.

The design of a pay range frequently permits the initial steps (often to midpoint) to relate specific growth periods to time on the job. Normally, as jobholders reach these time milestones, they have attained additional job knowledge and receive an automatic pay increase to the next step. The automatic progression is common where the new jobholders receive training in the operation of certain kinds of equipment or in working within well-defined procedures so that they reach acceptable degrees of competence within certain periods of time.

A relatively simple pay structure suitable for these conditions is one with three steps. The first step is the pay provided to the newly hired person or to an incumbent who has just been placed on the job. The time required to move from the first to the second step is normally called the *probationary period,* which may range from 30 days to one year. It is within this period that the incumbent demonstrates an ability to perform the job. At the successful completion of the probationary period, the incumbent receives the second step in the pay range. The third step is achieved when job performance indicates competence (Figure 11–6).

FIGURE 11–6   Three-Step Pay Grade

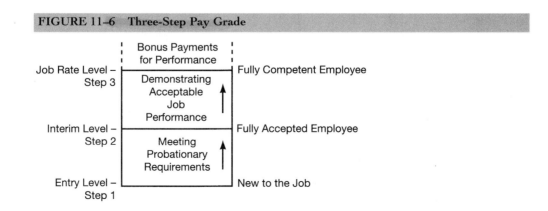

Step progression related to merit is not nearly so cut and dried. Theoretically, increases through these steps relate directly to performance and contributions. Many organizations use the steps beyond the midpoint for merit pay increases. If, for example, there are three steps beyond the midpoint, ideally 10 to 15 percent of those qualified will be in the first step beyond midpoint, 70 to 80 percent in the second step, and 10 to 15 percent in the highest step in the pay range. In many mature organizations with long-standing pay structure plans, it is not uncommon to find 70 to 80 percent of all employees at the maximum step in the pay range. This is a prime indicator that something may be wrong with the pay structure and that it requires some review and analysis.

The major problem in any progressive step procedure is the overwhelming influence of seniority (time in service). In real-world situations, growth and merit criteria frequently become subverted into a seniority system. This condition develops because of the difficulty organizations experience in recognizing growth or merit. The use of seniority measurements in lieu of understandable growth standards and acceptable merit standards is a trap every compensation manager must avoid at all costs. A possible first step is to recognize seniority outside the pay range by allowing fixed pay rewards for time in service and then developing workable standards for growth and merit.

In the 1970s, another major issue emerged relating to the improper use of in-step increases within a pay range—the use of in-step increases in lieu of economic or cost-of-living adjustments to the pay structure. When organizations did not provide adequate across-the-board increases or changes in the overall pay structure to maintain the real income or current living standards of employees, piecemeal changes were made by granting employees, when possible, in-step pay increases. These increases came about because of general inflationary trends in the economy and had nothing to do with either seniority or merit. Organizations can answer this problem by finding a way to relate pay structure design and changes to variations in cost of living.

Spread of Range and Steps   The spread of a range within a pay grade may vary from 10 percent to 50 percent on either side of the midpoint of a pay scale. Normally, a range of 15 to 25 percent on either side of the midpoint is common. With pressures to decrease the number of pay grades and to improve recognition of performance, pay ranges of 20 to 50 percent on either side of the midpoint are becoming more common.

The size of each pay step within a grade may increase arithmetically (absolutely), geometrically (by a constant percentage), or randomly. In most cases, geometric increases are preferable. There may be a deviation in the percentage of increase between steps at certain points in the structure (the lower half of the structure may have a 30 percent spread within the pay grades and the upper half a 50 percent spread). In this case, the structure may be called a *split structure*, or it may become two structures or substructures making up the major structure.

Identifying Pay Grade Dimensions   If the midpoint and the desired percentage spread of the range to the maximum and minimum limits are known, it is a matter of simple mathematics to identify the upper and lower limits of the pay grade. If the midpoint is $7.00 and the spread of the range to the maximum rate of the grade is 14.0 percent and the spread to the minimum rate is also 14.0 percent, the maximum is equal to $7.00 times (100 percent + 14.0 percent) or $7.00 × 1.14 or $7.98. The minimum limit is

$7.00 times (100 percent – 14.0 percent) or $7.00 × .86 or $6.02. The actual total percentage spread of the range is 32.6 percent.

$$\frac{\$7.98 - \$6.02}{\$6.02} = \frac{\$1.96}{\$6.02} = 3.26 \qquad .326 \times 100 = 32.6\%$$

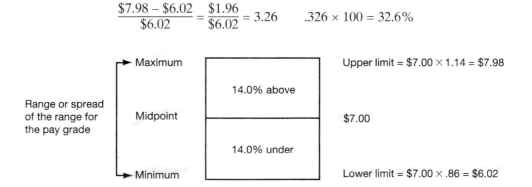

The value 32.6 percent does not equal the sum of the midpoint to maximum value of 14 percent and the midpoint to minimum value of 14 percent, which would be 28 percent.

When the midpoint and the percentage spread of the range are known, the following mathematical procedure can be used to obtain the maximum and the minimum of the pay grade. The first step is to determine the minimum of the pay grade. The minimum is obtained by first adding half of the percentage spread of the range to 100 percent and then dividing the midpoint by this amount. For example, the midpoint is $7.00 and the range is 33 percent. To obtain the minimum, the midpoint value ($7.00) is divided by 100 percent + ½ of the range (33 percent).

$$\frac{\$7.00}{\$1.00 + \frac{1}{2}(.33)} = \frac{\$7.00}{1.165} = \$6.01$$

The maximum is then obtained by multiplying the minimum by 100 percent plus the percentage spread of the range. If $6.01 is taken to be the minimum and the spread of the range is 33 percent:

$$\$6.01 \times (100\% + 33\%) \text{ or } \$6.01 \times 1.33 = \$7.99$$

After the minimum, midpoint, and maximum pay rates are determined, the number of steps in the range is the next concern. A fundamental concept here is that each step has true recognition value and makes some perceptual impact on the recipient. The smaller the incremental step, the less the recognition and the smaller the motivational force on the recipient. Pay steps have had incremental increases beginning with 2 percent, but again, recognition factors are resulting in greater increases between steps. Increases of 5.0 to 7.5 percent between the steps in this grade produce a seven-step pay scale (begin by multiplying $6.01 by 100 percent plus 5 percent or 1.05 and then each subsequent value by 1.05) (Figure 11–7). In this approach, the midpoint (step 4) is not quite $7.00 and the maximum is $8.05 which exceeds the actual maximum of $7.99. Slight adjustments to the step rates can be made so that the fourth step will equal the midpoint and the seventh step will equal the maximum of the pay grade.

The actual range of a pay grade is frequently an amount arbitrarily selected by an individual or individuals with compensation policy decision-making responsibilities.

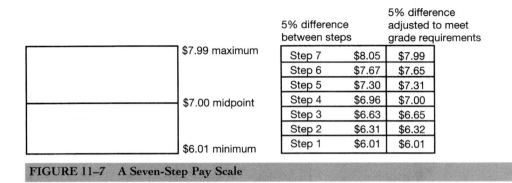

			5% difference between steps		5% difference adjusted to meet grade requirements
	$7.99 maximum	Step 7	$8.05		$7.99
		Step 6	$7.67		$7.65
		Step 5	$7.30		$7.31
	$7.00 midpoint	Step 4	$6.96		$7.00
		Step 3	$6.63		$6.65
		Step 2	$6.31		$6.32
	$6.01 minimum	Step 1	$6.01		$6.01

FIGURE 11–7   A Seven-Step Pay Scale

However, certain issues can affect the final value selected. If the range is small and the minimum or lower limit relates closely to the market, the entry rate of pay is more attractive to those looking for employment. There is also an unsatisfactory side to this story. When entry and maximum limits are too close, long-term employees feel that the organization does not recognize their services and loyalty, and, to individuals in these pay grades, there is an unsatisfactory compression of pay rates within the pay grade.

Pay Grade Overlap   Following the identification of the midpoint, upper limit, and lower limit of the pay grade, the next step is to establish the relationship between adjacent pay grades. The pay structure may have no overlap between pay grades and may look like Figure 11–8a or the pay structure may have overlapping pay grades and look like Figure 11–8b. The overlaps between pay grades are those pay opportunities that are identical in adjacent pay grades as in Figure 11–8c.

The difference in midpoints and the spread of the pay range then determine the amount of overlap between adjoining grades. An overlap of approximately 70 percent is not unusual between adjoining pay grades. A theory underlying overlap between pay grades is that the amount of overlap should equal the similarity of responsibilities, duties, knowledge, and skills that exist among jobs in the adjacent pay grades (80 percent overlap equates to an 80 percent comparability in responsibilities and duties, knowledge, and skills in jobs assigned to these pay grades).

For example, the pay structure of the Olympia Nursing Home has a difference of 15 percent between midpoints and a pay range of 33 percent within each grade. Grade level 2 has a midpoint of $7.00 an hour (see Figure 11–9).

An overlap between pay grades provides an opportunity for the excellent performer in the lower pay grade who has long tenure (high seniority) to earn more than the new, less experienced person in a more senior pay grade. The philosophy here is that the skilled, high performer in a lower-graded job may be making a greater contribution than the less experienced incumbent in the next higher grade. When there is minimal distance between midpoints (less than 5.0 percent) and the grades have limited spread (15 to 25 percent), overlap will extend for a number of grades. Some experts in pay structure design feel that overlap beyond three adjacent grades—four grades in total—should be avoided.

A major problem with pay grades that have a large overlap is that an employee already in the upper end of a pay grade who receives a promotion to a job in the next

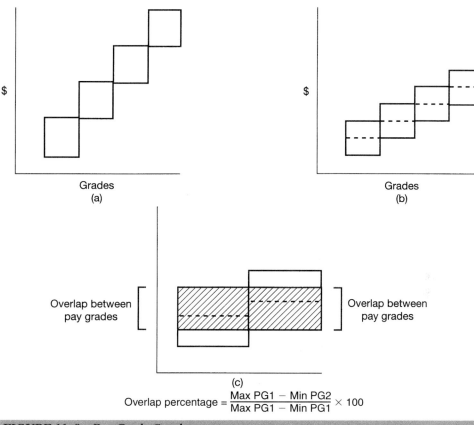

$$\text{Overlap percentage} = \frac{\text{Max PG1} - \text{Min PG2}}{\text{Max PG1} - \text{Min PG1}} \times 100$$

FIGURE 11–8   Pay Grade Overlap

FIGURE 11–9   Pay Structure to Olympia Nursing Home

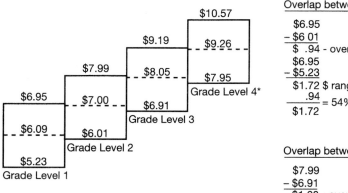

Overlap between GL 1 and GL 2

$6.95
$$- \underline{\$6.01}$$
$$\quad\underline{\$\ .94}\ \text{- overlap between GL 1 and GL 2}$$
$6.95
$$- \underline{\$5.23}$$
$$\quad\underline{\$1.72}\ \$\ \text{range of GL 1}$$
$$\frac{.94}{\$1.72} = 54\% \text{ spread of the range}$$

Overlap between GL 2 and GL 3

$7.99
$$- \underline{\$6.91}$$
$$\quad\underline{\$1.08}\ \text{- overlap between GL 2 and GL 3}$$
$7.99
$$- \underline{\$6.01}$$
$$\quad\underline{\$1.98}\ \$\ \text{range of GL 2}$$
$$\frac{\$1.08}{\$1.98} = 54\% \text{ spread of the range}$$

* With overlap of approximately 54%, no overlap exists between pay grades 1 and 4.

pay grade—even a promotion that results in an advancement two or three grades up the pay structure—may not receive much of an increase or have an opportunity to increase the amount of future pay. Many compensation policy decision makers feel that in order for a promotion to have a true incentive value, it should carry with it at least a 10 percent increase in pay. This is one of the major reasons for the warning that in a well-designed pay structure there should be no overlap between pay grades that are four grades apart. (The promotion guide chart in chapter 18 provides guidelines for pay-related promotion decisions.) An opposite situation arises when there is little or no overlap between pay grades. When an employee receives a promotion from one pay grade to another, the increase in the employee's rate of pay to just the minimum of the new grade is so large that it exceeds pay policy requirements.

Pay Rates below Minimum   Some organizations have a cap (limit) on any pay increase an employee can receive at one time. It is possible for an employee to be promoted to a new job in a pay grade considerably higher than the one occupied at present and have the cap on the pay increase prohibit that employee from immediately receiving the minimum level of pay for the new job. This same situation can occur when the pay structure has grades with little or no overlap. The term *green circle* applies to any incumbent receiving a rate of pay below the minimum of the pay grade. It is extremely difficult to explain to a promoted employee why he or she is receiving less than the minimum rate of pay of the pay grade. Some organizations pay newly hired employees with no experience rates 10 to 20 percent below the established minimum.

Pay Rates above Maximum   Some organizations provide superseniority pay increases to employees with long tenure. These superseniority pay increases may place the employee in a pay step that extends beyond the maximum of the pay range. The term *silver circle* identifies the incumbent in a superseniority pay step. Some organizations also allow for merit increases that could extend the pay of the incumbent beyond the established maximum. The term *gold circle* identifies incumbents receiving this kind of in-step pay increase. In cases of changes in pay structure architecture or demotion, some employees may be receiving rates of pay higher than the maximum of the assigned pay grades. Pay policies may state that these employees should receive no further increases until their rates of pay are within the pay structure. Employees receiving these above maximum rates of pay are called *red-circled* employees, or their rates of pay are *red circled.*

Mature organizations with many high-seniority employees frequently encounter a problem called "running out of range." In this case, an organization finds that a large number of its employees are at the top of the pay range, and morale suffers as they realize there is little or no opportunity for further increases. There is no easy answer to this problem. One solution may be some kind of 10-year, 15-year, or 20-year seniority cash bonus. Another solution is to ensure real income maintenance by some kind of cost-of-living adjustments.

Some organizations with many senior employees who are at the top of the pay grade—topping out—feel that these employees are worth more to the organization than their job-related skills indicate. At times, organizations facing this issue add one or more superseniority steps to the pay grade. This pay above the maximum could be considered *individual worth* payments. As previously mentioned, the maximum of the pay grade indicates the top dollar value of the jobs within the assigned pay grade. Superseniority payments recognize the value and worth of the individual to the organization. This value and worth can go beyond job-related contributions to organization-related contributions.

Shadow Range   A possible solution to the "market" pay demands for the job in high demand—the exotic job—where the internally evaluated worth of the job is out of line with the market demand rate is to establish a *shadow range.* If the vertical lines of the pay grade are extended, the exotic job can be paid at a higher rate than that normally paid to jobs of comparable worth to the organization but can still be placed in the proper internal worth dimension (the appropriate pay grade). This response to the pay demands of the exotic job is not a cure-all, but it does provide an alternative way of handling a difficult problem (the jobs having a market worth that is out of line with internally equitable considerations). If and when the demand for the job ceases or decreases, administrative efforts can be taken to place it within the proper limits of the pay grade. Current examples of exotic jobs are those found in the information technology field.

Broadbanding   In the 1990s, broadbanding became a major tool of the compensation specialist involved in the redesign of pay plans. There is a variety of definitions for broadbanding, but one that is commonly used is that it is the grouping of jobs of significant differences or worth or value within one band. This pay grouping or expanded pay grade may have a range varying from 50 percent to more than 100 percent and include jobs that have responsibilities and duties that vary in complexity and difficulty and require significantly different kinds and levels of knowledge and skills. Through broadbanding, an organization can reduce the number of pay grades included within the pay plan. In the discussion of an expanding pay structure later in this chapter, the pay sector designation could be equivalent to a broadband within a broadbanding plan. The rate of pay for the broadband could vary from the minimum rate of pay of the lowest pay grade in the sector to the maximum rate of pay of the highest pay grade in the sector.

Broadbanding can be useful in designing a pay plan for organizations that make extensive use of teams. New team members with minimum levels of required knowledge and skills could be paid at the lower end of the band and, as they acquire more knowledge and skills and perform more and different jobs, assignments, or workstations, their pay could be increased upward through the band.

The proponents of broadbanding have a number of reasons for moving away from pay structure design as presented in this chapter. With the reduction in numbers and levels of management and the expanded authority of nonmanagement workers through the use of empowered teams, the authority and concomitant responsibilities of involved employees have expanded. Some management and compensation experts feel that it is unwise, possibly impossible, to precisely identify and define the work of an individual employee because the work requirements can change significantly over a relatively short period. They justify their position by stating that in modern organizations, the concept of a job with rather specific boundaries has become obsolete and that the employee does what is necessary to achieve organization, work unit/team, and individual goals. In fact, they further state the idea of a job and its associated job description become barriers to improved organizational and individual performance. These advocates of broadbanding state that it is not only unwise but impossible to make "fine" distinctions among jobs (whatever "fine" may mean).

Because the employee, within situational restraints, makes and defines the job, the boundaries of the job become very hazy and difficult to establish. Because of increased flexibility at the workplace, a pay structure that better recognizes the dynamic situation is one that expands range and pay opportunities for the involved employee. By combining anywhere from three to eight pay grades within one band, workers can expand their knowledge and skill, successfully perform higher levels of assignments, and increase their rates of pay with less bureaucratic procedures than those that must be followed to be promoted from one job to another in a higher pay grade.

Broadbanding has also been used to give an immediate supervisor more authority to assign a rate of pay or give a pay increase to a subordinate. This transfer of authority reduces some of the bureaucratic control of the human resources department. This return of almost complete authority for subordinate pay increases to the immediate supervisor is, in reality, a return to pay practices of 50 or more years ago.

The value of broadbanding is yet to be proved. It will take some time to establish its usefulness, cost benefits, and limitations. Until there is sufficient time to review the effects of its possible widespread use, it will be unwise to "junk" the traditional approaches to the design of pay structures as described in this chapter. Problems such as "running out of range," in which there is a significant number of employees at the top of the range, that occur with typical pay structure design and administration as discussed earlier in this chapter can just as easily occur within broadbanding. However, the labor cost issue could be significantly enhanced within the broadbanding approach because the maximum rate within a band is considerably higher than the maximum rate of most of the grades that would be typically included within a band. Well-designed pay grades with proper pay administration can be a major force in controlling labor costs.

INTERLOCKING MULTIPLE PAY STRUCTURES

Organizations often use one evaluation method for determining the worth of lower-paid jobs (crafts and trades, clerical, nonsupervisory workers) and another for higher-paid jobs (technical, professional, administrative, and managerial). When more than one method is used, the scatter diagram is usually different, and in turn the pay policy line has a different slope and *y*-intercept.

The designers and the managers of a multiple pay structure system must have confidence in their structures and be able to justify the reasonableness and fairness of using more than one. The first step in developing a defense for such a system is to evaluate the higher-level, nonmanagement jobs using the managerial evaluation method and lower-level management jobs using the nonmanagerial evaluation method.

The second step in this process is to determine the monetary worth of these upper- and lower-level jobs in the opposite pay structure. This cross-evaluation identifies the differences in pay received by the jobs in each structure. Answering the following questions will identify the strengths and the weaknesses or differences in the design of multiple pay structures:

1. How does each job fare under each structure? Does it appear that under one structure a certain job receives a windfall or an undeserved higher rate of pay than in the other structure? Which jobs receive unduly harsh pay treatment?
2. Can these differences in pay be justified?

3. Can one structure be used in place of two structures?
4. Are the jobs being placed in the proper pay structure?

After performing a cross-evaluation, it is possible to develop a scatter diagram from the cross-evaluated jobs to establish a separate pay policy or trend line. The x and y paired coordinate points for each job are the evaluation points received under the evaluation methods used for developing the two pay structures. The lower-level pay structure evaluation method can be used to provide the y-axis data points, and the upper-level pay structure evaluation method can be used to provide the x-axis data points. Analysis of the data points may reveal a distribution that will produce a trend line that will "kink" or curve dramatically upward or downward, or it may identify a specific break area. The points of the scatter diagram may spread over such a wide area that it prohibits the development of a meaningful regression line.

An analysis of the trend line will assist designers of pay structures in testing the validity of their multiple-structure systems. If the adjoining or overlapping ends of a pay structure cannot be related, some weaknesses are probably present in the design of one or both structures. The weaknesses should be identified and corrected.[5]

THE EXPANDING OR FAN-TYPE PAY STRUCTURE: AN OPTIONAL APPROACH

Pay policy and job demands may require designers to develop a pay structure that varies the difference between midpoints and fans the spread within a pay grade from the lower-level jobs to the higher-level jobs. A single expanding pay structure can cover a wide number of jobs in an organization starting with entry-level jobs at the lowest end of the nonexempt group and ending with senior management jobs at the top end of the pay structure.

Expanding Pay Structure Architecture

Four critical data points control the design of an expanding pay structure:

1. Lowest rate of pay the organization wishes to pay any employee. This, in turn, will be the minimum or lowest rate of pay for Pay Grade 1 or the first pay grade in the pay structure.
2. Percentage range of pay for each pay grade or group of pay grades (see discussion that follows on pay sectors).
3. Midpoint-to-midpoint differences between pay grades.
4. Points (if using a point-factor job evaluation method) that establish the horizontal width of each pay grade.

Pay Sectors   An essential part of an expanding pay structure is the role of pay sectors. Pay sectors are groups of pay grades having identical or very similar pay structure architectural characteristics, that is, identical percentage ranges and midpoint-to-midpoint differences and identical or very similar horizontal point ranges. Each pay sector in an expanding pay structure is in reality a different pay structure. In the examples provided in Figure 11–10, the seven linear pay structures developed through

---

[5]Information on the interlocking of multiple pay structures is provided by Robert J. Greene, compensation consultant.

FIGURE 11–10 Expanding Pay Structure Design Characteristics for Organization Using FES

Pay Sector	Pay Grades	FES Point Range per Pay Grade	Percentage Spread of the Range	Midpoint-to-Midpoint Difference
I	1–4	50, 55	30	6.0
II	5–9	100, 110	35	6.5
III	10–13	125	40	7.0
IV	14–17	145	45	7.5
V	18–21	185	50	8.0
VI	22–25	220	55	8.5
VII	26–27	245, 470	60	9.0

FES Points	Pay Sectors	Range Spread %	Midpoint %	Pay Grade	Step #1	Step #2	Step #3	Step #4	Step #5	Step #6	Step #7	Step #8	Step #9
190–240	1	30	6	1	13,278	13,776	14,274	14,772	15,270	15,768	16,266	16,764	17,262
245–300	1	30	6	2	14,075	14,603	15,131	15,658	16,186	16,714	17,242	17,770	18,297
305–360	1	30	6	3	14,919	15,479	16,038	16,598	17,157	17,717	18,276	18,836	19,395
365–420	1	30	6	4	15,815	16,408	17,001	17,594	18,187	18,780	19,373	19,966	20,559
425–525	2	30	6.5	5	16,843	17,474	18,106	18,737	19,369	20,001	20,632	21,264	21,895
530–630	2	30	6.5	6	17,937	18,610	19,283	19,955	20,628	21,301	21,973	22,646	23,319
635–745	2	30	6.5	7	19,103	19,820	20,536	21,252	21,969	22,685	23,402	24,118	24,834
750–860	2	30	6.5	8	20,345	21,108	21,871	22,634	23,397	24,160	24,923	25,686	26,448
865–975	2	30	6.5	9	21,667	22,480	23,292	24,105	24,918	25,730	26,543	27,355	28,168
980–1,105	3	40	7	10	22,218	23,329	24,440	25,551	26,662	27,773	28,884	29,994	31,105
1,110–1,235	3	40	7	11	23,773	24,962	26,151	27,339	28,528	29,717	30,905	32,094	33,283
1,240–1,365	3	40	7	12	25,438	26,709	27,981	29,253	30,525	31,797	33,069	34,341	35,613
1,370–1,495	3	40	7	13	27,218	28,579	29,940	31,301	32,662	34,023	35,384	36,744	38,105
1,500–1,645	4	40	7.5	14	29,260	30,722	32,185	33,648	35,111	36,574	38,037	39,500	40,963
1,650–1,795	4	40	7.5	15	31,454	33,027	34,599	36,172	37,745	39,317	40,890	42,463	44,036
1,800–1,945	4	40	7.5	16	33,813	35,504	37,194	38,885	40,576	42,266	43,957	45,648	47,338
1,950–2,095	4	40	7.5	17	36,349	38,166	39,984	41,801	43,619	45,436	47,254	49,071	50,889
2,100–2,285	5	50	8	18	37,687	40,042	42,397	44,753	47,108	49,464	51,819	54,175	56,530
2,290–2,475	5	50	8	19	40,702	43,245	45,789	48,333	50,877	53,421	55,965	58,509	61,052
2,480–2,665	5	50	8	20	43,958	46,705	49,452	52,200	54,947	57,694	60,442	63,189	65,937
2,670–2,855	5	50	8	21	47,474	50,441	53,409	56,376	59,343	62,310	65,277	68,244	71,211
2,860–3,080	6	50	8.5	22	51,510	54,729	57,948	61,168	64,387	67,606	70,826	74,045	77,264
3,085–3,305	6	50	8.5	23	55,888	59,381	62,874	66,367	69,860	73,353	76,846	80,339	83,832
3,310–3,530	6	50	8.5	24	60,638	64,428	68,218	72,008	75,798	79,588	83,378	87,168	90,958
3,535–3,755	6	50	8.5	25	65,793	69,905	74,017	78,129	82,241	86,353	90,465	94,577	98,689
3,760–4,115	7	50	9	26	71,714	76,196	80,678	85,160	89,643	94,125	98,607	103,089	107,571
4,120–4,480	7	50	9	27	78,168	83,054	87,939	92,825	97,710	102,596	107,481	112,367	117,252

the seven pay sectors simulate a curved line. This simulation of a curved line recognizes that as job worth increases linearly, rates of pay for these jobs of increasing worth increase geometrically.

Jobs within pay grades of an assigned pay sector have similar knowledge and skill requirements and similar kinds of responsibilities. The jobs in pay grades within a pay sector may have some differences in the level of required knowledge and skills, some differences in scope and complexity of responsibilities, and differences in working conditions. The organization may wish to recognize these differences through assignment to different pay grades that provide differences in rates of pay. The example provided in Figure 11–10 of an expanding pay structure uses the Factor Evaluation System (FES) as the point-factor job evaluation method; however, almost all well-designed point-factor methods can be used to provide the same kind of structure. The points assigned to the total job evaluation method will determine the number of pay grades that can be established through a particular method.

Figure 11–11 uses the Hay Method for rating jobs. When using the Hay Method a slight modification was made to each sector by including only three pay grades in each sector. Also because of commonly used Hay pay structure design characteristics, all pay ranges are 50 percent in length. The three pay grade limit on each sector relates to the ±3 step up/down convention developed by Ned Hay, designer of the Hay Method, to recognize perceptible differences among jobs. (There is further discussion of the Hay Method in chapters 8 and 9.)

Midpoint-to-Midpoint Differences   The most critical pay data in an expanding pay structure is the midpoint of each pay grade. If an organization has established within its compensation policy the desire to meet the market, the midpoint of each pay grade should compare favorably (±5 percent) with market survey midpoints of benchmark jobs assigned to each pay grade or benchmark jobs within a select sample of pay grades within each pay sector.

If an organization wishes to pay above or below the market, it first must recognize market rates of pay, then perform the necessary calculations to establish midpoint rates of pay that match compensation policy requirements. It must be noted that initial steps in designing an expanding pay structure are quite mechanical; however, once a first draft pay structure is designed, it must then meet market-related pay criteria to establish the validity of the plan. Later in this section, there is a discussion of the use of computer-based spreadsheet software for designing and producing a variety of pay structure configurations in a very short period of time.

Point Variations   Because most point-factor job evaluation plans have a linear design relationship among levels or degrees of a factor, the width of a pay grade will depend on the job evaluation method. However, in moving from pay grades in one sector to pay grades in the adjacent sector, the point length of the pay grade will normally increase. The height of the pay grade depends on organizational preference for paying jobs with just perceptible differences, or possibly significantly perceptible differences, different rates of pay. An increasing width of the pay grade permits jobs with increasing linear differences in point scores to be assigned to the same pay grades. Here again, the pay structure designers are recognizing job value changes as a geometric perception, not

Pay Sector	Pay Grades	Hay Point Spread (15% within Pay Grade)	Percent Spread of the Range	Midpoint-to-Midpoint Difference
I	1–3	57–66, 67–76, 77–87	50	6.0
II	4–6	88–100, 101–115, 116–132	50	7.5
III	7–9	133–152, 153–175, 176–200	50	9.0
IV	10–12	201–230, 231–264, 265–304	50	10.5
V	13–15	305–350, 351–400, 401–460	50	12.0
VI	16–18	461–528, 529–608, 609–700	50	13.5
VII	19–21	701–800, 801–920, 921–1056	50	15.0

9 STEP FORMULA
7 Sector 21 Grades

ENTER PAY GRADE 1, STEP #5   15,270

Pay Sectors	Pay Grade	Step #1	Step #2	Step #3	Step #4	Step #5	Step #6	Step #7	Step #8	Step #9
I	1	12,216	12,979	13,742	14,506	15,270	16,033	16,796	17,560	18,324
I	2	12,949	13,758	14,567	15,376	16,186	16,995	17,804	18,613	19,423
I	3	13,726	14,584	15,442	16,300	17,157	18,015	18,873	19,731	20,589
II	4	14,755	15,677	16,599	17,521	18,444	19,366	20,288	21,210	22,133
II	5	15,862	16,853	17,845	18,836	19,827	20,818	21,810	22,801	23,792
II	6	17,051	18,117	19,183	20,248	21,314	22,380	23,446	24,511	25,577
III	7	18,586	19,748	20,909	22,071	23,232	24,394	25,555	26,717	27,878
III	8	20,259	21,525	22,792	24,058	25,324	26,590	27,857	29,123	30,389
III	9	22,083	23,463	24,844	26,224	27,604	28,984	30,365	31,745	33,125
IV	10	24,402	25,927	27,452	28,977	30,502	32,027	33,552	35,077	36,602
IV	11	26,964	28,649	30,335	32,020	33,705	35,390	37,076	38,761	40,446
IV	12	29,795	31,627	33,520	35,382	37,244	39,106	40,969	42,831	44,693
V	13	33,370	35,456	37,542	39,627	41,713	43,799	45,885	47,970	50,056
V	14	37,375	39,711	42,047	44,383	46,719	49,055	51,391	53,727	56,063
V	15	41,860	44,476	47,093	49,709	52,325	54,941	57,558	60,174	62,790
VI	16	47,511	50,481	53,450	56,420	59,389	62,359	65,328	68,298	71,267
VI	17	53,926	57,296	60,667	64,037	67,407	70,777	74,148	77,518	80,888
VI	18	61,205	65,030	68,856	72,681	76,506	80,331	84,157	87,982	91,807
VII	19	70,386	74,785	79,184	83,583	87,982	92,381	96,780	101,179	105,578
VII	20	80,943	86,002	91,061	96,120	101,179	106,237	111,296	116,355	121,414
VII	21	93,085	98,903	104,721	110,538	116,356	122,174	127,992	133,809	139,627

FIGURE 11–11 Expanding Pay Structure Design Characteristics for Organization Using Hay Method

one that is linear. (See chapter 8 for discussion on Weber's Law and the work of Ned Hay on just perceptible differences.)

Examples of an Expanding Pay Structure   Figure 11–10 is a pay structure for an organization that uses the FES point-factor job evaluation method. This method has nine factors with a minimum score of 190 points and a maximum score of 4,480 points. In designing the pay structure, there are seven pay sectors with 27 pay grades. (See chapters 8 and 9 for discussions of FES.)

Figure 11–11 is an expanding pay structure for an organization that uses the Hay Method (see discussion of Hay Method in chapters 8 and 9). The design of this pay structure includes seven pay sectors with 21 pay grades.

ARCHITECTURAL DESIGN HINTS

PG 1 Minimum Rate of Pay   As previously discussed, use state or federal minimum wage mandate, poverty-level income data, or rate of pay that meets compensation policy requirements of the organization.

Midpoint of PG 1   Using the policy-established minimum rate of pay for PG 1 and the range for the pay grade, it is possible to establish the midpoint for the pay grade. All following midpoints in the expanding pay structure are built upon this midpoint.

Midpoints for All Remaining Pay Grades   All remaining midpoint calculations depend on the established midpoint-to-midpoint differences. In many cases, midpoint-to-midpoint differences can vary from 5 to 15 percent. However, in most cases, differences of from 6 to 10 percent will satisfy the needs of most designers. Usually, a 0.5 percent step up from one sector to the next provides sufficient difference in rates of pay for jobs in each pay grade to meet market- or organization-related demands. In organizations that have large numbers of employees performing jobs requiring significantly different kinds and levels of knowledge and skills, a 1 or 2 percent midpoint-to-midpoint difference produces needed rates of pay for each pay grade. A possible example of an organization that may require 1 to 2 percent increases in midpoint-to-midpoint differences between adjacent pay sectors could be a hospital, or possibly a hospital specializing in research or performing state-of-the-art surgical procedures. These institutions hire relatively low-skilled janitorial, laundry, and food service workers, moderately skilled nursing aides and LPNs, skilled technicians and nurses, and highly skilled nursing specialists, researchers, and doctors. To include all of these kinds of jobs within one pay structure requires the organization to pay some employees close to government-required minimum wages and the highly paid in excess of $100,000 per year. The increase in pay between sectors can be significant, requiring more than a 0.5 to 1.0 percent increase from midpoint to midpoint. (Note the 1.5 percent midpoint-to-midpoint difference in pay plan presented in Figure 11–11.)

Pay Grade Range   For most jobs requiring unskilled and semiskilled workers, a range of 30 percent will usually be adequate. (A range less than 30 percent will often fail to provide rates of pay high enough for senior employees who have 10 or more years of service in these lower-level jobs.) Where jobs require relatively higher rates of pay—rates of pay in excess of $50,000 per year—it will be necessary to have ranges of 50 percent and greater as the upper limits of the pay grades exceed $75,000 per year.

Steps within a Pay Grade   An option available to pay grade designers is to establish steps within a pay grade. Two primary approaches are available for determining a rate of pay for each step in a pay grade. Depending on the number of steps (*n*) desired, the difference between the maximum and minimum can be divided by $n - 1$ and this amount added successively to each previous step until reaching the maximum. For example, PG 1 minimum is $10,920 and PG 1 maximum is $14,196. $14,196 − $10,920 = $3,276 ÷ 8 = $409.50.

Step 1	Step 2	Step 3	Step 4	Step 5	Step 6	Step 7	Step 8	Step 9
10,920	11,329.50	11,739	12,148.50	12,558	12,967.50	13,777	13,786.50	14,196

If a constant percentage increase is desired, divide the range percentage by the number of desired steps. Using the previous example of a range of 30 percent divided by nine steps, which equals 3.333 percent, start by multiplying 10,920 by 1.03333 (1 for the initial value and .03333 for the increase).

PG 1	PG 2	PG 3	PG 4	PG 5	PG 6	PG 7	PG 8	PG 9
10,920	11,284	11,660	13,049	12,450	12,865	13,294	13,737	14,195

PAY SECTORS AND LEVELS OF EDUCATION, EXPERIENCE, AND TRAINING

When developing pay sectors, an education criterion may be most valuable for grouping pay grades within one sector. After evaluating all jobs, it is useful to review the education, experience, and training requirements for jobs within each pay grade. A first hint for grouping pay grades within a sector may follow this route:

Pay Sector	Education, Experience, Training
I	Less than high school education; no prior experience to a maximum of 2 years in related kinds of work; little to no formal training
II	High school diploma, some prior experience in related work—minimum of one year; some formal training in technology related to job requirements.
III	Completion of associate degree program or at least 3 years' experience in related field of work; formal training in field or posession of appropriate registrations, certificates, or licenses.
IV	Completion of baccalaureate program or extensive experience (5 to 10 years) in related field of work. Must hold or be capable of acquiring required registrations, certificates, or licenses.
V	Completion of masters program or extensive experience (10 or more years) in jobs within related fields of work. Must hold required registrations, certificates, or licenses.
VI	Knowledge gained through formal education and work experience that exceeds levels acquired through a masters program. Must hold required registrations, certificates, or licenses.
VII	Knowledge gained through formal education and job experience that establishes jobholders as masters of a professional field of work.

Skill-Based Pay, Pay-for-Knowledge, and Broadbanding   The architectural factors developed within the expanding pay structure have a close relationship to the skill-based pay, pay-for-knowledge, and broadbanding methods that are currently being promoted. As mentioned in the discussion of broadbanding, the pay sectors developed in the expanding design could easily be proxies for the band in a broadbanding approach. In addition, a careful analysis of the change in skill and knowledge requirements from Sector I to Sector VII will closely relate to the increase in the kinds and levels of skills or knowledge in a job evaluation plan that focuses on either skills or knowledge. Chapter 12 contains a further discussion of these concepts within the context of a team-based organization.

SPREADSHEET SOFTWARE

In many cases, the initial selection of midpoint-to-midpoint differences and pay ranges does not meet compensation policy demands and labor market identified rates of pay. To meet these demands, designers of expanding pay structures will have to adjust their ranges set for each pay sector and the midpoint-to-midpoint differences for each sector. As previously discussed, designers have a wide latitude of options in varying these two areas of pay structure architecture. The expanding pay structure concept provides an ideal application for basic spreadsheet software. Figures 11–10 and 11–11 can be produced through software such as Lotus, Quattro Pro, or Excel.

The expanding pay structure developed in Figure 11–11 uses 21 rows and 13 columns. The actual number of rows and columns required to design a pay structure depends on number of pay grades to be included within the structure (rows) and steps within each pay grade (columns).

After establishing the range spread percentage and midpoint-to-midpoint percentage in columns 2 and 3, enter the midpoint rate of pay for pay grade 1 (see line 5 "ENTER PAY GRADE 1, STEP 5"). When the designer wishes to modify the proposed pay structure, all that must be done is to revise the range column (column 2) and midpoint-to-midpoint differences (column 3) or possibly reset the minimum pay for PG 1. With each revision, the program will recalculate a revised pay structure. Within a very short period of time and with minimal effort, the designer can perform several "what-if's" by changing the different variables of the pay structure. These revised pay structures can then be compared with pay data from market surveys and then used to facilitate the calculation of payroll costs. One-half percent midpoint-to-midpoint difference and 5 percent variation in range can provide significant pay grade differences. Spreadsheet software simplifies the administrative support work required to produce expanding pay structures. It is possible that no configuration will produce the results desired by the designers and, in this case, they must consider the use of multiple pay structures for their organization.

Summary

Pay structure designers must not operate in a vacuum. They must recognize market conditions. This does not mean that it is necessary to blindly follow market trends. It does mean that the designer must be able to recognize differences in his or her own pay structure compared with that being presented by market data and know why these differences may exist. No one set of rules informs any person how to develop a pay structure for an organization. Form is governed by organizational philosophy and compensation strategies. Refinement through careful review of existing data and design characteristics and iterative redesigns or intelligent editing will usually produce an acceptable product that has been designed by a skilled professional who understands and makes use of objective data. It is a process that moves from abstraction to precision.

The first step in building a pay structure is to set midpoint, minimum, and maximum rates of pay, including minimum and maximum rates of pay for each pay grade and for the organization as a whole. Then the number of grades, the range of pay within each grade, the amount of overlap between adjoining pay grades, and the difference between grade midpoints must be determined.

Much of the thinking in this area is now in a stage of transition. Whereas in the past it was not uncommon for a large organization to have three different pay structures with 30 to 40 grades within each, today the tendency is to simplify the process.

Pressures from both within and without the organization are forcing the redesign of the organizational structure. Such pressures as increased efficiency, equal pay for equal work, and recognition of performance are sparking a reduction in the number of levels within the organizational structure. These factors have the direct effect of reducing the number of pay grades. With such reduction, it is possible and even necessary to increase both the number and the size of steps within each grade. This, combined with improved performance appraisal techniques, provides the organization with a greater opportunity to recognize performance, to differentiate between the inexperienced and the proven, between those willing to provide the extra effort and those just willing to get by.

As an organization reduces the number of levels in its structure, it reduces the opportunity for its members to gain hierarchical promotion (grade to grade), but by increasing the spread of the range for a pay grade and the pay importance of each incremental step within the range, it provides an opportunity for upward movement within a grade. In this manner, the attention of the employee and the organization focuses in the proper direction—on the job itself.

Not only does the pay structure weave together internal requirements, it also enables the organization to compare itself with its competitors in the human resources marketplace. The ability to make market comparisons, as well as the ability to relate to economic changes, permits the organization to raise the entire level of the pay structure when necessary, making it competitive with its environment without changing internal relationships.

Review Questions

1. Describe various methods for developing a line of best fit.
2. Why would an organization use more than one pay structure?
3. Describe some of the factors that influence the design of a pay structure.
4. What is the value of having a 5 percent difference between midpoints? A 20 percent difference between midpoints?
5. What are some of the philosophical issues underlying overlap between pay grades?

Appendix 11A
The Least-Squares Method for Determining
Line of Best Fit (Trend Line)

The following steps make up the least-squares method for determining the line of best fit or trend line.

Step 1

The equation for a straight line will be used because most pay distributions approximate a straight line. This equation is $Y = a + bX$, where

Y = actual pay rate (or job rate of pay from survey data)

X = evaluated points for organizational job

a = constant—where line of best fit intercepts (crosses) Y-axis (Y value when x is zero)

b = constant—slope of line of best fit. (If line goes "uphill" from left to right, the slope is positive [+]; conversely, a "downhill" from left to right is a negative [−] slope.)

$$\frac{\Delta Y}{\Delta X} \text{ or } \frac{Y_2 - Y_1}{X_2 - X_1}$$

(The larger the value of the slope, the faster the rate of change! The impact of the slope on the pay structure is that the greater the slope of the pay policy line, the greater the difference in pay between jobs of similar [not same] worth.)

Step 2

The formula for the straight line must be developed by solving for the constants a and b for a particular distribution of actual pay and evaluated points or organizational job used for matching purpose and pay rate for comparable jobs. This is accomplished by solving two simultaneous equations.

(1) $\qquad\qquad\qquad \Sigma Y = Na + b\Sigma X$

(2) $\qquad\qquad\qquad \Sigma XY = a\Sigma X + b\Sigma X^2$

where

ΣY = sum of the pay rate column

ΣX = sum of the point cross column

ΣXY = sum of the cross products of pay rates and point values

ΣX^2 = sum of the squares of the point values

N = number of jobs evaluated

For example, the least-squares table shown here (Table 11A–1) lists nine jobs and their respective points. The mathematical manipulation of the evaluated points and the respective rates of pay provide the data necessary to solve these two simultaneous equations.

Jobs	X Points	Y Rate	XY	X^2
TABLE 11A–1 Least Squares				
A	50	2.00	100.00	2,500
B	75	2.30	172.50	5,625
C	100	2.65	265.00	10,000
D	125	3.05	381.25	15,625
E	150	3.50	525.00	22,500
F	175	4.00	700.00	30,625
G	200	4.60	920.00	40,000
H	225	5.29	1,190.25	50,625
I	250	6.08	1,520.00	62,500
Σ	1,350	33.47	5,774.00	240,000

Step 3

Solve the simultaneous equations by substituting the values from the least-squares table:

(1) $$\Sigma Y = Na + b\Sigma X$$

(2) $$\Sigma XY = a\Sigma X + b\Sigma X^2$$

(1) $$33.47 = 9a + 1350b$$

(2) $$5774.0 = 1350a + 240{,}000b$$

Multiply (1) by 1350/9 = 150:

(1) $$33.47\,(150) = 9a(150) + 1350b\,(150)$$

(1) $$5020.5 = 1350a + 202{,}500b$$

Subtract (1) from (2) and solve for b:

(2)
$$5{,}774.0 = 1{,}350a + 240{,}000b$$
$$5{,}020.5 = 1{,}350a + 202{,}500b$$
$$735.5 = \qquad\quad + 37{,}500b$$

$$b = \frac{753.5}{37{,}500}$$

$$b = .02$$

Substitute value of b in equation (1) and solve for a:

$$33.47 = 9a + 1350(.02)$$
$$9a = 33.47 - 27$$
$$a = \frac{6.47}{9} = .718 \text{ or } .72 \text{ (rounding off)}$$

Step 4

The equation for the line of best fit for this distribution is

$$Y = .72 + .02(X)$$

Step 5

To determine points for plotting the line, substitute X values for the highest-rated job, the lowest-rated job, and one intermediate point as a checkpoint.

$Y_L = .72 + .02(50)$
$Y_L = 1.72$
$Y_1 = .72 + .02(150)$
$Y_1 = 3.72$
$Y_H = .72 + .02(250)$
$Y_H = 5.72$

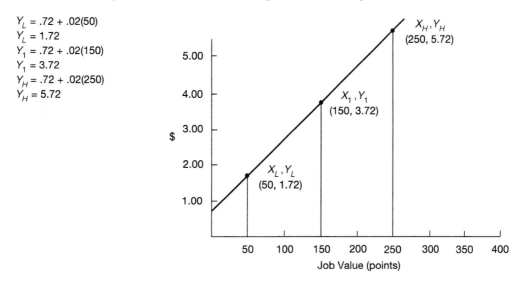

A curve may be plotted using these three sets of paired coordinates:

$$(X_L, Y_L) = (50, 1.72)$$
$$(X_1, Y_1) = (150, 3.72)$$
$$(X_H, Y_H) = (250, 5.72)$$

If only two points are to be used for determining the line, then only Step 1 of this process is necessary.

CHAPTER 12

Team-Based Pay in a Knowledge-Based World

Learning Objectives

In this chapter you will learn about:

1. The design of teams in contemporary organizations.

2. Analysis of the work of teams.

3. The kinds of pay plans useful for compensating team members.

4. The similarities and differences among skill-based pay, pay-for-knowledge, and competency-based pay plans.

Compensation Strategy

Integrate the development and understanding of work and role requirements to ensure team success.

In the 1960s, many organizations in the United States began to realize that they would have to make drastic changes in their organizational structure if they were to compete in a global economy and also provide U.S. customers with quality products at a competitive price. Recognizing that labor costs are a major part of the costs of doing business, intense efforts were focused on what could be done to make the workplace more cost efficient while improving the motivational environment for the workforce. These efforts combined the philosophical concepts of "economic man" and "social man" with the ever expanding concepts being developed and promoted by behavioral scientists. Review appendix 3A, "Economic Theories," for a detailed description of social wage theories and economic theories that have developed over the past 2,500 years or more.

As early as the 1950s, managers and human resources experts began using teams as a critical focus for improving workplace performance. By the 1960s, a number of major team-based operations were designed and operating within a team-based environment. Before analyzing these team operations and the compensation systems developed to support them, it will be helpful to take a quick overview of the basic concepts underlying economic man and social man and the concepts presented by the behavioral scientists.

With the advent of the Industrial Revolution, theorists and practitioners were promoting the use of money to direct and stimulate human behavior. These individuals felt that if money were, in some manner, linked directly to workplace efforts, employees would use their knowledge, skills, and efforts to provide outputs of sufficient quantity and quality to make the employer profitable and successful.

During this period, there were many experts on human behavior that cast doubt on the theories related to economic man. These promoters of social man downplayed the use of financial incentives to motivate human behavior. This battle between economic man and social man advocates has existed since the dawn of a money-based economy, but with the rise of capitalism within the Industrial Revolution, the differences between these two concepts rose to new heights.

The 1950s witnessed the rising influence of behavioral and social scientists on the world of pay and incentive system design. The behavioral and social science critics focused much of their attention on the inadequacies of industrial engineering–based wage systems. The work of Frederick W. Taylor and his industrial engineering (IE) colleagues was a major focus of criticism by these social scientists. The efforts of industrial engineers to identify and define fundamental work motions and establish time standards (motion and time study) in the manufacturing sector fed into the service world where jobs were often narrowly defined, had very restricted assigned rates of pay, and were the source of concern of some very vocal behavioral scientists.

Are human beings so socially oriented that financial incentives can only be a demotivating influence, or can social forces and economic forces be integrated in such a manner that human efforts at the workplace can be stimulated and directed to benefit the employee, the employer, and the customer? Interest in integrating social and economic forces gave birth to behavioral science theories developed by Henry Murray, Abraham Maslow, Frederick Herzberg, and others (see chapter 13 for extensive discussions of motivation theories).

A core concept developed by these behavioral scientists was that employer-provided rewards had different influences on human motivation. Some rewards related to survival of employees and their families; other rewards improved lifestyle opportunities; still other work-related rewards could significantly expand self-satisfaction. Such terms as *job enlargement, job enrichment, participation,* and *organizational democracy* promoted an expanded view of organizational design and employer-provided rewards. In an attempt to integrate these concepts, some practitioners and theorists began promoting the expanded use of teams within the organization.

KINDS OF TEAMS

In the world of work, team design will vary depending on the particular use of the team. In turn, the compensation program for team members will vary according to team design. Two major different kinds of teams are those that are temporary and those that are permanent parts of the organization.

Temporary teams are established to develop a specific product or solve a particular problem. With the completion of the assigned mission, the team is dissolved.

Permanent teams, on the other hand, are established parts of the organizational structure and produce a defined product. Teams can further be differentiated by the kind of supervision or management under which they perform. A team can function within a traditional management hierarchy, and the team leader is assigned through the established management process. In recent years, much attention has focused on the self-managed or self-directed work team. In this kind of work environment, the team members select their own leaders or managers.

Team design and team member roles are also significantly influenced by the kinds of output produced by the team. A temporary team of managers or professionals may consist of specialists who have extremely high levels of knowledge about specific subjects. These individuals then use their own levels of knowledge in some kind of a mutually interactive process to solve complex problems or possibly develop a new or innovative product. Temporary teams can also be established at the operating levels of an organization. At these levels, a team can be established to solve a problem facing employees and management when employee input can be of significant value in making an appropriate or useful decision. The kind of team, temporary or permanent, outputs to be produced, and knowledge and skills required of members directly influence the compensation program designed for them.

Team Design

Teams are far more than groups of people combining efforts to achieve some kind of an assignment (e.g., produce a product, gain a victory in a sport, or overcome an enemy in a military operation). Although there are examples in current literature regarding team operations and successes with teams ranging in size to more than 50 individuals, this is a very misleading description of a team. A basic team size is most likely 7 ± 2. It may be that a team can consist of as few as three individuals and have as many as 15, but from a practical, intellectual, and emotional perspective, the ideal team size should range from five to nine members. There are some very practical reasons for these limits, but possibly most important are the concepts developed in the 1950s by George A. Miller, a Harvard University professor of psychology, in his article, "The Magical Number Seven, Plus or Minus Two: Some Limits on Our Capacity for Processing Information." Using Miller's research, team designers must recognize that human beings possess a finite and rather small capacity for making unidimensional judgments. In terms of distinguishing alternatives, the mean corresponds to about 6.5 categories. One standard deviation includes from 4 to 10 categories, and the total range is from 3 to 15 categories.[1] To understand how Miller's efforts fit into team design, it is important to be able to differentiate a team from any other kind of group of individuals.

A team, as defined by Katzenbach and Smith, is a small number of people with complementary skills who are committed to a common purpose, set of performance goals, and approach for which they hold themselves mutually accountable.[2]

---

[1]George A. Miller, "The Magical Number Seven, Plus or Minus Two: Some Limits on Our Capacity for Processing Information," *The Psychological Review,* March 1956, pp. 81–97.
[2]Jon R. Katzenbach and Douglas K. Smith, "The Discipline of Teams," *The Harvard Business Review,* March–April 1993, pp. 111–120.

Katzenbach and Smith further define a team by these seven characteristics:

1. Shared leadership roles
2. Individual and mutual accountability
3. Specific team purpose that the team itself delivers
4. Collective work products
5. Open-ended discussion and active problem-solving meetings
6. Performance measured directly by assessing collective work products
7. Real work discussed, decided on, and completed together

The critical concepts in this definition are complementary skills and commitment to a common purpose. Where Miller's research supports Katzenbach and Smith's team design ("small number of people") is that in order for a team to be successful in completing assignments and achieving goals, all members must fully understand and accept the qualities, characteristics, and idiosyncrasies of each other team member. They must also have a good general understanding of what each member is doing and the problems and opportunities facing each member, and what each member can do to assist all other members to perform successfully their assignments. Miller is telling the world that there is a very definite limitation on what the human brain can recognize and relate to in a very efficient, goal-achieving manner. When too many people are part of a team (i.e., more than 9 or at most 15), individuals are unable to recognize and accept individual differences, strengths, and weaknesses, and cannot coordinate their efforts to maximize the opportunities for successful achievement of goals and commitment to the common purpose as stated by Katzenbach and Smith.

A major issue involved in designing a team is whether or not a supervisor should be a member of the team. A good estimate is that between 25 to 50 percent of teams include a supervisory employee.

Analyzing Team Work

Possibly one of the most important differences in organizing and developing a team and organizing within a traditional management structure is the focus on team member work assignments. Many promoters of team-based operations stress the need to eliminate job descriptions and narrowly defined work assignments. These individuals are often the opponents of any kind of "Taylorism"—scientific management approaches to work design. To those not intimately involved in team-based operations, it may appear that work analysis or its traditional organizational relative, job analysis, is not only unnecessary but is a barrier to improved performance. Nothing can be further from the truth.

At the center of team-based operations, especially with permanent teams established at the operating levels to produce specific products, the communication and documentation of work assignments are absolutely critical. A major difference between traditional job analysis and contemporary work analysis for team operations is that the team members themselves are the primary definers of workplace activities. One of the early functions performed by team members is the identification of all work activities performed within the domain of the team operations.

In the traditional organization, as discussed in chapters 6 and 7, the job analysis–job description functions are usually performed by job analysts operating out of the human resources (HR)/personnel department. In the team-based environment, the team members themselves perform the analysis, although HR specialists may provide consulting support throughout the work identification and definition phases of team development.

Instead of relying on the completion of job analysis questionnaires, team-based work analysis will often focus on a meeting of all team members in which a complete description of all team work activities is completed. In this process, it is not unusual for each team member to be given a premeeting assignment. This homework assignment is to list all the activities, tasks, or duties performed by the individual.

At the work analysis meeting, each employee presents his or her list of assignments (a first draft replica of a traditional and often berated job description). All team members review each member's list and ask such critical questions as, "Why do you do that?" or "When do you do that?" or make such comments as, "I didn't know you do that." Further discussion may lead to valuable additions to lists of tasks as one team member may say, "If I do this, would that help you?" During this stage of the work analysis process, members will attempt to better describe or refine some of the identified tasks and, possibly more important, search for missing tasks.

At this team meeting in which work activities are identified, defined, and refined, an outsider (nonteam member or frequently a member of the HR department or a consultant) will place each individual's list of work assignments on a flip chart. Other team members will modify and refine the statements as necessary. When each member's work statements are completed, the spreadsheets can then be posted on the wall for later review and analysis after all team members have completed their lists of work activities.

This analysis process not only provides a comprehensive overview and documentation of team work assignments, but it is one of the first processes used to develop team cohesiveness and understanding of the total work picture. It promotes an appreciation of what each member must do and the contributions all team members must make to ensure team success.

A basic factor underlying the successful operation of a team is that each member has a good, if not complete, understanding of what happens at each workstation and can make decisions and take action relative to some event that may not directly relate to current work assignments but does or would have an influence on continuing successful team operations. The team member is truly a fully functioning member of the knowledge-based world, and the more knowledge acquired and the more skills demonstrated, the more valuable the individual is to the team and to the organization.

The work analysis process is one of the first *activities* performed by all members as a team. It assists in establishing a positive work relationship. It promotes human interaction. Team members not only discuss what they do but, possibly more important, why they do it and even how they do it. This process not only promotes self-respect but mutual understanding and respect by all team members of the roles played by each member. It provides a basic building block for team success—communication and documentation of team activities.

The need to carefully and completely identify and define all team-related work efforts (i.e., tasks, duties, responsibilities) is of critical importance to those involved in establishing team-based operations and designing team-based pay systems. Following this work analysis, it is then possible to establish knowledge and skill requirements and to further define the knowledge and skills by kinds and levels (blocs or units). With the development of kinds and levels of knowledge and skills, it is then possible to develop tests to assess individual acquisition of specific kinds and levels of knowledge and skills and develop education and training programs to expand member acquisition of knowledge and skill competency. After completion of these efforts, it is then possible to establish pay systems that relate to team-required knowledge and skills.

Self-Managed Work Teams

In the 1950s, initial approaches to team-based operations began to appear in the apparel industry. Apparel factories that had to face short runs of a wide variety of garments began to eliminate their continuous assembly operations in which large numbers of sewing machine operators performed very short-run operations and received piece rate–based incentives determined by some kind of motion and time study. In the team operation, a group of 5 to 15 operators worked as a team to produce an entire garment. A rate of pay was set for each completed garment. The total pay for the day was determined by the number of garments produced and the rate set for each style of garment. The team members then divided the daily earnings among themselves. In some cases, team members decided on whether or not certain team members should receive a higher proportion of the daily earnings than other members. In almost all team efforts, certain positions or workstations require more skill than other stations, even when work is divided as fairly as possible. However, in these early efforts members seldom divided their daily earnings in any way other than equally.

A major contributor to the development and use of teams was Frederick Herzberg. A direct output of Herzberg's work on job enlargement and job enrichment has been the focus on teams, or more explicitly, *self-managed work teams*. To provide management with more flexibility in making workplace assignments while simultaneously increasing employee opportunities for work-related intellectual growth and advancement, the team concept became a critical component. Self-managed work teams emerged out of the manufacturing industries. Recognizing the demotivational aspects of narrowly focused jobs, motivational researchers and operating managers realized that if workers could be delegated more authority over their work, the opportunity for job-related interest and commitment could lead to improved quantity and quality of output. Recognizing these factors led to the development of teams that had collective authority to manage workplace efforts that included a wide variety of jobs. In turn, these teams had the authority and responsibility to train team members, make job assignments, schedule workplace job rotations, establish performance standards, inspect output to ensure meeting quality and quantity standards, enforce workplace standards of behavior, and identify employees who should be receiving team-related promotions and pay increases.

In the 1960s, General Foods opened a new dog food manufacturing plant in Topeka, Kansas, and the initial design of the plant included the concept of self-managed work teams. The entire plant was divided into a number of teams. Each team had a defined production process to complete within an established work area. Team members had assignments that ensured the efficient operation of equipment. Each team was responsible for doing its own work scheduling, assigning team members to certain positions/workstations, and training team members. Once the plant became fully operational and all teams were performing their assignments in a fully proficient manner, team members were granted the opportunity to select new employees and make recommendations for employees eligible for pay increases.

Underlying team-based operations is the identification and description of all major work activities and the knowledge and skills required to perform these activities—traditional job analysis efforts. However, instead of defining specific jobs and implementing some kind of classification or job evaluation plans to establish job rates of pay, these work activities are separated by skill levels or blocs of skills. Skill levels range from work efforts requiring minimal amounts of training and experience, for example, machines that require minimal skills to operate and machine loading and unloading that focus more on physical abilities than intellectual skills, to machines that require considerable observation and adjustment skills and even maintenance and repair skills. These skill requirements are then grouped into four to six levels with the possible highest level including or consisting of the skill to repair assigned equipment. A possible highest skill level includes skills to perform assignments in another team (e.g., multiteam skills). Each higher skill level or bloc is assigned a higher rate of pay. The term *skill-based pay* has been given to pay systems that recognize acquisition of different blocs of skills.

USE OF SKILL-, KNOWLEDGE-, AND COMPETENCY-BASED PAY

In the discussion in chapter 7 on defining the work of employees moving up through the organizational hierarchy, it was noted that higher-level jobs do *not* require more task statements for adequate definition. However, it was emphasized that the higher the level of the assignment within the organizational hierarchy, the broader or more general the meaning of the task statement. Task (activity) statements for lower-level jobs state in fairly precise terms what the employee does. At the lower levels in the hierarchy, the task statement can be almost as precise or specific as a statement defining a procedure, which not only defines *what,* but *how.* In moving upward through the hierarchy, activity/task statements become more general and allow the employee far more latitude in the actual how-to of work assignments.

This same reasoning process can be a major reason for the use of skill-based pay at the operating levels and, in particular, in manufacturing settings, whereas knowledge and competency are used to determine base rates of pay for employees in management, professional, and various service-providing teams.

The "funnel approach" (Figure 12–1) is useful in developing an understanding of the relationship between skill-based pay and pay for knowledge. Again, as discussed in chapters 6 and 7, job/work analysis begins with an identification and description of *what* an employee does. The next, more precise description is the translation from *what* the employee does (task identification) to *what* the employee must know to do the *what* (knowledge requirements). The third step in this process is moving from knowledge required to skill identification—what skill will a proficient or competent employee demonstrate in performance of work assignments? The final and most precise description involves the development of standards (tests) to measure knowledge and skill acquisition (at the educational level) and standards (performance) at the work level.

As discussed previously in this section, the higher the level of the job, the more general the description of the work to be performed. The generalized description of the higher-level jobs permits the jobholder (employee) to use more of his or her own

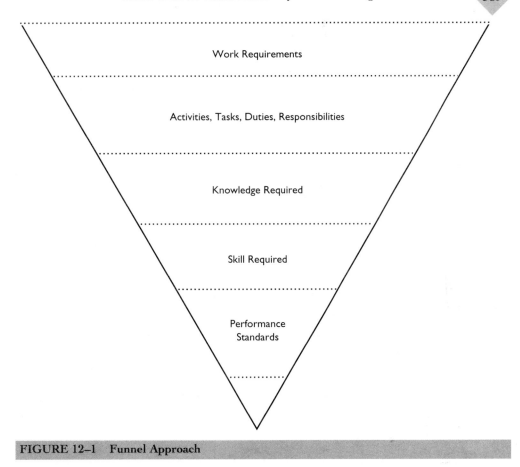

Work Requirements

Activities, Tasks, Duties, Responsibilities

Knowledge Required

Skill Required

Performance
Standards

FIGURE 12–1 Funnel Approach

knowledge, skills, and interests in the actual how-to in accomplishing work assignments. This same analysis process influences the use of the concept of skill-based pay and accompanying descriptive materials for establishing base pay for teams in a goods or precise service-providing operation. The concept of knowledge-based pay is used for teams involved in providing higher-levels of knowledge-based services. Competency-based pay can be used for higher-level managerial and technical/professional work where both activities performed and the results to be achieved are difficult to identify and measure precisely.

To assist in understanding the move from traditional pay plan operations, as discussed in chapters 6–11, to the use of skill-based pay and its counterparts, knowledge- and competency-based pay plans, it is critical to develop a solid definition for each of these three plans, recognizing where in the organization each plan would be used. Following their definitions, it is then possible to establish similarities and differences among these three approaches to pay setting and also to identify similarities and differences between traditional pay-setting practices (as described in chapters 6–11) and these relatively new plans that are currently receiving much attention and publicity in the management and human resources worlds.

A major difference between the job evaluation methods developed in the 1920s, 1930s, and 1940s and the skill/knowledge-based pay systems of the 1970s, 1980s, and 1990s is that the 1920s–1940s plans were extremely generic in design. They were developed to relate to all kinds of jobs in all kinds of organizations. The 1970s–1990s plans are usually unique to each organization and relate specifically to the kinds of work performed and the knowledge and skills required of employees within the organization.

Skill-Based Pay

In a *skill-based pay plan,* the base pay of an individual is determined by the kinds and levels of skills acquired by the individual. The organization's skill-based pay plan identifies kinds and levels of skills required of an employee in the successful completion of workplace assignments.

Workplace assignments for team members within a skill-based pay plan will cover a much wider variety of work assignments than those assigned to a specific employee in a typical job-based plan. In a team-based organization design, all of the more narrowly defined jobs within a traditional organization design are included within the work efforts of the team members. A major objective in a team-based environment is to promote knowledge and skill development of all team members to successfully perform all team assignments. Different kinds and levels of skills are given different sets of quantitative values. These quantitative values, in turn, relate to specific rates of pay. With acquisition and demonstration of a specific kind or level of skill, the employee receives the assigned rate of pay. However, the employee does not have to perform a work assignment requiring the specific kind or level of skill in order to receive the related rate of pay. A typical skill-based pay plan will have from four to eight steps, levels, or blocs. The employee advances from one step to the next with the acquisition of the established kind or level of skill or skill blocs.

At first glance, skill-based pay for work teams appears to be revolutionary, but with a closer, in-depth review, it is far more evolutionary than revolutionary. As just mentioned, a major effort involved in skill-based pay is job analysis. This activity may not be called job analysis, but team members, organization specialists, and even consultants spend considerable time at the start of a skill-based pay program analyzing and identifying work assignments and the knowledge and skills required to perform these assignments in a proficient manner.

As noted earlier, the knowledge and skill requirements are grouped into four, six, or sometimes more levels. In reality, these skill levels are not too different from the degrees or levels found within the skill, knowledge, judgment, or complexity compensable factors found in a traditional job evaluation plan. In fact, the four to six levels often found in a skill-based pay plan may be very similar to the knowledge requirements of a labor-trade series that includes laborer, Operator I, Operator II, Operator III; apprentice, journeyman, master; or some similar classification and grading scheme. The knowledge, skills, and ability model designed by the Communication Workers of America (CWA) and AT&T, as discussed later in this section, can be used to establish skill levels or blocs of skills for a skill-based pay or pay-for-knowledge plan.

Even when it comes to setting pay for each skill level, it is extremely helpful, even necessary, to analyze market pay practices for jobs requiring comparable skills and then relating these market practices to the levels within the skill-based pay program.

It is true that organizations using teams have far fewer job titles or classifications. The pay plan has a greater pay range if the team-required work is viewed as one integrated job with assignments ranging from basic and relatively simple and requiring minimal knowledge and skills to complex work requiring considerable knowledge and skills. When using a team-based pay plan with only four to six skill levels, the spread of pay for the plan will range from 70 to at times more than 100 percent. As discussed in chapter 11, pay grades that would include team-related jobs would most commonly have ranges from 25 to 40 percent.

A major difference between skill-based pay for a team and traditional job-based pay is the speed with which an employee can acquire additional job knowledge and gain relatively large increases in pay. In a skill-based pay plan, an employee is paid for what he or she knows, not necessarily what he or she does. It is possible for a highly skilled team member to perform an assignment (position or workstation) requiring low levels of knowledge and skills but receive the top rate of pay. As team members gain experience and receive training on more complex assignments, they become eligible for a higher rate of pay and do not have to wait for a job opening to receive a promotion to a higher-level job with a higher rate of pay. It must be recognized that the skill levels are those required in the performance of all assignments fulfilled by team members. However, an employee is paid for acquired skill proficiencies and not necessarily what the individual does that day or that pay period. The benefit to the organization is that all team members are more knowledgeable and skilled in team-related assignments. Because of this increase in skills, both quality and quantity of output increase and, because of variety in assignments, work becomes more interesting and leads to an enriched workplace environment.

An issue facing management is that in most cases skill-based pay plans have the potential to increase labor costs. Also employees reach the top or near the top skills (and pay) levels far more quickly than they would in a traditional pay system. In fact, a major drive for group incentive plans such as gainsharing (see discussion in chapter 14) is to provide additional cash amounts to teams in which the majority of the members have "topped out," reaching the highest or next to highest skill level.

One of the names assigned to the skill-based pay concept that may have the most impact is *pay for mastery*. Sandra Jewell of The Jewell Consulting Network coined this term in assisting various organizations to develop self-managed work teams. The importance of this term is that employees are not being paid higher wages or levels of pay simply because they have acquired more knowledge and skills but because they have become masters at the work they do. By acquiring job-related mastery, they are able to identify and perform work assignments Better, Easier, Simpler, and Timelier—BEST. In this manner, the employer provides its clients with a product that is on time and is of the highest possible quality. In addition, the organization achieves profitable levels of output. By having teams of master employees, everyone wins. The employees receive higher levels of pay while performing jobs that are more interesting and in which they have greater levels of authority. The users of the provided goods and services receive a quality product on time and at a competitive price. The employers are able to enjoy a profit while having minimum labor and client problems. This is a goal of most organizations in a capitalistic-democratic society.

A Knowledge, Skills, and Ability Model   An ideal starting place for an organization interested in developing a skill-based pay plan is an analysis and review of the

Knowledge, Skills, and Ability job evaluation plan developed by the CWA and AT&T in the early 1980s.

As a result of bargaining efforts in 1980, representative unions led by the CWA agreed to join AT&T in developing a job evaluation plan for their unionized members. In 1981, AT&T presented a list of 26 job requirements derived from Bell System testing and evaluation research based on the work of Edwin A. Fleishman. CWA and AT&T jointly combined, modified, and trimmed the list to the following factors and subfactors (the 17 factors and subfactors are defined in Figure 12–2):

1. **Communication Skills**
   a. Expressive
   b. Comprehensive
2. **Problem Solving**
   a. Fact-Finding
   b. Systems Reasoning
3. **Mathematics**

4. **Impacting Others**
   a. Adaptability
   b. Persuasion
5. **Coping**
   a. Mental Demands
   b. Physical Demands
6. **Safety Skills**

7. **Specialty Skills**
   a. Electrical and Electronic Knowledge
   b. Mechanical Knowledge
   c. Tools and Uses
   d. Graphics
   e. Coding
   f. Keyboard Skills
8. **Driving**

All subfactors and each factor that had no subfactors were described in one or two sentences. A scale with a range of 0 to 80 points was developed for each of these factors. For each of the following intervals—5–15, 20–30, 35–50, 55–65, and 70–80—qualitative descriptors were developed. See Figure 12–3 for an example of the subfactor Persuasion (B) within the factor Impacting Others (4).

In late 1982, an evaluation team consisting of representatives of the CWA and AT&T evaluated a set of benchmark jobs for one of the operating telephone company divisions of AT&T. The committee found that the factors and interval descriptions needed additional definition to differentiate between levels of work. Once the factors were refined, CWA and AT&T conducted a joint pilot study at Chesapeake & Potomac (C&P) of Maryland, implementing all aspects of the plan. The plan was to be used as a prototype for a job evaluation system to be utilized throughout the Bell System, covering 600,000 workers.

At C&P, the joint committee staff trained two workers and two first-level supervisors to document work. These job analysts spent eight months describing 25 job titles covering 80 percent of the workforce. A joint 12-member evaluation team consisting of a representative group of workers, managers, men, women, and minorities from a mix of geographic locations and job titles evaluated the 25 titles. A job incumbent or first-line supervisor was present to provide job expertise during each evaluation session. The group was able to produce an acceptable hierarchy of jobs using the jointly developed system. However, final agreement was not reached on the plan during national bargaining in 1983 because of the company's refusal to involve the union in the process over the long run.[3] The divestiture of AT&T operating units placed a cloud on the future implementation of this plan.

---

[3]Correspondence with Ms. Lorel E. Foged, economist statistician, Development and Research Department, Communications Workers of America and member of the joint national CWA/AT&T Occupational Job Evaluation Committee, January 17, 1984.

1. *Expression* is speaking and/or writing in words, sentences, or numbers so others will understand. It is measured in terms of the complexity of the information being expressed as well as the comprehension ability of the receiver of the information.
2. *Comprehension* is understanding spoken and/or written words, sentences, or numbers. It is measured in terms of the complexity of the information being received as well as the quality of the information being received.
3. *Fact-finding* is obtaining or selecting pertinent information through observation, research, or questioning. It includes organizing and combining different pieces of information into meaningful order to identify a problem. It does not include the application of this information to solve the problem. An unknown is the key element in fact-finding.
4. *Systems reasoning* is making decisions that involve the selection and application of appropriate business resources or usage of relevant facts to solve identified problems or to achieve a desired result. This is based on knowledge and understanding of products and services, materials, policies, practices, and procedures.
5. *Mathematics* is the selection and application of mathematical methods or procedures to solve problems or to achieve desired results. These systems range from basic arithmetic computations to the most complex statistical techniques or other applications such as occur in physics or engineering problems.
6. *Adaptability* is the need to adapt one's behavior to changing or unusual circumstances to achieve a desired result. This includes changes in personal interactions or work situations.
7. *Persuasion* is influencing the behaviors or actions of others. The changes in behaviors or actions may not be observed immediately.
8. *Mental demand* is mental effort associated with attending to or performing a task in the presence of distractions or work frustrations. Distractions and work frustrations arise from boredom, overlapping demands, exacting deadlines and output standards, lack of latitude to adapt behavior, discouraging circumstances, repeated unsuccessful attempts, and nonemployee-controlled work flow.
9. *Physical demand* is physical effort associated with activities such as handling weight repetition of work motions, maintenance of difficult work positions, or exposure to unpleasant surroundings.
10. *Safety skills* measures the adherence to prescribed safety and personal security practices in the performance of tasks involving exposure to hazard or risk in the work environment.
11. *Electrical/electronic knowledge* is the knowledge and application of the principles of electricity, electronics, electronic logic, and integrated transmission technologies such as lasers and fiber optics. This includes understanding of circuits, their component parts and how they work together, and understanding the output from devices or meters that register or display information related to these systems.
12. *Mechanical knowledge* is the knowledge and application of principles of how mechanical equipment such as gears, pulleys, motors, and hydraulics works. It includes the operation, repair, or maintenance of systems. It does *not* include knowledge of tools and their uses.
13. *Tools and uses* is the knowledge, appropriate selection, and application of hand tools, office machines, and mechanical and electrical tools (test sets). This does not include keyboard devices.
14. *Graphics* is reading and interpreting and/or preparing graphic representations of information such as maps, plans, drawings, blueprints, diagrams, and timing/flowcharts. It includes the preparation of visual artwork.
15. *Coding* is reading and/or writing and interpreting coded information. Codes may be identified by the fact that the ideas or concepts they represent may be translated, expanded, or expressed in English.
16. *Keyboard skills* is the operation of keyboard devices such as typewriters, data terminals, calculators, and operator equipment.
17. *Driving* is the maneuvering of a certain type of motorized vehicle. The factor does not measure the mental demand nor the safety skills in driving.

FIGURE 12–2   AT&T-CWA Factors and Subfactors

Impacting Others

PERSUASION

Influence the behavior or actions of others. The changes in the behaviors or actions of others may not be observed immediately.

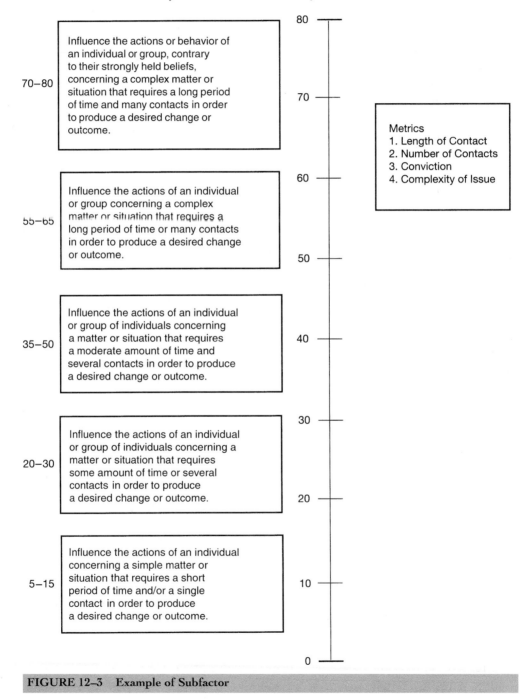

70–80	Influence the actions or behavior of an individual or group, contrary to their strongly held beliefs, concerning a complex matter or situation that requires a long period of time and many contacts in order to produce a desired change or outcome.
55–65	Influence the actions of an individual or group concerning a complex matter or situation that requires a long period of time or many contacts in order to produce a desired change or outcome.
35–50	Influence the actions of an individual or group of individuals concerning a matter or situation that requires a moderate amount of time and several contacts in order to produce a desired change or outcome.
20–30	Influence the actions of an individual or group of individuals concerning a matter or situation that requires some amount of time or several contacts in order to produce a desired change or outcome.
5–15	Influence the actions of an individual concerning a simple matter or situation that requires a short period of time and/or a single contact in order to produce a desired change or outcome.

80
70
60
50
40
30
20
10
0

Metrics
1. Length of Contact
2. Number of Contacts
3. Conviction
4. Complexity of Issue

FIGURE 12–3   Example of Subfactor

This CWA-AT&T plan is an excellent example of taking relatively generic factors and translating them into organization-specific factors. Possibly the only factor that is missing in the CWA-AT&T plan is a managerial-supervisory factor. This factor is missing because the CWA-AT&T plan was designed for unionized workers, and management authority and responsibility remain within the purview of nonunion workers. However, in many skill-based plans designed for teams, it is imperative to recognize managerial-supervisory skills.

Pay for Knowledge/Knowledge-Based Pay

With the development of skill-based pay, another modification in team or group pay plans emerged with the title *pay for knowledge.* While skill-based pay evolved in the manufacturing sector, pay for knowledge developed in the service sector. A number of the original pay-for-knowledge plans were within banks and insurance companies and similar kinds of organizations in which large numbers of employees processed records-producing data and information instead of goods.

In a *knowledge-based pay plan,* the base pay of an individual is determined by the kinds and levels of knowledge acquired by the individual. The organization identifies and defines the kinds and levels of knowledge an employee must possess to successfully perform work assignments. The kinds and levels of knowledge valued by the organization are assigned specific monetary worth to the organization. Rates of pay are established relative to specific kinds and levels of knowledge. Here, the basic difference between a skill-based pay plan and a knowledge-based pay plan emerges.

As discussed in the funnel approach (see Figure 12–1 and corresponding text), descriptive statements of knowledge are broader and more general than statements describing skills. When the work of teams can be defined rather precisely and the descriptions of the skills used are to be organization specific, the skill-based approach will be most appropriate. When the description of the work becomes more general and it is more difficult to describe precisely what each employee (team member) will do in a specific situation—that is, the how-to depends on situational requirements and the knowledge, skill, aptitude, and resources available to the involved individual—a knowledge- or competency-based pay plan will be more appropriate.

The CWA-AT&T model can also be used as a starting point for developing a knowledge-based pay plan. Now, the focus is on knowledge required of an employee and the knowledge requirements of all team members to successfully complete work assignments. The transition from a skill-based plan to a knowledge-based plan is that the more specifically defined skills are translated into more generally defined kinds and levels of knowledge.

The common thread linking skill- and knowledge-based plans is that both the skill and knowledge descriptors are organization specific and relate directly to the work performed by the employees within the involved organization. The use of involved employees in developing the CWA-AT&T plan can be critical in developing any skill- or knowledge-based pay plan.

Pay-for-knowledge plans that have existed for decades are the pay plans designed for public school teachers. Many of these plans vary the pay teachers receive based on the degrees they hold. A bachelor's degree receives the lowest rate of pay, with those holding a master's degree receiving a higher rate, and those with a doctorate, the highest rate. In recent years, these degree-related pay plans have been under intense fire, as many school districts feel there is minimal relationship between teacher classroom performance and the degree held. Also degrees in one knowledge area may receive higher rates of pay than degrees in other areas. A degree in mathematics or science may receive a higher rate of pay than a degree in social studies. These kinds of plans are often called credential-based pay plans.

Competency-Based Pay

In the 1980s and 1990s, a new term and pay determination process, *competency-based pay,* was introduced into the area of pay system design. Like other words and terms used to promote new and supposedly more appropriate methods for measuring job worth and determining rates of pay, the term *competency* has not had one commonly accepted definition. To develop a useful definition of the competency approach, it is helpful to start with an acceptable definition of competence.

> Competence is a combination of knowledge and skills required to successfully perform an assignment. Its attainment is evidenced by the ability of an individual to gather data, process it into useful information, assess it, and arrive at an appropriate and usable decision in order to initiate the actions necessary to accomplish that assignment in an acceptable manner.

Competency-based pay systems have been designed and used principally for employees in management and professional positions. The driving force underlying the development of a competency-based pay system is that the results expected of these management/professional jobs are difficult to define in precise terms. To simplify and clarify both descriptions of what the work consists of and results expected, broadly defined competencies are established for these jobs. These competencies are a combination of knowledge and skills required and results expected in the performance of work assignments.

In moving upward to the highest level of managerial and professional positions, the work performed becomes more and more influenced by the mission, policies, and strategies of the organization. The time dimension related to work assignments moves from the short term here and now to the much more indefinite future. In moving from tactical, day-to-day operations to long-term strategic operations, the work of those whose jobs influence and, in turn, are influenced directly by organizational strategies can only be defined in general or generic terms. Competencies become useful for establishing base pay for employees in these kinds of work settings.

The Compensable Factor Cube (Figure 12–4) developed by the author can be used as a starting point for designing a competency-based pay plan. Once again, the approach used by the CWA and AT&T in developing their knowledge, skills, and ability model are critical in transforming the factors presented in the Compensable Factor Cube to organization-specific competencies. The Compensable Factor Cube offers in general terms the requirements for almost any managerial or professional work. In moving from the generic factors to organization-specific competencies, an in-depth

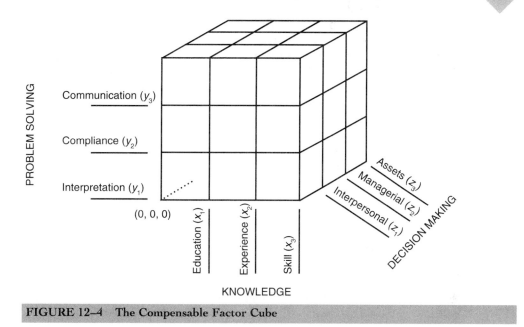

FIGURE 12–4   The Compensable Factor Cube

Universal factors, subfactors, and degrees comprising the Compensable Factor Cube.

analysis of the work performed by managers and professionals at various levels in different functional areas of the organization are required. Through an in-depth analysis of organizational work required, knowledge, problem-solving, and decision-making factors and their subfactors can be converted into pay determination competencies.

I. *Knowledge*—prerequisites for thinking and action required to perform assignment necessary to produce acceptable output.
  A. *Education*—formal learning necessary for the development of sufficient mental capabilities to perform assignments.
     1. High school diploma.
     2. Two-year college certificate (paraprofessional licensing).
     3. Four-year college degree (professional licensing).
     4. Education beyond undergraduate degree and/or professional licensing.
     5. Master's degree and/or advanced professional licensing.
     6. Doctorate and/or senior professional licensing.
  B. *Experience*—amount and complexity of direct participation in interaction with and training in use of equipment, materials, technology, processes, and systems necessary to perform assignment as measured by time.
     1. One month to less than 6 months required.
     2. Six months to 1 year required.
     3. More than 1 year to 3 years required.
     4. From 3 to 5 years required.
     5. From 5 to 10 years required.
     6. Over 10 years required.

C. *Skill*—dexterity, accuracy, alertness required relative to the flow of work or to levels of complexity in the use of and interaction with both human and nonhuman resources in performing assignments.

1. Skills requiring moderate accuracy or alertness in use of nonprecision tools, measuring devices requiring simple settings, simple operating equipment, basic applicators, assembling operations, or related operating methods and procedures, and interpersonal activities.

2. Skills requiring moderate accuracy or alertness in use of precision tools such as basic keyboard devices, advanced operating equipment, complex applicators, or assembling operations requiring advanced accuracy and alertness, or related operating methods and procedures, and interpersonal activities.

3. Skills requiring accuracy, alertness, and dexterity over an extended period of time in the use of precision tools, advanced keyboard devices, complex operating equipment, or related operating methods and procedures, and interpersonal activities.

4. Skills requiring accuracy, alertness, and dexterity over an extended period of time in the use of precision tools or equipment, or related methods and procedures, and interpersonal activities within a technological system whose operations influence the success of a unit or group.

5. Skills requiring extreme accuracy, alertness, and dexterity over an extended period of time in the use of precision tools or equipment, or related methods and procedures, and interpersonal activities within an advanced technological system where output is valuable and mistakes are harmful and costly.

6. Skills requiring extreme accuracy, alertness, and dexterity over an extended period of time in the use of precision tools or equipment, or related methods and procedures, and interpersonal activities within an advanced and complex technological system where output is of such importance that mistakes may jeopardize existence of operation if not organization.

II. *Problem Solving*—applying knowledge through interpretation, compliance, and communication to solve organizational problems in order to achieve desired levels of performance.

A. *Interpretation*—analyzing and evaluating action-oriented instructional information.

1. Requires moderate amount of interpretation. Complies with general policies, practices, and/or procedures within differing situations relative to a job or grouping of jobs to determine action.

2. Requires moderate amount of interpretation. Complies with broad policies, practices, and/or procedures relative to a variety of situations involving work group, team, or a number of work groups or teams operating as a well-identified unit to determine action.

3. Requires broad amount of interpretation as actions in changing situations involve a variety of problems determined by broad policies, practices, and procedures relative to the operation of a basic cost or profit center that combines the efforts of diverse functional groups.

4. Requires broad amount of interpretation in actions of constantly changing situations involving a variety of problems determined by broadest limits of

organizational policies and procedures relative to the operation of an independent division.

5. Requires extensive amount of interpretation in actions of nonrecurring, unique situations involving widest variety of situations determined by broadest limits of organizational policy and procedures relative to the operation of the entire organization.

6. Requires extensive amount of interpretation in actions in nonrecurring, unique situations involving wide variety of problems limited only by basic organizational philosophy and the impact of external forces on the operation of the organization.

B. *Compliance*—requirements for following instructions or orders of varying degrees of complexity necessary for implementation and coordination of resources of the organization within limits of existing policies and precedents.

1. Written, oral, or visual directives involving use of quantitative information from specifications, graphs, pictures, blueprints, dials, gauges, and so on.

2. Basic directives relating to technological processes or flow of work in some stage of operation.

3. Complex directives relating to technological processes or flow of work in some stage of operation.

4. Basic directives relating external forces with technological processes of the organization.

5. Complex directives relating external forces with technological processes of the organization.

6. Extremely complex directives relating external forces with technological processes of the organization.

C. *Communication*—transmitting directions, instructions, and suggestions in varying degrees of complexity necessary for the utilization and coordination of resources of the organization.

1. Provide simple and/or oral communications concerning a variety of situations following a general pattern. Requires moderate grammatical skills.

2. Provide written and/or oral communications concerning changing standards and procedures for output within constraints set by quality, quantity, and cost. Requires moderate grammatical skills as well as ability to use basic coded information necessary in performance of assignment.

3. Provide written and/or oral communications involving multiunit operation or processes within framework of broad organizational policies. Requires moderate grammatical skills as well as ability to identify varied components of output involving both quantitative and qualitative indicators including coded information.

4. Provide written and/or oral communication concerning basic operations of organization including processes or systems involved in its output. Requires comprehensive grammatical skills as well as ability to identify varied components of output involving both quantitative and qualitative indicators including advanced skills in coded information.

5. Provide written and/or oral communications concerning general long-range plans of organization relating organizational objectives, policies, and strategy

to both immediate and future output of the organization. Requires advanced grammatical skills as well as ability to use wide variety of information.

6. Provide written and/or oral communications concerning abstract and/or complex concepts relating to organizational philosophy, mission and strategies, financial and scientific processes; and external forces. Requires diverse as well as profound knowledge of grammar and composition.

III. *Decision Making*—intensity, scope, and complexity of interactions necessary to make decisions in order to achieve acceptable levels of performance.

A. *Interpersonal*—empathetic understanding and effectiveness in interaction with others in such areas as teaching, counseling, coaching, training, and development.

1. Frequent interchange of guidance information on nonroutine matters requiring some involvement in both counseling and instruction of members of work group or individuals outside the organization who provide direct assistance to the organization.

2. Frequent interchange of guidance information on nonroutine matters requiring frequent involvement in interviewing, counseling, and/or instruction with members of adjoining or linking groups, and individuals or outside groups who have direct relationships with the organization.

3. Very frequent interchange of nonroutine information requiring interviewing, counseling, and/or instruction of managers and professionals in adjoining or linking sections or departments as well as occasional contact with individuals and groups outside the basic confines of the organization.

4. Extensive interchange of nonroutine information requiring interviewing, counseling, and/or instruction of managers and professionals within a major division of the organization as well as occasional involvement with groups outside the normal operating limits of the organization.

5. Continuous interchange of complex, nonroutine information in a teaching and counseling capacity with senior officials throughout the organization as well as frequent involvement with groups outside the normal limits of the organization.

6. Continuous involvement in exchange of complex, nonroutine information in a teaching and counseling capacity with members at all levels of the organization as well as individuals and groups outside the organization including suppliers, clients, special interest groups, and the general public.

B. *Managerial*—quantity and quality of supervision provided and received.

1. Receives general supervision from superior. May provide moderate direction or supervision to at least 5 but less than 20 other employees. If involved with self-managed work team, number of employees may increase to 100 or more.

2. Receives general supervision from superior; has rather broad latitudes for actions involving methods, procedures, and controls in achieving objectives. May provide direction for work group(s) ranging in total size from 5 to 100 employees. If involved with self-managed work team, number of employees may be greater than 200.

3. Receives nominal supervision from superior; has broad latitude for actions involving methods, procedures, and control in achieving objectives. Provides direction for broad grouping of work units ranging in size relative to function or output.

4. Receives nominal supervision, functioning rather independently under general guidelines set by senior executives. Provides direction for all members of broad grouping of work units that vary in size relative to function or output.

5. Receives minimal supervision. Functions independently under general policies of organization or broad guidelines set by senior executives. Provides direction for all members or organizationwide work units that vary in size relative to function or output.

6. Receives no supervision and functions under general guidance from boards or public policy. Provides direction and/or supervision for organization—if not directly, then by normal chain of command.

C. *Assets*—degree of accountability for human and nonhuman resources in the planning, operations, and control of the job.

1. Responsible for actions of small group; responsible for and has interaction with organizational resources of moderate costs.

2. Responsible for actions of small group; responsible for and has interaction with organizational resources of considerable costs.

3. Responsible for actions of multigroup operations; responsible for and has interaction with organizational resources of moderate costs.

4. Responsible for actions of multigroup operations; responsible for and has interaction with organizational resources of considerable costs.

5. Responsible for organizationwide activities and resources.

6. Responsible for total resources and operations of the organization.

Competencies and Performance Appraisal

The previous discussion of competencies focuses primarily on their use in the development of a job-worth hierarchy. Competencies are also being promoted for more extensive use within the performance appraisal function and in making changes in base pay. Chapter 13 includes an extensive discussion of performance appraisal. A primary purpose of job evaluation is to establish the relative worth of jobs in an organization. Performance appraisal is the process whereby the contributions and results achieved by each employee are recognized and measured and then used to change or modify the rewards to be made available to each employee. One of the major contributions in the area of identifying and developing competencies lies with their enhancement of performance dimensions that can then be the basis for a useful and valid performance appraisal-rating instrument.

In a research project conducted by the American Compensation Association (ACA), the use of competencies for improving employee performance was investigated.[4] This research focuses on the use of competencies as performance dimensions. Competencies are defined at the organization, strategic business unit, and department levels. The following seven competencies are defined at the organization level:

1. Vision/communicate
2. Accountability/commitment/integrity

---

[4]*Raising the Bar: Using Competencies to Enhance Employee Performance* (Scottsdale, AZ: American Compensation Association in cooperation with Hay Group, Hewitt Associates LLC, Towers Perrin, William M. Mercer Inc., May 1996).

3. Global/teamwork
4. Passion for excellence
5. Boundaryless/empowerment/involvement
6. Receptivity to change
7. Energy/speed[5]

A major concept presented in this research is that by using competencies in performance appraisal and tying them directly to compensation administration, employee performance can be measured more effectively and individual and organizational performance can be improved.

The Market and Team-Based Pay

When establishing base rates of pay for team members, the market continues to be a powerful influence. At this time, a problem facing those responsible for establishing team-based pay is acquiring comparable work or job matches within team assignments and establishing competitive rates of pay or rates of pay the organization feels are appropriate, recognizing its pay philosophy and policy and market conditions. The factors discussed in chapter 10 regarding market rates of pay and pay surveys are relevant to team-based pay. The problem facing the compensation professional is determining the market rate of pay for team members when few or no other organizations in the labor market are using teams.

One solution is to acquire rates of pay for jobs in the labor market that require levels of knowledge and skill equivalent to the lowest levels required of team members to jobs in the labor market requiring knowledge and skills equivalent to the highest levels required of team members.

Broadbanding—Pay Structure Design

There is a discussion of broadbanding in chapter 11. Briefly, the principal difference between broadbanding in a team-based environment and pay structure design in a job-based organization is the use of fewer rates of pay or pay grades. In developing a broadbanded pay schedule for team-based pay, the work requirements and required skills and knowledge relate to as few as three to four rates of pay and usually no more than eight. The range from the lowest rate of pay for team members to the highest rate may be greater than 100 percent, in other words, the most knowledgeable or skilled team member can earn double or more than that offered to an entry-level, low-skilled team member.

The actual determination of rates of pay for the various skill or knowledge levels/ blocs differs minimally from the actual processes used in establishing a pay structure within a traditional organization (review discussions in chapters 10 and 11). Organization professionals (managers and compensation specialists) must determine what the organization wishes to pay for work performed. Here organizational philosophy, rev-

---

[5]Ibid., pp. 26, 27.

enue available, employee knowledge, skills, aptitudes and attitudes, and market conditions will influence rates of pay established for each skill/knowledge bloc.

Benefits for Team Members

The design and development of a benefits program for team members will vary little from the typical benefits program offered by most organizations. Whether an organization is job based or team based, a basic package of benefits, as described in chapters 15 and 17, will be offered to all employees.

Incentive Programs for Team Members

Incentive awards granted to team members vary by organization and team design. Some organizations vary the size of incentive awards by individual performance. Other organizations provide the same amount of money to all team members, whereas in other situations all members receive an incentive award based on an equal percentage of their base pay or salary. In most cases, the award offered to a team leader uses the same criteria as that used for awarding all other team members. Between 25 and 35 percent of the time, team leaders receive a larger incentive award than that offered to other team members.

The development of incentive programs within a team-based environment may be even more critical and important than in a job-based structure. When using a broadbanding approach for determining the base pay of team members, pay increase movement upward through the band for team members will normally be much faster than it will be for employees in a traditional pay-setting program. This increased speed in "topping out"—reaching the maximum rate of pay of the band—places pressure on the organization as to what opportunities are available to the employee for an increase in pay or compensation. Because in most cases team use of broadbanding will result in higher levels of pay, organizations are making greater use of some kind of performance-related incentive plans to supplement or complement team-based pay plans.

It must be recognized that a basic premise underlying the use of teams is that there will be significant improvement in the performance of team assignments versus an operation in which each employee performs a restrictive or narrowly defined assignment of work. Although these members will normally receive a base pay higher than that offered to individual jobholders, the improved team performance—quantity, quality, and timeliness of output—should overshadow the increased labor costs and result in improved organizational profitability.

Currently, a number of team-based operations have been using some kind of gainsharing plan to supplement their base pay plan. Chapter 14 discusses in detail such plans as Lincoln Electric's profit-sharing plan and the Scanlon Plan and other cost-reduction sharing programs. These programs may be absolutely essential to ensure the long-term success of any team-based operation.

By its very nature, a team-based operation focuses on team interaction and support. Individual incentive plans may be detrimental to the successful operation of any team. Any kind of gainsharing, profit-sharing, or bonus plan can be related to the base-pay earnings of each employee so that employee qualifications and contributions can be linked directly to an incentive plan distribution.

Summary

The use of teams is becoming increasingly popular and more widely used within contemporary organizations. Teams of employees can be delegated the authority to make a wide variety of work-related decisions that were once the domain of managers and professional staff personnel. Not only are team members making decisions related to day-to-day work assignments, but as team operations become institutionalized, the authority of the team continues to expand. Team members are often given the opportunity to inspect and review equipment and technology to be used by the team and make decisions on which equipment and technology should be acquired by the organization. The team has the authority to determine layout of equipment and design of workplace operations.

Traditional job analysis, job evaluation, pay structure design, and market pay analysis practices are being modified to support team operations. The modification efforts involve the development of skill- and knowledge-based plans that use limited numbers of skill or knowledge blocs that, in turn, have rates of pay with significantly greater ranges than those offered to jobs within a traditional job-based pay plan. In addition, organizations are taking an increased interest in developing some kind of performance-related incentive plan to reinforce desired team-related behavior that leads to improved organizational productivity.

Review Questions

1. Can money be used to stimulate employee performance that benefits the organization?
2. Discuss the relationship between the age-old economic theories and the recently developed behavioral science motivation theories. Are they in conflict or are they mutually supportive?
3. What are the major characteristics of a team?
4. How are organizations using teams?
5. Define the differences among skill, knowledge, and competencies.
6. What is meant by a skill or knowledge bloc?
7. How is broadbanding used in designing a pay system for team members?
8. How can broadbanding have an adverse influence on organizational labor costs?
9. How can team effort result in improved organizational profitability?

References

Extensive research on team-based operations has been conducted by the Center for Effective Organizations (CEO), School of Business Administration, University of Southern California. Edward E. Lawler III, the director of CEO, and members of CEO have produced a variety of publications regarding many aspects of team design and operation. In addition to books and articles produced by Edward Lawler, CEO members such as Gerald E. Ledford Jr., Susan A. Mohrman, Susan Cohen, Allan M. Mohrman Jr., Gary C. McMahan, and Ramkrishnan B. Tenkasi have produced a number of research reports, articles, and books that may be of value to those involved in team-based programs.

PART III

Micro- and Macroeconomic Compensation Concepts

The final chapters of the book discuss compensation components that add on to the employee's base pay. Particular attention focuses on the subject of pay for performance and the opportunities available to organizations to direct and increase employee motivation to the achievement of organizational goals and objectives. This part also includes discussions of compensation programs for specific groups of employees such as senior management and how their compensation opportunities differ from the great majority of the workforce.

Chapter 16 includes a discussion of compensation practices for executives and employees at foreign work sites. Chapter 17 includes an extensive overview of the benefits packages offered to employees. The final chapter analyzes the administrative processes that are involved in compensation management. Upon completion of the final chapter, the reader should have a strong foundation for designing, building, and administering a compensation system that rewards employee performance and enables the organization to be profitable and successful.

CHAPTER

Measuring and Paying for Performance

13

Learning Objectives

In this chapter you will learn about:

1. The importance of relating kinds and levels of employee-provided rewards to kinds and levels of employee contributions.
2. The problems related to measuring and rating employee performance.
3. Motivation and its influence on employee workplace contributions and results.
4. Merit pay and the critical need to relate pay to performance.
5. The relationship between a number of critical government regulations and the measuring and rating of performance.
6. The design of performance appraisal instruments.
7. The development of a performance appraisal instrument(s) best suited for a particular organization.

Compensation Strategy

Recognize performance that supports work unit and organizational efficiency by rewarding employee-achieved results and behaviors demonstrated.

Increasing organizational productivity is one of the hottest current topics in executive suites. Managers know that simply paying employees more will not result in increased output and improved quality. They frequently find that employees who may be overpaid or highly paid relative to others doing comparable work may be less productive than their lower-paid peers or counterparts. Rising costs during the 1970s, followed by the high inflationary period of the early 1980s, and continuing with the intense national and international competition of the 1980s and 1990s, taught U.S. executives a number of expensive and bitter lessons. Possibly the most important lesson learned by top management was that a high-cost workforce not only can destroy the profitability of the firm but also may lead to its demise.

During the same period, workers facing ever-increasing costs of living began to expect annual and even more frequent additions to their pay. These additions quite often had no relationship to individual performance and organizational productivity. The strong economy of the 1950s and 1960s and the inflation of the 1970s solidified the concept of job and pay entitlement in the minds of many workers. They were of the opinion that they had ownership rights to their jobs and were entitled to every cent they received in pay.

This feeling of job ownership disintegrated with massive restructuring and reductions in force beginning in the 1980s and continuing into the 1990s. The importance of the job took on a new light. All employees, union or nonunion, blue collar or white collar, exempt or nonexempt, recognized that the days of job ownership and entitlement were at an end. All employees began to recognize the importance of cooperative effort and the need to improve quantity and quality of organizational output.

Organizations began to realize that if they were to be more competitive, they would have to change this "I'm owed it" mentality to an "I earned it" mentality. A major opportunity available to organizations to bring about this change in attitude is to reduce the fixed part of compensation packages and increase the variable part. The variable components consist of all short- and long-term incentives and awards. The kind and amount of incentives and awards must be linked directly to desired employee behaviors, contributions, or results achieved. These incentives and awards comprise a pay-for-performance program.

PAY FOR PERFORMANCE IN A KNOWLEDGE-ORIENTED, SERVICE-SECTOR ECONOMY

Slightly over a hundred years ago, large numbers of workers in the United States moved from agricultural jobs into industrial jobs. In the factories and mills, workers produced an easily observed and measured output by performing a limited number of actions, frequently repeated daily, if not hourly, on a sequential basis. In these settings, industrial engineers were extremely successful in increasing output by relating employee pay to units produced. This factory work required limited database development and knowledge acquisition by workers, but placed significant demands on physical capabilities.

Now, in the first decade of the twenty-first century, factories and mills are providing employment for less than 20 percent of the U.S. workforce. Many of the heavy physical jobs in these factories and mills have now been replaced by individuals operating keyboards that control computerized robots that do the heavy work and the repetitive exercises. Although the great majority of workers are now finding employment in service-related organizations (banks; insurance companies; utilities; hospitals; transportation; food and lodging; local, state, and federal governments; schools), the differences between manufacturing and service industry jobs are becoming even more blurred because some of the most labor-intensive jobs today are found in service industries in which clerks sit at a terminal all day, entering data into a computer, or manually reviewing, sorting, and filing forms. These data entry and analyzing jobs in service-sector businesses may be the factory jobs of the twenty-first century.

The Knowledge-Directed Worker

In conjunction with this transition from a manufacturing workplace to an office or service-related work environment, the nature and kind of assignments performed by many workers have changed and are still changing. The term *knowledge-directed* or *gold-collar* worker is often used to describe modern-day employees. Instead of using physical strength within a restrictive motion-and-time-directed work environment, these workers must make much greater use of their intellectual faculties within a problem-solving, decision-making work environment. Although the lowest levels of data entry and data processing jobs provide some problem identification opportunities, jobs at succeedingly higher levels require incumbents to analyze data and disseminate information. These workers spend a significant part of their workday engaged in complex problem solving, rather than performing mechanistic, repetitive work assignments. An effective knowledge-directed service worker must develop within his or her brain large databases and acquire knowledge of more different kinds of activities in order to make the correct decisions required in the performance of job assignments.

Because so much of the work goes on inside the brains of these knowledge-directed workers, it is very difficult to identify, recognize, or quantify through observation the quality of their contributions or outputs. It is also difficult to determine with any degree of precision how many workers are required to produce a specific output. These definitional problems place more emphasis than ever before on the work to be done by each employee.

Barriers to Pay for Performance

A number of barriers block the design of incentives for these kinds of jobs. Some of the more critical are these:

1. The work of individual employees can vary significantly from day to day.
2. It may be quite difficult to observe a complete work cycle.
3. A number of activities may be performed once a week, once a month, once a quarter, or upon the occurrence of a specific situation.
4. The time required to perform an assignment may not be a good indicator of the importance of the assignment relative to all other assignments included within the job, or of the knowledge and skills required of the jobholder.
5. An individual may interact with different employees or clients at different times to complete a work assignment, and the results achieved may depend directly on the cooperation and skill of the other employees or clients involved in the interaction.

These barriers limit the use of industrial engineering motion and time practices for designing pay-for-performance programs for the knowledge-directed worker. Realizing this, by the 1950s, incentive plan designers began seeking assistance from behavioral scientists involved in developing motivation theories and concepts.

APPLICATION OF MOTIVATION THEORIES

Over the years, many scholars and researchers have made contributions to understanding why people behave the way they do. Those involved in designing reward systems or pay-for-performance programs also want to understand more about human behavior. Their goal is to design programs that direct employee behavior in a manner that benefits both the employee and the organization. Even so, much debate centers about the usefulness of motivation theories and their assumptions and recommendations.

Figure 13–1 presents a model of a number of motivation theories and their designers, and the following sections briefly review content and process theories of motivation and their contributions to the design of pay-for-performance programs.

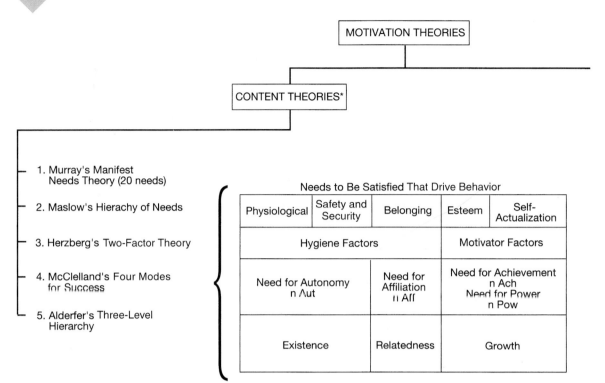

* Content Theories Based on Human Needs Satisfaction That Drive Behavior

NO ONE MODEL ACTUALLY OR COMPLETELY DESCRIBES WHY PEOPLE BEHAVE THE WAY THEY DO

* * * * * *

HOWEVER

WITHIN EACH MODEL IS A SEED THAT ASSISTS IN EXPLAINING AND PROMOTING UNDERSTANDING OF HUMAN BEHAVIOR

1. Henry A. Murray et al., *Exploration in Personality* (New York: Oxford University Press, 1938).

2. A. H. Maslow, "A Theory of Human Motivation," *Psychological Review*, vol. 50, 1943, pp. 370–396; and Abraham Maslow, *Motivation and Personality* (New York: Harper & Row, 1959).

3. Frederick Herzberg, Bernard Mausner, and Barbara Snyderman, *The Motivation to Work* (New York: Wiley, 1959).

4. David C. McClelland, "Achievement Motivation Can Be Developed," *Harvard Business Review*, November–December 1965, pp. 6–8, 10, 12, 14, 16, 20, 22, 24, 178; David C. McClelland and David H. Burnham, "Power Is the Great Motivator," *Harvard Business Review*, March–April 1976, p. 103.

5. Clayton P. Alderfer, *Existence, Relatedness, and Growth* (New York: Free Press, 1972).

FIGURE 13–1   Motivation Theories and Their Designers

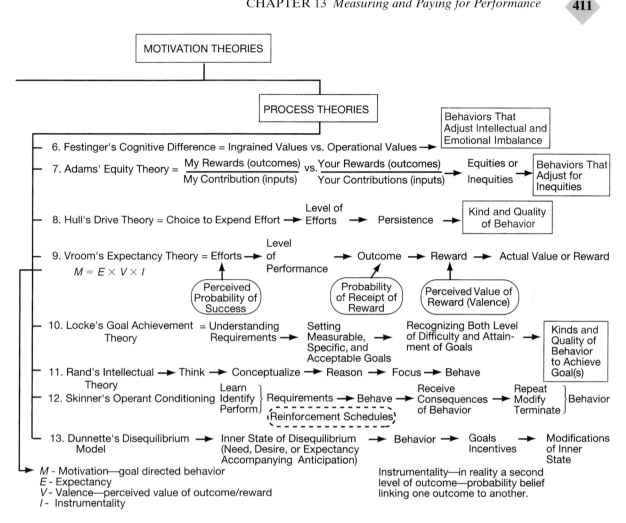

6. Leon A. Festinger, *A Theory of Cognitive Dissonance* (Evanston, IL: Row-Peterson, 1957).

7. J. Stacy Adams, "Toward an Understanding of Inequity," *Journal of Abnormal and Social Psychology*, October 1963, pp. 422–436.

8. Clark L. Hull, *A Behavior System: An Introduction to Behavior Theory Concerning the Individual Organism* (New Haven, CT: Yale University Press, 1952).

9. Victor H. Vroom, *Work and Motivation* (New York: Wiley, 1964).

10. Edwin A. Locke, "Toward a Theory of Task Motivation and Incentives," *Organization Behavior and Human Performance*, vol. 3, 1968, pp. 157–189; Edwin A. Locke, "The Ubiquity of the Technique of Goal Setting in Theories of and Approaches to Employee Motivation," *Academy of Management Review*, July 1978, pp. 594–601.

11. Ayn Rand, *The Virtue of Selfishness: A New Concept of Egoism* (New York: Signet Book, 1961), p. 21.

12. B. F. Skinner, *The Behavior of Organisms* (New York: Appleton-Century-Crofts, 1969); *Contingencies of Reinforcement: A Theoretical Analysis* (New York: Appleton-Century-Crofts, 1971).

13. Marvin D. Dunnette, "A Behavioral Scientist Looks at Managerial Compensation, in *Managerial Compensation*, ed. Robert Andrews (Ann Arbor, MI: Foundation for Research on Human Behavior, April 1965), p. 36.

Content Theories of Motivation

Content theories of motivation focus on the needs individuals attempt to satisfy through various kinds of actions or behaviors. This theory relates to a basic definition of *motivation*—activities undertaken to satisfy a need. Another meaning of motivation is the inducement or incentive to action. In both cases, motivation is a process, *not* a thing.

A primary contributor to the content theory of motivation is Henry A. Murray.[1] He identified an extensive set of needs. Then Abraham A. Maslow placed needs in a five-level hierarchy and developed the proposition that lower-level needs (needs that relate to physiological survival) must be reasonably satisfied before a person attempts to satisfy the higher-order needs (needs relating primarily to the emotional and intellectual makeup of an individual).[2] Frederick Herzberg repackaged Maslow's hierarchy of needs and developed the concepts of hygiene factors and motivators, creating the two-factor theory of motivation. In conjunction with these efforts, he promoted the idea of intrinsic and extrinsic motivators.[3] Herzberg's hygiene factors related to the first three levels of Maslow's hierarchy, and his motivators related to the upper two levels of the hierarchy. Herzberg developed the hypothesis that positive job satisfaction can occur only when job content makes it possible for the motivator factors to come into play (the job itself promotes employee responsibility, achievement, recognition, growth).

The concepts of intrinsic and extrinsic motivators added to the understanding and usefulness of motivators. *Intrinsic* motivators are those drives generated from within the individual; *extrinsic* motivators come from outside the individual. Self-esteem and increased responsibility coming from a *well-designed* job are intrinsic motivators. Pay that comes from the organization and the pat on the back from the supervisor in recognition of a job well done are examples of extrinsic motivators, or in Herzberg's terms, hygiene factors.

Content Theory Research and Application

Following up on the work of Maslow and Herzberg, R. DeCharms and E. L. Deci claimed that pay for performance could reduce employee motivation and block improved performance. DeCharms states that a task with intrinsic potential to motivate performance may actually yield lower task motivation when an extrinsic reward is offered for the task performed.[4] Deci states that he tested DeCharm's theory and found that pay for performance could actually reduce motivation in a task that has intrinsic motivational attraction.[5]

The work of Deci resulted in much debate, but Deci provided some valuable information. If a pay or incentive program does not have a strong relationship to the

---

[1]Henry A. Murray et al., *Explorations in Personality* (New York: Oxford University Press, 1938).

[2]A. H. Maslow, "A Theory of Human Motivation," *Psychological Review,* vol. 50, 1943, pp. 370–396; and Abraham Maslow, *Motivation and Personality* (New York: Harper & Row, 1954).

[3]Frederick Herzberg, Bernard Mausner, and Barbara Snyderman, *The Motivation to Work* (New York: Wiley, 1959).

[4]R. DeCharms, *Personal Causation: The Internal Affective Determinants of Behavior* (New York: Academic Press, 1968).

[5]E. L. Deci, "Effects of Externally Motivated Rewards on Intrinsic Motivation," *Journal of Personality and Social Psychology,* April 1971, pp. 105–115; E. L. Deci, "Intrinsic Motivation, Extrinsic Reinforcement, and Inequity," *Journal of Personality and Social Psychology,* April 1972, pp. 113–120; E. L. Deci, "The Effects of Contingent and Noncontingent Rewards and Controls on Intrinsic Motivation," *Organizational Behavior and Human Performance,* October 1972, pp. 217–229.

work performed, behaviors demonstrated, and results achieved, pay or money can act as a *demotivator*. Another issue that must be recognized is that a job consists of many tasks. Even in the most exciting and self-actualizing job, there are satisfying and dissatisfying tasks, but, for acceptable job performance, these unpalatable tasks must also be completed and completed properly. It is also true that some jobs have a preponderance of satisfying tasks and other jobs a preponderance of dissatisfying tasks.

Another scholar, Ernest J. McCormick, who is considered to be one of the foremost experts on job analysis and job content, reviewed Herzberg's concepts and stated: "What seems to be missing is some systemic analysis of the relationship between specific job characteristics on one hand, and job satisfaction on the other hand—taking into account also the pervading aspects of individual differences and individual interests."[6] What may be inferred from McCormick's review is that what may be satisfying and motivating to one person may be stressful and demotivating to another. Attempting to make broad general assumptions regarding the kind of work performed and levels of satisfaction gained may be misleading and possibly may even provide false information. Satisfaction is highly individualistic and situationally based.

A major dimension used by Herzberg to distinguish between hygiene factors and motivators is the *length of time* the particular factor continues to drive behavior. He noted that salary (base pay) has a very short motivational time span. An employee may receive a pay raise today, and 30 days later begin to question when the next raise will be coming. Meanwhile, the current salary has little influence on his or her willingness to improve performance. Few would argue with this analysis. Herzberg then stated that motivators have a long time span of motivation. However, he never placed a length of time on the influencing values of his motivators. The decay period for both hygiene factors and motivators is extremely individual and situation specific. Internally generated satisfaction for performing a task or job in a superior manner may last 15 minutes for one person but assist in driving behavior throughout the life span of another individual.

Herzberg's research did a very poor job in analyzing the total compensation package and how the various components influenced employee behavior. His attention was focused on base pay—salary or wages. It must be recognized, however, that his research used a limited sample of occupations and was conducted in the 1950s, when the design and administration—even the view—of a compensation system was far more simplistic than it is today.

Herzberg was probably correct in picking on pay/salary as a hygiene factor. When organizations implement an employee attitude or opinion survey that asks such questions as "How would you rate your salary, considering your responsibilities and duties?" "How would you rate your salary, considering what you would get for the same kind of work in other companies?" "How would you rate your opportunity to earn more money in your present job?" they receive disappointing results. Employee responses to these kinds of questions, even in extremely well-paying companies, are usually at a "barely satisfactory" or "moderately satisfactory" level. This kind of rating is received while questions regarding other organization-provided reward opportunities receive "extremely satisfied" and "well-satisfied" response ratings.

[6]Ernest J. McCormick, "Job and Task Analysis," in Marvin D. Dunnette, ed., *Handbook of Industrial and Organizational Psychology* (Chicago: Rand McNally College Publishing Co., 1976), pp. 651–696.

One of the best-known experts on compensation practices and employee workplace behavior, Edward E. Lawler III, performed some of his early research with Lyman Porter in testing Herzberg's theories. Lawler found that highly paid managers have more security and esteem needs than lower-paid managers.[7] From these research results, Lawler inferred that if employees had other means of satisfying these needs, money would have a lower value in motivating desired behavior. In a later report, Lawler stated that organizations could be more successful if they would (1) identify groups for which a differential need strength is evident and (2) devise selection strategies that will identify those individuals who have needs that can be satisfied through a pay system tied to performance.[8]

What Lawler recognized is that every part of the management and human resources system must interact in a positive and dynamic nature, or the reward system will have only minimal influence on employee behavior. There is no doubt that if employers could hire the right person for each job (properly match employee knowledge, skills, and abilities with job requirements) and the right person to match the organization's culture (select individuals with values that are similar and reinforce organizational values), the reward system would operate much more effectively.

Process Theories of Motivation

Process theories of motivation expand on the content theories by describing how the motivation process works. Behavioral science researchers have found it easier to defend and support process-related theories, and reward system designers have found process theories more helpful and useful than content theories. The greater acceptance of process theories of motivation lies with their implicit recognition of motivation as a process with identifiable and potentially observable parts.

To make use of need theory concepts, reward system designers must be able to recognize the actions occurring inside the brains of those participating in the rewards program. Process theories, however, provide information on how to develop each part and how to review the results of each part of the process.

One process theory, the *expectancy theory* developed by Victor H. Vroom, has received more acceptance among researchers than most other motivation theories. *Expectancy* represents ideas or thoughts an individual develops about the consequences that may result from a certain action.[9] Expectancy theory models provide these three guidelines for designing incentives:

1. The need to define or identify explicitly certain desired actions (activities).
2. The need to relate specific outcomes and consequences to the demonstration of certain actions.
3. The need to provide the consequence within some established schedule.

Possibly the most valuable research into employee behavior centers on the work of B. F. Skinner. Skinner's efforts focus on *operant* (learned) behavior—or, as he calls it,

[7]Edward E. Lawler III and Lyman W. Porter, "Perception Regarding Management Compensation," *Industrial Relations,* October 1963, pp. 41–49.
[8]Edward E. Lawler III, *Pay and Organizational Effectiveness: A Psychological View* (New York: McGraw-Hill, 1971).
[9]Victor Vroom, *Work and Motivation,* p. 17.

"operant conditioning." Skinner states that not only does operant behavior depend on its consequences but also that the environment shapes, changes, and directs behavior.[10]

Psychologists and behavioral scientists following in Skinner's footsteps increased the value of his concepts by developing reinforcement theory. Reinforcement theory sets forth these three views of human behavior:

1. Individuals take no active role in shaping their own behavior; they are merely agents responding to outside forces.
2. The concept of needs, drives, or goal-directed behavior is unacceptable because of the inability to observe, identify, and measure these forces.
3. Permanent change in individual behavior results from reinforcement of a particular behavior.

Four reinforcement approaches used to encourage and achieve desired behavior are (1) positive reinforcement, (2) punishment, (3) negative reinforcement, and (4) extinction. Because short-term incentives are designed and implemented to foster positive reinforcement, only this approach will be reviewed. This procedure maintains or increases the rate of a response by contingently presenting a stimulus (a positive reinforcer) following the response. Thus, when a stimulus such as an object or event follows or is presented contingently as a consequence of a response, and the rate of that response increases or is maintained as a result, the stimulus is called a positive reinforcer. Praise, attention, recognition of achievement and effort, pay for performance, and special events and activities serve as positive reinforcers. Nontechnical terms for a positive reinforcer include *incentives, rewards,* or *strokes.* Positive reinforcement takes the following three steps:

Step 1: The employer provides a cue (notification or assignment to do something).
Step 2: The employee behavior is acceptable (successful accomplishment of assignment).
Step 3: The employer provides a suitable reward-consequence (leading to repetition of the demonstrated behavior because of the importance of reward to employee. A reward is a positive reinforcer when the desired behavior increases in occurrence following the contingent presentation of the "reward").

Lessons from Process Theories   Skinner and reinforcement theories tell pay-for-performance designers that a reward (consequence or reinforcer) will have more motivational influence when the employee recognizes a direct relationship between activities performed, results achieved, and rewards gained. Motivational value also increases when the timing of the delivery of the rewards closely approximates the demonstration of a behavior, the completion of an assignment, or the achievement of a result. These elements of motivational theory support the concept that the most powerful short-term incentive is one that relates to individual performance, and the weakest is one that relates the individual to the overall performance of the organization. This

---

[10]B. F. Skinner, "Operant Behavior," *American Psychologist,* August 1963, pp. 503–515; B. F. Skinner, *Contingencies of Reinforcement* (New York: Appleton-Century-Crofts, 1969).

in no way implies that work unit[11] or organization-based short-term incentives have little motivational value. It just means that these two basic kinds of incentives are weaker than those relating to the contribution of the individual or those relating to team performance when the individual is a team member.[12]

A Lesson from F. W. Taylor   In the last decades of the nineteenth century, industrial engineers in the manufacturing sector developed incentive plans that were and continue to be excellent examples of process theories in operation. Frederick W. Taylor provides an example of process theory in operation in his description of "motivating" Schmidt, the little Pennsylvania Dutchman. Taylor craftily convinced Schmidt that if he followed instructions with no "back talk," he could become a first-class man and, as a first-class man, he would load 47 tons of pig iron a day instead of 12.5 tons (an increase in output of 376 percent). For this work he would receive $1.85 a day instead of $1.15 a day (an increase in compensation of 61 percent).[13] Most employers would consider this to be a very good exchange.

The process followed by Taylor in successfully accomplishing this dramatic increase in output used his four principles of scientific management. They are:

1. Analyzing the job in a comprehensive manner. (Taylor and his colleagues observed pig iron handlers loading railroad cars for three to four days. They identified the four work elements involved in handling a pig of iron—stoop down and pick up 92–pound pig of iron; walk a few feet up an inclined plank to a railroad car; drop pig to floor or on a pile; return to pick up next pig.)

2. Selecting the right person and training him how to perform the assignment properly. (As one of four finalists selected from among a group of 75 pig iron handlers, Schmidt was determined to be the person with the right stuff—he appeared to have the right work habits and physical ability. Schmidt was taught not only how to pick up the pig of iron, but when to pick it up and when to rest. The work and rest intervals related to the engineer's determination that 43 percent of the work day should be spent picking and walking and 57 percent of the day resting.)

3. Cooperating with employees to ensure that work is done according to identified assignments and production standards. (Cooperation means providing employees with the tools necessary to get the job done.)

4. Dividing the work to be done by management and the work to be done by employees.[14]

The efforts of the pig iron handlers and Taylor as described in these four steps provide an excellent example of what occurs in a motion-and-time-directed work environment.

Taylor's process, designed approximately 100 years ago, is also applicable for improving understanding and performance in a knowledge-directed work environment.

---

[11]In this context, a *work unit* is a unit consisting of a number of employees comprising more than a team. It may consist of a section, department, division, or whatever name an organization may wish to call it. Different operations are performed in the work unit, but there are criteria available for measuring and rating the performance of the identified work unit.

[12]In this context, a *team* is a limited number of employees, preferably no more than 11 or 12, working together to perform well-defined activities and achieve specific results.

[13]Frederick W. Taylor, *The Principles of Scientific Management* (New York: Norton, 1947), pp. 36–48.

[14]Ibid.

A review of the three guidelines provided in the expectancy model and the three steps in the positive reinforcement model fit neatly into Taylor's four principles of scientific management. All kinds of modern research continue to support the almost intuitive concept that workers at all levels of the organization and in all kinds of jobs believe that pay or at least part of their pay should be tied to performance (individual, team, work unit, or organizational).[15]

Using Incentives   Researchers investigating the relationship between pay-for-performance programs, employee motivation, and organizational productivity note that pay-for-performance programs have little positive effect when

1. Little trust exists in the program and in the manner in which it operates.[16]
2. The organization fails to communicate the procedures to be followed.[17]
3. Policies are not developed that relate specific pay increases with particular levels of employee performance.[18]
4. Performance ratings are viewed as being biased or relating poorly to actual performance.[19]

Anyone working with people recognizes that there is an almost unlimited number of factors available to influence individual motivation. Moreover, a motivating factor that turns on a person today can turn that same person off tomorrow. No one knows for sure how motivators work, how much of a motivator is required, and when it will work, let alone *why* it works. What is known is that a major reason an employee works is for a paycheck and the compensation package. The employee has a certain amount of discretion in how to use the money from the paycheck. The paycheck and other compensation components provide for today's current survival, growth, and recreational activities and also for security, growth, and the good life in the future.

These compensation components can in no way satisfy all the needs of an employee. However, organizations provide literally hundreds of other rewards that at times reinforce the compensation program and frequently satisfy needs a compensation program can never meet.

When properly designed and administered, incentive programs can relate to an entirely different set of employee behavioral factors than do wages and salaries. To have motivational value, incentives should be compensation components designed to recognize contributions normally considered to be beyond the call of normal duty assignments. These contributions require extra intellectual, emotional, and physical efforts. In addition to being organization and market driven, they are individual, team, and situation driven. Incentives are not a fixed cost; rather, they are an investment—a variable-cost

---

[15]Lee Dyers, Donald P. Schwab, and Ronald D. Theriault, "Managerial Perceptions Regarding Salary Increase Criteria," *Personnel Psychology,* Summer 1976, pp. 233–242; Gary F. Latham and D. L. Dossett, "Designing Incentive Plans for Unionized Employees: A Comparison of Continuous and Variable Rater Reinforcement Schedules," *Personnel Psychology,* Spring 1978, pp. 47–61.

[16]Jone L. Pearce, William B. Stevenson, and James L. Perry, "Managerial Compensation Based on Organizational Performance: A Time Series Analysis of the Effects of Merit Pay," *Academy of Management Journal,* June 1985, pp. 261–278.

[17]Clay W. Hamner, "How to Ruin Motivation with Pay," *Compensation Review,* Third Quarter, 1975, pp. 88–98.

[18]Ibid.

[19]Herbert H. Meyer, "The Pay-for-Performance Dilemma," *Organizational Dynamics,* Winter 1975, pp. 74–78.

item. By stimulating increased intellectual, emotional, and physical effort, incentives lead to improved individual and team performance that, in turn, result in increased work unit and organizational productivity. Productivity improvement can result in increased and improved outputs, lower costs, and higher profitability.

A major reason for the relationship between a well-designed incentive and improved performance is *ownership*. An incentive provides an employee with a "piece of the action"—a share of the profits earned by the organization or a share in the reduction in costs as a result of his or her efforts—not an entitlement but an earned right through ownership. In sharing profits or cost reductions, the organization takes a positive step in informing employees that they are not only key contributors but shareholders—part owners of the organization. When an employer shares its profits with its employees, the bond between them is significantly strengthened. As this bonding occurs, the magical quality of trust evolves. This, in turn, promotes employee involvement and commitment. These two qualities become the foundation for employee pride in performance and concern for craftsmanship. When this occurs, the employer's incentive investment pays off.

Another major reason underlying the success of incentives is through that somewhat ambiguous yet almost universal human desire for recognition. Incentives can provide all kinds of recognition. They act as the "gold star," the carrot, the pat on the back. Incentives are excellent communicators of the message, "We recognize what you did and are doing for us. Your contribution is essential to our success, and here is a 'thank you' from the organization."

MERIT PAY

A key part of pay for performance in many organizations is its merit pay program. The term *merit pay* has different meanings within different organizations. However, merit pay can have one critical organizational meaning—an adjustment to base pay that relates directly to the employee's performance. The actual amount of the adjustment depends to some degree on the level of the employee's performance. (Other factors may also be involved in determining the amount of the adjustment. These factors are discussed in detail in the section on merit guide charts in chapter 18.)

What most organizations wish to emphasize through their merit pay program is the fact that no employee is guaranteed an annual (or any) pay increase (thereby minimizing the "entitlement" mentality). Pay increases are made only if (1) the organization can afford it and (2) the employee deserves it. No employee receives an automatic increase in base pay by simply being a member of the organization. The organization wishes to avoid the "across-the-board" pay increase decisions promoted during the 1970s when sometime during the year, all employees received a "flat" increase or a given percentage increase in base pay. The merit increase program as developed within most organizations, however, has been and continues to be a regular annual increase of some amount to base pay. Whether or not merit pay plans are actually based on merit continues to be a debatable subject.

Merit Pay—Beneficial or Harmful?

Edward E. Lawler, one of the nation's experts in employee motivation and reward system design, has promoted the idea that most popular pay-for-performance (merit pay) arrangements will not work because they are plugged into antiquated pay systems—

"the workplace of, say, 1960." At a 1987 conference sponsored by the American Productivity Center and the American Compensation Association, Lawler stated: "If we've learned one thing after 30 or 40 years of research on pay and motivation, it's that *merit pay* is a terrible way to increase productivity. . . . The difference in merit pay between the outstanding and poor performers is so small that there's no incentive value at all. Not to mention the fact that it's so unclear how a person got a higher or lower raise that it takes an enormous leap of faith, or stupidity, for an employee to decide that pay and performance are really related." He further stated that more companies are scrapping subjective job appraisals and setting up bonus plans based on specific performance goals. When companies link bonus pay to individual performance instead of achievement of group or companywide goals, employees sometimes get an every-man-for-himself attitude that does little to boost productivity.[20]

However, a 1985 study of 16 California corporations conducted by Kenneth S. Teel analyzed the merit pay practices of these organizations for salaried, exempt employees.[21] Teel's findings appear to refute Lawler's arguments. Teel stated that the wide variations in activities and size of these 16 corporations made them a representative sample of U.S. private-sector industries. He noted that the eight smaller organizations had an average salary (merit) budget of 8.1 percent and that 68 percent of all involved employees in these organizations received pay increases within ±2 percent of the established budget. A large percentage of employees in the eight larger organizations also received merit increases within ±2 percent of a merit budget that averaged 8 percent. Teel also noted that merit pay adjustments ranged from 0 to at least 14 percent (a discussion of merit budgets is presented in chapter 18).

At first glance, it would appear that there is little pay discrimination among performers and that Lawler is correct in stating that merit pay plans provide little incentive for better performance. But before using Teel's ±2 percent as an affirmation of Lawler's arguments, it is useful to review Teel's data. Teel noted that these 16 organizations have been in existence for extended periods of time, that the employee groups consist of salaried exempt members (these individuals are probably older employees occupying higher-level technician, professional, and management jobs and earning between $30,000 and $70,000 per year), and that the ±2 percent range includes approximately ±1 standard deviation or 70 percent of the salaried exempt workforce. The first critical point to recognize is that the ±2 percent around the 8 percent average is a significant variation in annual base pay adjustments. This also means that 30 percent of the employees are receiving significantly more or significantly less than the 8 percent average.

By paying the best of the middle group of employees (those receiving +2 percent) 4 percent more than the bottom group (those receiving –2 percent), the better performers are receiving significantly more than their peers in that same middle group—the ±2 percent range. The actual variation in annual adjustments to base pay between the –2 percent and the +2 percent recipients can be more than $2,000 or greater than 50 percent. (From the perception of any employee, these differences are significant.) It

[20]Ray Alvareztorres, "Motivation Ideas Not Paying Off, Manager Says," *Atlanta Constitution,* August 17, 1987, p. 8C.
[21]Kenneth S. Teel, "Are Merit Raises Really Based on Merit?" *Personnel Journal,* March 1986, pp. 88–90, 93–95.

must also be remembered that pay increases compound from year to year, and an individual receiving just a 4 percent increase greater than a peer for 10 years would, at the end of those 10 years, be earning $20,000+ more than the peer (considering that the two employees were both initially earning $30,000 a year). Take, for example, two midlevel managers who were earning $30,000. Over the next 10 years, the one employee at the top end of the middle group received a 10 percent merit pay increase each year and the employee at the lower end of the middle group received a 6 percent increase. The employee receiving the 10 percent adjustment earned $77,812 at the end of the 10 years and the employee receiving the 6 percent adjustment earned $53,725, or 31 percent less. Now, if these two employees are ready to retire at the end of this 10-year period and will receive 50 percent of their base pay for the rest of their lives as retirement pay, it is quite possible the employee receiving $38,906 would be able to have a more comfortable lifestyle than the employee receiving $26,863. Lawler may find this difference insignificant; it is unlikely that the recipients will have the same feeling.

One of the most difficult problems related to the use of performance ratings in making pay decisions is to discriminate among the large group of employees in the organization who are the solid, everyday contributors. It is with this group of from 70 to 90 percent of the total workforce for most organizations that pay differences frequently are not made. Teel's research, however, indicated that in his 16-organization sample, significant differences in annual pay adjustments were being made. (Return to the difference in pay adjustments for the employee receiving the 10 percent increase and the employee receiving 6 percent.) By the way, few organizations have trouble identifying those employees who are among the 5 to 10 percent top and bottom performers.

PERFORMANCE APPRAISAL: ISSUES AND OPPORTUNITIES

In order for merit pay to truly pay for performance, some mechanism must be used to measure and rate the performance of all employees whose pay will be adjusted according to individual performance. For many organizations and their employees, the mechanism used to measure and rate performance is the performance appraisal system. *Performance appraisal* is the formal process, normally conducted by means of completing an instrument that identifies and documents a jobholder's contributions and workplace behaviors. A primary reason for appraising performance is to encourage employees to put forth their best effort so that the organization can reach its mission and goals. Through the appraisal process, the organization identifies and recognizes effort and contributions. Rewarding employees for effort and contributions reinforces their behaviors in a manner that increases the likelihood that they will achieve their own goals.

Performance appraisal occurs constantly in every organization. Even when it is not part of a formal system, individuals and groups informally appraise performance. Through the informal process, they identify individual and unit differences. At the same time, they frequently set informal limits or "bogies" on what individuals or units may produce or the way in which they behave, thereby intentionally limiting productivity.

The appraisal process should permit—in fact, promote—successful goal attainment. Without a formal process, appraisal will take an informal route. Although it is true that the organization has certain influences and opportunities within the informal processes, its influence and control (feedback) opportunities leading to coordinated, well-directed actions are much less in the informal system.

Organizations find that performance appraisal often fails to achieve its mission. When appraisal is done poorly, or even done well under unsatisfactory operating conditions, it may lead to increased employee anxiety and hostility, and eventually to poor use of both human and nonhuman resources, increased costs, and declining productivity. The ultimate result may even be the decay and death of the organization. If an organization is to grow and prosper, it must identify those outputs, and the individuals, teams, and work units responsible for their achievement, that will lead to successful operations. It must be able to reward and expand areas of strength and improve or at least minimize areas of weakness. Success in these areas depends on some form of performance appraisal.

Performance appraisal data and information are used for making decisions in the following major areas:

1. Organizational and human resource planning
2. Employee training and development
3. Compensation administration
4. Employee movement (lateral transfer, demotion, promotion, layoffs, and termination)
5. Validation of selection procedures

This chapter looks specifically at the performance appraisal process from a compensation administration perspective, focusing on the kinds of compensation decisions influenced by performance appraisal ratings. Answers to the following questions provide valuable insights into the kinds of decisions that must be made:

1. Is the employee eligible for a pay increase? If yes, how much should it be and, possibly, when should it be made?
2. Is the employee eligible for a step increase in the pay grade?
3. Is the employee eligible for an additional "quality" or superior performance step increase in the pay grade?
4. Is the employee eligible for a short-term bonus? Will the final rating score be a major or total determinant of the amount of the bonus?
5. Are employee increases determined by some kind of a merit guide chart?
6. Are there specific goals the employee must achieve in order to gain a certain long-term bonus or to acquire stock?
7. Are profit-sharing distributions tied directly to performance ratings?

Even the linking of training and promotion decisions to performance appraisal ratings has definite compensation-related elements—for example, the opportunity, based on performance in the current job, to attend a training program and, with successful completion of training, advancement to a better and *higher-paying* job or even a lateral transfer and eventual advancement.

Implementation Problems

It is unlikely that any managerial problem has attracted more attention, or has so successfully resisted solution, than that of arriving at a valid and useful method for measuring and rating performance. The measurement of performance is a complex assignment. Measurements currently in use are frequently imprecise and do not support the kinds of decisions organizations wish to make. Because of the many problems associated with the measurement of performance, many employees, including most union members, feel that the only solution is to replace appraisal with the one basic criterion that is relatively free of subjective bias—seniority.

To overcome the difficulties in performing appraisals, many organizations do one of two things: Either they do nothing, or they use meaningless appraisal programs, which provide the ratee with little constructive assistance in improving workplace behavior. If organizationally provided rewards are ever to stimulate improved performance, there must be a proper and direct relationship between demonstrated behaviors and rewards.

Jacob Bronowski, world-famous scientist and humanist, may have uncovered a basic barrier to success in appraising worker performance. From his research and studies, Bronowski concluded that man's biological makeup dictates his view of the world. The nature of the human eye and brain and the capacity to develop symbolic language allow the eye and the brain to provide an *interpretation* of what surrounds mankind as opposed to *absolute reality.*[22] Recognizing and accepting that what an individual sees is interpretive and not objective lends perspective to the appraisal process. Improvement will result when those responsible for the design and administration of the appraisal process use their skills and efforts to make it easier to identify performance realities. This effort will help to minimize the variances resulting from the natural individual tendency to provide a unique interpretation of reality that has deeper roots in imagination than in objective reality.

Government Regulations and Court Rulings

Employees constantly exert pressure on supervisors to learn where they stand and on compensation managers to provide an equitable relationship between pay and performance. As if these internal pressures were not enough for management to face, federal legislation and court rulings make the entire appraisal process even more complex and difficult to manage.

Title VII of the Civil Rights Act of 1964 and Equal Employment Opportunity Commission (EEOC) guidelines state that:

1. Employers must take affirmative action not to discriminate because of race, color, religion, sex, or national origin when making employment decisions.
2. Employment decisions include those involved in the selection, training, transfer, retention, promotion, and compensation processes.
3. Any paper-and-pencil or performance measure used in making employment decisions is a test.
4. A test must be fairly administered and empirically validated.

Most formal performance appraisal techniques rely on paper-and-pencil methods to identify demonstrated employee work behaviors. The information provided by these techniques assists management in making employment decisions. The EEOC and the

---

[22]Jacob Bronowski, *The Origins of Knowledge and Imagination* (New Haven, CT: Yale University Press, 1977).

courts recognize the impact that the appraisal process has on employment opportunities and the possibility of inherent bias in many parts of the process. The EEOC and the courts have played and will continue to play an important role in developing the process of performance appraisal.

A review of a few of the court rulings that have identified and defined the responsibilities management must accept in designing and managing its appraisal program indicates the direction organizations must take with performance appraisal.

***Griggs* v. *Duke Power Company,* 3 FEP Cases 175 (1972)**   In this landmark case, the disparate impact theory of discrimination was established. *Disparate impact* occurs where personnel policies and practices that are neutral on their face have an adverse impact on protected groups. Where disparate impact has occurred, proof of intent is not required. Intent will be inferred and a *prima facie* case proved if certain facts are established by the plaintiff. Facts can be established through the use of statistical analysis. After establishing a *prima facie* case, the burden of proof shifts to the defendant. In *Griggs,* the central issue was that an educational restriction on an employment decision is useless unless it can be proved that there exists a bona fide occupational qualification (BFOQ) between the test and actual job performance. The burden of proof is on the employer to show nondiscrimination in any employment decision related to discrimination. Here, the impact of an employer's actions becomes even more important than the intent of such actions.

Beginning with chapter 6, this book has stressed the need for an accurate and complete description of the work performed by each employee. In this chapter, this job content focus becomes the recommended center of the performance measurement and rating process. Measuring and rating performance based on the unique job requirements of each incumbent is a significant first step in complying with the court requirements set forth in *Griggs.*

***Rowe* v. *General Motors Corporation,* 4 FEP Cases 445 (1972)**   All-white supervisory recommendations were based on subjective and vague standards leading to a lack of promotions and transfers for black employees that, in turn, led to discriminatory practices. Of particular importance in this case are the five points the Court used as evidence of discriminatory practices that highlighted the inadequacy of the performance appraisal process:

1. The recommendation of the foreman was the most important factor in the promotion process.
2. Foremen received no written instructions pertaining to the qualifications necessary for promotion.
3. The standards that most influenced the ratings were vague and subjective.
4. Hourly employees were not notified of promotional opportunities.
5. The appraisal-promotion process contained no safeguards to protect against discriminatory practices.

The approach to performance measurement presented in this chapter accepts the concept that normally the immediate supervisor is the individual most aware of the ratee's performance and should be the one to do the performance rating. From the start of the job definition process to the establishment of performance standards, supervisor and incumbent must be involved in an open communication process in which both parties have the opportunity to identify and agree to job activities and performance standards. This process involves well-defined and established procedures that include training on the reasons for and the operation of the appraisal program. In this manner, the performance appraisal process becomes a major organizational communication tool—both a medium and a message.

McDonnell-Douglas Corporation v. Green, 5 FEP Cases 965 (1973) With the court's acceptance of a Title VII case based on *prima facie* evidence of discrimination, a defendant must only provide simple proof that discriminatory actions did not take place. For example, in employment, a selection test is job related; in pay, a "factor other than sex" defense is the use of a bona fide classification plan; in the termination of an employee over the age of 40, the termination is based on unsatisfactory performance documented by a bona fide performance appraisal program. With the defendant's articulation of some legitimate, nondiscriminatory reason for the employee's rejection, the burden of proof shifts to the plaintiff, who must then prove by a preponderance of evidence that the reason stated by the defendant was not a true reason.

By having a performance appraisal instrument based solidly on participatively established, well-communicated job responsibilities and duties, an employer/defendant can provide proof of job relatedness, overcoming the *prima facie* evidence of the plaintiff.

Brito v. Zia Company, 5 FEP Cases 1207 (1973) Performance appraisal ratings resulted in a layoff of a disproportionate number of Spanish-surnamed employees. The court ruled that the Zia Company had not developed job-related criteria for evaluating employees' work performance to be used in determining employment, promotions, and discharges that are required to protect minority group applicants and employees from the discriminatory effects of such failures. The court stated that the employment practices of Zia were illegal because (1) the ratings were based on subjective supervisory observations, (2) the ratings were not administered and scored in a controlled and standardized fashion, and (3) some raters had little daily contact with the ratees.

The *Zia* case stresses the importance of standardizing and regulating the appraisal process. It must not be subject to the individual interpretation of raters, and most important, the raters must have firsthand knowledge of employee behaviors and contributions. The entire process must minimize subjective influences.

Moody v. Albemarle Paper Co., 10 FEP Cases 1181 (1975) Supervisors rated employees, irrespective of the job they were doing, against each other using as a criterion which employee did the best work in the employee's current job. No criteria of job performance were established, and there was no way of knowing what criteria the supervisor used when making the rating comparison. The court concluded that supervisors must use criteria that are not vague and open to divergent interpretations in making employment decisions. Performance ratings that do not have a job content base have a built-in bias, and such tests must be validated statistically. Using job comparison, the process becomes suspect and opens involved organizations to unsatisfactory court rulings.

By developing a program in which, from inception (job definition phase), supervisor and incumbent have cooperated in defining the job and eventually in setting performance standards, opportunities for vagueness and divergent interpretations are minimized.

***Wade* v. *Mississippi Cooperative Extension Service,* 12 FEP Cases 1041 (1976)**   Trait rating systems can be subjective and biased and are usually not based on job content. There must be a BFOQ between trait and work performed. Data must be provided that show a relationship between appraisal instruments and job analysis and that the appraisal instrument is a valid predictor of job performance.

Although the performance appraisal process focuses on job content, another segment of employee behavior relates to how an incumbent influences the success enjoyed by other employees and work units. This second segment of employee performance appraisal makes use of traits, but these traits have a well-identified relationship to the successful operation of the work unit. To be acceptable, these traits must be operationally defined in terms of work activities and behaviors.

***McDonald* v. *Santa Fe Trail Transportation Co. Inc.,* 12 FEP Cases 1577 (1976)** Reverse discrimination is illegal. The Civil Rights Act covers all employees. The appraisal system proposed in this chapter can be used for all employees in all kinds of jobs. When critical employment-related decisions are based on demonstrated and documented employee behaviors and contributions, the appraisal system provides solid support for employee discrimination to be based on one factor only—performance, a legal approach for discrimination.

***Mistretta* v. *Sandia Corp.,* 15 FEP Cases 1690 (1977); 21 FEP Cases 1671 (1978); and 24 FEP Cases 316 (1980)**   The defendant was found guilty of age discrimination in using a stretch-out pay policy (length of time between increases "stretches out" as employee ages—see maturity curve in chapters 8 and 18) and in determining the employees who would be terminated in a reduction in force.

Because of the nature of the curve, employees (especially the poor performers among the more senior professionals) took a longer period of time to earn a substantial pay adjustment (at least 5 percent). Recognizing this fact, Sandia developed time charts that based the time interval for a pay adjustment on the earned percentage pay adjustment and the individual's age. The percentage pay adjustment was calculated by

1. Rating the employee's performance
2. Matching the performance rating with the appropriate maturity curve
3. Setting the new pay rate based on the employee's age and selected curve
4. Calculating the percentage difference in current pay and newly established pay

By locating earned percentage increase in pay and age of employee on the time chart, it was possible to identify the time period for that individual's next pay adjustment. The longer wait for pay adjustment was called a "stretch-out."

The court found that this stretch-out process discriminated against older employees. The maturity curve system that uses market data is based on an assumption that there is a "decline" stage in the later years of a professional's working life. It accepted the plaintiff's claim that literature on aging does not support such an assumption. The court also found that the performance ratings and a list of employees by "least contribution" were subjectively developed. Raters used an overall criterion—performance—to rank employees. Through a series of mergings, employees were rated from best to poorest as to contribution to the mission of Sandia. The two committees that reviewed the lists of employees to be terminated made no inquiry as to age as a factor in the performance ratings or in the selection process. No positive effort was made to see whether or not the termination decisions had any impact on older age groups.

The courts found that the actions of the defendant were neither malicious nor in bad faith, but were purposeful, designed, and intentional. The defendant's stretch-out policy for determining salary increases was age discriminatory; the stretch-out plan was not a bona fide occupational qualification.

Developing an appraisal program in which each employee is measured and rated on his or her own job requirements and established performance standards and then provided with a normalized final rating score minimizes the need for any kind of subjective and politicized merging process to establish a distribution of ratings. Once again, regardless of race, gender, or age, each employee is rated on his or her own unique contributions.

Complying with EEOC Guidelines and Court Rulings

The approach to performance appraisal presented in this chapter assists an organization in meeting the following Equal Employment Opportunity Commission and court-ruling-identified guidelines and requirements:

1. Performance rating methods must be job related or validated.
2. Content or performance rating methods must be based on thorough job analysis.
3. Raters must have been able consistently to observe ratees perform their assignments.
4. Raters must use the same rating criteria, and ratings must be scored under standardized conditions.
5. Criteria used for appraising performance must not unfairly depress the scores of minority groups.
6. Appraisal forms and instructions to raters are an essential part of the process and require validation.
7. Criteria such as regularity of attendance, tenure, and training time are usually not considered part of actual work proficiency. Because they are frequently used as performance appraisal criteria, they require validation evidence. For performance predictors to be acceptable to the EEOC and the federal courts, they must be valid and reliable.

Appendix 13B identifies and describes the various kinds of validity and reliability that may be used to justify legally a particular performance appraisal program or plan.

Performance Appraisal and the Americans with Disabilities Act of 1990 (ADA)
The federal government's interest in job content–related performance appraisal will continue into the twenty-first century. EEOC and local civil rights agencies have been given significantly more enforcement and penalty authority through ADA. Organizations must carefully examine each job to determine which functions or tasks (duties) are essential to performance. This investigation should determine the degree of skill required to perform the function (duty) and even whether or not the function (duty) is essential. To make these determinations, organizations will have to perform some kind of job analysis and job content-related performance appraisal to establish the essential requirements of the job. (See chapter 6 for discussion of essential job functions.)

PERFORMANCE APPRAISAL:
A COST-EFFECTIVENESS ANALYSIS

The same problems blocking the implementation of a job analysis program that provides complete, concise, and useful job data also affect the development of a valid and reliable performance appraisal program. That is, both are labor-intensive.

In job analysis, the labor-intensive part involves principally the time required of the incumbent or subject matter expert and a job analyst in defining what work is being performed. In addition, the job supervisor must devote time to reviewing and approving the developed job content and job requirement data. In performance appraisal, similar time problems can exist. Not only must job content be identified, but now time is required by the rater (supervisor) and ratee (incumbent) in defining and prioritizing job duties and establishing performance dimensions and performance standards. Even more time is required in face-to-face discussions of work performed, behaviors demonstrated, and results achieved. Because of the potentially "excessive" time drain on both rater and ratee and the potentially dissatisfying subject(s) to be reviewed, both parties are often unwilling to spend the time necessary to make performance appraisal work.

Performance appraisal has a strong "dissatisfaction" component because in some manner (not necessarily logical, rational, systematic, justifiable, or explainable), pay adjustments, short- and long-term incentives, and promotions are tied to performance ratings. There is little doubt that performance appraisals can be an extremely touchy issue for both employees and raters. Because of the problems involved, organizations implementing a formal performance appraisal program must make some hard decisions regarding the uses to be made of the outputs. If they are only to be used as a bureaucratic façade that permits managers to make whatever decisions they wish, then the generic performance appraisal instrument (see Figure 13–2) or some adaptation will do. The strength of this universally applicable or generic performance appraisal instrument is that it:

1. Covers a wide variety of jobs
2. Is easily and quickly completed
3. Requires minimal documentation
4. Is quantifiable
5. Is relatively easy and cheap to administer
6. Permits evasive actions to avoid unacceptable confrontations

However, when organizations use such an instrument, the following are some examples of employee concerns. From an employee's point of view, the form:

1. Is not precise enough to measure individual performance in different kinds of jobs. It does not permit the rating of performance on less global criteria or the use of job-related standards.
2. Fails to recognize the unique qualities, characteristics, and behaviors of each employee that lead to the successful performance of a job.
3. Does not relate to what the employee does; it does not measure every aspect of the job.
4. Fails to require an adequate definition of the job. Job duties that are not well established or that change during a rating period may not even be recognized.

Employee: _____ Evaluator: _____

Job Title: _____

Place a check in the column that most accurately reflects your evaluation in each category of the above-named person.

	Outstanding	Exceeds Job Requirements	Meets Job Requirements	Needs Improvement	Unsatisfactory
1. KNOWLEDGE OF JOB: Rate overall knowledge and understanding of assigned duties, responsibilities, relevant policies, and procedures.					
2. QUALITY OF WORK: Rate the accuracy, thoroughness, and neatness of work in comparison to the requirements or expectations for the position.					
3. QUANTITY OF WORK: Rate the amount of work successfully completed on a timely basis in comparison to the requirements or expectations for the position.					
4. ORGANIZATIONAL SKILLS: Consider how employee effectively manages time, properly sets priorities, and follows up on projects as necessary.					
5. COOPERATION AND FLEXIBILITY: Rate the extent to which the employee is willing to help others during peak work periods and how he/she responds to changing work requirements.					
6. JUDGMENT: Rate effectiveness in responding to problems with appropriate courses of action.					
7. EMPLOYEE/PUBLIC RELATIONS: Rate employee's communication skills, courtesy, and effective interaction with firm personnel, clients, and vendors, if applicable.					
8. ATTENDANCE AND PUNCTUALITY: Consider whether employee has a good attendance record, is basically on time, or has an attendance problem and is frequently late.					

FIGURE 13–2   Annual Employee Performance Appraisal Instrument

5. Provides little or no impetus or opportunity for prioritizing job duties—identifying the critical or important job activities requiring special effort or establishing relationships between time spent on a duty and duty importance.
6. Does not recognize situational differences that dictate what must be done. These events do not always relate to successful completion of job assignments or achievement of job goals.
7. Fosters employee beliefs that individual differences in skill, effort, and initiative make minimal to no difference in job-related results.
8. Does not promote employee participation in providing ideas or available knowledge for developing performance plans and setting performance standards.
9. Promotes employee feelings that performance ratings are based on criteria that may be hidden or at least unknown to the ratee.

From an employer's perspective, the problem is that

1. The data generated by this kind of performance appraisal instrument as a defense in a court case (breach of contract; age, race, gender, even disability discrimination) could quite possibly be more damaging than helpful.
2. The process and the data provide almost no assistance in organizational planning, even work unit or job design.
3. The instrument is of little use in identifying either overstaffing or overevaluated jobs that have occurred because of inflated and untrue job descriptions.

The job description (definition)–based appraisal process discussed briefly in this chapter is only one of literally hundreds of approaches available for rating employee performance. Appendix 13A briefly describes some of the other major approaches to performance appraisal.

DESIGNING A JOB CONTENT–BASED
PERFORMANCE APPRAISAL PROGRAM

The job analysis and job description chapters described an approach for developing a job definition. The job definition now becomes the basis for the performance appraisal rating instrument. The responsibilities and duties of the job definition become transformed into performance dimensions and rating items. After establishing performance dimensions, rating scales can be designed for each rating item. To assist in selecting the most appropriate rating scale interval, performance standards are established for each rating item. During the rating period, the supervisor documents observed behaviors and achieved results to support a selected rating score. Finally, all rating scores are entered into a computerized database, permitting the parties involved to analyze rating scores from a variety of critical perspectives.

Performance Dimensions

Performance dimensions are those qualities or features of a job or the activities that take place at a work site that are conducive to measurement. They provide a means for describing the scope of total workplace activities. Performance dimensions integrate the established requirements of the job with the specific knowledge, skills, efforts, and desires of the incumbent, the demands placed on the job through changes in environmental conditions, and organizational resources available to the incumbent.

To ensure a valid measurement of performance, a set of performance dimensions for a specific job must meet the same three tests required of responsibilities and duties that form a job definition (see chapter 7). There must be sufficient dimensions to eliminate any chance of *deficiency* in terms of covering the most important aspects of the job. Dimensions must not be included that would result in *contamination* of the performance measurement—that is, the inclusion of extraneous factors that are not important for overall successful performance. In addition, dimensions must be weighted to minimize *distortion* that occurs through improper or unacceptable emphasis.

A listing of performance dimensions must also consider their ordering and arrangement. Thought must be given not only to the influence that the dimensions have on each other but also to how the actual order of the items may bias rater perception and possibly the rating itself.

As mentioned in chapter 12, competencies are currently receiving significant attention for use as performance dimensions.

Over the years, behaviors, traits, and even generic types of activities have been used for performance dimensions. Once again, semantics becomes an issue. The words *responsibilities* and *duties, behaviors, competencies,* even *traits* may be defined in exactly the same way. The important point is that these descriptors emanate from the job and other workplace and organization requirements and that the same statement can be identified by any one of the terms. Whether the appraisal form uses responsibilities and duties, behaviors, traits, or competencies, the appraisal process must provide a solid bridge that connects the impersonal job content and organizational requirements to the extremely personal actions exhibited and results achieved by each incumbent.

Rating Scale Design and Development

After identifying the criteria (performance dimension rating items) to be used to rate employee performance, the time arrives to develop useful and valid rating scales. The desired strengths of all rating scale techniques are that they (a) be relatively easy to administer, (b) translate directly to quantitative terms, (c) permit standardization, thus allowing for comparability across various organizational lines (departments, functions, occupations, jobs), and (d) relate to various kinds of qualities or rating items.

A major problem any rater faces when using a measurement instrument consisting of rating items and adjacent rating scales is that the ratee may have demonstrated behavior that relates to more than one interval on the rating scale. In fact, it is not unusual for an employee to perform in a manner that relates to a number of scale intervals. A rater, from available observations, must select an interval (score) that best describes the overall performance of the ratee relative to the specific rating item for that period. It is here that the rater's observation opportunities, observation skills, and biases come together to form one specific selection. This final decision is a judgment made from available information. Opportunities for subjective judgments for or against the ratee are widely prevalent. A later section on documenting employee behavior and achieved results discusses the part of the process that facilitates improved rating objectivity.

Numerical Anchors

1   10

or Adjectival Anchors

Unacceptable   Acceptable

FIGURE 13–3   Terminal Anchors

Number of Rating Scale Intervals   Whether a scale should consist of two, three, or 93 intervals is a matter researchers still debate. It is common to find rating instruments that use a five-interval scale, but it is also common to find scales that have seven or nine intervals. For performance appraisal, the magic number seven plus or minus two seems to be an appropriate standard when determining the number of intervals to use on a specific rating scale.

Odd or Even Numbers of Intervals   When an odd number is used, raters are inclined to use the average or central tendency value. This is not necessarily unacceptable because most employees do behave in an average manner, but all too often the rater uses a neutral value or midvalue for rating a quality in order to escape making a decision or even to avoid conflict.

Rating Scale Descriptors   Rating scales use numbers, words, or phrases as labels to identify the degree or level of quality demonstrated. Each point on a rating scale must be meaningfully different. A rating scale may be an unbroken continuum with terminal anchors, such as those shown in Figure 13–3 or it may have discrete intervals such as those shown in Figure 13–4.

In each case, the rater receives instructions to place a check along the line at the point or within the interval that most accurately identifies the degree of the quality or trait as demonstrated by the employee. A point score can be identified by the location of the check on the continuum. An interval scale provides more specific reference points when rating.

Probably the most commonly used descriptors of intervals on a rating scale are adjectives. A simple adjective rating scale is one that measures a quality by descriptors

FIGURE 13–4   Discrete Intervals

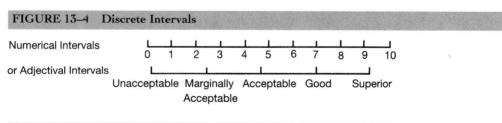

Numerical Intervals

0 1 2 3 4 5 6 7 8 9 10

or Adjectival Intervals

Unacceptable Marginally Acceptable Good Superior
Acceptable

Effort	Unacceptable 0-1	Meets Minimal Requirements 2-3	Acceptable 4-6	Fully Proficient 7-8	Superior 9-10

such as *unsatisfactory, marginal, satisfactory, commendable*, and *superior.* These descriptors may be defined as follows:

Unsatisfactory: Performance clearly fails to meet minimum requirements. (Other descriptors that may be used are *unacceptable, poor.*)

Marginal: Performance occasionally fails to meet minimum requirements. (Other descriptors that may be used are *needs assistance, below average, borderline, minimally acceptable.*)

Satisfactory: Performance meets stated job requirements. (Other descriptors that may be used are *average, proficient, acceptable, fully successful, competent.*)

Commendable: Performance consistently exceeds stated job requirements. (Other descriptors that may be used are *good, fully proficient, above average, highly successful.*)

Superior: All aspects of performance clearly and specifically exceed stated job requirements. (Other descriptors that may be used are *superlative, outstanding, excellent, exceptional, distinguished.*)

An example of how one firm developed a job description–based performance appraisal program can be found in James G. Woods and Theresa Dillon, "The Performance Review Approach to Improving Productivity," *Personnel,* March 1985, pp. 20–27. Of particular interest is their design of the performance appraisal instrument and their job rating scale and performance level descriptors, which are comparable but somewhat different from the approach presented here.

Performance Standards

What is a standard? The dictionary describes a *standard* as a means of determining what a thing should be: a criterion, a gauge, a yardstick. Standards play an important part in all aspects of life. Standards are used for applying moral and religious judgments and for deriving concepts of beauty, honor, and behavior. Standards are vital to the success of any communication program. No word-based language system yet devised has been able to overcome differences in human interpretation and perception. To minimize confusion and promote rational and logical understanding of words and terms, standards of measurement relating to all kinds of human activity have been developed. These standards of measurement provide a transportable method for identifying variations in results and differences in behavior.

A *performance standard* is a criterion used to measure an employee's performance. The performance standard may measure a defined part (when measuring a part of the job, multiple performance standards must be established) or the total job. The standard must be useful in identifying the achieved level of performance—less than, equal to, or more than an acceptable level or some point on a continuum of level of performance. It is impossible to determine the worth of anything without first having something with which to compare it. With job performance, as with other things, it is necessary to have a model—a reference point—for estimating relative value. People continually make assessments of job performance: "the most efficient secretary I've ever seen," "a topflight manager," "a lousy report." These statements imply standards, but it is unclear what criteria are being used for the comparison. Such measurements may be close to or wide of the mark, but there is no way to tell because the standard being applied is not evident.

Setting standards to measure performance is neither new nor unusual. What is different today is the need to be as objective and accurate as possible, to measure the right things, and to document the criteria used for measurement. Performance standards must be valid and must be able to support the accuracy of the measurement. Performance standards must measure results—the degree of accomplishment of job activities at a specified level. Because of increasing complexity, constant reduction in tolerance for error, and further expansion of division of labor, standards are absolutely critical to ensure that systems and parts work as designed.

From the very term *performance appraisal,* it becomes readily apparent that standards must be an integral part of the process. Performance appraisal standards provide both rater and ratee with a base for describing work-related progress in a manner that is mutually understandable. In the complex, highly interactive, and interdependent world of today, performance standards provide a degree of uniformity in the nonuniform world of work. A basic performance measurement problem facing all supervisors (raters) is that jobs cannot be made uniform; they cannot be made standard. Performance standards that mean the same thing to at least two people (the rater and the ratee) lead to an improved understanding of job requirements, job behaviors, and job outputs. In the current work scene, performance standards become useful only when they are commonly understood and voluntarily acknowledged and accepted. Performance standards provide a mandatory guideline for work output or a minimum acceptable level of employee behavior. Performance standards facilitate the trade between employee-provided availability, capabilities, and performance and employer-provided rewards.

Performance Standards at a Fully Acceptable Level of Performance   At a fully acceptable level of performance, a performance standard:

1. Should enable the user to differentiate between acceptable and unacceptable results
2. Should present some challenge to the employee
3. Should be realistic—that is, it should be attainable by any qualified, proficient, and fully trained employee who has the necessary authority and resources
4. Should be a statement of the conditions that will exist and will measure a job activity when it is performed acceptably, expressed in terms of quantity, quality, time, cost, effect obtained, manner of performance, or method of doing
5. Should relate to or express a time frame for accomplishment
6. Should at least be recognizable if not observable

Because there are significant variations both in the nature of jobs and in the way incumbents perform jobs, different dimensions of performance must be established. (When using the responsibility and duty approach for defining a job, the job responsibilities become performance dimensions and the duties become performance dimension rating items.) Standards must then be set for measuring performance dimensions and rating items. These standards must be accurate, observable, and documentable.

Documenting Employee Workplace Behaviors and Results   Practically all human beings remember most vividly things that occurred most recently. Because the performance of many employees is formally reviewed and rated only once a year, documentation related to behavior and results achieved throughout the performance review period must be made in writing. (Even when performance reviews are done more often—two to four times a year—documentation is essential.) This documentation can be an effective prod to assist the rater to develop a comprehensive and accurate view of total employee performance throughout the rating period. It can also be used at some future date to justify to any outside parties (defending a lawsuit) why a particular rating was made.

Kinds of Acceptable Documentation There are at least three kinds of acceptable documentation: (1) critical incidents, (2) ongoing demonstrated behaviors and/or activities, and (3) results obtained. Documentation may include a combination of any of the three. The following are definitions and examples of the three kinds of documentation.

1. *Critical Incidents.* These are brief descriptions of outstanding successes or failures or unusual problems the employee has encountered in doing the job. These incidents are called "critical" (or "significant") because they are the really good or really bad things an employee has done on the job; they stand out from the employee's regular job performance. Examples:

   On June 30, 1999, employee typed the entire budget report (100 pages) with no errors.
   On May 1, 1999, employee resolved quality problems in product ABC that eliminated an extremely sensitive and costly issue.
   On July 16, 1999, employee was involved in a traffic accident which was his fault and which resulted in $4,000 in damages to the company's delivery truck.

2. *Ongoing Demonstrated Behaviors and/or Activities.* These are specific samples of consistently demonstrated behaviors or activities by the employee that assist in supporting a specific performance rating. Examples:

   Always submits reports with sufficient time to correct any identified errors.
   I have overheard her explaining application procedures to applicants; she gives a clear, concise explanation.
   Always dresses neatly, presenting a professional appearance to clients.

3. *Results Obtained.* This is the final product of a project/assignment completed by the employee, or the final outcome of a situation in which the employee was involved. The employee may not have been personally observed working on the specific project/assignment or working in that specific situation, but a review of the final product and/or outcome permits an assessment of the level of performance. It is here that statistics become a valuable support for a rating. Examples:

   As a result of the presentation and follow-up efforts of this employee, National Account XYZ was obtained. The securing of this account has been a major marketing goal for the last five years.
   Employee personally responsible for clearing 50 cases during the rating period.
   Employee's error rate in processing applications was 1 percent during the rating period.[23]

---

[23]Kathleen C. Robinson, *Supervisor's Performance Appraisal Manual* (Marietta, GA: Cobb County Board of Commissioners, 1986).

In the completion of job duties, employees demonstrate various behaviors (actions). A documentation form can be used by the rating supervisor to describe the behaviors an employee demonstrates while on the job—good or bad, acceptable or unacceptable. When completing a behavior documentation form, raters should not give opinions; rather, they should describe the incidents or examples of behavior as completely and accurately as possible. The more specific the description of a behavior, the more useful it will be in developing a rating score and, if necessary at some future time, justifying that rating.

The performance documentation form presented in Figure 13–5 can be completed by each rater as the ratee/incumbent demonstrates a specific behavior or produces an output. These forms are kept in the supervisor's personal employee files and are reviewed when performance ratings are made.

Maintaining an Employee Documentation File Each supervisor should keep a file on each employee. This file should hold pertinent demographic data on each employee (address, telephone number, name of next of kin) and also contain all notes, records, and documents developed during the year that relate to employee-demonstrated behaviors and achieved results.

OTHER CRITICAL PERFORMANCE APPRAISAL–RELATED ISSUES

Other critical performance issues include the following:

1. Raters other than the immediate supervisor available to rate employees
2. Rater errors and rater training
3. Monitoring of performance appraisal ratings

Raters of Employee Performance

Although in the vast majority of cases the immediate supervisor does the rating, this is not always the case; at times, he or she may not be the only rater. Whoever does the rating, that individual should have had the opportunity to observe the employee in action or possibly to use that employee's output. Observers of employee behavior other than the immediate supervisor can include:

1. Supervisors of the ratee's immediate supervisor
2. Other supervisors with whom the ratee has had direct contact
3. Subordinates of the ratee
4. Peers of the ratee
5. Other members of the organization who interact with the ratee, or possibly clients of the organization who use product(s) provided by the ratee
6. The ratee himself or herself (Many current appraisal programs allow employees to rate themselves using the same instrument as used by the immediate supervisor. In some cases, rater and ratee exchange rating information prior to a formal performance rating interview.)

It is quite possible that when an organization uses multiple raters these raters will be observing and able to rate different kinds of ratee behaviors. If this is the case, it

436

Employee's
Name_____

Employee's
Job
Title_____

Date of
Occurrence

Time of
Occurrence

A. Location of
P. Occurrence _____

Identify Observed Behavior (If reporting hearsay information, identify source and location of actual observer.)

Date Form
Completed _____

Time Form
Completed _____

Signature and
A. Title of Person
P. Completing Form _____
_____

Items to be considered in identifying behavior (may be used as a checklist):

What specifically occurred?
Is there sufficient detail to support future judgment?
Have you described results of behavior?
What circumstances influenced behavior?
       Was there an emergency situation?
       Did unusual or adverse conditions exist?

Behavior Being Documented
       Insubordination
       Attendance
       Quantity of Work
       Quality of Work

Theft
Malicious Damage
Interpersonal Relations
Acceptance of Job-Enlarging
       Responsibilities

Other Factors Being Rated in the Current System:

Second-Party Observations:

       Remote Location
       Works Independently

Temporarily Assigned to Others

FIGURE 13–5   Performance Documentation Form (Identification of Employee On-the-Job Behaviors)

Richard I. Henderson, *Performance Appraisal,* 2nd ed. (Reston, VA: Reston Publishing Company, 1984), p. 327.

may be necessary to provide those raters with different kinds of rating instruments, or when using a job content–based performance appraisal rating instrument, to have raters rate only those items and performance dimensions they have been able to observe or, at a minimum, to identify results achieved. The use of multiple raters has increased in recent years. The term *360-degree performance appraisal* has been used to describe this process.[24]

Rater Errors and Rater Training

Over the years, rater errors have been identified as a major cause of ineffective performance appraisal programs. There are those who contend that if raters were provided with adequate training, most of these errors would occur far less frequently and might even be eliminated.

Common Rating Errors   Some of the typical rating errors that contaminate performance ratings are:

Halo effect: Rating an employee excellent in one quality, which in turn influences the rater to give that employee a similar rating or a higher than deserved rating on other qualities. A subset of the halo effect is the *logic error*. In this situation, a rater confuses one performance dimension with another and then incorrectly rates the dimension because of the misunderstanding. For example, an employee demonstrates a high degree of dependability (is never absent or late) and, from this behavior, a comparable high degree of integrity is inferred (would never use organizational property for personal use).

Horn effect: Rating a person unsatisfactory in one quality, which in turn influences the rater to give that person a similar rating or a lower than deserved rating on other qualities. (Frequently, the term *halo effect* is used to include both effects identified here.)

Central tendency: Providing a rating of average or around the midpoint for all qualities. Because many employees do perform somewhere around an average, it is an easily rationalized escape from making a valid appraisal.

Strict rating: Rating consistently lower than the normal or average; being constantly overly harsh in rating performance qualities.

Lenient rating: Rating consistently higher than the expected norm or average; being overly loose in rating performance qualities. This is probably the most common form of rating error. A major reason for this error is to avoid conflict; it provides a path of least resistance.

Latest behavior: Rating influenced by the most recent behavior; failing to recognize the most commonly demonstrated behaviors during the entire appraisal period.

Initial impression: Rating based on first impressions; failing to recognize most consistently demonstrated behaviors during the entire appraisal period.

---

[24]Mark R. Edwards and Ann J. Ewen, *360 Degree Feedback: The Powerful New Model for Employee Assessment and Performance Improvement* (Toronto: American Management Association, 1996).

Spillover effect: Allowing past performance appraisal ratings to unjustly influence current ratings. Past performance ratings, good or bad, result in a similar rating for the current period, although demonstrated behavior does not deserve the rating, good or bad.

Status effect: Overrating employees in higher-level jobs or jobs held in high esteem and underrating employees in lower-level jobs or jobs held in low esteem.

Same as me: Giving the ratee a rating higher than deserved because the person has qualities or characteristics similar to those of the rater (or similar to those held in high esteem).

Different from me: Giving the ratee a rating lower than deserved because the person has qualities or characteristics dissimilar to the rater (or similar to those held in low esteem).

Performance dimension order: Two or more dimensions on a performance instrument follow or closely follow each other and both describe or relate to a similar quality. The rater rates the first dimension accurately and then rates the second dimension similarly to the first because of their proximity. If the dimensions had been arranged in a significantly different order, the ratings might have been different.

Another kind of error frequently identified by performance appraisal researchers is one called *contrast effect*. This kind of error results when a rater measures a ratee against other employees he or she has recently rated or relative to the average performance of other members in the work unit or those performing in similar jobs rather than in comparison with established performance criteria. If the recently rated others were rated properly and their activities (behaviors) or results were correctly identified, the rater could be establishing credible performance behaviors or standards for measurement. On the other hand, if the individual received an undeserved higher or lower rating because the other rated workers were working at a lower or higher than expected level, or if the recently rated others were rated incorrectly and the rating errors can be attributed to the errors previously described in this chapter or to a lack of knowledge of performance criteria, the present ratee is the beneficiary or victim, as the case may be, of rater bias or incorrect/inadequate knowledge of ratee performance.

Minimizing Rating Errors   Although there are an infinite number of reasons why raters make errors, the first clue to why these errors are made is that raters are human. They are subject to the same problems and forces that influence all human behaviors. A major avenue to overcoming human error is education of individuals making the errors. Two educational opportunities available for reducing rater errors are (1) improving understanding of the entire performance appraisal process and (2) developing skills in observing employee behaviors and results achieved, writing documentation, and interviewing employees to provide constructive criticism. To minimize rater-based errors, organizations have the opportunity of designing information and training programs that support raters in their difficult responsibility of accurately measuring and rating employee performance.

At an absolute minimum, organizations should offer some kind of information exchange. Before a new performance appraisal program or even a new rating instrument is introduced, the program or instrument should be reviewed with each rater. If possible, prior to such a meeting, manuals or other directives should be given to all raters so that they will be prepared to ask questions and respond to the points, procedures, or issues discussed at the meetings.

Training programs designed to provide knowledge and develop skills in the following subject areas can be helpful in reducing rater errors:

1. Why the organization has a performance appraisal program and the uses it makes of performance appraisal–provided data and information
2. How to identify, describe, and prioritize job responsibilities and duties
3. How to develop and describe performance standards
4. How to keep job definitions current
5. How to observe and record workplace behaviors
6. How to measure and rate performance and make proper use of appraisal rating instruments
7. How to recognize rating errors and how to eliminate them
8. How to conduct an appraisal interview
9. How to interact with others and influence them in a positive manner
10. How to use subordinate performance appraisals to improve rater planning, doing, and control activities

Training alone will not eliminate all rating errors. A major reason for rater errors may relate to fear—the possibility of subordinate retaliation resulting in the sabotage of work efforts in the rater's work unit or even physical or emotional abuse of the rater. In these cases, experience gained through the continued rating and reviewing of employee performance may assist in overcoming these fears. Also, training can give the rater increased confidence in working with the kind of employee who may try to instill fear into the rater.

Monitoring Performance Appraisal Ratings

A job content–based performance appraisal process assists in overcoming a number of the understanding and perceptual issues related to performance rating, but it certainly does not overcome or eliminate all of them. Because of the important relationship between an employee's lifestyle (spendable income) and current and future job security, the entire appraisal process must be monitored. The computer can be an extremely useful tool for monitoring performance appraisal ratings and related actions. After all the work is done in designing an acceptable performance appraisal rating system and rating process, and after all raters and ratees receive adequate training in the operation of the system and their own roles in the process, a monitoring system must be implemented. It is impossible to believe that a program as important to both employees and employers will function as designed without "policing" actions. A number of major monitoring programs can be computer driven:

1. Tracking employee ratings over time
2. Identifying variations in ratings by performance dimensions
3. Recognizing differences in employee ratings by raters (if different raters have rated the employee)

4. Comparing rating score distributions by rater
5. Comparing rating score distributions by rater by (1) kind of job, (2) job levels in organization, and (3) ratee demographics such as race, gender, age, veteran's status, disability status
6. Comparing rater's ratings of subordinate by performance rating of rater's work unit by higher-level raters
7. Developing distribution of ratings by department, level, kind of job, and pay grade
8. Identifying departments, work units, teams, raters with unusually high (or highest) and unusually low (or lowest) performance ratings

By providing these kinds of data through reports given to raters, reviewers, and appropriate managers throughout the organization, it becomes possible to track performance ratings and develop an understanding of what is occurring throughout the organization on this critical issue.

Summary

More and more organizations are embracing and implementing some kind of pay-for-performance program. To be successful in this quest, performance management programs are linking employee behaviors and contributions to desired organizational results. Knowledge-directed workers in the first decade of the twenty-first century react to rewards and modify workplace behaviors in a manner not too different from their great-grandparents who performed motion-and-time-directed work in the mills and factories a century ago. However, the establishment of performance standards for knowledge-directed workers is a far more difficult process than that used by industrial engineers in the factories and mills.

Recognizing merit and paying for performance frequently require some kind of performance appraisal. Performance appraisal within a contemporary performance management system involves a clear understanding of job requirements and job expectations between those doing the rating and those being rated. Extensive communication and planning are essential ingredients of any program that leads to improved employee performance and organizational productivity.

The performance appraisal is a formal process that centers on the identification and measurement of employee contributions and workplace behaviors during a specified period. Although the performance appraisal is conducted primarily to rate employee performance, its ultimate purpose is to direct the efforts of all employees toward the achievement of organizational objectives and goals. Possibly most important, performance appraisal provides the opportunity for supervisor and subordinate to give each other feedback on performance-related issues. Although a performance appraisal should be fair, accurate, and objective, the philosophies, values, and culture of the rater and ratee often interfere.

Government regulations and court rulings have been applied to performance appraisal in attempts to maintain equity. Performance dimensions should facilitate accurate and objective measurement. The design process includes determining the number of intervals and the descriptors to be used in a rating scale and developing performance standards. There are various kinds of rater errors and also ways to minimize and correct them.

Review Questions

1. Why is it necessary for an organization formally to appraise performance? Describe some situations in which an organization would be wise if it did not formally appraise performance.
2. What are some prerequisite conditions that must exist before instituting formal performance appraisal?
3. Who performs appraisals?
4. Is there one best time for performing appraisal? Explain.
5. Describe the difference between trait-oriented and results-oriented performance appraisal instruments, identifying some of the instruments used in each case.
6. Develop a systems approach to performance appraisal that combines a group of appraisers, various times for appraisal, and a variety of instruments. Identify when each element would be best suited for a specific need.

Appendix 13A
Ranking and Rating Instruments and Formats

A key part of any performance appraisal process is the kind of instruments or formats used to rank and rate documented performance and observed or recognized results. This appendix provides a brief description of some of the more commonly used appraisal instruments and formats. The presentation moves from the most general to the more specific.

Ranking

A number of procedures are available for comparing the overall performance of one employee with another. (See appendix 8A for descriptions of paired-comparison procedures.) The result of ranking can be a hierarchical listing from best to poorest (1, 2, 3, 4, . . . n) or it can result in a distribution (5 percent in top and bottom categories; 15 percent in each of the adjoining categories; and 60 percent in the middle categories). None to significant amounts of documentation may be required to support the rating. Any one or a combination of the following instruments/formats can be used to provide required documentation.

Narrative Descriptive Review   This kind of instrument involves the rater in completing some form of an essay. The approach can be one that simply tells the rater to describe on a blank sheet of paper how the ratee performed during a specific rating period. The other extreme may include a listing of specific personal, job, or organizational related characteristics the rater must describe relative to the ratee's behavior and contributions. The narrative review may consist of a number of complex, critical-incident documents that contain narratives resulting from personal rater observations of ratee-demonstrated successful and unsuccessful work behaviors and contributions.

Checklist   This kind of instrument or format is the most commonly used. The actual design of the instrument can take a wide variety of forms. Whatever the form, the checklist includes rating or performance dimension and rating scales. Some of the kinds of checklists now in use are simple, adjective, weighted, forced choice, mixed standard scale, Behavioral Anchored Rating Scale, Behavioral Observation Scale, and Behavioral Expectation Scale.

1. *Simple checklist.* May include lists of job requirements, behaviors, or traits that act as performance dimensions. A simple binary rating scale is attached to each item—Yes or (1) the item listed occurred, or No or (0) the item listed did not occur. The final rating score is determined by number of items checked.

2. *Adjective checklist.* Involves the inclusion of rating scales with a number of intervals to performance dimensions included within a simple checklist. Each interval on the rating scale provides some kind of quantitative score regarding the relevant performance dimension. The rating scales using adjective descriptors can take the form of (1) not applicable, (2) fails to meet job requirements, (3) meets job requirements, (4) exceeds job requirements. Or the scale could be phrases that define differences relative to the specific performance dimension. The final rating score is determined by summing the scores of the selected/checklist intervals.

3. *Weighted checklist.* Adds a weight to each item included within an adjective checklist. When determining the final rating, each selected interval score must be multiplied by the weight assigned to each item. The weighted scores of all items are summed to provide final weighted ratings.

4. *Forced-choice checklist.* Involves combining performance dimension items into groups containing between two and five statements. There may be as many as 50 groups. A rater may be asked to select the items most descriptive and least descriptive of the ratee from each group. The rating scale in this case has three intervals: (1) not applicable, (2) most descriptive, (3) least descriptive. The final selection of most and least desired items are then grouped and scores are determined relative to index of discrimination and index of desirability.

5. *Mixed standard scale.* Includes a list of possible employee behaviors or traits. Typically, this list includes from 15 to 25 behaviors or traits. Each behavior or trait is further described by three statements that describe a good, an average, and a poor level of performance relative to each listed behavior or trait. A rater then rates each behavior descriptor statement using a +, 0, or – rating interval. The + indicates that the ratee performed better than the descriptor; 0 means that the ratee fit the descriptor; and – indicates that the ratee performed more poorly than the descriptor. Each descriptor statement is rated independently of all other statements. A final rating score is developed based on the +, 0, – rating arrays given to the descriptor statements of each behavior or trait.

6. *Behavioral Anchored Rating Scale (BARS).* Requires identification of the performance dimension that best describes total performance for a job. Examples of performance ranging from excellent to unsatisfactory are then established for each performance dimension. These examples form a rating scale, and each example is given a score. The rater then selects the example of performance that best describes the overall performance of the ratee relative to the specific performance dimension or selects a slot between two adjacent identified examples and establishes a score. The final employee performance rating is a sum of ratings given to all performance dimensions. (Each dimension could be weighted; then the rating procedure is similar to the one described under weighted checklist.) The Behavioral

Observation Scale (BOS) and the Behavioral Expectation Scale (BES) are offshoots of the BARS approach with slightly different scoring methods.

Goal Setting   Goal setting is most commonly known by the label *management by objectives (MBO)*. MBO was originally developed to be a participative process in which supervisor and subordinate at the start of a rating period jointly arrived at goals that would be used to measure the level of subordinate performance for the rating period. These goals would be job based but linked to the overall goals and objectives of the organization. The final rating would be based on the degree of success the ratee enjoyed in achieving the preset goals.

Appendix 13B
Validity and Reliability

Validity

Validity can be described as the degree of accuracy of an inference made about a direct relationship between a particular outcome of a testing device and the demonstrated performance of the individual being tested.

The three principal kinds of validity are content, criterion related, and construct.

Content Validity   Content validity provides a measure of the relationship between items on a test instrument (remember, a performance appraisal form is a test instrument) and the actual properties the test instrument is designed to measure. It shows through documentation of job data and methodology that the content of a testing procedure is representative of all important skills, job behaviors, or outputs required in the performance of a job.

Face validity is a form of content validity. It is the observed similarity between the content of the predictor of performance and actual job content; that is, on the surface, the items or content of the predictor *appear* to be job related.

Criterion-Related Validity   Criterion-related validity measures how well a test predicts an outcome. It is a statistical statement based on *empirical* data that describe the direct relationship between scores on a predictor (a selection procedure—résumé, completed application form, letters of reference, results of an interview, test results) and scores on a criterion measure (a performance appraisal instrument—performance dimension(s) on the instrument). For example, measures of job success as identified by various factors on a selection instrument must be relevant and critical to the job and must relate either positively or negatively to employee job performance (criterion) or some set of performance subfactors (criteria) and that may be identified in a performance appraisal instrument. (It must be recognized that the performance appraisal instrument can also be used as a predictor. For example, when performance appraisal ratings are used for making promotion decisions, the performance appraisal instrument is used as a predictor.) The inference is that individuals receiving high scores on the predictor actually perform better than those receiving low scores.

Construct Validity   A construct is a theoretical idea developed to explain and to organize some aspect of existing knowledge. Construct validity is the degree to which scores obtained through a test may be interpreted as measuring a hypothesized trait or property (the construct—motivation, intelligence, leadership). To demonstrate construct validity, the construct must, first of all, be well defined and understood, and the important components of job behavior must relate to the construct. The issue involved in measuring a psychological quality in performance appraisal is the ability to obtain an objective measure of the degree to which an individual possesses the quality. The appraisal instrument designer must clearly identify and describe what constitutes the psychological quality of the construct. For example, cooperation is a trait or construct on the form, and the assumption is made that employees rated high on cooperation actually are more cooperative than employees rated low. If it can be shown that this relationship is true, then it can be said that the measure has construct validity. The problem is how to get an objective measurement of cooperation. This would require extensive research on cooperation, including its meaning, its relationship to other constructs, and, possibly most important, the relationship between cooperation and the work done by employees. Accomplishing this kind of assignment that includes all kinds of jobs at all levels in an organization is quite difficult and costly.

Validation Establishment Procedures   Designing and implementing a performance appraisal procedure or system that has any chance of being "validated" must have its roots firmly planted in the content of the job. Chapters 6 and 7 provide detailed information on activities an organization can perform to assist it in developing a job content base to the appraisal process.

Reliability

Reliability is a measure of the consistency or stability of a test or other measure over time or with its use by different raters. Reliability is also defined by measurement experts as

$$\frac{\text{true variance}}{\text{true variance} + \text{error variance}}$$

A reliable test is one that provides similar or comparable results regardless of when it is used or who uses it. Because performance appraisal is considered a "test" by federal agencies responsible for enforcing legislation that relates to the personnel actions of organizations, the reliability of performance appraisal instruments is of serious concern. In almost all cases in which people are involved in making ratings, error is involved. Rater error is a distinct problem in performance appraisal. A review of the primary ways of estimating reliability and relating these reliability measurement opportunities to performance appraisal indicates the problems with establishing the reliability of performance appraisal instruments, let alone going any further into the performance appraisal process.

Three commonly used methods for estimating reliability of tests in general are the test-retest method, the subdivided test or split-half method, and the parallel test method.

Test-Retest Method   The test-retest method requires administering the same test at two different points in time. This method is the easiest to use of the three. It requires the rater, ratee, ratee performance, and instrument to be stable over time. When this method is used for measuring the reliability of a performance appraisal instrument, stability problems quickly arise. Few things are constant in the world of work; people change, and situations change. As a result, work-related behaviors change. These kinds of changes make it impossible to determine how well the appraisal instrument estimates true variance in performance.

Subdivided Test or Split-Half Method   The subdivided test method requires that a test be split into two equal parts. The test can be administered as one test. The comparable test items are split into equivalent halves for scoring purposes. If the test is reliable, each half will give the same or comparable ratings. The division can be by odd–even numbers, and the actual test items can be randomly placed or placed by any other method. It is only necessary that each part represent all types of test questions asked in the original instrument. The problem in performance appraisal is that measurement instruments seldom have items that measure the same qualities. This method of estimating reliability requires two sets of items that are able to measure the same qualities or characteristics. Performance appraisal instruments seldom, if ever, include two complete sets of items that measure the same quality. For this reason, this method is of no practical value in performance appraisal.

Parallel Test Method   The parallel test method uses two completely comparable or equivalent test instruments. The items included in each instrument do not have to be identical, but they must cover the same qualities and have a measuring scheme that permits a meaningful comparison of the qualities. The parallel instruments may be administered consecutively or after a lapse of a period of time. If the measurements are reliable, they will provide the same results. The main problem with this method is the difficulty of developing two instruments that are truly equivalent.

Tests must also meet intrarater and interrater reliability standards:

Intrarater Reliability   Intrarater reliability means that the same rater using the same instrument at different times produces the same results. The performance appraisal–related issues in this kind of reliability measurement arise from the fact that the performance-related conditions may have changed and that the rater is truly not measuring comparable behavior. This, in turn, makes it very difficult to arrive at comparable results.

Interrater Reliability   Interrater reliability means that different raters using the same instrument produce the same results over a similar period of time. In the world where performance appraisals are made, it is unlikely that any two raters will have the same opportunity to acquire and use the same information about any one person's performance.

Internal Consistency   Another issue to be considered in determining the reliability of a test instrument is internal consistency. A high degree of reliability (i.e., a coefficient that is equal to or greater than .70; 1.0 is a perfect coefficient) tends to indicate that the items on the instrument are (a) accurately measuring the qualities or characteristics being rated and (b) resulting in similar response patterns by different raters. Internal consistency can be estimated through various kinds of statistical procedures.

CHAPTER

Short-Term Incentives

Learning Objectives

In this chapter you will learn about:

1. The various kinds of short-term incentives used by organizations.

2. Various purposes for which organizations design short-term incentives.

3. The value and costs of suggestion plans.

4. Organizationwide short-term incentive programs, including gainsharing, Scanlon Plans, and profit-sharing plans.

5. The best times for providing awards and bonus payments.

Compensation Strategy

Improve organizational and employee productivity without increasing base pay fixed costs by using incentive programs that recognize improvements in employee, work unit, and organizational performance.

Recognizing both limitations and weaknesses in their merit pay programs, by the early 1980s many organizations began to review other short-term incentive opportunities. Short-term incentives are those additions to base pay provided to employees within the current operating year. Organizations sometimes call their short-term incentives variable pay. In the decade of the 1990s, with ever-increasing employer interest in controlling labor costs, the use of variable pay, or short-term incentive programs, for employees at all levels in an organization has received greatly increased interest and attention.

Short-term incentives can take a wide variety of forms. They can be a supplement to the paycheck. They can be separate amounts provided weekly, monthly, quarterly, annually; or they can be granted upon the achievement of a certain event or result. Short-term incentives range from premium and differential payments for employees who work in unusual situations, to incentive plans that pay for units produced, to bonuses for individual innovation and creativity, to awards or bonuses for achieving all kinds of desired results (perfect attendance, acceptance of a reduction in base pay), to the attainment of specific organizational goals (profits earned, reduction in costs).

Almost all organizations can offer one or more short-term incentive opportunities to employees. In reviewing opportunities for granting short-term incentives, employees must be viewed from four different perspectives: (1) as an individual contributor, (2) as a member of a team, (3) as a member of a work unit, and (4) as a member of the organization. It is certainly possible for an employee to receive more than one short-term incentive, depending on the level of aggregation for the particular incentive. One of the secrets in designing short-term incentives is to know when to provide an incentive for individual effort and when to provide incentives for some aggregate grouping.

PREMIUMS AND DIFFERENTIALS

Although some may question whether or not premiums and differentials are incentives, they are used to reward employees who make contributions beyond the ordinary. *Work premiums* or *differentials* provide extra compensation for effort that is normally considered burdensome, distasteful, hazardous, or inconvenient. These premiums cover areas such as pay for overtime work, shift work, weekend or holiday work, work that is offensive to any of the senses, or work that is potentially hazardous. A prominent characteristic of work premiums is that in certain cases they must comply with federal wage and hour law requirements. Most organizations must pay a time-and-a-half premium after 40 hours of work in a week. Practically all other premium considerations involve individual organizational decisions and union acceptance within a collective bargaining contract.

Overtime

Almost every firm, at one time or another, runs into a situation that requires its employees to work more than 40 hours in a week. Overtime is a useful device for cutting payroll costs, even though those working overtime receive premiums. In fact, a good rule of thumb to follow is that an organization that never pays overtime is overstaffed. Most organizations that pay time-and-a-half or even double-time premiums for overtime find these charges to be less than the cost of hiring a full-time employee for the purpose of eliminating the need for overtime. In addition, when overtime is not excessive, most employees appreciate the opportunity to earn more money. Today, some organizations require employees to work overtime. An employee within a "mandatory" overtime program can be terminated if he or she refuses to work overtime when requested. The cost savings related to controlling workforce growth are definitely being recognized in these mandated situations.

Beyond excessive overtime work requirements, the major problem encountered by most organizations is scheduling. Because of the potential problems in this area, many organizations take special care in making overtime policy. The policy may include such elements as (1) who must work overtime, (2) what kind of notice an employee should receive, (3) the way overtime is distributed, and (4) what premium rates are offered.

Because many jobs require specialized knowledge and skills, certain employees may be obligated to work overtime. In some cases, managers are responsible for giving due notice, but a sudden emergency may require the manager to have a certain latitude concerning overtime scheduling. The problem is to differentiate between the true emergency and managerial laxities.

Because many employees like to receive pay premiums from overtime work, the scheduling process, in addition to recognizing knowledge requirements and seniority, must also take into account those persons last receiving overtime work and those who *do not* desire overtime. One way to solve the scheduling problem is to make two lists: (1) the "green" list for those who voluntarily wish to work overtime and (2) the "orange" list for those who do not. As much as possible, only those on the green list should receive overtime. Those on the orange list should work overtime only after the green list has been exhausted. Workers may change from one list to the other at their request. To prevent scheduling chaos, however, it may be worthwhile to allow changes only at three-month intervals.

In addition to federal time-and-a-half requirements, overtime rates may vary according to the time of day or the day of the week (weekday, Saturday, Sunday, or holiday). Some organizations also vary in their definition of a regular workweek. Although most follow federal 40-hour workweek guidelines, a few have 35- and 37½-hour workweeks, and others have federally approved 80-hour pay periods. (A further discussion of overtime pay for exempt personnel appears in chapter 18, and chapter 5 includes a discussion of the Fair Labor Standards Act and its overtime provisions.)

Shift, Weekend, and Holiday Work

Most companies that require a second (4:00 P.M. to midnight) or third (midnight to 8:00 A.M.) shift pay some form of shift differential. A major exception occurs in the information systems area: Computer operators and programmers who work second and third shifts frequently do not receive shift premiums. For some employees, these nonstandard shift times meet other needs (they are attending college during the day). The third shift usually receives a higher premium than the second shift, and this pay is normally considered part of the employee's base pay. The shift premium may be a flat amount such as 30 cents per hour added to the normal shift (day) rate or a percentage increment such as an additional 10 percent of that rate. Salaried employees doing shift work usually receive an additional monthly increment to their base rate. A term sometimes used in place of shift is *turn* or *work turn*.

Employees who work a Monday-to-Friday schedule usually receive premium pay for work performed on weekends or holidays. Saturday pay is usually at the time-and-a-half rate; Sunday and holiday premiums are sometimes computed at a double rate. An employee seldom receives weekend or holiday pay in addition to overtime. When the premium rates vary, however, the employee will receive the highest rate for the day.

In its 1995/96 *Compensation Report*, Watson Wyatt Data Services/ECS identified the shift differential practices by major employment groups who normally receive such payments (Table 14–1). The WWDS/ECS Technician and Skilled Trades Personnel Report provides the data shown in Table 14–2 on survey participant practices regarding sixth working day, seventh working day, and holiday premiums.

Reporting, Call-Back, Standby, and Cleanup Time

Another group of premiums businesses provide to employees for their availability, knowledge, and job skills includes special payments for reporting, call-back, standby, and cleanup time.

TABLE 14–1   Shift Differential as a Percentage of Salary

	Supervisory Management Report	Office Personnel Report	Technician and Skilled Trades Personnel Report
	Median Percentage	Median Percentage	Median Percentage
2nd shift	7.0	10.0	6.0
3rd shift	8.5	10.0	10.0

TABLE 14–2   Sixth Day, Seventh Day, and Holiday Premium Pay Practices by Percentage of Respondents

	Sixth Day	Seventh Day	Holidays
Time and a half	97.9	58.0	39.4
Double time	0.0	39.3	31.5
Double time and a half	0.0	0.3	18.6
Triple time for holidays	0.0	0.0	6.1

Source: Technician and Skilled Trades Personnel Report, pp. 568, 569.

A *reporting* premium guarantees a certain amount of pay to a worker who reports and finds no work available. When a worker has not been given adequate notice of the unavailability of work because of weather conditions, lack of materials, or other such reasons, some organizations provide reporting premiums. A normal reporting premium is four hours of pay for being sent home without work. Many organizations state in their compensation policy that they are under no obligation to pay a reporting premium when the lack of work is due to conditions beyond their control. Some organizations have the following reporting time policy:

1. The worker receives a full day's pay if work has begun and is stopped through no fault of the employee.
2. The worker receives a full week's pay for working a full day on the first working day of the week and no work is available the rest of the week.
3. The worker receives pay for a minimum of four hours if scheduled or notified to report for work but no work is available.

Employees who have a certain skill that may be needed at any hour receive a *call-back* or *call-in* premium. In essence, this worker is on standby and must be available for a work assignment at any time outside normal working hours. Workers normally receive a call-back premium any time they are on a standby alert. Whether they work or not is unimportant. Once called in to work, they receive their regular pay and any other earned premiums or differentials.

Standby or idle time payments provide an employee with a guaranteed amount of pay even when there is no work to perform. The most common reasons for lack of work are a machine breakdown or a stop in the flow of work because of a shortage of materials. These conditions are usually temporary in nature, and the employer prefers to pay the employee to stand by until the problems are corrected. At that time, the employee returns to the normal assigned duties. The standby guarantee is usually equal to the employee's normally earned hourly rate of pay.

Workers who perform assignments that require them to change clothing, shower, or perform other such activities receive their regular rate of pay for a certain amount of cleanup time. The cleanup requirement may come from dirty working conditions, strenuous work activities, or conditions dangerous to health (working in radioactive areas requiring special clothing and cleaning activities).

Some organizations provide paid lunch periods. When this occurs, an employee normally receives credit for 30 minutes of work time. Employees who work in areas where it takes an extended period of time to reach the work site may receive a travel premium.

Fair Labor Standards Act (FLSA) and Reporting Time   From an FLSA perspective, there are two different situations related to reporting to work at a set time. These two situations fall under the titles *Engaged to Wait* and *Waiting to Be Engaged*. In an Engaged to Wait situation, an employer (typically in a fast-food operation) requires employees to report to work and, before being permitted to punch in or be on the clock, they wait to be assigned a job at the convenience of the employer. Normally, in this standby situation, the employee waits in a break room or waiting room until sufficient customer flow generates work. Not paying an employee in an Engaged to Wait situation is *illegal*. The waiting time is considered to be part of the employee's principal activity and, thus, work time under the FLSA. In a Waiting to Be Engaged situation, an employee arrives early and waits for the work day to start before punching in. This is legal.

Burdensome, Stressful, Distasteful, Hazardous Work   Offensive working conditions are those in which the environment of the work activities requires effort in excessively dirty or filthy conditions. Also included are conditions where radiation, dust, fumes, or other noxious odors, or excessive cold, heat, or dampness affect breathing, vision, hearing, taste, or the employee's general health. A recently identified problem area involves employees who must view a video display terminal (VDT) for extended periods of time during a working day. Eyestrain and other physical problems appear to be a significant issue for those working under such conditions. Also, employees who must work in what are normally considered unsafe areas such as extreme heights (e.g., 60 feet above a certain base), or where moving machinery or other physical conditions make the workplace hazardous, may receive work premiums.

These premiums vary proportionally with the degree of unsatisfactory or hazardous conditions involved. Some organizations provide a premium of one-and-one-half times the normal rate of pay for working under such conditions. In some cases, the premium is double the normal rate. One of the more extreme examples of premium pay for hazardous work is the job called a "jumper." Jumpers get $6 an hour to work 10 minutes for a paid 12-hour day and overtime for all hours over 8. Jumpers clean out and repair corroded and leaking pipes deep inside nuclear power generating plants. When jumpers "burn out"—get the maximum allowable radiation—they receive a bonus of several hundred dollars.[1]

---

[1]Mary Williams, "Ten Minutes' Work for 12 Hours Pay? What's the Catch?" *The Wall Street Journal*, October 12, 1983, pp. 1, 21.

In recent times, stress has become a working condition for all levels of employees who perform knowledge-based assignments. There is a movement toward providing premiums for these stressful conditions.

PAY FOR UNITS PRODUCED

Basing an employee's pay on some kind of measurable output is probably the oldest of all incentive programs. With the rise of the craft trades in medieval Europe and the building and decorating of churches and palaces came pay plans based on output. The fourteenth- to sixteenth-century shipbuilders of Venice, Italy, the tapestry weavers of Ghent, Belgium, and workers in "cottage" industries had elaborate pay systems based on units produced. However, it was not until the blossoming of the Industrial Revolution in the nineteenth century, with millions of workers employed in mills and factories, that major and systematic efforts went into the design and administration of pay-for-output incentive programs.

These millions of workers operated and tended machines; loaded, unloaded, and stored materials; and either performed manual assembly operations or assisted machines in product assembly. As large numbers of people came to work in these mills and factories, costs soared, requiring improved methods of doing work and better ways to pay employees. These productivity improvement requirements gave rise to the field of industrial engineering in the last quarter of the nineteenth century.

Early in his career in the last quarter of the nineteenth century, Frederick W. Taylor, a pioneer industrial engineer, recognized that a slight addition to the employee's earnings could significantly enhance the individual's output.[2] Although this concept is straightforward and simple, Taylor initially encountered many roadblocks in selling his ideas to management. By 1912, a congressional committee subpoenaed Taylor so that it could acquire firsthand knowledge of his theories of scientific management,[3] because to many industrial executives and politicians, his theories appeared to be Marxist or socialistic in design. Underpinning Taylor's scientific management was the concept that well-trained employees, performing expertly designed jobs and being paid incentives in which earnings increased with effort expended, would significantly increase the productivity and profitability of the firm. (See example of Schmidt in chapter 13.)

Designing Pay-for-Units-Produced Programs

When implementing a pay-for-units-produced program, industrial engineers first study the entire operation and develop the most efficient flow of work, processes, and methods for performing assignments. One of the final reviews takes place at each workstation.[4] Here, considerable effort goes into the basic three Ss of workplace efficiency programs: standardize, simplify, and specialize. In the process of standardization, simplification, and specialization, many jobs evolved that required employees to do almost

---

[2]Frederick W. Taylor, "A Piece Rate System," *Transactions of the American Society of Mechanical Engineers*, Vol. 16, 1895, pp. 856–905.

[3]Frederick W. Taylor, *The Principles of Scientific Management* (New York: Norton, 1967; originally published in 1911).

[4]A job and a workstation may be synonymous, or a workstation may be a part of a job. A workstation may be a single responsibility with a set of duties defining a specific assignment area where particular activities must be performed. In this case, more than one workstation comprises a job.

the same thing day in and day out. Once the three Ss were applied to the factory setting, it became possible to train individuals to perform these repetitive assignments and to measure the time required to complete the total assignment or each of its steps. By doing methods analysis and time measurements, engineers, analysts, and operating managers are able quickly and accurately to determine staffing levels—the number of employees required to produce an identified quantity of output. These time measurements also provide the foundation for establishing a variety of incentive programs.

Three building blocks provide the foundation for many pay-for-units-produced incentive plans: (1) establishing the time required for an employee to produce a unit of output, (2) determining what should be considered an acceptable level of performance in a standard work period, and (3) establishing an acceptable level of pay for an employee performing an assigned job in the specified time period. In most work situations in the United States, an employee will work 8 hours per day, 40 hours per week. It is item 1—establishing the time required to produce a unit of output—that has and continues to require much work and effort. Appendix 14A provides a detailed description of standard-setting procedures and incentive plan designs developed by industrial engineers in the late nineteenth and early twentieth centuries. These efforts can provide valuable insights to designers of service-sector incentive plans.

INDIVIDUAL-BASED BONUSES AND AWARDS

Employee behaviors that lead to improved organizational performance are almost limitless. However, some behaviors are critical, and it is on those behaviors that incentive designers focus. If an award is to have the greatest impact on employee behavior, it should follow that behavior as closely as possible. Here are examples of incentive plans designed to stimulate specific employee behaviors.

Attendee Bonus

A serious cost and quality problem that faces many organizations is absenteeism. Probably nowhere was this problem more prevalent than in automobile assembly plants. High rates of absenteeism required U.S. automobile manufacturers to hire large numbers of extra workers to substitute for absentees. The replacement workers frequently did not perform a specific assignment as well as the permanent jobholder. When sufficient numbers of regular workers report to work, there may be no need for replacement workers who are receiving a full day's pay for standing by. In addition, the absent employee costs the employer approximately $25 per hour whether on the job or absent. Reduction of absenteeism has been a major goal of all automobile manufacturers.

After trying various programs with its assembly-line workers, General Motors instituted an attendee bonus program. An employee with no unexcused absences during the quarter received a $50 bonus. If an employee had no unexcused absences in three out of the four quarters in the year, he or she received an additional $150, for a total of $300 in bonuses. An employee who had no unexcused absences during the entire year received, in addition to the four $50 bonuses, a year-end bonus of $300, for a total of $500 for perfect attendance.

Another approach used by a laundry to improve attendance is a weekly P.O.T. party. On the first break on Monday morning, all employees who are present and who were

*P*resent and *O*n *T*ime each day of the previous week place their names in a pot. One employee draws a name, and the employee whose name is drawn receives a $50 bonus.

Length-of-Service and Seniority Rewards

Although seniority rewards are normally a direct part of the compensation system, some organizations recognize long service—10, 15, 25, 30 years—through some form of recognition awards (the diamond-studded lapel pin or the gold watch, for example).

The most recent view is that seniority or length-of-service rewards should not be part of the base pay program, but rather an additional element in the total compensation-reward system. Many people (especially those in the union movement) believe that seniority is the one stabilizing factor available to all employees. It enables employees to know where they stand in relation to coworkers, where they have been, and where they are going. It makes the future easier to live with and more acceptable. It is still possible to recognize to some degree the importance of seniority through a separate years-of-service bonus and to achieve some of the other needs satisfied by seniority through improved objective recognition of performance by managers.

Referral Awards

Employees who refer applicants who accept employment and become full-time employees receive a small cash award for their efforts. This award is generally used only in tight labor market conditions; it is rarely a permanent part of a compensation program.

Patent Awards

Today, more than ever before, employers must tap the intellectual capabilities of each employee. Most jobs require employees to think about a variety of things and then relate these thoughts to work situations. It is difficult to fault the motto "Work smarter, not harder," but intellectual effort may actually consume far more human energy than physical effort, so requesting employees to "work smarter" is, in reality, asking them to "work harder." For a long time, organizations have recognized and rewarded such intellectual contributions. One way an organization rewards its best "thinkers" is through promotion, but promotion is not always a practical option. For the most creative of employees whose inventions result in patents, organizations provide patent awards. Although most U.S. organizations require research and development employees to sign preemployment contracts that give the firm all rights to their creations, employees who develop patentable ideas usually receive some kind of bonus or royalty.

For the professional who works in the research and development field, awards are usually provided for filed and issued patents. Patent awards may range from $100 to $500 at the time of filing for a patent to an additional $100 to $500 at the time of issuance, to an amount that may vary from a few hundred dollars to more than $10,000 for a patent that has commercial value to the company. Some organizations provide special awards for the number of patents issued to an employee. These awards may range from $200 to $1,000. A few firms are now offering the scientists who develop patentable ideas a percentage of all royalties generated as long as the individual remains with the company and sometimes even into retirement. In some cases, an inventor may receive royalties that range from 10 to 15 percent of profits earned by the product invented. These royalty earnings could easily exceed $100,000.

There are those who believe that U.S. organizations are falling behind Germany and Japan in rewarding inventions.[5] In Germany, federal legislation requires employee inventors to be rewarded for their contributions. The law separates employee inventions into two categories: (1) free inventions—those that are nonwork related, and (2) service inventions—those derived from work tasks. Service inventions include those kept as company trade secrets, patented inventions, and cost savings and technical improvements not eligible for patent. It is for these inventions that employees must be rewarded. To determine the amount of actual payment, the organization must take into account the value of the invention, the company's investment in development, the duties of the employee, and the employee's role in the creative process.

Suggestion Plans

Although only a small number of employees may have the spark of genius that results in a patent, within the brain of every employee is the capacity to develop suggestions that can lead to profitable innovations. Ever since the 1880s, when the suggestion box was introduced into U.S. organizations, the employee suggestion has been a major factor in improving operations, products, or services. In 1982, Oliver Hallett, executive secretary of the National Association of Suggestion Systems (NASS), claimed that a suggestion program will return $5 for every dollar invested in it. He warned, however, that it takes at least a year before the results of a suggestion program become obvious. NASS statistics show that an average of 25 percent of all suggestions were adopted. By 1991, this figure had increased to 37 percent according to a 1992 NASS Statistical Report. In 1992, NASS became the Employee Involvement Association (EIA), with headquarters in Arlington, Virginia.

A 1992 annual report of NASS based on 1991 data provided by 386 reporting organizations noted total savings dollars as a result of employee suggestions to be $20 billion.[6] In 1988, NASS also noted that about 87 percent of the private firms provided cash awards, whereas all federal agencies could provide cash awards. However, the average award paid per 100 eligible employees in private firms was $682, whereas the average award for federal employees was $299. Researchers stressed that money is a primary motivational factor in stimulating employee participation in any suggestion program. The NASS report further noted a 30 percent participation rate among eligible private firms, with a 3.9 percent participation rate of workers in federal agencies.[7]

A 1990–1992 investigation of the suggestion program within certain sections of the Internal Revenue Service (IRS) of the U.S. government revealed that approximately 25 percent of all suggestions evaluated in the fiscal years of 1987 to 1991 were approved. The IRS estimated an average savings of $31 for every dollar paid to employees.[8] The suggestion program in the federal government is part of the incentive-award program established under the Government Employees Incentives Awards Act of 1954. A review of the suggestion program in the early 1980s noted that in the first 25

---

[5]Neal Orkin, "Rewarding Employee Inventions: Time for Change," *Harvard Business Review*, January–February 1984, pp. 56, 57.

[6]*Overview of the 1991 NASS Statistical Report* (Chicago: National Association of Suggestion Systems, 1992), p. vii.

[7]U.S. General Accounting Office, "Federal Workforce: Federal Suggestion Could Be Enhanced" (Washington, DC: U.S. General Accounting Office, August 1989), pp. 9, 17, 18.

[8]U.S. General Accounting Office, "Tax Administration: Implementation of IRS Employee Suggestions" (Washington, DC: U.S. General Accounting Office, November 1992), p. 4.

years of its operation it produced $2.7 billion in first-year benefits. This review recognized a 10 : 1 return for the government suggestion program.

In 1985 General Motors paid out approximately $64 million for approximately 309,000 suggestions, while Eastman Kodak spent approximately $4.6 million for approximately 87,000 ideas.[9] Since George Eastman presented a $2 award in 1898, Kodak has accepted 740,000 ideas from a pool of 2.1 million suggestions. In 1980 four providers of suggestions each received $50,000.[10] In 1984 Eastman Kodak took a step forward in making use of employee suggestions by forming an eight-member "venture board" to evaluate ideas presented by employees for new businesses other than photography and chemicals. An idea approved by the venture board will be given budget money, space, and a manager to develop the idea.[11]

Practically every incentive plan recognizes the importance of the suggestion and provides rewards for stimulating employee creativity and innovation. The suggestion system has been a major element in any employer plan to encourage greater employee involvement. But many systems have failed because of the following factors:

1. Management lacks interest and fails to support the system.
2. There has been insufficient time to review and analyze the suggestions.
3. Those developing suggestions fear the impact of the suggestions on coworkers.
4. Supervisors consider suggestions a personal threat.
5. Some creative individuals are unable to describe or articulate their ideas accurately.

The 1992 GAO report of the IRS noted two additional factors that limited the success of the suggestion program in addition to lack of management emphasis. They were (1) failure to publicize the program and (2) untimely evaluations and lack of feedback to suggestion providers. To overcome these weaknesses, the IRS strengthened its training programs for suggestion evaluators. A major concern within the IRS was that only about 3 percent of its employees participated in its suggestion program. This number was considered very poor relative to an overall governmentwide average participation of 5 percent and a 13 percent participation in the private sector.[12]

To generate more suggestions and improve suggestion programs, organizations should always be specific when informing an employee about the reasons an idea was not adopted. Some organizations help employees prepare suggestions; others permit employees to present suggestions to evaluation committees. In some cases, a suggestion is never removed from the process by anyone other than the individual making it. In this case, it may be restated, modified, or better described to clarify it.

Federal Government Incentive Awards

The Government Employee's Incentive Awards Act of 1954 established a uniform governmentwide incentives award program. The Civil Service Reform Act of 1978 then made some modifications in its operations.

Incentive awards can be granted to any employee who proposes a suggestion or develops an invention. *Special achievement awards* are earned by performing in a superior manner over a specified period or by performing a special act or service. These

---

[9]*Annual Statistical Report*/1985 (Chicago: National Association of Suggestion Systems, May 1986), pp. 15, 16.
[10]"Suggestion Box: In Tough Times, Old Aid May Bring New Aid," *Industry Week,* March 22, 1982.
[11]"Kodak Forms Board To Consider Ideas From Its Employees," *Wall Street Journal*, February 3, 1984, p. 37.
[12]U.S. General Accounting Office, "Tax Administration," pp. 6, 7.

awards recognize employees' contributions to a significant reduction in costs or improvements in government operations or services. The awards can take the form of a cash bonus; a quality step increase, which is an additional within-grade increase granted to General Schedule employees; and/or a nonmonetary award, such as a medal, a plaque, or a certificate.

An agency head may grant a cash bonus award of $25 to $10,000 and, with prior approval of the Office of Personnel Management, up to $25,000. The award can be granted to a group or to an individual. When a group receives such an award, all members should receive a share. The share allocation can be of an equal amount to all members or divided in proportion to each individual's contribution.

The benefits gained by the government from employee contributions can be either tangible or intangible. Tangible benefits awards are determined by estimating the net first-year monetary benefit gained by the government after the suggestion is placed into operation. Table 14–3 is a schedule of awards that can be received by federal employees based on estimated benefits gained by the government as a result of the suggestions. The table identifies the estimated benefits that determine the amount of the award.

Special Achievement Awards

Like the federal government, some other organizations recognize outstanding employee contributions through special awards. Formal cash awards offered to outstanding contributors may range from $500 to $100,000. The number of prizes offered annually depends on corporate policy and the size of the prizes awarded. The special awards are usually granted to a small number of employees on an annual basis.

Some organizations reward members who are elected to office in professional organizations or who publish articles in professional journals. Awards of this nature frequently range from $100 to $300. Awards that are highly valued by professionals relate to professional development and growth. The opportunity to attend professional meetings, write a paper to be presented at such a meeting, take a spouse at company expense to those meetings, and receive professional journals and magazines is most desirable. Time off to prepare a paper for submission to a professional journal or for delivery at a professional meeting contributes to the individual's stature. The opportunity to attend special courses is also highly prized. Possibly most important is the opportunity to work on challenging assignments. Other on-the-job noncompensation rewards include

TABLE 14–3 Tangible Award Determinations in the Federal Government

Estimated First-Year Benefit to the Government	Amount of Award
Up to $10,000	10 percent of the estimated benefit (total possible $1,000)
$10,001 to $100,000	$1,000 for the first $10,000 plus 3 percent of the benefits over $10,000
$100,001 or more	$3,700 for the first $100,000 plus 0.5 percent of the benefits over $100,000
	Maximum award of $25,000 for benefit of $4,360.00 ($25,000 is the maximum award authorized by OPM)

better office space and equipment, increased technical or clerical assistance, and more influence over budget decisions.

The professional employee frequently looks outside the organization for growth and reward opportunities. Additional education, visibility at professional meetings and in professional journals, opportunities to participate in unusual or critical projects—all have very definite long-term monetary value to the professionals. This kind of professional growth may not only influence pay increase and promotion opportunities on the present job, but also lead to offers of better jobs in other organizations.

Contest Bonuses

Many organizations develop contests, games, or promotions to stimulate extra effort. These special goals may focus on productivity or quality improvement; development of a better safety record; or reduction of costs, absenteeism, or tardiness.

Most contests encourage some type of individual effort and foster a spirit of competition. Quite often, organizations design and implement contests to overcome boredom and offer the winners certain "bragging rights." The prizes offered to stimulate the special effort include merchandise, cash premiums, special trips, and even time off. Quite often, the prizes focus on rewards of interest to other family members (particularly the spouse). Recognition of the influence of the spouse assists in gaining greater interest in winning a particular premium.

The major difficulty with such contests is that in the design phase organizations fail to consider the full effect a contest may have. Quite often, contests have unanticipated results from misdirected efforts that produce unhealthy side effects. It is essential before implementing a contest that organizations attempt to identify and recognize its impact on overall objectives.[13]

Special Awards at IBM

To reinforce a desired, demonstrated employee behavior, employers recognize that the behavior should receive prompt recognition. Many organizations now offer a variety of one-time incentive awards that focus on the results of a particularly meritorious employee behavior.

An excellent example of this type of program was the awards plan used by IBM in the 1970s to recognize significant performance by an employee.[14] These one-time awards were in addition to any incentive or merit increase program that was part of the normal compensation program for IBM employees.

The IBM award plan had three distinct parts. The first recognized accomplishment at the local level. This award, called the IBM Informal Award Plan, allowed the immediate supervisor, with approval from the next highest level of management, to recognize an employee's exceptional diligence or contribution to a higher-level award (when that contribution was not significant enough to allow that employee to participate in the higher-level award). Cash bonuses were the most common of the informal awards. The informal award had a value limit of $1,500.

[13]David R. Hampton, "Contests as Misdirected Motivators," *Compensation Review*, Second Quarter, 1970, pp. 32–38.
[14]This information was provided by James M. Bridgman at the Eastern Regional Meeting of the American Compensation Association, Atlanta, GA, May 13, 1977.

One of the favorite awards, however, was what management in some areas called "Dinner for Two." By making this impromptu award, the immediate supervisor not only had opportunity to pat an employee on the back with some type of verbal praise but could say, "Thanks a lot for that splendid effort. Would you take your spouse out to dinner and send me the bill?"

The second category was the Outstanding Contribution Plan designed to recognize achievement of outstanding value to IBM. This plan had two parts. One was the Outstanding Innovation Award Plan that rewarded innovativeness and creativity resulting in outstanding economic or prestige value to IBM. The second was the IBM Division Award that recognized achievements having an economic, commercial, or industrial value. It was primarily nontechnical. The awards ranged from $2,500 to $20,000, with approximately 60 percent ranging from $2,500 to $5,000; 35 percent from $5,000 to $10,000; and the remaining 5 percent, up to $20,000.

The final category was the Corporate Award by which IBM recognized a previous outstanding contribution that was of extraordinary significance to IBM. These awards were almost totally technical and provided at least $10,000 to the recipient. They were made annually at a Corporate Recognition Event banquet. This company spent approximately $8 to $10 million a year on all three categories of award plans.

Few employers have the need or the opportunity to provide an incentive plan like that of IBM, but the basic philosophy is valuable and useful to every employer. An intrinsic reward every worker receives from working is recognition of a job well done. Everyone enjoys the feeling of being wanted, being a member of a select, successful group, being appreciated, and being able to make a contribution that enhances the opportunity for success of all the group members. There are still those who argue that money has a negative impact on the intrinsic rewards an employee receives in performing a job. However, what better way does an employer have to recognize above-average effort or exceptional contributions than to publicly provide a monetary or in-kind payment (dinner for two) that clearly demonstrates to all employees how much the organization values performance? To further promote employee participation and recognize contributions, IBM also had a strong suggestion program. In 1982, IBM received almost 213,000 employee suggestions and made award payments in excess of $12 million.[15]

AGGREGATING EMPLOYEES FOR INCENTIVE OPPORTUNITIES

A 1990 study of executive compensation by The Conference Board[16] revealed that almost all companies in all industries except insurance and utilities have incentive plans for their executives. Another study conducted in 1985 by The Hay Group revealed the spread of incentive plans from a typical manufacturing setting to use by banks, hospitals, and utilities. Incentive opportunities were provided not only to top managers and sales representatives, but also to middle managers, key professionals, and technical staff.[17]

---

[15]*Annual Statistical Report/1982* (Chicago: National Association of Suggestion Systems, 1983), p. 14.
[16]Elizabeth R. Arreglado, *Top Executive Compensation*, 1991 Edition (New York: The Conference Board, 1991), p. 13.
[17]Lance A. Berger and Thomas E. Tice, "Incentives: The Strategic Side of Compensation Planning," *Journal of Compensation and Benefits*, May–June 1986, pp. 325–329.

The Conference Board noted that the median CEO bonus for 1990 was approximately 50 percent of salary.[18] Like most other movements in the field of compensation, placing more of the executive total compensation package into variable components has a base in the historical development of the industrial empires of the late nineteenth and early twentieth centuries.

Until the late 1920s, executive compensation was basically a private affair between the board of directors and the involved executives. It was not unusual for the full board to delegate to the chairman authority to determine executive bonuses, with shareholders having practically no voice in any such actions. Executives in major corporations would often have relatively low base pay but extremely high annual bonuses. An example is the 1929 managerial profit-sharing plan for the president of Bethlehem Steel. Eugene G. Grace, president, received a salary of $12,000 and a bonus of $1,623,753.[19]

In various industries and organizations and for some employees, short-term incentive plans are thriving. For decades, many top managers have received a large percentage of their total compensation in the form of short- and long-term incentives. In some cases, the value of the incentive packages exceeds the annual salaries of these top executives. It is not unusual for executives to receive short-term bonuses equal to 50 percent of base pay and for other senior managers to receive bonuses equaling 25 to 50 percent of base pay. Prior to the 1980s, these kinds of incentive payments were restricted to senior management positions. Beginning in the early 1980s, however, short-term incentive programs began to descend through the management structure, and by the mid-1980s, considerable thought and effort focused on the development of variable-pay incentive programs for all employees.

However, the major recipients of short-term incentives continue to be the senior managers—the top 1 to 5 percent of the workforce who are responsible for providing overall direction and leadership for the organization. Different companies have different ways of identifying those eligible for managerial bonus plans. It can be by salary (all members having annual salaries greater than $125,000), or pay grade (all employees in pay grade 25 and above), or level in the organization (top three levels in the organization's hierarchy).

The size of the bonus pool from which management short-term incentives are taken is normally determined by some form of profit measurement. Measures used to determine the amount of the short-term incentive pool vary by organization, but many of the formula-driven plans use one or more of the following measurement dimensions:

1. Profit before taxes
2. Profit after taxes [profit for fiscal year after payment (allowance) for federal, state, and local taxes]
3. Return on equity: $\dfrac{\text{profit after taxes}}{\text{stock}}$
4. Return on invested capital: $\dfrac{\text{profit after taxes}}{\text{all paid-in capital plus all retained earnings}}$

The amount of the bonus is normally established as a percentage of base pay. This percentage is usually called the target award. If the organization achieves more profit

[18]Arreglado, *Top Executive Compensation*, p. 18.
[19]"Salary $12,000, Bonus $1,623,753," *The Literary Digest*, August 9, 1930, p. 10.

than expected with any accompanying increase in the bonus pool, the award can increase above the target. In a very profitable year, a short-term incentive award can increase by 1.5 to 2 times the target award. If profit drops below expectations, the actual bonus can drop to zero. The final bonus payment received by an executive can vary based on the individual's performance and, for a division executive, the performance of the assigned division.[20] Some organizations currently combine senior management performance with corporate performance in determining the amount of the short-term bonus. An example of how this program operates is through the use of a performance matrix in which the rows recognize personal contributions and the columns relate to corporate performance. (See Figure 14–1.)

Short-Term Incentives at TRW

During the 1980s, TRW, a major manufacturer of aerospace equipment, computers, and other products, had a three-level managerial short-term incentive plan. Level One included approximately 150 employees ranging from the CEO and vice president to division managers. Level Two, the Management Incentive Compensation Program (MICP), included 1,100 middle managers. Level 3 was a Management Bonus Plan (MBP) for all lower-middle-level managers, including plant managers.[21] An attitude survey of the 1,100 managers involved in the MICP provided some disturbing results to the top executives and designers of the TRW compensation program. Responses to the following attitude survey questions prompted management concern:

1. Does TRW have methods for measuring performance that are consistent with broad strategy? Only 34 percent of the responses were favorable.
2. Does the incentive compensation plan reward managers for success during economic downturns? Thirty-eight percent of the responses were favorable.
3. Does TRW pay off on financial versus nonfinancial objectives? Seventy-five percent of responses said yes to payoff on financial objectives, whereas 56 percent responded yes to payoff on nonfinancial objectives.

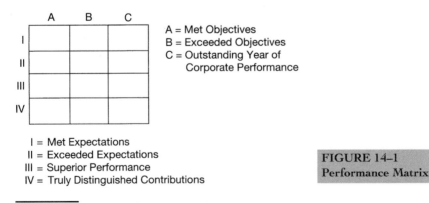

A = Met Objectives
B = Exceeded Objectives
C = Outstanding Year of Corporate Performance

I = Met Expectations
II = Exceeded Expectations
III = Superior Performance
IV = Truly Distinguished Contributions

FIGURE 14–1
Performance Matrix

---

[20]There is an excellent description of executive short-term incentives in Graef S. Crystal, *Questions and Answers on Executive Compensation* (Englewood Cliffs, NJ: Prentice-Hall, 1984), pp. 27–54.
[21]"Incentive Compensation for Middle Managers," *Personnel Management Compensation* (Englewood Cliffs, NJ: Prentice-Hall, June 11, 1986), pp. 6, 7.

4. Does TRW pay off on long-term and short-term goals? Eighty-seven percent of responses said yes to pay off on short-term goals, but only 25 percent said yes to pay off on short- and long-term goals.

Following the results of the survey and after conducting an in-depth review of general management systems, the company recognized a need to change the bases on which individual performance was measured relative to rewards granted. Individual performance had to be linked to long-term goals rather than annual short-term goals. A three-phase plan was then designed to achieve this goal: (1) a goal phase, (2) a performance appraisal phase, and (3) a reward decision phase. Possibly TRW officials agreed with Peter Drucker, a recognized management expert, who states: "Short-term earnings are quite unreliable, indeed grossly misleading, as measurements of a company's actual performance."[22]

Short-Term Incentives at AT&T

For a number of years prior to deregulation, AT&T and a number of its operating companies had instituted two pay-at-risk programs for its managers—an Individual Incentive Award (IIA) or Special Merit Award, and a Management Team Incentive Award (MTIA). The two programs were designed to change the managerial annual pay increase program from one that was primarily an across-the-board increase that folded into base pay to one that recognized performance and had to be earned each year. In 1986, when AT&T and the now independent regional operating companies negotiated with their unionized employees, a Team Incentive Award (TIA) appeared in a number of the contracts.

The IIA provided a lump-sum bonus to outstanding performers. From 3 to 25 percent of the managerial workforce was eligible. A specific percentage of employees was eligible at each pay grade or level of management (levels of management ascend from first to seventh level). Each grade or level was treated separately, and no IIA money was transferred from one level to another. In conjunction with this program, pay ranges were narrowed to shift the focus from increase in base pay to the one-shot bonus for excellence in performance. The lump-sum bonus was determined by the recipient level or pay grade (a first-level manager could be eligible for a bonus equaling 15 percent of base pay, whereas a fourth-level manager could be eligible for a bonus that equaled 30 percent of base pay). At the lower pay levels, 5 percent of the employee's pay was at risk, whereas at the upper levels, it was 20 percent. Individual performance ratings determined who were considered outstanding performers. Considerable documentation had to accompany an outstanding rating. MTIAs were granted to members of specific divisions or units. Appropriate division or unit goals were established at the beginning of the year. The goals included department service objectives and interdepartmental goals. Goal attainment results were published monthly.

An example of the 1986 TIA is the one negotiated between Bell South and the Communication Workers of America. The TIA called for a standard amount equivalent to 1.5 percent of wages (plus overtime) to be paid March 1, 1987, 1988, and 1989,

---

[22]Peter F. Drucker, "If Earnings Aren't the Dial to Read," *The Wall Street Journal,* October 30, 1986, p. 32.

based on the performance of the previous year. The standard amount was multiplied in accordance with corporate performance.[23]

ORGANIZATIONWIDE SHORT-TERM INCENTIVES

Possibly the easiest kind of incentive program to implement is one that includes everyone in the organization. Other than pay for output, these are the oldest of all incentive plans. For various reasons, organizations must generate broad indicators of performance that can be used to establish organizationwide incentive programs. Such indicators are profit, costs, sales, return on investment, return on assets, or the change in any of these indicators from one year to the next. Using these indicators and board of directors/top executive decisions, bonus pools can be established with various formulas to determine the actual payments to each participant.

Over the years, a variety of productivity improvement programs have focused on increasing profits or reducing costs. These plans allow the employee to share with the employer any benefits gained from improved profits or a reduction in costs. The philosophy underlying this type of program is that profit sharing and cost reduction are both an opportunity and the responsibility of every member of the organization. If responsibility for profit sharing and cost reduction has organizationwide acceptance and if each member seizes every opportunity to reduce costs, an employer can meet almost any competitive challenge, grant job security to each member, and provide high rewards for work efforts.

Productivity Gainsharing Programs

In recent years, a new term that has caught the fancy of many authors writing in the area of productivity improvement has been *productivity gainsharing*. (It is interesting to note that by 1895, Frederick A. Halsey was extolling the use of "gainsharing" to improve productivity in the industrial sector.) Productivity gainsharing is basically a sharing by the organization with employees of "bottom-line" improvements obtained through increased productivity. Gainsharing in this approach involves all or a significant number of employees in some kind of group sharing and total employee involvement. The purpose is to encourage employee involvement and commitment to improving the performance of the organization.

Each member has the opportunity to conserve both human and material resources. In addition, through the constructive use of innovation and creativity, better ways can be found to perform existing operations. By tapping the ingenuity of the entire workforce, it is possible to reduce costs through elimination of wasted materials and labor and also to develop new or better goods or services that strengthen the company and increase job security. Each cost-reduction plan provides a formula through which workers receive a share of the money saved as a result of improvements in work practices.

A first requirement for a gainsharing plan is determination of a standard measure of performance. Once management and the workforce agree to a standard, it is possible to compare actual performance with the standard. The difference between the two is at-

---

[23]Information on AT&T and Bell South Incentive Plans obtained from "Putting Pay At Risk," *Personnel Management–Compensation,* Prentice-Hall, Inc., July 9, 1986, pp. 2–4, and "Bargaining '86," *A Joint CWA–Bell South Bulletin,* No. 15, August 13, 1986.

tributed to the efforts of both workers and management. Because both groups have a direct impact on cost reduction, most gainsharing plans call for a sharing of savings. Some plans provide for a 50–50 split; others, 67–33; and some may require that 75 percent of the total savings go back to the workers and that 25 percent remain with the company.

To be successful, a gainsharing plan must have the complete support of senior management. Beyond mere approval of plan development and implementation, senior management must be certain that the plan is well conceived and executed. A gainsharing plan must relate business objectives to the standards identified as improvement targets. It must recognize the need to provide data that may, in the past, have been considered top secret. The plan must consider the variables that affect these standards and the way they will be managed when they change sufficiently to have an impact on the credibility or the viability of the plan. Some of the variables that can have an influence on the operation of a gainsharing plan are these:

1. New machinery or other technological changes
2. Changes in methods, procedures, or processes
3. Product mix
4. Raw material availability, quality, and cost
5. Labor cost
6. Customer service requirements
7. Delivery procedures
8. Inventory policy
9. Sales price of good or service
10. Financing and funding patterns

To develop a plan that has a chance to survive, thoughtful and lengthy planning must precede implementation. A review of the Scanlon Plan, a well-known cost-reduction (gainsharing) plan, provides insight into the underlying philosophy and basic design of gainsharing plans. Appendix 14B provides examples of two other kinds of gainsharing plans—the Rucker plan and the Improshare plan.

Scanlon Plan

In the late 1930s, Joseph N. Scanlon, then president of the local union at Empire Steel & Tin Plate Company in Mansfield, Ohio, developed a union–management cooperation plan that provided the concepts underlying what was to become known as the *Scanlon Plan.*[24] Scanlon's philosophy was that if the company would foster and use employee ideas and suggestions and, in turn, reward employees for their constructive efforts, the company would improve profitability and workers would gain through steady employment and increased pay. The plan as it is known today took shape in 1944 when Scanlon, who was then employed by the United Steelworkers as director of their production-engineering department, worked with the Adamson Company to improve its productivity. At Adamson, the bonus was added to his concept. In the first year of its operation at Adamson, workers received bonuses that increased their frozen pay by 41 percent, and the company stated that its profits were increased by 2.5 times what they would have been without the plan.

---

[24]Frederick G. Lesieur, ed., *The Scanlon Plan . . . A Frontier in Labor Management Cooperation* (Cambridge, MA: MIT Press, 1958).

The original plan developed by Scanlon required good management, mutual respect, integrity, and trust on the part of both management and labor, and a strong labor force that recognized its responsibilities for making its business stronger and more competitive. An ideal Scanlon Plan would include every member of the business, but among its many variations, it may include all production employees, all nonexempt employees, or all employees up to a certain level of management. Normally, once implemented, it is the only pay-for-performance plan operating in the business.

The basic elements of the Scanlon Plan are:

1. The ratio
2. The bonus
3. The production committee
4. The screening committee

The *ratio* or norm is the standard that serves as a measure for judging business performance. The ratio is

$$\frac{\text{total labor cost}}{\text{sales value of production}}$$

The 10 variables previously listed as having an impact on cost-reduction plans in general have an impact on this ratio as well. Many organizations find that this ratio is fairly stable over an extended period. A common value lies between 37 and 42 percent. (In most cases, management has more opportunity to influence labor costs than any other costs involved in the production process. It is critical to recognize that a 2 percent reduction in labor costs could result in a 10 to 15 percent improvement in profitability.) Prior to establishing such a ratio, it is wise for management to analyze its labor costs and sales value of production for at least the preceding two years. It is not uncommon for an organization to go back at least seven years. It is helpful if this analysis is done on a month-to-month basis to identify seasonal fluctuations. The ratio may be changed, but the number of changes must be kept to an absolute minimum.[25]

The amount of the *bonus* depends on the reduction in costs below the preset ratio. The normal method of distributing the bonus is for the first 25 percent to go into an escrow account to reimburse management when the ratio rises above the predetermined normal base. Any amount remaining in escrow at the end of the year becomes part of the Christmas distribution. Seventy-five percent of the remaining funds, or 56.25 percent of the total bonus, then goes to the workers on a monthly basis. The 18.75 percent remaining in the bonus pool goes to the company. In addition, the company gains from better use of its assets. The basis for each individual's share of the bonus is his or her monthly earnings as a percentage of the monthly total labor costs. The following procedure describes the steps involved in establishing a Scanlon Plan allocation.

A *production committee* is formed in each major department and consists of two to five worker representatives and one representative of management (normally the unit's foreman or supervisor). The purpose of the committee is to use the wealth of

---

[25]In a personal letter to this author, dated January 22, 1975, Frederick Lesieur stated that in the inflationary spirals of 1972–1974, as material costs outstripped wage increases, Scanlon ratios had to undergo frequent changes. Those involved in managing Scanlon Plans found, however, that these changes were made with minimal difficulty.

Ratio	= 42.5	This is an agreed-upon value based on records of previous year or an average number of previous years.
Net sales for month	= $4,083,500	From sales records
Net inventory change	= 584,000	This can be either a plus or minus value and is calculated by adding net change in sales value of inventory plus net change in sales value of goods in process.
Sales value of production	$4,667,500	

Ratio-based standard
= ratio × sales value of production labor cost
= .425 × 4,667,500
= 1,983,688

Actual monthly payroll	= 1,642,784
Monthly bonus pool	= 340,904
Reserved for potential deficits (25%) .25 × 340,904	= 85,226
Bonus balance	255,678
Company share (25%)	63,920
Employee share (75%)	191,758
Employee A's monthly earnings	= 1,689.99

Employee A's earnings as a percentage of total payroll

$$= \frac{\text{employee A's earnings}}{\text{total payroll}} = \frac{1,689.99}{1,642,874.00}$$

= .00103

Employee A's share of monthly bonus

= employee A's percentage of payroll × available bonus
= .00103 × 191,758
= $249.29*

---

*Employee will also share at end of year in all bonus pool funds remaining in deficit reserve pool.

imagination and ingenuity lying untapped in the workers' brains. The committee develops employee suggestions to increase productivity, improve quality, reduce waste, and improve methods of organizational operations. It also develops an understanding of all production costs and disseminates this information throughout the business. This committee normally meets twice a month. (In recent years, quality control circles—QC circles—have received much publicity. The purpose of the QC circle is similar to that of the Scanlon production committee.)

The *screening committee* consists of top members of the plant management and worker representatives, usually eight to twelve members. It reviews the monthly bonus, discusses current production problems, and considers all suggestions for organizational improvement. It discusses all aspects of business trends relative to the enterprise, from competitors for product and labor, to sales and shipment policies, orders, quality, customer problems, to the general business outlook. This committee normally meets once a month. The ultimate success of any Scanlon plan rests with these committees.

The Scanlon Plan© Today[26]

Today the Scanlon Plan is recognized as a system of total organization development, which consists of assumptions about human behavior, a set of principles for the

---

[26]The Scanlon Plan Today, produced by Scanlon Plan Associates®, Frost, Greenwood and Associates, 217 North Clippert Street, Lansing, Michigan 48912. Reprinted with permission.

management of organizations, and a participative process of implementation. It is a misconception to view the Scanlon Plan narrowly as an incentive system, quality-of-work-life program, suggestion plan, paternalistic employee relations activity, or antiunion strategy. In fact, it is not a plan at all in the sense that it does not specify a mechanistic procedure to be followed in standardized fashion; no two Scanlon Plans are alike. Rather, it is a demanding process to achieve organizational productivity and human self-fulfillment. Through research and experience, four principles have been validated that both define the Scanlon Plan and serve as conditions of Scanlon Plan success:

1. *Identity:* the continual process of clarifying and understanding the organization's "mandate" (i.e., requirements to serve customers, owners/shareholders, and employees.) This process includes recognition and affirmation by the majority of employees of the need to change in order to manage more effectively all the organization's resources: marketplace, financial, physical, and human.
2. *Participation:* acceptance by all employees of the responsibility for the mandate and the opportunity to responsibly influence the decision-making process. Participation includes accountability for one's own job and to all who have a vested interest in the enterprise.
3. *Equity:* the assurance of a fair and balanced return to customers (product value, quality, delivery, fair price), owners (profitability, return on investment, growth), and employees (job security, competitive wages and benefits, sharing in productivity gains).
4. *Managerial Competence:* the unequivocal requirement of leadership to define the "right job," to be open to influence, and to create a climate for productivity improvement. The identity, participation, and equity processes are demanding tests of managerial attitudes, abilities, and performance.

Implementation of these principles is accomplished through a rigorous organization development process, beginning with the top-level leadership responsibility to articulate the organization's mandate and then to gain the understanding, acceptance, and commitment by the executive staff, managers, supervisors, support personnel, and all other employees. Formulation of the specific components of any company's Scanlon Plan proposal becomes the assignment of an ad hoc committee, led by management and including elected employee representatives from all levels and functions. Acceptance of and commitment to implement the proposal is confirmed by a 90 percent or more affirmative secret vote of all people in the organization.

The Scanlon Plan reaches its potential only as it becomes the **primary** tool for managing the business. It is not an end in itself, but instead must become the means of defining and achieving the expectations of customers, owners/investors, and employees. It cannot be delegated. Indeed the first step tests the top leader's ability and willingness to define "the right job" as an absolutely necessary precondition for the participation of all employees in "doing the job right."

Profit Sharing

Profit sharing has developed hand in hand with the concepts of democracy and the worth and dignity of human labor. An early American sponsor of profit sharing was Albert Gallatin, who introduced it into his glassworks factory in New Geneva, Pennsylvania, in 1794. M. Le Claire, owner of a house painting and decorating business in Paris, France, has been credited with being the father of profit sharing. He earned this title not because his was the first such plan, but because it was one of the most successful. He introduced his plan in 1842.

Today, profit sharing is widely accepted as a fundamental part of the compensation program of over 150,000 American businesses. *Profit sharing* has been defined by the Council of Profit Sharing Industries as any procedure under which an employer pays or makes available to regular employees, subject to reasonable eligibility rules, in addition to prevailing rates of pay, special current or deferred sums based on the profits of business.

There are essentially three different types of profit-sharing plans in existence today:

1. Cash or current payment plan, which provides for the distribution of profits relative to some predetermined division by either cash or company stock, or both, within a short period following the earning of the profit and the determination of the proportionate shares.
2. Deferred plan, which provides for placement of earned funds into an escrow account for distribution at a future date (this plan usually provides the financial support for the pension program of the business).
3. Combined plan, which has the features of both.

With the enactment in 1974 of the Employee Retirement Income Security Act (ERISA), many additional financial responsibilities and burdensome administrative details have been placed on organizations that use profit sharing to finance pension plans. Because of this law and its associated problems, many firms changed their profit-sharing programs to provide for some form of annual payment, thus requiring their employees to develop their own retirement programs. With the development and popularity of 401(k) benefits plans (see discussion in chapter 15), profit sharing received increased recognition by relating employer contributions to an employee's 401(k) plan and to corporate profits.

A major philosophical issue behind all profit-sharing programs is the need to educate employees on the importance of profit, the employees' effect on profit, and how increased profits benefit them. A major weakness of many profit-sharing plans is that once they have been incorporated into the compensation system, they become institutionalized, accepted as permanent, unchanging fixtures, and have little to no motivational influence in improving work performance. If a profit-sharing program is to have motivational impact, the rewards offered to the employee must vary with the success of the business. A clear relationship must exist between rewards and performance. For this reason, payment for effort must have as close a time relationship to the performance period as possible. Monthly or bimonthly bonus payments are excellent; quarterly, semiannual, or annual payments are acceptable but certainly less a motivator unless the reward is very large or has worker recognition and acceptance. One of the premier profit-sharing plans that over the past 65 years has provided the type of stimulation desired by every business is the plan developed by James F. Lincoln of the Lincoln Electric Company, Cleveland, Ohio.[27]

---

[27]*Lincoln's Incentive System and Approach to Manufacturing* (Cleveland, OH: The Lincoln Electric Company, 1972). A compilation of various articles describes Lincoln's incentive plan and operation.

Lincoln's Incentive System   Upon being made general manager of the Lincoln Electric Company in 1914, James Lincoln established an incentive compensation plan. After 20 years of effort, the incentive plan evolved substantially into the plan that exists today. Its principal features are these:

1. The company guarantees 30 hours of work 50 weeks a year to each employee who has at least three years of service. (It guarantees no specific rate of pay, and the worker must be willing to transfer from one job to another and work overtime during periods of peak demand. The company reserves the right to terminate the agreement providing six months advance notice is given.)

2. Standard job evaluation procedures set the base wage, using the six compensable factors of mentality, skill, responsibility, mental application, physical application, and working conditions to determine the importance of each job. The combination of job evaluation and labor market requirements then sets the actual dollar worth of the job.

3. The majority of employees are on a piecework incentive plan. The factory products—arc welding equipment and electric motors—lend themselves to standardized operation and the setting of rates. Both workers and management, however, recognize labor's opportunity to improve both quality and quantity of output. Every possible job that can be standardized has a piece rate. Rates are set through the use of normal time-study procedures. The jobs that are not on piece rates include clerical work, tool room operations, maintenance and repairs, and experimental work. New employees and employees on new jobs receive a temporary exemption from piecework standards. Employees in a few small assembly operations work on a group piecework plan.

4. All employees may participate in the suggestion program with the exception of department heads and members of the engineering and time-study departments (suggestions for improvements are a fundamental part of their jobs). Any suggestions that lead to organizational progress (improved manufacturing methods, sales, procedures, waste reduction, or new or improved products) are considered during merit rating.

5. Twice a year, a merit rating program appraises the actual work performance of each employee. This program uses four report cards. Each card rates the work performance according to one of the four following work variables: (1) *dependability* (ability to supervise oneself, including work safety performance, orderliness, care of equipment, and effectiveness in the use of one's skills); (2) *quality* (success in eliminating errors and reducing scrap and waste); (3) *output* (willingness to be productive, not hold back work effort or output, and recognize the importance of attendance); (4) *ideas and cooperation* (initiative and ingenuity in developing new methods to reduce costs, increase output, improve quality, and effect better customer relations). The supervisor doing the rating informs subordinates of their scores. The individual scores for each group are posted by number only. It is possible, through process of elimination, to identify the score of a specific employee. Many employees openly state their scores. Managers at levels above that of immediate supervisor responsible for appraising performance take an active role in reviewing all merit ratings.

6. After the first year of service, each employee annually has the opportunity to purchase a limited number of shares of company stock. Upon retirement or termina-

tion of employment, the company has an option to repurchase the stock. Currently, about 75 percent of the employees own 40 percent of the stock.

7. Employees elect representatives to an "advisory board." This board has the opportunity to suggest changes in policies and operation; however, the final decision on all changes is made by management. This board meets every two weeks.

8. Independent work groups or "subcontractor shop" operations, in which employees have the opportunity to earn specified piecework rates, perform their own quality control and develop their own production procedures in completing subassembly operations within given cost, quantity, and quality parameters.

9. All profits of the business are split three ways: (a) the corporation retains a certain share for capital improvement and financial security; (b) shareholders receive approximately 6 percent to 8 percent dividends based on the book value of the three types of company stock; and (c) employees receive all remaining profits.

10. The annual cash bonus earned by the employees closely approximates their annual earnings. Recent bonus multipliers have ranged from 60 to 70 percent. The actual distribution an employee earns is a function of the employee's annual earnings as a percentage of the total labor cost, individual performance appraisal merit rating, and total amount of profit earned by Lincoln Electric.

The year-end bonus plan was initiated when James Lincoln turned down a request for a 10 percent increase in wages in 1933 because he felt the profit picture would not warrant such an increase. The workers then responded with the request for a year-end bonus if, through increased productivity and lowered costs, the year-end profits were larger. After some deliberation, Lincoln agreed to this efficiency-oriented proposal. To everyone's surprise (including Lincoln's), the bonus amounted to $350 instead of the $35 to $50 expected by Lincoln. In 1995, over 3,400 employees shared a bonus of $64 million. Over the past several years, the annual bonus has ranged from a low of 55 percent to a high of 115 percent of annual earnings. The total of all bonuses paid since 1934 is approximately equal to total wages and salaries paid over the same period. In 1995, the average bonus per eligible employee was nearly $19,000.

By many standards, Lincoln Electric is not an easy place to work. There is no room for the "I don't care" worker. The success of the entire business depends on a high level of contribution by each member. There is a mutual understanding of need and a mutual respect based on democratic principles espoused and lived by James F. Lincoln. The democratic principles go much deeper than the basic elements of the incentive system. For example, there are no reserved employee parking spaces; there is one cafeteria (with excellent food) and all employees—workers and managers alike—sit wherever spaces are available. In addition, there is a policy of promotion from within that requires all promotional opportunities to be posted (including many senior positions). There are no definite lines of promotion, and promotions are given by qualification only. The benefits program includes a two-week paid vacation for employees with one year of service, three weeks for 13 years of service, four weeks for 20 years of service, and five weeks for 25 years of service. There is a paid medical, surgical, and hospital plan; life insurance; and a retirement plan beginning at age 60 with pension based on years of service and total earnings excluding bonus should an employee choose to retire. Other benefits include an annual picnic, company dinner, and a Quarter-Century Club.

In addition, employees may challenge any time study. If a time study results in a lowering of a rate, the involved employee may request transfer to a job that pays an equal or higher rate. Piece rate is not a speedup tool but rather a tool of fair and equitable distribution of rewards for the effort of a motivated employee. There is no limit to earnings, and no rate can be changed unless there has been a change in method, design, or tooling. Employees challenge less than one-fifth of 1 percent of all rate changes. There is a periodic review of all rates.

The principles of incentive compensation are a fundamental part of the democratic process. Many believe that Lincoln Electric has the *highest-paid* factory workers in the world and, measuring in units of work produced, the *lowest-cost* workers in any factory in the world in a similar line of work.[28]

Since 1934, Lincoln has become a dominant force in its business. It has been able to maintain a stable price structure as a result of a significant increase in output per worker, even though, as mentioned, the workforce is highly paid. It is interesting to note that the hourly wage rate of Lincoln is competitive but not outstanding. The combination of annual wages and bonuses, however, is almost unbelievable.

Employees at Lincoln Electric Co. are not the only members of the workforce enjoying generous annual bonuses. On January 16, 1988, the 3,700 employees of Andersen Corporation of Bayport, Minnesota, participated in their 74th annual profit-sharing program. The profit-sharing pool for 1987 was $105.9 million, granting workers a bonus of 84 percent of their annual salary. The average bonus was $28,620.[29]

Profit Sharing at GM, Ford, and Chrysler[30]   In 1982, after several years of a severe decline in sales of domestic automobiles, the United Automobile Workers Union (UAW) granted GM and Ford major wage and benefits concessions in a 30-month accord. One of the major additions to the GM and Ford contracts was a profit-sharing plan. The GM plan called for employees to receive 10 percent of that portion of the company's U.S. pretax profit in excess of the sum of 10 percent of net worth and 5 percent of other assets. The Ford plan was more liberal, but UAW executives explained that GM workers would receive a larger distribution because GM historically generated greater profits.

In 1984, GM and Ford made the first profit-sharing payment from their 1982 agreement. In 1983, GM had profits of $3.73 billion and distributed $322 million to 350,000 UAW-represented employees and 181,000 "nonexecutive" salaried employees not covered by the UAW contract for an average bonus of $640 for employees who worked a normal schedule in 1983. In 1984, GM profits rose to $3.87 billion with a profit-sharing bonus of $515 (GM stated that the drop in the amount of the bonus was due to a recall of over 100,000 employees). UAW officials stated that GM-UAW members contributed $4,500 to $6,200 in wage and benefits concessions during the 30-month contract. They also complained that, at the same time, 5,800 GM executives throughout the world were receiving bonuses that averaged $31,000 (average bonus 50 times as large as that received by the average nonexecutive).

---

[28]J. F. Lincoln, "Incentive Compensation: The Way to Industrial Democracy," *Advanced Management,* February 1950, pp. 17–18.
[29]"Profit Sharing: Bonanza in Bayport," *Time,* February 1, 1988, p. 47.
[30]All data are from Bureau of Labor Statistics, *Current Wage Developments* (Washington, DC: U.S. Department of Labor, April 1982, March 1984, March 1985).

Meanwhile at Ford, 1983 profits were $1.9 billion and the average bonus for 158,000 employees was $440. In 1984, with Ford earning record profits of $2.9 billion, the average profit-sharing bonus for 170,000 employees jumped to $2,000. Ford's plan also includes low and mid-level white-collar nonunion members.

By early 1987, GM-UAW members became painfully aware that their UAW representatives may not have done a good job in designing their collectively bargained profit-sharing plan. Relative to Ford, GM was a poor second in the profitability race among the three major U.S. automobile manufacturers. In February 1987, Ford disclosed that it would make a $370 million payment to eligible hourly and salaried employees. This amounted to an average bonus of over $2,100 per worker. A 19-year veteran of a Ford assembly plant stated: "I'll do my part for the company because they deserve it. They're giving us their profits." In 1988, Ford workers received profit-sharing checks that averaged $3,700.[31] There was a different view at GM where, because of lower GM profits in 1986 and 1987 and the GM-UAW profit-sharing formula, GM assembly plant workers received no bonus. At the same time, GM distributed approximately $170 million to its executives. A GM worker and local UAW official stated: "I think it's pretty insulting for a corporation to be claiming poverty...and then have the audacity to say we have to pay our big shots a bonus."[32] In 1987, GM and UAW renegotiated their profit-sharing formula to improve the opportunity of GM-UAW members receiving a profit-sharing bonus. The difference in the operation of these two profit-sharing programs may help explain why to this very day Ford management has had better relations with the UAW than has GM.

The U.S. auto industry witnessed dramatic changes in profitability during the first half of the 1990s, significantly influencing the profit-sharing payout for auto workers. Profit sharing continues to be a very volatile issue between the unions and the automobile industry. Table 14–4 provides data on profit sharing paid to hourly workers in U.S. auto companies.

Timing of Bonus Payments

For employees, any time a bonus is provided is the right time. However, an old adage, "timing is everything," has significant applicability with incentive bonuses. In the discussion of motivational theories in chapter 13, the point was made that to reinforce a desired behavior, rewards should be provided shortly after the demonstration of that behavior. In an organization, this kind of timing is not always possible. Two times when the offering of an incentive may be extremely powerful are prior to Christmas and prior to the employee's annual vacation.

Christmas Bonus   One of the most common times for an organization to provide extra pay or a special bonus is immediately before Christmas. The Christmas bonus can range from a gift such as a ham or a turkey, to a gift certificate, or to a monetary payment computed in a number of ways. Some of the more common ways to calculate Christmas money bonuses are (1) a thirteenth-month paycheck (a cash payment equivalent to one

[31]"Ford Workers to Get Profit-Sharing Checks That Average $3,700," *The Wall Street Journal,* February 22, 1988, p. 5.
[32]Jacob M. Schlesinger and Paul Ingrassia, "Ford Schedules Profit-Sharing Payments for '86, Average Over $2,100 a Worker," *The Wall Street Journal,* February 19, 1987, p. 12.

TABLE 14–4	1994 and 1995 Profit Sharing for U.S. Auto Workers	
	1994	*1995*
Chrysler	$8,000	$ 3,200
Ford	4,000	1,700
General Motors*	590	800
Saturn	3,245	10,000

*Except Saturn

In preparing for its 1996 contract negotiations with Chrysler Corporation, UAW let it be known that it wanted Chrysler to share more of its profits with its hourly workers. In response to the UAW statement concerning profit sharing, Chrysler stated that for three years between 1993 and 1995 its hourly workers received profit-sharing bonuses averaging $15,500.[33]

month's earnings); (2) some percentage of annual earnings; (3) an award based on years of service; and (4) distribution of funds from a profit-sharing or cost-reduction plan.

Many employees look forward to their Christmas bonus as a source of money for shopping. Many of these employees live from paycheck to paycheck. Their established living patterns consume their total earnings with little to no funds available for savings. The Christmas bonus, in essence, becomes a Christmas savings plan that allows the employee to have the opportunity to make additional purchases at this time of year.

Vacation Bonus Organizations with a vacation period in which all employees receive their vacation at the same time often set the annual bonus payment to precede the vacation to permit employees with minimal cash reserves to make greater use of their time off. One organization provides a mini bonus by calculating vacation paychecks at a rate of 1.5 times base pay to provide more spending money for the vacation.

Annual Lump-Sum Bonuses Unionized firms having relatively high-paid employees began in 1982 to take a different approach to base pay programs. Recognizing the problem union officials have with rank-and-file members when attempting to obtain approval of a contract that calls for either wage concessions, no wage increase, or very small wage increases (2 percent or less), annual lump-sum bonuses began to appear in all kinds of union contracts. These lump-sum payments are usually not "folded" into the employee's base wage (do not increase the base wage of the employee), but they certainly add to annual spendable income. The lump-sum payments are designed to be a "sweetener" or inducement for union members to agree to what could easily be considered a very distasteful or unacceptable contract.

The most common lump-sum bonus is a flat dollar amount. The first-year bonus could average $759, with $616 in the second year, and $630 in the third year. The second most common form of lump-sum bonus is one in which the bonus is calculated as a per-

---

[33]Angelo B. Henderson, "UAW to Pressure Chrysler to Share More of Its Profit," *The Wall Street Journal*, June 6, 1996, p. B8.

centage of the pay of the previous year. The average is 3 percent each year, ranging from 1 to 12 percent in the first year and 2 to 5 percent in the second and third years. Some lump-sum bonuses are a combination of a fixed dollar amount and a percentage, and sometimes company stock is offered in lieu of a cash payment.

Even in nonunion settings, lump-sum bonuses are now being used. To slow the growth of base salaries, some firms provide a lump-sum bonus equaling any annual salary increase above the midpoint. This one-time payment is not added to base salary. In July 1987, Delta Airlines, the airline with the highest-paid employees in the industry, gave each of its nonunion employees a bonus or "pay supplement" based on length of service. The bonuses averaged about $1,428 for each of the approximately 35,000 eligible employees. Delta noted that it had not had a pay increase in 18 months because it was attempting to cut costs in an increasingly competitive industry. However, by providing this lump-sum bonus, the company was able to reward its workers without increasing its cost structure, and at the same time tell its workers that they had performed well and that the bonus was a sign of Delta's appreciation.[34]

Summary

Work premiums are forms of extra compensation for work considered burdensome, hazardous, stressful, distasteful, or inconvenient. Some examples of work premiums include pay for overtime, shifts, weekends, and holidays.

Performance-based awards are paid to those who contribute output beyond certain predetermined standards. These standards must be consistent and fair. A variety of methods can be used to develop standards. Kinds of performance-based awards include piecework, merit pay, and special awards. Cost-reduction plans such as the Scanlon Plan are witnessing a revival in popularity. Gainsharing plans and short-term profit-sharing plans, such as the Lincoln Electric plan, are receiving increased attention and interest. Short-term contest and suggestion plans continue to stimulate employee innovation, but they require management support and implementation.

To be effective, performance-based awards should follow employee behavior as soon as possible. The law of diminishing returns applies to the effective use of any reward. Rewards must be constantly monitored and changes must be made whenever their usefulness begins to diminish. Regardless of their responsibilities and duties, employees should be made to feel that their jobs contribute to the success of the organization. Work premiums and rewards should emphasize and reflect this fact.

Review Questions

1. What is a work premium? Describe some, giving the particular use and goal of each.
2. What is a performance incentive? Why do organizations use them?
3. Describe various approaches for setting standards that provide the foundation of performance incentive programs.
4. What are the major differences between a cost-reduction program and a profit-sharing program? What are the philosophic issues underlying each type of program? Give examples of each.

---

[34]Marilyn Geewax, "Analyst: $50 Million in Bonuses Planned for Pre-merger Workers," *Atlanta Constitution,* July 24, 1987, p. 1A.

5. Describe the major elements of (1) the Scanlon Plan and (2) Lincoln's incentive system.

6. Identify and describe different reasons for implementing a short-term bonus.

Appendix 14A
Setting Standards and Designing Incentives for an Industrial Economy

Nearly all output-based incentive programs involve operations in which workers have considerable control over their output.[35] In industries in which production operations are largely machine paced, such as automobile assembly lines, cigarette manufacturing, chemical processing, and pulp and paper production, individual output-based incentive programs are almost nonexistent. Because output-based programs reward extra effort, the first requirement of any such program is to set fair standards that define what an average worker under normal conditions should produce in a set period of time (normally on an hourly or daily basis).

Over the past 100 years, various methods have been developed to measure and determine standard output. No system is foolproof, and even the most scientifically contrived system includes some subjectivity. The major measurement procedures are stopwatch time studies, synthetic time studies, and work sampling. The development of standards is usually the responsibility of industrial engineers.

Measurement Procedures

Because work standards have a direct impact on one of the most important elements of the work cycle—the worker's paycheck—they are a source of problems and grievances. Before setting standards in an industrial environment, operating conditions at the workplace must have a degree of uniformity. These uniform conditions include methods of doing the work; procedures for delivering, handling, and removing materials; quality of raw materials; types of equipment and their maintenance; and quality standards of output. Workers must have control over work output, and there must be a clear relationship between effort and output. Variations in any of these areas have a direct impact on output, but it is practically impossible not to have them. Additional problems related to setting standards are those involved with (1) making allowances for fatigue and personal needs, (2) recognizing unavoidable delays, (3) determining the representative of jobholders being timed, and (4) leveling final findings. (*Leveling* occurs when the analyst reviewing the work rates the worker as being faster or slower than the average worker in doing the job or elements of the job.) Through the leveling process, the time required for the worker to do the work is increased or lowered, depending on the leveling rate assigned by the analyst.

If individual output-based incentive programs are to succeed, there must be some "give" on both sides. When variations occur, organizations must honor certain commitments. At the same time, workers must trust management and understand that changes must be made if the organization is to be competitive and provide a product that meets consumer demands. This can be accomplished with a bit of communication

---

[35]George L. Stelluto, "Report on Incentive Pay in Manufacturing Industries," *Monthly Labor Review,* July 1969, pp. 49–53.

between management and workers. Assurances made and followed through will produce astonishing results.

Two symptoms of error in setting standards show up in what are called *loose* and *tight* standards or rates. When a standard is loose, management contends that workers' earnings are excessive, taking into account the extra effort involved in producing the output. Employees complain of tight standards when, after producing the extra effort, they realize earnings lower than they expected.

Three commonly used techniques for setting performance standards are through the use of (1) motion and time study, (2) micromotion analysis, and (3) work measurement. A brief description of each technique follows.

Motion and Time Study   In the oldest and simplest of the three techniques—motion and time study—an analyst makes a time study by closely watching a worker and using a stopwatch to time performance. Most studies include a detailed analysis of each work element. The analyst then relates each element to the normal time required for the entire work cycle.

Motion and time study provides data on the time required by a "normal" worker to perform a specific operation. A "normal" worker refers to a qualified, experienced employee performing at an average pace while working under conditions that usually prevail at the workstation.

Time-study analysts who provide accurate data must have an understanding of the job and be able to develop a harmonious relationship with the employees being studied. Employees tend to be suspicious of anyone who studies their performance, and this distrust may manifest itself in many ways. Workers being appraised may attempt to inflate their performance or even deflate their performance. The skilled analyst must be able to "rate" employees. Rating is the establishment of the degree to which the employee being studied performs better or worse than a "normal" worker.

Micromotion Analysis   A more sophisticated approach is micromotion analysis, which requires photographing a worker performing a job. The camera operates at a constant speed—usually 1,000 frames a minute. By analyzing the film, the analyst can determine work patterns for each part of the worker's body. By studying each movement and counting the number of frames necessary to document a complete cycle of work, a methods analyst is able to determine acceptable methods and set standards. Using this approach, Frank and Lillian Gilbreth established basic elements that proved to be most valuable for analyzing physical work relationships.

Work Measurement   Following the work of the Gilbreths, time-study engineers devised methods for combining standard time value with each basic work element or fundamental motion. By assigning time values to these fundamental motions, engineers are able to work in a laboratory and synthesize the motions necessary to perform an assignment and to set a time standard for the work under study. Some of the better known synthetic time systems are Methods-Time Measurement (MTM), Work Measurement, Basic Motion Time-study (BMT), and Dimensional Motion Times (DMT). Each of these methods was developed primarily for industrial application and relates to jobs having observable and measurable manual labor inputs. They all provide work standards that come from an analysis of job content. However, they are not free of subjectivity; and all require personnel skilled in the method being used. Both a strength and weakness of work measurement is that each job standard requires an individual analysis, which is time-consuming and thus costly.

Incentive Plans

Using these different methods for studying workplace activities, industrial engineers have developed a number of different kinds of output-based incentive plans. The plans developed for the industrial workers in factories and mills took two basic forms: (1) piecework plans and (2) day work plans.

Piecework Plans   Piecework plans are used when the work of the individual (1) requires a short period of time to complete, (2) is repeated frequently, and (3) has as a standard a designated number of units to be produced in a given time period. A *piecework plan* is a plan that pays an employee for each unit produced. Most plans provide each worker with a guaranteed wage rate if standards are not met. Three of the most common methods used to determine the guarantee are (1) to set it equivalent to the federal or state minimum wage, (2) to use some form of a job evaluation process, or (3) to set the standard through collective bargaining if the organization is unionized.

After setting the guarantee, management must determine its base for standards of performance. Two systems are available: (1) setting the base on what an average worker produces, and (2) setting it on what a motivated worker produces. The definition for the *average worker production standard* is the output produced under normal conditions by an average worker with average education, experience, and skill who is physically fit for the job. The definition for the *motivated worker production standard* is the output produced by a motivated worker with sufficient education, experience, and skill who is physically fit for the job and who works at an incentive-induced pace that can be maintained day after day without harmful effect.[36] No matter which base is used, it usually receives a 100 percent value as the standard.

The next step is to decide on an *incentive rate*. Most organizations pay their motivated output rate at 25 to 35 percent above what they would consider to be a fair rate of the output of the average worker. An incentive rate of 30 percent appears not only to be a fair and equitable reward for the extra effort, but it also provides maximum motivational impact on most workers.[37]

The design of a piecework plan can have considerable variation. For example, a plan could be designed to pay the same amount for each unit produced. Another design would pay a specific amount up to a particular level, and beyond that threshold pay a lower rate for all additional units. A completely opposite approach would be to pay a higher rate for all additional units produced above the threshold. Another approach would be one in which an employee who exceeds the threshold receives a higher rate for *all* units produced (including the ones up to the threshold amount).

A piecework plan is commonly used when a short period of time is required to produce the unit of output and the work cycle is repeated continuously. Piecework plans are common in the textile and apparel industries and are also found in service-related industries, especially in data entry jobs.

---

[36]See Marvin E. Mundel, *Motion and Time Study: Improving Productivity,* 6th ed. (Englewood Cliffs, NJ: Prentice-Hall, 1985), for an excellent and in-depth discussion of the standard-setting process.

[37]Mitchell Fein, *Wage Incentive Plans* (Norcross, GA: American Institute of Industrial Engineers, 1970), p. 28.

Rewarding indirect labor. Piecework plans in general were born at the time of the rise of craft trades in the thirteenth and fourteenth centuries. At that time, the master craftsman received full rewards for his labor, whereas helpers and apprentices earned little more than subsistence wages. The thorny issue of fair and equitable payment for personnel who support and make possible the productivity improvement of the direct laborer (the person actually performing the measured task) confronts many organizations to this very day.

A major consideration that frequently blocks resolution of this problem is the variety of activities and jobs performed by indirect labor. In many cases, these workers assist a number of direct laborers. They may perform functions that include providing, sorting, or preparing raw materials; removing finished materials; inspecting; training; maintaining equipment or records; and general supervising. It is difficult to maintain a high level of performance among the direct laborers without providing those who support them with some type of reward.

Some pay-for-performance plans for indirect laborers provide the same percentage increase above normal as that earned by the direct laborer. Other plans develop standards based on hours worked to units of product produced or some variation thereof. When piecework programs are used in small group operations, the indirect labor jobs are often scheduled in the activity requirements of the group.

As with other elements of the incentive package, the indirect labor issue must not be set aside because of the difficulty involved in developing acceptable solutions.

Team use of piecework plans. Most of the discussion concerning piecework plans has involved individual effort, but these programs can be just as effective for stimulating the performance of a team.

There are two basic approaches for developing team plans. The first is identical to that described for setting individual piecework standards. It requires setting work standards for each member of the team and maintaining a count of the output of each member. The difference between this team approach and that related to individual piecework arises in the method of payment. The team approach may use one of the following payment methods: (1) all members receive the pay earned by the highest producer; (2) all members receive the pay earned by the lowest producer; and (3) all members receive payment equal to the average pay earned by the team.

The second and far more unique approach is to set a standard based on the team's final output. This approach does not relieve management of the responsibility of completing a detailed analysis of the work performed by each member. Work-flow and work-processing information are still necessary for establishing the initial balancing of work activities among the members. Once production is under way, the team may vary the distribution of tasks among members to meet its own demands, which will result in a change in the work-balancing system developed by management. This approach is more useful when all work together to complete a single product. The first approach would be applicable when members are performing similar or identical assignments.

The advantage of the team approach is not only the simplification of measuring output, but the support individual members provide one another. A well-knit, properly managed work team assists in training new and less experienced members. It also rotates jobs or workstation assignments so that it makes the most effective use of human resources. The members also aid one another in overcoming both on- and off-the-job problems that affect team performance. The piecework incentive plan provides a goal that assists in coordinating and directing team efforts for the benefit of the organization, the team, and its individual members.

In most well-functioning work teams, the total earnings (base pay plus any pay-for-performance earnings) are split equally among members. It is possible that the team itself may wish to grant a larger percentage to the more senior or experienced members, but this is the exceptional case and is strictly a team decision. (See chapter 12 for an in-depth discussion of team-based pay.)

Day Work Plans   Piecework plans were not appropriate for all industrial settings. Frequently, day work plans were designed when a piecework plan was impractical. A day work plan is used when a relatively long period of time is required to produce a unit of output, and the required activities and the order of performing them may vary. A day work standard is typically set in terms of time required to complete one unit of production.

A typical example of a day work plan can be found in a law firm. Today, it is possible to look in the classified section of almost any newspaper and check the prices some lawyers quote for a specific service. For example, uncontested divorces, $130; wills, $49; DUI, $175; Chapter 13 Bankruptcy Debt Repayment Plan, $135. Such an ad states that these are the charges no matter how much time is required to perform the services. The lawyer has identified how long it takes to provide a specific service, established the desired level of income, and then set the fee for the service relative to these two inputs. These charges also include payment for the services provided by all support personnel in the law firm.

Another common example of a day work plan involves mechanics in vehicle repair garages. For almost every possible problem that can occur with a vehicle, there is an established standard time to do the necessary repairs or adjustments. The mechanic identifies the problem, checks a readily available time allowance book for the standard time to perform the repair or adjustment, and then, by multiplying an established hourly rate of pay by the standard time, arrives at a total cost.

Day work plans vary in complexity. The simplest is a basic day rate plan (which is not an incentive plan). In a basic day rate plan, the employee receives a set wage regardless of output or performance. This plan is used where there is a need to emphasize quality, where the job is machine paced, where it is difficult to establish performance standards or measure output, or where the organization wishes to promote the economic security of the employee. Most employees in the United States today are paid through a basic day rate plan.

A *standard hour* or *differential day rate plan* is a variation of the basic plan. This plan involves setting the time needed by an average worker to complete one unit of output and a prescribed hourly rate of pay for that employee. When a worker completes the unit of work within the prescribed time, the worker receives the prescribed rate of pay. If the work takes longer, the worker still receives the prescribed rate of pay. If the worker produces the unit in less time, he or she receives additional payment. For example, if the allowed time is two hours and the prescribed rate of pay is $10 per hour and the worker completes five units in an eight-hour day, the worker would receive $5 \times \$20$ or $100, whereas the standard rate of pay for an eight-hour work day for an employee who produces four units would be $80. Individual job incentives negotiated between the United Steelworkers of America (USWA) and the major steel manufacturers use the standard hour plan. The previous examples of the lawyer and the automobile mechanic involve the use of standard hour plans.

Appendix 14B
Two Other Kinds of Gainsharing Plans

Rucker Plan

A plantwide, cost-reduction incentive plan, the *Rucker Plan of Group Incentives,* has been developed by the Eddy-Rucker-Nickels Company.[38] This incentive plan has a philosophical base similar to that of the Scanlon plan. The Rucker plan has been most successful in manufacturing companies that are already profitable, that have reasonably good employee–management relations, and that employ between 50 and 800 people. It has been used to add an incentive in "day rate" shops, to replace unsatisfactory piecework plans, or as a supplement to satisfactory piecework plans to provide incentive to those employees it does not cover.

A major difference between the Scanlon plan and the Rucker plan is the norm or base used to establish a measure of productivity. The Rucker plan's measure of productivity is called *economic productivity*. It is the output of value added by manufacture for each dollar of input of payroll costs. *Value added by manufacture* is the difference between the sales income from goods produced and the cost of the materials, supplies, and outside services consumed in the production and delivery of that output. *Payroll costs* are all employment costs paid to, because of, or on behalf of the employee group measured. Accounting procedures similar to those used for developing the ratio in the Scanlon plan are used to develop the economic productivity measure of the Rucker plan.

The following procedures are used to establish the Rucker plan:

1. Identify a base period that provides data that will be valid and useful for establishing standards.
2. Generate the following data (using past business records):
   - .1 Sales value of production (*SVP*)
   - .2 Cost of materials, supplies, service, etc. (*COM*)
   - .3 Cost of labor (*COL*)
3. Using these data, establish the following standards:
   - .1 Value added (*VA*) = *SVP* − *COM*
   - .2 Labor contribution to *VA* (*LCVA*) = $\dfrac{COL}{VA}$
   - .3 Economic productivity index (*EPI*) = $\dfrac{1.00}{LCVA}$
   - .4 Expected value of production (*EVP*) = *EPI* × *COL* (for bonus period)

For example, a firm identified the following business figures (all figures in millions of dollars):

1. *SVP* = $20
2. *COM* = $ 9

---

[38]Carl Heyel, ed., *The Encyclopedia of Management,* 2nd ed. (New York: Van Nostrand Reinhold, 1973), pp. 895–900.

3. VA $= \$11$
4. $COL = \$6$

5. $LCVA = \dfrac{6}{11} = .545$

6. EPI $= \dfrac{1.00}{.545} = 1.83$

The following business data were generated for the current bonus period:

$$SVP = 2.5 \qquad VA = 1.3$$
$$COM = 1.2 \qquad COL = .6$$

Actual Value of Production $(AVP) = SVP - (COM + COL) = 2.5 - (1.2 + .6)$

$AVP = .7$

$EVP = .6 \times 1.83 = 1.098$

$$\text{Savings or Loss} = EVP - AVP = 1.098 - .7 = .398 \text{ or } \$398,000$$

Labor contribution to Value Added is .545. Therefore, the money placed in the bonus pool for labor contribution to the savings is $\$398,000 \times .545 = \$216,910$

Labor's contributions to savings are deposited in a bonus pool, with two-thirds of the bonus paid out to the employees monthly and one-third held in reserve until the end of the year. This reserve provides a cushion for accounting adjustments or for periods when the standard is not met. After a final year-end audit, all the reserve is distributed to the employees.

Improshare Plan

The *Improshare* (IMproved PROductivity through SHARing) *plan*[39] is an industrial engineering–based productivity measurement and sharing plan developed in the mid-1970s by Mitchell Fein. This plan uses easy-to-obtain past production records to establish base performance standards. It may include both hourly and salaried employees, incentive and nonincentive employees, or any designated group. The organization and its employees share in a 50/50 division of all productivity gains.

The first step in the Improshare plan is to identify the groups to be included in the plan and the products to be produced. The next step is to establish the *base period,* the *base period product costs,* and the *base productivity factor (BPF)*. The base period is the period of time used to establish productivity standards. The base period product costs are those costs used by management during the base period that represent the direct labor hours to produce a product by major operations and by total products being produced. (This is represented in the following model by Standard Value Hours.) These costs are usually determined through some form of engineered time standards for all operations, totaled to obtain an overall engineered time standard for each product. The BPF represents the relationship in the base period between the actual hours worked by all employees in the plan and the value of work in standard man hours produced by these employees, as determined by the product costs used by management for the base period.

After establishing all required base period performance data, the organization then calculates current performance in hours worked and output produced. By comparing

---

[39]Mitchell Fein, *An Alternative to Traditional Managing* (Hillsdale, NJ: Mitchell Fein, 1980), pp. 28–41.

current output and hours worked against base period standards, hours saved (Improshare earned hours) are calculated. Then, the Improshare-designed hours gained are used to calculate the employee share of the improvements. The following example is a simple representation of the formulas and calculations used in an Improshare plan.

Olympia Company manufactures two products—Product A and Product B. From a review of manufacturing statistics, a base period was established. The base period data were:

$$
\begin{array}{ll}
\text{Production (Direct Labor) Workers —Product A} & = \ \ 60 \\
\text{Support (Indirect Labor) Workers —Product A} & = \ \ 25 \\
\text{Production (Direct Labor) Workers —Product B} & = \ \ 40 \\
\text{Support (Indirect Labor) Workers —Product B} & = \ \underline{\ 15} \\
\text{Total Production and Support Workforce} & = 140
\end{array}
$$

Base Period Hours Worked = 2,000 (50 weeks × 40 hours per week)
Base Period Units Produced = A – 15,000; B – 5,000

$$\text{Standard Value } (SV) \text{ Hours (per product)} = \frac{\text{Total Production Employee Hours}}{\text{Units Produced}}$$

$$SV \text{ Hours (Product A)} = \frac{60 \times 2,000}{15,000} = \frac{120,000}{15,000} = 8$$

$$SV \text{ Hours (Product B)} = \frac{40 \times 2,000}{5,000} = \frac{80,000}{5,000} = 16$$

$$\text{Base Productivity Factor } (BPF) = \frac{\text{Total Hours Worked (Production and Support Personnel)}}{\text{Total Standard Value } (SV) \text{ Hours}}$$

$$
\begin{array}{ll}
\text{Total Workers A = 60} & \text{B = 40} \\
\phantom{\text{Total Workers A = }}\underline{25} & \phantom{\text{B = }}\underline{15} \\
\phantom{\text{Total Workers A = }}85 & \phantom{\text{B = }}55
\end{array}
$$

Total Hours Worked = (85 + 55) × 50 × 40 = 280,000 Hours Worked
SV Hours (Product A) = 8 hours × 15,000 units = 120,000
SV Hours (Product B) = 16 hours × 5,000 units = $\underline{\ \ 80,000}$
$$BPF = \frac{280,000}{200,000} = 1.4 \qquad 200,000$$

Bonus Month Calculations:

Product A = 2,500 units produced
Product B = 300 units produced
Total Production and Support Personnel = 170
Hours Worked per Employee for Bonus Period = 21 days × 8 hours/day = 168
Total Actual Hours Worked = 168 × 170 = 28,560

Total Improshare Hours during Bonus Period:

Product A = SV Hours (Product A) × Units Produced × BPF
Product B = SV Hours (Product B) × Units Produced × BPF
Product A = 8 × 2500 × 1.4 = 28,000
Product B = 16 × 300 × 1.4 = $\underline{\ \ 6,720}$
Total Improshare Hours = 34,720
Total Actual Hours Worked = $\underline{28,560}$
Gained Hours = 6,160
50/50 Split Bonus Hours = 3,080

$$\text{Bonus Percentage} = \frac{\text{Bonus Hours}}{\text{Actual Hours}} = \frac{3,080}{28,560} = 10.78\%$$

Each employee would receive a bonus equal to 10.78 percent of monthly earnings.

Three controls established in the Improshare plan permit changes in the measurement standards: (1) a ceiling on productivity improvement of 160 percent, (2) cash buyback of measurement standards, and (3) 80/20 share of improvements created by capital equipment.

The employees receive the productivity monthly gain as a percentage increase in their regular pay. By using a 50/50 share of productivity gains and setting a 160 percent ceiling on productivity performance, the maximum employee gainsharing is 30 percent of regular wages. When gains of over 160 percent are achieved, that amount over the 160 percent is "banked." If in the next performance calculation period the productivity gain is less than 160 percent, the "banked gain" is added to the gain for the next payout period. When high productivity continues and the productivity calculation remains above 160 percent, management has the right to buy back the gain over 160 percent. If, for example, the gain for the year rests at 180 percent, employees receive 50 percent of the difference between 180 and 160 in a one-time annual bonus payment. If the employee's hourly rate of pay was $7 and the employee worked 2,000 hours in the year, the buy-back bonus for the employee would be calculated in this manner:

$$20\% \text{ (buy back)} \times 50\% \text{ (division of gain)} \times \$7 \text{ (hourly rate)}$$
$$\times 2,000 \text{ (hours worked)} = \$1,400 \text{ (buy-back bonus)}$$

Then, in turn, the base period standard for future calculation would be increased by 1.8/1.6 or 1.125.

When gains are made because of the introduction of new equipment or new technology, management receives 80 percent of all savings on technological improvements and the workers split the remaining 20 percent.

CHAPTER

Long-Term Incentives and Wealth Building

Learning Objectives

In this chapter you will learn about:

1. The relationship between long-term incentive programs and the future lifestyles of employees.

2. The influence of federal legislation on the long-term incentive programs of organizations.

3. The various features of a long-term compensation (retirement) program.

4. The increasing popularity of defined contribution plans and the decline in the use of defined benefits plans.

5. ESOPs and 401(k)s.

6. IRAs, SEPs, Keogh plans, and SIMPLE, Roth, and Education IRAs.

Compensation Strategy

Develop qualified deferred compensation programs that link future economic security of all employees to the economic survival and prosperity of the organization.

In attempting to predict the future, there is always some degree of uncertainty. Sometime between the ages of 25 and 30, and after 5 to 10 years in the workforce, employees start thinking about the future, and nagging questions begin to cause concern and anxiety.

Will I be doing this job the rest of my life?

What occupational opportunities will I have in the future?

What kind of security will I have when I no longer wish to work or am incapable of competing against younger members of the workforce?

Where will I obtain the funds to live a desired lifestyle once I no longer have a full-time job?

By the time an employee reaches the age of 40 and has 10 to 15 years of service, the very idea of having to look elsewhere for employment can be traumatic. At this stage of the employee's life, job security and future income, even into retirement, become critical concerns.

For most employees, their long-term security needs are provided for by the federal Social Security and Medicare programs, their employer's retirement plan, and the continuation of their employer's medical and life insurance plans. For a small group of employees, employer-provided long-term compensation arrangements can provide significant wealth to fund estates that can take care of the financial requirements of children and grandchildren.

WEALTH AND WORK IN THE UNITED STATES

Although there were some major flaws in a 1986 University of Michigan study, the statistics still appear to be valid. The study reported that the majority of the wealthy did not acquire their wealth through inheritance but rather through accumulated earnings. It indicated that approximately 9 percent of all households had wealth ranging between $206,340 and $1.4 million. This indicator is another criterion for identifying the upper middle class.

The United States has often been considered the Promised Land. Although the streets may never have been paved with gold, for many people the United States has been a land of opportunity. The University of Michigan study appears to support the premise that through hard work and diligent effort it is possible to accumulate large amounts of wealth.[1]

A number of avenues are available for achieving the American dream beyond short-term income—for example, making wise investments in which the capital is preserved and a significant return on the invested capital is recognized. The old adage, "It's not what you earn but what you don't spend that counts," is another basis for one useful strategy to accumulate wealth. Certainly, if an employer is paying all or a significant share of the costs of valued benefits including health and accident, disability, and life insurance; child and elderly care; and continuing or advanced education programs, even recreation and entertainment opportunities, it saves the employee from spending after-tax dollars to pay for these programs. Not only is the employer paying for these benefits, but for corporate and individual income tax purposes, the employer is usually able to deduct the benefit costs as an expense, and the employee does not incur the expenditure as an earning that would result in increased taxable income.

The relationship between both employer and employee tax obligations is a critical issue not only in the area of employee benefits but also with regard to long-term incentive and deferred income programs. Because many employees do not realize the value of their employer-provided benefits, let alone the avoidance of income tax obligations for the employer payments, the failure to understand the impact of tax legislation on the total compensation program becomes understandable. However, once

---

[1]Survey Research Center, *The Concentration of Wealth in the United States* (Ann Arbor: University of Michigan, 1986).

employees become deeply involved in a long-term incentive/deferred income program and the desire to accumulate wealth and develop an estate, federal tax legislation becomes a critical issue.

TAX LEGISLATION

Upon receipt of the first paycheck, an employee quickly learns that there can be a considerable difference between the granted rate of pay and spendable earnings. Federal, state, and local income tax withholdings and the Social Security and Medicare taxes can quickly remove 20 percent or more of earned income. These taxes are easy to calculate and are understood by most employees. They recognize that income tax withholding decreases with more dependents and that the withholding is a set percentage of base pay. Social Security and Medicare taxes are also easy to grasp, but when it comes to understanding the tax requirements of long-term incentives and deferred compensation, many new and more complex terms must be recognized. The new vocabulary includes *qualified: nondiscrimination rules, highly paid employees, key employees, top-heavy plans, safe harbor provisions, plan formulas, vesting schedule,* and *Social Security integration; nonqualified: doctrine of economic benefit, constructive receipt doctrine,* and *funding opportunities.* These terms are defined in appendixes 16A and 16B.

The federal income tax program is a major source of revenue for the federal government. Individuals, corporations, estates, and trusts may be required to pay income taxes. The major parts of a federal income tax program that affect an individual's income tax payments are (1) deductions from gross income to determine adjusted gross income and taxable income, (2) income tax rates and tax schedules to determine owed taxes, and (3) credits or deductions from calculated tax to determine tax due.

Corporate taxable income is the difference between gross income and deductions. Deductions are allowed for all ordinary and necessary expenses paid or incurred in carrying out a trade or business. Most deductions and credits granted to individuals are also applicable to corporations.

From 1861, with the passage of the Tax Revenue Act, until the passage of the Tax Reform Act of 1986 and subsequent tax legislation to date, income tax laws have witnessed many changes. The Tax Revenue Act of 1861 placed a 3 percent tax on all income over $800. At that time, there were no credits or deductions. Over the years, the maximum marginal rate has risen and declined depending on the revenue needs of the nation. After the passage of the Sixteenth Amendment in 1913, which granted Congress the right to collect taxes on income from whatever source, Congress passed the Income Tax Law of 1913. This law provided a $3,000 deduction for single taxpayers and a $4,000 deduction for a married taxpayer. The tax rate was 1 percent. Those having incomes greater than $20,000 paid a surtax of from 1 to 6 percent, depending on income. By 1917, the maximum marginal tax rate had risen to 77 percent, with deductions allowed for charitable contributions and tax credits allowed for children. In the 1920s, the maximum marginal tax rate declined to 24 percent. It rose to 77 percent in the 1930s, and during World War II, to 94 percent. In 1954, the rates ranged from 20 to 91 percent. Then, in 1964, the maximum tax rate was reduced to 70 percent. In 1968, a 10 percent surcharge on income tax was imposed, and in 1969, the maximum tax rate was reduced to 50 percent. By 1994 the maximum tax rate was 39.6 percent.

During these years, various deductions and credits were entered into the tax program. Such additions as capital gains, a minimum tax on tax preference items, and an alternative minimum tax became part of the income tax laws. Major modifications and simplifications were made with the passage of the Tax Reform Act of 1986 (TRA 86). The 15 income tax brackets were reduced to two with tax rates of 15 percent and 28 percent. Later a third tax bracket of 33 percent, subsequently reduced to 31 percent, was added. The top tax bracket is currently 36 percent. With income over a certain level, there is a 10 percent surtax.

The Taxpayer Relief Act of 1997 (TRA 97) reduced capital gains and wealth transfer taxes, added child credits, and provided new education and savings incentives. The Roth IRA and Education IRA were established under this act. Then in 1998, the Internal Revenue Service Restructuring and Reform Act of 1998 was passed. This act contained many provisions to correct technical errors contained in TRA 97. There are significant new provisions regarding capital gains taxation and estate and gift taxes.

To further ease the burden of income and payroll taxes, families with extremely low income receive an earned income tax credit (EIC), a rebate designed primarily to affect low wage earners' Social Security and Medicare tax payments. For example, in 1988, a two-parent family of four with an income equal to the poverty line of $12,351 paid $413.71 in federal income tax and $927.56 in Social Security and Medicare tax. Their total federal tax burden was $1,341.27. This family received an EIC of $1,031.71, and had a total federal tax burden of $309.56. By 1998, a worker having an earned income and adjusted gross income of less than $12,300 and having two or more dependent children living with him or her was eligible for as much as $3,756 in an EIC. These deductions and credits are designed to eliminate most of the income tax burden for low-income households.

Over the years, the U.S. Congress has used tax legislation to promote both individual and corporate behaviors that have social merit. One major way of accomplishing these social improvement goals is through the addition of a wide variety of deductions and credits to corporate and individual income tax obligations. These deductions and credits can promote the growth of certain businesses or enhance certain desired business activities. They can also promote individual security and enhance the lifestyles of all workers and their dependents.

DESIGNING A LONG-TERM INCENTIVE AND DEFERRED COMPENSATION PLAN

Before investigating the potential use of a long-term incentive and deferred compensation program, at least one important question must be answered: Why would anyone want to have any part of earnings delayed? In the past, income tax laws have been a major reason for the willingness of the highly paid to defer receipt of income. When income tax rates were as high as 90 percent, it was quite likely that a highly paid individual would, at some time in the future, be in a lower income tax bracket, and postponing receipt of income would be advantageous.

With the passage of TRA 86, there were predictions that long-term deferred compensation programs would become less attractive to employees. A major reason for these predictions was the talk of elimination of capital gains and the reduction of tax brackets from 15 to 2. By 1999, capital gains continued to be alive and well, with a maximum rate of 20 percent. It was felt that most highly paid employees would never be in a lower tax bracket than the top bracket of 39.6 percent, even after retirement, and for that matter, a much larger percentage of employees would now be in the highest tax bracket. These predictions, however, were based on narrow and possibly faulty conclusions. First of all, there is no guarantee that the maximum tax rate will remain at 39.6 percent, and, second, most long-term corporate deferral programs provide the recipient with an attractive rate of interest (higher than that obtained through conservative investment practices). In addition, the interest generated in a deferred program is tax deferred and compounded tax free. Also, neither the employer nor the employee may truly have a choice about taking all payments currently or receiving a significant share at some future date. In the last decades of the twentieth century, long-term survival and growth became major concerns of organizations of all sizes in all kinds of businesses, and most employees were aware that with the decline or the possible demise of their companies, they could lose both jobs and economic security.

This mutual concern is broadening and intensifying interest in an area of compensation that for many employee groups has received minimal attention—long-term income and protection. Other than for a very small group of employees in the executive suites, the focus of compensation programs has been, in the past, primarily both fixed and on the short term (with the exception of Social Security and pension plans). To integrate both employee and organizational needs for long-term survival and growth, the compensation system must now require employee contributions that will help achieve the long-term objectives of the organization and employer recognition of these long-term contributions through rewards that are based on the long-term success of the organization.

Fixed and Variable Long-Term Compensation

Chapters 13 and 14 focused on variable short-term compensation components. Now, this chapter and chapter 16 focus on both fixed and variable long-term compensation components. The increase in size and importance of long-term compensation will affect almost every segment of the workforce with the possible exception of the contingent employees—those who receive almost 100 percent of their compensation in short-term wages and salaries and whose only benefits are those that are government mandated. Recent court cases may allow contingent employees to receive incentives and benefits that have been previously unavailable to them.

Over the years, employers have offered various kinds of long-term compensation to employees. The most common arrangements have been those that provide retirement programs to supplement federal Social Security benefits. A long-term compensation plan may also involve the deferral of a certain amount of current pay until retirement (either a decrease in existing salary or deferral of a proposed increase). Upon retirement, the employee receives a stream of payments over a designated period or for life. If the individual dies before retirement or before the payment of installments as set forth in the contract, the beneficiary of the employee receives the amount owed.

Peter Chingos and colleagues provide a model for developing a useful long-term incentive program for almost any organization. Their model focuses on deferred compensation, which they define as "delayed payment for services; that is, the employee receives compensation after the period in which the services are performed." They further identify three types of deferred plans: (1) qualified deferred, (2) capital accumulation, and (3) other deferred and supplemental retirement income arrangements.[2]

The conventional wisdom espoused by many compensation experts is that they do not consider deferred arrangements as "incentive" plans. This author strongly disagrees but does recognize that organizations must do a far better job of communicating the value of deferred long-term compensation programs to their employees. This communication must link future economic security of all employees to the economic survival and health of the organization. An underlying premise of this view is that all components of a compensation program can be incentive related if properly designed and communicated to all employees. The three parts of the Chingos model can be used for developing a long-term incentive program that promotes employee wealth building.

Foundation of a Long-Term Compensation Program

The foundation of a long-term compensation program includes the use of various kinds of qualified deferred plans defined under Section 401 of the Internal Revenue Code (IRC). Plans meeting requirements established within Section 401 of IRC receive favorable tax treatment. Section 401 deferred compensation plans are usually pension, profit-sharing, and stock bonus plans. There are two important favorable tax treatments of Section 401: (1) The employer can recognize the deferred payment as an expense in the period in which it was earned and interest earned by such payments as an expense in the period accrued; and (2) employees need not report "qualified" (meeting IRC requirements) deferred compensation payments until actually or constructively received (definition in section on tax implications). This means that a deferred payment does not add to the employee's wage base in the year granted and is not part of the employee's taxable income.

Capital Accumulation Arrangements

Capital accumulation arrangements provide participating employees with "capital stock, or the right to purchase or receive capital stock under specified terms and conditions; or the right to receive cash under specified conditions or any combination of the foregoing."[3] Within the capital accumulation group of deferred compensation, Chingos and colleagues locate long-term incentive plans.

Graef Crystal, an expert on executive compensation, defines a long-term incentive plan as one intended to reward an employee for a performance accomplishment over a period of several years rather than just a single year.[4] The concepts presented in this chapter and chapter 16 expand on the definition espoused by Crystal. Even though a significant portion of the long-term arrangements provided in the foundation section is fixed, it is important to the organization to communicate the message to employees that the amount of the final retirement benefits relates directly to the employee's contribution to the organization, movement through the organization, and success of the organization. The availability and size of all long-term components, not just those dis-

[2]Peter T. Chingos et al., *Financial Considerations of Executive Compensation and Retirement Plans* (New York: Wiley, 1984), pp. 9, 10.
[3]Chingos et al., *Financial Considerations,* p. 21.
[4]Graef S. Crystal, *Questions and Answers on Executive Compensation* (Englewood Cliffs, NJ: Prentice-Hall, 1984).

cussed in this section, relate to the ability of the organization to meets its performance targets into the distant future.

Other Deferred and Supplemental Income Arrangements

The design of a long-term compensation program must relate and in some manner overcome the very critical income tax issue of constructive receipt and the nonmotivational influence of qualified retirement arrangements on highly paid employees. If an employer funds a nonqualified deferred compensation plan in any manner that guarantees the funds to the recipient, the doctrine of constructive receipt is met and the employee must recognize all employer contributions as current earned income and pay income tax on the contributions. The other side of the nonqualified deferred compensation issue then is that the employer's promises or contract to pay the recipient a specified amount at some time in the future may place the employee at considerable risk. An unforeseen or unfortunate situation could arise, making the promise, even the contract, almost worthless (the employer enters into bankruptcy or the employer is acquired in a hostile takeover and the new corporation refuses to recognize certain agreements made by the old employer).

There are, however, a number of opportunities available to employers for providing participants in a nonqualified deferred compensation plan with a significant amount of security that the promise to pay will be met. In these plans, the employer invests for the recipient. The investment generates gains that are not taxed to the recipient and, at some future date, the recipient can receive either a lump-sum payment or a series of installments. A wide variety of arrangements, including insurance-based plans, such as variable life, whole life, or universal life policies; variable annuities; escrow custodial accounts; internally funded revocable trusts; and externally funded nonexempt trusts can be established to provide participants in a nonqualified deferred compensation program with a reasonable amount of assurance that they will receive the agreed-to amount due at the specified date. In these funding arrangements, the employer normally does not receive an income tax deduction until the employee recognizes the income. These arrangements are discussed in detail in chapter 16.

There are additional advantages of a nonqualified pension arrangement: (1) It does not have to comply with IRS regulations requiring set-up or annual administration fees; (2) it does not require IRS approval; (3) there are no penalties for early withdrawal (before age 59½) and late withdrawals (after age 70½); (4) there are no excess accumulation taxes; (5) the plan need not comply with nondiscriminatory provisions that favor the lower-paid employees; (6) withdrawals can be made to fund a dependent's college education or assist in an emergency situation; (7) a participant can determine his or her own contribution level; and (8) there is no IRS tax for overfunding.

QUALIFIED DEFERRED COMPENSATION ARRANGEMENTS

For many employees, the good life, the golden years, are those coming after age 55 or at first eligibility for retirement. Not having to get up at 5 or 6 o'clock each morning, not having to do required activities that may no longer be challenging or enjoyable is the dream of many workers. This dream can be fulfilled only through wise and successful retirement planning.

The 1980s and 1990s witnessed a steady decline in retirement age. Many large organizations involved in restructuring and reducing numbers of employees of their staffs offered employees age 45 to 50 with 20 to 30 years of tenure lucrative retirement opportunities (add five years to age and tenure for retirement purposes; receive a $10,000 bonus; or receive an additional retirement payment each year until the employee becomes eligible for additional Social Security payment at age 62 or 65).

In the not too distant past, few workers gave the slightest thought to retirement prior to reaching the age of 55 or 60. This is no longer the case. In the not too distant future, those who retire at 55 or 65 will have, respectively, from 30 to 20 more years to enjoy. Many workers will spend as many years retired as they did working. However, as more and more workers and their families enjoy the life of the middle levels of the middle class, they realize that their retirement income must include more than Social Security benefits. They also begin to realize that the development of investments to supplement Social Security and employer pension plans is a long-term, if not lifetime, affair. Some of the major components of the foundation for a secure and enjoyable future are (1) Social Security and Medicare, (2) employer-provided qualified retirement plans, (3) savings or thrift plans, (4) cash or deferred arrangement (CODA)—401(k) plans, (5) IRAs, (6) SEPs, (7) SIMPLE plans, (8) Keogh plans, and (9) the continuation of employer-provided health and medical insurance.

Employer-provided retirement programs, including Social Security costs, in many cases, account for approximately 30 percent of the cost of all benefits. (Benefit costs for most employers range between 30 to 40 percent of total payroll.) Developing a cost-effective retirement program for employees usually requires the counsel of a specialist. Retirement plans must not only provide adequate retirement benefits but must also meet the approval of a number of federal agencies and, in many states, comply with a variety of state laws. In addition to the Internal Revenue Service tax codes, most retirement plans must now comply with the Employee Retirement Income Security Act of 1974 (ERISA), which places strict requirements on privately operated pension plans. The Taft-Hartley Act also requires the unionized company to permit its unions to participate in the administration of its pension plan.

To provide the employee with the best set of retirement benefits, each organization must design its own program, taking into consideration the kind of organization it is; the range in kinds of benefits offered; and the basic needs, characteristics, and demands of its employees. A critical element of any retirement plan is its funding. The employer's current contribution to a retirement fund (trust) helps ensure that money will be available at some future time to make the promised payments to the retiree. ERISA requires employers to pay the full cost of currently promised benefits. It also requires employers to make amortized payments on past liabilities. However, IRS codes do not allow all employers tax deductions for amortized payments of past liabilities established on a payment schedule that is less than 10 years long. Some organizations provide for the total funding of their group pension plans, whereas others require some employee contributions. Employee contributions make it possible to provide more liberal retirement benefits.

Social Security

Many retirees depend on Social Security for more than half of their retirement income. Although millions of Americans are the beneficiaries of the federal Social Security program, many more millions are paying premiums to qualify for Social Security benefits.

Social Security now provides retirement income to those electing to retire at the age of 62. Standard benefits become available after a worker reaches 65, although it is possible for an employee to increase benefits slightly by delaying receipt of payment until age 70. For each month Social Security payments are delayed after reaching age 65, the recipient can increase the earned payment by one-quarter of 1 percent (.0025) to age 70, for a maximum possible increase of 15 percent. In reverse, for each month a recipient requests payment to start before reaching the age of 65, the payment is decreased by one-quarter of 1 percent. If the recipient elects to begin receiving payments at age 62, the earned payment (at age 65) would decrease by 9 percent. Also, at age 65, Social Security recipients become eligible for Medicare. Currently, the age for a standard benefit will increase to age 66 in 2004 and then to 67 in 2027.

The actual amount of retirement benefits depends on the individual's age at the start of retirement, years of work, average earnings during that period, and number of eligible dependents at the time benefits start. Beginning in June 1975, Social Security benefits were linked to the consumer price index (CPI). If Congress increases benefits in a given year, there will be no cost-of-living adjustment for the following year. A wage earner who had always paid the maximum Social Security tax and retired in 1993 at age 65 received $13,536 a year while the average Social Security recipient received $7,548. A detailed discussion of Social Security legislation may be found in chapter 5.

Qualified Retirement Plans

At the present time, about 50 percent of the nonfarm U.S. workforce receive some form of retirement protection from employers through either private pension, deferred profit-sharing plans, or stock bonus plans. For these plans to receive any kind of tax preference treatment, they must meet requirements established by the IRS. Plans meeting IRS policies and regulations are called qualified plans. The Office of Pension and Welfare Benefits Programs (PWBP) within the U.S. Department of Labor also reviews and regulates private retirement programs.

There are three kinds of qualified retirement plans: pension, profit sharing, and stock bonus plans.

Pension Plans   Qualified pension plans are deferred arrangements that provide definitely determinable payments over a prescribed schedule. The actual amount of the benefit usually depends on the employee's base pay and some short-term add-ons (overtime, shift differentials) and years of service (these add-ons relate closely to W-2 earnings). A pension plan can be a *defined benefits plan,* a *defined contribution plan,* or a *cash balance plan.*

A *defined benefits plan* includes a formula that defines the benefits an employee is to receive. Average earnings in the highest three years of employment multiplied by 2 percent times the total years of service is one example. An employer with a defined benefits retirement plan must make annual contributions to the plan based upon actuarial computations to pay the vested retirement benefits. IRC, Section 415, dollar limit for a defined benefits plan was set at $90,000 and in 1988 became indexed to the CPI. In 1999, the limit was $130,000.

A *defined contribution plan* (also known as a *money purchase plan*) involves the payment of a specified annual amount to the account of each participant. The amount specified may be (1) a flat dollar amount, (2) an amount based on a special formula (an amount of corporate profit), or (3) an amount equal to a certain percentage of the participant's base pay (and stated add-ons). The employee's pension depends on the actual amount contributed and the increased earnings of the invested funds. IRC, Section 415, limits a defined contribution plan to $30,000. It will remain at $30,000 until the defined benefits limit reaches $120,000. After that, the defined contribution limit will be 25 percent of the defined benefits limit.

In the late 1980s and into the 1990s, more and more organizations converted their defined benefits plans into defined contribution plans. By 1998, 40.4 million workers were enrolled in defined contribution plans, while 24.6 million workers were enrolled in defined benefits plans.[5] Currently, because of past practices, approximately 76 percent of all pensioners receive benefits from a defined benefits plan.

In a defined contribution plan, the investment and management skills of the operators of the pension fund become a crucial factor in determining pension payments. In this kind of a plan, the employee assumes the investment risk. In a defined benefits plan, however, the employer assumes greater uncertainty when increases in benefits payments require larger contributions to a pension trust.[6]

Normally, payments made to a retiree are far less generous under a defined contribution plan than they are under a defined benefits plan. It is not unusual for an employee with 25 to 30 years of service within a defined benefits plan to receive 50 percent to 60 percent of salary until death. However, if this same employee had participated in a defined contribution plan and the employer had contributed 5 percent of the employee's salary, after 30 years, assuming retirement at age 65, the employee would have amassed enough to replace only about 15 percent of salary.[7]

In the late 1990s, many organizations switched their pension plans into a *cash-balance plan*. A cash-balance plan is much less expensive for the employer than the traditional plans. The plan looks similar to a defined benefits plan in that it pays a specific benefit at retirement based on years of employment and earnings. It is also a qualified plan and is federally insured.

The plan provides a hypothetical account for each employee and requires the employer to contribute a certain amount each year for each employee based on the employee's earnings. This feature makes the plan look like a 401(k) plan with each employee having a cash-balance account.

Because the cash-balance plan allows younger workers to earn pension benefits more quickly, when converting to a cash-balance account, organizations frequently protect older employees who may be 45 years of age or older or whose age and years of service total 70. These older individuals are permitted to remain in the existing plan. The reason for this provision is that in traditional plans, employers contribute significantly more to the benefit plan of older employees. In a cash-balance plan, the employer contribution is a certain percentage of the employee's earnings from the time the employee enters the program. In 1999, members of Congress and the IRS voiced concern over the design and use of many cash-balance plans.

---

[5]Robert Lewis, "Taking a risky turn? New pensions gain ground despite pitfalls," *AARP Bulletin,* November 1998, p. 6.
[6]U.S. Department of Labor, *Estimates of Participants and Financial Characteristics of Private Pension Plans* (Washington, DC: U.S. Government Printing Office, 1983).
[7]Steven P. Galante, "Aging Baby Boomers May Bid for Richer Retirement Plans," *The Wall Street Journal,* July 27, 1987, p. 19.

All pension plans are concerned with the following five basic issues:

1. *Standard retirement age.* The standard retirement age is generally taken to be 65. Some would like this to be reduced to 62, 60, and even 55. Some unions have demanded the 30-and-out option (retirement after 30 years of service) that permits some employees to retire in their late forties. Federal legislation enacted in 1978 and amendments effectively eliminated any mandatory retirement age.

2. *Size of benefits.* The size of benefits has been steadily increasing, and inflation of the 1970s and early 1980s caused some pension plans to be tied to cost-of-living indexes. Various methods are available for determining retirement income. One of these is the percentage formula method that includes a certain base pay and a base rate. Procedures for determining these two values include average pay earned by employees during total employment, or the pay of the last five years or even of the highest five years of pay. The base rate may be as low as 20 percent and as high as 75 percent. Some methods are related directly to length of employment; others are simply a flat rate after reaching a required number of years of employment. Many pension plans are providing from $1,000 to $2,000 a month to employees retiring at age 65 with 30 years of service.

3. *Discrimination in plan design.* Women have not only trailed men in the area of base pay, but they have also had less pension coverage and entitlement to benefits than men. Pension coverage for women was enhanced by women plaintiffs winning two major lawsuits.

   Pension premium payments and retiree pension annuities became a subject of discrimination when women took issue with both employer and insurance company practices requiring that the amount of premiums paid and benefits received relate to actuarial calculations. Because women as a group live longer than men as a group, either the contributions to the pension plans had to be greater or, if the contributions were the same, the benefits provided to female retirees were less than those received by male employees of the same status. In the case of *Manhart et al.* v. *City of Los Angeles, Department of Water and Power et al.,* 13 FEP Cases 1625 (1976), the court ruled that the employer violated Title VII by requiring female employees to make larger contributions to the retirement plan than male employees. The court further stated that because not all women live longer than all men, each woman must be considered as an individual, and because Title VII protects individuals, not classes of individuals, female employees must be treated the same as male employees.

   In 1983, in *Arizona Governing Committee* v. *Norris,* 32 FEP Cases 233 (1983), the court ruled that Title VII prohibits an employer from offering its employees the option of receiving retirement benefits from one of several insurance companies selected by the employer, all of which pay a woman lower monthly retirement benefits than a man who has made the same contribution. This ruling, in essence, requires insurance companies to use unisex actuarial tables for calculating pension premium payments and retiree annuities for tax-deferred annuity and deferred compensation plans.

4. *Early retirement.* Any retirement before age 65 has been considered early retirement. The 30-and-out program resulting in retirement opportunities for many in their fifties would warrant this designation. Some organizations permit employees to retire, with reduced pensions, as early as 10 to 15 years before the normal retirement

date. The major reasons for early retirement are to (1) open more jobs for younger employees and (2) trim staff levels where excess numbers of employees exist.

5. *Vesting.* (See discussion in appendix 16A.)

Profit-Sharing Plans   A qualified arrangement may also take the form of a profit-sharing plan. The employer's contributions to the plan are a percentage of corporate profits. Although an employer is not required to contribute a prescribed amount of profits to the plan, the employer must make substantial and recurring contributions to meet requirements. Because a profit-sharing plan may not be set up with retirement income as its primary purpose, lump-sum payments may be the normal method of distributing benefits. Special provisions are also established for plans that allow participants to elect to receive the employer's contribution as cash or to have it contributed to a qualified profit-sharing plan.

Stock Bonus Plan   Another form a qualified plan may take is that of stock bonus plan. In a qualified stock bonus plan, the employer contributes stock to the plan. The actual allocation among participants depends on the same requirements as a defined benefits plan and a defined profit-sharing plan, although the plan functions like a defined contribution plan.

Limitations on Qualified Plans   For the first time, with the enactment of TRA 86, a *limit was placed on the amount of pay* that can be taken into account for all qualified plans regardless of whether they are top-heavy. The limit in 1989 was $200,000, indexed to reflect CPI changes. By 1993, the limit was $235,840. In 1994, it was reduced to $150,000 and it now stands at $160,000. Beginning in 1987, the ratio of defined benefits to defined contribution limits changed from 3:1 to 4:1. The $30,000 defined contribution limit would not increase until the 4:1 ratio was achieved. Although the 4:1 ratio was achieved in 1995, no future change is contemplated in the defined contribution limit as the maximum defined benefits limit is currently fixed at $120,000. The $75,000 floor for early retirement under the defined benefit plan has been eliminated, and the maximum benefits will be reduced for all amounts paid before normal retirement age. The reduction will be 5/9 of 1 percent for the first 36 months of early retirement plus 5/12 of 1 percent for each additional month of early retirement after age 62. The reduction for ages before 62 will be based on actuarial factors using the plan's interest rate, but not less than 5 percent for early retirement. For purposes of determining when the maximum amount can be paid, normal retirement age has been changed to correspond with Social Security normal retirement age—65 for those born before 1938, 66 for those born from 1938 through 1954, and 67 for those born in 1955 and later. The dollar limit for defined benefits plans will be phased in on the basis of years of participation in the plan.

Many pension plans permit an employee to elect to receive a reduced pension upon retirement so that the pension continues in force after death, granting continued income to the spouse. Other plans allow the spouse to receive from 20 to 50 percent of the normal retirement income. This is more costly than the first option and has been considered unfair to those who have no spouse.

Employee Stock Ownership Plan (ESOP)

An ESOP is a defined contribution plan that operates like a qualified stock bonus plan. In an ESOP, the employer contributes stock to a *stock bonus trust (ESOT)* that qualifies as a tax-exempt employee trust under IRC, Section 401(a).

ESOPs take two primary forms—a stock bonus ESOP or a leveraged or leverageable ESOP. In a stock bonus ESOP, the employer contributes company stock to the ESOT and does not use the ESOT as a mechanism for obtaining funds. In a leveraged or leverageable ESOP, the employer uses the special tax privileges granted to an ESOT to obtain funding for various purposes (an owner wishing to reduce equity ownership and obtain cash for held stock; a company wishing to obtain money to purchase new equipment, build new facilities, or in some manner extend business opportunities).

Changes in federal tax laws beginning with the Tax Reform Act of 1976, followed by the Economic Recovery Tax Act of 1981 (ERTA), the Deficit Reduction Act of 1984 (DEFRA), and the Tax Reform Act of 1986 (TRA 86), have all stimulated interest in employee retirement programs that focus on employee ownership of stock in the company. ESOPs permit employers to take advantage of certain tax privileges when granting stock to employees. Past variations of the ESOP have been the retirement plan used by Sears, Roebuck and the plan known as the Kelso plan (used by companies to raise capital).

In a leveraged ESOP, a company borrows money from a financial institution, using its stock as security. Over a prescribed period of time, the company repays the loan. With each loan repayment, a certain amount of the stock that was used as security for the loan is placed into an ESOT for distribution at *no cost* to all employees. This stock then becomes part of an employee profit-sharing or retirement program. Not only do employees receive the stock upon retirement, but they also receive special tax credits for the value of the stock the company bought for them. The ESOP plans qualifying for tax benefits under the Tax Reform Act of 1976 are called TRASOPS.

Additional benefits of the plan to the company were these:

1. The company can sell its stock and redeem it without reducing the true value of the stock (because it is held by the financial institution as security for the loan).
2. The company can increase its working capital, cash flow, and net worth.
3. The company can pay off the loan and redeem the stock through the use of pretax dollars and at the same time receive special tax credits.

In the past, these TRASOP tax credits were a 1 percent investment-based tax credit and a possible additional 0.5 percent credit allotted to plan sponsors who permitted and matched voluntary employee contributions. This 1.0 to 1.5 percent tax credit favored capital-intensive firms. ERTA changed TRASOPs to PAYSOPs, which granted a payroll-based tax credit of 0.5 percent in 1983 and 1984 and was extended to December 31, 1987, by DEFRA. The payroll tax credit favored labor-intensive firms. Actual allocation to a specific employee PAYSOP was determined by the employee's salary as a percentage of total payroll.

TRA 86 placed additional restrictions on ESOPs but overall increased their attractiveness both as a qualified deferred compensation plan and a tool of corporate finance. Some of the major changes regarding ESOPs are these:

1. The tax credit for PAYSOP was terminated as of December 31, 1986.
2. Although ESOPs are designed to invest primarily in the employer's securities, organizations are now required to offer a diversification option to participants nearing retirement. Employees who have completed 10 years of participation in the plan and have reached age 55 must be given the right annually to diversify the

investment of their account over a five-year period. The portion of the account subject to this choice is 25 percent each year, but it becomes 50 percent in the final year of the election. The plan can actually distribute stock or cash to an employee who can then roll it over to an IRA; or the plan can provide a minimum of three optional investment programs, with the option of rolling the distribution over to another qualified plan that offers a choice of investments.

3. The assets of a terminated defined benefits plan could be transferred directly to an ESOP before 1989, provided that at least half of the employees in the terminated plans were covered by the ESOP. The assets from the terminated defined benefits plan could be used to buy employer stock or repay an outstanding ESOP loan. Securities attributable to the reversion amount had to be allocated within a maximum of seven years. TRA 86 changes included special distribution requirements—in most cases, members of an ESOP had to receive total distribution in equal installments over not more than five years.

4. DEFRA provided favorable funding options for ESOPs. DEFRA provisions permitted financial institutions to exclude half of the interest from an ESOP loan as earned income. TRA 86 permits regulated investment companies (mutual funds) to also receive favorable ESOP lending opportunities. TRA 86 permits an employer to borrow directly from the lender and still call it an ESOP loan, provided that securities equal to the proceeds are contributed to the ESOP within 30 days and are allocated within one year, and that the loan repayment period does not exceed seven years. This option essentially provides the employer with a line of credit.

5. Both DEFRA and TRA 86 encourage owner-employers of closely held companies to sell their stock to an ESOP in a number of ways. Of particular importance is a TRA 86 estate tax advantage. It allows an estate that sells employer securities to an ESOP to exclude 50 percent of the proceeds of the sale from tax. This provision does not apply if the stock originally came from a qualified plan or stock option plan.

6. Each participant in an ESOP is provided with one vote regardless of stock allocated to the participant's account and voting all shares held by the plan is in proportion to the vote. Employee participants in closely held companies must be allowed to vote on the following issues: mergers or consolidations, recapitalization, reclassification, liquidation, or dissolution or sale of assets.

7. The maximum dollar limit on an ESOP annual addition is $50,000 or 25 percent of pay, whichever is less.

In most ESOPs, the stock allocation to a participant's account is in proportion to the relative base pay plus other short-term add-ons from the employer corporation for that year. Whether from the aspect of sheer corporate survival, or improvement in profitability, or simply because owners think it is a right and proper thing, employee ownership is gaining interest in the United States. According to the National Center for Employee Ownership, by 1998 more than 10,000 companies had ESOPs that made approximately 9 million employees at least part owners of their companies. The median percentage ownership for ESOPs in publicly traded companies is about 10 percent to 15 percent, whereas the median percentage ownership for privately held companies is about 30 percent to 40 percent.[8]

---

[8]Corey Rosen, *An Overview of ESOPs, Stock Options, and Employee Ownership* (Oakland, CA: The National Center for Employee Ownership, 1998).

Past surveys indicated that companies with employee stock ownership plans were 1.5 times as profitable as comparable conventionally owned companies, and the more stock owned by employees, the greater the ratio became.[9] Companies with ESOPs had an average productivity growth rate one and one-half times greater than comparable conventional firms.[10] Current studies continue to show that ESOP providers outperform their peers.[11] A major reason for the profitability of companies with a significant amount of employee ownership may relate to the kind of management that first entertains employee ownership ideas, and then implements them and makes them work. Managers with such views and interests may also be the kinds of managers who lead their organizations in attaining significant shares of their markets and high levels of profitability.

Following are some benefits and costs of employee stock ownership plans from an employer and employee perspective:

Employer Benefits

1. An ESOP assists in establishing and maintaining a stable, high-performance workforce. It can act as golden handcuffs to retain desired employees.
2. The employer obtains certain tax benefits (deductions are permitted on dividends paid with respect to ESOP stock if the dividends are used to repay an ESOP loan; normally, dividends are not tax deductible but are taxable to both the corporation and to the individual recipient).
3. An ESOP permits the use of pretax dollars to purchase a desired employee benefit. (By being a qualified benefit, both principal and interest payments to the trust are tax deductible.)
4. An ESOP establishes a trust to hold more than 10 percent of assets in employer securities without having to prove the fiduciary soundness of decision.
5. An ESOP provides the owner with a way to sell equity interest without having to go public.
6. The leverage features of an ESOP may be highly desirable to an employer.
7. The owner can sell stock in any desired increment at any one time up to total holdings.
8. Companies currently not paying tax can carry ESOP deductions for 15 years.

Employer Costs

1. An ESOP may cause dilution of the value of stock and ownership rights.
2. "Cashed out" demands by employees in closely held companies may cause considerable drain on available cash. (Relates to requests by departing employees for cash value of stock.)
3. For even a small firm, ESOP installation costs range, at a minimum, from $10,000 to $15,000.
4. Fair market value of stock in a closely held company must be determined annually by an outside appraiser, which frequently costs at least $3,000.

---

[9]Michael Conte and Arnold Tannenbaum, *Employee Ownership: A Report to the Economic Development Administration* (Washington, DC: U.S. Department of Commerce, 1978), p. 19.
[10]Thomas Marsh and Dale McAllister, "ESOPs Tables," *Journal of Corporation Law,* Spring 1981, pp. 614–16.
[11]Daniel Eisenberg, "No ESOP Fable," *Time,* May 10, 1999, p. 95.

5. Proxy statements received by employee stockholders may provide sensitive executive compensation information.
6. Decline in price of stock may be considered an extreme loss in wealth by employees.

Employee Benefits

1. Participation in an ESOP gives employees equity opportunities with no cash investment. Provides excellent estate (wealth) building opportunities. (A 1983 study indicated that median wage earners—those earning $18,300—would accumulate $31,000 in company stock after 10 years of participation in a typical ESOP. The ESOP may be one of the best opportunities for a lower-middle-class worker to accumulate wealth and develop an estate.)[12]
2. Employees have a chance to voice their views at the policymaking levels of the organization.
3. Employees pay no tax on stock until distribution is made, either on leaving the firm or at retirement.
4. Employees can roll distribution over into an IRA, thus deferring any tax at time of distribution.

Employee Costs

1. Employer may pay lower wages or salaries, recognizing the possibility of significantly larger total compensation through stock acquisition opportunities.
2. Employer's stock may decrease in value or, possibly, become worthless in case of bankruptcy or business failure.

Savings or Thrift Plan

Possibly the most commonly provided defined contribution plan is the *savings or thrift plan.* Over the years, many organizations have developed savings or thrift plans that encourage employees to set aside certain amounts of earnings in order to have a more secure and happier retirement. The organization stimulates such a program by matching a certain percentage of the employee's savings—usually from 50 to 100 percent. Most programs specify a limit to the amount an employee can place in such a plan. An employee can contribute up to 6 percent of eligible annual compensation on a voluntary after-tax basis. These funds generate nontaxable interest and increase funds available upon retirement, but in no case can the total employer and employee contributions exceed $30,000 or 25 percent of salary, whichever is less.

The Average Deferred Percentage (ADP) tests established for determining elective contributions under a Cash or Deferred Arrangement (CODA) are also applicable to a savings plan. (See discussion of both CODA and ADP in next section.) The ADP tests include employee (after-tax) contributions, employer matching contributions, and voluntary employee contributions that are not matched by employer contributions to a savings plan.

With the introduction of CODA-401(k) plans, many savings and thrift plans have been modified to accept 401(k) salary reduction contributions.

---

[12]Corey Rosen and Jonathan Feldman, "Employee Benefits in Employee Stock Ownership Plans," *Pension World,* February 1986, pp. 34–39.

Cash or Deferred Arrangement (CODA)-401(k) Plans

Cash or Deferred Arrangement (CODA)-401(k) plans became popular with passage of the Revenue Act of 1978 and later Internal Revenue Service rulings under Section 401(k) of the IRC. The major feature of a 401(k) plan is that employees have the right to agree to a reduction in salary in exchange for a comparable employee contribution to a qualified trust. The amount deferred and accumulated investment earnings are excluded from current income and are taxed only when distributed. Lump-sum distributions are eligible for a 10-year averaging treatment.

Under TRA 86, an individual may defer no more than 20 percent of annual earnings with a maximum of $7,000 per year (indexed annually based on annual change in CPI beginning in 1988—$10,000 in 1999) under a CODA. This amount will be reduced by any Simplified Employee Pension (SEP) plan contribution and any salary reduction contribution under a tax-sheltered annuity. If a deferral exceeds the limit, the value of the excess contribution is taxable to the employee for the year in which it was made.

To ensure that 401(k) plans do not discriminate in favor of the highly compensated employee, the plan must be offered to a nondiscriminatory group of employees. A nondiscriminatory group might be determined, for example, by length of service (all employees with more than 4 years of service) or might consist of all nonunionized employees. After employees eligible to participate in a 401(k) plan are identified, the group must be divided into two sections. To determine the two groups, see the discussion on highly paid employees in appendix 16B. Organizations may require 401(k) participants to be 21 years of age and have one year of service.

Elective deferrals must meet a specific ADP test. The ADP tests established under TRA 86 specify that elective deferral of a highly paid employee may not exceed the greater of (1) 125 percent of the ADP for nonhighly paid employees, or (2) the lesser of 200 percent of the nonhighly paid ADP or this ADP plus 2 percentage points. For determining ADP tests, pay is defined as essentially W-2 earnings. There is a $150,000 limit to pay. The following is an example of the results of the ADP tests:

Average Deferral of Lower Paid (%)	Maximum Average Deferral for Highly Paid (%)	Test Used
1.0	2.0	200%
2.0	4.0	200%
3.0	5.0	plus 2%
4.0	6.0	plus 2%
5.0	7.0	plus 2%
6.0	8.0	plus 2%
7.0	9.0	plus 2%
8.0	10.0	plus 2%
9.0	11.5	125%
10.0	12.5	125%

Employers who match some percentage of their employees' contributions to a 401(k) plan find that employees are more willing to participate in the plan and also to contribute a larger percentage of their salaries. As in other employer matching plans, the most common form of match is a certain percentage of each dollar contributed by the employee. The most common match is 50 cents by the employer for each $1 contributed by the employee up to a cap of 5 to 6 percent of the employee's salary. Many plans permit the employee to contribute up to 10 percent, the amount above the cap being unmatched.[13]

Many employees are allowed to select the investment vehicle for their contribution. The investment funds are managed by a trustee. Fund options available to employees may be a conservative bond fund, government securities, a blue-chip stock fund, or a speculative stock fund. Some employers may use their own stock as an investing opportunity or possibly do the dollar matching with corporate stock, making the employee's investment even more diversified.

Individual Retirement Account (IRA)

Individuals who do not participate in an employer-sponsored retirement plan are allowed to have an IRA. In a traditional IRA, an individual can contribute $2,000 per year or 100 percent of earned income if less than $2,000. A married couple that files jointly can contribute $4,000. This contribution to an IRA is tax deductible—reduces taxable income, and the money invested in an IRA can grow tax deferred. The IRA owner can select his or her own investment program.

Simplified Employee Pension Plan (SEP)

Section 408(j) of the IRC established the *Simplified Employee Pension Plan (SEP),* which permits an employer to establish a qualified IRA program for employees if 100 percent of the employees who have reached the age of 25 during the calendar year and have performed services for the employer during the calendar year and at least three of the preceding calendar years participate. The employer may contribute an amount equal to $24,000 or 15 percent of each employee's earned income to a maximum of $160,000. An employer must contribute the same percentage of W-2 earnings for each eligible employee as the owner contributes to his or her own plan. An owner can vary or skip contributions from year to year. All contributions are immediately vested to the participant. TRA 86 restricts the use of SEPs to employers with fewer than 26 employees. SEP plans are subject to most of the same restrictions applicable to any qualified plan. SEP threshold earnings for participants is $400 annually.

Savings Incentive Match Plan for Employees (SIMPLE)

A *SIMPLE* is designed for employers with no more than 100 employees with no employee receiving less than $5,000 in pay. An employer using a SIMPLE may not use any other kind of qualified plan. Employees can contribute up to 100 percent of their pay on a pretax basis up to $6,000. Employers can match a participant's contributions on a dollar-for-dollar basis up to 3 percent of the participant's earnings or a maximum of

---

[13]"Popularity Grows for 401(k) Plans," *Pension World,* April 1984, p. 14.

$6,000 per year. The employer can also make a nonelective contribution of 2 percent of each employee's earnings whether or not the employee contributes to the plan.

Employers have the flexibility of contributing at least 1 percent of an employee's pay in two years of a five-year period and 3 percent in the other three years. An employer has minimal set-up cost, no administrative fees, and there is no discrimination test.

Employees can make withdrawals from the plan at any time but there is a 25 percent withdrawal penalty before age 59½ or within two years after becoming a plan participant. Employees may take loans against the plan and take withdrawal under certain hardship situations. The employee fund is 100 percent vested upon making the contribution.

A SIMPLE can be either a SIMPLE IRA or a SIMPLE 401(k). Although both kinds of plans are similar, differences relate to (1) administrative requirements, (2) employer contributions, and (3) access to assets.

Keogh (HR-10) Plan

Self-employed persons such as partners or sole proprietors can provide for their retirement by establishing a *Keogh (HR-10) plan.*

A Keogh plan can take three options: (1) profit-sharing plan, (2) money-purchase plan, or (3) paired plan. In a *profit-sharing plan,* the employer can (1) contribute from 0 percent to 15 percent of W-2 earnings up to a maximum of $160,000 each year, or (2) vary contributions from year to year and skip years.

In a *money-purchase plan,* the employer can (1) contribute 0 to 25 percent of W-2 earnings of up to a maximum of $160,000 each year, or (2) make contributions each year based on a fixed annual contribution percentage specified when setting up the plan.

A *paired plan* allows the employer to (1) contribute from 0 to 25 percent of W-2 earnings of up to a maximum of $160,000 each year or (2) contribute a fixed annual contribution percentage to a money-purchase plan and vary contributions to the participant's profit-sharing plan.

For any of these Keogh plans, the contribution to each eligible employee must be the same percentage of W-2 earnings as that contributed for the owner.

Roth and Education IRAs

With the passage of TRA 97, *Roth IRAs* and *Education IRAs* were offered to the U.S. taxpayer. Both IRAs permit certain individuals to contribute to the IRA and receive certain benefits.

Roth IRAs permit individuals who meet certain income requirements to contribute up to $2,000 ($4,000 if married and filing jointly). Roth IRAs do not allow any tax deductions for annual contributions. However, all earnings are income tax free upon withdrawal. There is no age 70½ forced distribution, and an investor can contribute to a Roth IRA as long as desired. Individuals who contribute to a SIMPLE or SEP IRA may also contribute up to $2,000 for a Roth IRA.

Education IRAs allow one or more individuals to contribute up to a maximum of $500 per year per child for the child's education. There is no up-front tax deduction, but all money earned through the investment is exempt from federal income tax as long as the money is withdrawn to pay for college expenses.

Summary

Most people and most organizations look to a future that provides better opportunities or, at a minimum, opportunities equaling those they currently enjoy. The long-term compensation opportunities provided by employers receive little recognition by many employees (long-term means compensation options that become available beyond the current operating year).

After spending 10 or so years in the workforce, many employees want to believe there is "life after work," not just daily after working hours, weekends, holidays, and vacations, but a comfortable retirement. For most workers, Social Security payments alone will not replace the income acquired from on-the-job earnings. Most large and medium-size organizations provide pension plans to supplement Social Security. In addition, select groups of employees (these groups are increasing in size every year) are being offered a variety of long-term compensation programs that can significantly enhance their Social Security and qualified pension plan earnings. Many employees have not considered long-term compensation arrangements to be an incentive. As more employees become affected by corporate streamlining, takeovers, and bankruptcies, they recognize that continuing viability, let alone the generosity of the pension plan, depends on the performance and success of their organizations. This recognition of the relationship between organizational survival and long-term security is promoting a willingness to perform in a manner that helps ensure organizational success. It is making long-term compensation a psychological imperative.

Review Questions

1. Discuss the kinds of patterns and actions federal legislators have taken regarding income tax, beginning with the Civil War.
2. Identify and describe the components included within long-term compensation.
3. Discuss some of the principal differences between defined benefits plans and defined contribution plans.
4. What differences are being identified between current retirement activities and projected retirement actions?
5. Discuss the operation of an ESOP and why it benefits both employer and employee.
6. How have 401(k)s in many ways replaced savings and thrift plans?
7. What is meant by a CODA and an ADP and what is the relationship between them?
8. What are cash-balance plans and why are organizations making increased use of them?

CHAPTER

Executive and International Compensation

16

Learning Objectives

In this chapter you will learn about:

1. The various components of executive compensation.

2. Long-term incentives provided to executives of U.S. organizations.

3. The benefits and perquisites provided to executives.

4. Legislation restricting kinds and amounts of executive compensation.

5. The major components of compensation at a foreign location.

6. Challenges facing organizations in providing compensation to employees in foreign work sites.

7. Differences in expatriate, host-country, and TCN employee compensation.

Compensation Strategy

Provide compensation incentive plans that link individual rewards to organizational objectives and performance and total returns to shareholders.

Chapters 14 and 15 discussed short- and long-term incentives that are provided to almost all employees. This chapter now will present additional materials on long-term incentives that are provided almost solely to the top executives of an organization. It is true that even some of these highly desired incentives are now beginning to be made available to those not occupying the executive suites, but this still occurs only in a minority of situations.

The last part of the chapter reviews some of the compensation challenges and opportunities available to organizations to attract competent and qualified personnel to foreign work sites.

EXECUTIVE COMPENSATION

In late 1991, President George Bush took a trip to Pacific Rim countries with a major objective of improving the economy of the United States, especially the manufacturing sector. His entourage included a number of the very top executives of the U.S. automobile industry. The last nation visited on this trip was Japan where the Japanese press launched a devastating attack on the compensation of these key automobile executives and the relatively poor international competitive performance of their American-based factories.

The Japanese attack on the compensation of U.S. executives was only one of a continuing series of front-page discussions of the executive compensation packages in the United States. These concerns are continuing to be voiced by top business-oriented newspapers and magazines, and one of the authors leading the charge against executive compensation packages is Graef S. (Bud) Crystal, a top consultant on executive compensation who changed jobs to become a college professor. His book, *In Search of Excess: The Overcompensation of American Executives,* has received national and international acclaim and has become a focal point for attacking executive compensation practices.

In defense of executive compensation packages, top management, members of the board of directors who approve these packages, highly specialized consultants who design the packages, and many writers who review the performance of U.S. organizations uniformly state that these components are needed and useful to attract and retain management personnel of outstanding ability and to encourage excellence in the performance of individual responsibilities. They state that these awards recognize the ability, efficiency, and loyalty of these executives whose efforts contribute to the success of the organization.

To those who claim that the kind and size of compensation granted to U.S. executives are not out of line in comparison with pay provided to top-of-the-line professionals and entertainers (including athletes), there is considerable validity. It must also be recognized that, historically, leaders of society have always had first claim to all things considered valuable by the other members of society. The top 1 percent received the dominant share of the riches, and the remainder received an existence share. So, writers and others who cry "greed" and hold in contempt the executives who are receiving huge compensation packages must realize this is nothing new. What is new and has been slowly evolving over the past 1,000 to 2,000 years is that more of the population is sharing in the wealth available to society, and this group has been growing slowly but steadily. As discussed in the first chapter of this book, this growing segment is called "middle class."

Social groups that have historically opposed the enormous differences between the pay, income, and wealth of the poorer members of society and those in the wealthier upper class have had a significant voice in the pay disparity issues of the 1990s. They contend that the increases in compensation received by U.S. executives are far out of line with those provided to the remainder of the workforce. To substantiate their claim of pay injustice, they note that the CEOs of large companies received a 36 percent raise in compensation, whereas white-collar workers had a 3.9 percent raise and blue-collar workers received a 2.7 percent raise. The AFL-CIO stated that a worker making $25,000 a year in 1994 would in 1999 be receiving an annual pay of $138,350 if his or her pay increased at the same rate as that of the average CEO.[1] It is possible that the exorbitant compensation of CEOs is a direct cause of the recent upsurge in union membership.

In addition, those defending the compensation of U.S. executives focus their defenses on the continuing rise in the success and worth of U.S. corporations. They contend that these business leaders have played a major role in the tremendous increase in value of the U.S. stock market. With U.S. executives receiving sizable increases in stock options and stock ownership over the past decade and the increase in value of stock on the U.S. stock market, their compensation has witnessed a steady rise. Exactly what influence the role of U.S. CEOs and other top executives has had on the increasing value of U.S. corporations can lead to heated debates. It can be accepted, however, that business, financial, and political leaders have certainly done something right relative to the booming stock market of the 1990s and the competitive position of the United States in the world economy. A defense for the high pay of U.S. executives can be found in Ira T. Kay's book, *CEO Pay and Shareholder Value: Helping the U.S. Win the Global Economic War.*

Before making any decisions as to the motivational or greed value of executive compensation, the following section identifies and briefly describes the major components of an executive incentive compensation package. Some of these components have been discussed earlier in this book, and some components are discussed in greater detail in this chapter and in the appendixes to this chapter. Major components of an executive compensation plan are:

1. Base salary
2. Short-term performance bonuses
3. Variety of equity (stock ownership) and equity-related components
4. Long-term performance bonuses
5. Severance packages (golden parachutes and other severance plans)
6. Retirement programs
7. Wide variety of benefits and perquisites

Base Salary

Chapter 4 provides an extensive discussion of base salaries provided to U.S. executives. By the late 1980s, many of the top executives of the major corporations in the United States began to receive annual salaries in excess of a million dollars. By 1992, the average salary of these top CEOs exceeded $1.5 million. As has been recognized by the press of the world, these million dollar plus salaries are only the tip of the iceberg of executive compensation.

The Omnibus Budget Reconciliation Act of 1993 placed a $1 million cap on deductible compensation of the top five executive officers of an organization. The act allows performance-based plans to be excluded from the cap. The performance criteria must (1) have shareholders' approval, (2) be approved by the outside directors of the compensation committee, and (3) be formula driven. Although the $1 million cap has

---

[1]"Executive Pay: Special Report," *Business Week,* April 19, 1999, p. 78.

promoted the use of performance-based bonuses for top executives, it has also promoted the concept that a base salary for a business executive should be $1 million.

Short-Term Bonuses

To augment the base salaries of executives of major corporations, short-term bonuses have ranged from 50 percent of base pay to 10 or more times base pay when their respective organizations have had a good year by recognizing some kind of financial indicators, for example, increase in value of stock or improvement in economic indicators such as return on equity, corporate profitability, and so on. Information on short-term bonuses is presented in chapter 4 and in chapter 14. In 1999, a review of proxies of 350 major U.S. companies by William M. Mercer, Inc., revealed that the median salary and bonus for the CEOs was $1,569,184.[2]

Equity and Equity-Related Components

Possibly the major wealth-building opportunity available to executives of U.S. corporations is through the opportunity to acquire stock in the organization or some combination of money and stock that relates to the improved price of organizational stock. The value and importance of stock-related awards above all link directly to the overall historical performance of the U.S. stock markets. Between 1926 and 1991 (this period includes the major depression of the 1930s and the many recessions from the 1950s to the 1990s), the U.S. stock market has witnessed a 10.4 percent increase in value annually of common stock.[3] Recognizing the Rule of 72, equity investments would double in slightly less than seven years. The beautiful part of equity-related awards is that the cost of the award to the recipient may range from zero to the fair market value of the stock at the time of the award or at the time of the exercise of an option. If and when the recipient does exercise the award (pay for the shares of stock made available in the award), he or she has the opportunity to recognize the negative or positive tax consequences of the value of the stock. Also when acquiring a "qualified" stock option, the recipient may not have to recognize the value of the stock award until such time as the stock is actually sold.

To add fuel to the fire regarding the unfairness and greed of executive pay, the value of stock option awards began to reach unbelievable heights. In 1992, Leon Hirsch, chairman of U.S. Surgical, was given options on 2.75 million shares that netted him a paper profit of $123 million by March 1992.[4] Also in March 1992 Roberto C. Goizueta, CEO of Coca-Cola, received a restricted stock option of one million shares worth $81 million.[5] Goizueta began to exercise this option in 1996. His cost per share was $57.5625. In February 1996, Coca-Cola was selling for $80.50.[6] By 1996, Mr. Goizueta held 2.3 million shares of common stock and 5.6 million shares of restricted stock. In addition to his stock holdings, in 1995 Mr. Goizueta received $1.60 million in salary and a $3.2 million bonus. He also received $1,463,616 in long-term incentive plan

[2]Joann S. Lublin, "Executive Pay: Lowering the Bar," *The Wall Street Journal,* April 8, 1999, pp. R1, R3.
[3]"The Case for Equities," Dean Witter Reynolds, Inc., 1992, p. 1.
[4]David Craig, "U.S. Surgical Chief's Options: $123 M," *USA Today,* March 26, 1992, p. 1B.
[5]Michael J. McCarthy, "Coca-Cola Gives Chairman Goizueta Restricted Stock Valued at $81 Million," *The Wall Street Journal,* March 20, 1992, p. A5.
[6]Robert Frank, "Coke's Chief Gets Options Covering One Million Shares," *The Wall Street Journal,* February 20, 1996, p. B10.

payouts. It is not unusual for top executives of U.S. corporations to receive stock awards of $500,000 to $1 million with over 90 percent of U.S. CEOs receiving some kind of a stock option.[7] In 1998, Michael Eisner of Disney received compensation of $575.6 million, principally in stock options.[8] In the 1999 survey by Mercer, 160 corporate CEOs exercised stock options in 1998 for a median gain of $2,770,185.[9] These stock awards have focused even more attention on the compensation packages of U.S. executives.

Stock awards include "qualified" stock awards such as incentive stock options (ISOs) and Employee Stock Purchase Plans and a variety of nonqualified stock and stock equivalent or related awards that include restricted stock options, stock appreciation rights (SARs), stock grants, restricted stock units, bonus units, dividend equivalent units, performance units, and similar kinds of awards that have many different corporate-provided titles. Appendix 16B provides a description of the features of the major different kinds of stock and stock-related awards.

Long-Term Performance Bonuses

These cash payments are very similar to the short-term bonus awards provided to corporate executives. The major difference is that the receipt of the award is two years or more into the future and the size of the award is based on multiyear achievement of established performance-related goals, for example, three-year cycle average or increase in the value of stock, return on equity, earnings per share, sales growth, and so on. When establishing these kinds of performance standards or goals, the actual size of the bonus often relates to achieved levels of performance. It is common to find that both short- and long-term bonus plans include three levels or tiers of performance: (1) threshold, (2) target, and (3) maximum. Achievement of a particular level of performance will determine the size of a bonus that may vary from 5 percent to 75 percent of salary. In 1990 the median direct compensation package for top U.S. CEOs was 39 percent base salary, 25 percent short-term incentive (bonus), and 36 percent long-term incentive (bonus).[10] By 1999, long-term compensation, mostly from exercised stock options, made up 80 percent of the average CEO's compensation package.[11]

Severance Packages

Many executive compensation components include features designed to keep the involved individual in the corporation, and at times "noncompete" requirements severely penalize financially an executive who leaves the organization and goes to work for a competitor. These severance packages specify awards to be provided if the employee is required to leave the organization under specific circumstances. A major part of a severance package may be an employment contract or, stated slightly differently, a major part of an employment contract may contain a specific severance opportunities clause.

Although not commonly offered to every CEO or key official, employee contracts are provided by a number of organizations to attract certain individuals and to retain key personnel. The executive contract may include specifications for front-end bonus,

---

[7]*1991 Executive Compensation Study* (New York: TPF&C, a Towers Perrin Company, 1991), Exhibit 12.
[8]"Executive Pay: Special Report," *Business Week*, April 18, 1999, p. 73.
[9]Lublin, p. R-3.
[10]TPF&C, Exhibit 7.
[11]"Executive Pay: Special Report," p. 74.

salary, pension, life and medical insurance, cash and deferred bonuses, stock acquisition opportunities, a variety of other benefits and services, widow's pension, and severance payments. These contracts normally stipulate the number of years and the option opportunities for renegotiation at the end of the contract period.

Key personnel who may be reluctant to leave a secure job are requesting and receiving the protection offered by an employment contract. In fact, some organizations now use these contracts to retain personnel by making it more difficult for them to be attracted to recruiting offers from other organizations.

In the late 1970s and early 1980s, low stock prices of many corporations gave rise to large numbers of corporate takeovers by other firms. Top executives of corporations that were good candidates for a takeover became extremely concerned about their job security. To protect these key officials when, due to a takeover, their jobs are terminated or their responsibilities are changed or reduced for any reason other than death, disability, or normal retirement, and also to make the takeover less attractive (by being more expensive), *golden parachute* clauses were added to existing executive contracts or became new contracts. Golden parachutes may be offered to anywhere from two to 20 key officials, although typically five or less receive such protection. Some plans include more than 20 participants.

The terms of golden parachute contracts vary significantly, but generally they guarantee the contract holder: (1) continuation of base pay for one to five years—it may be paid as a lump sum or over a specified period of time, (2) any bonuses that would normally have been granted during the time, (3) supplemental benefits, and, frequently, (4) immediate vesting of any stock option. (Normally, during a corporate takeover, the stock price of the firm being purchased enjoys a rapid and large rise.) The contract normally establishes a minimum level of income the recipient will receive during the term of the contract. A major variation among golden parachutes concerns "how fast they open." Different plans require different percentage changes in ownership before the benefits are available to the protected employees. A change of 20 percent in ownership would trigger some plans into operation.[12]

Retirement Programs

In addition to ERISA-controlled defined benefit and defined contribution retirement plans, corporate executives are provided with an array of supplemental retirement programs that ensures that they receive equal, if not better, retirement programs than those offered to the remainder of the work force.

When comparing the basic benefits received by the CEO and other key officials of the firm, a bias against these senior jobholders becomes evident. The problem frequently comes under the title of *reverse discrimination* in compensation practices. The discrimination occurs primarily because of the necessity for organizations to comply with IRS rules and regulations when designing "qualified" retirement plans (pension, savings and thrift plans), group life insurance plans, and long-term disability plans. In order for the company to be able to receive a tax deduction for the cost of these plans and for the employee to be able to defer any tax on employer contributions, the plans must be "qualified." A qualified plan must be (1) in writing and in effect in the tax year in which qualification is sought, (2) communicated to all employees, (3) established and

---

[12]Ann M. Morrison, "Those Executive Bailout Deals," *Fortune,* December 13, 1982, pp. 82–87.

maintained by the employer, and (4) operated for the exclusive benefit of the employees and their beneficiaries. A qualified plan must not discriminate in favor of officers, shareholders, or highly compensated employees (the prohibited group). A plan may, however, discriminate in favor of employees not in the prohibited group.

Under ERISA regulations, qualified plans may be either defined benefits or defined contribution plans. A defined contribution plan is one in which the employer provides a specific contribution to the account of each employee in the plan. In a defined benefits plan, the employee's benefits are first determined and the employer makes contributions sufficient to provide these benefits.

In addition to qualified plans discriminating against the highly paid employees regarding pension payments that relate directly to annual earnings, IRC qualifications further discriminate. For example,

1. By integrating the pension plan payment with a partially tax-free primary Social Security payment, the lower-paid employee receives a much higher percentage tax-free benefit in the pension payment.
2. Long-term disability (LTD) plans that have a cap or limit to the maximum monthly payments will severely restrict the monthly income of a disabled highly paid employee. (For example, in the third year of a disability, a typical LTD plan may call for the disability payment to be 50 percent of base pay to a maximum of $4,000 per month less Social Security. A $300,000 per year executive earning $25,000 per month would receive only 4,000/25,000 or 16 percent of base pay.)
3. Group life insurance plans frequently provide each employee with a benefit of two times base pay to a maximum of $250,000. (For example, the beneficiary of an employee who earned $25,000 per year would receive 200 percent of base pay, whereas the beneficiary of a $300,000 per year employee would receive 250,000/300,000 = 83.3 percent of base pay.) In addition, section 79 of the Internal Revenue Code limits tax-free life insurance to $50,000, and premium costs for insurance exceeding $50,000 are considered as imputed income to the employee.

To prevent discrimination against their more highly paid employees, many organizations develop executive benefits plans that permit the highly paid executives to be treated as well as the lower-paid employees. It is in the design of these kinds of executive benefits plans that knowledge of tax laws, insurance programs, estate building, and organizational compensation practices are skillfully combined. These plans are discussed in detail later in this chapter.

A tax-qualified defined benefits plan is subject to certain maximum and minimum provisions. In 1996, an employer could not recognize through qualified corporate contributions any earnings in excess of $150,000 per year. In 1991, David O. Maxwell, CEO of the Federal National Mortgage Association, a publicly owned but federally sponsored mortgage finance company, was able after slightly more than 10 years of service to receive a retirement plan that paid him $1,355,000 a year for the rest of his life and the life of his wife if she outlives him. Instead, Maxwell traded this annual pension payment in for a one-time lump sum payment of $19,590,485.[13] Although this may not be the typical pension payment received by a 10-year employee who rises to CEO, it is not unusual for top executives to have rolled into the calculation of the annual earnings for

---

[13]Peter Carlson, "Chairman of the Bucks," *Washington Post Magazine,* April 5, 1992, pp. 11, 12, 14, 15, 28–30.

determining retirement pay their base salary plus short-term and long-term bonuses earned that year plus any restricted stock options or performance unit awards received that year. There are further discussions of supplemental executive retirement plans later in this chapter and in appendix 16B.

Special Package of Benefits and Perquisites

Executives, like all other employees, have available to them all of the benefits organizations provide to their employees.

However, to maximize the time available to key executives for business-related purposes and, at the same time, enhance the quality of their lives, many highly desirable and special benefits and services are made available. These benefits and services are frequently grouped under the title of perquisites (perks). Perquisites are usually restricted to the CEO and that small group of key officials who comprise the senior management of the organization. In addition to the status relationship, perquisites provide benefits that either are not considered as earned income to the recipient or are taxed at a very modest level. The amount of tax liability incurred by the recipient depends to a significant degree on the design and the structure of the specific perquisite plan. The Tax Code definition of income includes moneys, property, and services received for services provided. Since the late 1970s, the IRS has recognized more "perks" as imputed income and has required organizations to place a value on them.

A brief description of some of the more common perks assists in identifying their desirability:

Company-provided car. The employee is able to use the car for both business and personal use. According to the IRS, the employee must pay a flat monthly maintenance charge or a mileage charge for personal use; cars costing more than $16,000 require detailed records as to their business and personal use.

Parking. Special no-cost, readily accessible to work site parking services.

Chauffeured limousine. Normally provided only to the CEO or key officials. The chauffeur may also act as a bodyguard.

Kidnap and ransom protection. A service of recent vintage aimed at protecting key officials who may be victims of such action.

Counseling service. Includes financial and legal services. Tax-related expenses are tax deductible; cost of nonbusiness-related services is considered taxable income.

Attending professional meetings and conferences. Opportunity to enhance professional knowledge and enjoy activities at selected sites.

Spouse travel. The company pays for expenses incurred in taking a spouse to a convention or on a business trip.

Use of company plane and yacht. Opportunity to mix use of company plane and yacht for personal enjoyment and business purposes.

Home entertainment allowance. Executives who do considerable entertaining are frequently provided with a domestic staff or given a home servants allowance. The allowance may include cost of food and beverages and payment of utility bills.

Special living accommodations. Executives required to perform business activities at odd hours or at a considerable distance from home are provided with an apartment or permanent hotel accommodations.

Club membership. Country clubs and luncheon club memberships are provided to executives who use such facilities in the performance of their jobs (personal use is recognized as imputed income by the IRS).

Special dining rooms. The business provides special dining facilities for key officials and their business guests.

Season tickets to entertainment events. The executive has free use of season tickets for family and business associates to a variety of entertainment events.

Special relocation allowance. A variety of relocation allowances is provided only to key officials. This includes low-interest loans to purchase a new home and complete coverage of all relocation expenses.

Use of company credit card. No waiting period for reimbursement of company-related charges and use of card for personal service and delay in repayment to the company.

Medical expense reimbursement. Coverage for all medical care.

College tuition reimbursement for children. Special programs that provide for college tuition.

No- and low-interest loans. Executives are provided funds at no interest or at interest rates well below market. (The Tax Reform Act of 1984 changed the tax status of such loans.)

A major perk offered to top executives is to receive loans at preferred rates of interest to assist them in exercising stock options (purchase stock options). Some corporations grant executives amounts of money to pay for any state or federal tax they may be obligated to pay upon exercise of a stock option.

Although reverse discrimination may be a valid concern when analyzing and designing the compensation program for CEOs and other key officials, it appears that the specialists working in this area have done an exceptional job in keeping their "clients" whole (i.e., maintaining their real income and current and future standard of living).

CAPITAL ACCUMULATION

With qualified deferred compensation arrangements, organizations are providing lifetime income opportunities that would otherwise cost an employee $200,000 or more to purchase. In this section, opportunities that build on the solid retirement foundation and can provide an extremely valuable estate for the employee will be explored and analyzed. The opportunities are categorized under the title of capital accumulation. These capital accumulation arrangements can, in turn, be further subdivided into equity and long-term cash compensation components. Some plans provide a mixture of both equity and cash components.

Providing employees with an opportunity to acquire stock in their employer's corporation is usually considered to be highly desirable. Over the past 50 years, however, the opportunity to acquire significant shares of stock in the corporation has been limited to an extremely small group of employees—the executives (those responsible for policy formulation and the long-term strategy of the organization). The move toward an expanded use of long-term incentive compensation will increase the importance of making shares of stock available to a wider range of employees.

Surveys by Frederic W. Cook & Co., Inc. of the top 200 industrial and top 200 service companies as identified in the April 22, 1991 issue of *Fortune* magazine substantiated the continuing use of these long-term incentives for corporate executives. To be classified as a long-term incentive, Cook required the corporate plans to meet the following criteria:

1. Be granted under a formal plan or practice, not just as part of an individual employment contract
2. Entail a vesting, performance, or exercise period of *over* one year
3. Not be primarily designed to accommodate foreign tax or securities laws
4. Not be merely a form of payment under an annual incentive plan

Cook places long-term incentives within two major groups: (1) market based and (2) performance based. Within the market-based group, Cook includes stock option and stock purchase plans, which further require an investment by the recipient, and stock appreciation rights (SARs) and restricted stock, which require no investment on the part of the recipient.

The second category, performance-based incentives, includes plans such as performance units and performance shares that involve some kind of goal attainment, and formula or dividend-driven plans such as purchase/appreciation grant, full value grant, and dividend equivalent.

Almost all large corporations provide long-term incentives for their executives. Stock options are the most common type of long-term awards, with restricted stock and performance shares increasing in usage.[14]

Stock acquisition plans permit corporations to achieve five goals. These are (1) permitting employees or select groups of employees to acquire shares of stock in the corporation; (2) promoting substantial ownership rights among employees or select groups of employees; (3) establishing through ownership a motivational work environment that stimulates superior performance; (4) enhancing employee willingness to save for the future; and (5) assisting employees to develop a substantial estate. These plans vary significantly as to eligibility, tax obligations to employer and recipient, and accounting treatment.

Corporate long-term incentive awards frequently have special organization-related design features and can have unique organization-provided titles. However, their specific features or requirements will determine whether or not these plans are qualified under IRC regulations. There is a lengthy discussion of various kinds of stock and stock equivalent long-term incentive compensation awards later in this chapter and in the appendixes to this chapter.

---

[14]Helaine Langenthal and Richard Kimball, *Long-Term Incentive Compensation Grants among the Service 200* (New York: Frederic W. Cook & Co., Inc., November 1991), pp. 2, 3; Leslie Lucania and Richard Kimball, *Long-Term Incentive Compensation Grants among the Top 200 Industrial Companies* (New York: Frederic W. Cook & Co., Inc., November 1991), p. 1.

Long-Term Bonuses

Long-term bonus plans are designed to provide awards that are earned over a specific period of time—2 to 5 or even 10 years into the future. The size of the bonus normally relates to the achievement or the continued achievement of certain well-defined results. The annual future awards may increase proportionally to the consistency and the improvement made in performance as measured by specific outcomes.

Organizations are now tying together their long-term bonuses with their long-range plans. The strategies established for achieving the long-range plans have specific corporate objectives. These corporate objectives, in turn, become the measures that determine the amount and the timing of the awards. The objectives may relate to some internal financing figures such as real growth in earnings per share (total growth minus allowance for inflation) or to some figures that compare results achieved with those of other organizations in a similar competitive environment. Over the years, many corporations have merged their long-term cash bonus plans into their stock and cash grant awards programs.

Just as with short-term bonus plans, payments for an earned bonus increment can be deferred until some later date (after retirement) and can be paid in cash, shares of stock, or both.

SEC Requirements

In addition to the Treasury Department regulations concerning the acquisition of corporate shares of stock by employees, the valuation of the stock and its disposition and taxation, the Securities and Exchange Commission (SEC) issues regulations regarding the communication and the acquisition of stock by certain key personnel. Under the Securities Act of 1933 and the Exchange Act of 1934, the SEC has the right to require corporations listing stock on national securities exchanges to disclose information about stock ownership, remuneration, and cash compensation received by certain individuals.

Remuneration is a term used by the SEC to identify specific compensation components. These include salary, fee, commissions, bonuses, stock and property payments, executive insurance, personal benefits, pensions or retirement plans, annuities, deferred compensation plans, short- and long-term incentive plans, stock purchase plans, and profit-sharing and thrift plans. *Cash compensation,* on the other hand, includes salaries, cash bonuses, commissions and fees, the vested portion of any deferred cash compensation earned during the fiscal year, and any other cash compensation.

The key personnel whose cash compensation must be documented on corporate proxy statements, registration statements, and periodic reports are the five most highly compensated executive officers who are involved in policymaking decisions and whose annual cash compensation is at least $60,000. Under a 1983 ruling, the SEC requires proxy disclosure information on: (1) cash remuneration of the five highest-paid executive officers earning at least $60,000, (2) stock option grants and exercises during the fiscal year, (3) incremental cost to the company of perquisites valued at $25,000 or more, (4) golden parachute valued at $60,000 or more, and (5) narrative description only for noncash and contingency remuneration plans, stock option plans, and perquisites.

In 1992, the SEC issued guidelines that required regulated corporations by 1993 to disclose the compensation of the chief executive and the four most highly paid senior executives. They must assign values to stock options received by these executives. They must prepare charts summarizing this information and the total return to investors in the corporation over five years. The charts must compare executive compensation with stock prices. Finally, employment and severance agreements for the five named officers must be made public.

Under sections 16(a) and 16(b) of the Exchange Act of 1934, officers, directors, and those individuals holding 10 percent or more of the stock in the corporation must disclose their stock ownership and provide monthly reports of changes in amount of ownership. This group is also known as "insiders."

Some special SEC requirements regarding the stock transactions of insiders are these:

1. Insiders cannot buy and then sell stock on the same day.
2. Insiders must comply to a 10-day window (they can buy and sell only for a 10 working-day period beginning on the third day following the end of a quarterly or annual financial reporting period).
3. Insiders are effectively prohibited from selling stock within six months of a purchase that includes the exercise of a stock option.

If an insider makes a buy-sell or sell-buy transaction within six months, any gained profit must be returned to the company. A mechanism that assists insiders to bypass the six-month purchase-sell restriction is a stock appreciation rights grant (SAR).

FASB

The Financial Accounting Standards Board has gained an increasingly more important role concerning compensation issues. FASB rulings on accounting treatment for different stock-based incentives have had a major impact on the particular kind of stock-based incentive program(s) organizations offer to their executives. For example, accounting treatment for performance shares plans is much more complex and difficult than accounting treatment for restricted stock options. Organizations must now review the executive compensation incentive plans from both an accounting expense and plan design perspective.

MAXIMIZING EXECUTIVE COMPENSATION OPPORTUNITIES

After making the best possible use of qualified and nonqualified long-term compensation arrangements, most organizations must take additional actions to complete their long-term compensation programs if they want these arrangements to act as incentives. The first major issue that must be addressed is the pension payment discrimination against highly paid employees. ERISA, as amended, places a maximum limit on pension payments of $90,000 indexed to the CPI, which in 1996 was $120,000. Highly paid employees could easily earn a higher retirement payment with regard to an organization's pension formula. A top executive with 25 years of service and a last five-year average pay of $600,000 who receives a 2 percent credit for each year of service would be due an annual pension of $300,000: $.02 \times 25 \times \$600,000 = \$300,000$. However, ERISA, as amended, limits the pension payments to $90,000 indexed to the CPI. In 1996, the executive had a shortfall of $180,000 ($300,000 – $120,000).

Additional issues surface regarding deferral of compensation and nonqualified compensation arrangements. When an employee decides to defer currently earned income to a later date or works to achieve a promised long-term cash, stock, or combination of cash and stock award, there must be a strong faith by the recipient that the organization will be financially capable of keeping its promises at the designated time. Trusts have also been used by organizations to provide a certain degree of security to an employee with a nonqualified deferred arrangement that funds will be available to make the promised payments, yet escape the constructive receipt doctrine.

In addition to obtaining strong assurances of ability to make payments at some future date, the recipient is also interested in the cash buildup of any deferred payment. By deferring current payments, the employee is able to escape current income and Social Security taxes and, if the deferred income is taken as an additional retirement payment, no Social Security tax will ever be paid. However, to be sure that constructive receipt does not occur and that the deferred compensation is not taxable to the recipient until actually received (1) the deferred amount must not be placed unconditionally in a trust or escrow for the benefit of the recipient, and (2) the promise to pay the deferred compensation must be merely a contractual obligation not evidenced in any way by notes or securities.

Over the years, organizations have used various kinds of programs to supplement retirement benefits for the highly paid, and to place funds in special accounts to pay for promised deferred arrangements. Corporate-owned life insurance (COLI) and grantor trusts have been used for these purposes.

Supplemental Executive Retirement Plans (SERPs)

One of the first steps taken by corporations to overcome ERISA-imposed limits on qualified pension plans was to develop ERISA excess benefit plans. An ERISA excess plan provides highly paid executives with payments that make up the loss in retirement benefits resulting from the ERISA-imposed maximum on the amount that can be paid under the qualified plan.

Since their development, ERISA excess plans have expanded to provide options that go far beyond their original goal of keeping the highly paid executive "whole." These modifications have given rise to Supplementary Executive Retirement Plans (SERPs). Unlike qualified plans, ERISA excess plans and SERPs do not require reporting and disclosure information. In organizations that initially had ERISA excess plans and then later developed SERPs, the ERISA excess plan became part of the SERP.

SERPs are unfunded, nonqualified retirement plans. An unfunded program is one that is simply based on a promise to selected individuals that the corporation accepts the obligation to pay certain deferred benefits from the general assets of the corporation at a specified time. The majority of these nonqualified plans are funded out of general company assets, although in recent years, until the passage of TRA 86, the COLI had become an extremely popular method for funding a SERP. With a COLI, the corporation owns and is the beneficiary of the policy. This means that the highly paid executive depends on the "naked" promise of the organization to make the future retirement payments. It also means that if the employee does not fulfill all contractual obligations relative to the SERP, all benefits are forfeitable. By using insurance policies to fund a SERP, there is a much greater likelihood that funds will be available for payments. Because the employer owns the insurance policy, the IRS considers the plan to be unfunded. Also, because the employer retains control of the assets, the employee does not violate IRS constructive receipt requirements.

Well-designed SERPs establish eligibility requirements and kinds and amounts of benefits to be provided to meet the plan's goals. A major goal of a SERP is to enable key officials to receive postretirement income that is commensurate with the compensation received by these top executives. A SERP may be valuable in recruiting key officials to a new organization in the middle to latter stages of a career in which a normal pension formula provides an inadequate pension due to the potential short service of the newly hired executive, or a SERP can be used to encourage early retirement. It can be useful in standardizing retirement benefits in a multinational corporation or a divisionalized firm with different kinds of retirement plans.

To increase retirement benefits and to offer more generous benefits than those granted to the rest of the workforce, those responsible for designing a SERP may recognize:

1. All taxable (W-2) earnings of the employee—this may include all short-term and even long-term incentive payments received during the years used for establishing base earnings. Many qualified pension plans count only base pay when determining annual earnings for the pension formula. For the nonexecutive employee—95 to 99 percent of the workforce—this means that overtime payments, other premiums and differentials, and short-term bonuses such as a Christmas bonus are not recognized in determining annual earnings for pension purposes. To maintain a plan as qualified, an organization cannot count either short-term or long-term incentives in determining the annual earnings for the highly paid employees.
2. All earned deferred income (using some kind of present value calculations) as part of annual earnings.

The plan may subtract retirement income coming from other sources when establishing the net payment to be made by the SERP. Other sources of retirement income to be deducted may be as follows: (1) income from Social Security and other currently available qualified and nonqualified plans, and (2) income from retirement plans of other employers (this will occur when the SERP recognizes years of employment with other employers).

"No-Cost" Executive Death Benefits

Over the years, the intense interest in the tax advantages made possible through a qualified retirement plan has caused those responsible for designing retirement plans to overlook the financial advantages possible through the use of insurance for funding specific features of nonqualified executive retirement plans. In recent years, insurance companies have become very active in designing policies that provide long-term (in excess of seven years) benefits that exceed the short-term tax advantages available through qualified plans. Recognizing the cost of capital and the long-term return on investment, cost-benefit analysis may now indicate that focusing on up-front tax deductibility may actually be extremely cost-inefficient. Employers interested in the best return on investment must recognize that plan design is one thing and the funding of the plan is a completely separate issue.

A major concern of many employees is to establish an estate that provides funds after their death to give their beneficiaries financial security. In recent years, an inconsistent practice in tax policy has made permanent life insurance (whole life or some variation) an extremely useful corporate investment. By purchasing permanent life insurance, corporations can provide large amounts of death benefits to executives at "no cost" to the corporation. This is possible because (1) insurance companies are now providing variable policy loan interest rates that closely approximate money market rates and crediting dividend interests at a rate similar to the policy loan rate; and (2) current tax policy permits a corporation to borrow money from the cash value of the policy to pay policy premiums and then to deduct interest payments on the first $50,000 of borrowed funds as a current business expense. This kind of plan is called a minimum deposit plan. The quirk in this tax policy is that in no other circumstance does the IRS permit a borrower to purchase a tax-exempt instrument through borrowed funds and then allow that borrower to deduct any portion of the interest costs of the borrowed funds. In addition to changes in tax laws that are minimizing the use of COLIs, recent court rulings are almost eliminating them.[15]

The "no-cost" opportunity to purchase large amounts of death-benefit insurance develops in this manner: A corporation purchases a permanent life policy (COLI) that equals at least two-thirds of a promised death benefit made to the executive. The corporation owns the policy and, upon the death of the executive, receives the proceeds. This money is then used to pay the promised amount to the estate of the deceased. The actual agreement between the corporation and the executive is treated as an entirely separate matter to eliminate any possibility of constructive receipt on the part of the executive and to prevent the executive from having to consider the insurance premium as earned income. The total tax implications of this kind of program are these: (1) The corporation can currently write off as a business expense the interest on the first $50,000 of funds borrowed from the cash value of the policy to pay premiums; (2) the corporation can charge off as business expense the total payment made to the estate at the time the payment is made; and (3) the estate must recognize the payment as taxable income. The premiums are not tax deductible, but the proceeds from the insurance policy are income tax free to the corporation.

As previously mentioned, the life insurance policy purchased by the corporation must equal at least two-thirds of the agreed-to life insurance death benefit. This amount assumes that the corporation is in the 34 percent corporate income tax bracket and that one-third of the payment will be income tax deductible. The other two-thirds will then come from the proceeds of the policy.

If the corporation wishes to have the policy return the cost of insurance and the "opportunity" cost of the premium payments, it must purchase a policy that is greater than two-thirds of the promised death benefit. The calculation required to determine the size of the policy must consider the opportunity cost of the funds used to make the premium payment—the income possible to the corporation if the funds used to make the premium payment were invested elsewhere. Depending on the ages of the executives to be included in the plan, the dates of retirement, and their physical condition, more than one insurance policy may have to be purchased to provide the kind of policy proceeds desired by the corporation.

With the passage of TRA 86 and its reduction of the corporate income tax rate and its restriction on deducting interest payments on money borrowed from a life insurance

---

[15]Tom Herman, "Tax Court Rules Winn-Dixie Can't Use Life-Insurance Program as Tax Shelter," *The Wall Street Journal,* October 21, 1999, p. B21.

policy to pay premium costs, the value of small COLI plans has almost been eliminated. Prior to TRA 86, it was not unusual to find a COLI for 10 to 15 executives. Today, however, most new COLI plans are written for organizations that wish to include 1,000 or even more than 10,000 plan participants. It is only with large numbers of participants that the aggregate funding opportunities available within a COLI make it an effective corporate financial vehicle. This is one more example of how government legislation democratizes corporate benefits programs. Appendix 16C includes a discussion of other insurance opportunities for funding executive retirement plans.

Insurance-Related Information

When developing a supplemental benefits plan for key personnel and using insurance to provide the additional benefits, answering the following questions will assist in making the wisest and most useful insurance selection:

1. How is the current group life insurance plan structured?
2. What are the differences between the pay (base pay plus short-term bonuses) of key personnel and the maximum insurance available through the group life plan?
3. What amount of extra life insurance should be offered to key personnel?
4. Is group life coverage provided after retirement? If yes, what is the amount?
5. Do the laws of the state in which the company is incorporated place a limit on group life insurance? If yes, what is the amount?
6. What opportunities are available to eliminate use of personal after-tax dollars to provide additional life insurance coverage?
7. How can group life insurance plans be utilized to give extra benefits on a tax-favored basis to select groups of employees?
8. How can group life insurance plans be redesigned or rearranged to reduce long-term costs to the company and also provide substantial benefits to select groups of employees?

Trusts

A trust is a temporary entity created to locate, maintain, and distribute assets and satisfy liabilities according to the wishes of the grantor. A trust is an arrangement created by a will or a lifetime declaration through which trustees take title to property for the purpose of protecting or conserving it for the beneficiaries. By this definition, a trust involves at least three parties: (1) the *grantor* who transfers certain assets to the trust, (2) the *trustee* who is charged with fiduciary duties associated with the trust agreement, and (3) the *beneficiary* who has rights to receive property from the trust. A grantor trust exists when the grantor is also the beneficiary or the trustee of the trust. In a grantor trust, some or all of the trust income is taxable to the grantor.

Corporations have been using a particular kind of grantor trust called a *rabbi trust* to offer a degree of assurance to individuals with deferred compensation arrangements that funds are set aside and will remain available to provide promised payments. In a rabbi trust, the employer makes contributions to an irrevocable trust but is prohibited from borrowing from the trust. Also, an acquiring corporation in a hostile takeover cannot prevent the trustee from making payments to the beneficiary without taking legal action to revoke the trust. However, the money in the trust is subject to the claims of the employer's creditors. Because it is a grantor trust, the employer must pay tax on any income the trust generates.

Trusts can also be used to minimize federal estate taxes and maximize transfer of an executive's wealth to his or her children. Although Section 401 of the IRC requires qualified pension plans to distribute payments that are more than "merely incidental" to the employees ("more than merely incidental" has been defined by the IRS as more than one-half of the funds accumulated for the benefit of the retired employee), the executive can transfer almost half of his or her pension funds to surviving children. Nonqualified plans provide even greater opportunities to transfer deferred payments to trusts set up for the beneficiaries of the highly paid executive. This transfer to the beneficiaries of an executive through trusts escapes federal taxes on the estate of the deceased executive. By first deferring receipt of income and then transferring funds into a trust, the executive may escape taxes on a significant amount of income and build an estate to support future generations.

This same kind of trust arrangement can also be used for a life insurance policy. As mentioned earlier, life insurance proceeds to a beneficiary are exempt from income tax. They are, however, included in the value of the general estate, and estate tax must be paid on the proceeds unless the beneficiary of the life insurance proceeds is an irrevocable trust. This kind of a trust arrangement is used in lieu of making an absolute assignment of the proceeds to the beneficiary.

INTERNATIONAL COMPENSATION

Compensation managers of many organizations are now facing an entirely new set of issues—designing and managing the compensation of employees who work for the company in a foreign nation. The unique compensation issues are in these areas:

1. Incentives provided to stimulate movement or expatriation to a foreign location or host country
2. Allowances for repatriation to home country
3. Additional tax burdens placed on employees working in a foreign location
4. Labor regulations in both host country and home country
5. Cost-of-living allowances in the host country
6. Home country and host country currency fluctuation
7. Formal and informal compensation practices unique to the host country
8. Determining home country for setting base pay of third-country nationals

There are a number of reasons for sending employees to a foreign work site. Among the most common and critical are:

1. Existing or potential employees who already live at the foreign work site do not have the necessary knowledge and skills and related work experience.
2. Existing or potential employees who already live at the foreign location do not have the knowledge of the business, its operations, plans, policies, and strategies.
3. The organization desired to develop a global perspective among employees and make it part of a career development program.

Home Country of Employee

An organization operating in one or more foreign nations may draw employees from three different places of residence: (1) the specific nation or host country where the operation is located; (2) the home nation of the parent operation; and (3) foreign countries other than the site of the operation.

The title given to those employees whose basic residence or home is the host nation is *nationals* or *locals.* Those who come from the home country of the operation are *expatriates* and those whose nation of residence is neither the host country nor the home country are *third-country nationals (TCNs).*

The compensation provided to locals, expatriates, and TCNs can vary considerably. Normally, the total compensation package provided to locals is the least costly whereas that provided to expatriates is most costly. From strictly a cost point of view, the more locals employed at the work site, the less the labor cost and the greater the return on invested capital. (There are cases, however, when TCN personnel are far less costly than host country personnel.) The expenses involved in stimulating an employee to move to a foreign site, the payment of relocation costs (both to the new site and return to the home base at the end of the foreign assignment), and, finally, the additional tax burden incurred by having expatriates and, at times, TCNs in foreign operations are substantial. These expenses often result in an excessive drain on the profitability of the foreign operation.

Attracting Individuals to a Foreign Work Site

Recruiting new employees with the requisite knowledge and skills, or influencing current employees to move to a foreign site, requires a wide array of compensation-related incentives. The kind of compensation components offered and the amount or quality of components available vary according to the desirability of the location.

Site Desirability Each site has its unique strengths and weaknesses, and these vary according to the way each individual perceives them. Some of these strengths or weaknesses relate to geographical location and climate. Others relate to social and political conditions.

Transfer Incentives Usually, the first compensation issue that confronts the compensation manager is the amount of additional pay required to induce an employee to move from the present job site to the new one in the foreign country. In some cases, the site may be so desirable that almost any job candidate would find it sufficient if the organization guaranteed that the individual would be as financially well-off in the host country as at home (keeping the employee "whole"). In most cases, however, the person asked to move to a foreign site will demand some premium over that earned in the present assignment.

The next set of compensation issues revolves around present housing. In many cases, the employee owns a house and looks to the employer to cover some or all of the expenses involved in selling it. These sale-of-residence expenses may include sufficient money to guarantee the employee no financial loss in the house sale or even some percentage of the profit. Because a house, in many cases, is currently one of the best investments a person can make, organizations now provide home rental assistance and absentee ownership management services for the homeowner who rents rather than sells while on foreign assignment.

In most cases, the organization again takes care of all moving expenses to the new site. In those cases in which it is impractical to move the family, special consideration must be granted for their maintenance at the present residence. In cases in which spouses or families do not make the move, the transfer will probably be for a limited period—a two-year contract, with at least one extended, completely paid leave at home at the end of the first year or at the end of the contract, or even a couple of completely paid holidays with the family in addition to the leave.

Developing a Compensation Program for Expatriates

Establishing a compensation plan for a job in a foreign location begins with the determination of base pay. The market or going rate of pay for a comparable job in the home country at the time of expatriation is normally used for setting this rate.

After setting base pay comes the determination of a *Foreign Service Premium (FSP),* which is an incentive bonus for performing the assignment in the *host* country. The FSP is usually expressed as a percentage of base pay and is part of the total pay received by the employee each pay period. Some organizations are now granting expatriates lump-sum bonuses in lieu of FSPs. These lump-sum payments are made at the time of expatriation and repatriation.

To maintain the employees' present standard of living in the foreign location, organizations provide a number of allowances to keep them "whole." A major one provides money for additional living costs (food, housing, transportation, and other consumables in the host country). Compensation managers obtain "ball park" figures from various sources on additional living costs to be incurred in moving an employee to a foreign location. These include (1) *U.S. Department of State Indexes of Living Costs Abroad and Quarters Allowances* on a quarterly basis, published by the Bureau of Labor Statistics, and (2) reports available from other organizations. Other major providers of international compensation data and information are Associates for International Research, Inc.; The Conference Board, Inc.; Organization Resources Counselors, Inc.; Runzheimer International; and Towers, Perrin. Living costs may include special allowances for utility expenses, servants, operation of the living quarters, and educational allowances for the children.

In host areas where conditions (climatic, political, social) are undesirable, a "hardship" or "location" allowance is added to base pay. Most pay plans include a cost-equalization allowance that includes cost-of-living and housing allowances. The equalization allowance consists of the *difference* between the costs of food, other consumable items, services, and housing in the home country and the costs of those items in the host country. In some cases, the cost-of-living allowance (COLA)—not to be confused with previously discussed COL*A,* cost of living *adjustment*—is tied to a change in the currency exchange rate between home country and host country. (It must be remembered that compensation *computations* are made in *home* country currency whereas actual *payments* are made in *host* country currency. This requires the use of some equivalency formula between home and host country currency.)

Many organizations also provide a tax equalization allowance. In computing such an allowance, the first step is to determine the hypothetical tax liabilities incurred by the employee. This is done by assuming that the employee is still working in the home country and receiving the established base pay (excluding all allowances and premiums for working in the foreign assignment) for a comparable job. Using the base pay and appropriate home base income tax rates, a hypothetical tax liability is established. Then the organization computes all tax liabilities (both those of the home and host countries) of the expatriate for all income earned on the job (base pay plus premiums plus all living cost adjustments). From these total tax liabilities, the hypothetical tax the expatriate would normally have paid on a comparable job in the home country is subtracted. This is the amount of tax burden assumed by the employer on the tax equalization allowance. Next to base pay and premiums, the tax equalization allowance until 1982 had been the highest cost incurred in sending an American to a foreign location. The tax burden for Americans employed abroad was considerably lightened by the Economic Recovery Tax Act of 1981, which allowed the first $75,000 of their income to be excluded from taxation. TRA 86 reduced this exclusion to $70,000 per year.

To minimize problems related to exchange of currency and to protect the employee, many organizations now "split" an expatriate's compensation between home country and host country compensation packages. A split-pay plan is one in which a certain amount of the total pay received by the expatriate is paid in home country currency and credited to a designated account in the home country. The expatriate receives the remaining pay in the host country in host country currency.

A procedure often used for determining the amount of the split that goes into the home country or domestic account and the amount that goes into the host country or foreign account takes this approach. First, a spendable income for the employee in the home country must be established. Spendable income is that amount of pay spent on goods, services, and housing. It represents total pay minus taxes (income and FICA), savings, investments, health and life insurance premiums, and any contributions made by the employee to benefit components.

Supplementing the spendable income are housing and cost-of-living allowances to ensure the expatriate the same standard of living in the host country as that enjoyed in the home country at the time of expatriation. These disposable income and living adjustment allowances are further supplemented during the period the expatriate is in the host country by the spendable portion of any pay increase granted and by any cost-of-living changes that occur (in the host country, using host country cost-of-living adjustment figures).

The domestic account consists of pay plus premiums minus spendable income and amount set aside for hypothetical income tax. It also includes that part of any pay adjustments (merit and general increases) granted to the individual or all employees of the organization not set aside for spendable income or additional tax liabilities.

In addition to the aforementioned compensation items, the following payments and services are provided to employees willing to accept a foreign assignment. These payments and services can be included within the following two groups:

1. Lifestyle enhancement services
2. Service allowances and premiums

Lifestyle enhancement services include a wide variety of programs that make living more acceptable and enjoyable at the foreign site. Some of these services are:

1. Provision for employee and family to learn the local language.
2. Education and training of employee and family on local culture, customs, and social expectations.
3. Counseling services for employee and family.

4. Assistance in finding a home at foreign work site.
5. Assistance in finding schools and suitable education programs for children and dependents.
6. Company car, driver, domestic staff, and child care.
7. Use of fitness facilities.
8. Subsidized health care services.
9. Assistance in joining local civic, social, and professional organizations.
10. Assistance to spouse in finding suitable and acceptable employment.

Allowances and premiums beyond the Foreign Service Premium and Tax Equalization Allowance could include:

1. Temporary living allowance
2. Hardship premium
3. Currency protection
4. Mobility premium
5. Home-leave allowance
6. Stopover allowance
7. Completion of assignment bonus
8. Assignment extension bonus
9. Emergency loan
10. Extended workweek payment

Summary

In recent years, the pay and benefits given to CEOs of U.S. corporations have received international notoriety. The total compensation packages for a large number of CEOs now reach values far in excess of a million dollars per year. Stock option plans offered to CEOs can reach values exceeding a hundred million dollars. An unresolved and very critical issue is: What effect does the high compensation given to CEOs have on the remainder of the workforce?

Another critical and unanswered issue is how much are these CEOs worth? Are they worth a combination of short- and long-term compensation that can run into the hundreds of millions, if not billions of dollars?

This chapter describes the various components of an executive compensation plan. Partly in response to federal tax legislation, a basic salary of a CEO of a major corporation is a million dollars. Then, moving beyond this base salary into performance-based short-term incentives, annual compensation can quickly exceed $2 million. By 1998, some top executives of major U.S. corporations were receiving annual compensation in excess of $10 million. With the linkage between various kinds of stock acquisition plans and the rise in value of the U.S. stock market, long-term compensation quickly moves into the multimillion-dollar range.

In addition to base pay and short- and long-term incentives, U.S. executives are also the recipients of a wide variety of benefits and perquisites that can assist in enhancing and enriching their lifestyles.

The federal government, through various pieces of tax and benefits-related legislation, has placed some controls and restrictions on the kinds and amounts of compensation provided to business executives.

Another issue facing some compensation professionals is what they can and must do to provide desirable and competitive compensation packages to employees in international locations. With the ever-increasing importance and expansion of global markets, U.S. businesses are placing employees at various work sites. Many components of compensation for employees at international sites relate to the compensation environment of that location. Other compensation components relate to the practices of the organization at its home site in the United States. International compensation is and will continue to be a more important part of the role played by many compensation professionals.

Review Questions

1. What are the components of an executive compensation plan?
2. What are golden parachutes?
3. Explain the difference between qualified and nonqualified pension plans.
4. Explain constructive receipt.
5. What is reverse discrimination and how does it influence the design of an executive compensation plan?
6. Why have stock acquisition plans become a major national issue?
7. How are various kinds of insurance plans used to fund an executive compensation program?
8. Identify compensation components offered to an employee of a U.S. business who is being offered the opportunity to take a job at a foreign work site.
9. When is a tax equalization program important to an employee accepting a job at a foreign work site?
10. Differentiate among home country, host country, and TCN employees.

Appendix 16A
Tax Legislation-Related Terms

A philosophical issue underlying income tax legislation is that it should promote equality, yet enhance equity. The equality issue underlies the various tax schedules or rates, or progressiveness, involved in designing income tax programs. The issue here is that those who can afford to pay taxes should shoulder the greatest burden, but at the same time, tax designers have not and do not want tax legislation to block individual initiative and stymie the spirit of free enterprise.

Following the 1913 passage of the federal income tax law (see chapter 5), the next piece of legislation that influenced corporate compensation practices was the Revenue Act of 1918. This act permitted corporations to deduct as an expense "reasonable" levels of compensation. Another influence on executive compensation came in 1921 when tax exemption was granted to profit-sharing and bonus plans.

The influence of the federal government on executive compensation began to evolve with the passage of the Revenue Act of 1934. This act required corporations subject to federal income tax regulations to submit the names and the salary amounts of all the executives who earned more than $15,000 a year. This salary disclosure figure was raised to $75,000 with passage of the Tax Revenue Act of 1938.

Chapter 5 lists and briefly describes the major pieces of tax legislation passed by the United States Congress that are of particular interest to CEOs and other highly paid employees. It must also be noted that a wide variety of state and local tax laws also directly influence executive compensation. These laws identify kinds of income and applicable tax rates that are included within earned income, capital gains, and ordinary income. Tax planning in conjunction with the development of an executive compensation plan must consider all tax consequences and the opportunity for reducing tax obligations. Tax consequences and tax savings are not only important to the employee but also to employers when calculating corporate income tax obligations. Any kind of executive compensation plan requires sophisticated tax computations. In 1993, the Financial Accounting Standards Board (FASB) issued an accounting standard that requires employers to recognize the value of fixed stock options granted after 1996 as compensation expenses when granted.

Tax Features   Tax consequences quickly become complex because of the impact of the maximum tax on earned or personal service income (currently, the maximum tax rate is 39.6 percent), minimum tax on items of tax preference, ordinary income tax, alternative minimum tax, income tax averaging opportunities, capital gains taxes, and special averaging rates on pension distributions.

In 1921, the Treasury Department adopted a capital gains tax rate. For the first time, different kinds of income were identified and defined. From 1921 until the present time, the tax rates on various kinds of income have moved up and down, and descriptions have varied as to what is to be included or exempted from specific kinds of tax obligations.

To relate tax legislation to executive compensation, it is essential to understand the following terms:

Earned or Personal Service Income: Employee income gained from direct wage payments, professional fees, cash or stock bonuses, pensions, annuities, and some forms of deferred compensation. The maximum tax rate on earned income is currently 39.6 percent.

Ordinary Income: That income gained from dividends, interest, rent, and some forms of deferred compensation. The maximum tax rate on ordinary income is currently 39.6 percent.

Capital Gains: Profits made from sale of an asset that appreciated in value since time of purchase. Net short-term capital gains are those net gains assets held for one year or less. These are taxed at ordinary income tax rates. Net long-term capital gains are net gains on those assets held for more than one year. These are taxed at 20 percent.

Alternative Minimum Tax: This alternative program was designed to ensure that taxpayers with excessive itemized deductions pay their fair share of taxes. It requires the individual to include all tax preference items in the calculations of taxable income. The alternative minimum tax rate is a flat 20 percent. The alternative minimum tax liability must be paid when it exceeds the regular tax liability.

Stock Award-Related Terms: The contractual language used in establishing stock award plans makes use of the following terms:

Board: Board of directors of the corporation.

Exercise Period: The period of time from and after a change in control (ownership rights) often 60 days in length, frequently called *window*.

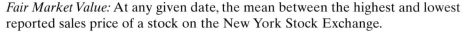

Fair Market Value: At any given date, the mean between the highest and lowest reported sales price of a stock on the New York Stock Exchange.

Methods of Exercise: Kinds of payment approved by the board that an optionee may use at time of exercise to obtain stock.

Option Price: The fair market value of the stock at the date of grant or a price designated by the board.

Performance Period: A two-year or greater period during which a long-term performance award can be earned as determined by the board.

Restriction Period: The period set by the board during which the recipient of a restricted stock award may not sell, assign, transfer, pledge, or otherwise encumber shares of the restricted stock.

Spread Value: The difference in the value of a share of stock, subject to a stock option, between the fair market value and the option price.

Qualified   This term can relate to a variety of employer-offered benefits. Within IRC Section 401(a), *qualified,* as related to pension, profit sharing, and stock-bonus plans, permits the employer to deduct all contributions to such plans in the year the contribution is made, and none of the employer's contribution is treated as employee taxable earnings until the employee receives the distribution (pension payment). To be qualified: (1) the plan must be in writing; (2) the employee's rights under the plan must be legally enforceable; (3) the employer must intend to maintain the plan indefinitely; (4) the employer must provide for reasonable notification to employees of benefits under the plan; (5) the plan must be maintained for the exclusive benefit of employees (or spouses and dependents, where applicable). A qualified plan must also meet these requirements: (1) benefits must be funded; (2) eligibility must not discriminate in favor of shareholders, officers, or highly compensated employees (see definition of *key employees* later in this section), (3) contributions and benefits covered by the plan must become nonforfeitable according to prescribed requirements and must not discriminate in favor of shareholders, officers, or highly compensated employees, but can discriminate in favor of the lower-paid employees.

Nondiscrimination   A *qualified* plan must be for the benefit of employees and be nondiscriminatory. It must cover all employees in the covered group who are 21 years of age and have completed one year of service. If a plan provides for 100 percent vesting, upon commencing participation, such participation may be postponed from the latter of three years from date of employment or from age 21.

To meet employee coverage requirements, the plan must include at least 70 percent of all employees or 80 percent of all eligible employees as long as at least 70 percent of the employees are eligible for participation.[16] In determining all employees, certain employees may be excluded. They are part-time employees who work less than 17½ hours per week or no more than six months per year, employees under the age of 21, and employees with less than six months of service. Nonresident aliens with no U.S. earned income and employees covered by a collective bargaining agreement must be excluded.

As of 1989, a plan coverage test must satisfy any one of three new tests: (1) a percentage test in which at least 70 percent of all nonhighly paid employees are included

---

[16]IRC, Section 410.

in the plan; (2) a ratio test in which the percentage of nonhighly paid employees who benefit under the plan must be at least 70 percent of the percentage of the highly paid employees who benefit under the plan; (3) the average benefits test, which includes two parts: (a) the plan must meet "fair cross-section tests" of the current law, and (b) the average employee-provided benefit for nonhighly paid (lower-paid) employees under all the employer's qualified plans (including an amount deemed to represent the employer-provided portion of Social Security) must be as a percentage of compensation at least 70 percent of a similar benefit for highly paid employees.

Contributions or benefits of or on behalf of employees under the plan must bear a uniform relationship to the total compensation or the basic or regular rate of compensation of such employees. To qualify the contributions or benefits of a pension, profit-sharing, or stock-bonus plan, the plan must not discriminate in favor of employees who are officers, shareholders, or highly compensated individuals.[17] This group is referred to as the *prohibited group* —those employees that the federal tax law prohibits qualified plans from discriminating in favor of regarding terms of coverage, contributions, or benefits.

Highly Paid Employees/Prohibited Group   A highly paid employee is defined as a 5 percent owner; a person earning over $100,000 a year in either the current or preceding year; a person earning over $66,000 a year in either the current or preceding year who is or was in the top 20 percent of all active employees for such year; or an officer earning over 150 percent of the dollar limit for annual additions to a defined contribution plan ($1.5 \times \$30,000 = \$45,000$ under the existing $30,000 dollar limit) in either the current or preceding year. The plan must include a minimum of one officer and a maximum of 50.

Key Employees   These may include only the smaller of (1) 50 officers, or three employees or 10 percent of all employees (whichever is greater); (2) 10 employees owning the largest interest in the employer; (3) a greater than 5 percent owner of the employer; and (4) a greater than 1 percent owner of the employer with annual compensation in excess of $150,000. A key employee does not include officers paid $45,000 or less a year.

Top-Heavy Plans   A defined benefits plan is top-heavy if the present value of accumulated accrued benefits for participants who are key employees for this plan exceed 60 percent of the present value of the accumulated accrued benefits for all employees under the plan, or if a defined contribution plan, the sum of the account balances of participants who are key employees for the plan exceeds 60 percent of the sum of account balances of all employees under the plan, or in either case, if the plan is part of top-heavy plans (two or more plans of a single employer may be aggregated to determine whether plans, as a group, are top-heavy).[18] Plans that are top-heavy must meet additional requirements such as (1) only the first $150,000 of an employee's compensation may be taken into account in determining plan contributions or benefits; (2) greater portability for plan participants who are nonkey employees; (3) specific benefits or contributions for nonkey employees; and (4) reduction on aggregate limit on contributions and benefits for key employees and other requirements.

---

[17]IRC, Section 416(i).
[18]IRC, Section 416(f), (g), (i).

Safe Harbor   With the development of cash or deferred arrangement (CODA) plans, two safe harbor provisions were established to prohibit the highly compensated from taking advantage of the opportunity through salary reduction to defer taxation on current and accrued earnings of their investments. These safe harbor provisions require that the actual deferred percentage of the highest-paid one-third of the employees must not exceed the actual deferred percentage of the lower-paid two-thirds: (1) by more than one and one-half times, and (2) by more than three percentage points, and not more than two and one-half times the actual deferred percentage of the lowest-paid two-thirds of the employees.[19]

An additional safe harbor provision appears under TRA 86. When an employer has separate lines of business (SLOBs) or operating units employing at least 50 employees for *bona fide* business reasons, and if the plan meets current "fair cross-section tests," any of the tests can also be satisfied separately for each line of business. To qualify as a "safe harbor," the percentage of highly paid employees at the separate facility must be not less than one-half nor more than twice the average percentage of highly paid employees companywide. Headquarters personnel are not considered as a separate line of business.

Vesting Schedule   To increase the mobility of a participant in a qualified pension plan, vesting schedules have been established within the IRC. A *vesting schedule* defines the participant's rights to the employer's contributions and the accrued earnings of these contributions. (Any employee contributions and the accrued earnings of these contributions are nonforfeitable from date of contribution.)

Beginning in 1989, only two vesting standards will be available: (1) a 5-year cliff vesting—all accrued benefits must be vested after 5 years of service; and (2) a 7-year graded vesting, requiring that 20 percent of accrued benefits be vested after 3 years of service. This percentage then increases in multiples of 20 percent each year until 100 percent vesting is achieved after 7 years. There will, however, be two exceptions: (1) multiemployer plans that are collectively bargained may continue to use the 10-year cliff vesting; and (2) vesting standards for top-heavy plans continue as in the past. If a plan requires more than one year of service for eligibility (up to 2 years is allowable), it must provide for 100 percent immediate vesting.

For top-heavy plans, there are two additional vesting schedules: (1) after 3 years of service, all nonkey employees have 100 percent vesting rights to all benefits accrued from employer contributions; and (2) nonkey employees receive 20 percent nonforfeitable rights to employer contributions with 2 years of service, and the rights increase by 20 percent for each additional year of service so that with 6 years of service, a nonkey employee is 100 percent vested.

Social Security Integration   To reduce pension costs, many corporations integrate employee Social Security retirement payments with their own pension programs. Because the organization is paying 7.65 percent of an employee's W-2 earnings—up to $72,600 as of 1999) plus 1.45 percent of all earnings beyond $72,600 (Medicare)—many organizations believe the two programs should be coordinated when making retirement payments. There is a relatively small spread between minimum and maximum Social Security payments, regardless of earnings, for employees who have worked and

---

[19]IRC, Section 401(k)(3).

participated in Social Security for an extended period (such as 35 years). Lower-paid employees receive a significantly greater percentage of their annual earnings in Social Security payments than do highly paid employees. Because of the relatively small spread in Social Security payments, when organizations do coordinate Social Security and qualified pension payments, the lower-paid employees receive a relatively smaller payment from the qualified pension plan.

For example, two employees, LP and HP, have both worked 35 years for an organization and retire. LP had a final average pay of $16,000 and HP had a final average pay of $100,000. Under a 2 percent per year pension formula, employee LP is eligible for a pension payment of .02 × 35 × $16,000 or $11,200. HP is eligible for .02 × 35 × $100,000 or $70,000. At time of retirement, LP is also eligible for a $7,000 Social Security payment and HP is eligible for a $10,000 Social Security payment (these Social Security payments are illustrative). If half of each employee's Social Security payment (employee and employer each paid half of the annual Social Security tax) is integrated into the final retirement payment, LP would have $3,500 of the Social Security payment integrated with $7,700 from the pension plan to provide the earned retirement of $11,200. HP would, in turn, receive $5,000 from Social Security and $65,000 from the pension plan for a $70,000 earned retirement payment. Social Security covered 31.25 percent (3,500/11,200), of LP's total retirement payment, whereas it covered 7.14 percent (5,000/70,000) of HP's retirement payment.

However, TRA 86 requires that any "offset" (amount of Social Security counted in a final retirement payment) in a defined benefits plan may not exceed 0.75 percent of the employee's final average pay or 50 percent of the benefits that would have been accrued without the offset. In the case of total benefits, the offset may not exceed 0.75 percent of the employee's final average pay × years of service (up to 35 years).

Returning to the example, the offset for LP cannot exceed .0075 × 35 × $16,000 = $4,200. In the example, LP's offset was $3,500, which is less than the maximum permissible offset of $4,200 and is acceptable. By integrating or coordinating Social Security benefits with organization retirement benefits, the organization can reduce the costs of a qualified defined benefits plan. However, because an integrated plan produces a total retirement income that is a relatively equal percentage for all employees, it is nondiscriminatory as long as it meets IRS offset requirements.

Nonqualified   Nonqualified deferred compensation components are those in which the employer does not receive a tax deduction until the employee is required to include the compensation as taxable income. Nonqualified deferred compensation takes many forms. It includes various kinds of stock acquisition plans, stock proxy plans (phantom stock plans), and programs to supplement Social Security and qualified retirement plans. These plans permit recipients to defer recognition of taxable income to some future date. At the same time, the recipient may not receive actual ownership rights to the particular compensation component. For recipients of nonqualified deferred compensation plans to be able to defer income tax, the income must not be constructively received.

Constructive Receipt Doctrine   To be sure that income promised through a deferred compensation plan is not taxable, the recipient must not take *constructive receipt* of the compensation. Constructive receipt recognizes control over funds even though the funds may not be in the physical possession of the employee. An example of constructive receipt is the interest earned on a savings account. Constructive receipt relates to a broader doctrine—the doctrine of economic benefit—that underlies the entire concept of income tax. This doctrine states that anyone who receives a benefit that is equivalent to or can be converted to cash can be taxed on this benefit currently. Recognizing the doctrine of constructive receipt, the tax treatment of a nonqualified deferred compensation plan depends on whether it is funded or nonfunded or forfeitable.

Nonfunded–Funded   A nonfunded, nonqualified deferred compensation plan is one in which the employee relies on the mere promise of the employer to make the compensation payment in the future. In a nonfunded plan, the employee does not have ownership to any of the plan funds. The assets of a nonfunded deferred compensation plan are commingled with the other assets of the employer, and guarantees of payment are subject to normal business risks. (An employer can own and pay premiums on a life insurance policy that pays death benefits in a deferred compensation plan. The employee, however, has no ownership vested rights in the contract or its funding. The policy must be accessible to general creditors of the employer.)

Nonqualified deferred compensation plans can be funded through the use of escrow custodial accounts or internally funded revocable trusts, or through externally funded nonexempt trusts. Generally, however, funded nonqualified deferred compensation plans must be forfeitable in order to keep the compensation from being immediately taxable.

Forfeitable   IRC, Section 83, states that a substantial risk of forfeiture exists when a person's rights to full enjoyment of such property are conditioned upon the future performance, or the refraining from the performance, of substantial services by an individual. A risk of forfeiture could relate to maintaining employment for a specific number of years, meeting certain profitability-related goals, or breaching a covenant not to compete.

Appendix 16B
Stock and Stock Equivalent Acquisition Plans

Prior to World War II, human resources management was just beginning to evolve as a distinctive staff function in the larger and more progressive organizations in the nation. Compensation administration, however, was barely a gleam in the eyes of some of the more innovative leaders in the fields of personnel administration and industrial engineering. Although the entire field of personnel administration received a huge boost from the employee rights and protection legislation of the 1930s, the influence of legislation on senior management compensation practices was negligible. Prior to 1945, the major influence of government legislation on senior management compensation was how stock options were classified and taxed. At this time, there were two classes of stock options: *proprietary options* and *nonproprietary options.*

Proprietary options provided no income to recipients at the time of exercise; and at the time of sale, gains were treated as long-term capital gains. Nonproprietary options created immediate income for the recipient and were treated as ordinary income upon exercise of the option (maximum ordinary tax rate then was 90 percent).

In 1945, the IRS took the position that all options were compensation and effectively eliminated proprietary stock options and almost eliminated the use of stock options as a compensation tool. During the period between 1945 to 1950, corporate leaders claimed that there was a need to expand proprietary interest to corporate leaders by providing opportunities for acquiring equity interests at nominal cost. With the passage of the Tax Revenue Act of 1950 and subsequent amendments to the Internal Revenue Code, profits from *restricted* stock options were recognized as long-term capital gains, which then had a maximum tax rate of 25 percent. At that time, an individual with an income of $1 million was taxed at a rate of 85.7 percent. The 1950 restricted stock option plans had the following features:

1. Options could be granted only to employees.
2. Recipients must be employed for a lengthy period of time on a continuous basis.
3. Option price could be as low as 85 percent of fair market value at time of grant.
4. Options could be exercised up to 10 years after grants (exercise period).
5. Sale of stock could be 2 years from the date of the grant or six months from time of exercise (holding period).

By 1964, the IRS, Congress, and corporate shareholders felt that top executives who were the recipients of restricted stock options had betrayed the intent of the 1950 code change. Therefore, the Revenue Act of 1964 replaced restricted stock options with qualified stock options. The 1964 qualified stock option plans had the following features:

1. Options must be granted within 10 years of the date of the plan adoption.
2. Option price of the stock is 100 percent of fair market value at date of the grant.
3. Stock option plans must be exercised within 5 years of the grant (exercise period).
4. Stock options must be exercised in order of grant unless the earlier granted option has expired.
5. Stock options must be in possession of the recipient for 3 years in order to obtain long-term capital gains treatment (holding period).
6. After making a grant, the recipient cannot own more than 5 percent of the outstanding corporate stock unless the equity capital in the corporation is less than $2 million.
7. The right to shares terminates at death or three months after resignation.

The Tax Reform Act of 1969 did not change the requirements for a qualified stock option, but it did raise the maximum tax rate on capital gains to 35 percent. It also introduced a 10 percent minimum tax on preference items, and the untaxed half of the capital gains was identified as a preference item. This change in the tax law reduced the value of the qualified stock option.

Then the Tax Reform Act of 1976 killed qualified stock options. The act forbade the granting of any more qualified stock options and set the date of May 20, 1981 as the last day any previously granted stock options could be exercised and take advantage of qualified stock option tax provisions. This act then set into motion great interest in and expanded use of nonqualified stock options.

The major features of a nonqualified stock option are:

1. Options must be granted pursuant to an approved corporate plan, and the purpose of the plan must be clearly identified.
2. An option can be granted at any price.
3. There is a 10-year limitation on the duration of the option (exercise period).

4. There is no sequential exercise restriction.
5. There is no restriction on the amount of stock a recipient can own.
6. After exercise, shares must be held for 1 year to receive long-term capital gains treatment (holding period).
7. Gain between option price and market price at time of exercise is considered earned income for that year and is, therefore, taxed at the applicable earned income rate (up to 50 percent). At time of sale, any additional gain is taxed as capital gains.

With the passage of the Economic Recovery Tax Act of 1981, a new kind of stock option—the incentive stock option (ISO)—was provided. The ISO is a substitute for the eliminated qualified stock option, but returns those wishing to use stock options almost full circle to the restricted stock option program of 1950.

Some of the major features of the ISO are:

1. The option holder must be an employee from the date of the grant of the option until 3 months before the date of the exercise. (A disabled employee has 12 months after leaving employment to exercise the option.)
2. Option price must equal or exceed the fair market value of the stock.
3. Option must be exercised within 10 years after the grant (exercise period).
4. To be eligible for capital gains tax rates, the stock must be held for at least 2 years from the date of the grant and at least 1 year after exercise of the grant. (No tax consequence results at the time of the grant or exercise of an incentive stock option.) (Holding period.)
5. Outstanding stock options must be exercised in order of grant.
6. Maximum value of stock option granted to an employee in any calendar year generally shall not exceed $100,000.
7. Terms of the option must forbid transfer other than at death and must be exercisable only by the optionee and during that person's lifetime.
8. Recipients of an option must not own more than 10 percent of the combined voting power of the employer or its parent or its subsidiary immediately before the granting of an option.
9. The option plan must be approved by stockholders within 12 months before or after the adoption of the plan.
10. The option must be granted within 10 years of the date of adoption or date of approval.

The Tax Reform Act of 1986 (TRA 86) eliminated the requirement that a holder of a stock option must hold shares gained for six months after an exercise before being permitted to sell these shares.

Major points of interest to recipients of a stock option are:

1. Number of shares of stock they are granted the right to purchase.
2. Purchase price (normally stock market price at time of grant).
3. Latest date option can be exercised (most stock prices tend to increase over time, thus the longer the exercise period, normally the more valuable the option. There are certainly cases in which the price of a company's stock has declined since the grant and it is worthless to the recipient—the stock option is "underwater").

4. Tax consequences at time of (a) exercise of the option or (b) sale of the stock. The important considerations here are (a) the effective personal service income tax rate of the recipient at the time of exercise or sale and (b) the tax implication—personal service, capital gains, and alternative minimum tax.

Like any reward to be received in the future, stock options have at least two shortcomings to the recipient. One is the inability to predict future tax consequences. This includes the inability to predict both income and tax rates at time tax payments are due. In fact, it is quite likely that those who receive lucrative stock options will also have substantial postretirement incomes, thus nullifying the tax advantage of deferred stock option gains. Second, there is always the chance that the business will decline in value, possibly fail, and make the stock options worthless.

Stock and stock equivalent acquisition plans vary significantly as to eligibility, tax obligations to employer and recipient, and accounting treatment for corporate financial records. The following review and brief description of some of the more common stock and stock equivalent acquisition plans, their unique features, and the purposes they serve will assist in gaining an appreciation of the variety of stock-related compensation components available and their relationship to tax legislation.

Stock Purchase Plans

Stock purchase plans are the most common kind of stock acquisition plans. A qualified stock purchase plan is one that permits almost all employees of an organization to acquire corporate stock. Internal Revenue Code Section 423 defines the requirements a corporation must meet to qualify a stock purchase program. A qualified stock purchase plan, similar to a nonqualified stock purchase plan, permits the purchase of corporate stock over a relatively short period of time. A qualified stock purchase plan, however, requires the recipient to purchase the stock within five years from the date of grant of the purchase option. The price of the stock can be as low as 85 percent of the market price at the time of offer or the market price at the time of purchase, if lower. No employee has the right to accrue more than $25,000 worth of stock at the fair market value in any one year. Many organizations permit their employees to purchase their stock through a payroll deduction. Usually, payroll deductions may not exceed 10 percent of an employee's compensation. Some employers combine a profit-sharing or awards program with the stock purchase plan by matching 50 percent to 100 percent of the employee's contribution to purchase additional stock.

If the employee meets IRS employment regulations (is employed by the corporation granting the option at all times during the period starting with the date of the grant and ending on the date three months before the option is exercised), no tax liability results at the time of the exercise. If the employee does not sell the stock within two years after the granting of the option or within one year after acquiring the stock, the difference between the option price and the fair market value of the stock at the time of sale is considered ordinary income and the remainder is capital gains.

Because of the limitations inherent within qualified stock purchase plans, some corporations use nonqualified stock purchase plans for executives. The various kinds of executive stock purchase or nonqualified stock purchase plans provide corporations with the flexibility of blending specific organizational requirements with key personnel demands. Depending upon the specific features of the plan, recipients of the nonqualified stock purchase plans are able to acquire stock at prices ranging from full market value to a flat one dollar per share for stock having a fair market value 10, 20, or more times that amount. In addition, the corporation may provide special loan arrangements so that the recipient has minimal financial burden when purchasing the stock. These stock purchase plans normally carry some restrictions. Typical restrictions are (1) the stockholder must be employed for a certain period of time; (2) the corporation has the right to buy back the stock; and (3) stockholders cannot sell for a definite period of time. There is, normally, no waiting period to purchase the stock. Among the various kinds of executive stock purchase plans are (1) full market value, (2) earn-out or performance, (3) discounted, and (4) formula value.

Full market value stock purchase plans require the recipient to pay the full market price for the stock, but, normally, the corporation provides favorable loan or pay arrangements to assist in the purchase of the stock.

Earn-out or *performance stock plans* permit key employees to receive a loan to purchase the stock. The employee then satisfies the loan (does not have to repay) by meeting certain performance requirements such as (1) continued employment or (2) specific organizational performance measures.

Discounted stock purchase plans are plans in which the purchase price is less than the fair market price of the stock. A typical restriction with this kind of plan is that the corporation has the right to repurchase the stock if the recipient leaves the firm within a specific period.

Formula value stock purchase plans relate the price of the stock to some special formula and not to the fair market price. Two commonly used formulas are (1) book value and (2) price earnings multiple. To establish the book value or stockholder's equity, the corporation must (1) determine net worth (total assets less total liabilities) and (2) divide net worth by number of shares of outstanding common stock. (The basic intent of any kind of book value–based plan is to minimize the influence of the speculative aspects of the stock market and focus the recipient's attention on the growth of the firm.)

A special kind of formula value stock purchase plan is the *book purchase plan.* In this plan, the corporation provides the recipient with low- or no-interest loans to purchase the stock. The recipient can, after a specific period of time, sell the stock back at the then-existing book value.

Stock purchase plans grant the recipients immediate ownership. They enable the recipient to pay capital gains on all appreciation. Stock dividends are taxable at personal service income tax rates (39.6 percent maximum). The stock offer is a capital transaction for the corporation, not a compensation expense. Thus, it is a business expense and not a profit-and-loss charge (charge against earnings).

Stock Option Plans

Stock option plans are similar to stock purchase plans with one major variation: Stock options are granted to key personnel over a period of time that exceeds the time periods granted for stock purchase plans. Just as with stock purchase plans, the employee receives the right to purchase a specific amount of corporate stock at a stipulated price within a specified period of time. The employee is under no obligation to purchase the stock. In working with stock options, two important words to recognize are *exercise* and *window.* The word *exercise* means the time when the stock option recipient actually acquires or purchases the stock. The word *window* refers to the specific period of time set by government regulation after the granting of the option that the recipient has the right to purchase the stock (this may also be called the *exercise period*). Under certain kinds of stock options, the recipient is required to report any difference between the fair market price of the stock and the price of exercise and is subject to tax at personal service income rates and must pay tax on that amount during the applicable tax period. When meeting capital gains time requirements, all other appreciation at the time of sale is taxed at long-term capital gains rates. See the earlier discussion of Economic Recovery Tax Act of 1981 and ISOs.

From a nonqualified perspective, tax laws do not impose any limitation on the amount of stock a corporation can option to an individual or individuals. The only limitation relates to practical business considerations. The shares of stock authorized for stock options are usually functions of (1) the size of the corporation, (2) the shares outstanding, and (3) the number of employees provided stock option rights. The actual size of an option granted to a specific employee usually depends on that individual's base pay, level in the hierarchy, and value to the organization.

A wide variety of nonqualified stock option plans has been designed over the years to meet various employee and employer demands. The nonqualified stock option plans are very similar to the previously described stock purchase plans. The major kinds of nonqualified stock option plans are:

1. Full price stock option plans.
2. Discounted stock option plans.
3. Variable-price stock option plans (including the nonqualified yo-yo plan).
4. Tax offset stock option plan.
5. Formula value stock option plan.

The *full price, discounted,* and *formula value stock option plans* have features comparable to the stock purchase plans with the same titles. The *variable-price stock option plan* permits the price of the stock in the option to vary according to some stock market determined value, financial performance measure, or other indicators of corporate performance. A particular kind of variable-price plan is the *yo-yo plan.* The unique feature of this plan is that each dollar increase in the market price of the stock reduces the option price of the stock by an identical amount. The initial option price is usually 100 percent of the fair market value.

The *tax offset stock option plan* requires the corporation to pay the recipient upon exercise of the option an amount of money sufficient to offset assessed tax liability. (See the discussion of additive SAR later in this section.) As in all nonqualified stock option plans, the corporation is able to declare a tax deduction equal to the amount the recipient declares as income at the time of the exercise of the option. By granting the recipient money sufficient to pay incurred taxes, the corporation, in effect, returns the tax savings to the employee.

A special kind of stock option plan is the granting of *stock warrants* to an employee. A warrant is a right to buy a specific number of shares of stock at a specified price within a definite time period. Warrants are normally transferable, can be sold by the warrant holder, and have a fair market value.

A third kind of stock acquisition plan is the *stock grant.* A stock grant provides selected employees with stock at *no* cost. Stock grants take two basic forms: stock appreciation grants and full-value grants.

Stock appreciation grants entitle the recipient to receive payments that equal the appreciated value of the stock (or number of shares or units of stock granted) over a designated period of time. A *full-value stock grant* entitles the recipient to receive the total value of the worth of a share of stock (or number of shares or units of stock granted) over a predetermined period of time. Total value includes base value of stock at time of initial grant, dividend, and appreciation of stock value during the period when the grant is in force.

Most stock grant plans take place over a period of time in excess of five years. Usually, the recipient or the firm must meet certain predetermined performance standards.

Some of the more common kinds of stock grant plans are the (1) restricted stock plan, (2) performance share plan, and (3) phantom stock plan. Each of these three kinds of plans may have a number of different features.

In a *restricted stock plan,* the corporation awards a specified number of shares of its common stock to certain individuals who have demonstrated continued superior performance. These individuals must continue employment with the corporation for a specific time period. In some cases, the employee may be required to pay a specific amount for the stock. When this occurs, the restricted plan becomes, in essence, a nonqualified stock option. The recipient has stockholder voting privileges and rights to all dividends, but, during a stipulated (restrictive) period, may not sell, transfer, or use the stock as a pledge or security for a debt. When a restriction is not met, the recipient may be required to sell the stock back at a penalty. The restrictive period may range from two to ten years in duration. Normally, restrictions lapse following retirement or involuntary termination. (See the Coca-Cola–Goizueta example earlier in the chapter.)

With all stock grant plans, the recipient must pay at personal service income tax rates the fair market value of the acquired stock. Dividends are also taxed at personal service income tax rates. All gains realized from the sale of the stock are taxed as long-term capital gains. Dividend payments made by the company on restricted stock may be charged as a business expense, and it can amortize the value of the stock on the restricted period. The amortized value is a charge to earnings. The corporation receives a tax credit for any increase in the value during the restricted period.

Restricted stock plans can be modified to have not only certain time restrictions, but may also include the meeting of certain performance measures before the actual granting of the restricted stock. The size of the grant may also be predicated on the reaching of certain goals or measures. This kind of grant is called a *restricted stock performance plan.*

A *performance share plan (PSP)* is similar to the restricted stock performance plan except that there is *no* holding period determining when the stock can be sold. These PSPs usually set grants for medium time periods—3 to 5 years. However, the holding periods for some plans may range from 6 to 10 years in length.

When reaching certain predetermined performance goals, the recipient has the right to specified shares of stock. For example, an employee may be eligible for a grant of 5,000 shares of stock if stockholder equity is increased by 10 percent, or 3,000 shares if it is increased by 6 percent, and nothing if less than 6 percent. The performance goals may be earnings per share over a specified time period or return on assets. The actual amount of stock granted may relate to some formula such as the price of stock at the time of payment and the actual goal achieved by the recipient.

Another kind of stock grant plan that gained popularity in the 1970s is the *phantom stock plan.* A major reason for the development of phantom stock plans was the difficulty some executives had in obtaining the funds necessary to exercise stock options. In this plan, stock or stock appreciation awards are made in artificial units. These units become a credit to the recipient against an equivalent number of shares of stock in the corporation. The actual payment value, which can be made in stock or cash or a combination of the two, is established by some predetermined formula that relates to either the market or some nonmarket value of the stock.

A typical phantom stock plan may take this form: In five years, it grants a specified number of units that are equal to shares of stock in the firm. The value of the units may equal the price of the stock at the time or the appreciated value of the stock from the time of the grant to that predetermined future date. It may also include the value of all declared dividends earned by the equivalent shares during the waiting period. The total value of the plan is then paid out in cash to the recipient in five years.

A special kind of phantom stock plan is a *stock appreciation rights (SAR)*. An SAR may take three distinct forms. An SAR may be linked directly to a stock option plan (a tandem plan), it may be freestanding or it may be an additive SAR. A stock option linked in tandem with an SAR permits the optionee to receive a stipulated payment that can be made in cash, stock, or a combination of the two in lieu of all or a designated part of the option. The amount of the option covered by the SAR may be a specified number of, or a certain percentage of, the option shares and be payable only in money. The value of the SAR may be limited to the appreciated value of the stock option from the time of the grant of the option to the time the SAR is available. Or the SAR value may be the full value of the stock at the time the option can be exercised and all dividends earned since the stock option was granted. The SAR may have a limit such as a certain percentage of the initial value of the option. A freestanding SAR is similar to the previously described phantom stock plan. An additive SAR provides award rights in addition to a stock option. When a stock option (or some part) is exercised, the recipient receives an SAR payment in addition to the stock grant. The funds from the additive SAR can be used to offset income tax obligations related to the stock option gain. Additive SARs can be used in conjunction with a tandem SAR. An SAR also limits the recipient's tax consequences because the gains are taxed as capital gains.

A plan that combines the features of a phantom stock plan with a performance share plan is a *performance unit plan (PUP)*. Similar to a phantom stock plan, the grant is made in some number of artificial units with each unit usually being the equivalent of one share of company stock. The actual dollar payout of these units is equivalent to the value of the stock at some future date stipulated in the plan.

Like the performance share plan, the recipient or the corporation must meet certain performance measures in order for the recipient to acquire the grant units. Although the PUP unit awards are made at the time of the grant, the units acquire a cash value only at the end of a stipulated period and upon the meeting of prescribed performance measures. The major difference between a PUP and a PSP is that a PUP has a prescribed and definite limit while a PSP is open-ended.

A *formula value appreciation rights plan* is a phantom grant plan in which the actual number of stock units used for determining appreciation gains is based on a predetermined formula rather than on the fair market value of the stock. The predetermined formula may be based on the number of years of continuous employment or on certain performance criteria.

A *formula value stock grant* is another kind of phantom grant plan in which the value of the stock unit awards does not relate to the stock's fair market value, but rather to some other evaluation procedure. A specific kind of formula value stock plan may grant the recipient a specified number of units equivalent to the book value of the stock at some specified future date (five years, upon retirement, etc.). This kind of grant is called a *book unit plan (BUP)*.

An offshoot of the phantom stock plan is the *phantom convertible debenture*. This plan grants phantom corporate bonds that pay interest and, upon maturity, will pay the recipient the face value of the bond or be convertible to shares of stock.

Reload Option   This stock option agreement entitles the optionee to a further option in the event the optionee exercises the option, in whole or in part, by surrendering already owned shares of common stock in accordance with the option plan. The new reload option will be equivalent to the number of shares tendered as payment in the stock-for-stock exercise and is priced at the fair market value at the time of the grant and expires at the same time as the original grant. A reload option encourages early exercise of a valuable stock option by permitting the optionee to capture the option profit in shares while retaining the same upside leverage as if the option is encouraged because the optionee will need shares to exercise other options in a reload fashion. This stock option is also known as a *restoration stock option*.

Appendix 16C
Special Corporate Insurance Programs

Section 79 Insurance   Section 79 of the IRC establishes income tax regulations that permit employers to provide employees with up to $50,000 of tax-free, group term life insurance. Income tax regulations also permit employers to provide group term life insurance in amounts above $50,000 if the amount of group insurance is computed under a formula that "precludes individual selection" (if the organization provides *all* employees with group term insurance equal to 1.5 times annual salary, an employee whose annual salary is $100,000 can be provided with $150,000 of insurance). In the case of the employee with a $100,000 annual salary and a $150,000 group term life income, the employee would receive the first $50,000 tax free, and the annual gross income of the employee would include the cost of the additional insurance as computed through the use of IRS Table I (Group-Term Life Insurance Uniform Premium Table), as revised on July 1, 1999. For example, if the employee receiving $150,000 in insurance is 48 years old, the monthly cost *per $1,000* of coverage is 15 cents according to Table I, age 45–49 column. The additional monthly charge to the employee's gross income would be $100,000 ÷ $1,000 × .15 = $15.00. Nondiscriminatory tests apply to Section 79 insurance.

Section 79 group life insurance plans must meet various nondiscriminatory rules to determine the amount of premium a highly paid employee must report as imputed income. A highly paid employee must consider as imputed income all premiums paid for any amount of insurance determined to be over the nondiscriminatory level, which is calculated by following nondiscriminatory rules. The actual value of a plan is determined by using IRC, Section 79, Table I rates for an employee age 40. If the nondiscriminatory level is less than $50,000, then the highly paid employee must consider all premiums paid beyond the nondiscriminatory level as imputed earnings. There is a $200,000 limit on pay when using a Section 79 group life insurance plan.

Section 79 insurance can include a whole life feature with stable costs and no possibility of cancellation. Both employer and employee contribute to the plan. The employer contribution pays for the "risk assumption" portion of the premium; the employee contribution builds the cash value of the policy. Upon retirement, the employee can select (a) a lump-sum cash payment, (b) an annuity income, (c) reduced paid-up death benefit, or (d) elect to continue insurance at the full face amount of the policy and pay premiums at the original age rate.

Additional advantages of Section 79 insurance are that (1) it is a less expensive way to provide postretirement insurance than through normal corporate group insurance; (2) premiums are tax deductible to the corporation; (3) income upon retirement is taxed as personal service income; (4) death benefits are income tax free; and (5) the employee can borrow on the cash value of the policy.

Split Dollar   Split-dollar life insurance plans involve both employer and employee in the purchase of a cash value or permanent life insurance policy. The employer usually pays that part of the premium that equals the increase in the cash value of the policy for the current year. The employee pays the balance, which is the term element of the premium. The resulting cash value of the policy can be used for funding a deferred compensation agreement. The cash value is retained or assigned to the employer while the employee designates the beneficiary for the remaining part of the death benefit—that amount which exceeds the cash value. At death, the insurance proceeds are received tax-free by the employer and the employee's beneficiary. The beneficiary may escape paying estate taxes if the employee makes an absolute assignment of the proceeds to the beneficiary.

The employee gains by being able to purchase insurance at a lower price than if the purchase has been made by the employee alone. The employee pays taxes on any amount by which the term value of the benefit and any dividends received exceed the employee's premium payment. The Internal Revenue Service P.S. 58 one-year term rate table identifies the premium value of the insurance protection for the year for tax purposes, or the lesser of the insurance carriers lowest-published term rate.

Salary Continuation Plans   Another approach available for providing key personnel with a stream of income for a period of years after retirement, or for the life of the individual, or to the surviving spouse, beneficiaries, or estate of the employee (if death occurs prior to retirement), is through the use of a salary continuation plan.

A salary continuation plan may involve an agreement between the key executive and the corporation whereby the executive agrees to be available for advisory or consulting services after retirement and also to refrain from entering the employment of a competitive company while receiving continued salary payments. The contract terminates if the executive is discharged for a cause as defined in the employment agreement.

Another plan used to provide salary continuation is the *supplemental income plan (SIP)*. A SIP is a future income contract between employer and employee. Like a deferred compensation plan, it provides supplemental income payments for a specified period of time or until death or upon incurring permanent disability. The amount of the payments can be based on some formula using years of service, final salary, certain performance goals, or any combination of these.

The employer can either fund the contract or can let it be unfunded and make payments out of future earnings. A funded SIP commonly uses some form of life insurance for financing the payment. A special kind of multipurpose life insurance policy has been developed to fund SIPs. A policy is issued on the life of each employee participating in the SIP, and the policy is owned by and payable to the corporation. The policy covers the expenses incurred in case of preretirement death of the employee. Or, after the retirement of the employee, the company can surrender the policy and use the funds collected or the loan value of the policy to offset the cost of installment payments for the employee. The company may also maintain the policy and upon the employee's death recover the face amount of the policy. The company pays no taxes on the face amount of the policy. Employee-received payment is considered earned income, and the employee is taxed at ordinary income tax rates in the years the payments are received.

In addition, split-dollar insurance plans can be used to fund salary continuation plans to escape income taxation upon the employee's death and remove any proceeds from the estate of the deceased for estate tax purposes.

The corporation can use its share of the anticipated proceeds from the split-dollar policy to fund the cost of providing salary continuation benefits. When using split-dollar insurance for this purpose, the plan should be executed separately from any other split-dollar plan to eliminate any suggestion that the employee has an interest in the employer's investment and to prevent current taxation based on constructive receipt.

Group Universal Life Insurance Plan (GULP)   A GULP combines low-cost term insurance with a tax-sheltered investment fund. GULPs are offered to employees as a supplement to a basic group life or as a replacement for other kinds of supplemental life insurance plans. GULPs gained popularity after the passage of TRA 86 because this law established extremely restrictive withdrawal rules for plan participants who wish to use 401(k) funds for the purchase of a home, payment of college tuition, or some other economic hardship. A GULP can be designed in a way that provides participants with a desired level of death-benefit coverage while also providing the participant with the opportunity to invest after-tax dollars in a tax-deferred cash value fund. Any gains achieved by the fund are tax sheltered until the time when the money is withdrawn. A properly structured GULP is not subject to ERISA regulations. Premiums are almost always paid by the employee through payroll deductions. A GULP could be in competition with a 401(k), and it also places an additional administrative cost on the employer.

CHAPTER

Benefits and Services

Learning Objectives

In this chapter you will learn about:

1. The kinds of benefits and services employers offer to their employees.

2. The costs to employers in providing benefits and services.

3. The role of federal and state legislation in the design of a benefits program.

4. The administration of a benefits and services program.

5. The importance of communicating the components of a benefits program to employees.

6. The various kinds of health care plans offered to employees.

7. The design and usefulness of a flexible benefits program.

Compensation Strategy

Provide organizational resources that link employee needs for both short- and long-term survival and recognize differences in individual and family requirements.

The very expensive but often forgotten stepchild of the total compensation package is that segment called *employee benefits and services,* which in the past was called *fringe benefits.* These benefits are primarily the in-kind payments employees receive in addition to payments in the form of money. At one time, the fringe benefits were of marginal importance, but this is no longer true. The Chamber of Commerce of the United States estimated that in 1929 total wages and salaries paid in the United States were $50.5 billion and that total benefit payments were $1.5 billion. Thus, in 1929 benefits were approximately 3 percent of wages and salaries. In 1994 wages and salaries were estimated to be $3,279.0 billion and benefits $1,308.3 billion.[1] By 1994

---

[1]U.S. Chamber of Commerce, *Employee Benefits 1995,* Table 17. Growth of Employee Benefits 1929 to 1994 (Washington, DC: U.S. Chamber of Commerce, 1995), p. 38.

benefits had risen to be 40.7 percent of wages and salaries.[2] If these estimates are accurate, wages and salaries increased more than 65-fold from 1929 to 1994, whereas benefits increased 872 times.

In many organizations today, benefits account for approximately 40 percent of payroll cost for each employee, and possibly by early in the twenty-first century they will reach 50 percent. (Some organizations have already exceeded this point.) In fact, the 1995 Chamber of Commerce study of employee benefits noted that approximately 2 percent of survey participants spent less than 18 percent of total payroll on benefits, whereas about 2 percent of survey participants spent 60 percent or more of payroll on benefits. The amount of benefits paid yearly per employee ranged from less than $3,500 to more than $24,000.[3] When a part of the compensation package reaches these proportions, it is no longer marginal. The fringe benefits of yesterday have evolved into the employee benefits and services of today.

The rapid expansion of the benefits program over the past five decades has been attributed to five causes:

1. The imposition of wage ceilings during World War II forced organizations to offer more and greater benefits in place of wage increases to attract new employees and to keep current workers.
2. With the increasing unacceptability of autocratic management and the decline of paternalism, instead of using threats or a variety of protective procedures, organizations have used benefits to gain employee compliance and loyalty, which has resulted in a more acceptable form of paternalism.
3. From the late 1940s into the 1970s, unions were able to gain a steady increase in wages for their members. The increases reached such a high level that the pressure for advancements in pay declined. This, in turn, led to greater interest and bargaining for more and expanded benefits.
4. Income tax legislation has had and continues to have a critical influence on the design of the benefits package. Employers are interested in benefit expenses that include pretax business costs and employees want to receive the benefits without the cost being included as taxable earnings. The federal government provides special tax treatment for benefits that are specifically included within a group titled "welfare benefit plans."
5. More recent changes in public policy to shift the cost burden from the federal government to private-sector employers regarding health care services and protection and continuing public concern over the long-term viability of Social Security and Medicare have placed even greater pressure on employers to provide more protection in these already costly areas.

In addition to paying employees fairly and adequately for their contributions in the performance of their jobs, organizations assume a social obligation for the welfare of employees and their dependents. Although these benefits are not directly related to product or service output, employers expect that they will improve productivity—first, through increased job satisfaction leading to improved quality and reduction in

---

[2]U.S. Chamber of Commerce, *Employee Benefits, 1995 Edition* (Washington, DC: U.S. Chamber of Commerce, 1995), pp. 7, 8.
[3]Ibid., Table 5, p. 15.

turnover and absenteeism and, second, by instilling in each employee a sense of security. Although many compensation and motivation experts question whether employee benefits and services stimulate improved worker performance, there is little doubt that an unacceptable or limited package may deter high-quality workers from seeking employment with a particular employer or may cause a worker to move to an employer who offers a better package. A good program assists in developing a motivational atmosphere that will stimulate an individual to join an organization and stay with it.

Benefits and services become complicated very quickly because of the number of available components, the variety of optional features within a component, and their legal and financial interactions, thus requiring the full-time efforts of specialists. It is, however, the responsibility of the compensation manager to call on these specialists, to be able to communicate with them, and to use their talents for the benefit of all members of the organization. To communicate effectively, the compensation specialist must know the components that comprise employee benefits and services, their distinguishing features, and what they provide to employees.

Employee benefits are those compensation components made available to employees that provide (1) protection in case of health and accident-related problems and (2) income at some future date or occasion (upon retirement, termination of employment, or meeting of certain objective criteria). *Employee services* are compensation components that contribute to the welfare of the employee by filling some kind of demand. These services usually enable the employee to enjoy a better lifestyle or to meet social or personal obligations while minimizing employment-related costs. Table 2–1 provides the majority of compensation components as listed in the compensation classification plan in this book. This classification of benefits and services is not universal. For instance, the Chamber of Commerce survey classifies benefits under seven major categories. Table 17–1 lists employee benefits by type of benefit for 1996. Table 17–2 presents the growth of employee benefits from 1929 to 1996. Another major benefit survey produced by the Hay Group is called the Hay Benefits Report. Its major benefits groups are (1) executive benefits and perquisites, (2) group life coverage, (3) sickness and disability benefits, (4) health care plans, (5) defined benefits and pension plans, (6) capital accumulation plans, (7) holiday and vacation policies, (8) flexible benefits programs, (9) benefit trends, and (10) personnel policies. The federal government's welfare benefits plan includes (1) health and accident plans; (2) group life insurance plans; (3) dependent care plans; (4) educational assistance plans; (5) group legal service plans; (6) no-additional-cost services, including qualified employee discounts and employer-operated eating facilities; (7) welfare benefits funds such as VEBAs, SUBs, GLSTs (discussed later in this chapter); and (8) cafeteria plans.

Tax legislation plays as critical a role in employer-provided benefits as it does in the qualified and nonqualified deferred arrangements discussed in the previous chapter. Many of the same terms and requirements appear in the discussion of welfare benefits plans as in the discussion of the long-term arrangements. Federal legislation continues to make major changes in the design of welfare benefits plans, especially in restricting the value of tax-favored benefits being delivered to highly paid employees. Recent legislation significantly tightened eligibility and benefit tests. Some of the major provisions of this legislation are discussed in the sections appropriate to the specific welfare benefits plan.

TABLE 17–1 Employee Benefits, by Type of Benefit: All Employees, 1996

Type of Benefit	Total, All Companies	Total, All Manufacturing	Total, All Non-manufacturing
Total Employees benefits as percent of payroll	41.3	44.1	40.7
1. Legally required payments (employers' share only)	8.8	9.7	8.7
a. Old-Age, Survivors, Disability, and Health Insurance (employer FICA taxes) and Railroad Retirement Tax	7.0	7.3	7.0
b. Unemployment compensation	0.7	1.0	0.6
c. Workers' compensation (included estimated cost of self-insured)	1.1	1.4	1.1
d. State sickness benefit insurance and other	0.1	0.0	0.1
2. Retirement and savings plan payments (employers' share only)	6.3	6.2	6.3
a. Defined benefit pension plan contributions	3.4	4.0	3.2
b. Defined contributions plan payments (401K type)	1.5	1.3	1.6
c. Profit sharing	0.5	0.6	0.4
d. Stock bonus and employee stock ownership plans (ESOP)	0.1	0.1	0.1
e. Pension plan premiums (net) under insurance and annuity contracts (insured and trusted)	0.5	0.0	0.6
f. Administrative and other costs	0.3	0.2	0.4
3. Life insurance and death benefit payments (employers' share only)	0.4	0.4	0.3
4. Medical and medically related benefit payments (employers' share only)	9.6	10.4	9.5
a. Hospital, surgical, medical, and major medical insurance (employers' share only)	7.0	7.7	6.9
b. Retiree (payments of retired employees) hospital, surgical, medical, and major medical insurance premiums (net)	1.0	1.1	0.9
c. Short-term disability, sickness, or accident insurance (company plan or insured plan)	0.4	0.6	0.4
d. Long-term disability or wage continuation (insured, self-administered, or trusts)	0.3	0.3	0.3
e. Dental insurance premiums	0.5	0.3	0.6
f. Other (vision care, physical and mental fitness benefits for former employees)	0.4	0.5	0.4
5. Paid rest periods, coffee breaks, lunch periods, wash-up time, travel time, clothes-change time, get ready time, etc.	3.7	4.6	3.5
6. Payments for time not worked	10.2	10.2	10.2
a. Payment for or in lieu of vacations	5.3	5.1	5.3
b. Payment for or in lieu of holidays	3.1	3.7	3.0
c. Sick leave pay	1.2	0.3	1.4
d. Parental leave (maternity and paternity leave payments)	0.0	0.0	0.0
e. Other	0.6	1.1	0.5
7. Miscellaneous benefit payments	2.3	2.6	2.2
a. Discounts on goods and services purchased from company by employees	0.4	0.0	0.4
b. Severance pay	0.3	0.1	0.4
c. Employee education expenditures	0.4	0.9	0.3
d. Child care	0.0	0.0	0.0
e. Other	1.2	1.5	1.1
Total employee benefits as cents per hour	679.9¢	887.8¢	646.4¢
Total employee benefits as dollars per year per employee	$14,086	$19,217	$13,299

TABLE 17–2 Growth of Employee Benefits, 1929 to 1996

Type of Payment	1929	1955	1965	1975	1986	1988	1989	1991	1992	1993	1994	1995	1996
	(Percent of Wages and Salaries)												
Legally required	0.8	3.3	5.3	8.4	11.1	11.6	12.2	12.2	12.1	11.8	11.8	12.0	11.7
Old-Age, Survivors, Disability, and Health Insurance (FICA taxes)	0.0	1.4	2.3	4.6	5.9	6.1	6.5	6.3	6.4	6.2	6.4	6.4	6.3
Unemployment compensation	0.0	0.7	1.0	0.8	1.2	1.0	0.9	0.7	0.9	0.9	0.9	0.9	0.8
Workers' compensation	0.6	0.5	0.7	1.0	1.0	1.6	1.7	1.7	1.8	1.6	1.6	1.6	1.4
Government employees retirement	0.2	0.5	1.0	1.7	2.8	2.7	2.9	3.2	2.7	3.1	2.9	3.1	3.0
Other	0.0	0.2	0.3	0.3	0.2	0.2	0.2	0.3	0.3	0.2	0.2	0.2	0.2
Agreed-upon	0.4	3.6	4.6	7.4	9.7	10.6	11.0	12.7	13.1	15.1	15.6	16.5	15.5
Pensions	0.2	2.2	2.3	3.6	2.8	4.1	4.0	5.1	5.3	5.8	6.0	6.7	5.8
Insurance	0.1	1.1	2.0	3.4	5.6	5.9	6.4	6.7	7.2	8.3	8.3	8.3	8.1
Other	0.1	0.3	0.3	0.4	1.3	0.6	0.6	0.9	0.6	1.0	1.3	1.6	1.6
Rest periods	1.0	3.0	3.1	3.7	3.3	2.9	3.0	2.5	3.1	2.4	2.2	2.2	3.7
Time not worked	0.7	5.9	7.3	9.4	10.2	10.4	10.2	9.9	10.2	9.7	9.7	10.2	10.2
Vacations	0.3	3.0	3.8	4.8	5.2	5.5	5.4	5.2	5.4	5.2	5.1	5.4	5.3
Holidays	0.3	2.0	2.5	3.2	3.1	3.2	3.2	3.1	3.2	2.9	3.1	3.3	3.1
Sick leave	0.1	0.8	0.8	1.2	1.4	1.3	1.2	1.2	1.2	1.2	1.2	1.2	1.2
Other	0.0	0.1	0.2	0.2	0.5	0.4	0.4	0.4	0.4	0.4	0.3	0.4	0.6
Bonuses, profit-sharing, etc.	0.1	1.2	1.2	1.1	1.2	1.1	1.1	0.9	0.6	0.6	0.7	0.8	0.8
Total benefit payments	3.0%	17.0%	21.5%	30.0%	35.5%	36.7%	37.5%	38.2%	39.1%	39.6%	4.0%	41.8%	41.9%
Wages and salaries (billions $)	$50.50	$212.10	$363.70	$814.70	$2,093.00	$2,431.10	$2,573.30	$2,827.00	$2,985.40	$3,090.60	$3,241.10	$3,419.70	$3,633.60
Total benefit payments (billions $)	$1.50	$36.10	$78.20	$244.40	$743.00	$813.90	$964.98	$1,080.14	$1,164.31	$1,223.88	$1,296.44	$1,429.44	$1,522.47

Source: Estimated by U.S. Chamber of Commerce from U.S. Department of Commerce data and U.S. Chamber of Commerce Survey.

The classification scheme provided in this book was devised to identify and describe compensation features and components as they provide lifestyle enhancement opportunities for employees and their dependents. Many major components have features that relate to a number of these lifestyle opportunities. On the other hand, the Chamber of Commerce surveys and other benefits surveys group components in a manner that eliminates double counting, since they are primarily interested in identifying benefits costs.

BENEFITS ADMINISTRATION

Because of the ever-increasing complexity, importance, and cost of employer-provided benefits, many organizations have a special unit responsible for the design and administration of their benefits program. In large organizations, the benefits manager may report to the vice president or director of compensation and benefits. In smaller organizations, the manager of compensation and benefits is responsible for practically all items identified and described in this book. However, in some organizations, benefits responsibility is fragmented. Pension, life insurance, and disability programs may be assigned to the finance department, and medical insurance, claims processing, and the completion of government reports related to mandated benefits to the accounting department, while top management retains authority for the entire time-off-with-pay program. Two important parts of benefits administration are (1) benefits planning and design and (2) benefits communication.

Benefits Planning and Design

By the early 1970s, some organizations began to recognize the importance of benefits planning and design when they began developing cafeteria or flexible benefits plans. In the design stage, each benefit must be carefully analyzed to determine its features. Design criteria include establishing (1) minimum age or length of service requirements before becoming eligible for a benefit; (2) possible employee contributions and vesting schedule for the pension plan; (3) coinsurance, deductible, ceiling requirements, and dual coverage for medical insurance; (4) options to be included in medical insurance (dental plan, psychiatric or psychological counseling, dependent coverage, and AIDS coverage). The organization must decide if temporary and part-time employees will be included as well as regular full-time members. What kind of benefits will be offered to retirees? Which dependents, if any, will be covered?[4]

Some of the critical issues in benefits planning are (1) current and future role of government-mandated benefits; (2) employee demographics and employee preferences; (3) possible use of self-funding and third-party administration; (4) employer ability to pay and employee contributions; and (5) monitoring and auditing programs.

Current and Future Role of Government Mandated Benefits   Possibly the first topic to be reviewed in benefits planning concerns the current and future role of the government. Government intervention in benefits plan design has been less in the United States than in almost any other industrial nation. Most Western industrialized nations require employers to pay significantly higher "social security" payments. In the

---

[4]Jerry Rosenblum and G. Victor Hallman, *Employee Benefit Planning* (Englewood Cliffs, NJ: Prentice Hall, 1981), pp. 427–431.

United States, employers are required to pay 7.65 percent of the first $72,600 a worker earns in 1999 for Social Security and Medicare payments. Employers must also pay unemployment and workers' compensation insurance premiums. The employer share of all legally required payments is less than 10 percent (Table 17–1). In Western European nations, it is not unusual for employers to pay over 25 percent of a worker's wages in "social security" tax.[5] However, the benefits accruing from these European plans are broader than those accruing to U.S. workers from mandated benefits. In many countries, the employee receives medical insurance, whereas in the United States the employer provides this benefit separately from those mandated by the government.

Beginning in the 1980s and continuing into the present time, certain members of Congress have campaigned actively to increase the role of the government in mandated benefits. Benefits to be required by the government include (1) severance pay, (2) minimum health insurance for all workers, and (3) maternity leave. If even one or more of these proposed programs becomes law, the costs of benefits and even total operation can increase significantly for many organizations.

Employee Demographics and Preferences   The day of providing almost unlimited benefits to employees is over. Organizations recognize that they should offer only those benefits that a prudent organization should provide and these benefits must be demanded by the majority of the employees. If an organization hires many younger people, it may investigate opportunities for child care. If it hires many middle-aged and older employees, the continuation of medical care for retirees may be a sensitive issue. Requiring employees to pay all or part of the premium for dependents may be considered when many employees are members of a dual-earner family in which the other wage earner may quite likely be the recipient of a medical insurance program. The design and implementation of a flexible benefits program may permit needed individualization and the opportunity to reduce employer costs.

Employer Ability to Pay and Employee Contributions   With the ever-increasing cost of nonmandated benefits and the potential of significantly higher costs of mandated benefits, employers recognize that they have to limit these costs. Employers must search for every available option to reduce these costs. One option is to shift as much of the cost as possible to the employee. This is accomplished directly by requiring the employee to contribute to the pension plan, having the employee pay part of the medical insurance premiums (coinsurance), increasing employee payments (the deductible) before the insurance pays for a claim, and reducing time-off-with-pay opportunities.

Self-Funding and Third-Party Administration   With certain kinds of insurance plans, self-funding may be a cost-reduction opportunity. Some organizations are finding cost savings by hiring outside parties (outsourcing) to administer their medical plans and other parts of their benefits program. This includes reviewing all submitted medical bills and second- and third-party reviews of elective surgery, and paying employee claims.

Monitoring and Auditing   The last phase of any planning process is to review what is happening. Employers must monitor every part of the benefits program. Is it operating as designed? Is it accomplishing its intended goals? Are there any areas or parts

---

[5]"Metal Workers' Pay Buys More in U.S. Than Abroad," *AFL-CIO News,* August 15, 1987, p. 8; *International Comparisons of Hourly Compensation Costs for Production Workers in Manufacturing, 1975–90* (Washington, DC: USDOL, Bureau of Labor Statistics, November 1991), p. 12.

of the program that are being abused? Feedback in these and other areas assists those responsible for planning and design to make necessary changes.

Benefits Communication

By the late 1960s and early 1970s, benefits administrators were well aware of the limited motivational value of their programs. Employees were unaware of what employers were providing. They viewed their benefits program as an entitlement. Employers began developing sophisticated communication programs to inform employees of how much they were receiving through the benefits program.

A basic benefits communication program consists of these elements:

1. Sometime within 90 days after employment, the new employee receives an oral and visual presentation of the benefits program. The employee is told when he or she is eligible for each benefit, kinds and amount of dependent coverage, and how to file an insurance claim. The employee receives a personal benefits booklet or manual. The oral presentation covers all major components included in the booklet or manual.

2. Each year, the employee receives a benefits statement that provides a detailed description of the employee's benefit account (see Figure 17–1 for an example of a section from an employee's Annual Benefits Statement). A number of commercial firms currently provide benefits booklets and annual statements at very low cost for employers.

3. The employee has access to as-needed services from an in-house benefits consultant reviewing particular problems or issues that may be covered by the organization's benefits plan or even benefits available in the community that are not provided by the organization.

4. Ad hoc employee meetings cover (1) new benefits, (2) cost containment opportunities, and (3) other critical or important benefits issues.

5. Continuing notices of provided benefits and services and topics of interest appear in all kinds of organizational communication devices. Online communications enable HR benefits personnel to communicate more closely with employees. Employees can use Internet services to identify problems, and HR specialists in return can respond to those employee issues.

EMPLOYEE BENEFITS

Most compensation components included within employee benefits are made available through some type of insurance plan. A very important group of benefit components, however, is frequently noninsurance based and provides income to the employee at some future date.

Employee benefits can be further classified under these seven major groups: (1) disability income continuation, (2) loss-of-job income continuation, (3) deferred income, (4) spouse or family income continuation, (5) health and accident protection, (6) property and liability protection, and (7) a special group of benefits and services called perquisites. Each of these groups contains a number of compensation components, which may have a variety of features that may be made available only to certain

Mr. JOHN Q. EMPLOYEE   B0-0004-4

YOUR SECURITY IF YOU ARE ILL

IF YOU BECOME SICK OR INJURED AND
CANNOT WORK YOU CURRENTLY HAVE:

*** SICK LEAVE***

34.7	DAYS OF SICK LEAVE AVAILABLE AT FULL SALARY. THIS PROVIDES
$ 4,894	OF SALARY PROTECTION.

*** SHORT-TERM DISABILITY***

$ 1,200 PER MONTH SHORT-TERM
DISABILITY FOR A MAXIMUM
OF FIVE MONTHS. THIS
BEGINS ON THE:
- EIGHTH DAY OF DISABILITY
  DUE TO ILLNESS.
- FIRST DAY OF DISABILITY
  DUE TO HOSPITALIZATION, OR
- FIRST DAY OF DISABILITY
  DUE TO ACCIDENTAL INJURY

*** LONG-TERM DISABILITY ***

$ 2,024 PER MONTH LONG-TERM
DISABILITY AFTER FIVE MONTHS
OF DISABILITY T0 AGE 65
UNDER CERTAIN CONDITIONS.

THIS BENEFIT IS COORDINATED
WITH DISABILITY BENEFITS YOU
MAY RECEIVE FROM TEACHERS
RETIREMENT, SOCIAL SECURITY,
WORKERS' COMPENSATION, AND
OTHER STANDARD FORMS OF
INCOME TO PROVIDE A MINIMUM
MONTHLY INCOME OF YOUR
70% SALARY.

PLUS IF YOU REMAIN ON LONG-TERM
DISABILITY, THE DEKALB
SCHOOL BOARD WILL CONTINUE
TO PAY INTO YOUR BOARD TAX
SHELTERED ANNUITY ACCOUNT
WHILE YOU ARE ELIGIBLE FOR
DISABILITY/

*** WORKERS' COMPENSATION***

BENEFITS AS PROVIDED BY
GEORGIA LAW.

*** YOUR MEDICAL SECURITY ***

YOU HAVE SELECTED THE HIGH OPTION
STATE HEALTH BENEFIT PLAN FOR YOU
AND YOUR FAMILY WHICH PROVIDES:

100% OF COVERED HOSPITAL EXPENSES
AFTER A $100 DEDUCTIBLE PER
CALENDAR YEAR.

100% OF INSTITUTIONAL CHARGES
FOR AMBULATORY SURGERY.
(NO DEDUCTIBLE)

90% OF USUAL AND CUSTOMARY
CHARGES FOR SURGERY.
(NO DEDUCTIBLE)

90% OF OTHER COVERED SERVICES
AFTER A $150 DEDUCTIBLE.

LIMIT FOR PSYCHIATRIC
CARE BENEFIT OF $2,500 ON
INPATIENT AND $2,500 ON
OUTPATIENT SERVICES PER
PERSON, PER CALENDAR YEAR.

THE STOP-LOSS LIMIT IS:

$ 400 PER PERSON PER CALENDAR
YEAR.
$1,000 FOR THE ENTIRE FAMILY:

THE MAXIMUM BENEFITS ARE:

$250,000 PER PERSON PER CALENDAR
YEAR AND
$500,000 PER PERSON, LIFETIME.

FIGURE 17–1   Annual Benefits Statement (Example)

employees or certain groups of employees. An identification of the major compensation components within each of the seven groups and a brief description of some of the more significant features follow.[6]

---

[6]Throughout this chapter, there are figures that provide average or usual practices for a specific benefit or service. These figures come from a wide variety of commonly available sources, which the author took the liberty of identifying as average practices. It must be recognized that the field of benefits and services is in a state of dynamic change, and the program of any one organization may vary significantly from the data provided.

Mr. JOHN Q. EMPLOYEE

B0-0004-4

YOUR SECURITY IF YOU ARE ILL

*** ACCIDENTAL DEATH AND DISMEMBERMENT INSURANCE ***

THIS PAYS:

$1,000	FOR ACCIDENTAL LOSS OF ANY TWO MEMBERS OF THE BODY.
$ 500	FOR LOSS OF ONE MEMBER OF THE BODY OR ONE EYE.

*** TRAVEL ACCIDENT INSURANCE ***

COVERS AN ACCIDENT OCCURRING ON OR IN A PUBLIC CONVEYANCE DURING AN AUTHORIZED BUSINESS TRIP.

THIS PAYS:

$100,000	FOR LOSS OF ANY TWO MEMBERS OF THE BODY.
$ 50,000	FOR LOSS OF ONE MEMBER OF THE BODY OR ONE EYE

*** DENTAL ASSISTANCE PLAN ***

YOU HAVE SELECTED THIS PLAN FOR YOU AND YOUR FAMILY WHICH PROVIDES:

90%	WITH NO DEDUCTIBLE OF THE COST OF PREVENTIVE DIAGNOSTIC, EMERGENCY OR PAIN RELIEVING SERVICES, AND SOME CORRECTIVE SURGERY (TYPE A).
$ 50	AFTER A DECUCTIBLE OF FOR DENTAL CARE BY THE PREFERRED PROVIDER, OR
$100	FOR DENTAL CARE BY OTHER THAN THE PREFERRED PROVIDER, THE PLAN PAYS:
80%	OF THE COST OF RESTORATIVE DENTISTRY AND SURGICAL PROCEDURES (TYPE B): AND
50%	OF THE COST OF PROSTHODONTIC PROCEDURES (TYPE C).

THE MAXIMUM BENEFITS ARE:
$1,000	PER PERSON PER YEAR:
$2,000	PER FAMILY PER YEAR.

*** SPECIFIED DISEASE INSURANCE ***

YOU HAVE SELECTED THIS COVERAGE FOR YOU AND YOUR FAMILY.

FOR DISEASES SPECIFIED YOU RECEIVE:

$ 90	PER DAY FOR FIRST 10 DAYS OF HOSPITALIZATION, AND
$ 50	PER DAY THEREAFTER.
	IF READMISSION IS MORE THAN 30 DAYS AFTER DISCHARGE, BENEFITS START WITH THE $90 PER DAY FOR FIRST 10 DAYS, AS SET OUT ABOVE.
100%	OF USUAL AND CUSTOMARY HOSPITAL CHARGES BEGINNING ON 91ST DAY OF CONTINUOUS CONFINEMENT.
$6,000	PER MONTH MAXIMUM. CONFINEMENTS OF LESS THAN 30 DAYS PRORATED AT $200 PER DAY.
PLUS:	FROM 15% TO 100% OF OTHER COVERED EXPENSES.
NOTE:	DIRECT QUESTIONS REGARDING YOUR EXACT COVERAGE TO THE AGENT LISTED IN THIS STATEMENT.

FIGURE 17–1 *(continued)*

Reprinted with permission of DeKalb County, Georgia, School Board.
Developed by Franklin Dean Grant.

Disability Income Continuation

Disabilities may be classified as regular, temporary, total, or partial. When employees are unable to work because of an accident or some health-related problem, disability income continuation payments assist them in maintaining their existing lifestyle without major modification. Various disability income continuation components provide weekly or monthly payments in lieu of the regular earned income paycheck. The following 11 components are among the more commonly available disability income continuation plans. Although all components will seldom be available to employees, components can be packaged to maximize employee protection while maintaining costs within reasonable limits for the employer. The major components are:

1. Short-term disability
2. Long-term disability (LTD)
3. Workers' compensation
4. Nonoccupational disability
5. Social Security
6. Travel accident insurance
7. Sick leave
8. Supplemental disability insurance
9. Accidental death and dismemberment
10. Group life insurance: Total permanent disability (TPD)
11. Retirement plans

Short-Term Disability or Sickness and Accident Plans (S&A)   This component provides payment while the insured is absent from work because of an accident or illness. The benefits provided by these plans usually range from 50 to 75 percent of the employee's base pay. Most plans have a waiting period before payment begins. For example, many contracts require a seven-day waiting period with regard to sickness. In other words, the employee does not collect any benefits until the eighth day of absence due to an illness. On the other hand, there frequently is no waiting period for an accident claim, and when there is one, it seldom exceeds three days. Often, there is a limit to the number of weeks of payment per disability; 26 weeks is a commonly used period for this short-term income maintenance program.

Long-Term Disability (LTD)   Long-term disability insurance is an alternative method for providing incapacitated employees with long-term security. These employees are probably in need of most assistance because they have the burden of added medical expenses with reduced or no income.

Many LTD plans are funded in conjunction with the pension plan of the organization, although some LTD plans use self-insurance funding procedures, and many more use the normal insurance approach with specific premiums and reserves to cover all claims. The LTD claims for a large group averages slightly less than five years.[7] LTD plans usually replace between 50 and 75 percent of base pay. Payments usually graduate in size, the largest payments occurring in the first two years and then leveling off for the remaining years. Normally, in the first two years, disabled workers receive disability payments when they are unable to work in their own occupations. If, after two years, disabled workers are still unable to work in any occupations in which they may use their education, experience, and abilities, they may continue to receive disability payments until age 65.

---

[7]James H. Brennan Jr., "What Makes LTD a Special Benefits Problem?" *Compensation Review,* First Quarter, 1974, pp. 26–34.

Workers' Compensation   State laws now require almost every employer to provide employees with occupational disability insurance. Although income benefits vary among the 50 states for permanent total disability, most states will pay lifetime benefits, although a few limit payment periods from 330 to 650 weeks. In the early 1990s, the payments ranged from a minimum of $20.00 a week to a maximum of $733.00 a week depending on the wages of the disabled employee and the state laws.[8] Some states also have a maximum limit for payments. Most states use a formula of two-thirds of the average weekly wage to calculate disability payments. The benefits for a temporary disability are, in most cases, similar to those for permanent total disability, except that the period of payments is limited to the time of disability. In 1981, the average cost to an employer for each employee for workers' compensation was $162. Employers in the state of Alaska had the highest average cost of $432, and employers in the state of Indiana had the lowest average cost of $71.[9]

Each state has its own schedule of income benefits for types of injuries, dismemberments, or loss of use. Funds are also available for rehabilitation and for maintenance expenses while the worker is undergoing retraining. (An extensive discussion of workers' compensation appears in chapter 5.)

Nonoccupational (Temporary) Disability   Workers in Puerto Rico and in five states—California, Hawaii, New Jersey, New York, and Rhode Island—who incur temporary disability arising from nonoccupational illness, injury, or pregnancy receive partial income maintenance through these disability laws. The duration of these payments is normally 26 weeks. The actual amount of payment depends on the wage of the employee before being disabled. *Employee* contributions provide a major funding source for these plans. The employee contributions range from an annual low of $27 in Puerto Rico to a high of $261.80 in California.

Social Security   The Social Security Act of 1935 established the federal Old Age, Survivors, Disability, and Health Insurance System (OASDHI). Under this system, totally and permanently disabled employees may be eligible for cash disability payments and Social Security. To qualify for Social Security-OASDHI Act benefits, workers must have spent a sufficient period of time in covered employment or self-employment and must be disabled as defined by the law. Payments begin after a worker has waited 5 full calendar months and continue to age 65. At that time, the worker is transferred to the retirement rolls. In 1996, the average disabled worker with spouse and children received a monthly Social Security payment of $1,262, whereas the average monthly payment to a single disabled worker was $704.[10]

Travel Accident Insurance   Organizations that require employees to travel frequently protect these workers by providing travel accident insurance. This plan provides additional protection in cases in which employees are disabled or killed on a work assignment. Payments usually start the first day of the disability and are usually either

---

[8]Survey Research Center, Economic Policy Division, *Analysis of Workers' Compensation Laws 1991,* "Income Benefits for Total Disability" (Washington, DC: Chamber of Commerce of the United States), Chart VI.

[9]"Workers Compensation Costs," *The Wall Street Journal,* May 1, 1984, p. 1.

[10]U.S. Department of Commerce, Bureau of Economic and Statistical Analysis, *Statistical Abstract of the United States, 1998* (Washington, DC: U.S. Government Printing Office, 1998), no. 610, p. 382.

a fixed schedule that varies disability payment by base earnings or a flat percentage of the regular rate of pay.

Sick Leave   Sick leave assures employees of pay when they are unable to work because of illness. Many organizations allow a specific number of days of leave each year, with 12 days (or 1 day a month) being a fairly common figure, although average granted sick leave in the United States is approximately 10 days per year. Some limit is usually set on the number of days an employee can accumulate. Many organizations limit the time to a 10- to 20-day accumulation of earned sick leave days to provide protection in case of an illness of 2 to 4 weeks or more. Short-term health and accident disability insurance then takes over and, for even longer periods of illness, long-term disability insurance and Social Security come into effect. Some organizations now pay employees for the accumulation of sick days up to a set number—for example, up to 6 months' base pay upon retirement.

A recent trend has been for organizations to "buy back" unused sick leave time by paying their employees a daily equivalent pay for each day of sick leave not used. When organizations feel that sick leave is encouraging absenteeism, policy is tightened by such measures as requiring a doctor's written explanation of the illness, not paying for the first day, and in some cases, reducing the number of days allotted. One organization has what it calls a "well pay" benefit. An employee with perfect attendance during the month receives an extra day's pay for that month. (See "A Different Approach" later in this chapter.) Other organizations, however, object to providing double payment simply to make sure employees report to work. They feel they are already paying for employees to be there and that those who come to work receive a "presenteeism" bonus—their pay. The complaint about double payment may be justified, but absenteeism and abuse of sick leave are also legitimate concerns. There is no doubt that sick leave pay does encourage unjustified absenteeism.

Supplemental Disability Insurance   Some organizations provide a small and select group of top management employees with supplemental disability income plans. These plans are designed to bring the disability income available to highly paid executives more closely in line with what they receive as regular pay and are designed to minimize reverse discrimination. See discussion of disability income plans for executives in chapter 16.

Accidental Death and Dismemberment   This plan provides a range of benefits in case of accidental loss of limbs or sight. The actual amount of benefits varies according to the extent of the injury or dismemberment. Most employees required to travel in the performance of company business receive a full range of life and accident insurance while away from their home base.

Group Life Insurance: Total Permanent Disability (TPD)   Many group life insurance plans have a total permanent disability feature. This feature grants an employee equal monthly payments over a period ranging from 60 to 120 payments. When the face value of the policy is small, the number of payments may be below 60.

Retirement Plans   Many retirement plans have some form of disability retirement benefits. These plans often have some service and age requirements. A common service requirement is 10 years, and the age limit may be 50. To limit the undesirable possibility that the disability benefit might reduce the average retirement benefits, many organizations have added a long-term disability option to their benefit programs.

Loss-of-Job Income Continuation

Loss-of-job income continuation plans are designed to assist workers during short-term periods of unemployment due to layoffs and termination. The eight major compensation components that make up this group of benefits are

1. Unemployment insurance (UI)
2. Supplemental unemployment benefit insurance (SUB)
3. Guaranteed annual income (GAI)
4. Guaranteed income stream (GIS)
5. Individual account plan
6. Severance pay
7. Job contract
8. Short-time compensation program

Unemployment Insurance (UI)   In September 1998, approximately 34 percent of jobless workers in the United States were receiving UI payments.[11] The average UI payment was $199 or 34 percent of the national average weekly wage. Most states relate their maximum UI payments to state average weekly wages.[12]

A typical computation of unemployment payment is 50 percent of base pay up to 66.7 percent of the weekly wage for employees in the state. Six requirements determine eligibility for unemployment insurance payments. An individual must (1) be able, available, and actively seeking work; (2) not have refused suitable employment; (3) not have left a job voluntarily without good cause; (4) not have been terminated for misconduct; (5) not be unemployed because of a labor dispute (except in Rhode Island and New York); and (6) have been previously employed in a covered industry or occupation earning a designated minimum amount for a designated period of time.

By 1998, Hawaii had the lowest possible minimum benefit amount (WBA) of $5, and Washington had the highest possible maximum WBA of $410 (excluding any dependents allowance).

Employer UI tax costs vary significantly among the 50 states. Some of the major reasons for differences in employer costs are (1) variations in economic conditions among states, (2) variation in restrictions against eligibility for receiving UI, and (3) variations in benefit payments. Table 17–3 lists the five highest and five lowest unemployment cost states. There is a lengthy discussion of UI in chapter 5.

Supplemental Unemployment Benefit Insurance (SUB)   Another major breakthrough in the area of income security was the guaranteed annual income plan developed between the Ford Motor Company and the UAW in 1955.[13] This plan became known as a supplemental unemployment benefits (SUB) plan because it supplemented unemployment benefits instead of providing a guaranteed annual income. Unions rep-

---

[11]US DOL, *UI Data Summary*, 3rd Quarter, 1998.
[12]Ibid.
[13]Norma Pope and Paul A. Brinker, "Recent Developments with the Guaranteed Annual Wage: The Ford Settlement," *Labor Law Journal,* September 1968, pp. 555–562.

TABLE 17–3	Average Per Employee Unemployment Tax Liability, 1995		
Five Highest		*Five Lowest*	
Rhode Island	729.40	Nebraska	$84.00
Alaska	610.30	New Hampshire	88.00
Washington	573.50	South Dakota	98.00
Hawaii	531.20	Virginia	104.00
Connecticut	511.00	Florida	119.00

Source: U.S. Department of Labor. ETA/UIS. Division of Actuarial Services, compiled by Laurdan Associates, Inc., 1998.

resenting workers in the manufacture of steel, rubber, flat glass, and farm equipment added SUB programs to their union contracts in the mid-1950s. The SUB program adopted by Ford and the UAW has been accepted as standard by the UAW and has been copied by other businesses interested in such a program. Approximately 50 percent of all manufacturing workers have some kind of a SUB plan.

The initial 1955 program guaranteed qualified workers (qualified relates strictly to seniority) 62 percent of their annual pay plus $1.50 a week per dependent (up to four) in addition to their regular state unemployment insurance. This program was modified in 1965, and those modifications are still in effect. The 1965 program allows each worker to receive half of a GAI unit for each week worked from the date of hire to a maximum of 52 units. Normally, a worker receives one week of SUB payment for each unit given up. A worker with less than 1 year of employment is not eligible for SUB payment. The guarantee period increases until the worker has 7 years of employment, at which time all the benefits of the plan accrue. Although the program basically permits a worker to receive one week of SUB payments for each earned GAI unit, it also requires that the SUB fund be at a prescribed level before this happens. The 1974 General Motors SUB fund required that it have $382.50 per employee in reserve before any worker with 52 GAI units can receive a full year of benefits. In September 1974 the fund had been reduced to $291 per employee. This reduction below the $382.50 minimum required employees with less than 5 years of service to give up 1.43 units per benefit week, thus allowing them only 36.4 weeks of SUB benefits. It required workers with 5 to 10 years of service to give up 1.25 credits and receive 41.6 weeks of SUB benefits. Workers received 95 percent of their after-tax weekly pay less $7.50 for nonincurred, work-related expenses, such as their lunch and transportation to and from work. (Most plans set a level of payment of 60 to 65 percent of take-home pay.) Because of the unexpected large layoffs in the automobile industry in 1974–1975, both the Chrysler and General Motors SUB fund accounts were depleted in 1975, with the result that the auto workers had to depend completely on state unemployment benefits.[14] By 1988, the GM-UAW national agreement provided SUB payments for hourly employees on the payroll for at least 1 year. These workers receive approximately 80

---

[14]"GM Fund Runs Dry This Week," *The Atlanta Constitution,* May 5, 1975, p. 9A.

percent of their take home pay for varying lengths of time depending on their seniority. A 10-year veteran receives SUB payments for 1 year in addition to unemployment benefits, while a 20-year veteran receives SUB payments for 2 years.

Guaranteed Annual Income (GAI)   GAI plans are normally found within a collective bargaining situation. An agreement reached in 1950 between the National Sugar Refining Company and the union representing its employees at the Long Island refinery was an early development in this area. This contract required that an employee working on Monday be assured wages for at least 4 days in that week. The next year at its Philadelphia refinery, the first guaranteed annual wage program went into operation. This program guaranteed each member of the bargaining unit 1,936 hours or 242 days of work a year. On an average, they work between 230 and 245 days a year, depending on their vacations and paid holiday programs.[15]

In the mid-1960s, the International Longshoremen's Association negotiated a GAI plan to provide income security for workers displaced by the change to containerization. To receive GAI pay, a dockworker must conform to the following requirements: Dockworkers who have not been notified of a job for the next day must appear at the union hiring hall by 7:00 A.M. and insert a plastic badge into a computerized system; if they do not receive a call for work, they can check out by 9:00 A.M. and still receive 8 hours of pay for that day. Employees who fail to badge-in or to report for their daily assignments receive a debit. The accumulation of a certain number of debits can result in total loss of GAI for the year in which it occurs.

By the early 1980s, the hours of guaranteed work for dockworkers varied among the seaport cities. In New York, dockworkers received 2,080 GAI hours, whereas dockworkers along the western Gulf of Mexico were guaranteed an average of about 900 hours of pay a year. The GAI benefit of 2,080 hours provided by New York port employers was estimated to cost them between $40 and $47 million annually.[16] This benefit provided a competitive cost advantage to southern ports and may have accounted for the fact that these ports had a faster freight tonnage growth than northern ports during the late 1960s and 1970s. In 1984, employers in Philadelphia tried to gain a reduction in GAI hours from 1,900 to 1,600, and in Boston from 1,800 to 1,500.[17] After complex negotiations in 1986, the GAI hours were reduced from 1,900 to 1,700 with further reduction on October 1, 1988, to 1,600 for East Coast dockworkers. The GAI hours were also reduced for South Atlantic dockworkers. In the West Gulf region, negotiations led to elimination of the GAI.

Guaranteed Income Stream   An addition to income programs is the guaranteed income stream (GIS) negotiated between Ford and the UAW in its 1982 bargaining. Under GIS, Ford workers who lose their jobs after 15 years of service receive 50 percent of their base pay until they are eligible for retirement.

---

[15]Harvey A. Young and Michael F. Dougherty, "Influence of the Guaranteed Annual Wage upon Labor Relations and Productivity: National Sugar Refinery's Experience," *Management of Personnel Quarterly,* Winter 1971, pp. 27–32.

[16]John D. Williams, "Dock Workers Slated to Vote Tomorrow on New 3-Year Contracts, May End Strike," *The Wall Street Journal,* November 28, 1977, p. 26; John D. Williams, "Dock Union Says Workers Voted End to Walkout," *The Wall Street Journal,* November 30, 1977, p. 30.

[17]John D. Williams, "Dock Workers Strike Four Atlantic Ports Over Local Issues," *The Wall Street Journal,* February 10, 1984, p. 50.

Individual Account Plan   This plan requires the employer to make certain predetermined and negotiated contributions to the account of each covered employee. The fund provides payments to the employee when there are work suspensions other than disciplinarian layoffs or labor disputes.

Severance Pay   Severance plans are becoming far more common. These provide a one-time payment or a series of payments over a limited period upon termination of employment at no fault of the employee. When workers are permanently displaced as a result of plant closings, technological advances, or economic depressions, they may receive a payment to assist in maintaining their standard of living until new employment is found. Unions have been active in obtaining severance pay protection for their members. The actual amount and timing of receipt of such payments vary significantly. A severance payment may be equal to two or three days of work or as much as the pay for six months or one year of work. Small severance payments are usually made the last day of work, whereas large payments may be made at two or three different times. With the combination of rapid and extensive technological changes and extreme worldwide competition in the sales of goods and services, severance pay protection is becoming an increasingly important issue.

A special kind of severance payment—the *golden parachute*—was introduced to the world of work in the late 1970s. The relatively low stock prices of many corporations gave rise to large numbers of corporate takeovers by other firms. Top executives of corporations that were good candidates for takeover became extremely concerned about their jobs and sought the security provided by severance payments. To protect these key officials when, due to takeover, their jobs are terminated or their responsibilities are changed or reduced for any reason other than death, disability, or normal retirement, and also to make the takeover less attractive (by being more expensive), golden parachute clauses were added to existing executive contracts or became new contracts. Golden parachutes may be offered to anywhere from 2 to 20 key officials, although typically 5 or less receive such protection. In a few cases, more than 100 employees have been given golden parachutes. See additional discussion of golden parachutes in executive compensation in chapter 16.

The Deficit Reduction Act of 1984 (DEFRA) places restrictions on tax treatment of golden parachutes. Corporate tax deductions are not allowed for parachute payments (defined to include *all* amounts paid as a result of a change of control) in excess of an amount equal to the recipient's average annual compensation. The recipient must pay a 20 percent excise tax on this excess amount. The law also provides tests to determine whether this special tax treatment is applicable. TRA 86 further defined highly compensated individuals who could be penalized for receiving "excess parachute payments." They are current or former employees who are among the highest paid 1 percent of the corporation's and its affiliates' employees, but must not exceed 250.

In 1986, Herman Miller, Inc., a major manufacturer of office furniture, introduced a silver parachute plan designed to provide security for all of its employees who might be adversely affected in the event of a hostile takeover. To be a participant, an employee must have at least two years of continuous full-time employment. The silver parachute severance payment for employees with fewer than five years of continuous full-time employment equals the employee's annual compensation during the year immediately preceding the termination of employment. Employees with five or more years of continuous full-time employment receive a severance payment equal to two and one-half times annual compensation received during the year immediately preceding termination. Annual compensation equals participant's wages, salary, bonus, Scanlon Plan bonus, and other incentive compensation. Another name attached to these employee-based severance payments is tin parachutes.[18]

Beginning in 1990, the U.S. military began to downsize. From 1990–1992, this reduction was accomplished through attrition and reduced recruiting. However, by 1992, with a rapid deescalation of worldwide military confrontation and a critical need to redirect government spending toward social and nonmilitary economic improvement programs, the U.S. military—principally the Army and the Air Force—began programs to reduce their military personnel by nearly one-third by 1997. To promote voluntary separation, the military designed two severance pay options that were far better than a lump-sum payment to those *involuntarily* terminated through the reduction in force. The two voluntary separation packages, which were given the title "copper handshakes," were the special separation bonus (SSB) that provided the terminated individual with a lump-sum bonus equal to 15 percent of basic annual pay multiplied by years of service; and the voluntary separation incentive (VSI) that offered the individual a payment of approximately 2 percent of basic annual pay multiplied by years of service for twice the number of years served. In the early stage of this separation program, over 75 percent of those requesting voluntary separation took the lump-sum bonus option.[19]

Examples of Severance Pay Options

Rank	Years of Service	Annual Pay	Involuntary Separation Lump-Sum Bonus	Voluntary Separation	
				SSB	VSI
Army Captain	10	$45,493	$36,090	$54,135	$9,022 for 20 yrs
Army Sergeant	12	$22,496	$21,349	$32,024	$5,337 for 24 yrs

In 1987, the U.S. Supreme Court affirmed a State of Maine law requiring severance payments for workers who lose their jobs when a plant closes or relocates. The Maine law requires employers in such situations to make a lump-sum payment of one week's pay for each year worked to employees with at least three years' service. The law applies to firms with more than 100 workers that close a plant or move operations more than 100 miles from the original site.

In February 1989, the Worker Adjustment and Retraining Notification Act of 1988 took effect. This act required employers with 100 or more employees to provide a 60-day notice of plant closings and layoffs. Plant closings involving 50 or more employees at one site are covered. Layoffs involving either 500 employees or a third of the workforce, if at least 50 employees, are also covered. Failure to comply permits employees to sue for up to 60 days of back wages and benefits.

---

[18]Herman Miller, *The Silver Parachute: A Plan to Protect the Interests of the Participative Owners of Herman Miller, Inc.* (Zeeland, MI: 1986).
[19]Bruce Van Voorst, "You're Out of the Army Now," *Time,* March 9, 1992, p. 30.

In 1989, the State of New York implemented a termination notice law. This amendment to the New York State Labor Law requires employers to give any employee employed in New York State written notice, no later than five working days after termination of employment, of (1) the exact date of termination of employment and (2) the exact date(s) of the cancellation of "employee benefits connected with such termination."

Job Contract   This kind of plan is usually made available to senior-level management employees and highly skilled and desired professionals. Individuals receiving such a contract are guaranteed a certain income for a specific period of time with certain obligations normally required of the recipient. If, for any reason, the employer terminates employment, the employee receives the payments due on the unfinished terms of the contract.

Although not commonly offered to every key official, employee contracts are provided by a number of organizations to attract certain individuals and to retain key personnel. The executive contract may include specifications for front-end bonus, a "no strings attached" offer to a key individual for recruiting purposes. Normally, this kind of bonus replaces the value of stock options, accumulated bonuses, and other benefits the individual must give up when moving to the new employer. In recent years, highly desired individuals have received front-end bonuses that have exceeded $1 million. An executive contract can also include salary, pension, life and medical insurance, cash and deferred bonuses, stock acquisition opportunities, a variety of other benefits and services, widow's pension, and severance payments. These contracts normally stipulate the number of employment years and the option opportunities for renegotiation at the end of the contract period.

Desired key personnel who may be reluctant to leave a secure job are requesting and receiving the protection offered by an employment contract. In fact, some organizations now use these contracts to retain personnel by making it more difficult for them to be attracted to recruiting offers from other organizations.

Short-Time Compensation Program   Unemployment compensation in the United States took a new form with the introduction of a *short-time compensation plan.* Although short-time compensation programs have been used by several European nations since the 1920s, these programs were not implemented in the United States until 1978, when California adopted its work sharing unemployment insurance program (WSUI). The program works this way: Employers forced to cut production during a downturn reduce the number of hours worked by all affected employees instead of laying off a certain number of workers. Employees who have their hours reduced can then apply to the state for unemployment compensation assistance to make up a part of the difference between normal pay and the reduced pay. The unemployment assistance is provided on a pro rata basis. A person who works three days instead of the normal five days is eligible to receive 40 percent of the maximum benefits available to the worker for a given week of unemployment benefits.

Deferred Income

The opportunity to retire with economic security after completing a useful work life is a basic goal of almost all employees. Chapters 15 and 16 discuss in detail many of the compensation components that are included within the deferred income program of an organization. Over the years, employers have established the following kinds of compensation components to help employees accumulate capital and meet future financial goals:

1. Social Security
2. Qualified Retirement Plan
   Pension Plan
   Profit-Sharing Plan
   Stock Bonus Plan
3. Simplified Employee Pension Plans (SEPs)
4. Keogh Plans
5. Supplemental Executive Retirement Plans (SERPs)
6. Supplemental and Executive Group Life Insurance Plans
   Corporate-Owned Life Insurance (COLI)
   Section 79
   Split Dollar
   Group Universal Life Plans (GULPs)
7. Stock Purchase Plan
8. Stock Option Plan
9. Stock Grant
10. Deferred Income Plans
11. Grantor Trusts (Rabbi Trusts)

Spouse and Family Income Protection

Most employees attempt to ensure the future welfare of their dependents in case of their death. One component, life insurance, and a number of other components previously identified and described have specific features to assist a worker's dependents in the event of such a calamity. The major components available to protect workers' dependents are these:

1. Life insurance
2. Retirement plans
3. Social Security and Medicare
4. Tax-sheltered annuity
5. Workers' compensation
6. Accidental death and dismemberment
7. Travel accident insurance
8. Health care coverage

Life Insurance   This component provides financial assistance to the family upon the death of the insured. Possibly the most important benefit of a life insurance policy is that its proceeds transfer tax free to the beneficiary(ies) of the policy. Most organizations provide group term life insurance to their employees. IRC, Section 79, permits employers to provide up to $50,000 worth of life insurance tax free to their employees. As a rule of thumb, most employers provide group term life insurance that equals two times the employee's annual earnings at no cost to the employee.

Some organizations also increase life insurance coverage with increasing years of service. Some policies permit employees to increase their coverage at a nominal amount and to purchase life insurance for dependents. If many employees request such options, they can usually take advantage of some group feature that permits a reduced rate.

Most companies pay 100 percent of the base premium, with employees paying for any additional available options. When employees contribute to the plan, the split ranges from 50-50 between employer and employee to 80-20, with the employer paying the 80 percent.

Most life insurance plans have standard features that

1. Include all employees regardless of health or physical condition
2. Permit an employee to convert to an individual life insurance policy without a physical examination upon leaving the organization (within a prescribed time limit)

3. Insure employee and dependents for 30 days after separation
4. Continue coverage for retired employees

Some group life insurance plans provide for life insurance for dependents. These group plans normally cover both spouse and children. In most cases, the employee pays the total premium. A common maximum spouse coverage is $5,000, whereas maximum child coverage is $2,000. A feature currently being added to life insurance policies is called a "living benefit." This feature permits terminally ill employees to collect a portion of their life insurance benefits.

Retirement Plans   Many retirement plans have joint and survivor life income features that normally grant the spouse certain postretirement monthly income payments. When an employee selects such an option, the monthly retirement payments to the employee are actuarially reduced. Preretirement spouse and family death benefits are a feature in most retirement plans. Eligibility requirements for such benefits are usually age and service.

Social Security   Social Security also provides beneficiaries of deceased workers covered by Social Security with certain payments. These survivors can be the spouse, dependent children, dependent parents, and, under certain conditions, the divorced spouse. The amount of the payments depends on the (1) earnings of the worker, (2) length of time in the Social Security program, (3) age when benefit payments started, (4) age and number of recipients other than worker, and (5) state of health of recipients other than worker. In 1991, an average monthly Social Security benefit for a widowed mother and two children was $1,203. (See discussion of Social Security in chapters 5 and 15.)

Tax-Sheltered Annuity   See discussion of cash or deferred arrangements (CODA) in chapter 15.

Workers' Compensation   Workers' compensation insurance also provides burial expenses and income benefits for widows and children.

Accidental Death and Dismemberment (AD&D)   This component provides a fixed lump-sum benefit to a beneficiary when the death of an employee is accidental.

Travel Accident Insurance   This plan provides a lump-sum payment to beneficiaries of an employee killed while on a work assignment.

Health Care Coverage   Many employers provide health care coverage for survivors of deceased employees. This coverage usually lasts from 3 to 12 months. About half of the time, the employer pays for the premiums of such a plan.

ERISA and Employee Welfare Benefits Plans

The Employee Retirement Income Security Act (ERISA) of 1974 was designed to correct serious problems regarding the solvency of employer-funded pension plans. Since its passage, ERISA has been extended to cover employee benefits including plans providing health benefits. ERISA protects employers who offer benefits plans in many jurisdictions from potentially conflicting and inconsistent state and local laws by preempting laws related to health benefits.

One state, Hawaii, has been granted limited exemption from ERISA requirements related to health benefits plans. The exemption granted to Hawaii is limited to its

Prepaid Health Care Act that took effect in June 1974, while ERISA became law in September 1974. No other state has received similar exemption. ERISA imposes few requirements on employee health plans. However, the expansion of ERISA regulations into employee benefits programs came with a 1996 Supreme Court ruling that required employers to comply with statements they make about the continuation and extent of health coverage.[20] States cannot require self-insured companies to include mandated benefits in their plans or provide a particular health plan.

Health and Accident Protection

Organizations provide their employees with a wide variety of insurance services to help them and their families maintain a normal standard of living when unusual or unexpected health-related adversities occur. These health care–related insurance plans cover medical, surgical, and hospital bills resulting from an accident or illness. For these health plans to be recognized as a tax-deductible expense by an employer and not be considered taxable income to the employee, they must meet three eligibility requirements and one benefits nondiscriminatory requirement. These tests are:

ELIGIBILITY TESTS:

1. *50 percent test.* Fifty percent of all eligible employees are lower paid, or the percentage of lower paid employees eligible is greater than or equal to the percentage of highly paid eligible employees.
2. *90/50 test.* Ninety percent of lower-paid employees are eligible for health benefits worth at least 50 percent of the highest value of benefits available to any highly paid employee.
3. *Plan provision test.* No provision relating to eligibility discriminates in favor of the highly paid.

BENEFITS TEST:

The value of the average benefit to the lower-paid employee for all health plans combined is at least 75 percent of the value of the average benefit to the highly paid. (The definition for highly paid employees is the same as that provided in chapter 16.)

In the past, most employers recognized expenses for the cost of health care benefits when they occurred and as they paid premiums and other costs. However, by December 15, 1992, the Statement of Financial Accounting Standards (SFAS) No. 106 required organizations that provide life insurance and health care benefits to recognize these costs through an accrual basis. This change to the accrual method of accounting requires recognition of the expected cost of providing future benefits during the year the employee rendered services. SFAS 106 also required a measurement of the obligation owed to current and retired employees as of the date of adoption. The obligation can be recognized immediately or amortized over a period of up to 20 years.[21]

---

[20]Paul M. Barrett, "Justices Back Workers Suing over Benefits," *The Wall Street Journal*, March 20, 1996, pp. A3, A5.
[21]"New Study Offers Insight on How Companies Are Responding to FAS 106: Impact, Timing, Disclosure, Plan Design, and Funding," *News and Information* (Lincolnshire, IL: Hewitt Associates, January 30, 1992).

Most organizations use one of the two following plans to provide medical benefits for their employees and their dependents. These plans are titled (1) fee-for-service plans and (2) managed care plans.

Fee-for-Service Plans

Fee-for-service (FFS) plans allow patients to choose any provider and pay for specific medical procedures as expenses are incurred. FFS plan benefits are financed three different ways: (1) self-insured plans, (2) commercial insurance plans, and (3) Blue Cross/Blue Shield plans. Commercial insurance companies typically establish an experience-based rate for each employer, whereas Blue Cross/Blue Shield plans establish rates based on the medical experience of the entire community.

The most common way of financing an FFS is through self-insurance. With self-insurance, the sponsor—usually the employer—accepts the risk for paying for all covered medical services. Most FFS participants are in a self-insured program.

In many self-insured programs, the employer contracts with an insurance company to pay claims beyond a specified amount. These plans are called minimum premium plans (MPP). In an FFS plan, the participant must make the following payments: (1) a *deductible* must be met before the sponsor pays any medical bill. A deductible can typically be a flat dollar amount ranging from $100 to $300 per year per individual; (2) the plan will pay a specified percentage of covered medical expenses with the employee paying the remainder—*coinsurance* (most plans pay between 80 and 90 percent of the medical charges); and (3) in many plans, after the employee pays a specified dollar amount for medical expenses, the coinsurance cost is eliminated. This annual limit on employee payment is a stop-loss feature and is called *out-of-pocket expense limit.* It is frequently set between $1,500 and $2,500. FFS plans usually place a lifetime ceiling on the amount the plan will pay for. This ceiling can range from $250,000 to $1 million.

Managed Care Plans

In the past, FFS plans were the most common medical benefit plans offered to employees. However, in the past decade, *managed care accounts* have become the major provider of medical care insurance for employees. Managed care organizations direct their attention to providing users with mainstream medical care while, at the same time, containing health care costs.

In a managed care plan, the plan manager directs participants to specific providers of services. Managed care plans may have one or more of the following features:

1. Preadmission review of all hospital admissions for nonemergency and nonmaternity care.
2. Utilization review to monitor care while hospitalized.
3. Discharge planning to coordinate a continued course of treatment in a more cost-effective health care setting.
4. Mandatory second surgical opinions for selected procedures.

Managed care plans take three basic forms: (1) health maintenance organization (HMO); (2) preferred provider organization (PPO); and (3) point of service (POS) plan.

HMOs   The Health Maintenance Organization (HMO) Act of 1973 is a federal initiative for stimulating the development of a nationwide, prepaid health care system.

This act furnishes a meaningful alternative to organizations for providing health care services to their employees.

HMOs are financed through independent organizations, commercial insurers, or Blue Cross/Blue Shield organizations. Independent organizations such as Kaiser Permanente are most common. HMOs provide services 24 hours a day, 365 days a year out of a central facility, or they can use individual practice associations (IPAs) in which the providers work from their own offices.

Built-in forms of utilization reviews, including second surgical opinions, are automatically provided. Participants in an HMO must select a primary care physician (PCP) who may be salaried or paid on a per capita basis (often called a "capitated" system). The PCP acts as a "gatekeeper" for all medical services. The gatekeeper refers the individual to a provider within the network if special services are required.

HMOs provide a fixed set of medical benefits for a prepaid fee, which gives rise to another name for HMOs—the prepaid services approach. Most medical services are either covered in full or require patients to pay a nominal copayment. Typical copayments for an office visit to a physician is $5 to $10. Most HMOs assist in paying for physician-prescribed drugs, with a participant making a copayment of $3 to $5 for each prescription.

PPOs   The focus on health care cost control has given birth to another form of health delivery services—the preferred provider organization (PPO), an alternative to an HMO. PPOs are a network of independent physicians, hospitals, and other health care providers who contract with an insurance entity to provide care at discounted rates. The health care provider(s) agree(s) to offer strict cost-utilization controls and fee discounts to the employer, with cost efficiency being the greatest advantage. Employers attempt to influence their employees to use the most cost-effective provider. PPOs work closely with employers in promoting preventive medical care and health services. Participants may choose their own provider of services or receive care from designated hospitals, physicians, laboratories, or dentists. Individuals choosing their own providers will normally receive a lower rate of reimbursement. Like FFS plans, PPOs require participants to pay a deductible, coinsurance, and plan maximum. When using a physician inside the network, the costs to the participants are very similar to those of an HMO.

POSs   Point-of-service (POS) plans are in many ways similar to PPOs but with less structure. These plans allow participants to use care providers within or outside a given network. An open enrollment option allows POS plan participants to use either HMO service providers or non-HMO providers. If the outside network provider charges a higher fee than the HMO provider, the participant may have to pay the additional cost of the outside network provider.

A POS is also called an open-ended HMO. It includes a network of gatekeeper managed care providers who may be partially capitated or paid for each service delivered. A POS also may allow participants to choose their own providers. When selecting an out-of-network provider, there is a higher employee copayment.

In a 1998 study conducted by William M. Mercer, Inc. (a benefits consulting firm), it found that total per employee health care costs increased by 6.1 percent in 1998, following five years of minimal growth. The study also found that from 1997 to 1998, HMO membership fell from 30 percent to 29 percent and POS membership dropped from 20 percent to 18 percent. Meanwhile, membership in PPOs increased from 35 percent to 40 percent.[22]

Features of Health Care Insurance Plans

Medical coverage included in *medical insurance plans* continues to expand every year. Basic medical coverage includes payments for *diagnostic visits* to the doctor's office, *outpatient X-rays*, and *laboratory coverage*. Recent additions include *home visits* by the doctor and *ambulatory or outpatient surgery*. Although still rare among medical benefits, the *annual physical* is beginning to appear in more health insurance programs. Another recent addition to health care insurance plans is the extension of comprehensive health care benefits to include some of the survivors of deceased company employees and retirees. A relatively new provision covers outpatient and nonhospital *psychiatric care*.

Opening the door to emotional health benefits also includes *alcohol and drug rehabilitation services*. Employees suffering from alcohol and drug abuse problems are receiving medical treatment under these recently developed psychiatric outpatient benefits programs.

The Mental Health Parity Act of 1996 and the Taxpayers Relief Act of 1997 drastically influence mental health services. They prohibit group health plans that provide both medical and surgical benefits and mental health (psychiatric care) benefits from imposing either aggregate lifetime dollar limits or annual dollar limits on mental health benefits unless the plan also imposes the limits on "substantially all" medical and surgical benefits.

Substance abuse and chemical dependency are specifically excluded from the definition of what constitutes "mental health benefits." Prior to passage of these acts, mental health programs frequently had some form of coinsurance requirement ranging from 10 to 15 percent. Usually provisions limited the number of visits permitted in a fixed period of time as well as the charges accrued in one year.

Major Medical   Major medical is a group insurance plan designed to help employees pay medical bills incurred because of serious or prolonged illness. A feature found in many major medical plans is *skilled nursing care* or *extended care facility coverage*.

Hospitalization Plans   *Hospitalization plans* offered by commercial insurance companies usually provide fixed cash benefits for hospital room and board, in-hospital doctor visits, and certain other hospital charges. These plans pay directly to the insured who, in turn, pays the hospital. On the other hand, *hospital service plans* provide service rather than direct cash payments, paying for room, board, in-house doctor visits, and other necessary hospital services. The major national provider of these services is the Blue Cross system.

Surgical   The *surgical expense benefits* are similar to the hospitalization plans. Both the commercial insurance companies and the service plans follow a similar procedure of listing a schedule of payments for different types of operations. Some plans allow doctors' charges to relate to the patient's income. Patients having an income below a certain level pay nothing more than that listed on the schedule of payments, whereas patients having an income above the prescribed level may be charged a higher fee and

[22]Ron Winslow, "Measure of HMO Membership Falls for First Time," *The Wall Street Journal,* January 26, 1999, p. B7.

may be responsible for the difference between the charged fee and the scheduled payment. Currently, most plans reimburse surgical fees on a 100-percent-of-reasonable-and-customary-charge basis. Blue Shield is the surgical counterpart of the Blue Cross hospital service plan.

Comprehensive Physical   Some organizations now provide all employees with an annual comprehensive physical. This has long been a benefit for senior management in many organizations.

In-House Medical Services   Some large organizations have their own medical staff. When such staff is available, employees may receive not only free medical care but also pharmacy services at little to no cost. More and more large organizations are using this approach to reduce overall medical costs.

Postretirement Medical   To provide health care protection for retired employees many organizations have extended their health care plans to their retired employees. The loss of health care insurance 30 days after retirement has been a serious concern to employees. Today, most plans provide retirees with coverage comparable to what they received as active employees. Many employers pay the entire premium cost for their retirees. These plans provide a critical link in enhancing the financial security of their workforce.

AIDS Coverage   *AIDS* coverage in health care insurance has become a major issue. The increase of health care costs related to the AIDS epidemic is having a critical effect upon the health care plans of organizations. Most health care plans fall under ERISA, and its regulations control an employer's rights to amend its health and welfare plans. However, courts have held uniformly that, absent an implied or express agreement to the contrary between the employer and employee, the employer is free to alter, amend, or even eliminate group health benefits.[23] In recent years, employers have specifically removed AIDS from their catastrophic illness coverage. These catastrophic illnesses frequently have high amounts ($500,000 to $1 million) of overall lifetime maximum benefits. Some organizations now place a $5,000 lifetime maximum benefit for AIDS-related claims. Some organizations have even removed AIDS coverage from their health benefits plans and established a separate, self-insurance health benefits plan with a $5,000 to $25,000 cap on lifetime coverage.

In 1992, the U.S. Supreme Court, in the case of *McGann* v. *H & H Music Co.*, refused to review a lower court decision that permitted an organization to terminate an existing medical plan (1988) after learning that one of its employees had contracted AIDS. The terminated plan had provided a maximum lifetime medical benefit of $1 million; the replacement plan, however, included, among other changes, a $5,000 cap for AIDS treatment.[24]

Medical Savings Accounts (MSAs)   The Health Insurance Portability and Accountability Act of 1996 established a four-year pilot program that allows for the creation of up to 750,000 tax-free MSAs for workers in businesses with fewer than 50

[23]Rory Judd Albert and Neal S. Schelberg, "AIDS Has Damaging Effects on Employee Health Plans," *Pension World,* March 1992, pp. 52–54.
[24]Anthony J. Gajda, "Health Insurance after McGann," *The Wall Street Journal,* November 11, 1992, p. A-10.

employees. It allows employees or employers to make an annual payment into an MSA (but not both in the same year).

Contributions to an MSA by an individual are tax deductible to the employee, and an employee's contributions do not count toward gross income and are not subject to federal taxes. MSA funds can be placed in a passbook savings account, a money market, or a mutual fund account. The money placed in an MSA can be used to pay for out-of-pocket expenses, including deductible cost for a high-deductible medical insurance policy. A high-deductible insurance policy can have a deductible chart that ranges between $1,500 and $2,250 for an individual and $3,000 and $4,500 for family coverage. A typical MSA high-deductible policy can have an annual premium cost of $100 in addition to the $2,250 deductible. For individual coverage, up to 65 percent of the deductible of the medical insurance plan can be contributed to an MSA and up to 75 percent of deductible for a family plan. Until age 65, MSA funds can only be used to pay for deductible and qualified medical expenses, including doctor visits, prescription drugs, and vision and dental care. After age 65, MSA funds can be used any way the insured individual desires.

Dental   A major added medical coverage is that of comprehensive *dental care benefits.* Three basic kinds of dental protection plans have been developed: (1) schedule plans, (2) comprehensive plans, and (3) combination plans.[25]

The *schedule plan* lists payments for each dental procedure performed. There is no deductible in this plan.

The *comprehensive plan* provides a percentage reimbursement of 50 to 80 percent on covered expenses after an initial deductible (the insured pays the first $25 to $50). The plan may contain an annual (a few hundred dollars) and lifetime ($5,000 or more) limit to benefits.

The *combination plan* provides a fixed fee schedule for some dental expenses and a deductible on some or all types of dental expenses with a possible limiting coinsurance clause in which the insured pays some percentage of the fee up to 15 to 25 percent.

Although the cost of most dental plans was initially totally covered by employers, many new plans require employee contributions. Preventive care will usually receive the best coverage.

A number of different methods have been developed for organizing dentists. In some cases, the insurance carrier enlists a panel of dentists to provide services. In other cases, the labor union or employer may do the organizing. In still other cases, a group of dentists may form their own private corporation and provide services to the employer or union on some contractual agreement.

Vision   Recently, *vision care* has been added to some plans. Many vision care plans provide employees with one eye examination and one set of prescription glasses each year. An employee may be required to pay a set fee for each eye examination and new pair of glasses. This benefit may be of limited value, however, as most vision care claims are under $100. Growth in vision care plans has been very slow.

Hearing Aid   Although it affects a smaller number of employees than the vision aid plan, a benefit that may be of greater value is the hearing aid plan because the cost for a hearing aid ranges from $400 to $2,000.

---

[25]J. F. Follman, Jr., "Dental Insurance," *Pension & Welfare News,* August 1973, pp. 20, 22, 24, 72.

Workers' Compensation   These previously described state laws also provide medical benefits and hospital care for insured and disabled employees.

Social Security   Through its *Medicare* program, Social Security provides significant benefits for a wide range of health care services to almost everyone aged 65 or older. This program protects those individuals against costs of extended hospitalization, convalescent care, and major doctor bills. The Medicare program enables employers to reduce their cost of extending health care insurance to retirees or active employees 65 or older. There is, however, no age limit to Medicare benefits to people with kidney disease who require dialysis or to individuals who have received Social Security disability benefits for two years. Many corporate retirement plans include a Medicare offset feature and also reimburse retirees and their spouses for Medicare Part B premiums. In 1999, the Medicare Part B monthly premium was $45.50.

Additions to Health Care Coverage   The Health Insurance Portability and Accountability Act of 1996 made significant additions to health care coverage for American workers. Major features of this act are (1) workers who change jobs are guaranteed eligibility for insurance coverage in their new jobs; (2) workers cannot be denied coverage by their employer's insurer for more than one year because of a preexisting condition; (3) premiums must be the same regardless of an employee's health condition; (4) individuals who have been covered in a group plan for at least 18 months have access to individual insurance coverage.

Play-or-Pay Plans

In the early 1990s, a few states began to implement play-or-pay health care insurance programs.[26] Play-or-pay plans focus primarily on employers who have many low-wage and part-time employees and do not offer these employees health care insurance. Employers who do not offer or "pay" for employee health care insurance are required to "play" in a state-directed health care program. Most play-or-pay plans require employers to contribute a set amount based on a fixed percentage of the payroll.[27]

Although the state of Hawaii had required employers to contribute to a state insurance fund prior to the interest in play-or-pay programs, it does provide a useful example regarding employer contributions to a state fund. When an employer does not provide health care insurance, the employer and employee must contribute to the state fund. The employee must contribute the lesser of half the premium cost or 1.5 percent of his or her gross wages. In 1990, the average annual wage of a worker in Hawaii was $23,192. This resulted in $29.00 per month contribution which was about one-third of the premium cost for individual coverage. Health care insurance costs in Hawaii are much less than in most other states.

Health Care Cost Containment

Possibly no compensation topic has created more interest among both human resources specialists and top levels of management than the continued increase in health care costs. By 1990, personal health care expenditures in the United States totaled $2,255 per

---

[26]Pay—provide health insurance to their employees.
  Play—pay a tax that goes to a government-sponsored health insurance fund to insure those not covered by the employer plan.
[27]Peter Magowan, "A Great Prognosis for 'Play or Pay,' " *The Wall Street Journal,* March 26, 1992, p. A3.

person and represented 10.7 percent of the U.S. gross national product. In 1970, this expenditure was 6.4 percent of the gross national product. Between 1990 and 1992, total health care expenses increased from $585 billion to approximately $800 billion,[28] and by 1997 reached $1,035.0 billion.[29] Between 1987 and 1991, corporate health care spending per employee increased from $1,985 to $3,605. In the period between October 1990 and October 1992, the medical care component of the consumer price index (CPI) increased by 8.2 percent. The annual increase between April 1998 and April 1999 was 3.5 percent, continuing as one of the highest component increases in the CPI.[30]

For employers, escalating health care costs have resulted in drastic increases in health care insurance premiums. In response to these rising costs, some employers have discontinued providing health care coverage, others have required employees to make copayments, still others have reduced offered health care services, and others have required their employees to join some kind of a managed care program.

At the federal and state government levels, efforts have been taken to slow down the growth of Medicare and Medicaid costs. Between 1985 and 1993, Medicaid costs tripled and the number of beneficiaries increased by more than 50 percent. It is predicted that Medicaid and Medicare costs will continue to be the fastest growing component of both federal and state budgets. In 1997, Medicare enrollment was 37.5 million with a cost of $206.1 billion, whereas Medicaid had 35 million enrollees with a cost of $121.4 billion.[31]

The rapid increase in health care costs and health insurance has resulted in more and more small- and medium-size firms doing what in the past had been done primarily by large firms—establishing self-insured health plans. By 1991, 65 percent of employers had self-insured medical plans. This was up from 46 percent in 1986.[32]

Because of the dramatic increase in health care costs, employers who only a decade ago strongly opposed any form of a national health plan have become supportive of some form of a national insurance plan. With the escalation of health care costs, more and more Americans find themselves without health insurance. By 1996, it was estimated that 42 million Americans had no health care coverage.[33] As medical insurance premiums continue to escalate, more employers (especially employers with less than 100 employees) do not provide medical insurance coverage.

Health care cost containment options have been developed by employers seeking alternative ways of limiting or containing rapidly escalating costs of health care benefits. The most direct approaches are to (1) require employees to make a contribution (share in the premium cost) to the benefit or to increase the contribution if already doing so; (2) increase the amount of the deductible or require a deductible payment where none exists; (3) increase the coinsurance percentage or establish coinsurance where none exists (share in cost for a medical treatment); and (4) add no new features

[28]*Health Care Spending: Non-policy Factors Account for Most State Differences* (Washington, DC: U.S. General Accounting Office, February 13, 1992).

[29]U.S. Department of Commerce, Bureau of Economic and Statistical Analysis, *Statistical Abstract of the United States, 1998* (Washington, DC: U.S. Government Printing Office, 1998), No. 165, p. 118.

[30]U.S. Deptartment of Labor, Bureau of Labor Statistics, Consumer Price Index, April 1999.

[31]*Statistical Abstract,* No. 174, p. 122.

[32]Edward Felsenthal, "Self-Insurance of Health Plan Benefits Firms," *The Wall Street Journal,* November 11, 1992, pp. B1, B12.

[33]*Statistical Abstract,* p. 115.

to a benefit plan unless others are removed or reduced in cost. Other cost containment opportunities include utilization reviews, health maintenance, and self-insurance.

Utilization reviews require employers or their designated agents to check the health care services received by their employees and the quality of these services. They identify the benefits employees are actually using and what it is costing employers to provide them. This review process must be ongoing because it should analyze what happens to employees after they receive health care services. An offshoot of the utilization review is to have in-house staff review all claims for accuracy of payment or to hire an outside claim review service to do the necessary monitoring and auditing. A special kind of utilization review committee is a peer review organization (PRO). PROs consist of health care professionals who are responsible for analyzing Medicare costs of designated related groups (DRGs)—groups of related kinds of medical services for which Social Security will provide a specific reimbursable amount to a hospital for their Medicare patients. PRO reviews of DRG costs include total number of discharges, average length of hospitalization, matching rates, average patient age, and percentage of female patients. PROs provide data to guide consumers, physicians, and hospitals in evaluating the quality of hospital medical services.

Health maintenance, that is, preventing illness, is far less costly than curing illness. Encouraging employees to invest in staying well provides immediate and long-term benefits to both employees and the employer. Stress reduction, exercise, proper diet, antismoking programs, and minimization of substance abuse (reducing dependence on alcohol, narcotics, and other drugs) all pay off by increasing the energy level of healthy employees. A payoff to the organization may be less costly insurance premiums.

Other actions being taken by employers to contain rising health care costs are (1) increased use of preemployment physicals, (2) periodic physical examinations, (3) preadmission testing coverage, (4) requiring second surgical opinions, and (5) providing premiums to employees who stay healthy. Additional preventive services include routine prenatal care, immunization of infants, well-baby care for infants up to age 2, PAP smears for women, and routine mammography screening for women 50 years of age and older.

Self-insurance as an alternative is being used by more employers as they assume responsibility for certain health-related risks. Health-related risks now being covered by employers themselves through self-insurance are short-term disability benefits, basic group health insurance, long-term disability, survivor income, and group term insurance. Commercial insurance supplements self-insurance programs for risks that seldom occur or catastrophic events that could result in substantial financial loss. Self-insuring employers may use a third party to pay claims under an administrative service contract.[34]

Universal Health Care

Providing adequate health care to every American while containing the growth of health care costs became one of the major issues facing the United States in the 1990s. In some manner, all employers, state and federal governments, private health care insurers, and providers of health care services must coordinate their efforts to provide

---

[34]Carlton Harker, "Self-Insurance—An Employer's Option," *Personnel Journal,* May 1977, pp. 251–252.

adequate, cost-effective health care for all Americans. The play-or-pay programs are serious approaches to combining (1) state Medicaid programs (that involve both federal and state funding), (2) employer-provided health insurance, and (3) state health care plans funded by special state taxes that cover individuals not covered by (1) and (2).

The efforts of the state of Hawaii and play-or-pay programs in Massachusetts and Oregon, initiatives in a number of states to provide health care to low-income children and adults, the success of the State of Maryland in lowering the increase in health care costs through a hospital rate regulation, and the creation of high-risk pools by some states to make insurance available to the medically uninsurable are all worthwhile approaches for solving the health care problem. However, in the coming years, much more effort must be taken by all parties to make health care affordable to all residents of the United States.

Property and Liability Protection

Of rather recent vintage is the addition of compensation components that provide employees with personal property and liability protection. These property and liability protection components include:

1. Group auto
2. Group home
3. Group legal
4. Group umbrella liability
5. Employee liability
6. Fidelity bond insurance

Group Auto   Pioneers in this field have been Traveler's Insurance Company, the American Postal Workers Union, and the National Association of Letter Carriers. Within the next 10 years, auto insurance will probably become a more common benefit. The current pattern is for an employer and an insurance company to develop a group plan through which the employee saves approximately 15 percent of the premium cost because of the group rate reduction. Payments are normally made through a payroll deduction. As group auto insurance develops, employers may make some contribution.

Group Home   A new benefit is a homeowner's insurance plan developed by the employer and an insurance company. The employee makes a savings in the premium cost through a mass purchase and the payment of premiums through a payroll deduction.

Group Legal   Although some organizations with legal departments have always provided employees with legal advice concerning tax problems and garnishments, a full range of legal counseling through legal insurance plans is relatively new. Unions have been a key stimulus in gaining legal insurance for their members. An amendment to the Taft-Hartley Act in 1973 permitted private companies to join with unions to offer legal insurance. After the law was amended, prepaid legal insurance became an additional collective bargaining issue. Then the Tax Reform Act of 1986 and its attendant IRC, Section 120, provided favorable tax treatment to employees who receive legal services under a qualified group legal plan. IRC, Section 120, includes group legal plans within welfare benefits plans.

In the 1990s over 70 percent of all Americans and 50 percent of all lawyers were involved in group legal plans. These plans were completely separate from other qualified welfare benefits plans. The major uses have been for auto claims, divorce cases, and child custody contests.

Two types of prepaid legal insurance plans now exist. One is the "open panel," which permits an employee to seek an attorney who will perform the legal service for the fee scheduled in the policy. The other is the "closed panel," which requires the use of one of a number of specified attorneys.

Most plans require some amount of employee contribution; annual fees range from $10 to $25, and total policy costs range from $100 to $150 annually. Employees can exclude from income tax up to $70 per month in employer provided coverage.

Group Umbrella Liability   With lawsuits granting ever-higher settlements, liability coverage beyond that found in the normal auto and homeowners' policies becomes more important to many employees. Commercial insurance companies are now offering employers group umbrella liability plans that provide increased liability coverage for employees at minimal cost.

Employee Liability   Because of the greater likelihood of lawsuits and the increased liability of employees for actions they take when performing their jobs, organizations now provide their top decision makers with liability insurance. These insurance plans provide coverage in the millions of dollars. Employees in sensitive positions such as top executives and members of the board of directors are now receiving such protection.

Fidelity Bond Insurance   Organizations may make the premium payments for the fidelity bond insurance required of employees who must be bonded in order to perform certain job assignments.

EMPLOYEE SERVICES

Employers provide a wide array of services that enhance the lifestyle of employees. In some cases, these services grant employees time off with pay. In other cases, the services include highly valued in-kind benefits, which, if purchased by employees themselves, would require the expenditure of after-tax dollars. In providing these services, the employer usually receives a tax deduction and, in most cases, the good or service is not considered an earned income item. Even in cases in which employees may be charged with additional earned income for the receipt of the good or service, the charge to income is considerably less than the cost that would have been incurred by the recipient. The three major sets of components that constitute the employee services group are (1) pay for time not worked, (2) time off without pay, and (3) income equivalent payments and reimbursements for incurred expenses.

Pay for Time Not Worked

Over the past 35 years, the drive to reduce working hours and total time spent at work has focused on providing workers with more paid holidays and longer vacations. In negotiations with the automobile industry in 1947, the UAW made a major breakthrough when it gained six paid holidays for its members in that industry. From an employee's perspective, possibly the most desired but frequently unrecognized benefit is time off with pay. There are numerous time-off-with-pay components and employees usually receive their daily base pay rate as the rate paid for these time-off opportunities. The more common time-off-with-pay components are these:

1. Holidays	11. Paternity leave
2. Vacations	12. Maternity leave
3. Jury duty	13. Sick leave
4. Election official	14. Wellness leave
5. Witness in court	15. Time off to vote
6. Civic duty	16. Blood donation
7. Military duty	17. Grievance and contract negotiations
8. Funeral leave	18. Lunch, rest, and wash-up periods
9. Illness in family leave	19. Personal leave
10. Marriage leave	20. Sabbatical leave

Holidays   Most organizations now provide employees with nine to twelve paid holidays a year (see Table 17–4). Some organizations also offer from one to three floating holidays a year in which the selection is left to the discretion of the employee or is mutually agreed on between the employer and the employees. Some organizations allow employees to observe a holiday on their birthdays.

Most employers determine holiday pay in the same way they determine vacation pay. Those employees who are required to work on holidays because of the nature of the business are usually given compensatory time off (alternative time off with pay at the discretion of the employee with the approval of the organization) and/or premium pay for the day worked. Most organizations observe a holiday on Friday if it falls on a Saturday, and on Monday if it falls on a Sunday.

TABLE 17–4 Common Holidays

Most Commonly Offered	*Other*
New Year's Day	President's Day (third Monday in February)[a]
Martin Luther King, Jr., Day	Columbus Day (second Monday in October)[a]
Good Friday	Presidential Election Day
Memorial Day (last Monday in May)[a]	Veterans Day
July 4th	Friday after Thanksgiving
Labor Day	Day before or after Christmas
Thanksgiving Day (fourth Thursday in November)	Day before or after New Year's
Christmas Day	

[a] These are Monday holidays observed by federal employees and by some state and private enterprise employees.

Vacations   Although vacations vary widely, some plans have been liberalized in recent years. Many organizations provide a vacation package similar to the following:

1. One week after 6 months to 1 year of service.
2. Two weeks after 1–5 years of service.
3. Three weeks after 5–10 years of service.
4. Four weeks after 15–25 years of service.
5. Five weeks after 25 years of service.

The method of computing vacation pay often depends on the type of work and the manner of compensating an employee. Those receiving a regular weekly salary usually receive their base salary rate. Some organizations pay two percent of the employee's annual earnings for each week of vacation. Those employees paid on an incentive basis may have their vacation pay based on some average weekly earnings for a specified period before the vacation. Some organizations are now providing their employees with a *vacation banking plan*, which enables employees to trade off all or part of the value of an unused vacation, which is then collected upon termination or retirement. In many cases, organizations allow employees to carry over up to two weeks of vacation to the next year.

Jury Duty   Many employers pay their employees who serve on juries. The employees usually receive the difference between their regular eight-hour pay and the amount they receive for each day of jury duty. Some employers permit employees to receive their regular pay in addition to jury duty pay. Some states require employers to pay employees who are on jury duty.

Election Official   Some employers grant employees who work as election officials time off with pay at the difference between their base rate of pay and the amount received as an election official.

Witness in Court   When employees are required to appear as a witness in court, some employers grant these employees time off with pay during their courtroom appearance.

Civic Duty   Some organizations provide a specified number of days off with pay to employees providing services to civic organizations.

Military Duty   Many employers provide from one to two weeks off with pay, depending on the military obligation of the employee and the length of service with the organization. Some states require employers to pay employees who are performing military duty.

The 1990 activation of military reservists and National Guard personnel for Operation Desert Storm raised the issue of employment and benefits rights of these personnel and the obligations of their employers. Federal law does not require employers to pay wages and salaries and to continue to offer welfare and pension benefits to employees called to active duty. In the Desert Storm operation, many employers continued benefits coverage for their called-up employees and seniority time was granted for employees while on active duty. The Veterans Reemployment Act requires reemployment of employees called to active duty and the crediting of military service for certain benefit purposes. Because of these requirements, personnel called to active duty are considered to have been on a leave of absence during the period of active duty and receive all of the benefits offered to any employee granted a leave of absence.

Funeral Leave   Many employers grant employees one to five days off to attend the funeral of a member of the immediate family.

Illness in Family Leave   Many employers grant one to five days off to employees to allow them to assist in caring for members of the immediate family.

Marriage Leave   Some employers grant up to five days of paid absence for those planning to continue employment after marriage.

Paternity Leave   Some employers grant up to five days of paid absence for the father to assist his wife after the birth of a child. (See discussion in chapter 5.)

Maternity Leave   Few organizations provide specific paid days off for maternity leave, but most organizations permit pregnant employees to use sick leave and annual leave for paid time off while on maternity leave. (See discussion in chapter 5.)

Sick Leave   Previously discussed under "Disability Income Continuation." Also read the section "A Different Approach."

Wellness Leave   A recent addition to the time-off-with-pay classification is a feature aimed at combating absenteeism. Each employee receives a half hour of paid leave for each week of perfect attendance during all regularly scheduled work hours.

Time Off to Vote   Some employers grant employees a paid hour or two of time off to vote in local, state, and national elections.

Blood Donations   Some employers grant employees paid time off to donate blood. The time may vary from that sufficient to go to a mobile unit to up to four hours to go to a blood bank.

Grievance and Contract Negotiations   Most unionized organizations permit time off with pay to employees who are involved in a grievance procedure or in certain union activities, specified by contract.

Lunch, Rest, and Wash-Up Periods   Some organizations grant employees wash-up time (organizations may allow employees involved in extremely dirty work up to 30 minutes to clean up prior to leaving their jobs for the day), rest periods and/or coffee breaks (usually a 10 to 15 minute break twice a day), and lunch periods (usually 30 minutes).

Personal Leave   A variety of special personal excused absences are permitted for time off with pay.

Sabbatical Leave   A few organizations now permit certain employees to have up to one year of sabbatical leave for performing work that has value to society or enhances the professional qualifications of the employee.

A Different Approach

Over the years, many organizations have found sick leave to be a much abused benefit. Sick leave was established to give employees paid time off when they were unable to work because of illness or injury. Many employees have looked upon sick leave as so many more days off with pay. An early morning headache, some time in the sun, or time just to get some odd chores done are reason enough to take a day of sick leave. Organizations have taken various steps to minimize sick leave abuses, including eliminating sick leave programs.

A recent innovation to the time-off-with-pay programs that may be one of the more useful plans yet developed has been instituted by a number of organizations—in many cases, hospitals—that have employees working 24 hours a day, 7 days a week. This new program is variously known as earned time, personal time, or no-fault time off.

In these plans, employees work to gain time off with pay. They earn a certain amount of time off with pay for every hour worked. The actual amount of time off for each hour worked is calculated in this manner:

1. The organization decides how many days off with pay it wishes to grant to employees. It may wish to provide different amounts according to the employee's job or seniority.
2. After calculating the number of granted days off, a ratio is developed between these days off and hours worked. The organization includes time off with pay in this calculation, as granted days off with pay are used to earn additional days off with pay.

Consider, for example, employees who work 40 hours per week for 52 weeks a year, or 2,080 hours. For a 5-year employee, the organization has been granting 3 weeks or 15 working days paid vacation, 8 holidays, and 12 days of sick leave. This equals 35 days off with pay. Dividing 35 days by 2,080 or 35/2,080 = 0.0168 days off for each hour worked. If the organization wishes to give 26 days, the ratio would be 0.0125 days off for each hour worked. Earned time (ET) hours can be calculated daily by multiplying hours worked times ET ratio. A simple computer-based program can be developed to maintain ET hours for each employee.

Various rules have to be established with regard to such plans. Examples of ET rules are

1. Overtime is counted toward ET.
2. To gain ET, an employee must work at least 32 hours of ET in any one scheduled workweek.
3. All ET used must be scheduled and approved in advance by the immediate supervisor except when this is impossible because of illness or injury. Abuse of supervisory notification may result in disciplinary action.
4. Employees may accumulate up to a maximum of 90 ET days.
5. ET will not count as time worked for the purpose of calculating overtime.
6. Employees, with permission of their supervisor, may take advances on ET. However, employees who leave the firm and have taken advanced ET will have the monetary value of the advances deducted from their final paycheck.
7. Shift differentials and premiums will be used in calculating rate of pay for ET. Weekend and holiday differentials will not be counted.
8. Employees may "cash in" up to 50 percent of accumulated ET once a year. The "cashed in" rate will be 75 percent of base pay plus earned differentials and pre-

miums. (The reason for the 75 percent is that, for most employees, pay advances almost annually and the reduction recognizes the difference in what the employee was earning when the ET was accumulated and what the employee receives when "cashing in" the ET.[35])

Time Off from Work without Pay

For years, some organizations have provided employees with sabbaticals without pay. Here, an employee has an opportunity to pursue a special interest area. Although the employee is not paid, he or she continues to be covered by the employer's medical and life insurance and disability programs.

In 1987, the U.S. Supreme Court upheld the constitutionality of a State of California pregnancy disability leave statute. The California law requires 12 weeks of unpaid leave for pregnant women and reinstatement to their jobs upon return to the work force. Other states have enacted similar parallel leave statutes. Typical features of such plans are (1) offering up to 12 weeks of parental leave and (2) leave available upon the birth, adoption, or serious illness of a child. In 1993, the first major piece of legislation enacted under the Clinton administration was the Family and Medical Leave Act. It granted employees 12 weeks of unpaid leave for a variety of purposes, including a worker's own illness or that of a spouse, child, or parent. The hidden costs underlying any unpaid leave is not simply holding a job open for these employees, but continuing their benefits coverage while they are on a nonpay status.

Income Equivalent Payments and Reimbursements for Incurred Expenses

The ever-increasing diversity and popularity of employee benefits have given rise to a significant number of benefits that can be grouped under a category called nonstatutory benefits. The majority of benefits previously described are either mandated by legislation or permitted by statutes and given preferential tax treatment. These include the qualified arrangements discussed in chapter 15 and the welfare benefits plans discussed in this chapter. However, as organizations provide more and different kinds of benefits and services, the nonstatutory group continues to expand. There are no specific pieces of legislation affecting the nonstatutory benefits. They usually involve the payment of a particular expense by the employer or the provision of goods or services to the employees. Over the years, court cases, Internal Revenue Service rulings, and administrative customs have provided a particular tax or nontax status regarding most of these benefits.

This group of compensation components includes some of the most diverse and most desirable kinds of goods and services employees receive from their employers. Many of these components and new ones that appear almost daily have been introduced in response to changes in the economic situation and to tax demands. This broad

---

[35]The ET program described here is modeled after that implemented by David A. Williamson, Director, Human Resources of St. Joseph Hospital, Nashua, NH.

group of services provides employees with the opportunity for an improved and more enjoyable lifestyle. Some of the more common components are

Tax-Free or Tax-Preferred Benefits or Services

1. Charitable contributions	7. Elderly care	14. Travel expenses
2. Counseling	8. Subsidized food service	Car reimbursement
Financial	9. Discounts on merchandise	Tolls and parking
Legal	10. Physical awareness and	Food and entertainment
Psychiatric	fitness programs	reimbursement
Psychological	11. Social and recreational	15. Clothing reimbursement/
3. Tax preparation	opportunities	allowance
4. Education subsidies	12. Parking	16. Tool reimbursement/
5. Child adoption	13. Transportation to and	allowance
6. Child care	from work	17. Relocation expenses
		18. Emergency loans
		19. Credit union
		20. Housing

Charitable Contributions   Many employers now match, either totally or by some percentage, contributions made by employees to their favorite charities or educational institutions. There may be a limit to the contribution the organization makes to a specific charity of any employee.

Counseling   Organizations often ask to what extent they should counsel employees. Some experts feel that counseling is acceptable only when employees are unable to function on their jobs because of a problem that impairs their work activity, or when they specifically request it.

Counseling activities include attentive listening by a supervisor to an employee's problem in an attempt to identify and understand what is blocking acceptable performance. Often, the problems identified by the employee only camouflage more serious, hidden ones. When a supervisor is unable to help an employee resolve a conflict, the next step is referral to an in-house specialist who is able to provide additional counseling skills. When more serious psychological problems arise, the employer may refer the employee to a private practitioner. (See health-related benefits mentioned earlier in this chapter.)

Some of the counseling benefits now provided, in addition to *medical* and *psychological services,* include *financial* counseling (on how to make up a family budget and live within it to overcome existing indebtedness problems, and how to maximize use of current income in developing a future estate), *family* counseling (on a wide range of family activities, including marital, child, financial, and other personal problems), *career* development (encouraging and assisting employees to look toward the future and to where their best opportunities lie), *outplacement* (helping those who lose their jobs involuntarily and those disenchanted with their present jobs to find new ones), and *legal* counseling (on how to protect oneself when having legal problems). Currently, many employers are offering these services under an umbrella program called *employee assistance (EA).*

Tax Preparation   This service assists employees in meeting tax requirements and may include the identification of legal methods for reducing or deferring tax liabilities.

Educational Subsidies   Educational opportunity provisions are appearing in more and more benefits plans. In the past and moving into the future, the federal government has promoted education subsidies by permitting tuition aid plans to be nontaxable (to the employee) and considering tax credits for those paying college tuition for family members. In the past, large organizations have provided tuition aid plans for employees who have completed their second year of college or who wish to continue in a graduate program. Traditionally, these programs have ranged from the total payment of all tuition and benefits to the payment of some percentage (50 to 75 percent), to a flat fee per year ($250 to $350). New programs provide educational benefits to (1) employees who wish to complete their high school education, (2) those who would like to start their college programs, and (3) those who are interested in enrolling in a vocational-technical program.

In addition to these external education and training programs, many firms are implementing a wide variety of in-house educational programs ranging from remedial work on basic literacy to training aimed at improving job opportunities.

Child Adoption   Recently, a few firms have been providing employees with financial assistance for legal and other service costs incurred in adopting a child. One employer reimburses its employees as much as 80 percent of the adoption cost up to $800; another provides total reimbursement up to $500.

Child Care   Child care as an employee benefit is just beginning. Some of the programs started over the past 10 years have had poor employee participation because of the high cost, transportation problems, or competition from other more convenient child care centers. Some successful programs are close to the employee's workplace (frequently in the same building), and the employer provides 50 to 75 percent of the operating costs; however, many employees prefer child care facilities close to their homes. With increasing numbers of both parents working, this will become one of the most demanded services. See Employee Spending Accounts at end of chapter for a preferred method of paying for this service.

Elderly Care   With the "graying of the United States" comes the other end of the dependent care problem. Employees with infants and young children have one problem, whereas employees with elderly relatives have another, but in many ways similar, kind of problem. Caring for an older relative can be as much if not more of an emotional and financial strain than child care. With increasing costs related to nursing home and extended skill care, more aged dependents will be receiving home care. A few companies are now beginning to assist employees with this problem. A first step is to provide employees with information on ways of coping with the problem. A second step is to provide financial assistance for dependents.[36]

Employees receiving benefits under an employer's dependent care assistance plan may exclude from income up to $5,000 of benefits, if single or married filing jointly, or $2,500 if filing separately.

---

[36]Dana E. Friedman, "Eldercare: The Employee Benefit of the 1990s?" *Across the Board,* June 1986.

An employer has the option of choosing whether to consider dependent care as a statutory or nonstatutory benefit. If the benefit is considered a statutory benefit, the following tests must be met:

1. The three eligibility tests and the benefits test described in the Health and Accident Protection section, or the alternative 80 percent test.
2. The plan may be aggregated with other welfare benefit plans to help the dependent care plan or other plans pass the tests.

If the nonstatutory route is selected, the plan must meet these tests: The average benefit to the lower-paid employee must be at least 55 percent of the average benefit received by the higher-paid employee. If this plan is combined with a salary reduction agreement (see CODA in chapter 15), employees with pay of $25,000 or less are excluded from the test.

Subsidized Food Services   Many companies provide employee dining facilities. Furnishings and equipment range from benches and vending machines to elaborate cafeteria services. Some organizations now allow their employees to order food to take home for their evening meal. Most food operations are nonprofit, and vending machine profits usually go into some type of additional employee benefits fund. Some firms provide food services below cost and absorb these costs because they consider that well-fed employees are healthier and, thus, able to work more effectively. This is one of the most sought-after company-provided services.

A common feature in smaller companies, offices, and the service type of business is free coffee, soft drinks, and snacks. Some firms have set up free coffee and soft drink stands and eliminated the traditional coffee break in an attempt to minimize some of its adverse effects. For example, the normal scheduling of coffee breaks frequently occurs when the work efficiency cycle of the employee is at its highest peak, and the break destroys this cycle.

Discounts on Merchandise   Many firms, on their own or in conjunction with merchandising businesses, provide discounts for employees on a large range of products. In addition, businesses that produce desirable products frequently make them available to employees at a liberal discount. Some organizations have equipment that some employees find extremely useful. When replacing it, instead of selling to companies involved in the resale of such equipment, the organization offers it to employees. The price is usually about what the organization would receive for it on the used equipment or used machinery market.

Physical Awareness and Fitness Programs   More and more organizations are now providing educational and training programs to help participants enhance their understanding of what they must do to improve their physical and emotional health. In addition, some organizations provide facilities and even grant time off to participate in physical fitness activities.

Social and Recreational Opportunities   Social and recreational opportunities are probably the oldest of the benefits and the ones that cause the greatest concern over whether benefits are worth the costs. These programs include the annual summer picnic and Christmas party, company-sponsored athletic events, dancing clubs, card and game parties, craft activities, and social service activities that provide a valuable solution to a community need. The major considerations an employer faces here are the following:

1. Do employees really want them?
2. How many will benefit?
3. Are activities sufficiently varied to cover the diversity of employee desires?

With extended amounts of time off and greater employee interest in travel, many organizations work with travel agencies to acquire flight and tour services at reduced costs so that employees may have additional leisure-time services.

Parking   Over the years, many companies have provided parking facilities; those in downtown areas frequently pay for employee parking. Because parking has become an ever-increasing and irritating problem, employees give this benefit high priority. Employees involved in carpooling frequently receive preferential parking treatment.

Transportation to and from Work   As transportation costs increase, employers are becoming involved in various benefits to help reduce employee transportation costs. In some areas, large employers have supported commuter bus services that operate between the company facility and selected stops close to the residences of many employees. Other employers provide mileage allowances for employees who carpool or share with the employee in the cost of public transportation.

Travel Expenses   Employees who use their own automobiles while performing work assignments may receive a specified allowance or a mileage reimbursement. These employees normally receive reimbursement for all toll and parking expenses. Many employees who travel on company business may also receive either a food and entertainment allowance or reimbursement for all such incurred expenses.

Clothing Reimbursement/Allowance   When dangers are inherent in the job, some companies require employees to wear safety clothing, which they provide at either no cost or a discount, or they may grant an allowance that the employee can use to purchase the necessary clothing. This minimizes the costs related to accidents and also saves on the wear and tear on personal clothing. In addition, many employers grant an allowance for or provide work clothing (coveralls) to employees involved in rough and/or dirty work. In recent years, many service-related organizations have provided employees with well-styled career clothing. There is often a choice among a number of daily apparel options. Employees sometimes participate in the original design and selection of the items. The management of airlines, restaurants, banks, hotels, automobile rental agencies, and the like, feel that career clothing permits the public to identify more easily with their employees. Well-styled, free clothing in which the employees have selection opportunities overcomes some of the dissatisfactions they may have about wearing uniforms.

Tool Reimbursement/Allowance   Organizations hiring employees to do specific kinds of work that requires the use of small or hand tools frequently reimburse employees who must purchase these tools to do their work assignments or grant an allowance for tool purchases.

Relocation Expenses   Many organizations are attempting to reduce the number of transfers of their employees, but it is still necessary occasionally to move employees from one location to another. Moving is frequently a traumatic experience for a family. To ease the burden, employers not only pay the cost of moving the household goods and the family but also frequently provide financial assistance in selling the previous residence and buying the new one. Companies use many different procedures. In some cases, they purchase the old home, and in others they provide a fixed fee for any differences incurred in mortgage costs. Another procedure involves the development of an "eligibility schedule," which lists the reimbursement a transferred employee receives. The amount depends on the length of residence at the previous location and any cost-of-living differential between the previous and new locations. These payments are made over a number of years.[37]

Emergency Loans   A service some employees find very useful is the opportunity to obtain emergency loans at little or no interest. To minimize the abuse of such a privilege, limits are set on the size and the number of times an employee can obtain such loans.

Credit Unions   Normally, credit unions are separate businesses made up of members of a particular company or group of companies to provide benefits for the members. Credit unions are organized in a number of ways, but one of the more common ways is that each employee of a company who wishes to become a member must purchase a share of stock for $5 to $10. This stock and additional savings deposits accrue interest at a rate determined by the board of directors. Quite often, members can make savings deposits through payroll deduction plans (in most cases, interest begins on the first day of the month of the deposit) as well as through direct deposits (if made by the tenth of the month, direct deposits draw interest from the first, otherwise from date of deposit).

Any employee who is a member of the credit union can apply for loans at a rate determined by the board of directors. Loan eligibility terms and loan rate of interest are normally more favorable than those offered by commercial institutions.

Housing   With the high cost of housing, some organizations (frequently those with available and choice property) are building homes, condominiums, and rental units for a select group of their employees. Rental costs or purchase prices are normally below existing market prices. Employers use this service to attract individuals who might otherwise be reluctant to join or remain with the organization.

Perquisites

To maximize the time available to key executives for business-related purposes and, at the same time, enhance the quality of their lives, many highly desirable and special benefits and services are made available. These benefits and services are frequently grouped under the title of perquisites (perks). Perquisites are usually restricted to the CEO and that small group of key officials who comprise the senior management of the organization. In addition to the status relationship, perquisites provide benefits that either are not considered as earned income to the recipient or are taxed at a very modest level. The amount of tax liability incurred by the recipient depends to a significant

---

[37]Raymond W. Speck, Jr., "Tailoring the 'Extras' That Go with Transfers," *Compensation Review,* First Quarter, 1970, pp. 29–35.

degree on the design and the structure of the specific perquisite plan. The Tax Code definition of income includes moneys, property, and services received for services provided. Since the late 1970s, the IRS has recognized more "perks" as imputed income and has required organizations to place a value on them.

A brief description of some of the more common perks are identified in chapter 16.

FUNDING BENEFITS THROUGH A VEBA

A funding vehicle used by many organizations to reduce benefit costs is the Voluntary Employee Benefits Association (VEBA). A VEBA is a tax-exempt trust designed to meet the specific needs of an organization. Both employer and employee contributions are turned over to the trustee of the fund. The trustee then pays benefit claims and expenses and invests excess funds. Employer contributions to the fund are deductible business expenses, and benefits are usually not considered taxable income to the employee members of the VEBA. The trust can accumulate funds tax free.

To operate under 501(a) of IRC, the fund must meet the following requirements:

1. The organization is an association of employees.
2. The membership of the employees into the association is "voluntary."
3. The organization is operated only for the purpose of providing for life, sickness, accident, or other benefits for its members and their dependents.
4. No part of the net earnings of the organization (other than payment of life, sickness, accident, or other benefits) goes to the benefit of any private shareholder or individual.

VEBA reduces benefits costs by (1) having lower operating expenses than insured programs, (2) requiring small reserves, and (3) paying minimal to no state insurance premium taxes (frequently 2 to 4 percent of net premium). VEBAs are frequently used to fund long-term disability plans and retired life insurance reserves (reserve fund for future insurance premiums after retirement). They can also be established to provide vacation benefits, recreational benefits and facilities, child care facilities, severance payments, and educational benefits.

Other specialized trusts are the Supplementary Unemployment Compensation Trusts [SUB or 501(c)(17)] and the Group Legal Service Trusts [GLST or 501(c)(20)]. The SUB trust is used to fund SUB programs, and GLSTs fund group legal plans.

Both DEFRA and TRA 86 place limitations on employer deductible contributions and accumulation of tax-free reserves. To ensure IRS approval of VEBAs, SUB trusts, and GLSTs, employers must meet nondiscriminatory tests similar to those established for various welfare benefits plans. A plan must not discriminate in favor of highly paid employees. DEFRA also imposes limits on amounts set aside on a tax-exempt basis in a VEBA, SUB, or GLST. These welfare benefit trusts must make certain that employers do not receive a refund, credit, or additional benefits based on their claims, administrative costs, or investment experience. VEBAs are also prohibited from funding retiree health benefits. However, legislation has been proposed that would permit employer-deductible contributions and tax-free buildup assets in a *voluntary retiree health plan* (VRHP—pronounced VERP). Retired employee health insurance has been one of the major benefits cost issues of the late 1990s and will continue to be a problem into the twenty-first century. It has been estimated that private employers who provide retiree health benefits may be liable for an estimated $60 billion in unfunded commitments to retirees.[38] (See discussions of retiree medical issues earlier in this chapter.)

COSTING BENEFITS

A central issue relating to the communication of benefits to employees is that many organizations have never performed an in-depth cost analysis of their programs and so have never developed accurate and valid figures to describe them. Costing is an absolutely essential prerequisite to any worthwhile benefits communication program.

Four methods are available for costing benefits and services. Although each has a particular value, it is frequently more effective to combine two or more. The four commonly used costing methods are the following:

1. Annual cost of benefits and services for all employees.
2. Cost per employee per year.
3. Percentage of payroll (annual cost divided by annual payroll).
4. Cents per hour (cost per employee per hour).[39]

Annual Cost   The annual cost method provides total annual cost figures for each benefit. An organization should develop accounting procedures that compute such costs. The continued growth of computerized accounting and bookkeeping procedures will help to capture these costs. This method is especially valuable in developing budgets and in describing the total cost of the benefits program.

Cost per Employee per Year   Simple bookkeeping procedures permit the development of annual costs per employee of particular benefits (especially those benefits and services in the category of pay for time not worked and in some of the employee security and health benefits). However, bookkeeping is more complex for other benefits (particularly those involving group insurance, for example, and components provided to special groups of employees, for example, a bowling team). In these cases, firms must maintain accurate records of total costs of each program per year and of those employees who are recipients. It is then possible to divide the total cost of the program by the number of employees receiving the benefit or the service and to allocate the costs to each employee.

In addition to determining the cost of each benefit, companies may also wish to know the aggregate cost of benefits per employee. Here, the employer simply accumulates the total cost of all benefits and services and divides that figure by the average number of workers employed during the year.

When an employer tells employees of the amount the organization has paid to obtain the annual benefits offered, this figure probably has some impact. However, to achieve the greatest effect, the information should be given to the employees along with a cents-per-hour total and a cents-per-hour breakdown per benefit. (See discussion on communication of employee benefits earlier in this chapter.)

---

[38]"Employers' Liability for Current Retiree Health Care Could Total $60 Billion," *Pension World,* September 1987, p. 39.

[39]Harold Stieglitz, *Computing the Cost of Fringe Benefits: Studies in Personnel Policy,* no. 128 (New York: National Industrial Conference Board, 1952), pp. 4–19.

Percentage of Payroll   Computing the percentage of payroll costs requires a determination of just what the organization includes as payroll costs for work performed. Some firms include only straight-time costs and consider premiums to be part of the benefits costs. This problem emphasizes the importance of identifying and defining benefits and services and often requires major policy decisions by senior management.

After identifying and classifying all compensation costs, nothing more is necessary than a simple mathematical computation to determine the cost of each component and the total cost of benefits and services as a percentage of payroll. This figure is valuable in comparing benefit and service costs with those of other organizations.

Cents per Hour   The cents-per-hour figure also varies among organizations because of the different ways to identify and define the term *hour*. To one organization, hours may mean an arbitrary figure calculated by multiplying the days the organization operated during the year by 8 hours (260 × 8 hours = 2,080 hours); to another company, it may mean the total of actual hours worked by the employee. In the latter case, it is possible to calculate cents per hour by dividing the total benefits costs by the total number of hours worked during the year.

The cents-per-hour method probably is most frequently used in expressing the cost of benefits. It is especially valuable to an organization that must bargain with unions over wages, hours, benefits, and other issues. In discussing the total compensation package, it is then possible to relate direct wage rates to benefits costs and to develop a cost for the total package.

The cents-per-hour method is also valuable in communicating the cost of benefits to employees because they can relate this figure to their hourly pay. The major problem here is that this figure may not have an impact on the employee because it is still a relatively small number. A service worker being paid $6 an hour may not attach much significance to the fact that the company paid $2 in benefits costs for each hour worked. On the other hand, the significance of the benefit may seem greater if the figure is given as $4,160 a year ($2 × 2,080 hours/year).

In 1997 the Chamber of Commerce reported that benefits costs in 1996 were $14,086 per hourly paid employee, and 41.9 percent of payroll.[40]

FLEXIBLE COMPENSATION/BENEFITS PLAN (CAFETERIA PLANS)[41]

The flexible compensation/benefits plan was originally designed to enable senior executives, top professionals, and managers to choose individually many of their benefits and services. Today, however, organizations are looking to flexible compensation/benefits as an opportunity to (1) contain the costs of the benefits package, (2) provide benefits desired by the employee on a more tax-effective basis, and (3) give employees a choice as to the benefits they receive.

---

[40]U.S. Chamber of Commerce, *Employee Benefits—1997 Edition*, Table 4A, p. 14 and Table 17, p. 41.
[41]These kinds of plans were initially called Cafeteria Plans because employees had choices among a number of options. Over the years, "flexible" has replaced "cafeteria." Under IRS regulations, the term *cafeteria* continues to be used.

The flexible benefits plan permits an employee to select benefits and services within certain limits. These include total benefit dollars available and those benefits that are mandatory for all employees because of legal requirements, security needs, or majority rule. Before involving the employee in the selection process, however, the employer must identify the available alternative benefits and services and then determine the cost of each benefit and service as well as a total permissible cost for the entire package.

Basically, the flexible compensation and benefits plan accomplishes four goals that are fundamental to the development of a successful program. It increases or improves employee

1. Appreciation of the interest and desire of the employer to improve the quality of life of each employee.
2. Loyalty and motivation, which, in turn, enhance productivity.
3. Understanding of the value and the cost of each benefit and service component.
4. Understanding of the value and the cost of the total benefits program.

By 1995, over half of all full-time employees in medium and large private establishments were offered flexible benefits plans. The number of firms offering flexible benefits continues to increase each year.[42]

Appreciation of Employer Interest

Although companies and managers are spending more time and money to improve their benefits programs, not enough has been done to inform employees of this effort and to explain its impact on their lives. If employers are to realize any motivational value from the large sums spent on their compensation programs, they must recognize that such spending in itself has little or no motivational value. It is one thing for an employer to exchange pay for the efforts of employees; it is another to develop a variety of procedures that enables workers to have some voice in how they perform their work and in the rewards they receive for their contributions. A central theme of this text is that, through involvement opportunities in well-conceived, well-designed, and well-implemented compensation programs, employees can improve their understanding of why and how they receive rewards for their work.

The rapid increase in benefits offered is no mystery because it is in this segment of the compensation system that the organization has the opportunity to provide some stability to the quality of the worker's life and to promote opportunities for improving it.

To provide these advancement opportunities in the employee's work life, as well as to enhance its stability, management must understand the value and the cost of each part of the compensation system. Unfortunately, the one area in which minimal value and cost analysis has been performed is that of employee benefits—here the "fringe" mentality lingers. Through the communication of the classification and costing of benefits, the employee is able to recognize their true importance and value.

---

[42]*Employee Benefits in Medium and Large Private Establishments, 1995,* U.S. Department of Labor, Bureau of Labor Statistics (Washington, DC: April 1998), p. 143.

To develop a benefit value and cost analysis, organizations must first classify their benefits and services, then identify those available within each classification, and, finally, cost each in terms understood by those involved. After classifying and costing benefits and services, the next step is to provide employees with this information. Informing employees of their opportunities for participating in the selection of available benefits and services increases the motivational value of the benefits program. In taking time to recognize the large amounts of money it spends on benefits, an organization is made more aware of the need to spend some small percentage of these funds in communicating their value and costs to its workers. The flexible compensation benefits plan is ideal for this purpose. It lays the groundwork that enables employees to recognize more fully how important the employer considers them as contributing members and what the employer is attempting to do to improve the quality of their work lives.

Currently, a number of professional organizations are providing benefit analysis services at a reasonable cost that can provide both the organization and its members with critical and valuable benefits information. For example, BeneTrax, a total benefits communication and analysis software tool produced by the U.S. Chamber of Commerce, allows companies to provide their employees with a detailed report that identifies benefit costs and relates these costs to salaries and the total compensation package. It produces a personalized benefits statement for each employee while giving the employer specific costs of each provided benefit.

Worker Expectations and Preferences

Because of increased employer interest in identifying what employees want in the way of benefits and services, researchers are developing new and better ways to examine employee attitudes, expectations, and preferences.

Even when well designed, properly implemented, and carefully analyzed, the traditional attitude survey has inherent weaknesses that make its usefulness questionable. A typical, well-designed survey probes for employee views on specific subjects. In the case of employee attitudes on benefits and services, it focuses on such issues as (1) employee expectations concerning prospective benefits, (2) opinions about the way benefits received compare with those offered by other employers, (3) use and understanding of currently available benefits, and (4) employee desires for currently unavailable benefits.

An attitude survey investigating such issues may use open-ended questions or require the employee to select one of a number of responses such as "strongly disagree," "satisfactory," or "strongly agree." Open-ended questions provide the opportunity to submit a wide range of opinions, but they take much time, both for the respondent to complete and the investigator to review. Forced-choice questions are easy to score, but they limit response opportunities.

A better way to determine employee benefit desires is to use preference surveys. The principal difference between the traditional attitude survey and the preference survey is that in the attitude survey employees normally identify their positions on a subject, whereas in the preference survey they make selections among alternatives.

John Foley, president of Compac Systems, Inc., has developed a preference survey procedure using a series of matrices that require respondents to order by rank their benefit choices among a number of options.[43] The three underlying considerations identified by Foley are valuable to anyone interested in analyzing employee benefit preferences.

1. What does the employee now have? An addition to a currently available benefit is usually less valuable than an entirely new benefit.
2. What can the employee use? Use depends on current lifestyle. It is difficult to identify any long-term utility.
3. What is the employer prepared to provide? This is the primary issue. It relates to what an employer can afford and is willing to offer.

A preference survey requires that more information be provided than that usually offered in an attitude survey. Preference survey design assumes that employees do not have information available at their fingertips. To make choices, they must be able to identify clearly what they must sacrifice in order to gain something else.

Foley states that to obtain high-quality preference information, employees must be treated as intelligent adults. A well-designed survey (1) informs the respondent what the procedure is all about, (2) states how the information will be analyzed, (3) maintains confidentiality, (4) furnishes feedback, and (5) tells respondents what they can expect from the survey.

Because a benefits preference survey relates so closely to employees' current lifestyles, demographic data profiles on respondents are critical (age, gender, marital status, job level in organizational structure). The "here and now" consideration also limits the life expectancy of preference information. Foley states that it is good for about two years. To have any degree of confidence in pay preference data, a sample should include at least 100 respondents.

Benefits preference information reveals that there is no direct relationship between what a benefit costs an employer and the value an employee places on it.[44] In fact, the amount an employer spends on a specific benefit is of little importance to an employee.

Although employee demographic data do reveal some interesting general patterns with respect to benefits preferences, the number of variables having an impact on a group of workers in a given situation makes it difficult to identify any fixed pattern of responses or to assume that the responses of one group would be those of another group. A major difficulty here is that employee values are conditioned by the opportunities available to a specific employee at any point in time.

Another approach used for obtaining employee inputs to the design of a flexible compensation program is through the use of a focus group. Some progressive organizations have found that one or more focus groups of employees representing various groups of employees can be given in-depth instruction on existing benefits, benefits that could be made available, and benefits offered by competitors. This training could include strengths and weaknesses of each benefit, its value, and cost. The focus group then makes recommendations that would represent the entire organization.

---

[43]Presentation by John Foley at the American Compensation Association Eastern Regional Meeting, Atlanta, GA, May 12, 1977.
[44]Wilbur G. Lewellen and Howard P. Lanser, "Executive Pay Preferences," *Harvard Business Review,* September–October 1973, pp. 115–122.

Micro Approach

By allowing employees to select their level of benefits as well as the composition of these benefits, both management and specialists can gain a better understanding of what employees want in their package and how benefits can satisfy some of their needs.

It is highly unlikely that one program will satisfy all or even a majority of employees. Young married workers may value some type of maternity or paternity benefit and child care, whereas older employees look for a pension plan that will provide reasonable security. A single female may be interested in a travel club, but an older bachelor may place far more value on a stock option. Members of two-earner families certainly do not require identical or even similar benefits from their employers, even when they work for the same employer. Is it possible to develop a benefits program that reflects the needs and the values of each employee?

The Mix   Any such plan must contain *nonoptional* items, including the mandated benefits of Social Security, workers' compensation, and unemployment insurance, as well as certain group life, health, medical, accident, and pension plans that require full participation before an insurance company will provide them. These items form a core group.

Most likely, there will be a set of *semioptional* items, including benefits provided principally by insurance companies (or other companies in certain areas) for which they charge a flat rate after analyzing certain organizational features. For example, if an insurance company offers a flat fee for life insurance but more of the older employees select this option, the skewed distribution may require a change in the rate. An answer is to change the rate relative to the age of the applicants or to make the benefit nonoptional if it is desired by many employees. (A major drawback for flexible benefits from the perspective of insurance companies is that when employees have the opportunity to select insurance programs or options, only employees most in need will select a specific program or option. Such employee choice behavior, which is called *adverse selection,* will cause the cost of the program or option to skyrocket. Adverse selection has not been a major problem with flexible benefits plans that have been implemented to date.)

Optional items include many of the components previously listed. Whether the components are nonoptional, semioptional, or optional, each will carry a price tag. Employees can choose the component they desire within total cost limits set by the organization. This micro approach permits employees to weigh the cost and value of each component against every other component.

Another approach in developing a flexible benefits program is to design it around a Section 125 spending account. These stand-alone programs are differentiated from a full flexible plan that includes choices in the areas of medical, dental, long-term disability, employee and dependent life, AD&D, vacation trading, and Section 125 spending accounts for health, dependent care, and other approved services. There is a further discussion of a flexible spending account later in this chapter.

Macro Approach

The flexible or cafeteria benefits plan does not give management the right to abdicate its responsibility to develop and present a benefits and services program that provides each employee with a certain degree of security and opportunity for growth. No doubt, the flexible benefits plan will emphasize for many employees its micro aspects, but it will also understate its overall impact. A number of procedures are open to organizations for minimizing this negative effect. First, administrative costs will prevent employees from changing benefits at will. Employers must establish time schedules for stopping or exchanging benefits.

Second, organizations will probably have to expand their benefits counseling program to advise employees about the value of benefits and to assist them in making selections that are in their own best interests. This service could be the beginning of a broader and more valuable full-service counseling program that could bring employer and employee closer together.

Establishing a Flexible Compensation/Benefits Plan

Much planning and deliberation are necessary before a flexible benefits plan is started. A number of groups must have a voice in its initial design. Three major groups that must participate are (1) senior management (for setting objectives and determining policy), (2) compensation and human resources specialists (for guiding the development of and assisting in the construction of a program that meets organizational objectives and the perceptions and demands of the employees), and (3) the employees (for providing initial inputs about what should be included in a benefits program, ranking by value, and, finally, making choices).

Senior Management   Senior managers must first decide what they would like their benefits program to accomplish. If it is to provide essential security needs, they must define what these needs represent to employees at a point in time. Should the program provide security for today? Or should it include tomorrow and many tomorrows? Should it cover only the employees, or also their immediate families? Should it cover practically all health-related problems? Should it cover legal and financial problems? Should it include social and leisure activities?

After considering these issues, policymakers can outline the kinds and the depth of benefits they wish to provide. With increasing interest in employee participation in the benefit selection process, policymakers now must decide whether to permit such employee selection. They must then determine the limits of the benefits package (nonoptional versus optional and total cost of package).

Another policy decision relates to whether employer and employee share the costs. What contribution, if any, will the employee make for each benefit? How much can the employer afford to pay?

Many benefits have eligibility requirements built into their initial design; others have government restrictions; still others have organizational requirements. Determining who qualifies, the length of service requirements, and the quality and the quantity of benefits are all policy decisions.

Compensation Specialists   Compensation specialists form the functional group that spearheads the task force. The task force, consisting of members from throughout the organization, is responsible for developing data and information that assist senior management in making correct decisions. These decisions, in turn, provide the groundwork for developing a workable and acceptable benefits program.

The task force includes many specialists. Some are experts in project management with experience in directing the planning, operations, and control efforts of a variety of individuals with a variety of interests and skills toward the accomplishment of predetermined objectives and goals. Others are systems and computer software specialists who have expertise in developing systems and providing mechanisms for collecting, analyzing, and disseminating a wide variety and masses of data. Also included are specialists who have expertise in the financial and accounting areas of the organization. There are legal specialists who understand the implications of specific benefits that must comply with certain state or federal statutes. And there are external benefits specialists who have specialized knowledge of the particular benefits under review.

Employees   Through a variety of mechanisms (counseling, attitude and preference surveys), employees provide operating management (including the task force) and senior management with their thoughts on the kinds and the variety of benefits and services needed and their priorities.

To ensure acceptance by employees, significant attention must be given to information programs to expand and improve employee understanding of the value and strength of a flexible benefits program.

In recent years, some companies have used live telemeetings. They broadcast to employees in scattered locations through the use of satellite video equipment. A two-hour telemeeting conducted by New York Life Insurance Company consisted of live presentations by human resources specialists and pretaped vignettes with colorful graphics, ending with a live question and answer period. Other communication methods used by New York Life include a series of newsletters, an enrollment kit, a telephone hot line, and an interactive software disk. The disk allows employees to compare options, calculate costs for different combinations of benefits, and estimate the effect of various choices in their take-home pay. New York Life found the disk to be extremely popular. They estimated that 70 percent of the employees used the disk.[45]

Collecting Data   Data may be collected in a number of ways. If the organization is not too large and has a relatively homogeneous workforce in one general location, it is possible to begin with an attitude or preference questionnaire developed initially by the task force. The form can secure and rank data on the benefits desired by the workforce. If the organization is large, it may be necessary first to study the work group through an analysis of such characteristics as

Age	Spouse eligibility or opportunity for benefits
Gender	Number of dependents and their ages
Base salary	Amount and sources of other income
Step or location in pay grade	Years of service
Geographic location	Years on present job
Marital status	Bonus eligibility
Employed spouse	

By using a number of these characteristics, it is possible to develop a stratified random sample of the entire work group that can provide the task force with a good idea of employee expectations, perceptions, and demands.

---

[45]*On Flexible Compensation* (Chicago: Hewitt Associates, January 1992), pp. 4, 5.

Depending on convenience as well as on time and cost considerations, the sample group can meet with members of the task force or provide benefit needs and priority data through a questionnaire. From data collected through the stratified random sample, it is then possible to develop a questionnaire that can be used by 100 percent of the workforce.

Administration   In 1984, Hewitt Associates offered FlexSystem,™ a computerized system for flexible benefits programs. This program permits employer access on a time-sharing basis for such administrative functions as enrolling applicants, maintaining transaction histories, recording contribution accruals, processing claims, and handling disposition of unused funds at year end. The system can also prepare account balance statements for employees, process new hires and terminations, update employee coverage, and add new employee groups. It can also issue a variety of employer-valued reports.

Changes in Legislation   The Revenue Act of 1978 and the Miscellaneous Revenue Act of 1980 provide additional options to flexible benefits plans. The 1978 legislative changes make it possible for eligible employees to select between cash or other currently taxable compensation components or one or more nontaxable components (medical expense insurance, group life insurance plans, disability insurance) and only those components subject to taxes are taxable. (Prior to 1978, having the option to select taxable items could make the entire benefits program taxable.)

The 1980 act further broadened flexible benefits opportunities by granting with this kind of plan the option of having cash or deferred profit sharing arrangements. This enables companies to offer employees a choice under qualified stock bonus or profit-sharing plans between currently taxable cash payments or tax-free deferrals that become taxable when actually paid.

However, DEFRA restricted the benefits that can be offered under a flexible benefits plan. It permits employers to offer only tax-free benefits. Rollovers or cash paybacks of unused benefits to finance future benefits are prohibited. This 1984 legislation was designed to block employers from providing employees with tax-free income. The legislation allows most current tax-free benefits to remain in effect, but it does make it more difficult to qualify new benefits as tax free.

DEFRA noted that cash, group term life insurance for employees and dependents, accident and health coverage, dependent care assistance, deferrals into 401(k) plans, and vacations can be offered to participants in a cafeteria plan. Benefits that cannot be offered are any noncash benefit that is taxable income to the employee, scholarships and fellowships, van pooling, educational assistance, employee discounts, free parking, and meals and lodging furnished for the convenience of the employer. TRA 86 clarified a major issue regarding cafeteria (flexible) benefits plans. This issue concerned the "taxability" of qualified benefits if the employee has the right to select between taxable and nontaxable benefits under a cafeteria plan. TRA 86 notes that the constructive receipt rule does not apply to a cafeteria plan unless it discriminates in favor of the highly compensated as to either eligibility or benefits.

Other TRA 86 clarifications and requirements are these:

1. A cafeteria plan includes all plans that offer a choice between two or more benefits consisting of cash and qualified benefits, or two or more qualified benefits.

Qualified benefits include health, group term life (including amounts over $50,000), disability, 401(k), and any other benefits permitted under the regulations.

2. Salary reduction [e.g., 401(k)] included within a cafeteria plan is not subject to FICA or FUTA taxes.

3. No more than 25 percent of nontaxable benefits provided under a cafeteria plan may be provided to the highly paid.

Examples of Flexible Compensation Programs

Coopers & Lybrand, a national accounting consulting firm, has identified five basic flexible compensation plans: (1) the modular plan, (2) the core plan, (3) the benefits bank, (4) the unlimited choice plan, and (5) the mini-flex plan.[46]

The *modular plan* consists of "modules" or packages of benefits. All of the modules have the same kinds of benefits but offer various kinds of coverage. A major strength of this plan is that it is relatively simple and easy to administer. A major disadvantage is that *adverse selection* may occur (only employees with the greatest need select a specific option and those who may make minimal use do not select it).

The *core plan* provides a certain core of benefits to all employees and then offers a certain number of benefit dollars to purchase additional benefits. This kind of plan requires in-depth analysis to establish proper pricing.

The *benefits bank* is a modification of the core plan. Only a core package of benefits is provided and all savings between the cost of the core package and the cost of the original benefits package is placed in a bank. Each employee receives a certain dollar credit that permits him or her to purchase a variety of compensation components. This plan may provide the best opportunity for cost containment.

The *unlimited choice plan* grants each employee a fixed dollar amount of credit and all available benefits are priced. The employee then matches available funds with selected benefits. There is no core of benefits. This plan may be very dangerous because employees may not select proper or adequate protection. (It is possible that a survivor of an employee who died without having selected life insurance coverage as an option could sue the employer for the amount available but not selected.) It also fails to recognize the costs incurred by the employer in providing government-required benefits.

The *mini-flex plan* uses salary reduction to pay the employees' share of contributory benefits. This allows employees to make contributions with pretax dollars rather than after-tax dollars. The plan is easy to administer but does not offer employees a choice of the benefits.

A. S. Hansen, an actuarial and management consulting firm that is now part of William M. Mercer, Inc., developed a plan called flexcomp. As in the mini-flex plan, employees may elect to convert a portion (up to 10 percent) of their annual base salary into flexible dollars by taking advantage of 401(k) salary reduction opportunities.

The salary reduction money contributed to flexcomp escapes federal and, when applicable, state and local income tax. Vacation days in excess of five days may also be converted into flexible dollars in whole-day increments. Finally, if the deductible on the

[46]National Technical Services Unit, *Flexible Compensation: Giving Employees a Choice* (Washington, DC: Coopers & Lybrand, 1983).

medical-dental program is increased, the savings in the cost of the plan can produce flexible dollars. The flexible dollars for each employee can then be deposited in a "bank"—a special employee expense account (SEEA). Each employee can accumulate up to $10,000 in his or her SEEA.

A wide range of compensation components can be purchased with flexible dollars or through the flexible dollars in the SEEA. They range from payment of the deductible part of the medical-dental plan to legal expenses to financial planning to child care. Flexible dollars can be used directly to purchase extended sick leave or they can be deposited in a savings and profit sharing plan, which operates very much like an IRA and is a qualified retirement plan. (The options available in this kind of plan must be carefully reviewed because of the restrictions established in 1984 tax legislation that prohibit using rollovers and cash paybacks of unused benefits to finance future benefits.)

Employee Spending Accounts—IRC, Section 125, Plans

An addition to the benefits field that may be used in place of or added to a flexible benefits program is the employee spending account (ESA). The ESA is a tax-free reimbursement account designed to moderate or possibly reduce the rising cost of benefits for the employee while at the same time giving the employer greater control over benefit expenditures. Employees who qualify for an ESA are normally permanent employees working more than 1,000 hours per year. Since enactment of IRC, Section 125, in 1978, and further clarifications in 1984, employees are allowed to convert a portion of taxable wages or salaries into nontaxable dollars to be used to pay for specific benefits. While reducing their taxable income, they can use the funds to pay for (1) medical expense reimbursement (including dental and optometry); (2) premiums for accident, health, hospitalization, disability, and group term or universal life insurance; (3) dependent care assistance; (4) legal services; and (5) personal financial planning. This program permits organizations to shift some of the premium costs and increase deductibles and copayments without serious financial burdens to employees. Also, when employees place these funds into an ESA, neither the employee nor the employer must pay Social Security tax, and the employer escapes FUTA tax on this money.

The IRS requires that employees who are granted the opportunity to participate in such a plan (1) make any election before the beginning of the plan year; (2) not change elections during the plan year except in case of change in family status (divorce, death); (3) make separate elections for medical expenses and other services such as dependent care and legal benefits; (4) use elected benefits in the plan year and forfeit any unused amount in an elected category at the end of the plan year (rollovers for contributions into 401(k) plans or taking cash of leftover elections are prohibited).

Family-Oriented Benefits

The 1990s witnessed ever-increasing employer controls to reduce the growth of benefits packages. One group of benefits, however, is receiving favorable employer support. This group is called *family-oriented benefits*. Family-oriented benefits include such previously mentioned items as (1) employee assistance (EA) programs, (2) child and elderly care assistance, (3) paternity leave, (4) adoption expenses, (5) long-term care, and (6) living benefits (life insurance benefits paid to the terminally ill). These benefits have been discussed earlier in this chapter. In addition, family-oriented programs may include such organization design and policy related issues as (1) flexible hours and (2) work-at-home opportunities. Flexible benefits, Section 125 options, and VEBAs permit such highly desirable family-oriented benefits to grow without unacceptable costs to the employer. Employers then benefit by being able to attract and retain staff that, in turn, reduces recruiting and training costs for new employees and results in improved productivity.

Basic Issues

Senior management has the responsibility for determining the total value of benefits and approving the percentage breakdown of this total into optional and nonoptional items. Senior management must also determine the number of optional components and the monetary value that an employee may select (in this case, such criteria as a percentage of base income or a fixed amount per year by length of service and base income are useful).

Other questions that usually have to be resolved in flexible benefits plans are these:

1. Will the flexible benefits plan comply with Internal Revenue Service standards by not discriminating in favor of highly compensated employees and by providing only legal tax-free benefits?
2. Will overloading the plan with nonoptional items to guarantee employee security negate the intent and the value of the plan, leaving few opportunities for individual choice?
3. Will the plan recognize change in employee basic levels of pay during the benefit year?
4. Will the plan recognize change in employee dependents or marital status?
5. Will the plan recognize changes in premium or benefit cost?
6. When, during the year, will an employee be permitted to make changes in a benefit?

Summary

Employee benefits protect employees in case of health-related problems and provide income at some future date or occasion. Employee services fill various kinds of employee demands; they enable employees to enjoy a better lifestyle and help them to meet social and personal obligations.

Since the end of World War II, employee benefits and services have increased in importance as part of the total compensation package. In fact, they have increased to such an extent that, in some cases, the benefit components cost the employer more than the wage payments, including base wages, premiums, and differentials. There appears to be no end to the kind and amount of benefits employees seek. Income taxes continue to take a big bite of earned income and employees recognize the value of having the employer provide benefits that, if purchased, would require the expenditure of after-tax dollars.

With the changes brought about through legislation, the federal government is taking an active role in promoting greater use of flexible benefits plans that will also increase the desirability and motivational value of the benefits package. At the same time, compensation managers must take advantage of every available option to bring the rapidly escalating costs of the benefits package under control.

Review Questions

1. With benefits consuming approximately 40 percent of the compensation dollar of most organizations, among many managers the "fringe benefit" concept still exists. Develop a detailed outline of the various components of a typical benefits program, indicating their importance and scope. Develop the outline so that it may be used as a presentation.
2. Analyze benefits from the point of view of (1) employee security and health, (2) time not worked, and (3) employer-provided services. Describe some of the major items within each of these components.
3. Describe opportunities available to management to contain health care costs.
4. Describe what you believe to be some of the more important employee benefits offered by an employer. Why?
5. Describe various methods for costing benefits. Why may it be necessary to use more than one costing method?
6. What is a flexible or cafeteria benefits plan? What hurdles must be overcome before such plans will achieve greater acceptance and use? What impact does the Revenue Act of 1978 have on flexible benefits plans?

C H A P T E R

Pay Delivery Administration

Learning Objectives

In this chapter you will learn about:

1. The organizational budgeting process.

2. Individuals who have direct influence on the budgeting process.

3. The relationship between pay structure change and market conditions.

4. Adjusting employee pay to changes in the market.

5. Tools that can be used for compensation planning and administration.

6. The influence of compensation on QWL programs.

7. The meaning of due process and its effect on organizations.

Compensation Strategy

Maintain and adapt compensation programs to ensure alignment with marketplace practices and recognition by employees of the connection between workplace practices and organizational performance.

O nce hired, and after working for a week or at the most a month, the employee receives a paycheck for work performed. Experience is gained from performing job assignments and with continuing orientation to the organization and its various reward practices. As a result, the employee develops a unique view of the relationship between pay and the assigned job, pay and performance, pay as a part of the total compensation package, and compensation as a part of total membership rewards.[1]

---

[1]Donald J. Petrie, "Explaining the Company's Pay Policy," *Personnel,* November–December 1968, pp. 20–26.

Pay and compensation policy now become real and important considerations. The employee begins to search for answers to such basic questions as the following:

1. When is the next pay day?
2. When is the first increase possible?
3. What are the criteria for raises?
4. What are the eligibility requirements for vacations?
5. How long is the first vacation?
6. How many paid holidays are there? What are they? Are there eligibility requirements?
7. What are the criteria for promotions?
8. Are cost-of-living adjustments provided?
9. How are overtime opportunities determined?
10. Is an employee's pay ever reduced?

Answers to these questions help to acquaint the employee with the organization. After they have been answered, a second group of questions arises that affects worker performance and organizational productivity and profitability even more critically. The employee now recognizes that the job not only dictates a standard of living, but it also defines the social status and economic worth of the individual. Among such questions are these:

1. Is this a regular, full-time job?
2. Will the job and its rewards offer income security?
3. Will the job and its rewards provide a satisfying lifestyle?
4. Does the job permit extra effort, and will the organization recognize special contributions?
5. Will the job provide opportunity for self-growth and career development?
6. Do the job and its rewards compare favorably with those available in this area, or in this profession, or in this line of work?

Organizational success depends to a significant degree on the assumptions and the expectations employees develop concerning the intellectual, emotional, and physical efforts they exert and the rewards they receive for improving productivity of the organization.

TYING IT ALL TOGETHER

The reasons behind the time and the costs expended in designing and implementing job analysis, job evaluation, compensation surveys, pay structures, pay-for-performance programs, including short- and long-term incentives, and benefits packages now become apparent. The employer must pay the employee for services rendered. A compensation program that develops internal equity, permits the organization to compete in the labor market, and stimulates employees to exert extra effort has a bottom line meaning—fair pay to employees and, it is hoped, profit to the organization.

Skilled administrators keep a well-designed compensation program alive and current and improve those parts of it that do not meet employer needs and employee demands.

Above and beyond all other influences, the amount of money an organization is able to spend for compensating its employees is the limiting factor. A new organization in a competitive environment may have only limited funds. One in a monopolistic situation may have fairly substantial amounts for this purpose. Many employers feel that the more they restrict these costs, the greater will be their opportunity to increase profit.

Some industries have traditionally paid their employees low rates of pay. Employees in these industries have, at times, made demands for pay increases that must be covered by increases in the price of goods and services. If the consumers of the goods and services are not willing to pay the increased prices, the employer may be forced out of business. Other firms have exceedingly high markup (profit potential) on their output and are able to pay employees at much higher levels than those that operate within very narrow profit constraints.

A small percentage change in human resources costs can result in a significant change in profitability. Although a difficult issue, personnel costs and their relationship to productivity and profitability still provide greater opportunities for employer influence than almost any other cost of doing business.

For most companies, human resources costs consume much of the money available for staying in business. For the average company, these costs consume between 35 and 45 percent of total revenues. For labor-intensive, service-sector organizations, human resources costs may easily exceed 60 percent, whereas for some industries that are capital-intensive and spend a major share of income on raw material, preassembled products, and plant, human resources costs may drop to 10 to 15 percent. Whether 15 percent or 60 percent, these costs have a significant impact on organizational profitability. The proper design and administration of the compensation program is, therefore, very important.

Employee confidence in the stability and the fairness of the compensation system develops by setting pay levels that ensure each person a rate of pay and total compensation that are internally fair compared with that received by every other member and externally competitive with that received by others performing similar jobs in other organizations in relevant labor markets. Serious differences in pay levels (either internally or externally) often result in the (1) loss of competent employees to other organizations providing better compensation opportunities, (2) inability to attract qualified personnel, and (3) destruction of a work environment that stimulates superior performance.

Because of the many parts of a compensation system, it is inherently complex; yet it must be made as understandable as possible to all employees. Its administration can increase the system's complexity, or it can be a positive force toward increasing understandability. All employees should be aware of what the organization is providing in money and in-kind payments to obtain their services. They should know why they are receiving these payments, how they are determined, who makes the determinations, when payments are available, and what opportunities are available to each employee to influence the amount.

Of all the processes with which compensation becomes involved, possibly no single one is more important than the activities that make inputs into organizational budgets. Through the budgeting process, a significant part of the financial resources is allocated to personnel costs.

Cost allocations for human resources take many forms and frequently compete for the limited funds of the organization. Compensation managers should have a major influence on the allocation of funds for human resources to such diverse areas as base pay, benefits, and incentive programs. It is not only critical that allocations be correctly proportioned among these areas, but also that proper decisions be made among allocations to various compensation components within each area.

THE BUDGET PROCESS

Compensation personnel have an important role to play in the development of the organization's budget. The budget defines how the organization will spend its money for the coming planned period or plan year. Budgets are written plans expressed in terms of dollars or some kind of units (number of employees in a specific department), or both. An organizational budget will include a capital budget, an operating budget, and a cash budget. The operating budget is of primary importance to compensation professionals because it identifies the operating revenues and expenses for the budget period. A significant part of operating expenses is the human resources costs of the organization.[2]

At the topmost levels of the organization, those same individuals who set overall organizational objectives, approve the strategies necessary for achieving these objectives, and establish the policies that act as guidelines for acceptable employee behavior also approve the annual salary budgets. The personnel budget consists of all kinds of staffing-related expenses such as wages and salaries; merit increases; pay structure adjustments; general increases (including cost-of-living adjustments); benefits; upgrades; bonuses, commissions, and other incentives; overtime and other various premiums and differentials; and, frequently, allowances for contract or outside labor.

The Personnel Budget

The *personnel budget* includes all labor costs in gross figures. It identifies the total number of employees in each unit and the money necessary to pay them for the coming budget year. The *merit* or *salary increase budget* normally represents the largest share of the increase in the personnel budget over the preceding year. It permits the organization to reward superior performance and maintain its position in the market relative to its established pay philosophy and policy.

The budget for personnel costs is developed by each operating or division manager and submitted to the controller (chief financial officer—CFO) for consolidation. The controller submits the personnel cost budget, along with all other budgets, with recommendations as to the financial feasibility to the chief operating officer (COO) or to the CEO, depending upon the individual company. The controller's recommendations are the result of reviewing projects and programs for the coming year, projections of revenue, costs involved in producing the revenue, and the compensation committee's desires. The human resources (HR) department, at times, is given the responsibility of overseeing the personnel cost budget after its approval by the CEO or the COO.

---

[2]George W. Torrence, "Who Approves Salary Increases?" *Management Record,* July–August 1960, pp. 11–13; "The Budgeting of Salary Increases," *Management Record,* March 1961, pp. 2–7; "Individual vs. General Salary Increases," *Management Record,* May 1961, pp. 18–20; "Explaining Salary Programs to Salaried Employees," *Management Record,* July–August 1961, pp. 15–17; "Administering Merit Increases for Salaried Personnel," *Management Record,* November 1961, pp. 9–12.

The Compensation Committee   A major organizational unit involved in the development of the personnel budget is the *compensation committee* of the board of directors. A small, select group of usually three to five directors makes up the committee. Although outside members are preferred, it is not unusual to find at least one member who is an employee of the firm. These committee members should be capable of exercising judgment and reasonable care in an area in which conflict of interest may abound. They have significant influence on the compensation received by the chief executive officer and other members of senior management. They may also review the compensation opportunities made available to all employees. However, the compensation committee can exercise almost total authority over the compensation practices of the entire organization.

Compensation personnel may provide the committee with information on current market practices, or the committee may use the services of contracted outside compensation consultants. The compensation committee may perform all or a select group of the following activities:

1. Periodically review and appraise the performance of the chief executive officer and top management.
2. Set compensation for the chief executive officer.
3. Review compensation of competitive companies.
4. Review and approve proposed increases in compensation for officers and directors.
5. Monitor executive perquisites and expenses.
6. Review and approve criteria used for determining amounts of performance-based bonuses for executives.
7. Review general policies and procedures relating to director and officer compensation and total compensation for all employees.
8. Ensure compatibility of the long-term strategic objectives of the corporation and the performance goals used as a base for determining long-term incentive awards.
9. Develop special supplemental awards in cash, stock, or a combination of both for extraordinary accomplishments.
10. Review and approve personnel-related budgets.
11. Report findings to the full board.

Others Involved in Budget Decisions

The *chief executive officer* (CEO) has ultimate responsibility for all decisions made in the operation of the organization. This officer, as final decision maker, reviews, makes recommendations for necessary changes, and approves personnel budgets and all compensation strategies. It is quite possible that a very strong CEO can dominate the board of directors and, in reality, control the entire personnel budget process.

The responsibility for the development of the initial amounts to be described in the personnel budget normally rests in the *finance department* or the *office of the controller,* but at times the HR department is given this responsibility. Financial analysts review projects and programs for the coming year, develop projections of revenue, identify major costs involved in producing outputs that result in revenue, and allocate a certain amount of money to personnel budgets.

Some organizations have established a *salary administration committee,* which typically consists of from three to seven members, usually including the chief financial officer, the senior human resources officer, and other senior management officials. This committee reviews the total budget and makes allocation recommendations and decisions. In analyzing the allocations made to the various major units of the organization, the committee reviews historical records regarding past outputs and incurred human resource costs by department, projected outputs for the coming year, and economic conditions that may affect projected operations. It reviews recommendations made by department heads and supervisors that fall outside the scope of standing operating procedures and gives required approval or makes necessary adjustments. This committee also functions as a review body on existing compensation policy and makes recommendations for necessary changes.

Decisions made by this committee then go to the HR and compensation departments. Specialists now transmit personnel budget opportunities to the respective division or department heads. With the information on funds available for employee compensation, the HR department makes available a variety of information that assists major division or department heads and their subordinate managers in making the best decisions possible for allocating funds to specific groups and units and for individual compensation.

Some organizations have *job evaluation committees,* which usually consist of various management representatives and may also include nonmanagement personnel. Their main responsibility is to ensure internal fairness among jobs by determining job worth according to some evaluation plan. Organizations that have point-factor job evaluation methods frequently use job evaluation committees. Many organizations do not use these committees because they find them slow and cumbersome in operation and too political.

Figure 18–1 describes the flow of compensation information among the various individuals and groups responsible for compensation decisions.

The final step in the determination and the allocation of pay to employees rests with the *immediate supervisor* and his or her *higher-level managers.* Ideally, these individuals usually have the closest contact with the employee. They review the requirements of their units and the performance of the employee. They analyze the performance of each employee relative to established standards and the performance of others and, within limits set by policy or compensation guidelines, recommend the allocation of the merit increase portion of the budget among their subordinates. Table 18–1 describes pay adjustment and promotion recommendation responsibilities.

ADMINISTRATION OF PAY

The administration of pay includes three distinct steps:

1. Providing merit or salary increase budget data and information.
2. Adjusting the pay structure in line with the compensation policy, the market, and the approved merit or salary increase budget for the planned year.
3. Moving employees in the pay grade relative to such factors as (a) level of performance, (b) seniority on the job or in the organization and time since last adjustment, and (c) location in the pay grade.

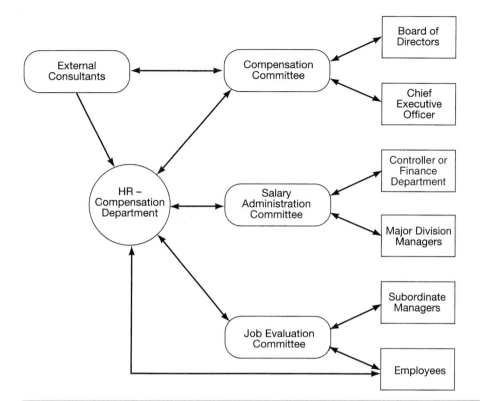

FIGURE 18–1   Possible Compensation Information Flow and Compensation Decision Points

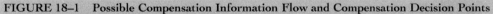

TABLE 18–1   Typical Pay Adjustment and Promotion Recommendation Responsibilities

Immediate supervisor	Appraises performance; makes pay adjustment or promotion recommendations.
Reviewing manager of managers	Reviews recommendations of subordinate supervisors and changes, endorses, approves, or initiates action for pay adjustment and promotion.
Human resources and compensation departments	Reviews department head recommendations for compliance with compensation policy and budget, merit increase, and promotion guidelines. Advises department heads on propriety of actions. Processes all necessary recordkeeping data and information.
Senior management	Grants final approval for all compensation adjustments and job changes. Approves or denies requests that extend beyond policies and guidelines. Approves policy changes. Sets annual personnel budget and department allocations.

Forecasting Personnel Costs

Anywhere from three to eight months prior to the start of the next fiscal year, the HR department is asked to submit a merit, adjustment factor, or salary increase budget for the coming year. Although both salary increase and merit budgets identify projected increases in the personnel budget for the coming year, the term *merit* carries with it a very specific meaning that goes beyond the implication of a salary increase budget. Merit adjustments to employees' pay reflect the employer's desire to recognize performance and to ensure that those who perform in a creditable manner will receive pay that will stay abreast of market changes consistent with the financial condition of the organization. It also implies that the organization does not guarantee the "real" income of its members—it is not providing cost-of-living adjustments. However, if all employees work together and if the organization is able to pay, it will reward through merit pay adjustments those whose contributions have helped the organization reach the level of success it has enjoyed.

The compensation department uses a number of data sources and processes to develop data for making adjustments to the changes that have occurred during the current operating year. One source of data is the marketplace. Surveys that identify past situations and projected changes allow the compensation specialists to make their own determination regarding changes in market levels of pay and the influence the market will have on the merit budget.

Internally, an entirely different set of data requests is initiated. The collection of internal data frequently starts with a request to all department heads to submit a merit budget for their respective departments. To assist these individuals to respond in an acceptable manner, the HR department must instruct managers on how policies and guidelines affect the adjustment of pay of each employee. Pay increase policies and guidelines may cover areas such as (1) employee's position in the pay grade, (2) employee's performance ratings, (3) employee's tenure, (4) the overall pay level of the department, and (5) timing of individual pay adjustments.

Accompanying the request for merit pay data may be an up-to-date list of all employees in the department; their job titles; current rates of pay; pay grade minimums, midpoints, and maximums; and recommended increases. Today, many organizations include all relevant compensation data in computer-based personnel data files. Each department head should be provided with as much pay-related data as necessary.

The department head is requested to list projected pay increases for the next year, identify any employees who are due to be promoted during the coming year, those who are eligible for any special increase (completion of a specific training program that results in an increase in pay), and possibly any other personnel changes that are projected to occur, such as additions, deletions, or, possibly, reclassification of positions.

The requests forwarded by each department head provide only a first estimate of the pay treatment each employee will receive for the coming year. There is no guarantee that all adjustment requests will be granted. The department head also will be able to make adjustments within certain limits once the merit budget is approved and allocations are made to each department, but as just mentioned, a manager may try to force results based on something planned or written at an earlier time.

The department head requests are returned to the HR department, reviewed to assure compliance with established pay policies, and summarized. The summary data, the data generated from market analyses, and the end of year payroll projections are reviewed. From this analysis, the compensation manager recommends the amount of additional merit money that will be needed for updating the pay program and for maintaining a desired competitive position. The merit budget is then sent to the chief financial officer or controller who, after reviewing it for compliance with established policy, forwards it to the chief executive officer for approval.

At the executive level, approval or recommendations for change of the merit budget will be strongly influenced by the profitability of the organization and any changes that may have occurred at this level with respect to their compensation philosophy and policy.

If economic conditions are favorable and the organization's financial position is strong, top management may want to know if additions could or should be made to the merit budget requests. On the other hand, if financial conditions are unsatisfactory, the merit budget could be cut to zero or requests could be made for reductions in the personnel budget, which could mean a negative merit budget.

Using Merit Increase and Pay Structure Survey Data

In the late summer of each year, a number of major consulting companies and associations survey organizations regarding their proposed merit increase budgets for the coming year. They may also collect data on proposed pay structure adjustments and general increases. These data are then reported in the fall of the year. It is during this time that many organizations are developing their various budgets for the coming year. Compensation personnel can use the various surveys to assist in fine-tuning their own merit budget and pay structure adjustment recommendations.

Watson Wyatt Data Services (WWDS)/ECS collects various kinds of budget-related data, along with the pay and benefits data in each of its annual surveys. The Watson Wyatt Data Services/ECS 1998–99 Salary Budget Survey, pages 6 and 10, reported 1998 merit increases for the following employee groups: Officer/Executive–2.7 percent, Exempt Salaried–2.9 percent, Nonexempt Salaried–2.7 percent, and Nonexempt Hourly–2.6 percent. Nonexempt hourly employees were major recipients of general or cost of living (COLA) and step increases. In addition to WWDS/ECS, many local organizations perform annual surveys to provide this kind of information.

Table 18–2 is a compilation of salary budget data for 1998 and 1999. An HR/compensation specialist could use these data to compare the performance of his or her organization with WWDS/ECS-provided prior year actual, budget year, and projected budget data. These kind of data not only assist in making merit budget recommendations, but the value of using data collected by a reputable organization from over 18,000 participants assists in supporting recommendations made to senior management.

The American Compensation Association (ACA) has been conducting total salary increase budget surveys for 25 years. The 1998–1999 survey included data from over 2,900 firms in the United States and Canada. Table 18–3 is a summary of total salary increases for 1997, 1998, and 1999. ACA noted that with more employees being included within variable pay plans and stock offerings, salary growth between 4.0 and 4.5 percent is likely to continue into the coming years.

TABLE 18–2 Average Salary Increase Budgets

Entire Sample Combined/ Employee Group	Average 1998 Salary Increase Granted		Average 1999 Salary Increase Budget	
	Percentage of Salary	*Number of Responses*	*Percentage of Salary*	*Number of Responses*
Executive	5.0%	872	4.3%	859
Exempt	4.4%	1,029	4.1%	1,001
Nonexempt	4.1%	1,034	4.0%	1,013
Overall (All Employee Groups Combined)*	4.3%	987	4.1%	977

*This overall figure was supplied by participants in response to a separate question. It is not calculated from the data supplied regarding the other employee groups.

Source: Watson Wyatt Data Services, Rochelle Park, NJ: Watson Wyatt Worldwide, 1999/2000.

Allocating Merit Budget Funds

After top management approves the merit budget, compensation specialists then have the responsibility of (1) making any necessary changes in the pay structure(s) and (2) allocating the merit budget pool to the various departments of the organization.

Designing Pay Structure Adjustment Most organizations that have an orderly administrative procedure for adjusting the pay structure make such an adjustment once a year. In making pay structure adjustments, organizations have to recognize two issues. The first relates to established compensation policy and the second relates to amount of the approved merit budget.

A strategy that underlies compensation policy concerns how the organization wishes to meet its competitors in the labor market.

Does senior management wish to use its compensation dollars to attract the highest-quality personnel available? It may not be necessary to have superior performers for successful operation. Competent employees with average or even below-average education, experience, skill, interest, and attitudes may be sufficient to meet personnel

TABLE 18–3 Total Salary Budget Increase

	Total Salary Increases				
	Projected 1997	*Actual 1997*	*Projected 1998*	*Actual 1998*	*Projected 1999*
Nonexempt Hourly Nonunion Employees (NHNE)	3.9%	4.1%	4.0%	4.1%	4.1%
Nonexempt Salaried Employees (NSE)	4.1%	4.1%	4.2%	4.2%	4.3%
Exempt Salaried Employees (ESE)	4.1%	4.3%	4.3%	4.5%	4.4%
Officers/Executives (O/E)	4.3%	4.5%	4.4%	4.6%	4.6%

Source: Reprinted from *Report on the 1999–2000 Total Salary Increase Budget Survey* with permission from the American Compensation Association (ACA), Scottsdale, AZ 85260 U.S.A.; telephone (480) 951-9191; fax (480) 483-8352. ©ACA, http://www.acaonline.org <http://www.acaonline.org>.

TABLE 18–4 Pay Posture Guideline Chart

Quality of Personnel Desired	Pay Rate Offered
Superior	Premium—15% to 25% or more above market rates
Above average	Fully competitive—10% to 15% above market rates
Average	Competitive—Meets market rates
Below average	Marginal—10% or more below market rates

needs. The critical demand made by these types of employers is for the employee to be present at work and perform assigned duties.

After identifying what the market rate of pay is for a job or job family, an organization may use the pay posture guideline chart in Table 18–4 to establish its pay schedule. Now the organization makes some decisions relative to the timing of pay structure adjustments. Does it wish to *lead* the market, or pay its employees more than the identified market rate; does it wish to *match* the market, or pay at the "going" rate; or does it wish to *lag* the market, or pay below the established market rate? There are various opportunities available in both pay structure design and administration to accomplish lead, match, lag policy requirements. The organization can set its pay policy (midpoint) line at the 60th or even the 75th percentile of the identified market, in theory paying the average or fully proficient employee a significant percent above the market. A second opportunity arises when determining the time during the plan year for forecasting the market that will be used as the base for determining pay adjustment requests. Will the forecast be based on the market at the beginning, the middle, or the end of the plan year? Because most costs, including most personnel costs, escalate constantly throughout the year, the projected personnel costs at the end of the year will normally be higher than those at the beginning of the year (see Figure 18–2).

1. An annual adjustment to the pay structure that is based on the projected market a year into the future will mean that the organization has a pay level higher than the market throughout the year. This *lead* position diminishes throughout the year until it matches the market at the end of the year.
2. An annual adjustment to the pay structure that is based on the projected market at the middle of the year means that the pay level of the organization will *lead* the market for the first six months and *lag* the market for the second six months, thus theoretically matching the market for the year.
3. When the pay structure is adjusted to the market at the beginning of the year, the pay level of the organization will *lag* the market throughout the year.

This process does not give as precise lead, match, lag data as does the design approach using percentiles. It is effective, however, in relating compensation policy to labor market conditions. Once again, survey data can be extremely useful in identifying relationships in market conditions for making pay structure adjustments. Table 18–3 can provide needed data.

Implementing Pay Structure Adjustment   Following senior management's approval of the merit budget, the compensation administrators are ready to adjust the pay

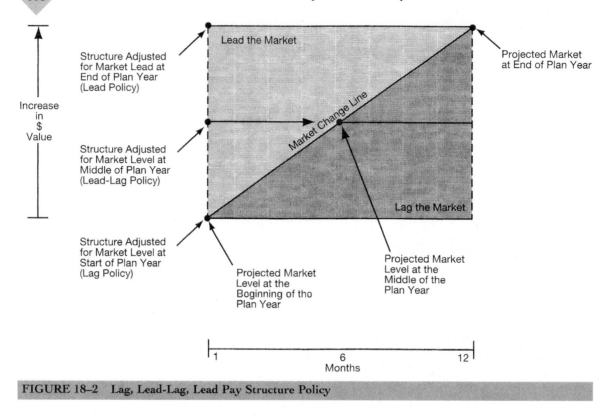

FIGURE 18–2   Lag, Lead-Lag, Lead Pay Structure Policy

structure(s). A good starting point in this process is to calculate the percentage relationship between the approved merit fund and the end-of-year payroll. This percentage or a close approximation may be used to adjust the pay structure. If, for example, after reviewing the merit budget a decision is made to adjust the pay structure by 5 percent, the value of the minimum, midpoint, and maximum rates and the steps within each pay grade are increased by that amount (see Figure 18–3). This procedure grants management room within the structure to upgrade the employee's pay. The employee does not necessarily receive a pay increase of 5 percent; the actual individual increase is a management decision.

Large national organizations may have national, regional, and local pay structures for different groups of employees. National pay structures will most likely include management, sales, and professional employees. Organizations that have regional pay structures are likely to include all groups of employees (managerial, sales, professional, technicians and skilled trades, and administrative support personnel), whereas those with local pay structures focus primarily on jobs in the administrative support, technician, and skilled trades occupations. Some large organizations have separate pay structures for each business unit.

If an organization has multiple pay structures such as previously described or one for the nonexempt, nonsalaried workforce; a second for the nonexempt, salaried work-

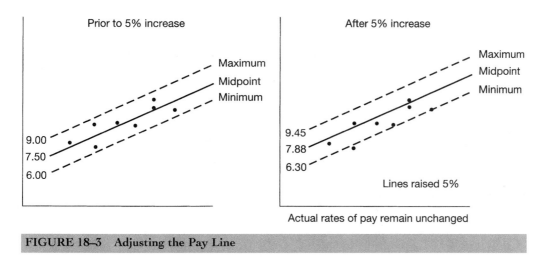

FIGURE 18–3   Adjusting the Pay Line

force; and a third for the exempt workforce, it may make somewhat different adjustments to each structure relative to a perceived imbalance between the specific pay structure and its relevant market. Merit budget adjustments may also differ.

For example, if the overall merit pool provides a 6 percent increase over the previous year's average annual payroll, the nonexempt, nonsalaried pay structure may receive a 4 percent upward adjustment; the nonexempt salaried structure may be moved upward by 5.5 percent; and the exempt structure adjusted upward 6.5 percent. If the compensation manager thinks there are some problems in the design of the pay structure (i.e., range of the grades or midpoint-to-midpoint difference), these adjustments should be made at this time. This pay grade adjustment has *not* at this time resulted in any change in the pay of any employee. When more than one pay structure is used, care must be taken that certain groups of employees are not adversely affected.

Department Allocation of Merit Funds   The next step in the administration process occurs in dividing the merit pool among all the departments. Beginning at this step, the administrative process becomes far more complex. Some organizations may allocate the merit pool among the departments by giving each department a percentage of the merit pool equal to that department's payroll as a percentage of the total payroll of the organization. Many organizations, however, carefully review the pay structure practices of each department. The analysis will include a calculation of the compa-ratio of the department or possibly a compa-ratio analysis of employees in specific pay grades or a compa-ratio using such demographic qualities as compa-ratio within each job or pay grade by race, gender, age, or handicap status. (An in-depth discussion of the compa-ratio and its use for planning and control appears later in this chapter.) A compa-ratio analysis may indicate that one unit or possibly one group of employees is underpaid relative to other groups and that this group should receive larger percentages of the merit pay than they normally would if a distribution were made equal to the unit's share of the total payroll.

Adjusting the Pay of Each Employee   After the CEO approves the merit budget and the HR department has adjusted the pay structure and allocated specific amounts of the merit budget pool to each department, the time arrives to make decisions regarding the amount of pay adjustment to be granted to each employee. Compensation policy guidelines now assume a very critical role in the decisions to be made regarding these pay adjustments.

The major issues that require consideration are the employee's: (1) current level of performance, (2) tenure on present job, (3) common review date or anniversary date—date hired or promoted to present job, (4) date of last adjustment, (5) reason for last adjustment, (6) location in the pay grade—at midpoint, between the 25th and 50th percentile, and so on.

The issues of seniority and merit have been discussed from a variety of viewpoints throughout the text. A well-designed compensation system recognizes and addresses these vital issues. Seniority provides a certain amount of security to all employees. Length of service identifies to some degree loyalty to the organization. Most organizations try through their compensation system to recognize seniority—that is, employee loyalty. The amount of such benefits as vacation time, pensions, and, at times, thrift plans varies directly with increased length of service. In-step pay grade progressions often are tied to time in grade. Many merit plans are misnamed. When 90 to 100 percent of the employees receive a similar merit increase, the likelihood is that the merit plan is truly a seniority plan. When a superior performer receives a 6 percent increase; a commendable performer, 5 percent; and the great majority of the remainder, 4 percent; superior performance, in reality, may be receiving minimal recognition. Organizations would be far better off to call their pay adjustment programs by more appropriate titles. If the program is truly based on seniority, it should be called a seniority or length-of-service plan.

An alternative to tying pay increases to length of service is using a one-time seniority bonus. This practice is becoming more appealing to employers. Such a plan may call for a 5 percent bonus based on highest annual earnings on the anniversary date of completion of five years of service, with possibly a 7.5 percent bonus after 10 years, and a 10 percent bonus after 15 years. A bonus of this size may have a strong incentive impact on the employee. Another advantage is that the organization is not adding seniority to its base pay plan and making seniority payments a permanent part of the employee's base pay.

It is much more difficult to develop a merit pay program based on individual performance. A step in the right direction is the design and the development of an appraisal program that recognizes individual contributions. However, employers must recognize the problems and costs involved in developing reliable and valid performance appraisal procedures and instruments. Chapter 13 discusses this subject in detail. Employers must also recognize that all employees deserve the right to know where they stand and how well they are doing. Some kind of performance appraisal is a necessity for most organizations. Without a formal process, implementation of a merit or pay-for-performance program is almost impossible.

Figure 18–4, a performance-pay grade profile, describes various levels of performance and an incumbent's location in a pay grade. This kind of model can be used to inform both supervisors and employees of the kind of performance and time period necessary to move upward through a pay grade.

Quartiles	Percentiles	Performance Level
Maximum	100	
4th Quartile		Performs in a superior manner for sustained periods of time; must maintain this level of performance to remain in the 4th Quartile of the pay range.
	70	
3rd Quartile		Performs in a commendable manner; consistently exceeds fully satisfactory levels of performance for extended periods of time (e.g., at least 2 years).
	54	
Midpoint	50	Consistently performs all responsibilities in a fully satisfactory manner; is fully trained and normally has from 2 to 4 years' experience on the job.
	46	
2nd Quartile		Performs responsibilities between a marginal and a satisfactory level. Incumbent is still in a learning stage and has not performed all responsibilities at a fully proficient level for a reasonable period (e.g., 6 months).
	25	
1st Quartile		Performs responsibilities at a marginal or less level. Normally, incumbent is new to this job. If in this pay bracket for more than 24 months, should be reassigned or terminated.
Minimum	0	
Probationary Range		Placed in job with less than minimal qualifications. Should not be at level of pay for more than 6 months (90 days is a normal probationary period).

FIGURE 18–4   Performance—Pay Grade Profile

Modified from Robert J. Greene, "Auditing Your Pay Programs: Are They Equitable, Competitive, and Defensible?" Handout III.

To ensure a complete range of performance ratings, raters may be required to distribute their ratings according to some predetermined mix. A typical forced distribution may take the order shown in Table 18–5.

Table 18–6 provides another possibility for distributing performance ratings and the range of merit increases that may be granted relative to a specific rating. The specific

TABLE 18–5   Forced Distribution of Employee Performance Ratings

Performance Rating Level	Percentage of Rates at Each Level (approximating a normal distribution)	Percentage of Rates at Each Level (top-heavy distribution)
Distinguished	5	10
Superior	10	20
Commendable	35	40
Competent	35	20
Marginal	10	5
Unacceptable	5[a]	5[a]

[a] This rating percentage is not mandatory and may be combined with that in the marginal level.

amount of the range of permissible merit increase may vary, and it may be established anew each year depending on the fiscal condition of the organization and the state of the economy.

In conjunction with performance appraisal many organizations are turning to *merit guidecharts* for determining pay adjustments and for ensuring differentiation of pay based on demonstrated employee performance. Merit guidecharts vary among organizations, but they have similar basic characteristics. Guidecharts usually identify the employee's (1) current performance rating and (2) location in a pay grade. (At times, a factor that varies receipt of merit increase relative to received rating and time interval since last merit pay adjustment is added to the guidechart.) The intersection of the dimensions—current performance rating and location in pay grade—identifies a percentage of pay increase based on the performance level and location of the employee in grade (see Table 18–7). (In some cases, instead of a percentage increase the guidechart identifies a specific dollar adjustment. In these cases a guidechart may be designed for each grade.)

The rationale for paying different rates of pay to individuals receiving identical performance ratings is that those in the upper quartiles are already receiving more pay and this permits those in the lower levels of the pay range to improve their situations relative to the midpoint or the organization's established competitive position.

Actual percentage values in the performance pay adjustment boxes of the merit guidechart shown in Table 18–8 may have two components. One is a value that is re-

TABLE 18–6   Merit Pay Distribution Schedule

Performance Rating	Distribution	Merit Range Increase
Superior	Top 5 to 10%	10% or higher
Commendable	Next 10 to 15%	7 to 10%
Satisfactory	Middle 60 to 75%	3 to 6%
Marginal	Next 5 to 10%	0 to 3%
Unacceptable	Bottom 0 to 5%	0%

TABLE 18–7 A Simple Merit Guidechart[a]

| | Location in Pay Grade | Performance Rating | | | |
| | | Superior | Commendable | Satisfactory | Marginal |
			(percent adjustment to current pay)		
Maximum—100th Percentile					
	4th Quartile	4	2	0	0
75th Percentile					
	3rd Quartile	5	3	0	0
Midpoint— 50th Percentile					
	2nd Quartile	6	4	2	0
25th Percentile					
	1st Quartile	7	5	3	0
Minimum— 0 Percentile					

[a] The following statement may also be included with the guidechart: In no case will the percentage increase shown multiplied by the current pay of the employee result in an amount of pay that exceeds the maximum of the assigned pay grade for the job of that employee.

lated to a market-required or cost-of-living adjustment to the pay structure, and the second is the performance adjustment.

The x in the guidechart represents the percentage change in the pay structure. If, for example, the structure were increased by 5 percent, then each employee receiving an x increase would receive 5 percent plus the performance rating increase. Those receiving no x increase would be receiving a relative pay cut and would regress within the pay grade. Those receiving a fraction of the x ($x/4$, $x/2$) would also not be receiving the full benefit of the pay structure change.

Combining the structure and merit components in the annual pay increase program has some significant implications when the pay structure adjustment—the x value—equals the change in cost of living (e.g., change in CPI). From a perspective of

TABLE 18–8 Merit Guidechart Combining Performance Ratings and Pay Structure Adjustments

| | Location in Pay Grade | Performance Rating | | | |
		Superior	Commendable	Satisfactory	Marginal
Maximum—100th Percentile					
	4th Quartile	$3 + x$	$1 + x$	0	0
75th Percentile					
	3rd Quartile	$4 + x$	$2 + x$	0	0
Midpoint— 50th Percentile					
	2nd Quartile	$5 + x$	$3 + x$	$1 + \dfrac{x}{4}$	0
25th Percentile					
	1st Quartile	$6 + x$	$4 + x$	$2 + \dfrac{x}{2}$	0
Minimum— 0 Percentile					

real income, employees receiving less than an *x* percent increase are actually receiving in real terms a reduction in pay (taking the view that the organization feels that an *x* percent adjustment is necessary to meet general labor market advancements or changes in cost of living). Without instituting an actual pay cut, this provides an opportunity to retard the pay of the overpaid employee, the poor performer, or the one who has retired on the job. It also allows for a more rapid increase in pay for the employee in the lower portion of the pay grade who is performing well.

An additional element frequently inserted into this kind of process is to vary the performance review dates relative to the location of the employee in the pay grade or relative to the performance rating of the employee (discussed in a later section). Employees in the lower quartiles of the pay grade are reviewed more frequently and, thus, have the opportunity to receive more frequent pay increases. A schedule of performance review and subsequent pay adjustments may take this form:

Location in Grade	Minimum Period until Next Review
Above maximum	By exception only
Fourth quartile	15–18 months
Third quartile	12–15 months
Second quartile	9–12 months
First quartile	6 months
Below minimum	3 months

Some of the more widely used pay adjustment guidelines are these:

1. Fixed time period, in-step set pay adjustment with acceptable performance. Example: The General Schedule of the federal government has 10 steps in each pay grade. The waiting period for advancement to steps 2 and 3 is 52 weeks; the waiting period for advancement to steps 4, 5, and 6 is 104 weeks; and advancement to steps 7, 8, and 9 is 156 weeks. In order to gain an in-step rate increase, the employee must be rated as a satisfactory or better performer. (This is also an example of using an employee's *anniversary date* for timing the award of a merit increase.)
2. Fixed time period with pay adjustment based on level of performance. (When the time period has the same beginning and ending dates for all employees, this is an example of using a *common review date* for timing the award of a merit increase.) Example: Unstructured (Open) Pay Grade

Rating	Percentage Range
Superior	10–12
Commendable	7–9
Satisfactory	4–6
Marginal	0–3

Maturity Curves and Pay Administration

Through the use of surveys that provide market data on relevant professional jobs using years since BS degree, an organization can modify or design its pay structure in line with its compensation philosophy and market considerations. There is truly very little difference between the maturity curve approach discussed in chapter 8 and a pay structure in which the grades are adjusted relative to changes in the market and in which individual pay is a function of job worth and performance on the job. The maturity curves can be used similarly to the compa-ratio or control point for pay administration purposes.

Various surveys provide the data necessary to relate the pay practices of an organization to the market. A premier survey that uses years since BS degree for collecting pay data of engineers is one conducted by the Engineering Workforce Commission of the American Association of Engineering Societies. It has been conducting these surveys since 1953. In 1995, 235 participating organizations provided more than 105,000 rates of pay. The data are separated by all-manufacturing and all-nonmanufacturing industries and by supervisor-nonsupervisor categories. There is also a geographic/ regional breakdown of data. Figure 18–5 and Table 18–9 provide examples of the kind of data and figures found in the Engineering Workforce Commission surveys.

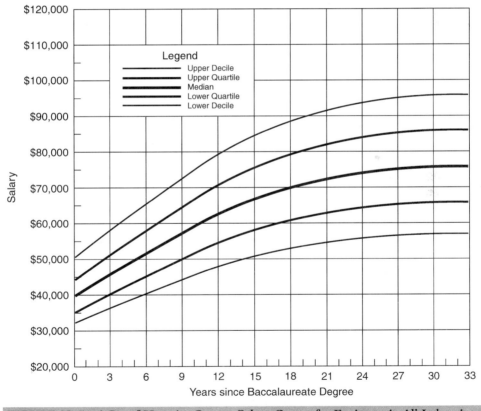

FIGURE 18–5   A Set of Maturity Curves: Salary Curves for Engineers in All Industries, Nonsupervisors, All Degree Levels

See associated data in Table 18–9.

Source: Engineering Workforce Commission (EWC) of the American Association of Engineering Societies (AAES), *Engineers' Salaries: Special Industry Report, 1998* (Washington, DC, 1998), p. 5.

TABLE 18–9 Maturity Curve Data: 1998 Engineering Salary Statistics: All Industry, Nonsupervisory

Years Since B.S.	0	1	2	3	4	5	6	7	8	9–11
Smooth Curve Data										
Upper Decile	48450	50800	53250	55700	58200	60750	63250	65750	68200	73000
Upper Quartile	43150	45500	47850	50200	52550	54900	57200	59450	61600	65750
Median	38700	40700	42700	44700	46700	48700	50700	52600	54500	58150
Lower Quartile	34950	36650	38400	40100	41850	43600	45350	47100	48750	51950
Lower Decile	31700	33400	35050	36650	38250	39800	41250	42650	44000	46500
Mean	39650	41700	43750	45800	47800	49800	51800	53700	55600	59150
Raw (Unsmoothed) Statistics										
Upper Decile	51150	50500	51300	54600	57500	61300	62050	64750	66800	74350
Upper Quartile	45600	45650	46400	49600	50750	53550	55500	59300	61200	66150
Median	40600	40600	42450	43550	44650	46900	50450	53250	53500	58600
Lower Quartile	36100	35350	39050	40700	40350	42600	44950	48150	48400	52350
Lower Decile	32050	32900	36400	37100	36500	38500	41250	43050	43500	46550
Mean	41500	41400	43300	45300	46200	48700	51100	53800	54900	59550
Supporting Data										
Total Number	1223	1458	1804	1744	1701	1807	1698	1925	1989	6656
$125,000 or More	0	0	0	0	0	0	0	0	0	0
Less than $30,000	59	26	29	0	17	15	6	7	6	18

Source: Engineering Workforce Commission (EWC) of the American Association of Engineering Societies (AAES), *Engineers' Salaries: Special Industry Report, 1998* (Washington, DC, 1998), p. 5.

As with any kind of survey data that are used for pay administration purposes, the curves can be used as "true" examples of the real world and compensation professionals can adjust their pay structures to fit the market as identified by the sample, or they can use the survey to reflect market movement and then finely tune their own internally developed curves to reflect market changes and the organization's compensation policy.

Some organizations may have 10th, 25th, 50th, 75th, and 90th percentile curves, while other organizations may have as many as 50 curves. There are no established or consistent practices as to the number of curves desired or required. These curves provide a salary range for each designated level of performance.

Organizations that use maturity curves for salary administration will typically assign each employee to the curve that best fits his or her level of demonstrated performance. For the new employee, a proxy to *performance* may be established by giving a score relative to undergraduate grades, courses taken, and university attended. As the individual receives some kind of performance review, the performance ratings replace the education-based standard for placing the employee on a particular curve. A good performance review system is critical to the success of a maturity curve program. Many

TABLE 18–9 *(continued)*

Years Since B.S.	12–14	15–17	18–20	21–23	24–26	27–29	30–32	33+	Totals	Z
				Smooth Curve Data						
Upper Decile	79550	85050	89350	92400	94300	95350	95750	95600	85050	2.2
Upper Quartile	71300	75950	79550	82250	84150	85350	86050	86600	75300	4.0
Median	63000	67150	70400	72900	74600	75700	76350	76850	62950	4.0
Lower Quartile	56250	59650	62200	63800	64700	65000	64950	64400	51350	2.2
Lower Decile	49600	52050	53850	55150	56000	56550	56850	57100	42450	4.0
Mean	63900	67900	71100	73500	75200	76300	77000	77550	64050	3.8
				Raw (Unsmoothed) Statistics						
Upper Decile	81650	84900	88100	90900	94800	93200	96300	97000	85050	
Upper Quartile	74350	77600	78800	81300	83600	84300	86750	84100	75300	
Median	65150	68400	70250	72000	73600	76200	76600	74250	62950	
Lower Quartile	56700	59800	62000	62800	63350	66200	66350	64100	51350	
Lower Decile	49950	52250	55250	54650	56050	58800	56250	54300	42450	
Mean	65550	68850	70900	72750	74750	76600	77100	75650	64050	
				Supporting Data						
Total Number	6507	6398	5355	4236	3900	3441	2523	4115	58482	
$125,000 or More	0	12	2	14	28	37	18	61	173	
Less than $30,000	6	21	0	5	0	3	0	1	220	

companies use maturity curve market surveys as a secondary consideration for scientists and engineers in a salary grade system.[3]

One approach an organization may take for placing employees into an appropriate curve is to first grade employees into five levels according to performance—distinguished, superior, commendable, marginal, or marginal or less. Then, using the maturity curves, the organization pays the distinguished performers, who comprise the top 10 percent of the rated employees, at approximately the 90th percentile. The superior group, which includes 15 percent of the rated employees, receives pay in the 75th percentile. The commendable performers, who comprise the middle 50 percent of the rated employees, are paid at approximately the 50th percentile. The marginal group is paid at approximately the 25th percentile and represents the next 15 percent of those rated. The marginal-or-less group is paid at around the 10th percentile and makes up the remaining 10 percent of the employees (see Figure 18–5). Dividing a workforce into five distinct

---

[3]The following three articles provide an in-depth review of the maturity curve method, its strengths, weaknesses, and uses: George W. Torrence, "Maturity Curves and Salary Administration," *Management Record,* January 1962, pp. 14–17; Edward A. Shaw, "The Maturity Factor as an Aid in Administering Professional Salaries," *Personnel,* September–October 1962, pp. 37–42; and Ralph Kulberg, "Relating Maturity Curve Data to Job Level and Performance," *Personnel,* March–April 1964, pp. 45–50. Personal correspondence with Eugene K. Hamilton dated January 10, 1984, provided insight into maturity curves.

groups with approximately 15 percent in a marginal category and 10 percent in a less-than-acceptable category may be extremely hazardous to employee morale. In a well-managed, established organization, it is quite possible that 25 percent of the workforce will not fall into a marginal-or-less category. It is also possible that even 5 percent will not be unacceptable performers. The need to identify a certain percentage of the workforce as less than acceptable may not only be inappropriate but wrong.

If a performer is measured at three levels—superior, competent, or marginal, then the superior group (the top 25 percent of all employees) would be paid at around the 75th percentile; the competent (the middle 50 percent) around the median or 50th percentile; and the marginal (the bottom 25 percent) at around the 25th percentile.

The actual construction of maturity curves may utilize any of a wide range of methods. Often, the literal application of raw salary statistics across experience levels fails to yield satisfactory results due to sampling or other sources of error. Most analysts employ curve-smoothing procedures to deal with this problem. Methods for smoothing range from simple pencil-and-paper plots based on scatter diagrams to relatively advanced mathematical procedures such as banded splines. For many years, the Engineering Workforce Commission (EWC), formerly known as the Engineering Manpower Commission (EMC) has used an iterative least-squares approach to compute smooth curves with minimal deviations from raw data. Originally developed at Bell Laboratories, this approach has been refined by EWC staff in recent years. A major reason for seeking refinements was the observation that for some data sets—for example, smaller samples dominated by two employers with very different salary scales—the original least-squares approach sometimes yielded results that defied common sense, such as U-shaped curves in which starting and ending rates were infinitely high, whereas mid-career compensation estimates dipped to zero.

In the process of eliminating such obviously senseless results, EWC's programmers also incorporated several other refinements including the use of "anchor points" to tie all curves for any data set to the starting values for persons with a minimal level of academic preparation and experience, and adjustment of the iterative process to ensure that curves tend to rise most rapidly during the early stages of experience and flatten out at the later stages. In addition, EWC has been reporting both its smooth-curve results and the raw salary statistics on which those results are based, which allows users of its data to experiment with their own approaches. The commission also reported the final values of a key variable in its curve-smoothing equation, the exponent z, in the hopes that inspection of this statistic may lead to better understanding of relationships between data and the curve-smoothing process. The broad conclusion is that users of maturity curves should be aware of the approach used to generate data, especially when smoothing techniques are employed, because these methodological decisions can have quite pronounced effects on salary estimates.[4]

Annual Performance Bonus

Instead of using a merit guidechart and an associated increase to base pay as a manner of recognizing differing levels of performance, some organizations are now finding one-

---

[4]Letter dated May 6, 1992, from Richard A. Ellis, Director, Manpower Studies, Engineering Manpower Commission of the American Association of Engineering Societies, Washington, DC.

time, lump-sum performance bonuses to be a more effective and less costly kind of reward. Such a bonus may be paid once or twice a year. It must be reearned by meeting identified performance criteria and does not become a permanent part of the employee's pay. Another advantage to using short-term bonuses is that these earnings are not typically built into a base for calculating benefits, thus providing a savings in benefits expenses.

Timing of Pay Adjustments

The pay adjustment options just described provide organizations with significantly different ways of determining the amount and the timing of performance-based awards. Although merit guidecharts provide timing recommendations for granting performance-based awards, most organizations adjust pay annually, either on the employee's *anniversary date* (the date the employee entered the job or the date of last increase), or on a *common review date* (an identical period for reviewing the performance of all employees). The organizations then follow the review with a pay adjustment.

The anniversary date is normally the date the employee was hired or promoted into the position, and adjusting pay on this date allows for individualized pay treatment. Organizations using a merit pay plan, however, may find it best to review the performance and the pay of all employees in a segment of the organization or pay classification on a common review date. This practice allows for improved comparisons among employees who perform similar kinds of work or who are members in the same work unit, as well as the tying of pay adjustments to certain natural breaks in the manner in which business is conducted. This approach also makes it easier to budget for these increases.

This kind of rating and pay adjustment behavior, however, may not be in the best interest of the organization. When a pay adjustment almost always follows a performance rating (even when the adjustment varies according to the received rating), a message is being sent to all employees that the annual raise is an established compensation policy practice. As organizations attempt to improve their control over pay practices, one change they may want to institute is the lengthening of the intervals between adjustments. The pay practices of the 1970s of annual (at times even more frequent) pay increases to almost all employees was frequently far more "tenure-with-the-organization related" than performance or merit based.

By lengthening the time between merit increases for the marginal or even satisfactory performer, larger adjustments can be granted to the top performer and managers can still keep their adjustments within the merit budget allocations for their respective departments. If all or the great majority of employees receive a 4 to 6 percent annual pay adjustment, and if merit budgets average from 4 to 7 percent, there is little available with which to differentiate the pay of the superior performers.

Time of the year can also have a critical effect on an employee's reaction to a pay adjustment. An example of a poor time to give a pay increase is at the first of the year. Deductions for Social Security payments drastically decrease for some employees (those earning more than $72,600 in 1999) at some time during the fourth quarter of the previous year and the increase on their paychecks reflects that the deductions have become less. The first paycheck of the new year includes a resumption of the full Social Security deduction. An employee could possibly receive a 10 percent increase in pay and with increased income tax withholdings, Social Security deductions, and other deductions arising at the start of the year, receive less spendable earnings than in the last paycheck of the past year. Pay adjustments should be timed to have the greatest psychological impact on the employee, improve management decisions, and ease administration.

Compa-Ratio: A Tool for Planning and Administration

A favorite planning and administration tool of many compensation managers is the *compa-ratio*. The compa-ratio provides an index number that permits management to do an analysis of the anatomy of the pay grade or salary range. It is calculated by dividing the total *actual* pay received by all employees (or groups to be analyzed) in a pay grade by the midpoint of the pay grade multiplied by the number of employees (or number of individuals in the group) in the pay grade, or total pay divided by total midpoints. A compa-ratio can also be determined for each individual salary in the organization. The very design of the compa-ratio requires the setting of midpoints and the assignment of jobs to pay grades. When an organization operates a pay program with a structure that uses pay grades and the pay grades have minimums and maximums, the compa-ratio index numbers can be extremely useful.

The spread of the range determines the maximum and minimum limits for a compa-ratio. The compa-ratio limits (*CRL*) can be calculated by using the following formula:

$$CRL = 1 \pm \frac{\text{range}}{2 + \text{range}}$$

If the range of a pay grade is 50 percent, then

$$CRL = 1 \pm \frac{.5}{2 + .5} = 1 \pm \frac{.5}{2.5} = 1.20 \text{ and } .80$$

If the range is 40 percent,

$$CRL = 1 \pm \frac{.4}{2 + .4} = 1 \pm \frac{.4}{2.4} = 1.167 \text{ and } .833$$

Desired Spread of the Range	*Compa-Ratio Limits*		
Percent	*Minimum*	*Midpoint*	*Maximum*
50	.800	1.000	1.200
40	.833	1.000	1.167
30	.870	1.000	1.130
25	.890	1.000	1.110

The compa-ratio is most often used in organizations having a uniform 50 percent spread for all pay grades. When an organization varies the spread of the range among the pay grades, the range index (see a later section) may be a much more useful pay analysis tool.

If, for example, an organization uses a 50 percent spread of the range, a 1.00 compa-ratio indicates that the average rate of pay equals the midpoint. An index value of 1.20

indicates that all rates of pay are at the maximum or that the average rate of pay (if some rates are higher than the maximum) equals the maximum of the pay grade. An index value of 0.80 indicates that all rates of pay are at the minimum or that the average rate of pay (if some rates of pay are less than minimum) equals the minimum of the pay grade.

If an organization has a compensation policy in which its midpoint reflects what the organization wishes to pay for its fully proficient employees, then an index number of 1.0 would normally indicate an acceptable distribution of employees in the grade. An index that moves down toward 0.80 indicates (1) possible underpayment of employees in the pay grade or (2) a significant number of employees in the grade who are new to the jobs within it. An index moving toward 1.2 may indicate (1) a very senior workforce in the grade, (2) a low rate of turnover, (3) possible inflation (overly high ratings) of employee performance when merit is being recognized by in-step movement through the grade, (4) cost-of-living adjustments being made through the use of instep pay increases, and (5) a pay structure that is not being adjusted to reflect market requirements. Compa-ratios can be used not only to identify the level of actual pay for all jobs in a grade, but also to identify pay practices of specific jobs within a grade.

Of current significant interest is the fact that the compa-ratio can be used to analyze the pay treatment of specific groups of employees. Segregating employees by such demographics as gender, race, disability status, or age group, a compa-ratio analysis could provide a first indication that there is potential bias for or against certain groups of employees.

The compa-ratio can be used for all kinds of planning and control purposes. The following are some examples.

1. *Pay grade analysis.* Distribution of incumbent rates of pay in a pay grade. Can be further analyzed by job in work unit or by employee group demographics such as gender, age, race in a pay grade.
2. *Department analysis.* Comparison of pay distributions among departments by computing the sum pay of all employees in the department divided by the sum of the number of employees in each pay grade times their respective midpoint rates of pay.
3. *Relating performance appraisal rating to pay adjustments.* Replacement of percentiles or quartiles in previous merit guidechart examples with compa-ratio values: less than .88; .88 to .96; .96 to 1.04; 1.04 to 1.12; 1.12 to 1.20.
4. *Merit budget decisions.* Use of the compa-ratio or its reciprocal to establish merit budget allocations if the organization wishes to make departmental budgets more equal from the perspective of a compa-ratio balance.
5. *Pay structure analysis.* Chapter 11 contains an extensive discussion on how to design a pay structure using such pay structure design statistics as lowest and highest rates of pay to be paid, desired range(s) for pay grades, midpoint-to-midpoint difference(s), overlap, and survey data for identifying competitive (market) midpoints and pay grade ranges (competitive hiring and maximum rates of pay for all jobs). Although the following discussion focuses on the use of the compa-ratio for monitoring purposes, the described procedures can just as easily be used to evaluate the effectiveness of a newly created pay structure.

After obtaining pay data for benchmark jobs, actual rates of pay (highly preferred) or average rates (easier to obtain), and assigned pay grade maximum and minimum, a table can be developed that identifies each survey participant's actual pay practice (behavior). This kind of table provides a compa-ratio value for each benchmark job for each participant and a summary or average compa-ratio for each benchmark job for all participants. The table can be designed to further separate jobs by such groupings as senior management, operating management, nonexempt hourly. This is useful because compa-ratio interpretations will vary by such groups because of variations in spread of the range of pay practices.

By developing a compa-ratio that compares market (average or median) pay data with midpoint of relevant current pay grade, the compensation specialist can quickly identify the competitive posture of the organization. (Depending on the compa-ratio limits, a movement somewhat above 1.0 indicates the possibility of too low a midpoint; below 1.0, too high a midpoint.) This procedure can be used for analyzing each benchmark job included in a pay grade and for identifying whether or not the organization has any problem with the location of the midpoint.

The next analytical step uses the compa-ratio data to analyze the competitive posture of the minimum and maximum of the pay grade. In this step, the analysis involves a review of the assigned pay grade minimum and maximum of each benchmark job. This analysis is dependent on the reliability of the provided pay data and whether or not the range data provided are actually used by the participant (the participant actually hires or pays new employees close to or at the identified minimum and does not pay employees more than the maximum—espoused minimums and maximums are actually minimums and maximums used). This analysis informs a compensation specialist whether or not the minimum and maximum are set properly (competitively), or where they may be out of line with certain competitors in the marketplace and, if there is a misalignment, how serious it is and what if anything must be done to correct it.

Control Point: A Tool for Planning and Administration

Some organizations use the term *control point* to indicate a rate the organization wishes to set as the going or pay policy rate that reflects its relationship to the market. The control point can be considered a proxy to the compa-ratio. The following procedure can be used to establish a control point:

Step 1. Evaluate the job and obtain a point score.
Step 2. Assign to the point score a specific rate of pay that the organization wishes to pay to a fully proficient employee in the job.
Step 3. Call the assigned dollar rate the *control point* for the job.

This same procedure could be performed relative to a pay grade. Instead of assigning a dollar value to a specific point score, simply assign a dollar value to a specific place in the pay grade. (As discussed in chapter 11, the pay grade will have its horizontal dimensions identified by point scores and a job can be located in an appropriate pay grade relative to its own point score.)

By using the control point, the organization can eliminate the need of formally setting minimum and maximum rates of pay. All it must do is establish the monetary value of its appropriate pay policy midpoint and then relate a control point to this value. The organization establishes a number of values around its control point that, in effect, control its pay practices.

For example, the following index numbers could be used in conjunction with the midpoint value of 1.00:

.83—The minimum amount an entry-level employee can be paid

.88—The maximum rate of pay to be paid to a marginal employee

.93—The maximum rate that can be paid to a satisfactory employee

.97—Control point. The rate of pay paid to a fully proficient employee (In this case, the organization is paying its average performer .03 under its established market or going rate—from the organization's perspective, it has made a conscious policy decision to pay less than the market.)

1.00—Going market value

1.10—The maximum that can be paid a superior-performing nonexempt or first-level operating manager

1.15—The maximum that can be paid a superior-performing mid-level operating manager

1.25—The maximum that can be paid a superior-performing upper-level operating manager

The described control point model closely approximates a pay structure with a 40 percent spread with regard to the minimum rate of pay. By using a control point for managing the pay system, the organization has extreme flexibility in both the design of the pay structure and the administration of the pay plan.

Range Index: A Tool for Planning and Administration

A third approach available for analyzing and managing a pay program is through the use of the range index. The *range index* is computed by dividing the actual rate of pay minus the minimum rate of pay by the spread of the range. Range indexes can be calculated for various groups of employees (exempt, nonexempt, by pay grade, by specific occupation or classes of jobs, or by employee demographic characteristics such as gender, race, or age). The range index keeps compensation managers informed of employee movement through the pay grade.

An employee earns $14,250. Using a pay scale with a $12,000 minimum salary and an $18,000 maximum salary, a 37.5 percent range index number can be computed with the following equation:

$$\text{range index} = \frac{\text{actual rate of pay} - \text{minimum rate of pay}}{\text{maximum rate of pay} - \text{minimum rate of pay}}$$

$$= \frac{14{,}250 - 12{,}000}{18{,}000 - 12{,}000} = \frac{2{,}250}{6{,}000} = .375 = 37.5\%$$

A range index value will always carry with it the same relative meaning. A range index of .50 means that an employee (or designated group of employees) is at the midpoint of the pay grade. A value between 50 and 100 percent indicates how closely the employee is moving toward the maximum of the pay grade, and index values between 0 and 50 percent indicate the movement between minimum and midpoint.

Target Salary

Some organizations use the term *target salary* to describe their approach to pay (salary) administration. A target salary program, like the three previously described tools, can be used for both pay planning and administration. A target salary program combines the individual's current rate of pay, location of the rate of pay in the pay grade (or compa-ratio, or value relative to control point, or range index) and level of performance. A target salary program can be used to budget and monitor the pay of an individual or all employees in a specific work unit. Such a program can use an approach described by one of the various merit guidecharts or any of the three pay planning and administration tools.

QUALITY OF WORK LIFE AND PAY ADMINISTRATION

Pay for knowledge is an outgrowth of the quality of work life (QWL) programs that originated in Europe (more specifically, the work done primarily at the Tavistock Institute of London) following the end of World War II. QWL is simultaneously a philosophy, a process, and a goal. The underlying philosophy of a QWL program is that if organizations grant employees significantly more authority over their workplace operations and then provide sufficient administrative and technical support, employee involvement will increase. Increased involvement will then lead to increased commitment and, with these kinds of positive emotional and intellectual interactions, performance and organizational productivity will improve. Currently, the term *employee empowerment* is being used to describe this process. QWL includes the interactions of all the parts and components necessary to gain the cooperative participation of knowledgeable employees who actively seek to achieve organization goals and to gain satisfaction from the work they perform.

Key to many QWL programs has been the development of teams. Employees as team members teach each other, assist in identifying and solving production and quality problems, make better use of available resources, and support each other emotionally as well as physically and intellectually. A major tool of team development and operation has been the design of pay systems that support teams and QWL programs. These QWL pay delivery systems have been given many labels. The two most common are skill-based pay and pay-for-knowledge. Other titles have been knowledge-based-pay, pay for learning, and multiskill-based pay. In 1984, the U.S. Department of Labor authorized the most comprehensive review of these kinds of pay delivery systems to date. The study was conducted by the College of Business Administration of the University of Arkansas.[5] (See chapters 8, 12, 13, and 14 for discussion of these pay processes.) Chapter 12 focuses on team-based pay systems.

At this relatively early stage in the development of QWL-based pay delivery systems, no one approach has been identified as a standard or basic plan. Designers of these plans develop unique qualities within their own plans and place their own distinct labels on the plans and plan design characteristics. However, these plans do appear to have some common design features: (1) Each plan adjusts an employee's rate

---

[5]Bureau of Labor Management Relations and Cooperative Programs, U.S. Department of Labor, *Explorative Investigation of Pay-for-Knowledge Systems* (Washington, DC: U.S. Government Printing Office, 1986).

of pay according to the demonstrated skills used in the activities required in the performance of work assignments over an extended period. (2) The employee will normally be required to perform a number of assignments requiring different kinds and levels of knowledge/skills. (3) In addition to the acquisition of specific "doing" skills, the employee will be involved in planning and scheduling work activities/assignments; the establishment of quality, quantity, and timeliness standards; and the measurement of results.

Nothing presented in this book is foreign or in opposition to these kinds of plans. The word *job* may be given a broader description, such as all the work performed by all members of the team—a work assignment, workstation, or work module may be more comparable to the way some organizations traditionally define a job. Whatever the title, however, work activities and work procedures may have to be defined and described even more precisely and accurately within a QWL program than in a more conventional setting. With increased job rotation, it is imperative that each employee know exactly and completely what must be done at each work station.

Although pay is related to skill modules (skill units, skill blocs, skill levels), organizations must still relate the pay of their employees to workers in other organizations performing similar kinds of work in a more traditional setting. This places more pressure on surveys than in the past. It increases the inference-making problems in relating pay survey data to specific organizational pay decisions. Because worker pay increases with the acquisition of more knowledge and the demonstration of additional skills, pay structures must be designed to recognize these acquisitions. Once again, many of the issues addressed in chapter 11 on pay structure design face those involved in establishing different rates of pay for different skill acquisitions. Although many of these "new" pay programs have only a few steps or pay increase opportunities, some plans have as many as 12 to 20 steps. Movement from bottom to top in some plans may take from three to five years. Even five years to the top is a shorter period of time than in many common pay structure designs and the old problem of "hitting the top of the range" appears sooner. Once employees reach the top of the pay plan, administrators begin searching for and developing additional incentive plans—gainsharing, team incentives/bonus plans, and so on.

Possibly the most serious problem in a pay-for-knowledge or skill-based pay plan is who determines when a skill has been acquired and when the determination is to be made so that an employee can receive a pay adjustment. This places designers of these programs face-to-face with the difficult issue of performance appraisal. What has been learned to date is that QWL pay delivery systems take more intense and skilled effort than pay systems in conventional settings. Successful employee involvement programs require managers who know what they are doing and the development of administrative processes that support employee and team interaction without blocking them with stifling bureaucratic processes and layers of unnecessary management. Possibly the one important difference in designing and operating a pay program in a traditional organization and one that is QWL-centered is the emphasis both on the individual and the team. The individual is paid for developing and using skills, and teamwork is recognized for helping and supporting the growth of individual skills. Protecting and promoting team effort must be given primary consideration at every stage in the development of the pay system.

OTHER COMPENSATION ADMINISTRATION ISSUES

In addition to the development and administration of the labor-personnel budget, other issues the compensation department may be concerned with are these:

1. Guidelines for promotion and demotion adjustments
2. Available options for keeping employees whole
3. Attracting workers with knowledge and skills that are in short supply
4. Paying all employees a salary
5. Overtime for exempt employees
6. Adjusting pay for nonunion employees
7. Compensating temporary part- and full-time employees and regular part-time employees

Guidelines for Promotion and Demotion Adjustments

Similar to many other compensation practices, policies and guidelines regarding promotion increases vary significantly. Promotional differences begin with the way organizations define promotions. Some of the more common definitions are these:

Kind of Promotion	Description	Promotion Increase
Within-grade promotion (transfer)	A lateral transfer in which responsibilities and duties have changed but are similar in scope and complexity. Overall job requirements are similar with new job in the same pay grade as the old job.	5%
In-class promotion	Moving from a junior to a more senior job in a class-series in which knowledge and skill requirements are upgraded but are in the same domain.	5% to 10%
Organization promotion	Moving to a job requiring different sets of knowledge and skills with major differences in the kinds, scope, and complexity of responsibilities.	Maximum of 15%

Promotion guidelines can also be set relative to (1) the individual's location in the pay structure, (2) pay grade movement, and (3) increase in point scores from current job to promoted job. Location in the pay grade may use these guidelines:

Current Pay Relative to New Pay Grade	Percentage Increase Granted
Below minimum	15 unless within 5 of minimum, then at least 5
Between minimum and midpoint	5 to 8
Between midpoint and maximum	7½ to 10 or maximum, whichever is less

When an organization uses a job evaluation method that provides a point score, it can relate its promotion increases directly to the change in the points. The points assigned to different jobs can also be linked to personnel policies relative to demotions and transfers. A change in total point score from current job to new job reflects the size of a promotion. In using the Hay Method, for example, if an individual's new job is less than 15 percent smaller or greater in total points than the current job, this will be considered a lateral transfer. An increase of 15 percent in total point score is considered to be a normal promotion, whereas an increase of 30 percent is considered a significant promotion. A point score change greater than 45 percent is extremely unusual, and it is unlikely that a person would have the knowledge or skill to move from one job to another with this great a point difference. Also, movement to a job that has a point score 15 percent or more less than the previously assigned job would be considered a demotion. (Note the use of the 15 percent or the just perceptible differences that provide the conceptual foundation for the design of the Hay charts.) The following table could be used to relate pay adjustments to change in point scores in the Hay Method:

Increase in Points (%)	Transfer or Promotion Pay Increase (%)	
1–9	4	Lateral transfer
10–14	7	Lateral transfer
15–29	9	Promotion
30 or greater	11	Promotion

In addition to promotion increases, many organizations also establish adjustment procedures for employees whose jobs are downgraded or who have been transferred to a lower evaluated job or a job in a lower pay grade. The demotion may require the employee to be paid at a rate not higher than the maximum of the new pay grade, or the demotion guidelines may take the following approach.

> When an employee is transferred to a position in a lower pay grade because of inadequate performance in the current position and the employee's current base pay is above the midpoint of the new pay grade, the employee's pay will be reduced to equal the midpoint of the new pay grade.
>
> If the employee is transferred to a position in a lower pay grade because of an organization change, the employee will keep his or her current pay grade for a period of two years. During that time, the individual and the organization will make every effort to move the individual to a position in a pay grade equivalent to or higher than the pay grade of the employee's previous position. If, at the end of two years, the employee's pay is above the maximum of the current pay grade, the pay of the employee will be reduced to the maximum of the pay grade.

Options for Keeping Employees Whole

To many employers, the very term *cost-of-living adjustment* (COLA) conjures up the image of the devil. It is for this reason that the concept of the merit budget has become so important over the past decade. The employer wants to maintain an acceptable market relationship and recognize employee performance, but under a merit budget philosophy, keeping an employee whole is not an organizational responsibility. However, for many organizations, even some with merit budgets, this issue does not disappear.

There are a number of ways an organization can assist its employees in maintaining their real purchasing power. Among these are (1) an equal dollar pay adjustment for all employees, (2) an adjustment to the pay policy (pay structure) line, (3) cost-of-living adjustments, (4) area wage differentials, and (5) in-step pay grade or pay grade advancements.

Equal Dollar Pay Adjustment   The term *across-the-board pay increase* normally means that all employees are granted an equal amount pay raise. For example, if an organization provides a $500 annual pay increase, the employee's normal time payment schedule is adjusted relative to this $500 increase. Hourly employees receive $500/2,080 hours = $0.24 per hour pay increase. Those on a weekly salary receive $500/52 weeks = $9.62 per week pay increase. An across-the-board pay raise provides an identical raise to employees in all jobs. When this occurs, and because the design of most pay structures uses relative relationships (percentage difference from minimum to maximum of a pay grade or percentage difference between midpoints), the entire structure becomes distorted and relationships become invalid.

A basic part of the philosophy that underlies across-the-board increases relates to the issue that the increase in the price of bread is the same for everyone. The problem here is that most workers design their lifestyles around job-related earnings. Lifestyle includes subsistence (food, clothing, shelter, and transportation), luxuries, and savings for the future. Considering all of these complex issues, the argument for across-the-board pay raises becomes much weaker.

The underlying strength of an across-the-board pay increase is that it supposedly is the most democratic action to take because it treats every employee equally. This has a sweet ring to employees in the lower end of the pay scale, but what about the employees who perform jobs requiring more responsibility and greater levels of knowledge and skill? A basic feature of any well-designed compensation system is that it provides compensation on an equitable basis. It offers compensation rewards that relate to the contributions made or offered by the employee.

Cost-of-Living Adjustment (COLA)   Most COLAs are clauses included within a collective bargaining contract that provide periodic wage increases for the covered employee. The COLA increase recognizes changes in the prices of goods and services. The term *keeping an employee whole* refers to the need for employees to have their pay adjusted to meet inflationary pressures at the marketplace. The consumer price index (CPI) is the major index used to determine COLAs.

The CPI is a mathematically based index designed and produced by the Bureau of Labor Statistics (BLS) of the U.S. Department of Labor. This index measures the relative change in a representative sample of goods and services over a period of time. The sample of goods and services includes an array of items within the following major categories: (1) food and beverages; (2) housing; (3) apparel and upkeep; (4) transportation; (5) medical care; (6) recreation; (7) education and communication; and (8) other goods and services. Within the eight major categories there are more than 250 items.

Throughout the history of the CPI, BLS has conducted Consumer Expenditure Surveys that identify the consumer expenditure items and establish weights for the items to be included within the CPI. A product of the 1972–73 survey was the identification of two population groups that had somewhat different expenditure patterns. They were the All Urban Consumers and the Urban Wage Earners and Clerical Workers.

Beginning January 1, 1978, BLS began producing two CPIs for these two groups. They are (1) the CPI for All Urban Consumers (CPI-U) and (2) the CPI for Urban Wage Earners and Clerical Workers (CPI-W). The weights of the basket of goods and services for the CPI-W closely match the pre-1978 concept based on the buying habits of wage earners and clerical workers in urban areas, whereas the CPI-U has differing item weights based on the buying habits of *everyone* who lives in an urban area. Since that time, there have been periodic changes in the items and the weights of items included within both CPIs based on surveys of consumer purchasing practices. BLS personnel collect prices on items included within the CPI in 85 different urban areas and produce CPI-Us and CPI-Ws for the nation and for 29 urban areas. The CPI for the United States is based on an average value of all items for the 1982–84 period and has a value of 100 for this period. The change in the CPI from one period to the next is expressed as a percentage of the previous value. For example, the CPI-U for January 1996 was 154.4 and for December 1995 was 153.5. The percentage difference between January 1996 and December 1995 was (154.4 – 153.5)/153.5 = .9/153.5 = .0059, or approximately one-half of 1 percent (.05 percent). For the year 1995, the CPI-U had a change of +2.7 percent.

The CPI is used to determine changes in such major government programs as Social Security benefits, retirement programs and food stamps, and various floors and ceilings in income tax computations.

Area Wage Differentials   Some nationwide firms that have employees performing similar jobs in different locations provide an area wage differential based on differences in living costs. Here, the 29 major metropolitan area CPIs produced by BLS are of value. The BLS also regularly produces approximately 90 on an annual or biennial basis and 120 additional Occupational Compensation Surveys on an irregular schedule. These area surveys are useful for establishing area wage differences. There are also a number of private-sector firms that produce area-specific cost data.

By using area wage differentials, an organization can have a national pay structure and then modify with appropriate wage differences, thus eliminating the need for regional or local pay structures. (See chapter 10 for additional discussions of pay surveys.) In compliance with locality pay regulations, the federal government modified its GS wage schedule using the data provided in Table 18–10.

In-Step Pay Grade or Pay Grade Advance   Although it is a very unsatisfactory approach, many organizations grant their cost-of-living adjustments through in-step advances within the pay grade. This practice corrupts the intended purpose of in-step pay grade advances, which is to recognize merit and seniority.

Attracting Workers with Knowledge and Skills That Are in Short Supply

An extremely difficult problem for compensation administrators occurs when workers with specific kinds of knowledge and skills are in short supply. If the shortage is temporary, it may be possible to provide some type of bonus to recruit employees with the required knowledge and skills. This, however, opens up the problem of what to do with employees currently performing the jobs. It may be possible to bring the new employees into the job at an advanced step or location in the pay grade or even to add a

TABLE 18–10 Locality-Based Comparability Payments (effective on the first day of the first applicable pay period beginning on or after January 1, 1999)	
Locality Pay Area[a]	*Rate*
Atlanta, GA	6.67%
Boston-Worcester-Lawrence, MA-NH-ME-CT	9.32%
Chicago-Gary-Kenosha, IL-IN-WI	9.98%
Cincinnati-Hamilton, OH-KY-IN	8.21%
Cleveland-Akron, OH	6.92%
Columbus, OH	7.46%
Dallas-Fort Worth, TX	7.47%
Dayton-Springfield, OH	6.67%
Denver-Boulder-Greeley, CO	9.16%
Detroit-Ann Arbor-Flint, MI	10.13%
Hartford, CN	9.85%
Houston-Galveston-Brazoria, TX	12.92%
Huntsville, AL	6.31%
Indianapolis, IN	6.08%
Kansas City, MO-KS	6.51%
Los Angeles-Riverside-Orange County, CA	11.14%
Miami-Fort Lauderdale, FL	8.51%
Milwaukee-Racine, WI	6.74%
Minneapolis-St. Paul, MN-WI	7.92%
New York-Northern New Jersey-Long Island, NY-NJ-CT-PA	10.55%
Orlando, FL	5.87%
Philadelphia-Wilmington-Atlantic City, PA-NJ-DE-MD	8.30%
Pittsburgh, PA	6.68%
Portland-Salem, OR-WA	7.80%
Richmond-Petersburg, VA	6.61%
Sacramento-Yolo, CA	8.27%
St. Louis, MO-IL	6.17%
San Diego, CA	8.62%
San Francisco-Oakland-San Jose, CA	13.06%
Seattle-Tacoma-Bremerton, WA	7.96%
Washington-Baltimore, DC-MD-VA-WV	7.86%
Rest of United States	5.87%

[a]Locality Pay Areas are defined in 5 CFR 531.603.

"shadow range" to the pay grade (extend the upward limits of the pay grade beyond its normal maximum) and then assign the employee an above-maximum rate of pay within the shadow range. Any of these courses of action can cause conflict with employees currently on the job who are at lower levels of pay. This situation may also be a sign of an improperly evaluated job, and it may be that a reevaluation could place the job in a higher pay grade. It may be possible to add some responsibilities and duties to the job, resulting in a higher evaluation and grade assignment.

The final solution may require the establishment of a separate pay structure for exotic or high-demand jobs. Possibly the only administrative procedure that satisfies problems related to these types of jobs is to pay these jobs what the market identifies as the going rate and then to carefully follow market trends or practices in the coming years and make future adjustments that recognize changes in the market.

Paying All Employees a Salary

Placing all employees on salary is one of the more recent applications of egalitarianism. Some employees being paid by the hour feel they are second-class citizens. They feel that if they themselves are to receive fair treatment, all employees should be on salary.

The basic impetus in this direction is that a salaried employee receives a prescribed amount of money every two weeks or each week that does not depend primarily on the number of hours worked. For this process, hourly rates of pay are converted to a weekly salary. It is important, however, to recognize that nonexempt salaried employees are still paid by the hour as far as those responsible for enforcing wage and hour requirements of the Fair Labor Standards Act are concerned. Employers must keep a record of hours worked by each employee (this does not require the use of a time clock) and pay time and a half to all nonexempt employees who work more than 40 hours in any one week, whether or not they are on a salary. Employees working under some type of pay-for-performance system may find it a disadvantage to be on a salary.[6]

Overtime for Exempt Employees

Many organizations frequently provide some kind of overtime payments for first-level management (supervisory personnel) and, less frequently, professionals and middle managers who are required to work more than 40 hours a week.

Most such personnel are exempt under Fair Labor Standards Act requirements, but employers are providing overtime pay for reasons of fairness. Overtime may not start until the exempt employee has worked 45 hours, there may be a cap to overtime hours, or a limit may be set by base pay (employees receiving base pay greater than $45,000 a year are not eligible for overtime payments). Some organizations pay exempt overtime at a straight hourly rate, while others provide a rate of overtime pay equivalent to time and a half. Possibly the most common kind of overtime payment is to grant qualified employees compensatory time off. Some organizations are now providing middle-level management employees and professionals year-end bonuses in lieu of overtime payments. Each organization, depending on its particular requirements, is wise to devise its own standards in this area.

Adjusting Pay for Nonunion Members

Unionized companies may also find it important to review compensation adjustments to nonunion employees. If an organization almost always adjusts the compensation of its nonunion members to meet changes made during contract negotiations, many nonunion members will secretly hope that the unionized members will receive the best settlements. They know that in a short while their own compensation will reflect these improvements.

[6]Robert D. Hulme and Richard V. Bevan, "The Blue-Collar Worker Goes on Salary," *Harvard Business Review,* March–April 1975, pp. 104–112.

This, in turn, may lead to an extremely strong prounion sentiment among nonunion members of the organization that may not be in the best interests of management.

Differences in Compensation for Regular, Temporary, Full-Time, and Part-Time Employees

The rapid increase in the use of temporary (contingent) and part-time employees by all kinds of organizations is forcing compensation system designers and administrators to investigate the differences in compensation for these employees. Everything in this book relates primarily to regular full-time employees. *Regular full-time employees* are those hired and scheduled to work the number of hours per week and weeks per year that are standard for that work unit. A standard work year normally consists of 52 weeks per year, with a workweek ranging from 32 to 40 hours. An average workweek in the United States today consists of approximately 37 hours. The U.S. Department of Labor considers full-time workers as those who work 35 hours or more per week on their sole or principal job.

Part-time employees, on the other hand, work less than a full workweek. Normally, they are scheduled to work from 20 to 32 hours per week, although, in some cases, part-time employees work less than 20 hours per week. The U.S. Department of Labor considers any person working less than 35 hours as a part-time worker.

Temporary or casual employees are hired to perform assignments that usually do not extend beyond six months in duration. A temporary worker may work on either a full-time or a part-time basis. Some organizations, however, hire almost all new employees on a temporary basis. These workers may work at this temporary status until the organization is certain the employee has the work habits and qualifications to perform the job in a fully proficient manner and the organization will be able to provide continuing employment with minimal threat for layoff for lack of work. This temporary status could last from one to five years. The term *contingent employee* is frequently being used in lieu of the terms *part-time, temporary,* or *casual employee.*

Regular part-time and temporary full-time and part-time employees frequently receive a compensation package that differs significantly from that provided to regular full-time employees in the same job classification. Usually, the hourly rate of pay for the job is the same no matter what the employment status of the incumbent. (Paying different rates of pay for the same job because of employment status could possibly lead to Equal Pay Act or Title VII violations.) Regular part-time and temporary employees usually receive entry-level rates of pay for the job and may receive some kind of pay adjustments (depending on their length of service and performance in the job) similar to that offered new regular full-time employees.

Regular part-time employees frequently earn vacation, holiday, and sick pay benefits in direct proportion to their scheduled hours of work (a 20-hour part-time employee working in a unit that normally schedules full-time employees for a 40-hour workweek would receive one-half the vacation, holiday, time-off-with-pay benefits earned by the full-time worker).

A recent and dramatic change in pay practices has occurred with some organizations and some occupations in their compensation practices regarding regular part-time employees. Whereas in the past most part-time work was the result of a slack in demand, today part-time workers are being hired to assist during periods of peak demands or for work schedules that are not desired by the regular full-time staff. Those employees who are willing to provide support under these circumstances work 30 hours or less a week but receive premium hourly rates of pay. Examples are bank tellers who may receive up to a 25 percent premium for evening or Saturday work, or nurses who work a 12-hour shift on both Saturday and Sunday and are paid for a 40-hour workweek.

Medical, disability, and life insurance plans vary dramatically among organizations. In some cases, part-time workers receive none of these benefits. It is more common, however, to find some kind of pro rata receipt of benefits, based on a proportion of hours worked, scheduled for regular full-time employees. With regard to retirement programs, ERISA requires that employees who work at least 1,000 hours in any calendar year, regardless of classification, be eligible for retirement, thrift, and stock plans.

Temporary employees frequently receive few or no benefits unless they meet ERISA requirements for retirement programs. Many organizations today hire their temporary work staff directly through second-party employers. In this case, those employers who provide the workers on an "as needed basis" pay all personnel costs. The temporary employee negotiates a pay rate directly with the second-party employer who then bills the client employer for all temporary help provided.

DUE PROCESS

For 30 years following the end of World War II, many workers in the United States viewed their jobs as an inalienable right. Not only did they have a right to their jobs, but they believed they owned them (i.e., a person's job was his or her own property), and they were *entitled* to whatever rewards they were already receiving and any additional ones they could influence their employers to provide. In the early 1980s, the meaning of *entitlement* began to return to its original definition—a property right that must be earned. Up until this time, survival generated through job security had been taken for granted. In the 1970s and in the early 1980s, however, some very unsettling events occurred in the United States and in the rest of the world. Employers and employees alike recognized that resources had become truly limited. Not only that, there was worldwide competition for these resources. It came as a shock that the desired and expected "good life" may only be available to those who work for it, and that there is no such thing as a free lunch.

Do two recessions, rapid and devastating inflation, and extreme worldwide competition in the industrial area mean an end to a claim for due process and a worker's bill of rights? No one can accurately predict the future, but if history can teach us anything, due process and the concept of job ownership are both very much alive and kicking.

What is *due process*? It is a legal concept that relates to the carrying out of certain legal proceedings for the purpose of ensuring individual rights in accordance with established rules and procedures. Citizens of the United States are guaranteed the right to due process under the Fifth and Fourteenth Amendments to the Constitution. Because employment at will is still very much alive, employees are not guaranteed due process rights as far as the employee–employer exchange process is concerned unless they are stated and described in specific pieces of legislation or within a contractual obligation. The employment at will doctrine is, in fact, being adjusted at times by judicial notice of public interest. The "at will" doctrine is not as absolute as it has been in the past.

Although the employer continues to own the job, these ownership rights have been eroded over the past 50 years by an ever-lengthening number of legislative actions and contractual obligations.

These acts and accompanying case law are establishing a body of due process in human resource jurisprudence that provides protection to employees in all kinds of work situations. However, unless specifically stated through legislation, employers are not required to provide individual rights to employees on the job. Nevertheless, good management practices necessitate additional considerations.

Although employees do not have full *legal* ownership of their jobs, it is in management's favor to recognize that a contract is being established when it provides a wide array of rewards in exchange for employee-provided availabilities, capabilities, and performance. To ensure that both parties understand the stipulations of the contract, instruments must be developed that identify certain obligations.

Recognizing the historical trend toward increasing due process rights, employers may be wise to develop and implement programs that provide due process opportunities to their employees. Demands on the part of both the employer and employee for improved understanding of what job requirements are and what they are not are increasing daily.

When a job applicant is hired and becomes a member of the organization, a first step in providing due process to this incumbent occurs by clearly identifying and describing job requirements. Many organizations have a probationary period of employment. During this period, the employment contract can be terminated with minimum explanation of the cause or minimal use of due process. Even in the probationary period, however, more organizations are taking the time and effort to establish and implement a well defined process to observe and measure the on-the-job performance of the probationary employees.

Training employees about what the company expects and in areas that improve job knowledge and skills is a second step. Permitting and assisting employees to set job performance standards is another step in expanding due process at the workplace. Active and valid participation in performance appraisal reviews continues due process. Providing rewards that relate to observed and demonstrated workplace behavior and achieved results ensures continuation of due process to a logical workplace conclusion.

Possibly the most important documents management can prepare and use are those that identify job content and job requirements and those that identify and analyze job performance. The job description, in essence, becomes a deed and title to the job. It actually provides *substantive due process*. The responsibilities and duties identified in the job description describe the assignments that must be performed for acceptable accomplishment of the job—they establish conditions or reasons for the existence of the job. The performance appraisal system and its accompanying instruments provide *procedural due process* that identifies and communicates the desired and actual results. They describe acceptable ways of performing the job. Performance dimensions and performance standards recognize contingencies that develop because of environmental influences and the variations in contributions arising because of the unique qualities of each incumbent. To ensure continuing possession of their jobs, employees must accept responsibility and recognize their accountability for satisfactory performance of these workplace obligations. In turn, they have every right to expect due process in protecting ownership rights to their jobs.

Ensuring Due Process in the Organization

Auditing, monitoring, and appeals processes in an organization provide a high level of quality control to the administration of the compensation program.

The auditors act as the eyes, ears, even noses of top management. They provide top management with information on how well the compensation system is operating. They identify deficiencies that may otherwise go unrecognized. Like all kinds of organizational auditing, it is a watchdog activity that reviews what is required by regulations, procedures, and rules as compared to what is actually happening. Auditors' reports assist top management in enforcing its policies, procedures, and rules. They make recommendations for additions when necessary, for changes in those that are either unenforceable or in need of modification, and for removing those of no value.

Monitors, on the other hand, work with each unit in the organization to ensure operation of programs as planned. Monitoring is a continuing operation that involves all levels in the organization. It identifies any discrepancies between what is supposed to occur and what actually does occur. Monitoring information should feed into the auditing system.

The third leg of this check-and-balance system is the appeals process. By granting each employee the right to appeal organization-related issues (a job evaluation score or a performance rating), the organization informs all employees that rules and procedures will be enforced in a fair and impartial manner. A compensation program with auditing, monitoring, and appeals components informs everyone that their actions are being reviewed. It forces all programs and processes to be explicit, clearly communicated, and understood. It permits everyone to know where he or she stands with regard to organization-related criteria and reward opportunities.

Auditing Report Information   Auditors' reports go directly to top management and provide this level with such information as this:

1. Purpose of the audit
2. Units audited
3. Critical issues or problems that require further review
4. Overall results or summary of the findings of the audit

Areas to Be Audited   To ensure compliance with established compensation policies and guidelines, the following areas require audit reviews:

1. Completeness and accuracy of job descriptions
2. Adequacy and use of performance standards for reviewing and rating employee performance
3. Proper classification and grading of jobs, searching for any possible Equal Pay or Title VII violations
4. Compliance with ADA requirements
5. Pay policy lines that reflect the compensation philosophy and policies of the organization
6. Relationship between pay adjustments and performance and between performance and current level of pay
7. Provision of pay adjustments that reflect compensation policies and guidelines

8. Analysis of base pay, performance ratings, and pay adjustments for any kind of illegal discrimination

9. Consistency of use of actual merit pay adjustments and funds budgeted for merit pay

(Currently, few organizations audit these activities. Lacking such capabilities, the compensation department should perform them.)

Monitoring Report Information   Monitoring report activities cover all parts of a work unit. The assignment here also is to identify problem areas and make recommendations for improving the program. The following kinds of information come from a monitor's report:

1. Which individuals/units are not implementing compensation programs as designed? Is there proper and consistent application of compensation and pay policies? Are all employees treated fairly?

2. Are job activities and performance standards accurately stated in understandable terms?

3. Are requested pay adjustments and current levels of pay in line with policy guidelines and received performance ratings?

4. Are raters' ratings being reviewed by higher-level managers?

5. Are performance appraisal schedules and standing operating procedures being followed?

6. Do managers have documentation to support the actions they take that influence employee compensation opportunities?

7. Are rater performance ratings indicative of some kind of rating errors?

8. Do employee rating and work unit productivity measures coincide or conflict?

9. Are jobs properly evaluated, classified, and graded?

10. Are most appropriate methods and tools being used to identify market levels of pay and other compensation opportunities?

Appeals Process   The essence of due process rests with the right to appeal. Many employees have minimal on-the-job guaranteed rights. Frequently, the immediate supervisor plays the role of arresting officer, jury, and judge. This may not be the best situation for all involved parties. The appeals process lets everyone know that:

1. There is a body of rules that must be followed.

2. Each person has the right to voice his or her side.

3. Decisions will be made on the basis of fact, and the burden of proof rests with all parties.

4. Every effort will be made to treat everyone the same.

This kind of check-and-balance system facilitates the movement of critical information throughout the organization. Problems that require resolution are identified. Attention focuses on what is right, what is wrong, and what can be done to improve things. Compensation is an extremely complex and sensitive issue. It has a direct impact on the life of the employee and the life of the organization. To ensure compliance with a program that is both complex and critical to the survival of the employee and the organization, procedures must be established and safeguarded that will allow employees to provide feedback to the organization with their related problems and concerns. Major appeals opportunities that some organizations are now granting employees are these:

1. Disagreement with received performance ratings and pay adjustments.
2. Failure to receive requested transfers and promotions.
3. Disagreement with evaluation of job.
4. Dissatisfaction with description of job content and established performance standards.

Guidelines to Due Process

In 1978, David W. Ewing identified seven guidelines organizations should follow that will result in all employees being treated in an equal and equitable manner.[7] These guidelines, which have been paraphrased here, can be most helpful to those responsible for designing and operating a compensation system that provides due process rights to all members of the organization. In essence, they state that the compensation system must:

1. Follow set procedures—prohibit arbitrary actions.
2. Be visible and known—both potential violators of rights and victims of abuse must know it.
3. Be predictable—engender confidence that certain employee behaviors will lead to specific actions by the organization.
4. Be institutionalized—be a relatively permanent part of the organization.
5. Be perceived as equitable—a majority of employees accept the actions as fair.
6. Be easy to use—neither complexity in administration nor potential ill effect prohibit use.
7. Be applicable to all employees—all employees from lowest to highest can expect to receive similar treatment.

Properly implemented in both letter and spirit, due process may be the most important action organizations can take to improve productivity.

Summary

Pay practices should evolve directly from organizational objectives. They should allow the organization to be competitive in its respective labor markets, promote pay equity among all jobs, recognize individual contributions, and adjust to local and national economic conditions. This chapter first focuses on the budget process and the role of compensation in ensuring that future financial expenditures are coordinated and controlled and support the accomplishments of organizational objectives. Three steps in pay administration are collecting merit/salary increase budget data; adjusting the pay structure relative to company compensation policy; and moving employees within the pay structure relative to performance, seniority, and location within the structure. The timing of any adjustments can be critical.

The chapter continues with a review of the compa-ratio and how it can be used to monitor how effectively pay grades are being used in an organization. In addition, there is a discussion of the wide variety of issues the compensation department must be

[7]David W. Ewing, *Freedom Inside the Organization: Bringing Civil Liberties to the Workplace* (New York: McGraw-Hill, 1978), p. 156.

concerned with, including formulating guidelines for promotions and demotions, choosing between options for keeping employees whole, and recognizing differences in employee contributions. Auditing, monitoring, and appeals procedures should be part of any well-designed compensation program.

Review Questions

1. Identify the major groups that have an impact on compensation-related decisions and the particular areas they influence.
2. Discuss the major issues and subissues that influence the pay of each employee.
3. What is meant by real income (wages or pay)? What is the relationship between real income and the term *keeping our employees whole*?
4. Discuss the meaning of compa-ratio and how the compa-ratio can be used for merit budget cost controls.
5. What is a merit guidechart? How may an organization use a merit guidechart to relate to both merit and pay structure adjustments?
6. Discuss the opportunities available for an organization to relate pay to (1) job worth, (2) seniority, (3) merit, (4) cost-of-living adjustments, and (5) area (geographic) differentials.
7. In what ways will organizations compensate regular versus temporary and full-time versus part-time employees differently?

Action Words

The following words are valuable for identifying and defining precisely the functions of a job. Through the use of concise terminology, it is possible to minimize ambiguity or misunderstanding relative to what is being done. It is not a complete list, however, and job description writers may find other verbs to be more suitable.

Accentuate: To accent; to emphasize.

Accept: To receive as true; to regard as proper, normal, inevitable.

Accomplish: To execute fully; to attain.

Account: To give a report on; to furnish a justifying analysis or explanation.

Accumulate: To collect; to gather.

Achieve: To bring to a successful conclusion.

Acknowledge: To report the receipt of.

Acquaint: To cause to know personally; to make familiar.

Acquire: To come into possession of

Act: To perform a specified function.

Activate: To mobilize; to set into motion.

Actuate: To put into mechanical action or motion.

Adapt: To suit or fit by modification.

Adhere: To give support or maintain loyalty; to be consistent; to hold fast or stick; to bind oneself to observance.

Adjust: To bring to a more satisfactory state; to bring the parts of something to a true or more effective position.

Administer: To regularly and customarily exercise discretion and independent judgment; to make important decisions.

Adopt: To take up and practice as one's own.

Advance: To bring or move forward; to accelerate the growth or progress of; to raise to a higher rank-promote; to bring forward for notice, consideration, or acceptance; to make progress; to raise in rate.

Advise: To recommend a course of action; to offer an informed opinion based on specialized knowledge.

Advocate: To recommend or speak in favor of.

Affirm: To assert positively; to confirm.

Affix: To secure an object to another; to attach.

Align: To arrange in a line; to array.

Allot: To assign as a share.

Alter: To make different without changing into something else.

Amend: To change or modify for the better.

Analyze: To separate into elements and critically examine.

Answer: To speak or write in reply.

Anticipate: To foresee and act in advance so as to prevent.

Apply: To put to use for a purpose; to employ diligently or with close attention.

Appoint: To name officially.

Appraise: To give an expert judgment of worth or merit.

Appropriate: To take exclusive possession of, to set apart for or assign to a particular purpose or use; to take without permission.

Approve: To accept as satisfactory; to exercise final authority with regard to commitment of resources.

Arise: To get up; to come into being or attention.

Arrange: To prepare for an event; to put in proper order.

Articulate: To pronounce distinctly; to express in coherent verbal form; to form or fit into a systematic whole.

Ascend: To move gradually upward; to rise from a lower-level; to go back in time or in order of genealogical succession; to succeed to.

Ascertain: To find out or discover through examination; to find out or learn for a certainty.

Aspire: To desire a lofty object.

Assemble: To collect or gather together in a predetermined order from various sources.

Assert: To state or declare positively.

Assess: To determine value of; to evaluate.

Assign: To specify or designate tasks or duties to be performed by others.

Assist: To help or aid others in the performance of work.

Associate: To bring into relation, as thought, memory, etc.; to join as a partner or ally; to unite or combine; to unite or join.

Assume: To undertake; to take for granted.

Assure: To give confidence; to make certain of.

Attach: To connect; to bind or affix to.

Attain: To come into possession of; to arrive at.

Attempt: To make an effort toward; to try.

Attend: To be present.

Audit: To examine officially with intent to verify.

Authorize: To approve; to empower through vested authority.

Avert: To turn away or aside; to see coming and ward off.

Award: To confer or bestow.

Balance: To compute the difference between the debits and credits of an account; to reconcile accounts.

Batch: To assemble into a group for one operation.

Budget: To plan expenditures.

Build: To construct.

Calculate: To make a mathematical computation.

Call: To communicate with by telephone; to summon; to announce.

Cancel: To mark out; invalidate. (Printing—to delete.)

Capitalize: To write or print with an initial capital or in capitals; to convert into capital; to compute the present value of; to supply capital for.

Carry out: To put into execution; to bring to a successful issue; to continue to an end or stopping point.

Categorize: To classify.

Certify: To confirm as accurate or title.

Challenge: To demand as of right; to take exception to; to question the legality or legal qualifications of; to invite into competition.

Change: To alter or transform.

Chart: To draw or plot data (as on a graph); to make a detailed plan.

Check: To verify; to compare with a source.

Circulate: To pass from person to person or place to place.

Clarify: To make easier to understand; to explain.

Classify: To arrange or organize according to systematic groups, classes, or categories.

Clear: To gain approval of others; to free from obstruction; to authorize; to get rid of.

Close: To bring to a conclusion; to bar passage; to shut; to suspend or stop operations.

Code: To use symbols (letters or numbers) to represent words.

Collaborate: To work jointly with; to cooperate with others.

Collate: To organize or assemble in a predetermined sequence.

Collect: To gather.

Combine: To bring to close relationship; to unite or to act together.

Command: To direct authoritatively; to order or request to be given; to give orders; to dominate from an elevated position.

Communicate: To impart an oral or written message; to transmit information.

Compare: To examine for the purpose of discovering resemblances or differences.

Compile: To put together information; to collect from other documents.

Complete: To finish; to fully carry out.

Comply: To act in accordance with rules, requests.

Compose: To make by putting parts together; to create; to write (an original letter, report, instructions).

Comprehend: To grasp the meaning of mentally.

Compute: To determine or calculate mathematically.

Concentrate: To bring or direct toward a common center or objective; to gather, collect.

Conclude: To bring to an end; to complete; or to form a final judgment.

Concur: To agree with a position, statement, action, or opinion.

Condense: To make more compact.

Conduct: To carry on; to direct the execution of.

Confer: To compare views; to consult.

Confirm: To give approval to; to assure the validity of.

Conform: To bring into harmony or agreement; to adapt oneself to prevailing standards or customs.

Consider: To think about with care or caution.

Consolidate: To bring together.

Construct: To make or form by combining parts; to draw with suitable instruments and under specified conditions.

Consult: To seek advice of others; to give professional advice or services.

Contact: To communicate with.

Contemplate: To view or consider with continued attention; to meditate on.

Continue: To maintain without interruption a condition, course, or action; to remain in existence.

Contrast: To compare to show differences; to exhibit unlikeness.

Contribute: To supply or give something; to submit for publication.

Control: To measure, interpret, and evaluate actions for conformance with plans or desired results.

Convert: To alter the physical or chemical nature of something; to alter for more effective utilization.

Convey: To move from one place to another; to transport; to communicate.

Convince: To persuade; to cause others to believe something, using evidence and/or argument.

Cooperate: To associate with another or others for mutual benefit.

Coordinate: To regulate, adjust, or combine the actions of others to attain harmony.

Copy: To duplicate an original.

Correct: To make or set right; to alter or adjust to conform to a standard.

Correlate: To establish or demonstrate a causal, complementary, parallel, or reciprocal relation.

Correspond: To communicate with.

Counsel: To advise; to consult with.

Count: To check one by one to determine the total number; to calculate or compute; to consider or regard; to list or name numerals in order.

Create: To bring into existence; to produce through imaginative skill.

Critique: To evaluate or analyze as to merit.

Debug: To detect, locate, and remove mistakes from a routine of malfunctions from a computer.

Decide: To arrive at a solution; to bring to a definitive end.

Dedicate: To set apart to a definite use; to become committed to.

Deduce: To derive a conclusion by reasoning; inference in which the conclusion follows necessarily from the premises; to reach a conclusion by mental deduction.

Defend: To take action against attack; to act as an attorney for.

Define: To state the exact meaning—(i.e., of a word); to fix the boundaries; to make clear the outline or form of.

Delegate: To commission another to perform tasks or duties which may carry specific degrees of accountability and authority.

Delete: To strike out or remove.

Deliver: To set free; to convey; to send to an intended destination.

Demonstrate: To illustrate and explain, especially with examples.

Describe: To represent by a figure, model, or picture; to trace the outline of; to given an account of in words.

Design: To conceive, create, and execute according to plan.

Detect: To discover the presence or fact of.

Determine: To resolve; to fix conclusively or authoritatively.

Develop: To disclose, discover, perfect, or unfold a plan or idea.

Devise: To form in the mind by new combinations or applications of ideas or principles; to invent.

Devote: To center the activities or attention of, to give up wholly or purposefully.

Diagram: To explain by a graphic design.

Dictate: To read or speak information to be recorded or written by another.

Differentiate: To make a distinction; to form or mark differently from other such things; to perceive the difference in or between.

Direct: To guide work operations through the establishment of objectives, policies, rules, practices, methods, and standards.

Disassemble: To take apart.

Discipline: To penalize individuals or groups whose behavior is contrary to established rules and regulations.

Discover: To make known.

Discriminate: To mark or to distinguish.

Discuss: To exchange views for the purpose of arriving at a conclusion.

Dispatch: To send off, or forward, to known destination or on specific business.

Display: To show; to spread before the view.

Dispose: To sell or get rid of.

Disseminate: To spread or disperse information or ideas.

Distinguish: To perceive as being separate or different; to separate into kinds, classes, or categories.

Distribute: To deliver to proper destination.

Divert: To turn from one course or use to another.

Divide: To separate into classes.

Document: To provide with factual or substantial support for statements made or a hypothesis proposed; to equip with exact references to authoritative supporting information.

Draft: To prepare papers or documents in preliminary form.

Draw: To compose or write up, following a set procedure or form (as in a contract); to pull or move something.

Edit: To revise and prepare material (written, film, tape, sound track) for publication or display.

Effect: To bring about; to accomplish.

Elaborate: To work out in detail; to give details.

Elect: To choose or select carefully.

Eliminate: To get rid of; to set aside as unimportant.

Emphasize: To stress.

Employ: To make use of, to use or engage the services of; to provide with a job that pays wages or a salary.

Encompass: To form a circle about; to envelop, include.

Encourage: To inspire with spirit, hope; to give help or patronage to.

Endorse: To support or recommend.

Enforce: To execute vigorously; to exercise executive or police power. Refers to laws and statutes.

Engage: To interlock with; to mesh; to provide occupation for; to arrange to obtain the use or services of.

Enlighten: To furnish knowledge to.

Endorse: To engage for duty; to secure the support and aid of.

Ensure: To make sure, certain, or safe; to guarantee.

Establish: To bring into existence.

Estimate: To forecast future requirements.

Evaluate: To determine or fix the value of.

Evidence: To prove.

Examine: To inspect closely.

Exchange: To give or take one thing in return for another.

Exclude: To shut out; to bar from participation, consideration, or inclusion.

Execute: To put into effect; to carry out.

Exercise: To exert influence; to train by drills and maneuvers; to use repeatedly in order to strengthen and develop.

Expect: To look forward; to consider probable or certain.

Expedite: To accelerate the process or progress of.

Explain: To make clear; to give reasons for.

Express: To represent in words; to make known one's feelings or opinions.

Extend: To total columns (bookkeeping term).

Extract: To draw forth; to withdraw; to separate; to determine by calculation.

Extrapolate: To infer (an unknown) from something known.

Facilitate: To make easier.

Feed: To move into a machine or opening in order to be used or processed; to furnish with something essential for growth, sustenance, maintenance, or operation.

Figure: To compute.

File: To arrange in a methodical manner; to rub smooth or cut away with a tool.

Finalize: To put in finished form.

Find: To encounter; to come upon by searching or effort.

Flag: To mark in some distinctive manner.

Focus: To concentrate; to converge; to adjust one's eye or camera to a particular range.

Follow up: To pursue closely in order to check progress.

Forecast: To predict; to estimate it, advance.

Formulate: To develop or devise.

Foster: To promote the growth or development of.

Fulfill: To put into effect; to bring to all end; to measure up to; to develop the full potentiality of.

Function: To act or operate as; to serve.

Furnish: To provide what is needed; to supply.

Gather: To collect; to harvest; to accumulate and place in order.

Generalize: To derive or induce from particulars.

Generate: To bring into existence; to originate by vital or chemical process.

Give: To grant or bestow; to administer; to make a present of.

Govern: To exercise continuous sovereign authority over; to control and direct the making and administration of authority over; to hold in check; to have decisive influence.

Grade: To rank; to prepare the surface of a road.

Grasp: To make the motion of seizing.

Group: To form together persons or things considered to be related.

Guarantee: To secure; to answer for the debt, default, or miscarriage of.

Guide: To show or lead the way to; to manage the affairs of; to influence the conduct or opinions of.

Handle: To touch, hold; to manage with the hands; to deal with, act on, or dispose of.

Help: To be of use to; to relieve; to remedy; to serve.

Hire: To engage the service of for a set sum.

Identify: To establish the characteristics of, to associate with some interest.

Illustrate: To make clear or intelligible, as by examples.

Implement: To carry out; to execute a plan or program.

Import: To bring from a foreign or external source.

Impress: To apply with pressure so as to imprint; to affect forcibly or deeply.

Improve: To make something better.

Indicate: To show, demonstrate with precision.

Infer: To conclude by reasoning from premises or evidence.

Inform: To communicate information to.

Initiate: To start; to introduce; to originate.

Innovate: To exercise imagination in introducing something new of in making changes that lead to improvement.

Insert: To put (something) into, between, or among other materials.

Inspect: To examine or determine; to critically analyze for suitability.

Inspire: To influence, move, or guide by divine inspiration.

Install: To place in office; to establish in an indicated place, condition, or status; to set up for use in office.

Institute: To establish in a position or office; to originate.

Instruct: To teach; to coach; to communicate knowledge; to direct or order.

Insure: To cover with insurance; to make certain.

Integrate: To unify; to make whole by putting all parts or elements together.

Interpolate: To alter or corrupt (as a text) by inserting new or foreign matter; act of inserting (words) into a text or conversation; to insert between other things or parts.

Interpret: To give the meaning of, to explain to others.

Interview: To obtain facts or opinions through inquiry or examination of various sources.

Invent: To think up or imagine; to create.

Inventory: To catalog or to count and list.

Invest: To spend or use time, money, or effort to achieve a future benefit.

Investigate: To observe or study by close examination and systematic inquiry.

Issue: To put forth or to distribute officially.

Itemize: To list; to write down in detail.

Join: To put or bring together.

Judge: To form an authoritative opinion; to determine and pronounce after inquiry and deliberation.

Justify: To prove or show to be right or reasonable; also, to align words such that both left- and right-hand margins are in line (typing term).

Keep: To hold or retain; to maintain.

Label: To distinguish; to designate; to assign a name to.

Lead: To guide or direct on a course or in the direction of, to channel; to direct the operations of.

Learn: To gain knowledge or understanding of.

Lend: To give for temporary use on condition that the same or its equivalent be returned.

Let: To allow; to rent or lease; to assign, especially after bids.

List: To enumerate; to enter into a catalog with a selling price.

Load: To place in or on a means of conveyance; to increase the weight of by adding something heavy.

Locate: To find, determine, or specify by means of searching, examining, or experimenting (to seek or find).

Look up: To search for and find.

Maintain: To continue; carry on; or keep in an existing state.

Make: To cause to happen to; to cause to exist, occur, or appear; to create; to bring into being by forming, shaping, or altering material.

Manage: To contrive or arrange; to make submissive to one's authority, discipline, or persuasion through planning, organizing, staffing, directing, and controlling.

Manipulate: To operate manually; to manage or utilize skillfully; to control by unfair or insidious means.

Map: To make a survey of for the purpose of representing; to plan in detail.

Market: To expose for sale; to sell.

Match: To set in competition with; to provide with a worthy competitor; to cause to correspond.

Measure: To determine length, width, or quantity of.

Mediate: To interpose with parties to reconcile them; to reconcile differences.

Meet: To cope with; to come together from different directions; to provide for.

Merge: To combine items from two or more similarly ordered sets into one set that is arranged in the same order.

Mix: To unite or blend into one group or mass.

Model: To teach by personal example; to instruct by demonstration.

Modify: To make less extreme; to limit or restrict the meaning of; to make minor changes in.

Monitor: To watch, observe; to check for a specific purpose.

Motivate: To arouse or stimulate to action.

Move: To go from one point to another; to begin operating or functioning or working in a usual way.

Name: To nominate; to speak about.

Necessitate: To force; to compel.

Negate: To deny the existence or truth of, to cause to be ineffective or invalid.

Negotiate: To confer with others with a view to reaching agreement.

Neutralize: To destroy the effectiveness of; to nullify.

Note: To observe; to recognize.

Notify: To make known.

Nullify: To make of no value or consequence; to cancel out.

Observe: To see, notice, or watch something or someone.

Obtain: To acquire or gain possession of.

Occupy: To take possession of; to fill.

Omit: To leave out; to disregard.

Open: To make available for entry or passage; to make accessible; to expose to view; to disclose.

Operate: To perform an activity or series of activities.

Oppose: To resist; to withstand; to place opposite or against.

Orchestrate: To arrange or combine so as to achieve a maximum effect.

Order: To arrange or classify; to request services or goods.

Organize: To arrange; to systematize or methodize.

Orient: To cause to become aware of familiar with, or adjusted to facts, principles, procedures, or situations.

Originate: To create; invent.

Outline: To make a summary of significant features.

Overcome: To get the better of, to gain superiority.

Oversee: To watch; to superintend, supervise.

Pace: To move along, proceed; to set or regulate the progress or speed of.

Participate: To take part in.

Perceive: To attain awareness or understanding of.

Perform: To fulfill or carry out some action.

Permit: To consent to; to authorize; to make possible.

Perpetuate: To cause to last indefinitely.

Persuade: To move by argument or entreaty to a belief, position, or course of action.

Pinpoint: To locate or aim with great precision or accuracy; to cause to stand out conspicuously.

Place: To locate and choose positions for.

Plan: To devise or project the realization or achievement of a course of action.

Point: To indicate the position of; to furnish with a point, as a pencil; to call attention to.

Post: To record data in ledgers or other forms from another source (accounting term).

Practice: To perform or work at repeatedly in order to gain proficiency.

Predict: To declare in advance; to foretell on the basis of observation, experience, or scientific reason.

Prepare: To make ready for a particular purpose.

Prescribe: To establish as a rule or guide.

Present: To introduce; to bestow; to lay as a charge before the court; to offer to view.

Preserve: To keep, guard, observe; to keep safe, protect; to keep free from decay; to maintain.

Prevent: To stop something from occurring; to take advance measures against.

Price: To fix, to establish, or to find out the value of.

Proceed: To begin to carry out all action.

Process: To subject to some special treatment; to handle in accordance with a prescribed procedure.

Procure: To obtain possession of; to bring about.

Produce: To grow; to make, bear, or yield something; to offer to view or notice; to exhibit.

Program: To arrange or work out a sequence of operations to be performed.

Project: To throw forward; to present for consideration; to communicate vividly, especially to an audience.

Promote: To advance to a higher level or position.

Propose: To form or declare a plan or intention.

Provide: To supply what is needed.

Pull: To haul, tow; to remove, as in filing.

Purchase: To buy or procure by committing organizational funds.

Qualify: To moderate; to alter the strength or flavor of; to limit or modify the meaning of.

Quantify: To make explicit the logical amount of; to determine or express the amount of.

Question: To interrogate; to doubt; to dispute; to inquire.

Quote: To repeat as from a book; to state a price as for merchandise.

Radiate: To shine brightly; to proceed in a direct line from or toward a center.

Rank: To arrange in regular formation; to assign to a particular position or class.

Rate: To assess the value of; to appraise; to arrange in sequence of rank.

Read: To interpret; to scan; to study the movements of, to understand the meaning of, to utter aloud the printed written words of.

Realize: To understand clearly; to get by sale, investment, or effort.

Reason: To use the faculty of reason; think; to reason (the power of comprehending, inferring or thinking, esp. in orderly rational ways).

Recall: To bring back to; to summon to return; to revoke or withdraw; to call back.

Receive: To acquire, come into possession of.

Recite: To repeat from memory; to tell in detail.

Recognize: To perceive clearly; to acknowledge with a show of appreciation.

Recommend: To advise or counsel a course of action; to offer or suggest for adoption.

Reconcile: To adjust; to restore to harmony; to make congruous.

Reconstruct: To rebuild; to reorganize or reestablish.

Record: To register; to set down in writing.

Recruit: To seek out others to become new members or personnel.

Rectify: To correct by calculation or adjustment; to remedy; to set right.

Reduce: To narrow down; to diminish in size or amount; to abridge; to lower in grade or rank.

Refer: To send or direct for aid, treatment, information, or decision; to direct attention; to make reference to.

Refine: To improve or perfect; to free from impurities.

Reflect: To think calmly and quietly; to give back as an image, likeness, or outline; to make apparent.

Regard: To pay attention to; to take into consideration; to relate to.

Register: To enter in a record.

Regulate: To govern or direct according to rule; to bring under the control of law; to fix or adjust the time, amount, degree of.

Reinforce: To strengthen with additional forces or additions.

Reject: To refuse to have, use, or take for some purpose; to refuse to hear, receive, or admit.

Relate: To show or establish logical or causal connection between; to have meaningful social relationships.

Release: To set free as in releasing information; to permit the publication or dissemination of.

Rely: To depend.

Remit: To spend money in payment of; to submit or refer for consideration, judgment, decision, or action.

Remove: To change the location, station or residence of, to dismiss from office.

Render: To furnish an opinion; to answer.

Repeat: To do or say something again.

Represent: To act in the place of or for.

Report: To give an account of; to furnish information or data.

Request: To ask for something.

Require: To claim by right and authority; to call for as suitable or appropriate; to demand as necessary.

Requisition: To ask in writing for something that is needed.

Rescind: To make void; to repeal; to abrogate a contract by restoring preexisting conditions.

Research: To inquire specifically, using involved and critical investigations.

Resolve: To clear up; to find an answer to; to reach a decision about; to change by resolution or formal vote.

Respect: To have reference to; to refrain from interfering with.

Respond: To make an answer; to show favorable reaction.

Restrict: To confine within bounds; to restrain.

Retrieve: To regain; to rescue.

Review: To consider; to reexamine.

Revise: To rework in order to correct or improve; to make a new, improved, or up-to-date version.

Route: To forward; to schedule to dispatch.

Salvage: To rescue or save (as from wreckage or ruin).

Satisfy: To carry out the terms of (a contract); to meet financial obligations; to make reparation to; to please.

Scan: To examine; to search a series of punched cards, tapes, or a memory bank to locate specific data (computer usage).

Schedule: To plan a timetable; to fix time.

Screen: To examine in orderly fashion to determine suitability or acceptability (as in appraising potential employees); to cull.

Search: To examine, to probe; to make a thorough examination or investigation of.

Secure: To gain possession of; to guarantee; to make safe.

Seek: To look for; to ask for; to try to acquire or gain.

Select: To choose the best suited.

Sell: To give up property to another for money or other valuable consideration.

Send: To dispatch by a means of communication; to convey.

Separate: To set apart.

Serve: To assist; to be of use; to hold office.

Service: To adjust; to repair or maintain.

Set up: To cause a condition to come into effect; to put in operation.

Show: To display; to give indication; to point out to someone.

Sign: To formally approve a document by affixing a signature.

Simplify: To clarify; to reduce to basic essentials.

Solicit: To approach with a request or plea; to strongly urge.

Solve: To find a solution for.

Sort: To separate or arrange according to a scheme; to rank by kind, class, division, etc.

Spark: To set off in a burst of activity; to activate.

Speak: To utter words; to express oneself before a group.

Specify: To state precisely in detail or to name explicitly.

Spend: To use up or pay out.

Stack: To pile up.

Standardize: To bring into conformity with something established by authority, custom, or general consent as a model or criterion.

State: To set forth definitely in speech or in writing.

Stimulate: To excite to activity; to urge.

Strengthen: To make stronger.

Strive: To endeavor; to devote serious effort or energy.

Structure: To give arrangement or form to; to arrange or organize.

Study: To contemplate; to carefully examine or investigate; to deliberate.

Subdivide: To separate or divide into parts.

Submit: To present data for the discretion or judgment of others.

Summarize: To restate material (facts, figures, etc.) briefly.

Supervise: To personally oversee, inspect, or guide the work of others with responsibility for meeting certain standards of performance.

Supplement: To add to.

Supply: To furnish something that is needed; to provide; to equip.

Support: To promote the interests or cause of; to argue or vote for; to pay the costs of, to hold up or serve as a foundation for.

Survey: To examine as to condition, situation, or value.

Sustain: To give support or relief to; to prolong; to support by adequate proof.

Synthesize: To put together; to compose or combine parts or elements so as to form a whole; to produce a substance by the union of elements; to combine often diverse conceptions into a coherent whole; to reason deductively.

Systematize: To arrange methodically.

Tabulate: To put in table form; to set up in columns, rows.

Take: To assume possession of; to grasp; to gain approval of; to undertake or perform.

Tend: To act as an attendant.

Tender: To present for acceptance.

Terminate: To bring to an end; to conclude.

Test: To put to proof, to examine, observe, or evaluate critically.

Tolerate: To endure.

Total: To add up; to compute,

Trace: To locate something by searching or researching evidence.

Trade: To give in exchange for another commodity; to make a purchase.

Train: To each, demonstrate, or guide others in order to bring tip to a predetermined standard.

Transact: To carry on business; to negotiate.

Transcribe: To transfer data from one for in of record to another or from one method of preparation to another, without changing the nature of data.

Transform: To change inform or structure; to change in condition, nature, or character.

Translate: To turn into one's own or another language.

Transmit: To transfer or send front one person or place to another; to sent out it signal either by radio waves or over a wire.

Transpose: To change the usual order of.

Treat: To regard and deal with in a specified manner; to provide care for or deal with medically.

Turn: To make rotate or revolve; to cause to move around so as to effect a desired end (as locking, opening, shutting); to reverse the sides or surfaces of.

Type: To write using a typewriter; to arrange by categories.

Uncover: To expose to view by removing a covering; to reveal.

Understand: To grasp the meaning of, to have thorough or technical acquaintance with or expertness in the practice of.

Update: To make current.

Use: To put into action or service; to consume or take; to act with regard to.

Utilize: To make use of.

Verify: To confirm or establish authenticity; to substantiate.

Weigh: To ascertain the heaviness of; to consider carefully.

Withhold: To hold back; to refrain from granting, giving, or allowing.

Withstand: To stand up against; to resist successfully.

Write: To set down letters, words, sentences, or figures on paper or other suitable material; to author; to draft.

Glossary of Terms

Many items in this glossary are described in much greater detail in the text. Check the index and contents for the location of the description in text.

Compensation specialists frequently must use the words and terms in this glossary in performing their assignments. To facilitate its use, it has been divided into three major sections: (1) compensation administration, (2) employee welfare and pension benefits, and (3) legislative-related terms.

COMPENSATION ADMINISTRATION

Ability: A general trait or quality acquired by an individual.

Ability to pay: The ability of an organization to meet the pay demands of its employees or their representatives.

Accountability: A term used in job analysis to denote the end results to be achieved by the employee.

Across-the-board increase: An identical increase in wages given to the majority of workers. Sometimes known as a general increase.

Activity: Action requiring human effort. (In this book, the word *activity* is used as a generic term.)

Actual hours: The actual number of hours worked in a period by an employee.

Adjective checklist: A performance appraisal instrument consisting of a set of adjectives or descriptive statements of traits or behaviors demonstrated by an employee.

Administration: Commonly used term indicating the top levels of management in industry and business, or its functions. Occasionally used in an opposite sense to mean the routines of lower management levels.

Adverse impact: A term used to describe an unfavorable effect of employment practices with regard to minorities or women. A basis for a finding of discrimination.

Affected class: A group of employees who continue to suffer the effects of past discrimination.

Affirmative action: Requirements of an employer to take positive steps to end underrepresentation of minorities and women.

Agency theory: A theory of motivation that depicts exchange relationships in terms of two parties: agents and principals. According to this theory, both sides of the exchange will seek the most favorable exchange possible and will act opportunistically if given a chance.

Agreement increase: An increase in pay given to all workers or to a majority of workers as a result of contract negotiations.

All-salaried workforce: Both exempt employees (exempt from provisions of the Fair Labor Standards Act), who traditionally are paid a salary rather than an hourly rate, and nonexempt employees receive a prescribed amount of money each pay period that does not primarily depend on the number of hours worked.

Alternation ranking: A job evaluation method that involves ordering the job description alternately at each extreme. All the jobs are considered. Agreement is reached on which is the most valuable, then the least valuable. Evaluators alternate between the next most valued and next least valued and so on until the jobs have been ordered.

Amortization: Paying off an interest-bearing liability through a series of installment payments.

Annual bonus: A lump-sum payment made in addition to an employee's regular salary or wage.

Annualize rate: Transforming an investment rate of return for a period greater than or less than one year to a rate in terms of 12 months.

Appeals procedures: Mechanism created to handle pay disagreements. They provide a forum for employees and managers to voice their complaints and receive a hearing.

Area differential: An allowance paid to an employee because of differences in living costs from one area to another (sometimes called area rate differential); allowance paid to an expatriate for medium-term cultural and hardship factors present in country of assignment. (See *Hardship allowance*.)

Authority: (1) The right to take independent action. (2) The right to direct the actions of others. As applied to functional or staff authority, it is the right to direct another unit of the organization *only* with regard to the functional specialty of the directing party.

Automatic wage adjustment: Increasing or decreasing wages in accordance with some specific plan independent of external influence or control.

Automatic wage progression: Increasing wages after specified periods of service independent of external influence or control (also *length-of-service increases*).

Automation: A combination of several machines or other automatic devices performing a coordinated sequence of operations.

Average earned rate: An hourly rate arrived at by dividing hours worked into the equivalent earnings paid for a calendar quarter for use in the next quarter. Excludes overtime bonuses and other payments not considered to be earnings.

Average hourly earnings: Hourly pay determined by dividing hours worked per period into the total wages paid for the period.

Average straight-time hourly earnings: Hourly pay determined by dividing the hours worked per period into the total straight-time earnings for the period (excluding overtime).

Balance sheet: An organization's financial statement showing assets, liabilities, and capital on a given date.

Base country: The country in which the employee is hired but not necessarily the country of citizenship.

Base wage rate or base rate: The hourly money rate paid for a job performed at standard pace. Does not include shift differentials, overtime, or incentive premiums.

Basic pay policies: Include decisions on the relative importance of (1) internal consistency, (2) external competitiveness, (3) employee contributions, and (4) the administration of the pay system. These policies form the foundation for the design and administration of pay systems and serve as guidelines for managing pay to accomplish the system's objectives.

Bedeaux plan: Individual incentive plan that provides a variation on straight piecework and standard hour plans. Instead of timing an entire task, a Bedeaux plan requires determination of the time required to complete each simple action of a task. Workers receive a wage incentive for completing a task in less than a standard time.

Behavior: What a person does.

Behaviorally Anchored Rating Scales (BARS): A performance rating scale that has each level of the scale linked directly to behavioral descriptions that are applicable to the job of the rated employee.

Benchmark: A standard with characteristics so detailed that other classifications can be compared as being above, below, or comparable to it; refers to jobs used for making pay comparisons within or outside the organization.

Benchmark conversion: Matching survey jobs by applying the employer's plan to the external jobs and then comparing the worth of the external job with its internal "match."

Blue-collar workers: These include skilled and semi-skilled craftworkers, unskilled laborers, and their immediate supervisors; these workers are usually paid on an hourly basis.

Board of directors: A governing body of a corporation that is elected by stockholders to represent them.

Bonus earnings or bonus: Extra compensation in addition to regular wages.

Bonus eligible: A group or a class of employees granted the right to participate in a bonus program.

Bonus eligibility: Rules that define employee bonus participation rights.

Bootleg wages: Wages above market rate that an employer must pay in a tight labor market to attract and hold skilled workers.

Bottom-up approach to pay budgeting: Under this approach individual employees' pay rates for the next plan year are forecasted and summed to create an organization's pay budget.

Broadbanding: A pay structure consisting of a few (four to eight) pay grades/bands with each band having a relatively wide range.

Budget: A definite financial plan for sales, output, and expenditures that imposes goals and limitations on various activities of an organization or an individual.

Business necessity: A basic defense of an employment practice alleged to have adverse impact.

Call-back pay: Payment given to an employee who is called back to work after his or her regular working hours; normally, there is a guaranteed amount regardless of number of hours worked.

Call-in pay: Guaranteed pay for workers who report to work at the usual time and for whom there is no work.

Career paths: Refers to the progression of jobs within an organization.

Cash: Ready money; payment for goods or services in money.

Cash equivalents: Payments easily and quickly converted to money.

Central tendency error: The overuse of average ratings.

Centralized: The condition in which a firm is organized so most authority for planning and decisions is retained by top management.

Checkoff: The deduction of union dues or assessments from employees' pay for the purpose of turning them over to the union.

Chief: The head of an activity. In an organization, it is usually coupled with the name of a department or activity (e.g., chief engineer).

Class of positions: A group of positions, regardless of location, that are alike enough in duties and responsibilities to be called by the same descriptive title, to be given the same pay scale under similar conditions, and to require substantially the same qualifications.

Classification: The assignment of a job to a pay grade.

Class-series: A grouping of job classes, regardless of location, having similar job content but differing in levels of skill, responsibility, knowledge, and qualification requirements.

Commission: A form of compensation for the sale of products or services; usually an amount figured as a percentage of the sale.

Commission plan—single goal: A plan in which key managers receive a bonus based on business or "profit-center" profits or some other quantitative measure of performance.

Committee: A group that meets as a body or through communication, usually in an advisory capacity. Some high-ranking committees have authority to direct action.

Communication: Generally refers to the transmittal of thoughts, ideas, instructions, orders, and so on, from one person to another. Within an organization, it often applies particularly to relations between superior and subordinate.

Comparable worth: The concept of measuring a job's value to the firm. This value is important to determine rates of pay for jobs having dissimilar job content and making different requirements on the jobholder. An issue that states that men and women who perform work of comparable value should receive comparable pay.

Compa-ratio: The ratio showing the relationship of total actual pay in a pay grade to the midpoint or some other control point of that pay grade. A ratio of 1.0 normally indicates adequate distribution of employees in that grade.

Compensable factors: Elements that describe and differentiate among jobs. Used to analyze jobs to develop their worth to the organization.

Compensation: All forms of financial returns and tangible services and benefits employees receive as part of an employment relationship.

Compensation budgeting: A part of the organization's planning process; helps to ensure that future financial expenditures are coordinated and controlled. It involves forecasting the total expenditures required by the compensation system during the next period as well as the amount of the compensation increases. Bottom up and top down are the two typical approaches to the process.

Compensatory time off: Time off given in lieu of overtime. Under the Fair Labor Standards Act, it must be given in the same workweek.

Competency: Basic units of knowledge and skills employees must acquire or demonstrate in order to successfully perform work assignments.

Competency-based pay: Pay related directly to the kinds and levels of competencies (knowledge and skills) required in the performance of the work/job.

Competitive compa-ratio: Ratio of market or survey midpoint job rates of pay to the organization's midpoint for that job.

Competitiveness: The ability of an organization to provide rates of pay comparable to that of labor market competitors.

Compression: The narrowing of the differences in rates of pay to the degree that purported differences between values of jobs are not recognized.

Conglomerate: A large collection of enterprises, often dissimilar, combined by merger or purchase by a parent or holding company.

Congruency: The degree of consistency or "fit" between the compensation system and other organizational components such as the strategy, product-market stage, culture and values, employee needs, and union status.

Constant: A fixed or invariable value or data item.

Consumer price index (CPI): A listing of price changes in a selected list of products and services purchased by a hypothetical family in representative cities that is prepared by the Bureau of Labor Statistics. Sometimes mistakenly called the "cost-of-living index."

Consideration: A legal term meaning the compensation to be realized by a party to a contract for performing contract provisions.

Content theories: Motivation theories that focus on *what* motivates people rather than on *how* people are motivated. Maslow's need hierarchy theory and Herzberg's two-factor theory fall in this category.

Contingency workforce: That part of the workforce that includes flexible workers, temporaries, part-time employees, and independent contractors. The pay and benefits of contingent workers tend to be about half the pay and benefits of noncontingent workers.

Contingent employees: Workers whose employment is of a limited duration (part-time or temporary).

Control: In management, the function of seeing that policies and plans are carried out. Can be a specialized activity such as production control or inventory control.

Control point: A point used to identify where average rates of pay should be centered for salary administration purposes.

Controller: An executive who is responsible for accounting and the control of expenditures (also, *comptroller*).

Conventional job analysis methods: Methods (e.g., functional job analysis) that typically involve an analyst using a questionnaire in conjunction with structured interviews of job incumbents and supervisors. The methods place considerable reliance on analysts' ability to understand the work performed and to accurately describe it.

Cooperative wage study (CWS): A study undertaken by 12 steel companies and the United Steel Workers to design an industrywide point plan (the Steel Plan) for clerical and technical personnel.

Corporation: A business that exists by charter from a government, is owned by stockholders, and is subject to control by those who possess the majority of voting shares.

Cost-of-living adjustment (COLA): Pay adjustments devised to bring wages and salaries in line with changes in the cost of living. Generally based on changes in price indexes published by the Bureau of Labor Statistics.

Cost-of-living allowance: An adjustment to an expatriate's pay that recognizes differences between cost of living at foreign work site and at base location in home country.

Cost-of-living index: A measure of the average changes in the cost of goods purchased by consumers against the cost during some base period.

Coverage: The number of jobs or the number of personnel whose jobs have been assigned a standard during the reporting period.

Criterion: A standard or measure used to appraise an employee's job proficiency or effectiveness.

Culture: The informal rules, rituals, and value systems of an organization that influence employee behavior.

Decentralized: The condition in which authority, responsibility, facilities, or work are dispersed among several units or locations.

Deferred compensation program: Provides income to an employee at some future time as a compensation for work performed now. Types of deferred compensation programs include stock option plans and pension plans.

Department: An individual or a group that operates as a distinctly separate unit, usually one of considerable size or importance.

Differentials: Pay differences among levels within the organization, such as the difference in pay between adjacent levels in a career path, between supervisors and subordinates, between union and nonunion employees, and between executives and regular employees.

Direct compensation: All forms of compensation that are paid directly to and received immediately by an individual.

Direct labor: Work performed on a product that advances it toward its ultimate specifications.

Director: (1) A member of the board of directors. (2) Title given to the head of an important activity, such as director of human resources.

Discount: A selling price below an established price.

Discount stock option: Rights to a stock option at a price less than 100 percent of fair market value.

Disparate (unequal) impact standard: An illegal application of pay practices that may appear to be neutral but have a negative effect on females or minorities, unless those practices can be shown to be business related.

Disparate (unequal) treatment standard: Illegal application of different standards to different classes of employees unless they can be shown to be business related.

Dispersion: Distribution of rates around a measure of central tendency.

Distributive justice: Fairness in the amount of reward distributed to employees.

Dividend: A proportion of a business' net earnings paid to its stockholders.

Dividend equivalents: An amount of money paid to key employees that equals dividends paid per share.

Division of labor: In general, the assignment of tasks or responsibilities to an individual or a group within an organization. Often applies to dividing work into relatively small tasks among individuals as in mass production.

Double-track system: A framework for professional employees in an organization whereby at least two general tracks of ascending compensation steps are available: (1) a managerial track to be ascended through increasing responsibility for supervision of people and (2) a professional track to be ascended through increasing contributions of a professional nature. Also known as dual-track system.

Downgrading: The demotion of an employee to a lower-rated job.

Drive theory: A motivational theory that assumes that all behavior is induced by drives (i.e., en-

ergizers such as thirst, hunger, sex), and that present behavior is based in large part on the consequences or rewards of past behavior.

Duty: An activity performed in carrying out a responsibility.

Earnings: Total wages of compensation received by an employee for time worked or services rendered (includes all compensation, overtime, premium pay).

Earnings per share: Net income less preferred dividends divided by share of common stock outstanding.

Earnings yield: A ratio found by dividing the market price of a stock into its earnings.

Effort: The will to perform productive work, either mental or manual.

Efficiency: (1) In an energy-consuming apparatus or process, the ratio, output/input, expressed as a percentage or a decimal. (2) A ratio that compares actual performance with a standard, as in performance rating.

Employee benefits: Tangible compensation given to employees other than wages.

Employee stock ownership plan (ESOP): A stock bonus plan that allows employers to take advantage of certain tax privileges while encouraging employee ownership of the company by granting stock to employees.

Entitlement: Employee belief that returns and/or rewards are due regardless of individual or company performance.

Environment: The external conditions affecting an individual or a group.

Equal pay for comparable work: The principle that, regardless of age, gender, color, or religion, an individual should be paid the same wage for the same kind of work.

Equalization component: As a part of an expatriate compensation package, equalization is one form of equity designed to "keep the worker whole" (i.e., maintain real income or purchasing power of base pay). This equalization typically comes in the form of tax equalization, housing allowances, and other allowances and premiums.

Equities: Ownership of property.

Equity: Absolute or relative justice or "fairness" in an exchange such as the employment contract. Absolute fairness is evaluated against a universally accepted criterion of equity, while relative fairness is assessed against a criterion that may vary according to the individuals involved in the exchange, the nature of what is exchanged, and the context of the exchange.

Equity pay objective: Fair pay treatment for all the participants in the employment relationship. Focuses attention on pay systems that recognize employee contributions and employee job requirements.

Equity theory: A theory proposing that in an exchange relationship (such as employment) the equality of outcome/input ratios between a person and a comparison with a standard or relevant person or group will determine fairness or equity. If the ratios diverge from each other, the person will experience reactions of unfairness and inequity.

Escalator clause: Provision in a labor agreement for making wage adjustments upward or downward in accordance with cost-of-living fluctuations.

Essay: An open-ended performance appraisal format. The descriptors used could range from comparisons with other employees through adjectives, behaviors, and goal accomplishment.

Exchange rate: A term in economics that identifies a rate of pay where labor demand and labor supply functions intersect in the external market.

Executive compensation: The special components of compensation provided to executives. Tax considerations are critical in the design of these plans.

Expatriate: An employee working at a foreign work site for a period in excess of one year.

Expectancy theory: A motivation theory that proposes that individuals will select an alternative based on how this choice relates to outcomes such as rewards. The choice made is based on the strength or value of the outcome and on the perceived probability that this choice will lead to the desired outcome.

Experience factor: A ratio of planned compa-ratio to actual compa-ratio indicating unanticipated changes in personnel, pay structure, etc.

External competitiveness: Refers to the pay relationships among organizations and focuses attention on the competitive positions reflected in these relationships within established or defined job markets.

External equity: Fairness in relation to the amount paid in the relevant external market.

Face validity: The determination of the relevance of a measuring device on "appearances" only.

Factor: One of a number of relatively distinct and underlying variables that combine to bring about a certain result.

Factor-comparison: A job evaluation method in which relative values for each of a number of factors of a job are established by direct comparison with the values established for the same factors on selected or key jobs.

Factor scales: Reflect different degrees within each compensable factor. Most commonly five to seven degrees are defined. Each degree may also be anchored by the typical skills, tasks, and behaviors, or key job titles.

Factor weights: Indicate the importance of each compensable factor in a job evaluation system. Weights can be derived either through a committee judgment or statistical analysis.

Fair day's work: The amount of work performed by an operator or group of operators that is fair to both the company and the operator, considering wages paid.

Family: The grouping of two or more class-series in an organization that have related or common work content.

Fat grades: The wide range of pay permitted in broadband pay structures. Fat grades support redesigned, downsized, or seamless organizations that have eliminated layers of managerial jobs. Employees may move laterally across a band in order to gain depth of experience.

Federal Insurance Contributions Act (FICA): The source of Social Security contribution withholding requirements. The FICA deduction is paid by employer and employee.

First impression error: Developing a negative opinion of an employee early in the review period and allowing that to negatively color all subsequent perceptions of performance.

First-line supervisor: The manager closest to nonsupervisory employees in the organization's hierarchy. Also called front-line supervisor.

Flat increase: An across-the-board increase that is either the same absolute amount or the same percentage amount for all positions.

Flat rates: A single rate, rather than a range of rates, for all individuals performing each job. Ignores seniority and performance differences.

Flexible compensation: The allocation of employee compensation in a variety of forms tailored to organization pay objectives and/or the needs of individual employees.

Foreign service premium: A percentage addition to base pay provided to compensate an expatriate for foreign environment factors.

Foreman: Head of a department in a factory.

Forms of compensation: Pay may be received directly in the form of cash (e.g., wages, bonuses, incentives) or indirectly through benefits (e.g., pensions, health insurance, vacations).

Function: (1) In industrial operations, an activity performed by a machine, an individual, or a group; (2) a specific purpose of an entity or its characteristic action in communications; (3) a machine action such as a carriage return or line feed.

Functional: A classification of an activity.

Functional job analysis (FJA): A conventional approach to job analysis developed by the U.S. Department of Labor. Five categories of data are collected: what the worker does; the methodologies and techniques employed; the machines, tools, and equipment used; the products and services that result; and the traits required of the worker. FJA constitutes a modification of DOL methodology and is widely used in the public sector.

Gainsharing: Any method of wage payment in which the worker participates in all or a portion of the added earnings that result from his or her improved performance.

Gantt plan: Individual incentive plan that provides for variable incentives as a function of a standard expressed as time period per unit of production. Under this plan, a standard time for a task is purposely set at a level requiring high effort to complete.

Garnishment: A legal action whereby a portion of an employee's wages are attached by a creditor to pay a debt.

Geographic differential: Differences in pay for the same job based on cost-of-living differences in geographic locations.

Glass ceiling: A subtle barrier that keeps women and minorities out of executive positions.

Global approach: Substitutes a particular skill and experience level for job description in determining external market rates. Includes rates for all individuals who possess that skill.

Going rate: An employer's best estimate of the rate of pay of the labor market to acquire needed personnel.

Golden handcuffs: Compensation components earned over a period of time that assist in retaining an employee.

Golden parachute: Compensation components payable to a key executive upon dissolution of the organization or termination of the job. Other names are silver parachute or tin parachute when payments are made to lower-level employees.

Goods: The tangible products of the economic system that can satisfy human wants or desires.

Green-circle rate: Rate of pay less than the minimum for that pay grade.

Grossing up: Supplements to an employee's pay to cover added tax expenses incurred by receiving some other addition to taxable income.

Group bonus: A bonus payment based on the performance of a group of workers operating as a unit.

Guaranteed annual wage: A plan that guarantees a minimum income to employees annually.

Guaranteed wage rate: The rate of pay an employer guarantees to his employees on incentive work.

Halo effect (error): The tendency of one factor to upwardly influence the rating of all other factors of whatever is being rated.

Halsey 50–50 method: Individual incentive method that provides for variable incentives as a function of a standard expressed as time period per unit of production. This plan derives its name from the shared split between worker and employer of any savings in direct costs.

Hardship allowance (premium): An addition to base pay granted in recognition of extraordinarily difficult living conditions, or physical hardships, or unhealthy environmental conditions.

Hay system: A point-factor system that evaluates jobs with respect to know-how, problem solving, and accountability. It is used primarily for exempt (managerial/professional) jobs.

Heredity: Genetically acquired psychological or physiological factors that establish characteristics or tendencies of the individual.

Hierarchies (or job structures): Jobs ordered according to their relative content and/or value.

Hiring rate: A beginning rate of pay at which people are hired into a job.

Hit rate: The ability of a job evaluation plan to replicate a predetermined, agreed-upon job structure.

Home leave: A periodic leave to country of domicile for employees in a foreign assignment.

Horn effect: The opposite of a halo effect; downgrading an employee across all performance dimensions exclusively because of poor performance on one dimension.

Housing allowance: A differential paid to adjust for differences between housing costs at foreign worksite and cost for similar housing at home base.

Human factors: The physical, mental, and emotional constraints that affect operator performance.

Human resources: All employees of an organization.

Human resource accounting: An approach to placing a dollar value on the organization's employees and its customer goodwill. (Also called human asset accounting.)

Implicit contract: The unwritten implied agreements, or patterns of reciprocal obligations and returns, between employers and employees. This includes reciprocal understandings about the nature of risks involved in wages, benefits, and employability.

Improshare (IMproved PROductivity through SHARing): A gainsharing plan in which a standard is developed to identify the expected hours required to produce an acceptable level of output. Any savings arising from production of agreed-upon output in fewer than expected hours are shared by the firm and the workers.

In-basket exercise: A specific type of work sample test often used in managerial selection. An individual is given a "basket" of work to respond to, using all possible resources.

Incentive: A reward, financial or otherwise, that compensates the worker for high and/or continued performance above standard. Also, a motivating influence to induce effort above normal (wage incentive).

Incentive stock options (ISOs): A form of deferred compensation designed to influence long-term performance. Gives an executive the right to pay today's market price for a block of shares in the company at a future time. No tax is due until the shares are sold.

Increase guidelines: Inherent compensation system controls. They specify amount and timing of pay increases on an organizationwide basis.

Incumbent: An individual occupying a job.

Indirect compensation: Compensation components normally included within an employee benefits package.

Indirect labor: Labor that is necessary to support the manufacture of a product, but does not directly enter into transforming the material into the product.

Individual-based systems: Pay systems that focus on employee rather than job characteristics. Pay is based on the highest work-related skills employees possess rather than on the specific job performed.

Individual incentive plans: Incentive compensation that is tied directly to objective measures of individual performance.

Inflation: A phase of a business cycle characterized by abnormally high prices and a decrease in the purchasing power of money.

Instrumentality: The perceived contingency that an outcome (performing well) has another outcome (a reward such as pay).

Integrated manufacturing strategies: Organization strategies designed to gain competitive advantage such as just-in-time manufacturing, statistical quality control, and advanced technologies.

Internal consistency: Refers to the pay relationships among jobs or skill levels within a single organization and focuses attention on employee and management acceptance of those relationships. It involves establishing equal pay for jobs of equal worth and acceptable pay differentials for jobs of unequal worth.

Internal pricing: Pricing jobs in relationship to what other jobs within the organization are paid.

Internal equity: The ranking of all jobs to each other relative to their value to the organization.

International compensation: Compensation practices related to employees in foreign work sites.

Interquartile range: In an array of data the distance between the first and third quartiles. A range containing the middle 50 percent of the data.

Interrater reliability: The extent of agreement among raters rating the same individual, group, or phenomena.

Interval rating: A measurement process in which differences among intervals are equal, permitting addition and subtraction.

Job: A collection of responsibilities and duties that, considered as a whole, constitute the established assignment to one or more individuals.

Job analysis: The process of carefully observing and appraising a job and then recording the details of the work performed. (Also referred to as *job study*.)

Job analyst: An individual who by reason of education and training performs job analysis studies.

Job bidding: Method of allowing employees to bid for (apply for) job vacancies. (Also called job posting and bidding.)

Job classification: A grouping of jobs of similar content, responsibilities, and so on into classes or grades usually having similar rates of pay.

Job cluster: A series of jobs grouped for job evaluation and wage and salary administration purposes on the basis of common skills, occupational qualifications, technology, licensing, working conditions, union jurisdiction, workplace, career paths, and organizational tradition.

Job content: The various assignments or activities that comprise a job.

Job description: A summary of the most important features of a job in terms of the general nature of the work involved and the kinds of workers required to perform it efficiently. It describes the job, not the individual who fills it.

Job design: The process of determining and specifying the content, methods, and relationships of a job in order to satisfy, in the most effective and efficient manner, the technological and human considerations within organizational constraints.

Job duties: A group of employee work activities or tasks which, taken together, describe a major purpose (responsibility) of that job.

Job enlargement: The process of adding more tasks (more "doing" functions) to a job to reduce overspecialization.

Job enrichment: The process of adding more responsibilities (planning and control as opposed to "doing") to make the job more meaningful and challenging.

Job evaluation: A formal process for determining the relative worth of various work assignments.

Job evaluation committee: A group representing all important constituencies within the organization that may be charged with the responsibility of (1) selecting a job evaluation system, (2) carrying out or at least supervising the process of job evaluation, and (3) evaluating the success with which the job evaluation has been conducted. Its role may vary among organizations.

Job evaluation manual: Information on the job evaluation plan that is used as a "yardstick" to evaluate jobs. It includes a description of the job evaluation method used, descriptions of all jobs, if relevant, a description of compensable factors, numerical degree scales, and weights. May also contain a description of available review or appeals procedure.

Job family: A collection of jobs that require common skills, occupational qualifications, technology, licensing, working conditions, and so on.

Job pricing: The assignment of a rate of pay to a job or to job grades; the practice of establishing rates of pay, making judgments that combine internal equity and market value data.

Job ranking: The ordering of jobs from most difficult/important to least difficult/ important.

Job rating: A proportional ordering of jobs from the most difficult/important to the least difficult/ important.

Job responsibility: A major purpose or end result of an employee's work activity; one of the primary reasons for the job's existence.

Job specification: Normally that part of the job description that includes the requisite qualifications of the jobholder. In the past, called *man specification.*

Job structure: Relationships among jobs inside an organization, based on work content and the job's relative contribution to the achievement of organizational objectives.

Key jobs (benchmark jobs): Selected jobs about which data may be gathered from other employers to provide the basis for setting pay.

Knowledge or skill blocs: The different kinds and levels of knowledge or skills competencies required to perform successfully work assignments.

Knowledge systems: Process that links pay to additional knowledge related to the same job (depth) (e.g., scientists and teachers) or to a number of different jobs (breadth) (e.g., technician).

Labor demand: In economic models, the demand for labor is a curve that indicates how the desired level of employment varies with changes in the price of labor when other factors are held constant. The shape of the labor demand curve is downward sloping. Thus, an increase in the wage rate will reduce the demand for labor in both the short and long run.

Labor market: A place where labor is exchanged for wages.

Labor supply: The people who are available for employment in a given occupation.

Lag, lead, or lead-lag policy: The timing of an adjustment to wage structure; if you lag, structure change matches market at start of year; if you lead, rate projected at end of year and adjustment made at beginning of year are in line with projection. Lead-lag—projection made for market at mid-year and adjustment at beginning of year are in line with projection. (Lead market—first six months; lag market—second six months.)

Learning curve: A graphic representation of human learning that shows rapid increases in learning in the early periods of time. Also used to indicate changes in performance over periods of time. A graphic presentation of the progress in production effectiveness as time passes.

Least-squares line: In regression analysis, the line fitted to a scatterplot of coordinates that minimizes the squared deviations of coordinates around the line. This line is also known as the *best fit line*.

Leniency error: Consistently rating someone higher than is deserved.

Leveling: Weighting market pay survey data according to the closeness of the job matches.

Level of aggregation: Refers to the size of the work unit for which performance is measured (e.g., individual work group, department, plan, or organization) and to which rewards are distributed.

Level rise: The percentage increase in the average wage rate paid.

Percent level rise =

$$100 \times \frac{\text{avg. pay year end} - \text{avg. pay year beginning}}{\text{avg. pay at the beginning of the year}}$$

Lifetime employment: Most prevalent in Japanese companies, this refers to the notion of an employee staying with the same company for his or her entire career, despite possible poor performance on the part of either the employee or the company.

Line: Employees directly involved in producing and/or selling the products or services of the organization. Compare line vs. staff.

Linear regression: A statistical technique that allows an analyst to build a model of a relationship between variables that are assumed to be linearly related.

Living wage: A term referring to a wage rate that permits the employee to maintain a given standard of living in the face of inflation.

Local country nationals (LCNs): Citizens of a country in which a U.S. foreign subsidiary is located, LCNs' compensation is tied either to local wage rates or to the rates of U.S. expatriates performing the same job. Each practice has different equity implications.

Locality pay: Adjusting pay rates for employees in a specific geographic area to account for local conditions such as labor shortages, housing cost differentials, and so on.

Long-term bonus: A component of deferred compensation that provides income in the form of a bonus over time—usually two years or longer.

Long-term incentives: Inducements offered in advance to influence longer rate (multiyear) results. Usually offered to top managers and professionals to focus on long-term organization objectives.

Low-high approach: Using the lowest- and highest-paid benchmark jobs in the external market to anchor an entire skill-based structure.

Lump-sum award: Payment of entire increase (typically merit based) at one time. Amount is not factored into base pay so any benefits tied to base pay also don't increase.

Management by exception: Confining an executive's attention to matters commensurate with his rank and ability. Accomplished by delegation of authority and the assignment of responsibilities to subordinates.

Management by objectives (MBO): A formal planning, operations, and control program in which supervisor and subordinate mutually discuss and agree on the achievement of certain desired results and in which the performance of the subordinate is measured by the relationship between goals set and results achieved.

Manager: A person engaged in management functions. A title usually applied to a position of considerable rank and often coupled with an adjective or phrase to define areas of responsibility (factory manager, sales manager).

Man specification: See *job specification*.

Manning tables: Classifications of all employees by job, age, gender, skill, experience, and so on, to provide information concerning manpower requirements. With the desexing of language, this should probably be called "human resource tables."

Marginal product of labor: The additional output associated with the employment of one additional human resources unit, with other factors held constant.

Marginal productivity theory (MPT): By contrast with Marxist "surplus value" theory, MPT focuses on labor demand rather than supply and argues that employers will pay a wage to a unit of labor that equals that unit's use (not exchange) value. That is, work is compensated in proportion to its contribution to the organization's production objectives.

Marginal revenue of labor: The additional revenue generated when the firm employs one additional unit of human resources, with other factors held constant.

Market pay lines: Summarize the distribution of market rates for the benchmark jobs under consideration. Several methods to construct the lines can be used: a single line connecting the distributions' midpoints (means or medians), or the 25th, 50th, and 75th percentiles. Often the lines are fitted to the data through a statistical procedure, such as regression analysis.

Market pricing: The setting of pay rates that reflects the best estimate of what is being paid in the market.

Maturity curve: A method of setting rates of pay for professionals using survey data based on age, or years since last degree, or years of experience.

Mean: A simple arithmetic average obtained by adding a series of numbers and dividing by the sum of the number of items in the series.

Median: The middle value in a distribution, with an equal number of values above and below it. An important statistic in evaluating groups of salary figures.

Merit increase: An individual's pay increase based on performance, seniority, or other equity criteria.

Merit pay increase guidelines: Guidelines that tie pay increases to performance. They may take one of two forms: The simplest version specifies pay increases permissible for different levels of performance. More complex guidelines tie pay not only to performance but also to position in the pay range.

Merit progression: A formula for progressing an employee through a wage structure according to time and grade, performance, or some other individual equity basis.

Merit rating: A method for appraising the worth of an employee with respect to his/her job. Serves as a basis for pay rating, promotion, or reassignment of work.

Merrick plan: Individual incentive plan that provides for variable incentives as a function of units of production per time period. It works like the Taylor plan, but three piecework rates are set: (1) high—for production exceeding 100 percent of standard; (2) medium—for production between 83 percent and 100 percent of standard; and (3) low—for production less than 83 percent of standard.

Method: A term used to signify the technique used for performing an operation.

Metropolitan statistical areas: A designation of the 194 largest communities in the nation consisting of counties or multiple counties to be used as benchmarks by the Bureau of Census of the U.S. Department of Commerce.

Middle and top management: Employees above the supervisory level who have technical and administrative training and whose major duties entail the direction of people and the organization.

Midpoint: The salary midway between the minimum and maximum of a pay range.

Midpoint progression: The percentage difference between adjacent midpoints in a pay structure obtained by dividing the midpoint of the higher pay grade by the midpoint of the lower pay grade.

Minimum wage: The minimum wage level set under the Fair Labor Standards Act.

Mode: The item in an array that occurs most frequently.

Model: A pattern of conceptual or mathematical relationships that, in some way, imitate, duplicate, or illustrate real-world conditions.

Multiple regression: A statistical technique used to build a model that describes the joint impact of several x (independent) variables on a y (dependent) variable.

Multiskill systems: The linking of pay to the number of different kinds of jobs/work assignments an employee is certified to do, regardless of the specific job he or she is currently performing.

Mutual commitment compensation: A pay strategy that combines high wages with an emphasis on quality, innovation, and customer service. Based on the belief that high wages are essential to reinforce cooperation and participation and will provide a better living standard for all employees.

Mutual rating: The rating of each person by everyone in the immediate working group.

National Electrical Manufacturing Association (NEMA): The NEMA plan is a point-factor job evaluation system that evolved into the National Position Evaluation Plan sponsored by NMTA associates.

National Metal Trades Association Plan (NMTA): A point-factor job evaluation plan for production, maintenance, and service personnel.

National Position Evaluation Plan: A point-factor job evaluation system that evolved from the NEMA plan. Today, the plan is sponsored by 11 management/manufacturing associations and is offered under the umbrella group, NMTA associates.

Needs theories: Motivation theories that focus on internally generated needs that induce behaviors designed to satisfy these needs.

Nominal rating: Identifying by a label.

Nonexempt employees: Workers subject to the provisions of the Fair Labor Standards Act.

Nonfinancial incentive: Any incentive to reward increased productivity other than monetary remuneration.

Nonqualified stock options: A right given to an executive to purchase stock at a stipulated price; the excess over fair market value is taxed as ordinary income.

Nonquantitative job evaluation: A traditional way of grouping job evaluation methods that includes classification and job ranking.

Normal distribution: The common bell-shaped or parametric distribution frequently used as a basis for making statistical inferences.

Occupation: A generalized job common to any industry and area.

On-call employees: Employees who must respond to work-related assignments/problems 24 hours a day. This group includes technical workers such as software service personnel and equipment repair and maintenance personnel.

Operational definition: Defining an abstract concept in terms of simple, observable procedures.

Option: An agreement or privilege which conveys the right to buy or sell a specific property (security) at a stipulated price in a stated time period.

Ordinal rating: Identifying by a specific position in an array.

Organization: (1) A systematically grouped body of individuals assembled for the accomplishment of a common objective. (2) The process of arranging units of the group and assigning responsibilities to each.

Organization chart: A diagram depicting an organization's structure including the names of the units, titles and names of individuals, their relative ranks, and interrelationships as to authority and responsibility.

Organization structure: The relative rank and relationship among organization units as defined in an organization chart.

Organizational culture: The composite of shared values, symbols, and cognitive schemes that tie employees together within the organization.

Outlier: An extreme value that may distort some measures of central tendency.

Output: The total production of a machine, process, or worker for a specified unit of time.

Outsourcing: The practice of hiring outside vendors to provide goods or services needed by the business at a competitive cost.

Overtime: Time worked by an employee in addition to regularly scheduled hours and in excess of the legal maximum hours of work.

Package: A term frequently used to describe a combination of pay and benefits received by workers as a result of collective bargaining. A package may include wage increases and additional employee benefits.

Paired-comparison: A technique used for ranking items.

Par: The value that appears on the face of a certificate (stock, bond). The value the issuing company promises to pay on maturity.

Par value: Price set by either the articles of incorporation or the corporation's directors below which a share may not be originally issued by the corporation.

Pay: Money received for work performed.

Pay adjustment: A general revision of pay rates. May be either across-the-board, such as "cost of living," or spot adjustments for revisions in prevailing rates.

Pay bands: The combination of two or more pay grades, frequently five to seven, into one expanded grade or band.

Pay compression: See *Compression*.

Pay differentials: Differentials in pay among jobs across and within organizations, and among individuals in the same job in an organization.

Pay-for-knowledge system: A compensation practice whereby employees are paid for the number of different jobs they can adequately perform or the kinds and levels of work-related knowledge they possess.

Pay-for-performance plans: Pay that varies with some measure of individual or organizational performance, such as merit pay, lump-sum bonus plans, incentive plans, and variable pay plans.

Pay grade: A specific component of a pay structure.

Pay grade differential: The difference in rates of pay between two adjacent pay grades. Usually defined by the percentage differences in their midpoints.

Pay grade overlap: The degree of overlap between two adjacent pay grades.

Pay increase guidelines: The mechanism through which different performance levels are translated into pay increases. They establish the size and time of the pay reward for good performance.

Pay level: An average of the array of rates paid by an employer.

Pay level policies: Decisions concerning a firm's level of pay vis-à-vis product and labor market competitors. There are three classes of pay level policies: to lead, to match, or to lag competition.

Pay mix: Relative emphasis among compensation components such as base pay, incentives, and benefits.

Pay objectives: The desired results of the pay system. The basic pay objectives include efficiency, equity, and compliance with laws and regulations. Objectives shape the design of the pay system and serve as the standard against which the success of the pay system is evaluated.

Pay plan: A schedule of pay rates or ranges and a list showing the assignment of each class in the classification plan to one of the rates or ranges. May extend to rules of administration and the benefit package.

Pay plan design: A process to identify pay levels, components, and timing that best match individual needs and organizational requirements.

Pay policy line: The trend line, or line of best fit, that shows the middle pay value of all of the jobs plotted on the scatter diagram.

Pay range: In a pay structure, the distance between the minimum and maximum rates of pay that are set for a pay grade. The range may be stated two different ways:

1. Range as a percent of the minimum:

$$\frac{\text{maximum} = \text{minimum}}{\text{minimum}} \times 100$$

2. Range as a ± percent of midpoint:

$$(+)\ \frac{\text{maximum} - \text{midpoint}}{\text{midpoint}} \times 100$$

$$(-)\ \frac{\text{midpoint} - \text{minimum}}{\text{midpoint}} \times 100$$

Pay satisfaction: A function of the discrepancy between employee perceptions of how much pay they *should* receive and how much pay they *do* receive. If these perceptions are equal, an employee is said to experience pay satisfaction.

Pay steps: The internal design characteristics of a pay grade.

Pay structure: An ordering of rates of pay for jobs or groups of jobs within an organization. A pay structure may be defined in terms of pay grades, job evaluation points, or pay policy lines.

Pay structure change: Change in pay structure calculated by dividing the sum of all midpoints of the new structure by the sum of the midpoints of the old structure and multiplying by 100.

Pay survey: The gathering of data on wages and salaries paid by other employers for selected key classes or positions.

Pay system controls: Basic processes that serve to control pay decision making. They include (1) controls inherent in the design of the pay techniques (e.g., increase guidelines, range maximums and minimums), and (2) budgetary controls.

Pay techniques: Mechanisms or technologies of compensation management, such as job analysis, job descriptions, market surveys, job evaluation, and the like, that tie the four basic pay policies to the pay objectives.

Pay trend line: A line fitted to a scatter plot that treats pay as a function of evaluation points and assigned monetary value.

Pay with competition policy: This policy tries to ensure that a firm's labor costs are approximately equal to those of its competitors. It seeks to avoid placing an employer at a disadvantage in pricing products or in maintaining a qualified workforce.

Percent change: A change in some variable from time 1 to time 2 expressed as a percentage of the value of that variable at time 1.

Percentile: A measure of location in a distribution of numbers that defines the value below which a given percentage of the data falls.

Performance: The ratio of the actual production produced by an operator to the standard production.

Performance appraisal: A system for rating the contributions of an employee with respect to his or her job. This rating serves as a basis for merit increases, promotions, and/or reassignment of work.

Performance dimension training: Training performance appraisers about the performance dimensions on which to measure and rate employee performance.

Performance fund: Total performance increase dollars expressed as a percentage of payroll at end of preceding period.

Performance share plan: A stock grant plan that stipulates the achievement of certain predetermined performance goals before the recipient has the right to the stock.

Performance shares: Grant of stock units that entitle the recipient to actual shares of stock or their cash equivalent value at the time of payment and contingent upon prescribed performance criteria.

Performance standard training: Training that gives performance appraisers a frame of reference for making ratee appraisals.

Performance standards: Established end results used for rating an individual's performance.

Periodic review: A plan of regularly reviewing the status of an employee or reviewing the contents of a job.

Perquisites: Also called "perks." Usually noncash compensation for top-level executives; extra benefits above regular salary such as club memberships, cars, and legal/financial counseling.

Personnel department (division): A staff concerned with securing and maintaining the manpower of the organization. Functions may include employment, compensation, training, safety, health, and other activities that contribute to satisfactory employer-employee relations (more commonly titled Human Resources Department).

Personnel manager (director): Staff executive in charge of personnel administration. Head of personnel or human resources department.

Phantom stock: An award of artificial shares of stock that have a value equal to an equivalent number of shares of stock in the corporation. The unit's actual cash or stock payout value is set by some predetermined formula that relates to either the market or nonmarket value of the stock.

Pink-collar workers: These are workers who occupy jobs in which 70 to 80 percent of the incumbents are female.

Plan: A basic division of accomplishment involving the mental process of determining the next action.

Planned compa-ratio budgeting: A form of top-down budgeting in which a planned compa-ratio rather than a planned level rise is established to control pay costs.

Planned level rise: The percentage increase in average pay that is planned to occur after considering such factors as anticipated rates of change in market data, changes in cost of living, the employer's ability to pay, and the efforts of turnover and promotions. This index may be used in top-down budgeting to control compensation costs.

Planned level rise budgeting: A form of top-down budgeting under which a planned level rise rather than a planned compa-ratio is established as the target to control pay costs.

Point-factor method: A method of job evaluation in which a range of point values is assigned to each of several compensable factors.

Policy: A code or guide for action that stipulates, in a general way, the preferred method of handling a situation or responsibility.

Policy line: A pay line that reflects the organization's policy with respect to the external labor market.

Position: (1) An element of work consisting of locating an object so it will be properly oriented in a specific location. (2) A job performed by a particular employee.

Position analysis questionnaire (PAQ): A highly structured job analysis technique that captures more than 150 aspects of a job.

Position classification: A whole-job method of job evaluation that uses narratives to identify an appropriate location for a position/job under review.

Premium: A selling price above an established price.

Premium pay: Extra pay over the regular wage rate for work performed outside or beyond the regularly scheduled workday (Sundays, holidays, night shifts).

Present value: The current worth of a series of amounts payable or receivable in the future after discounting each amount by an assumed rate of interest and adjusting for the probability of its payment or receipt.

Prevailing rate: The amount paid for like work by others in the labor market. The Davis-Bacon Act requires most federal contractors working in construction to pay wages and benefits prevailing in the area.

Price earnings ratio: The current stock market price of stock divided by its current or estimated future earnings.

Procedural equity: Concerned with the process used to make and implement decisions about pay. It suggests that the way pay decisions are made and implemented may be as important to employees as the results of the decisions.

Procedural justice: Fairness in the procedures used to determine the amount of reward employees will receive.

Procedure: A listing of the steps to follow in performing a given assignment—a specific work sequence.

Process: Any arrangement of events, machines, methods, resources, and/or personnel that forms a recognizable pattern to accomplish a predetermined goal or produce goods and services.

Process theories: Motivation theories that focus on *how* people are motivated rather than on *what* motivates people (e.g., drive, expectancy, and equity theories).

Product market: The market (or market segments) in which a firm competes to sell products or services.

Profit sharing: A method of compensation to employees based on the profit realized from the organization.

Profit-sharing plan: A defined contribution plan that provides for employee participation in the profits of an organization. Normally, the plan includes a predetermined and defined formula for allocating profit shares among participants and for distributing funds accumulated under the plan.

Program: A series of actions proposed in order to achieve a certain result.

Progression through the pay ranges: Three strategies to move employees through the pay ranges: (1) automatic or seniority-based progression, which is most appropriate when the necessary job skills are within the grasp of most employees; (2) merit progression, which is more appropriate when jobs allow variations in performance; and (3) a combination of automatic and merit progression. For example, employers may grant automatic increases up to the midpoint of the range and permit subsequent increases only when merited on the basis of performance appraisal.

Promotion: The upgrading of an employee to a higher job classification.

Purchasing power: The ability to buy goods and services in a certain currency, determined by exchange rates and availability of goods. Companies must determine purchasing power when allocating allowances to expatriates.

Qualified deferred compensation plan: To qualify for tax exemption, a deferred compensation program must provide contributions or benefits for employees other than executives that are proportionate in compensation terms to contributions provided to executives.

Quality control: A function of management, the object of which is to maintain a quality of product in line with established policies and standards. Broader in scope than inspection.

Quantitative job analysis (QJA): Job analysis method that relies on scaled questionnaires and inventories that produce job-related data that are documentable, can be statistically analyzed, and may be more objective than other analysis.

Quartile: A percentile measurement defining the values that divide an array of numbers into four equal parts.

Range maximums: The maximum values to be paid for a job grade, representing the top value the organization places on the output of the work.

Range midpoint: The salary midway between the minimum and maximum rates of a salary range. The midpoint rate for each range is usually set to correspond to the pay policy line and represents the rate paid for satisfactory performance on the job.

Range minimums: The minimum values to be paid for a job grade, representing the minimum value the organization places on the work. Often, rates below the minimum are used for trainees.

Range overlap: The degree of overlap between adjoining grade ranges is determined by the differences in midpoints among ranges and the range spread. A high degree of overlap and narrow midpoint differentials indicate small differences in the value of jobs in the adjoining grades and permit promotions without much change in the rates paid. By contrast, a small degree of overlap and wide midpoint differentials allow the manager to reinforce a promotion with a large salary increase. Usually calculated as

Percentage overlap =

$$100 \times \frac{\text{maximum rate for} \atop \text{lower pay grade} - \text{minimum rate for} \atop \text{higher pay grade}}{\text{maximum rate for} \atop \text{lower pay grade} - \text{minimum rate for} \atop \text{lower pay grade}}$$

Range spread: The difference between the minimum and maximum pay rates of a given pay grade expressed as a percentage of the minimum.

Ranking format: A type of performance appraisal format that requires the rater to compare employees against each other to determine the relative ordering of the group on some performance measure.

Ranking method: In job evaluation, a method in which jobs are listed in order of rank or relative value without attempting exact numerical rating.

Rate range: The range between the minimum and maximum hourly rates for a particular job classification.

Rater error training: Training performance appraisers to identify and suppress psychometric errors such as leniency, severity, central tendency, and halo errors when evaluating employee performance.

Rating errors: Errors in judgment that occur in a systematic manner when an individual observes and evaluates a person, group, or phenomenon. The most frequently described rating errors include halo, leniency, severity, and central tendency errors.

Rating formats: A type of performance appraisal format that requires raters to evaluate employees on absolute measurement scales that indicate varying levels of performance.

Ratio rating: A measurement process that permits multiplication and division because the distance between intervals is equal and there is an absolute zero.

Recency error: The opposite of first impression error. Performance (either good or bad) at the end of the review period that plays too large a role in determining an employee's rating for the entire period.

Real wages: The purchasing power of the money received as wages.

Red-circle rates: Rates that are above the maximum rate for a job (also *ringed rate*).

Reengineering: Changes in the way work is designed to include external customer focus. Usually includes organizational delayering and job restructuring.

Reinforcement theories: Theories such as expectancy and operant conditioning theory grant a prominent role to rewards (e.g., compensation) in influencing behavior. The theorists state that pay influences behavior to the extent merit increases and other work-related rewards are allocated on the basis of performance.

Relative value of jobs: Refers to their relative contribution to organizational goals, to their external market rates, or to some other agreed-upon rates.

Relevant markets: Those employers with whom an organization competes for skills and products/services. Three factors commonly used to determine the relevant markets are: the occupation or skills required, the geography (willingness to relocate and/or commute), and the other employers involved (particularly those who compete in the product market).

Reliability: The consistency quality of a measurement device.

Reopener clause: A provision in an employment contract that specifies that wages, and sometimes such nonwage items as pension/benefits, will be renegotiated under certain conditions (changes in cost of living, organization, profitability, and so on).

Reservation wage: A theoretical minimum standard below which a job seeker will not accept an offer.

Responsibility: A group of duties that identifies and describes a major purpose or a primary reason for the existence of a job.

Restricted stock plan: Recipient of stock grant does not receive right of full ownership until certain predetermined conditions are satisfied.

Reward system: The composite of all organizational mechanisms and strategies used to formally acknowledge employee behaviors and performance. It includes all forms of compensation, promotions, and assignments; nonmonetary awards and recognitions; training opportunities; job design and analysis; organizational design and working conditions; the supervisor; social networks; performance standards and reward criteria; performance appraisal; and the like.

Right-to-work laws: State laws prohibiting any type of union security arrangement between an employer and union that makes union membership a requirement.

Risk sharing: An incentive plan in which employee base wages are set below a specified level (e.g., 80 percent of the market wage) and incentive earnings are used to raise wages above the base. In good years an employee's incentive pay will more than make up for the 20 percent shortfall, giving the employee a pay premium. Because employees assume some of the risk, risk sharing plans pay more generously than success sharing plans in good years.

Routine: An ordered set of instructions that may have some general or frequent use.

Rowan plan: Individual incentive plan that provides for variable incentives as a function of a standard expressed as time period per unit of production. It is similar to the Halsey Plan, but in this plan a worker's bonus increases as the time required to complete the task decreases.

Rucker plan: A cost reduction program in which specific cost savings due to employee effort are shared with employees.

Rule of 72: A technique used to identify the number of years required for an investment to double in value. In using the Rule of 72, the number 72 is divided by the interest rate, ignoring the decimal point, and this gives the years necessary to double the value.

Salary: Money received for work performed for a given period of time, such as weekly or monthly, rather than hourly.

Salary continuation plans: Benefit options that provide some form of protection for disability. Some are legally required, such as workers' compensation provisions for work-related disability and Social Security disability income provisions for those who qualify.

Salary level change: The change in average salary from one period to the next in terms of a percent.

Salary range: See *Pay range.*

Salary sales compensation plan: Under this plan, the sales force is paid a fixed income not dependent on sales volume.

Salary structure: See *Pay structure.*

Salary structure change: See *Pay structure change.*

Sales compensation: Any form of compensation paid to sales personnel.

Savings/thrift plan: A plan established and maintained by an employer that provides for the accumulation of capital by the employee in which the employee makes stipulated rates of contributions and the employer supplements these contributions on the basis of some formula.

Scaling: Determining the intervals on a measurement instrument.

Scanlon plan: A cost-reduction program in which specific cost savings due to employee effort are shared with employees.

Scattergram: A mathematical technique designed to display a relationship between two variables.

Scientific management: The type of management that employs principles derived from research, from analysis of extensive records and other pertinent data, and from objective study of methods and results. A concept developed by F. W. Taylor in the late nineteenth century.

Secretary: (1) A company officer in charge of corporate records, bylaws and minutes of meetings, the corporation seal, meeting notices, and lists of stock- and bondholders. In smaller concerns, often combined with the job of treasurer. (2) A title usually applied to the assistant of an executive or organization unit.

Seniority: Rights and privileges accorded employees over other employees based on length of service.

Seniority increases: These tie pay increases to a progression pattern based on seniority. To the extent performance improves with time on the job, this method has the rudiments of paying for performance.

Service: Work done for others.

Severance pay: A compensation payment made beyond the normal base pay when an individual leaves the organization.

Severity error: The opposite of leniency error. Rating someone consistently lower than is deserved because of a behavior or result of performance in one area that was lower than expected.

Share: In a corporation, a unit of ownership interest. See *Stock.*

Shareholder: The owner of one or more shares of stock.

Shift differentials: Extra pay allowance made to employees who work on shifts other than the regular day shift.

Short-term incentives: Inducements offered in advance to influence future short-range (annual) results. Usually very specific performance standards are established.

Sick leave: Pay for time when not working due to illness or injury.

Single rate system: A compensation policy under which all employees in a given job are paid at the same rate.

Skewed distribution: A distribution of data that is not symmetric. (This is true of pay data found in most surveys.)

Skill: Proficiency at following a prescribed method.

Skill analysis: A systematic process to identify and collect information about skills required to perform work in an organization.

Skill based: Links pay to the depth and/or breadth of the skills and knowledge a person acquires or demonstrates that are relevant to the work. Typically applies to operators, technicians, and office workers where the work is relatively specific and defined. The criterion chosen can influence employee behaviors by describing what is required to get higher pay.

Skill-based/global approach to wage survey: This approach does not emphasize comparison of pay for specific jobs. Instead, it recognizes that employers usually tailor jobs to the organization or individual employee. Therefore, the rates paid to every individual employee in an entire skill group or function are included in the salary survey and become the reference point to design pay levels and structures.

Skill-based pay system: See *Pay-for-knowledge system.*

Skill blocs: Basic units of knowledge employees must master to perform the work, satisfy customers, and achieve business objectives.

Skill requirement: Includes experience, training, and ability as measured by the performance requirements of a particular job.

Sliding scale: Automatic wage adjustments (upward or downward) according to some specified agreement.

Slotting: The act of inserting an item within an array relative to specific criteria.

Social information processing theory (SIP): Counters need theory by focusing on external factors that motivate performance. According to SIP theorists, workers pay attention to environmental cues (e.g., inputs/outputs of coworkers) and process this information in a way that may alter personal work goals, expectations, and perceptions of equity. In turn, this influences job attitudes, behavior, and performance.

Soldiering: The premeditated, deliberate waste of productive time by a worker.

Source document: A record prepared at the time, or place, a transaction takes place.

Special groups: Employee groups for whom compensation practices diverge from typical company procedures (e.g., supervisors, middle and upper management, nonsupervisory professionals, sales, and personnel in foreign subsidiaries).

Speed-up: Forcing workers to increase production without extra compensation.

Spillover effect: This phenomenon refers to the fact that improvements obtained in unionized firms "spill over" to nonunion firms seeking ways to lessen workers' incentives for organizing a union.

Spot award: One-time award given to individual employees for exceptional performance; also called a spot bonus.

Staff: Employees who provide assistance or services to other employees rather than producing the basic good or service of the organization. See *Line.*

Standard deviation: A measure of dispersion of a set of numbers around a central point.

Standard hour plan: Individual incentive plan in which rate determination is based on time period per unit of production, and wages vary directly as a constant function of product level. In this context, the incentive rate in standard hour plans is set based on completion of a task in some expected time period.

Standard Metropolitan Statistical Area (SMSA): Geographic divisions consisting of counties or multiple counties as established by the U.S. Department of Commerce.

Standard rating scales: Characterized by (1) one or more performance standards being developed and defined for the appraiser and (2) each performance standard having a measurement scale indicating varying levels of performance on that dimension. Appraisers rate the appraises by checking the point on the scale that best represents the appraisee's performance level. Rating scales vary in the extent to which anchors along the scale are defined.

Statistical approach to factor selection: A method that uses a variety of statistical procedures to derive factors from data collected through quantitative job analysis from a sample of jobs that represent the range of the work employees (or an employee group) perform in the company. It is often labeled as *policy capturing* to contrast it with the committee judgment approach.

Statistical quality control: A type of quality control that makes use of mathematical statistics in sampling inspections and in the analysis of quality control data.

Step rates: Progression rates established within a pay grade.

Stock: (1) In corporation financing, the form in which an owner's interest is represented; (2) in an industrial enterprise, the stored finished goods ready for sale.

Stock appreciation rights (SARs): A phantom stock plan that normally provides a recipient with the cash equivalent to the appreciation of the stock and declared dividend during a stipulated period.

Stock grant plans: Plans that grant stock to employees without cost to them.

Stock purchase plan: A plan that allows employees to purchase stock.

Stock purchase plan (nonqualified): A plan that is, in effect, a management stock purchase plan. It allows senior management or other key person-

nel to buy stock in the business. This plan has certain restrictions: (1) the stockholder must be employed for a certain period of time, (2) the business has the right to buy back the stock, and (3) stockholders cannot sell the stock for a defined period.

Stock purchase plan (qualified): A program under which employees buy shares in the company's stock, with the company contributing a specific amount for each unit of employee contribution. Also, stock may be offered at a fixed price (usually below market) and paid for in full by the employees.

Straight piecework system: Individual incentive plan in which rate determination is based on units of production per time period; wages vary directly as a constant function of production level.

Straight ranking procedure: A type of performance appraisal format that requires the rater to compare or rank each employee relative to each other employee.

Straight time: Regular wage rate for work performed at a nonpremium time (regularly scheduled workday).

Strategy: The fundamental direction of the organization. It guides the deployment of all resources, including compensation.

Supervisor: In general, any person who directs the activities of immediate subordinates. Often a title applied to a group leader who heads a section within a department.

Surplus value: The difference between labor's use and exchange value. According to Marx, under capitalism wages are based on labor's exchange value—which is lower than its use value—and, thus, provide only a subsistence wage.

Synthetic feature: A composite, not naturally related to job content, used for identifying and defining job worth. See *Compensable factors*.

System: An assembly of methods, procedures, or techniques united by regulated interaction to form an organized whole. An organized collection of people, machines, and methods required to accomplish a set of specific functions.

Systems analysis: The analysis of an activity to determine precisely what must be accomplished and how to accomplish it.

Take-home pay: Wages minus any tax deductions or other deductions that the employee is required to make.

Task: Identifiable human effort exerted for a specific purpose and completed within a prescribed period of time.

Task inventory: A listing of all tasks performed on a job.

Tax equalization: A method whereby an expatriate pays neither more nor less tax than assumed home country tax on base pay.

Team incentive: An incentive plan restricted to team members with payout usually based on improvements in productivity, customer satisfaction, financial performance, or quality of goods and services directly attributable to the team.

Third country nationals (TCNs): Employees of a U.S. foreign subsidiary who maintain citizenship in a country other than the United States or the host country. TCNs' compensation is tied to comparative wages in the local country, the United States, or the country of citizenship. Each approach has different compensation implications.

Time span of discretion: The maximum period of time an employee can perform assignments without seeking or receiving supervisory review.

Top-down approach to pay budgeting: Also known as unit-level budgeting. Under this approach a total pay budget for the organization (or unit) is determined and allocated "down" to individual employees during the plan year. There are many approaches to unit-level budgeting. They differ in the type of financial index used as a control measure. Controlling for a planned level rise and controlling for a planned comparatio are two typical approaches.

Top management: The directors and top executives who control the major divisions and the enterprise as a whole. The chain of command includes the board of directors from the heads of primary divisions.

Topping out: When employees attain the top pay rate for the job or work performed.

Total compensation system: The complete pay package for employees including all forms of money, benefits, services, and in-kind payments.

Total reward system: Includes financial compensation, benefits, opportunities for social interaction, security, status and recognition, work variety, appropriate work load, importance of work, authority/control/autonomy, advancement opportunities, feedback, hazard-free working conditions, and opportunities for personal and professional development. An effective compensation system will utilize many of these rewards.

Tournament theory: The notion that larger differences in pay are more motivating than smaller differences. Like prize awards in a golf tournament, pay increases should get successively greater as one moves up the job hierarchy. Differences between the top job and second highest job should be the largest.

Treasurer: The company officer responsible for financing, banking relations, disbursements, and the like. Responsibilities may include records of and payments to holders of stocks and bonds of the company. May have direct or staff authority over, or parallel with that of, the controller.

Turnover: (1) In general labor terms, turnover is the number of persons hired within a stated period to replace those leaving or dropped; also, the ratio of this number to the average workforce maintained. (2) In pension plans, turnover refers to the ratio of participants who leave employment through quits, discharge, and so on, to the total of participants at any age or length of service. Also called *withdrawal* or *withdrawal rate*.

Turnover effect: The difference in actual salary level change versus expected salary level change. The difference is caused by changes in employee status, employee departures, and new hires. Turnover effect can be a plus or a minus, more often a minus, because lower-paid, shorter service employees replace more senior, higher-paid employees.

Two-tier pay plans: Wage structures that differentiate pay for the same jobs based on hiring date. A contract is negotiated that specifies that employees hired after a stated day will receive lower wages than their higher seniority peers working on the same or similar jobs.

Underutilization: The term used especially by federal EEO agencies meaning an employer is employing minorities and/or women at a rate below their percentages in the relevant labor market.

Universal compensable factor: Certain qualities which might be considered common to all jobs, such as mental, physical, and skill requirements. See *Compensable factors*.

Upgrading: The advancement of an employee to a higher classification (commonly called a promotion).

Validity: The quality that defines how well a device measures what it is supposed to measure.

Valuation discrimination: Focuses on the pay women and minorities receive for the work they perform. Discrimination occurs when members of these groups are paid less than white males for performing substantially equal work. This definition of pay discrimination is based on the standard of "equal pay for equal work." Many believe that this definition is limited. In their view, valuation discrimination can also occur when men and women hold entirely different jobs (in content or results) that are of comparable worth to the employer. Existing federal laws do not support the "equal pay for work of comparable worth" standard.

Variable: A quantity that can assume any or a given set of values.

Variable pay: Tying pay to productivity or some measure that can vary with the firm's profitability.

Wage adjustment provisions: Clauses in a multilayer union contract that specify the types of wage adjustments that have to be implemented during the life of the contract. These adjustments might be specified in three major ways: (1) deferred wage increases—negotiated at the time of contract negotiation with the time and amount specified in the contract, (2) cost-of-living adjustments (COLAs) or escalator clauses, and (3) reopener clauses.

Wage contour: A stable group of wage determining units that have common wagemaking characteristics used for identifying market pay relationships.

Wage curve: A series of wage rates shown graphically.

Wage differentials: Differences that exist in wage rates for similar jobs because of location of company, hours of work, working conditions, or type of product manufactured.

Wage level: The average of all the wage rates paid to workers in an occupation, an industry, or a group of industries.

Wage movement: Increase or decrease in an identified wage level.

Wage rate: The money rate expressed in dollars and cents paid to the employee per hour.

Wage survey: The systematic process of collecting information and making judgments about the compensation paid by other employers. Wage survey data are useful to design pay levels and structures.

Wages: Compensation paid to hourly workers (including those on incentive pay) for service rendered.

White-collar workers: "Nonmanual workers," like office, clerical, sales, or administrative personnel.

Work: Disciplined and persistent activity devoted to achieving a goal.

Work physiology: The specification of the physiological and psychological factors characteristic of a work environment.

Work station: The area where the worker performs the elements of work in a specific operation.

Worker or behavioral data: Include the behaviors required by the job. Used in job analysis.

Worth: The value of something measured by its qualities or by the esteem in which it is held.

Zones: Ranges of pay used as controls or guidelines within pay bands that can keep the system more structurally intact. Maximums, midpoints, and minimums provide guides to appropriate pay for certain levels of work. Without zones employees may float to the maximum pay, which for many jobs in the band is higher than market value.

EMPLOYEE WELFARE AND PENSION BENEFITS

Actuarially sound: A pension fund is considered "actuarially sound" when the amount in the fund and the current levels of contributions to the fund are sufficient, on the basis of assumptions made concerning interest and other factors, to meet the liabilities already accrued and accruing.

Actuary (pensions and insurance): A person trained in mathematics, statistics, and legal accounting methods, and the sound principles of operation of insurance, annuities, and pension plans.

Administrator (pension): The trustee of a jointly administered labor management pension (for purposes of the Federal Disclosure Act). In its usual meaning, it denotes the person or organization that performs the routine clerical operations of the plan.

Aggregate funding method: A method of accumulating money for future payment of pensions whereby the actuary determines the present value of all future benefit payments, deducts from this value whatever funds may be on hand with the insurance company or trustee, and distributes the cost of the balance over the future on a reasonable basis.

Annuity: Periodic payments made to a pensioner over a fixed period of time or until his or her death. *To purchase an annuity* means to pay over a lump sum or make periodic payments to an insurance company. In return, the insurance company guarantees to provide certain periodic payments to the participant as long as he or she lives beyond the first due date of the annuity.

Annuity, joint and survivor: An annuity payable as long as the pensioner lives and continued either in whole or in part after his or her death to a named survivor or contingent annuitant, if living, until the latter's death. Also called *contingent annuity.*

Annuity, modified refund: An arrangement commonly used under a contributory pension plan. If an employee dies after retirement, his or her beneficiary or estate will receive a sum equal to the accumulated value of his or her own contributions to the pension fund, with or without interest up to his or her retirement date, less the total retirement benefits he or she received prior to death.

Approved pension plans: Those plans that qualify for certain tax exemptions under provisions of the Internal Revenue Code and regulations of the commissioner of Internal Revenue.

Beneficiary: A person named to receive death or other specific benefits from an insurance policy, pension plan, will, or other source.

Benefit ceiling: A maximum payout for specific benefit claims (e.g., limiting liability for extended hospital stays to $150,000).

Benefit cutbacks: Similar to wage concessions, negotiations by some employers with employees to eliminate or reduce employer contributions to selected benefits options.

Cafeteria (flexible) benefit plan: A benefit plan in which employees have a choice as to the benefits they receive within some dollar limit. Usually a common core benefit package is required (e.g., specific minimum levels of health, disability, retirement, and death benefit) plus elective programs from which the employee may select a set dollar amount. Additional coverage may be available through employee contributions.

Claims processing: Begins when employee asserts that a specific event (e.g., disablement, hospitalization, unemployment) has occurred and demands that the employer fulfill a promise for payment. As such, a claims processor must first determine whether the act has, in fact, occurred.

Class year pension plan: A plan in which each year's contributions vest separately. Under ERISA, the employee must be 100 percent vested for any plan year within five years.

Coinsurance: A provision of a policy by which both the insured and the insurer share in a specified ratio the covered losses under a policy.

Contributory plan: A plan in which the employee contributes part of the cost.

Coordination of benefits: Efforts to ensure that employer coverage of an employee does not "double pay" because of identical protection offered by the government (private pension and Social Security coordination) or a spouse's employer.

Cost containment: Attempts made by organizations to contain benefits costs, such as imposing deductibles and coinsurance on health benefits or replacing defined benefit pension plans with defined contribution plans.

Death benefit: Amount paid or payable to the beneficiary of a pension plan or insurance policy on the death of the employee or insured.

Deductibles: Employer cost-saving tool by which the employee pays first x number of dollars when a benefit is used (e.g., hospitalization). The employer pays subsequent costs up to some predetermined maximum.

Deferred compensation: Any of a number of compensation payments that accrue to an employee at some future time.

Deferred full vesting: A plan in which the employee retains a right to all accrued benefits of a pension plan if terminated after reaching a certain age and/or after completing a certain period of service or participation in the plan.

Deferred graded vesting: A plan in which the worker acquires a right to a certain percentage of accrued benefits of a pension plan when he or she meets the requirements set down in the plan.

Defined benefit pension plan: A pension plan that specifies the benefits or methods of determining the benefits but not the level or rate of contribution. Contributions are determined actuarially on the benefits expected to become payable.

Defined contribution plan: A pension plan in which the contributions are fixed and the amount of benefits received depend on the funds accumulated in the participant's account.

Dual coverage: In families in which both spouses work, dual coverage refers to coverage of specific claims from each spouse's employment benefit package. Employers cut costs by specifying payment limitations under such conditions.

Employee contributions: Contributions made by employees to the premiums for various kinds of benefits.

Employee services and benefits: Programs that include a wide array of alternative pay forms ranging from payments for time not worked (vacations, jury duty) through services (drug counseling, financial planning, cafeteria support) to protection (medical care, life insurance, and pensions).

Equity funding: The funding of a portion of a retirement plan by investment in equities. It affects the employer's contributions but not the employee's benefits.

Excess pension funds: Since 1980, at least 1,406 pension plans with surpluses of more than $1 million have been terminated, allowing employers to recover $15.65 billion. In terminating a plan, employers provide replacement funds to cover obligations for promised retirement payments to current employees. Remaining funds or excess assets are recovered by the employer.

Experience rating: Insurance premiums vary directly with the number of claims filed. Experience rating is applied to unemployment insurance and workers' compensation, and may be applied to commercial health insurance premiums.

Fiduciary: Any person who (1) exercises any discretionary authority or control over the management of a plan or the management or disposition of its assets, (2) renders investment advice for a fee with respect to the funds or property of a plan, or has the authority to do so, or (3) has any discretionary authority or responsibility in the administration of a plan.

Fixed benefit retirement plan: A defined benefits pension plan that provides retirement benefits in a fixed amount or at a fixed percentage.

Flat benefit retirement plan: A defined benefits pension plan that provides benefits unrelated to earnings. For example, a certain amount per month per year of service.

Flexible benefits: See *Cafeteria (flexible) benefit plan.*

Floor plan: A kind of defined benefit pension plan or capital accumulation device that can be coordinated with a defined contribution plan to provide minimum floor benefits when a shortfall exists in a defined contribution plan.

Fringe benefits: An obsolete or inappropriate term first coined about 1943 by the War Labor Board to describe such benefits as vacations, holidays, and pensions.

Fund: Money and investments held in trust, or share of insurance company assets for payment of pension benefits. (Verb: to accumulate money necessary to pay off a pension benefit.)

Funding method: Manner of accumulating money for future payment of pensions.

Group annuity: A type of pension plan designed by insurance companies for a group of people, usually employees of a single employer, covering all qualifying individuals under one contract for the benefit of the members of the group.

Group life insurance: A life insurance plan, usually without medical examination, for a group of people under a master policy.

Group permanent insurance (pensions): A retirement plan that usually combines life insurance with retirement benefits and uses the level premium method, under a contract between the employer and the insurance company.

Health maintenance organization (HMO): An independently or federally funded organization that provides comprehensive health care service at a fixed monthly fee for a specified group of members.

Immediate full vesting: A provision that entitles employees to all the retirement income that has been accrued by employees on company contributions during their years of service with the company.

Individual contract pension trust: A pension plan under which a trust is created to buy and hold title to individual insurance or annuity contracts for those covered under the plan. The trust receives the premium payments from the employer and transmits them to the insurance company, receiving in turn the individual policies.

Individual retirement account (IRA): A defined contribution plan that provides additional retirement opportunities.

Insured plan: A plan funded with a life insurance company. The life insurance company guarantees the payment of annuities purchased.

Integration: With the significant increases in Social Security premiums paid by employers and employees and Social Security payments indexed to the CPI, many companies integrate the benefits provided by their pension plans with those available through Social Security. The IRS requires the use of offset plan integration rules to protect the pensions of lower-paid employees.

Joint and survivor annuity: An annuity payable as long as the pensioner lives and continuing in whole or in part after death to a named survivor or contingent annuitant, if living, until the latter's death.

Joint and survivor option: A pension plan provision in which, based on the age of the designated survivor, a reduced pension is paid as long as one of the two parties is living.

Keogh plan: A retirement plan designed for self-employed individuals and their employees. (Also referred to as H.R. 10 plan.)

Key man insurance: A health and/or life insurance policy taken out on essential employees, usually to benefit the employer and compensate for the employee's lost services.

Legally required benefits: Benefits that are required by statutory law: Workers' compensation, Social Security, and unemployment insurance are required in the United States. Required benefits vary among countries. Companies operating in foreign countries must comply with host country compensation and benefits mandates.

Level annual premium funding method: A method of accumulating money for payment of future pensions under which the level annual charge for a particular benefit is determined by the actuary for each age of entry, and is payable each year until retirement so that at that time the benefit is fully funded.

Life expectancy: The average number of years an individual of any given age may be expected to live, based on averages obtained from a mortality table.

Long-term disability (LTD): An insurance plan that provides payments to replace income lost through an inability to work because of illness or accident.

Major medical insurance: Protection for extensive surgical, hospital, or other medical expenses and services that are paid once a specified deductible is met. Normally written in conjunction with a basic medical plan.

Managed care: Health care services provided at a prescribed cost by a third-party organization to a group of individuals—or employees. These health care costs are usually significantly lower than those imposed in a fee-for-service program.

Modified refund annuity: See *Annuity, modified refund.*

Money-purchase benefit formula: A type of plan under which contributions of both employer and employee are fixed as flat amounts or flat percentages of the employee's salary. Either at retirement, or as contributions are paid, a benefit is provided for the employee of whatever amount the accumulated contributions, or current contributions, for him or her will produce according to the premium or actuarial tables adopted.

Mortality experience: The rate at which participants in a pension plan have died or are assumed to die. Also, the financial effect of the actual deaths that have occurred on the operation of a plan.

Mortality table: A listing of the mortality experience of individuals by age. A mortality table permits the actuary to calculate, on the average, how long a male or female of a given age may be expected to live.

Noncontributory pension plan: A plan in which the employer pays the entire cost of the premiums or of building up a fund from which pensions are paid.

Nonqualified benefit plan: Any kind of a benefit that does not qualify for favorable tax treatment because it usually provides benefits in excess of or differing from those allowable for deduction under the Internal Revenue Code.

Occupational diseases: Diseases that arise out of the course of employment, not including "ordinary diseases of life," for which workers' compensation claims can be filed.

Old-Age, Survivors, Disability, and Health Insurance Program: An omnibus federal social bill including retirement, survivors and disability insurance, hospital and medical insurance for the aged and disabled, black lung benefits, unemployment insurance, and public assistance in welfare systems.

Ordinary life pension trust: A trust-funded pension plan that provides death benefits through the purchase of ordinary or whole life insurance contracts for covered employees. The trust pays premiums on the insurance coverage until the employee reaches retirement age. The trust also accumulates, in an auxiliary fund, the additional sums necessary to purchase the retirement benefits of the plan for the employees, using the paid-up cash value of the life insurance policy for each employee as part of the purchase price of the annuity.

Pension: The amount of money paid at regular intervals to an employee who has retired from a company and is eligible under a pension plan to receive such payments.

Pension administrator: The person or organization designated by the terms of the instrument under which a pension or welfare plan operates as defined by ERISA.

Pension Benefit Guaranty Corporation (PBGC): A federal corporation established under ERISA located in the U.S. Department of Labor to guarantee vested pension rates. Employers pay a specified premium for each member in a covered pension plan.

Pension plan: A form of deferred compensation. All pension plans usually have four common characteristics: (1) They involve deferred payments to a former employee (or surviving spouse) for past services rendered; they all specify (2) a normal retirement age at which time benefits begin to accrue to the employee, (3) a formula employed to calculate benefits, and (4) integration with Social Security benefits.

Pension trust fund: A fund consisting of money contributed by the employer and, in some cases, the employee, to provide pension benefits. Contributions are paid to a trustee who invests the money, collects the interest and earnings, and disburses the benefits under the terms of the plan and trust agreement.

Portability: In a pension plan, an arrangement under which the contributions of employers who are parties to the plan pool their pension contributions in a central fund where they are ear-

marked for the individual employees to whom they are credited. In this way, the employee who changes jobs within a group of participating employers doesn't lose his or her pension rights because either (1) he or she leaves the job before he or she has service enough to acquire rights or (2) he or she hasn't stayed long enough for his or her benefit to become vested.

Preferred provider organization (PPO): Health care delivery system in which there is a direct contractual relationship between and among employers, health care providers, and third-party payers. An employer is able to select providers (e.g., selected doctors) who agree to provide price discounts and submit to strict utilization controls.

Present value: The current worth of a series of amounts payable or receivable in the future after discounting each amount by an assumed rate of interest and adjusting for its probability of payment or receipt.

Qualified benefit plan: A benefit plan that meets IRS requirements. It may be either a defined benefit or a defined contribution plan. It must not discriminate in favor of officers, shareholders, supervisory personnel, or highly compensated employees.

Self-administered trustee plan: A retirement plan under which contributions to purchase pension benefits are paid to a trustee, generally a bank, which invests the money, accumulates the earnings and interest, and pays benefits to eligible employees under the terms of the retirement plan and trust agreement. This plan is administered by the employer, or by a committee appointed under the terms of the plan, and the trustee.

Self-insurance: An organization funding its own insurance claims, for either health or life insurance or workers' compensation.

Sickness and accident insurance: An insurance program that provides short-term income for injured or sick workers for a period that usually does not exceed two years.

Simplified employee pension (SEP): A retirement income arrangement intended to markedly reduce the paperwork for regular pension plans.

Single-premium funding method: A method of accumulating money for future payment of pensions under which the amount of money required to pay for each particular benefit, or each year's unit of benefit, without any further contribution requirement, is paid to the insurance company or paid to the trust fund.

Social Security option: An option under which the employee may elect that monthly payments of annuity before a specified age (62 or 65) be increased and that payments thereafter are decreased to produce as nearly as practicable a level total annual annuity to the employee, including Social Security.

Split-dollar insurance: An agreement by two parties to share annual insurance expenses and, in turn, share in the equity of the death benefits of the policy.

Supplemental unemployment benefits (SUB) plan: A supplement to unemployment insurance; payments granted to workers for a specific period of time and funded through employer payments. Normally part of a union contract.

Thrift savings plans: A savings plan designed to help workers meet savings goals. A common plan involves a 50 percent employer match on employee contributions up to a maximum of 6 percent of pay.

Top heavy: A pension plan is determined to be top heavy if more than 60 percent of the present value of total accrued benefits is provided to co-owners and others who are defined as key employees. Both TEFRA 82 and TRA 86 contain top-heavy provisions.

Trust fund: See *Pension trust fund.*

Unemployment insurance: A payment made by the state to workers during periods of temporary unemployment. The program is funded principally through employer payments.

Unit benefit plan: A type of pension plan providing retirement benefits expressed as a definite amount of percentage for each year of service with the employer. The plan may define the benefit as a small unit of annuity for each year of membership in the plan, usually a percentage of the employee's earnings, such as 1 percent. The total of these units is the amount the employee will receive each year upon retirement. Sometimes referred to as a unit-purchase type of plan.

Variable annuity: An annuity under which the benefit varies according to the investment results of the funds set aside to provide it.

Vesting: In pension plans, vesting means that a participant who leaves the employ of the company for any reason not excepted by the plan does not lose all of the equity built up on his or her behalf, but may, at a designated time, receive either a stated lump-sum payment or payments, or a reduced or pro rata pension at the time he or she reaches retirement age.

Welfare plan: A plan that provides medical, surgical, or hospital care or benefits in the case of sickness, accident, disability, death, or unemployment. May also include benefits such as vacation or scholarship plans.

Workers' compensation: State laws that require most employers to provide employees with insurance protection from employment-related disabilities.

LEGISLATIVE-RELATED TERMS

Access discrimination: Staffing and allocation decisions made by employers that deny particular jobs, promotions, or training opportunities to qualified women or minorities. This type of discrimination is illegal under Title VII of the Civil Rights Act of 1964.

Age Discrimination in Employment Act (ADEA) of 1967 (amended 1978, 1986, and 1990): Makes nonfederal employees age 40 and over a protected class relative to their treatment in pay, benefits, and other personnel actions. The 1990 amendment is called the *Older Workers Benefit Protection Act.*

Bona fide occupational qualification (BFOQ): The phrase used in Title VII of the Civil Rights Act of 1964 to allow an exception to the equal employment law. BFOQ exceptions are rare and do not include race or color.

Civil Rights Act: Title VII of the Civil Rights Act of 1964 prohibits discrimination in terms and conditions of employment (including benefits) that is based on race, color, religion, sex, or national origin.

Civil Rights Act of 1991: Reestablishes the standards for proving discrimination that had been in general use before the 1989 Supreme Court rulings. Allows jury trials and damage awards.

Consolidated Omnibus Budget Reconciliation Act (COBRA): Employees who resign or are laid off through no fault of their own are eligible to continue receiving health coverage under employer's plan at a cost borne by the employee.

Davis-Bacon Act of 1931: Requires most federal contractors to pay wage rates prevailing in the area.

Employee Retirement Income Security Act of 1974 (ERISA): An act regulating private employer pension and welfare programs. The act has provisions that cover eligibility for participation, reporting, and disclosure requirements, establish fiduciary standards for the financial management of retirement funds, set up tax incentives for funding pension plans, and establish the Pension Benefit Guaranty Corporation to insure pension plans against financial failures.

Equal employment opportunity commission (EEOC): A commission of the federal government charged with enforcing the provisions of the Civil Rights Act of 1964 and the EPA of 1963 as it pertains to sex discrimination in pay.

Equal Pay Act (EPA) of 1963: An amendment to the Fair Labor Standards Act of 1938 prohibiting pay differentials on jobs that are substantially equal in terms of skills, efforts, responsibility, and working conditions, except when they are the result of bona fide seniority, merit, or production-based systems, or any other job-related factor other than sex.

Exempt jobs: Jobs not subject to provisions of the Fair Labor Standards Act with respect to minimum wage and overtime. Exempt employees include most executives, administrators, professionals, and outside sales representatives.

Fair Labor Standards Act of 1938 (FLSA): A federal law governing minimum wage, overtime pay, equal pay for men and women in the same types of jobs, child labor, and recordkeeping requirements.

Family and Medical Leave Act of 1993: Entitles eligible employees to receive unpaid leave up to 12 weeks per year for specified family or medical reasons, such as caring for ill family members or adopting a child.

Federal Employee Pay Comparability Act of 1990 (FEPCA): Seeks to close any pay gap between federal employees and employees of local and state government as well as private industry. The act phases in wedge adjustments when rates differ from local market rates by more than 5 percent.

Federal Insurance Contribution Act (FICA): The source of social security contribution withholding requirements. The FICA deduction is paid by both employer and employee.

Health Maintenance Act: Requires employers to offer alternative health coverage options (e.g., health maintenance organizations) to employees.

Occupational Safety and Health Act (OSHA) of 1970: Designed to improve working conditions in industry, thereby reducing worker accidents and job-related illnesses.

Pay discrimination: It is usually defined to include (1) access discrimination that occurs when qualified women and minorities are denied access to particular jobs, promotions, or training opportunities and (2) valuation discrimination that takes place when minorities or women are paid less than white males for performing substantially equal work. Both types of discrimination are illegal under Title VII of the Civil Rights Act of 1964. Existing federal laws do not support the "equal pay for work of comparable worth" standard.

Pension Benefit Guaranty Corporation: To protect individuals from bankrupt companies, employers are required to pay insurance premiums to this agency. In turn, the PBGC guarantees payment of vested benefits to employees formerly covered by terminated pension plans.

Pregnancy Discrimination Act of 1978: An amendment to Title VII of the Civil Rights Act. It requires employers to extend to pregnant employees or spouses the same disability and medical benefits provided other employees or spouses of employees.

Prevailing wage laws: A government-defined prevailing wage is the minimum wage that must be paid for work done on covered government projects or purchases. In practice, these prevailing rates have been union rates paid in various geographic areas. The main prevailing wage laws are

(1) Davis-Bacon (1931), (2) Walsh-Healey Public Contracts Act (1936), and (3) McNamara-O'Hara Service Contract Act (1965).

Revenue Act of 1978: Primarily simplified pension plans, added tax incentives for individual retirement accounts (IRAs), and adjusted requirements for ESOPs. The act also provided that cafeteria benefit plans need not be included in gross income and reaffirmed the legality of deferring compensation and taxes due on it for an employee.

Revenue Reconciliation Act of 1993: Limits employer deductions for executive compensation to $1 million and caps the amount of executive compensation used to compute contributions to and benefits from qualified retirement plans.

Social Security: The Social Security Act of 1935 established what has become the federal old-age, survivors, disability, and health insurance system. The beneficiaries are workers that participate in the Social Security program, their spouses, dependent parents, and dependent children. Benefits vary according to (1) earnings of the worker, (2) length of time in the program, (3) age when benefits start, (4) age and number of recipients other than the worker, and (5) state of health of recipients other than the worker.

Title VII of the Civil Rights Act of 1964: A major piece of legislation prohibiting pay discrimination. It is much broader in intent than the EPA, forbidding discrimination on the basis of race, color, religion, sex, pregnancy, or national origin.

TRASOP (Tax Reduction Act Employee Stock Ownership Plan): A form of employee stock ownership plan (ESOP) that meets specific requirements of the Tax Reform Act of 1975, as amended.

Unemployment insurance (UI): State-administered programs that provide financial security for workers during periods of joblessness. These plans are wholly financed by employers except in Alabama, Alaska, and New Jersey, where there are provisions for relatively small employee contributions.

Wage and price controls: Government regulations that aim at maintaining low inflation and low levels of unemployment. They frequently focus on "cost push" inflation, limiting the size of the pay raises and the rate of increases in the prices charged for goods and services. Used for limited time periods only.

Walsh-Healey Public Contracts Act of 1936: A federal law requiring certain employers holding federal contracts for the manufacture or provision of materials, supplies, and equipment to pay industry-prevailing wage rates.

Workers' compensation An insurance program, paid for by the employer, designed to protect employees from expenses incurred for a work-related injury or disease. Each state has its own workers' compensation law.

Name Index

Subject Index